THE VICTORIA CROSS WARS

THE VICTORIA CROSS WARS

Battles, Campaigns and Conflicts of All the VC Heroes

Brian Best

Frontline Books

First published in Great Britain in 2017
and republished in this format in 2020 by
by Frontline Books,
An imprint of
Pen & Sword Books Limited
Yorkshire - Philadelphia

ISBN 978 1 52678 147 5

A CIP catalogue record for this book is available from the British Library

Printed and bound in England by CPI Group (UK) Ltd, Croydon, CR0 4YY
Typeset in 10/12 point Palatino

Pen & Sword Books Limited incorporates the imprints of Atlas,
Archaeology, Aviation, Discovery, Family History, Fiction, History, Maritime,
Military, Military Classics, Politics, Select, Transport, True Crime, Air World,
Frontline Publishing, Leo Cooper, Remember When, Seaforth Publishing,
The Praetorian Press, Wharncliffe Local History, Wharncliffe Transport,
Wharncliffe True Crime and White Owl.

For a complete list of Pen & Sword titles please contact
PEN & SWORD BOOKS LIMITED
47 Church Street, Barnsley, South Yorkshire S70 2AS, United Kingdom
E-mail: enquiries@pen-and-sword.co.uk
Website: www.pen-and-sword.co.uk

Or
PEN AND SWORD BOOKS
1950 Lawrence Rd, Havertown, PA 19083, USA
E-mail: Uspen-and-sword@casematepublishers.com
Website: www.penandswordbooks.com

Contents

Introduction

The institution of the Victoria Cross in 1856 came two years after the introduction of the Distinguished Conduct Medal, which had been approved by Queen Victoria in December 1854. This was awarded for bravery to those of the rank of sergeant and below and followed the French example of the *Médaille Militaire,* which was formed in 1852. Many have incorrectly claimed that the Victoria Cross was the first award for gallantry and that we were following the example of similar awards made by France and Prussia. In 1813, King William Frederick III of Prussia ordered a new medal to be struck to replace all existing military decorations; the Iron Cross. It proved to be a brilliant public relations stroke as it equally rewarded men of all ranks. Napoleon had instituted a similar decoration in 1804 with the *Légion d'honneur*. It took until 1856 before Britain introduced a medal for all ranks; the Victoria Cross.

The Crimean War was the first European war to involve Britain since Waterloo and the first to receive blanket newspaper coverage. The now more readily available newspapers highlighted the case for a truly democratic recognition of all outstanding gallantry acts. So was set in motion an award would recognise all ranks from Privates to Officers of lower grades.

There are several people who could legitimately claim to have first suggested the awarding of an all-ranks gallantry award. One to have the strongest claim was *The Times* special correspondent, William Howard Russell, who accompanied the Army to the Crimea. He was to witness the three major battles of September to November 1854; Alma, Balaclava and Inkerman. He was given free rein by his editor, John Delane and filled the paper with his eyewitness accounts. As early as 30 October 1854, he received a generous letter from *The Times'* proprietor, John Walter acknowledging the emphasis on highlighting the plight of the ordinary soldier; 'the credit due of having added another laurel to the crown of the 'Fourth Estate' by the fidelity and zeal with which you have "reported", even on the field of battle, and evidently at considerable peril, the glorious achievements of our troops; while you have certainly earned their gratitude by making known their needless hardships'.

Russell learned from conversations in the camps of the bravery displayed by the British soldier. He wrote suggesting the Queen might create an order of merit or valour and that it should bear her name. He was gratified, when, in 1856, the Victoria Cross was instituted.

His reports may have influenced the Bath MP, Captain George Scobell, to raise the question in the House of Commons on 19 December 1854 requesting the bestowal of an 'Order of Merit' to; 'every grade and individual'.

Another who was instrumental in establishing the VC in its present form was Queen Victoria's husband, Prince Albert. He was a man who relished order and it was he who composed the first Warrant laying out the rules for its bestowing. Since the first Royal Warrant others have been issued modifying and limiting the VC provisions. One such Warrant was issued in 1858 and stated it may be awarded to those; 'who may perform acts of conspicuous courage and bravery … in circumstances of extreme danger, such as the occurrence of a fire on board ship, or of the foundering of a vessel at sea, or under any other circumstances in which life or public property may be saved'. It was a short-lived Warrant that did not find favour with the War Office and in 1881 it was replaced with a new Warrant that made it clear; 'the qualification shall be "Conspicuous bravery or devotion to the country in the presence of the enemy"'.

The design of the medal was altered and approved by the Queen. She suggested using the motto 'For Valour' rather than 'For the Brave' on the grounds that all her soldiers were brave. The design resembles the Peninsular Gold Cross and is often referred to as a *cross pattée*. A copper sample was sent to the Queen for approval but she rejected the choice of metal as it; 'would soon look like an old penny'. Instead she suggested that bronze would be more attractive and that it should be coated with a greenish varnish to protect it.

It was soon found that bronze was too hard and broke the steel dies at Hancocks, who had been appointed to supply the new award. There was little option but to resort to the wasteful process of sand casting. The crude casting required the Cross to be finished by hand-chasing and careful filing to bring out the detail. The completed Cross was unique in the same way that finger-prints are to each of us. Appropriately the bronze used was supplied by the cannon captured from the Russians during the Crimean War.

By the beginning of the First World War, the supply of bronze was running out. An apocryphal story has it that a couple of fitters at the Woolwich Arsenal were told to go and cut the cascables (the large ball-like projection at the breech-end around which recoil ropes were secured) from a couple of Russian cannon. Unable to identify the Russian pieces, the fitters cut the cascabels from the two nearest cannon, which turned out to be Chinese, possibly captured during the First Opium War of 1840. Apart from a period in the latter part of the Second World War, when the Chinese bronze could not be located and scrap bronze was used, this has been the metal from which the crosses have been made. Since then all VCs are made from the Chinese cascabels with enough to make a further sixty Crosses.

Apart from the Crimean War, the British Army was involved in fighting unsophisticated foes during the period up to the First World War. An exception can be made for the Boer War but even this conflict did not involve fighting in conventional European formations. This produced a Victorian-style of fighting which ended within a year of the start of the First World War. This latter conflict called for a more ruthless attitude, and more humanitarian deeds were rewarded with fewer acts of gallantry being recognised. Also, the bar has been progressively raised so that the VC act is verging on the suicidal, with a high incidence of posthumous awards.

The decision of the Commonwealth countries of Australia, New Zealand and Canada to institute their own version of the Victoria Cross during the latter part of the twentieth century has rather muddied the waters. The Victoria Cross and George Cross Association invites the current recipients of these new awards to its bi-annual Rededication Service at St Martin-in-the-Field, which would bring the current total of VCs award to 1363. For the sake of clarity, this book covers only the British or Imperial VCs awarded totalling 1358, including three double VCs.

As a biographically detailed book of all recipients would be impossible to produce, this book sets out to write about every war, campaign, battle and skirmish where an Imperial Victoria Cross was awarded. The origins of the conflict are examined, sometimes to the detriment of Britain, but whatever the causes the displays of gallantry performed by the soldiers, sailors and airmen merited being recognised with the Victoria Cross.

Chapter 1

Crimean War, 1854–56

Number of VCs awarded	111
Number of VCs awarded to officers	41
Number of VCs awarded to other ranks	70
Total awarded to Royal Navy	24
Total awarded to Royal Marines	3
Total awarded to British Army	84

Origins of the War

The Crimean War was caused by long-term tensions that had developed in Europe since the signing of the Treaty of Vienna in 1814 after Napoleon Bonaparte's defeat at Waterloo. The objective of the Treaty was to restore old boundaries and preserve the *status quo* by upholding stable and orderly monarchies. The new Czar, Nicholas 1, reverted to an autocratic rule and an expansion of her empire.

Russia began nibbling away at the Ottoman Empire and fought a series of wars on her borders beginning with Georgia, Chechnya, Armenia and Azerbaijan. She also cast her eyes to the east, and had reached the northern borders of Persia and Afghanistan, something that unsettled British India.

In 1848, Europe was rocked by a series of revolutions which in the main affected France, the Netherlands, Germany, Austria, Denmark, Poland and Italy. Britain and Russia were unaffected by this upheaval, although they were considerably uneasy about any spread over their borders. It did little to alter Russia's ambitions to further expand to the south into Europe. Czar Nicholas was again casting covetous eyes at the 'sick man of Europe', Turkey, and the declining power of the Ottoman Empire. His ambition was to gain control of the Straits – the Bosphorus, Sea of Marmara and the Dardanelles – to allow his Black Sea naval fleet access into the Mediterranean Sea. The most direct route was to advance through the Ottoman-ruled countries on the west of the Black Sea; Moldova, Rumania and Bulgaria.

One of the beneficiaries of the 1848 uprising in France was Louis Napoleon Bonaparte, who was elected President of the Second Republic. Within four years he felt strong enough to suspend the assembly and establish the Second French Empire, with himself as the new emperor, Napoleon III. As a usurper, he sought swift prestige to uphold his new 'Second Empire'.

To maintain Papal support, he championed the Catholic cause wherever he could. One such place was the holy places in Ottoman-controlled Palestine. Napoleon put pressure on the Sultan and managed to secure concessions for the Catholic Church, which enabled the priests to have control of the keys to the Church of the Nativity in Bethlehem.

Russia reacted with a demand for the Orthodox Church to also have shared control of the keys. In a series of clashes, several Orthodox monks were killed and Czar Nicholas insisted that he be appointed protector of the Orthodox Christians in the Ottoman Empire, something to which the Sultan could not concede. This gave the Czar the excuse he was looking for. In July 1853, Russia occupied the Turkish Danubian provinces of Moldova and Walachia. In October, Turkey declared war and Russia responded by sending her Black Sea fleet to attack and destroy a Turkish flotilla in the port at Sinope.

Britain supported Turkey as a buffer against Russian expansion in the region, fearing any Russian presence in the Eastern Mediterranean could threaten her route to India. Although large, the Russian army was badly led, poorly equipped and tactically out-of-date but, because of her record against Napoleon, she was still regarded as militarily invincible.

Initially reluctant to get involved in a war, especially allied with France, Britain finally agreed to go to Turkey's aid in the Danubian provinces. Along with France, Britain declared war with Russia in March 1854. After decades of peace, the British public was now in a mood for another war. Recruiting was brisk as young men were attracted by the colourful uniforms, the new weaponry and the chance to join the great adventure and 'to give the Russian bear a bloody nose'.

The first regiments set sail for the Eastern Mediterranean and soon some 60,000 allied troops were camped on the Bulgarian coast around Varna. Very quickly it became apparent how especially unprepared the British were to conduct a war. Failures in the commissariat and medical department soon surfaced, exacerbated by a virulent outbreak of cholera that swept through the camps. As the allies suffered in their tented camps, the Turkish had inflicted a stunning defeat on the Russian army at Silistria, seventy-five miles north on the Danube River. Ten thousand Turks, who had been besieged by 90,000 Russians, had routed the invaders who completely withdrew from the Danubian Provinces.

Though the immediate cause of the war had been resolved, the French and British governments were reluctant to return home without inflicting some sort of punishment of the enemy. Without accurate maps and with no intelligence, the British and French commanders, Lord Raglan and General St. Arnaud, planned to cross the Black Sea, land their troops on the southwest coast of the Crimean Peninsula and destroy the Russian fleet at Sebastopol.

Leaving the Bulgarian coast on 7 September, the allied troops endured a terrible week-long voyage until they were deposited on an open beach in Calamita Bay, some 35 miles north of Sebastopol. Weakened by cholera and dysentery they had brought from Varna, the mighty army marched south and fought the first battle of the campaign at the River Alma.

With little in the way of leadership from Lord Raglan, other than an order to advance, the British marched under fire to the river, crossed it and steadily advanced up the steep slopes on the far bank, where the Russians were dug in. It was here that the first half dozen Victoria Crosses were awarded for this hard-fought battle. Four were awarded to the Scots Fusilier Guards for gallantry while carrying their colours into battle; Captain Robert Lindsay, Sergeant John Simpson Knox, Sergeant James MacKechnie and Private William Reynolds. Captain Edward William Derrington Bell of 23rd (Royal Welch) Fusiliers won his for capturing a Russian gun that was being withdrawn from a redoubt, while Sergeant John Park of 77th (Middlesex) Regiment won his VC for Alma and other gallant acts during his Crimean service.

Another member of a colour-party was Sergeant Luke O'Connor of 23rd (Royal Welsh) Fusiliers who is acknowledged as the first military Victoria Cross winner.

LUKE O'CONNOR VC (1831-1915)

Luke O'Connor is often cited as an example of how a common soldier could prosper in the nineteenth century British Army, rising from the rank of private to that of major general. In 1900, he wrote a magazine article about his recollections of his service and early life.

Early Life

'I was born near Elphin, Co. Roscommon, in 1832 (he was actually born on 20th February 1831), and owing to the troubles in those days my parents, with a large portion of their numerous family, emigrated to Canada in order to go in for farming, and took me, being one of the youngest children with them. Crossing the Atlantic was a tedious business then, and we did it in a slow sailing vessel. During the long voyage my father died at sea. My widowed mother reached Quebec in the midst of a small-pox epidemic and fever, when she too, was taken ill and died, also one of my brothers, leaving me to the care of an elder sister, who brought me back to Ireland.

'My first recollection in life is my return to Boyle, a military town containing barracks … Here I was handed over to an uncle, as my sister returned immediately to America, where many of my relations still are;

some of them attained high positions during the American (Civil) War. It was not strange that my earliest ideas had a military tendency, for Roscommon is famous for giving soldiers to the service, and, indeed, many of my relatives have served in the Army all over the world … Little did I then think that later in life I should become a captain commanding a two-company detachment in the same quarters?'

The O'Connors were not without some financial standing in their homeland. This is confirmed by Luke's description of how he came to enlist in the Army.

'It was intended at first to make me a priest, and the notion sometimes took hold of my fancy. My uncle, however, wished me to return to Canada to join my people; but all at once he died. There was a first cousin of mine, however, in London in medical practice, who had served as a surgeon under Sir de Lacy Evans in Spain. (This would be the Carlist Wars of the 1830s in which British volunteers participated). I resolved to visit this relative, and see what he could do for me…In spite of this my wish to soldier became too strong for me, and shortly afterwards when again in Westminster I was struck by the gallant appearance of a fine-looking recruiting sergeant of the Royal Welch Fusiliers, a regiment I had never heard of before, and its title caught my fancy. I took the shilling once more, a few of my young friends followed my example, and we enlisted in the same regiment. I said nothing to my cousin this time, and in a few days found myself in the barracks at Winchester, where the Royal Welch were quartered in July 1849.'

Military Career

'Within a fortnight of joining I had so mastered my drill that I was noticed by my adjutant and sergeant-major and called out to drill a squad in their presence to see if I could do it just as I had been taught. Proud of the opportunity, I repeated the necessary cautions and gave the words of command completely to their satisfaction.

'Next day I was brought to the orderly-room before my colonel, Arthur Wellesley Torrens, a man well known in the service. Formally adjutant to the Guards, very much to the disgust of the older officers of the Royal Welch he had been promoted to command their regiment … To my great delight, on that day he gave me my stripe as lance-corporal, which I am always proud to remember. In June 1850, I was promoted full corporal and to lance-sergeant the same year, and twelve months later on, when the regiment was at Plymouth, I became a sergeant, just two years after joining it.'

O'Conner's natural intelligence and ability had made him stand out amongst his comrades and the rate of his promotion was quite exceptional and a clear indicator of things to come. In 1853, he was detached from the regiment to drill and train three militia units before embarking with his regiment on SS *Trent* for bound for Turkey and the war with Russia.

Crimea Landing

Along with their comrades, the 23rd Regiment sat and suffered in the unhealthy camps around Varna, losing one officer and thirty-six other ranks to cholera. In August, the British and French governments issued directives that their armies in Bulgaria were to embark at Varna and then endeavour to capture the Russian naval base at Sebastopol in the Crimea. On 14 September, the British army began to land troops at Calamita Bay, north of Sebastopol and the first regiment ashore was the 23rd Regiment. The unopposed landings lasted four days and on 19 September the advance south began. Blocking their route to Sebastopol was a Russian force under the command of Prince Menchikov which was posted on high ground behind the River Alma. Early on the morning of 20 September, the French, who were on the right of the line between the British army and the sea, began their advance against the Russian positions, expecting to be closely supported.

The British Staff, however, due to generally poor organisation, failed to order the advance until 15.00 hours when Lord Raglan ordered the 2nd and Light Divisions, supported by the 3rd and 1st Divisions, to advance up the slopes directly in front of them. The Royal Welch formed part of the Fusilier Brigade of the Light Division. As they advanced towards the river they passed through vineyards and scrambled over stone walls, which broke up their formation and they became the target for a heavy bombardment from the Russian guns on the heights ahead of them. Crossing the Alma River, they trudged up the slope which had no natural cover.

VC Action

Almost immediately, the advance slowed and, in places, began to falter. General Codrington, commanding the Fusilier Brigade, ordered his men to fix bayonets and attack the Russian positions. The 7th Regiment (Royal Fusiliers) on the right of the line was forced to form to the right to repel a large Russian column that was attempting to outflank them. The Royal Welch and the 33rd Regiment were joined by a regiment from the 2nd Division and the 19th Regiment and pushed on up the hill.

In the lead as a member of the colour escort, Sergeant Luke O'Connor, who recalled the assault: 'Early on the morning of 20th … the Light Division was deployed into line, and halted for some time. Our adjutant came to my captain and asked him to let me go as one of the escort for the colours. He replied I was wanted where I was. The adjutant returned with the colonel's commands for me to be sent as directed. I went away delighted with the distinction of being with the colour party, and was appointed centre sergeant. On the line being told to advance, I took the usual six paces to the front as guide to the right brigade of which the Royal Welch was the battalion of direction.

'The general, however, called me back, as we were now under heavy fire of shot and shell, and told me to take the usual place between the colours

... We pushed through the river, which was very deep in some places ... here the men began to drop very fast.'

As they reached the Russian line which was protected by an earthwork, the Colours of the Royal Welch were being carried by eighteen-year old Lieutenant Anstruther and Ensign Butler. Although this duty was deemed a great honour it drew much enemy fire and consequently heavy casualties. Garnet Wolseley later wrote that; 'a general who could condemn anyone to carry a large silk colour under close musketry fire ought to be tried for murder'.

Just how dangerous it was can be judged by the sequence of killed and wounded members of the colour party. Within minutes, Ensign Butler was shot dead and the pole broken by a musket ball. The fallen Regimental Colour was then picked up by Lieutenant Colonel Chester and then passed to Sergeant Honey Smith, who carried it for the remainder of the day. Lieutenant Anstruther, carrying the Queen's Colour, was urged by Sergeant O'Connor to move forward, believing that it was safer close to the earthwork than it was lower down the slope. Suddenly, the Russians began to limber up their artillery and Anstruther charged forward leading a number of men intent on foiling the enemy's plan.

'We then ran up the slope until about eighty yards from the redoubt when I remarked: "If we go further the colours may be taken, for we were far ahead of the men." We halted; at that moment, the poor officer was killed and I was knocked over at the same time by a bullet striking me in the breast and breaking two ribs. Private Evans came up and helped me on my legs; I then snatched up the flag, rushed to the earthwork and planted it on the parapet...The silk standard was riddled with shot, but the redoubt itself sheltered my body.'

When O'Connor fell, the Queen's Colour had been taken up by Private William Evans and he held it up to indicate that the Royal Welch were the first to reach the enemy positions, before passing it to Corporal Luby, who then relinquished it back to O'Connor. Captain Bevil Granville urged the wounded sergeant to relinquish the Colour and go to the rear for medical treatment but he refused until loss of blood forced him to pass it to the captain. Following further heavy fighting, the Russians finally withdrew, leaving the body-strewn battlefield to the Allies. The Royal Welch had eight officers and forty-four men killed and five officers and 154 men wounded, amongst whom was Sergeant Luke O'Connor, whose battlefield promotion to Colour-Sergeant was confirmed two days later. It was discovered that the Queen's Colour carried by O'Connor had been pierced by twenty-six bullets.

Promotion

O'Connor was one of the fortunate men who, having been severely wounded in action, managed to survive the ministering in the field and the notorious Barracks Hospital at Scutari. On 19 October, he had been commissioned without purchase as an ensign in the 76th Regiment of Foot (2nd Battalion, Duke of Wellington's) in recognition of his action at the Alma. It was normal to commission an NCO into another regiment as it was felt that such a promotion within the same regiment would place him in a difficult position with regard to his former comrades. Despite this the losses sustained by the Royal Welch meant that he was exchanged back into his old regiment on 5 November. A further promotion to lieutenant followed on 9 February 1855.

'I reached Scutari Hospital on 26th (September) and discharged on 20th October. I again embarked for the Crimea but caught a fever on board, was landed at the Balaklava Hospital and sent back to Scutari, where I received much kind attention from Miss Nightingale and the Sisters of Charity... Meanwhile, in February, I received the good news I had been promoted to an ensign's commission in the Royal Welch Fusiliers and this was subsequently antedated to 5th November 1854.'

On 8 September 1855, Lieutenant O'Connor took part in the second British assault on the Redan, one of the two major Sebastopol defensive works. With the Russians prepared to meet the attack, the storming party dashed across nearly 300 yards of open, fire-swept ground towards a twenty-foot wide and fourteen-foot deep ditch. Unfortunately, when they began their attack, the men of the 23rd Regiment who were in support were still some distance from the front line.

Lieutenant Boscawen Trevor Griffith wrote in a letter home: 'We rushed madly along the trenches … Several officers we met coming back wounded said that they had been in the Redan and that the supports were only wanted to complete a victory … We gained the 5th parallel, our most advanced trench, and "On, Twenty Third! This way!" cried the staff officers. We scrambled out of the trench on to open ground. That was a fearful moment. I rushed across the space…shot striking the ground all the way and men falling down on all sides. When I got to the edge of the ditch…I found our men all mixed up in confusion but keeping a steady fire against the enemy … over the next glacis – here were lots of men of different regiments all huddled together – scaling ladders placed against the parapet crowded with our fellows. Radcliffe and I got hold of a ladder and went up it to the top of the parapet where we were stopped by the press – wounded and dead men kept tumbling down upon us …

'Well, do as we could, we could not get the men to come up the parapet in sufficient numbers … Suddenly a panic seized our men and I grieve to say they deserted their comrades inside and retreated in confusion towards our trenches.'

O'Connor volunteered to command one of the storming parties which had to run 180 yards, straight into intense enemy fire. Half his men fell before they reached the parapet but he managed to reach the top before being shot through both thighs, falling back into the ditch and being knocked unconscious. He was carried back to the British lines where, for a while, it was considered that he would have to have one leg amputated. Invalided home, arrived at Portsmouth on 10 November. After recuperation at the Haslar Hospital, he was able to rejoin his regiment at Aldershot in December.

Command of the 23rd Regiment had devolved on Edward Bell. He had been a captain at the beginning of the Crimea War but, due to the high number of casualties amongst the officers, including the death of their commanding officer, Lieutenant Colonel Chester, Bell had assumed command of the regiment. During the advance up the Alma heights, Captain Bell had managed to capture a Russian 16-pounder artillery piece before it could be ridden away. Bell had seized the reins and led the team down the slope towards the British rear.

As Bell made his way down the hill, he was confronted by his divisional commander, the irascible Sir George Brown, who was furious that the captain had left his company during a crucial point in the battle in order to claim the gun as a prize. Suitably admonished, Bell pointed the horses towards the rear and returned to his company.

During the war there had been much debate in Britain about rewarding their gallant soldiers with a truly democratic medal. By the time the war ended in 1856, an appropriate gallantry award had been established and named after the Queen. In the autumn of 1856, all regiments who had taken part in the fighting were invited to submit the names of men considered to have performed with exceptional gallantry. Edward Bell's name was put forward along with Luke O'Connor's. Sir George Brown's disapproval of Bell leaving his company to secure the gun carried some considerable weight. Bell obviously thought this was unfair and argued, as the regiment's commanding officer, he could and would not support the nomination of Sergeant O'Connor unless his own nomination also went forward. As things transpired, both nominations were submitted and approved.

Both Brevet Lieutenant Colonel Edward Bell and Lieutenant Luke O'Connor appeared in *The London Gazette* on 24 February 1857 in the first list of Victoria Cross recipients. In view of Bell's intransigence regarding his own award, justice was done when Luke O'Connor had the privilege of being presented with his Cross by Queen Victoria at the first investiture on 26 June 1857. He had been given permission to delay his new overseas posting to receive his monarch's personal award. As commanding officer, Edward Bell was duty bound to accompany the 23rd Regiment on their way to China. Like other regiments sent to fight the Chinese, they were diverted to a new seat of conflict, the Indian Mutiny.

Further Campaigns

Luke O'Connor re-joined the 23rd Regiment in time to be part of the Lucknow relief column under the command of General Sir Colin Campbell. The regiment's crucial part in this operation was to hold a bridge over the river Gumti at the Secundra Bagh to enable the main force to evacuate the defenders of the Residency. During this phase, two Royal Welch Fusiliers, Lieutenant Thomas Hackett and Private George Monger, rescued a wounded soldier and were both awarded the VC.

Having brought the women and children to safety from Lucknow, Campbell's weakened and exhausted force was confronted by Tantia Topi's overwhelmingly superior Gwalior army at Cawnpore. On 6 December, in a fierce battle that proved to be the turning point of the Indian Mutiny, Campbell's men saved Cawnpore and defeated the Gwalior Contingent.

O'Connor and his comrades were involved in the final capture of Lucknow in March 1858. There followed much hard marching as the rebels were hunted down and finally defeated. In August, Luke O'Connor was promoted to captain and went with the regiment to Gibraltar for three years.

There followed a brief posting to Canada and another advance to brevet major. In January 1874, Sir Garnet Wolseley led a force composed of the Rifle Brigade, 23rd Regiment, 42nd Regiment and the West India Regiment to West Africa. This was to punish the Ashanti tribe for attacking the British trading post at Cape Coast. In what was a well-executed campaign, the 23rd helped defeat this war-like tribe in dense jungle and oppressive heat. This was to be O'Connor's last experience of action as he was brevetted Lieutenant Colonel in April.

His final overseas posting was to Gibraltar and on 21 June 1880, he was confirmed as Lieutenant Colonel. On 24 June 1884, he was made Commanding Officer of 2nd Battalion and retired on 2 March 1887. A week later, he was elevated to Major General.

Retirement

In retirement, along with Lord Roberts, he became Patron of the Bristol Indian Mutiny Veterans Association. More honours were bestowed upon him; he was made Companion of the Bath in 1906 and on 3 June 1913, he was knighted.

This remarkable old soldier died, unmarried, at his Mayfair home at the age of eighty-four on 1 February 1915. He was buried at St. Mary's RC Cemetery, Kensal Rise (Plot 1100). In a demonstration of the increasingly warm relations between Britain and Ireland, a ceremony honouring Luke O'Connor took place on 14 October 2007. A plaque was unveiled at King House, Boyle, Co. Roscommon, the former British Army HQ and where O'Connor served. In attendance for the first time were the General Officer Commanding Northern Ireland, Major General Phillip Trousdell and his Irish counterpart, General P. O'Callaghan, who jointly unveiled the plaque.

Despite Luke O'Connor's claim to be the first Victoria Cross winner, the man who could genuinely be said to be the very first VC was another young Irishman, Midshipman, or Mate, Charles Davis Lucas.

CHARLES LUCAS VC (1834-1914)

In what was a largely naval operation in the Baltic Sea, the Royal Navy planned to entice the Russian Fleet to leave their sanctuary at Kronstadt on the approaches to St Petersburg and do battle. Instead the Russians were content to remain in their fortified harbours and fortresses and watch the increasing frustration of the Royal Navy.

Instead of a straight forward Nelson-type battle, the Royal Navy had to be content with bombarding the Russian outposts, particularly the Åland archipelago that stretched across the Gulf of Bothnia between Finland and Sweden. It was here that three Victoria Crosses were won; Lieutenant John Bythesea, Stoker William Johnstone and Mate Charles Lucas. The latter performed his gallant act on 20 June 1854, in what was probably the first British action of the war against Russia.

Early Life

Charles Davis Lucas was born into a wealthy landowning family on 19 February 1834 at Drumargole, County Armagh. He joined the Navy in 1848 at the age of fourteen, the year the Irish Potato Famine was at its height. Serving first aboard HMS *Vanguard,* it was in his second ship, the forty-gun *Fox,* that he saw his first action in the Second Burmese War of 1852. Under the command of Commodore G. Lambert, *Fox* was part of the small squadron that attacked the heavily fortified enemy town of Martaban to great effect. Led by Commander Tarleton of *Fox,* a landing party attacked and captured the enemy stockades, spiking their guns and destroying their ammunition. Further action followed against Rangoon and Pegu. The end of the war resulted in the annexation of most of Burma to the East India Company.

With the outbreak of war with Russia in 1854, the greatest naval danger was seen as the Baltic Sea, where Russia's main fleet and her principle arsenals were situated. It followed that the main Anglo-French fleet was sent to the Baltic, but any hope that the Russians would oblige with a set piece naval battle was thwarted by the enemy's refusal to leave Kronstadt, their heavily-defended home port. The monotonous task of operating a blockade was alleviated by the occasional raid against land targets.

Before war had been declared, the Admiralty had the foresight to reconnoitre the Baltic area and despatched the new steam sloop, *Hecla.* Mate Charles Lucas had recently transferred to the *Hecla,* which left Hull on 19 February 1854. In a voyage of some 3,000 miles, she carried a team of surveyors, who drew charts and sought suitable anchorages for the large Anglo-French fleet. Several times *Hecla* used her superior speed to outrun Russian frigates; for she was better suited to speed than fighting, something later her captain seemed to forget.

Hecla's commander was the energetic and resourceful William Hutcheson Hall, a man who would play a prominent role in Lucas's life. As a young lieutenant, Hall had commanded the East India Company iron steam ship *Nemesis* during the First China War of 1840. With its shallow draught and armed with rockets, the Chinese called it the 'devil ship', as it created havoc amongst the enemy junks in Anson Bay. Hall further came to the Lordship's attention when he, and two other like-minded officers, proposed the establishment of a sailor's home in Portsmouth.

When *Hecla* returned from her Baltic mission, she joined the main fleet at Dover. The surveyors distributed their charts and briefed the commander, Sir Charles Napier, and his captains. The fleet, including *Hecla*, then set course for the Baltic.

VC Action

After the disappointment of the Russian fleet's refusal to fight, lesser targets were sought. It was *Hecla*, together with *Arrogant*, that first engaged the enemy amongst the Åland Islands at the mouth of the Gulf of Bothnia. Capturing the crew of a fishing boat, they compelled them to guide them through the shoals and scattered islets to look for enemy merchant ships which they suspected were at anchor. The Åland Islands were described by a naval officer:

'This granite archipelago encloses a perfect labyrinth of straits and bays studded with minor islands, and so fringed with reefs and banks as to make the navigation often impossible – always hazardous.'

As they were negotiating a narrow waterway, a Russian battery opened fire, but was quickly silenced by the forty-six-gun *Arrogant*. The following morning *Hecla* found herself in range of the guns of a Russian fort and, although she returned fire, she was no match for it. Fortunately, *Arrogant* arrived in time and, despite running aground, was able to silence the enemy guns. Finally, they found the three merchant ships, two of which had run aground. The third was taken by *Hecla* who, under fire from shore batteries and Russian infantry, took her in tow and steamed away with her prize. In the process, one man was killed and Hall was wounded in the leg by a spent musket ball.

This minor success received the thanks of the admiral-in-chief as well as the British Government and no doubt spurred Captain Hall to undertake a foolhardy attack against the formidable fortress of Bomarsund on the east coast of the main island in the Åland chain. In what should have been a reconnaissance led by Captain Hall, developed into a bombardment by three lightly armed ships against the solid walls of the three granite-built fortress towers and heavily fortified casements. The Russians had considerable superiority in firepower with over 100 guns against just thirty-eight (*Hecla* eight, *Odin* sixteen and *Valourous* sixteen).

Early in the fight, a live shell landed on *Hecla's* upper deck. A cry went up for all hands to fling themselves on the deck. One man ignored this advice. Twenty-year-old Charles Lucas ran forward, picked up the round shell with its fizzing fuse, carried it to the rail and dropped it overboard. It exploded with a tremendous roar before it hit the water and two men were slightly hurt. But for Lucas's prompt action, the consequences would have been far more serious.

Captain Hall showed his gratitude for the saving of his ship by promoting Lucas on the spot to Acting Lieutenant and, in his report, Hall was fulsome in his praise for Lucas's great presence of mind. In turn, Sir Charles Napier echoed this praise and recommended confirmation of Lucas's promotion.

Hall also exaggerated the damage inflicted upon the Russians and earned a stiff rebuke from the Admiralty for putting his ship in unnecessary danger and expending all his ammunition to little effect. Nonetheless, the news was well received by a British public hungry for some offensive movement from their much-vaunted navy. For a while, the name Bomarsund was the topic of conversation and a new coal mining village near Newcastle was even named after this obscure Baltic fortress.

For his bravery in saving the lives of his fellow crewmen, Charles Lucas was awarded the gold Royal Humane Society Medal. This large 51mm diameter medal was not intended for wearing, but Lucas had a ring and blue ribbon fitted. In 1869, official permission was granted for the wearing of the medal and a 38mm diameter medal was produced with a scroll suspension and navy blue ribbon. Just three years later, on 26 June 1857, Lieutenant Charles Lucas stood fourth in the line of recipients at the first investiture of the Victoria Cross and received his award from Queen Victoria. In effect, he received two awards for the same action.

Later Service

Lucas did not see any further combat but steadily climbed the promotion ladder. He served on *Calcutta, Powerful, Cressy, Edinburgh, Liffey* and *Indus.* In 1862 he was promoted to Commander and then to Captain in 1867, before retiring on 1 October 1873 as a Rear-Admiral. He moved to Argyllshire and shared a farm with his sister and her husband. He also owned a marble quarry and a half-share in a slate quarry. It was here that he received a message from his old commander from HMS *Hecla,* now Admiral Sir William Hutcheson Hall, summoning him to his death bed. Hall made an extraordinary request. He begged Lucas to take care of his wife Hilare and marry his only daughter Frances. Lucas, an incurable romantic, agreed.

They married in 1879 but the marriage was not a success. Frances proved to be arrogant, violent-tempered and far too aware of her position as a member of the Byng family, being the grand-daughter of the 6th Viscount Torrington. They made their home at Great Culverden, on the edge of Tunbridge Wells in a Decimus Burton-designed house. Charles Lucas occupied himself as a Justice of the Peace for both Kent and Argyllshire. It was after a train journey that Lucas found to his dismay that he had left all his medals in the carriage and they have never been recovered. Instead, he was issued with a duplicate group. The Indian General Service Medal with clasp to 'Pegu' is engraved with his details, as are both gold Royal Humane Medals. The Baltic Medal is blank, as is the reverse of the Victoria Cross.

Charles Lucas died peacefully at his home on 7 August 1914, just as Europe plunged into the madness of the First World War. He was buried the Byng's family plot in St Lawrence's Churchyard at the nearby village of Mereworth.

The main theatre in the war against Russia, however, was not in the Baltic, but in the Crimean Peninsula. Following the Battle of the Alma, the next major confrontation was the Russian advance on the British supply port of Balaclava. A field force of 25,000 commanded by Lieutenant General Pavel Liprandi appeared from the north-east, threatening the weakly-defended positions south of Sebastopol. The Russian assault began at 06.00 hours, on 25 October 1854, with the attack on the Turkish-manned redoubt on Canrobert Hill. In an unequal battle, the Russians overwhelmed the isolated redoubt and put the Turks to flight. Number 2 Redoubt on the Causeway Heights took the brunt of the next attack before capitulating. The brief resistance put up by the outnumbered Turks had bought time for the British to organised themselves to face the numerically superior enemy. As Redoubts 3 and 4 were overwhelmed, the Russian cavalry galloped down into the South Valley and probed towards Balaklava.

All that stood in their path was Sir Colin Campbell's 93rd Highlanders backed by Royal Marine artillery, 'W' Battery Royal Artillery and a few Turkish soldiers, who had been persuaded to stand and fight. At the extent of their range, the 93rd fired a volley, followed by another. Although it emptied a few saddles, it was the artillery fire that drove the horsemen back to the Causeway Heights. None the less, the line of Highlanders standing resolute in the path of a large cavalry charge was immortalised by *The Times* correspondent William Howard Russell who wrote of 'that thin red streak topped with a line of steel', later shortened to the more familiar 'thin red line'.

The Russians continued to probe the British defences and, having taken Redoubt 4, confronted General Scarlett's Heavy Brigade. In an almost slow-motion clash, the Heavies infiltrated the halted ranks of great-coated Russians and heaved their way through the mass. There were very few casualties but it was enough to cause the Russian cavalry to retreat from the field.

There was now a hiatus as the Russians appeared content to hold the area they had taken. Lord Cardigan's Light Brigade was assembled at the head of the North Valley and had been spectators of the Heavy Brigade's successful charge. They were drawn up below the Sapoune Heights where Lord Raglan and his staff were viewing the unfolding battle. From where they were watching they could see the Russians removing the Royal Artillery's cannon from the captured redoubts. Raglan sent a series of increasingly ambiguous and unclear messages to the Cavalry Commander, Lord Lucan, who was unable to see the redoubts from his position in the valley.

Exasperated by Lucan's inaction, Raglan dictated a note that was handed to an aide, Captain Lewis Nolan, a noted horseman. He had already shown contempt of the two Cavalry commanders and had grown impatient with Raglan's handling of the Light Cavalry. Skilfully descending the steep slope, the hot-headed Nolan handed Raglan's scribbled order to Lucan, who remained mystified as to where the cannon were. Contemptuously Nolan said: 'There, my lord, is your enemy, there are your guns!'

With that, he flung out an arm and pointed vaguely down the North Valley. All Lucan could see was a line of Russian cannon spread across the valley floor about a mile away. With no alternative but to obey, he conveyed the message to Cardigan to advance and attack the Russian battery. It was utter madness for there was also enemy artillery sited on the Fedioukine Hills to the left and batteries, infantry and cavalry on the Causeway Heights to the right. It is highly unlikely that the ranks of the under-strength regiments were informed of what they were about embark upon; an unsupported suicidal frontal attack on artillery, with both flanks held by the enemy.

As far as can be ascertained, the composition of the Brigade was made up of 126 men of the 4th Light Dragoons, 115 of the 8th Hussars, 142 of 11th Hussars, 126 of 13th Light Dragoons and 147 of 17th Lancers. Sickness, poor and scarce food, had taken a toll on the Brigade strength. The patched, dirty and tarnished clothing had replaced their once bright and colourful uniforms and their mounts had lost their parade-ground sleekness.

Early in the advance, Nolan, perhaps sensing the cavalry was heading in the wrong direction, spurred his horse across the front of the Brigade to divert them onto the Causeway Heights. A chance long range shot from a Russian cannon killed him and with it any chance of saving the doomed Brigade. As the advance gathered momentum and the Russian cannon began firing, the full magnitude of their task must have come as a shock to the soldiers, who had no alternative than to be swept along with their comrades. Saddles began to empty and horses went down with horrific wounds. Despite this, the gaps were closed up and the regiments kept their formations until they rode through the enemy battery and joined in a mêlée of confused fighting.

Confronted with an overwhelming force of Russian cavalry in rear of the cannon, the survivors were ordered to retreat. It was during this arduous and dangerous return that acts were performed that were later recognised with the awarding of the VC.

THE LIGHT BRIGADE VCs

The Charge of the Light Brigade was the result of confusion, human error and frustration. There was no strategic gain and afterwards the Light Brigade ceased to exist as a fighting unit. When the British public read of the Charge as reported by William Russell in *The Times*, their imagination was fired by the sheer bravery of British soldiers charging into the mouths of Russian cannon.

The poet laureate, Alfred Lord Tennyson, reinforced this view when he wrote his epic poem in praise of the Charge. In fact the death toll was only 110 out of the 666 men who took part in the charge, many of whom had their horses killed under them and returned on foot. Queen Victoria, ever proud of her 'unconquerable army', readily supported the idea that was gathering momentum, of a new gallantry award for all ranks. It would be nearly three years before the Queen presented the VC to two of the Light Brigade heroes.

When the Victoria Cross was instituted, rules or warrants were implemented to prevent the award from being diluted by being over-bestowed. The Charge was the earliest case where there had been so many examples of exceptional bravery against huge odds that the participating regiments were asked to vote for just one representative from each unit. Prince Albert wrote a memo as early as 22 January 1855 in which he made such a point:

'How is a distinction to be made, for instance, between the individual services of the 200 survivors of Lord Cardigan's Charge? If you reward them all it becomes merely a Medal for Balaclava, to which the Heavy Brigade and the 93rd have equal claims'. He then suggested:

'That in cases of general action it (the VC) be given in certain quantities to particular Regiments, so many to the Officers, so many to the sergeants, so many to the men (of the last say 1 per Company) and that their distribution be left to a jury of the same rank as the person to be rewarded … The limitation of the Numbers to be given to a Regiment at one time enforces the necessity of a selection and diminishes the pain to those who cannot be included.'

It was not until late 1856 to early 1857 that the commanding officers of all regiments who served in the late war were asked for their candidates for the Cross. In the case of the Light Brigade, just a single name per regiment was asked for initially, though none was submitted by the 8th Hussars and eventually the 17th Lancers had three men rewarded with the Victoria Cross. The Light Brigade VCs are:

SAMUEL PARKES (1813-1864)

Born in Wigginton near Tamworth, Staffordshire, in September 1815, Samuel Parkes was baptised at St Ethida's Church, Tamworth on 24 December 1815. He enlisted into the 4th Queen's Own Light Dragoons at the age of eighteen and was described as 6ft 2in tall, fair and well-built. Prior to enlistment, he gave his profession as labourer.

Parkes served with the regiment in India for nine and half years and participated in the Ghuznee campaign of 1839, for which he received a medal (the first Victorian campaign medal). After a three month voyage,

Parkes arrived back in England in March 1842. The Regiment was then sent to South Wales to keep civil order during the Rebecca Riots, a violent popular movement against the high tolls levied on the turnpikes in the country.

On 25 October 1854, Parkes was acting as Orderly to his commanding officer, Lord George Paget. In this role, Parkes needed to stay close to Paget and his Trumpeter, Hugh Crawford. During the retreat back to the Allied lines, Crawford's horse collapsed from exhaustion and he lost his sword. Parkes saw the helpless trumpeter being attacked by two mounted Cossacks and ran to defend him. Aggressively wielding his sword, Parkes managed to drive off the Russians. The two men then set off on foot and were joined by another trooper, John Eddon. They came upon their severely wounded Major Halkett, who urged them to save themselves, but Parkes hefted the officer onto his shoulder and attempted to carry him to safety.

Exhausted, Parkes was forced to lay down his burden just as a Russian officer called on him to surrender. Parkes refused and the Russian fired a pistol, which wounded him in the right hand. The three troopers made another run for their lines, but both Parkes and Crawford were captured and escorted back to the Russian lines. When the Russian commander, General Liprandi saw the tall Parkes, he commented; 'If you are a Light Dragoon, what sort of men are your Heavy Dragoons?'

After almost a year in captivity, Parkes re-joined the regiment at Balaclava. When it was learned of his outstanding exploits during the retreat, the regiment voted that Parkes should receive the newly-instituted Victoria Cross. His citation appeared in *The London Gazette* on 27 February 1857 and read:

'In the Charge of the Light Cavalry Brigade at Balaclava, Trumpet-Major Crawford's horse fell, and dismounted him, and he lost his sword; he was attacked by two Cossacks, when Private Samuel Parkes (whose horse had been shot) saved his life by placing himself between them and the Trumpet-Major, and drove them away by his sword. In attempting to follow the Light Brigade in the retreat, they were attacked by six Russians, whom Parkes kept at bay, and retired slowly, fighting and defending the Trumpet-Major for some time until deprived of his sword by a shot.'

Samuel Parkes had the honour to be the first Charger to receive his Cross from Queen Victoria at the Hyde Park Investiture on 26 June 1857. On 1 December 1857, Parkes was discharged from the Army at Aldershot after serving twenty-six years and 121 days.

After returning briefly to Tamworth, Parkes moved to London, where he married Ann Jeffry at St George's Church, Hanover Square. He was then employed as a park keeper or, more formally, 'Inspector of Hyde Park Constabulary'. It was while he was at work that he collapsed and died on 15 November 1864 at the age of forty-nine. The cause of death was given as 'Apoplexy' and he was buried in an unmarked grave in Brompton

Cemetery. A new marble gravestone was dedicated in 1999 and Parkes' VC group is on display at the Redoubt Fortress Museum, Eastbourne.

ALEXANDER DUNN VC (1833-1868)

Born 15 September 1833 at York (now Toronto), Alexander Roberts Dunn was the fifth son of John Henry Dunn, the Receiver-General of Upper Canada. His early education was at Upper Canada College, but he attended Harrow School when his father moved to England. In March 1852 at nineteen years of age, he was purchased a commission into the 11th (Prince Albert's Own Regiment) Hussars. Although it was the finest dressed of the Light Cavalry, the 11th was commanded by Lord Cardigan, notorious for falling out with his officers. When the regiment was sent to the Crimea, Cardigan was made Commander of the Light Brigade and the command of the regiment devolved on Lieutenant-Colonel John Douglas.

Alexander Dunn was another tall light cavalryman, at 6ft 2in, and described as handsome, good-natured and a dandy. To accommodate his height and reach, he had Wilkinson Sword make him a four-foot-long sabre, several inches longer than the regulation weapon. This formidable side arm was used to good effect as the 11th began to withdraw up the North Valley. Colonel Douglas had managed to keep his men together as they forced their way clear of the encircling Russian cavalry.

As they attempted this, Dunn spotted Sergeant Robert Bentley wrestling with his horse, which had been severely wounded, and was falling behind. The Russians sought him out as a straggler and closed in. Three of them concentrated their efforts to unseat him and as Bentley slid from his saddle, they prepared to finish him off. Seeing his predicament, Dunn wheeled round and spurred through the confusion of bodies, living and dead, to rescue him. With his thoroughbred mount rearing and side-wheeling in panic, Dunn slashed and thrust at the three assailants until he had killed them. With Bentley's mount unable to carry him, Dunn dismounted and placed him into his own saddle, slapped the horse on the rump to send it galloping after the rest of the 11th.

Now on foot, Dunn rushed to the assistance of Private Harvey Levitt from his troop, who had lost his horse and was being attacked by an enemy hussar. A quick powerful thrust dispatched the Russian and both men made their escape.

Whether or not he was sickened by the loss of so many of men, but Dunn applied to sell his commission just two weeks after the Battle of Balaclava. Despite Cardigan's attempt to block his resignation, Dunn did leave the Army. He then returned to his family's large estates in Canada. There may have been another reason for departing England and the regiment so precipitously, for he absconded with Colonel Douglas's wife, Rosa, some years' senior to him. A hurt and humiliated Douglas refused to grant her a divorce.

It must have been a most awkward situation when the 11th voted Alexander Dunn as their VC recipient and the sorely-tried Colonel Douglas submitted his own recommendation. The errant hero returned to England to receive his Cross from the Queen at Hyde Park on 26 June 1857. There is a story that he was loaned a uniform by Douglas, an honourable act indeed! Certainly, the 11th Hussars were in attendance at the ceremony and led by Lord Cardigan, to the delight of the huge crowds.

Returning to Canada, Dunn soon tired of wealthy inactivity and responded to Britain's call to help her stretched army quell the mutiny that broken out in India. He helped form a new regiment, the 100th (Prince of Wales Royal Canadian) Regiment and returned to England in 1858. Disappointingly, it was not required to go to India, being sent to garrison Gibraltar instead. By 1864, Dunn became a full colonel and was both the youngest colonel in the British Army and the first Canadian to command a regiment.

In 1864, Dunn exchanged into the 33rd (Duke of Wellington's) Regiment, described as a 'hard drinking' regiment. The Regiment was serving in India when they were ordered to Abyssinia as part of General Napier's punitive expedition against King Theodore. On 25 January 1868, the headquarters of the regiment had reached Senafe, about sixty miles from their base on the Red Sea. It was here that Alexander Dunn died in controversial circumstances.

That evening Dunn, accompanied by the regimental surgeon, James Sinclair, went out to shoot some game. They each took an Indian hospital orderly and shortly separated. Soon afterwards, Sinclair heard a shot and then saw Dunn's orderly running towards him shouting that the colonel had been shot. Sinclair found Dunn lying dead. The Regimental court of enquiry found that:

'The opinion that the death of Colonel Dunn was purely accidental caused by his own rifle exploding while he was in the act of using his brandy flask, when sitting on a stone, out shooting.' Given the inherent unreliability of hammer guns and the many shooting accidents that occurred, it seems the most likely explanation. However, this did not stop the rumours of foul play, as Dunn left a considerable fortune.

Alexander Dunn was buried at Senafe, in what is now Eritrea. Although his medals were bought by the Canadian authorities in 1894, the whereabouts of his grave became forgotten. Then in 1945, a British-led patrol of the Eritrean Mounted Police came upon a long neglected cemetery. The one grave that appeared to have been tended was that of Alexander Dunn and this was thanks to the occupying Italian army. There would be another long period of neglect, due in part to the war between Ethiopia and Eritrea, before Canadian soldiers serving as peacekeepers with the United Nations, accidentally came upon the grave. They cleaned up the area and erected a substantial cairn over the grave. There are now moves by the authorities to have the remains exhumed and brought back to Canada

JOSEPH MALONE VC (1833-1883)

Of Irish descent, Joseph Malone was born on 11 January 1833, in Eccles near Manchester. At the age of eighteen he joined the 13th Light Dragoons on 31 March 1851. Although he is often referred to as a corporal, in fact he leap-frogged this rank to become Lance Sergeant by the time he was sent to the Crimea.

Malone distinguished himself a month before the Charge, when he volunteered to lead three privates in the capture of a small baggage train and its escort. During the Charge, Malone's horse was killed and he was forced to retreat on foot. He came upon the badly wounded Captain Augustus Webb of the 17th Lancers and, despite the danger of marauding Cossacks and heavy fire from the flanks, remained with him until he was soon joined by two lancers, Berryman and Farrell, and fellow-light dragoon, Private James Lamb. Together, they carried the mortally-wounded officer back to the British lines. Sadly, their selfless act did not save Webb, for he died of his wounds at Scutari on 6 November.

Malone had an active war and was involved in the battles of Alma, Balaclava, Inkerman, Tchenaya and the expedition to Eupatoria. When it came to allotting one VC, Lamb and Malone drew lots and the latter won.

Malone was appointed Acting Quartermaster and Adjutant on 3 September 1855 and on 25 September 1857, *The London Gazette* announced his award. Queen Victoria presented him with his Cross at Windsor Castle on 21 November 1857. Promotion soon followed and he was appointed Riding Master of the 6th (Inniskilling) Dragoons on 7 September 1858 and sent to India. Coincidentally, he was joined by newly-commissioned ex-Chargers, Robert Davies, 11th Hussars and Charles Wooden, 17th Lancers. Malone married the daughter of Captain Weir, also a former 13th Light Dragoon ranker. His period in India was not pleasant, for he became embroiled in the notorious 'Crawley Affair', which culminated in the death under house arrest of the Regimental Sergeant Major and the court martial of the CO, Lieutenant Colonel Thomas Crawley.

The regiment returned in 1868 and served in Ireland. In 1881, Malone was promoted to Captain and the following year, the regiment was sent to Natal. On 28 June 1883, while sitting in the Officer's Mess at the Rugby Hotel, Pinetown, an ailing Captain Malone VC collapsed and died (some accounts state he died of bronchitis and others, typhoid). As was often the case in hot climates, he was buried the following day at St. Andrew's Churchyard. Nowadays, half the churchyard has been concreted over and made into a car park. Joseph Malone's VC group is held by the 13th/18th Royal Hussars Museum, Barnsley.

JOHN BERRYMAN VC (1825-1896)

Born at Dudley, Worcestershire on 18 July 1825, Berryman apprenticed as a cabinet maker. Thirsting for adventure, he enlisted in 'Bingham's Dandies', the 17th Lancers, who were then commanded by George Bingham, better known as Lord Lucan, the Cavalry Commander during the Crimean War. Berryman arrived in the Crimea as a corporal but was soon promoted to sergeant.

After the battle of the Alma, Berryman single-handedly captured three prisoners in an attack on the Russian baggage train. During the Charge, just as he reached the guns, his horse stopped dead, and Berryman was slightly wounded. Dismounting, he found that his mount's hind leg had been broken. He caught a riderless horse and as he swung into the saddle, the animal was hit in the chest throwing Berryman to the ground. As he retreated up the valley, he came upon Captain Webb and here his version of events varies from that of Joseph Malone's.

According to Berryman, he found Webb sitting stationary on his horse, unable to ride because of his painful leg wound. With the help of Lieutenant George Smith, who stood at the horse's head, Berryman eased the wounded officer out of his saddle. Smith then mounted the horse to ride for a stretcher. Amidst heavy firing, Berryman remained with Webb, despite being ordered to leave and save himself. When Sergeant Farrell came by, Berryman called to him to make a chair with their hands and carried Webb for about 200 yards, but the pain was too much and they were forced to stop. Joseph Malone was then asked to support Webb's leg and in this way, they managed to bring Webb to safety.

Farrell and Berryman then procured a stretcher and as they were carrying their wounded officer, the French Cavalry Commander, General Morris, met them and said to Berryman: 'Sergeant, if you were in the French service I would make you an officer on the spot!'

The regiment put forward Berryman's name for the new award and he was amongst the first list to be gazetted on 24 February 1857. His citation reads: 'John Berryman Troop Sergeant Major, 17th Lancers. Served with his regiment the whole of the war; was present at the Battle of the Alma, and also engaged in the pursuit at Mackenzie's Farm, where he succeeded in capturing three Russian prisoners, when they were in reach of their own guns. Was present and charge at the Battle of Balaklava, where his horse being shot under him, he stopped on the field with a wounded officer (Capt. Webb) amidst a shower of shot and shell, although repeatedly told by that officer to consult his own safety and leave him; but he refused to do so, and, on Sergt. Farrell coming up, with his assistance, carried Capt. Webb out of the range of the guns. He has also a clasp for Inkerman.'

On 26 June 1857, John Berryman received his Cross from Queen Victoria at the Hyde Park Investiture. The regiment was soon sent off to help quell the Indian Mutiny, but arrived too late to participate in any of the major engagements. It did, however, capture the ringleader, Tantia Topi. Berryman was commissioned in 1864 to Lieutenant and Quartermaster and, along with his fellow Charger VCs, Wooden and Malone, attended the First

Balaclava Banquet on 25 October 1875 at Alexander Palace. Over the years he was a great supporter of the Balaclava Commemoration Society and attended most Annual Dinners.

When news of the British disaster at Isandlwana on 22 January 1879 reached England, there was an urgent call for reinforcements, particularly cavalry. On arrival at Durban in early April, the 17th Lancers marched to Dundee in northern Natal, which was the jumping-off point for the Second Invasion of Zululand. Berryman accompanied the regiment and was present at the final defeat of the Zulus at Ulundi.

After thirty years' service in the same regiment, Berryman exchanged into the 5th (Royal Irish) Lancers, where he was made an Honorary Captain. When he retired in 1883, he did so as an Honorary Major. He died at his home on 27 June 1896 and was interred at St Agatha's Churchyard, Woldringham, Surrey.

JOHN FARRELL VC (1826-1865)

Born in Dublin in March 1826, John Farrell enlisted around 1842. He is one of those Victorian soldiers who left few clues to his background and there is no known photograph of him. In the Charge, his horse was killed and he teamed up with his fellow sergeant, John Berryman, in carrying Captain Webb back to the British lines. It is a curious thing that a second VC was bestowed to a 17th Lancer, when the rules had restricted the award to just one to each regiment. In any event, Farrell was gazetted on 18 November 1857 in an inaccurate citation that managed to both promote and demote fellow VC recipients:

'For having remained amidst a shower of shot and shell, with Capt. Webb, who was severely wounded, and whom he and Sergt-Major [*sic*] Berryman had carried as far as the pain of his wounds would allow, until a stretcher was procured, when he assisted the sergeant-major and a private of the 13th Dragoons [*sic*] (Malone) to carry that officer off the field'.

The regiment further rewarded him with promotion to Quartermaster Sergeant in March 1857. His taste for drink caused him to be reduced to private on 10 January 1858. This demotion lasted a matter of hours, for he was made up to sergeant again before the day ended. On 30 November 1864, he volunteered to exchange into the 18th Hussars but did not actually serve with them. Instead, he joined the Indian Army and the 2nd Light Cavalry.

Farrell's service with this regiment did not last long for he died of an abscess of the liver on 4 August 1865. He lies buried in an unmarked grave in Secunderbad and the whereabouts of his medals is unknown.

CHARLES WOODEN VC (1827-1876)

Born in London to German parents on 24 May 1826, Charles Wooden appears to have retained all his family's Teutonic traits. In 1845, he enlisted in the 17th Lancers and had attained the rank of sergeant by the time he was sent to the Crimea. He was not popular amongst his fellows, despite being regarded as a good soldier. Large, ginger-bearded, short tempered and humourless, he spoke with a strong German accent, despite being born in England. He gained a singular nickname, 'Tish me, the Devil', the answer he gave to a sentry who challenged him when returning to barracks after a drinking session. Somehow, the name seemed appropriate to his comrades.

During the Charge, Wooden had had his horse shot under him and managed to return to the British lines unscathed. Not so his temporary Commanding Officer, Captain William Morris, who had been badly cut about the head, captured and escaped and had two horses killed. The second fall had broken his right arm and some ribs, but he had managed to stagger almost to the British position, where he collapsed in great pain. It is not clear just how long he lay there; the time varies from a matter of hours to the following day. At length, an attempt was made by Turkish troops to carry Morris to safety, for he was laying just in range of the Russian guns on the Fedioukine Hills. The attempt ended when the Russians opened fire and the Turks bolted for cover.

Word reached the Light Brigade camp and Sergeant Wooden volunteered to accompany Surgeon James Mouat, 6th Dragoons, to bring in Captain Morris. The two men reached Morris and came under sporadic fire from the hills across the valley. Mouat managed to bind up the wounded officer's wounds and together he and Wooden carried Morris back into the Cavalry camp. Morris recovered from his wounds, but died four years later in India.

Wooden was promoted to Regimental Sergeant Major on 18 April 1856 and campaigned with the 17th Lancers during the Indian Mutiny. He probably had no aspirations of being awarded the Victoria Cross for what had not been a particularly hazardous rescue. In 1858, four years after the event, it must have come as a surprise when he learned that Surgeon Mouat had been awarded the Victoria Cross for saving Captain Morris. On 12 July, Wooden wrote to Mouat reminding him that he had assisted and shared in the danger they had braved together. Dr Mouat duly passed on Wooden's claim to the Horse Guards, together with his own recommendation. Horse Guards were reluctant but conceded that, for the sake of fairness, Wooden should also receive the VC. The citation read:

'*The London Gazette*, 26 Oct 1858. Charles Wooden, Sergeant-Major, 17th Lancers. Date of Act of Bravery; 26 Oct 1854. For having, after the retreat of the Light Cavalry, at the Battle of Balaclava, been instrumental, together with Dr James Mouat CB, in saving the life of Lieut-Colonel Morris CB, of the 17th Lancers, by proceeding under heavy fire to his assistance, when he was lying very dangerously wounded in an exposed situation.'

Note the date of the act of bravery – 26 October 1854 – the day after the actual Charge. The same date appears on Mouat's citation, which was either a clerical error or Morris did lay unattended overnight? It could be argued that Wooden's VC was not actually won during the Charge and, therefore, was not subject to the same rules that applied to the other recipients. It could also explain why the 17th Lancers ended up with three VCs for Balaclava, while the other regiments were represented by just one apiece.

Charles Wooden's pride in being awarded the Cross does not seem to have brought him either satisfaction or respect. Like many senior NCOs, he was granted a commission and joined the 6th (Inniskilling) Dragoons as Quarter-Master in 1860 at the cavalry station at Mhow, India. The Regiment was an unhappy one and had a large turnover of field officers. Ex-rankers like Wooden and his fellow VC, Joseph Malone, would find it nigh impossible to be accepted as equals in the class-conscious Officer's Mess. The following year, the atmosphere became positively poisonous with the arrival of a new Commanding Officer, Colonel Henry Crawley. Within a short period, Crawley had provoked a series of incidents that alienated most of his officers and led to the death of the RSM. Over the next four years, Wooden was repeatedly called upon to give evidence in the inquiries and trials that followed.

It must have been something of a relief when he transferred in 1865 into the 5th Lancers and then, finally in 1871, into the 104th (Bengal Fusiliers) Regiment. It was when the latter were stationed at Dover Castle that Wooden died in bizarre circumstances.

On the afternoon of Sunday, 25 April 1876, Wooden was found in his quarters, bleeding heavily from a head wound. A small pocket pistol, which had been fired twice, was found nearby. According to the doctor who attended him, Wooden managed to explain that he had a severe toothache and had attempted to shoot out the offending tooth. This extreme form of dentistry had resulted in the bullet being deflected into his brain. Wooden lingered until the following day before he died.

The other explanation offered was that he had committed suicide in either a fit of depression or because he suffered from blinding headaches. In the event, it was decided not to use suicide as the cause, so as to allow Wooden to have a Christian interment. The Regiment laid on a burial in St James Cemetery, with full military honours and the officers paid for the erection of a substantial headstone.

8th HUSSARS

There is one strange omission from this gallantry list; the 8th Hussars apparently did not submit a candidate for the Victoria Cross. The reason for this could be the fact that the Commanding Officer, Lieutenant Colonel Frederick Shewell, died at his home while on sick leave on 1 October 1855. This was around the time that the regiments began submitting their lists of recommended recipients and it could be that, with a change of commanding officer, this was overlooked or given a low priority. Two 8th Hussars Chargers were subsequently awarded the Cross; Lieutenant

Clement Heneage and Private John Pearson for gallantry at the Battle of Gwalior 17 June 1858.

The Battle of Balaklava was followed the following day a Russian attack on the 2nd Division on the extreme right flank of the British line before Sebastopol. Consisting of six battalions of infantry and four artillery pieces, the Russian advanced from the Karabelnaya suburb at the southern end of Sebastopol Bay on the afternoon of 26 October. Quickly overcoming the picquets, the Russians met stiff opposition from the Naval Brigade and units of infantry. In the brief skirmish, which became known as 'Little Inkerman', VCs were awarded to Lieutenant John Connolly, 49th Regiment, Sergeant Ambrose Madden, 41st Regiment, Major Gerald Goodlake, Coldstream Guards and Lieutenant William Hewett Naval Brigade.

This Russian foray had shown just how weak was the British right flank. Lord Raglan was conscious of this and appealed to the French for reinforcements for his depleted line. On the advice of their chief engineer, who thought the ground too difficult to defend with its scrubland and ravines, the French declined to help.

At dawn on 5 November, some 60,000 Russians with 234 guns and supported by two warships in Sebastopol Bay advanced up the scrub-covered heights at Inkerman on the British right flank. In mist-shrouded fighting by largely small formations of British infantry, the Russian were defeated and retreated back to Sebastopol. In this bitterly contested battle a total of twenty VCs were awarded including four for other actions in the war.

The bombardment of Sebastopol continued but the severe winter of 1854-55 all but destroyed the British army as a fighting force. Fresh recruits were sent and two bungled attempted in the summer to storm one of the main Russian strongpoints, the Redan, resulted in horrific casualties.

The date for the first attack chosen also had a political significance; 18 June, the fortieth anniversary of the Battle of Waterloo. A glorious allied victory would surely help to heal the wound that still festered between the former enemies. As the first troops scrambled out of their trenches, another blow to any chance of success was made when the artillery ceased their firing on the Redan. The Russian guns were now able to fire on the defenceless infantry as they staggered up the dusty slope. Soon the grapeshot and musketry was cutting the attackers down as soon as they left their starting positions. Great clouds of dust were thrown up adding to the confusion. It was a massacre from the very start. The survivors began to run back through the dust and smoke, chased by grape and canister fire, which added to the toll of dead and dying. Belatedly, the British artillery resumed firing, which helped cover the retreat.

A total of eighteen VCs were awarded but many were given for an accumulation of brave acts and not credited just for the Redan assault.

Similarly, the last attempt to take the Redan on 8 September failed mainly because the French launched their successful night time attack earlier than expected and Raglan felt honour bound to launch the British assault the following morning but to disastrous ends. In just two hours, 2,447 men were killed or wounded. As with the 18 June assault, twelve VCs were awarded but with the accumulation of previous gallant acts. The following day, the Russians withdrew across Sebastopol Bay leaving the city for the Allies to enter and so signalled the end of the war.

There was one Victoria Cross recipient who is overlooked as he did not participate in any of the well-known battles of the war, yet his story is a most remarkable one:

CHRISTOPHER TEESDALE VC (1833-1893)

When one thinks of the 1854-56 war with Russia, one thinks of the famous battles on the Crimean Peninsula or the naval actions in the Baltic Sea. It was for outstanding gallantry in these areas that 110 out of 111 VCs were awarded for that war. The odd man out was for an almost forgotten exploit on a front hundreds of miles from the main focus of the war. Yet, if the Russians had swept aside this tenuous defence, the war could have had a different outcome.

Kars was a fortified town on the Caucasian frontier in Eastern Turkey, some 1,800 kilometres from the capital, Constantinople. It lay in the path of the invading Russian army, who had routed the Turks in two battles. The demoralised remnants of the Turkish army fell back on Kars and it seemed only a matter of time before the Russians would take this strategically important town.

The British were aware that this remote region was important to them as the Russians could control the region and with it the vital overland route to Persia. From there, they could threaten India's North-West frontier. With this in mind, the Foreign Secretary, Lord Clarendon, appointed Colonel William Fenwick Williams as British Commissioner to the Turkish Army, Asia Minor, to report on the political and military situation in Kars and surrounding region.

Early Life

An officer in the Royal Artillery, Williams became one of the unsung heroes of the war. He was Canadian-born of Welsh stock and had considerable experience of the Armenian-Persia area to which he was being sent, having been seconded to the Ottoman army earlier in his career. He took with him as ADC, the twenty-one-year-old Lieutenant Christopher Charles Teesdale of the Royal Artillery. Christopher had been born 1 June 1833 to George and Rose Teesdale. George was serving as an officer in the Royal Horse Artillery at Grahamstown in South Africa, thus making Christopher the first South African-born VC. Two years later, the family moved back to England.

In 1848, Christopher entered 'The Shop', as the Woolwich Academy was known, and followed his father's footsteps into the Royal Artillery in 1852. It was during his first posting to Corfu, that he was appointed ADC to Colonel Williams. When Williams and Teesdale arrived in Kars on 24 September 1854, they found the situation and conditions about as bad as it could be. Poorly fed and clothed, the Turkish soldier was in no state to oppose the Russians. Corruption amongst the officers and politicians had robbed the common soldier of pay and food. A concerted attack by the Russian army would have undoubtedly taken Kars.

While Williams travelled the region, weeding out corruption amongst the pashas and trying to organise supplies and more troops, Teesdale was left at Kars. Largely by example and force of personality, he managed to instil discipline amongst the demoralised and listless soldiers. Kars itself was on a plateau dominated by an old fortress on a high crag. Around the town were a series of small forts and redoubts linked by breastworks. Teesdale organised work parties to build up those parts which had fallen into disrepair.

The following spring, the responsibility of these fortifications was taken over by the experienced Colonel A.T. Lake of the Madras Engineers and the widespread defences were strengthened and communications between the scattered strong points was greatly improved. The deplorable medical facilities were tackled by another Briton, Dr Sandwith, who did manage to ensure that the water supply was uncontaminated.

Fortunately the winter passed without the Russians being able to launch an assault. Promoted to the local rank of General, Williams continuously bombarded the Turkish authorities and the British Ambassador, Lord Stratford de Redcliffe, with requests and complaints, with no success. It was only when he appealed directly to Lord Clarendon that the situation marginally improved. In doing so, Williams made himself very unpopular with Constantinople.

With the siege of Sebastopol a priority, Kars was regarded very much as a side-show and there was very little chance of their situation significantly improving. Even when Sebastopol fell in September 1855, there was no thought of diverting resources to relieve the plight of the thousands of Turks and a handful of British holding a Russian army at bay.

In June, the Russians, under General Mouravieff had resumed operations against Kars. After a series of probes, he found that the defences were well organised and capable of withstanding an attack. Instead, he decided to start a blockade, cutting all communications and bringing up heavy siege artillery.

The Turkish infantry was in such a weakened state that there was no question of going on to the offensive. The only corps who was well trained was the artillery who outmatched their Russian opponents. Another positive point was that, despite their poor condition, the Turks were stubborn fighters when properly led and defending their own property. This was born out on 29 September, when the Russians launched their long anticipated assault.

VC Action

The following day, Christopher Teesdale wrote a long and detailed letter of the battle to his father. He had been patrolling around the line of works to the north-west of the town when, at 04.30 hours, he was startled by the flash and boom of a gun fired from a redoubt called Tachmash tabia. Spurring his horse to the redoubt he ascertained that the Russians were approaching across the valley below. Peering into the gloom, he saw a huge black mass making for his isolated position. The defenders fired rounds of case shot into the Russian columns, who diverted to the Turkish right and overwhelmed a small open breastwork. The Turkish soldiers took refuge in Teesdale's position in the Tachmash tabia. Teesdale then directed fire into the captured interior, which forced the Russians to take cover on the reverse side of the parapet. Teesdale wrote:

'Whilst this conflict occupied our attention on our left front, that part of the Russian column which had passed by on our right silently reformed amidst the darkness and, led by an intrepid officer rushed upon an almost unguarded point in our rear. So sudden was this assault that almost before I could rally a company to resist it, the Russians were swarming like bees upon the parapet and were already inside the work ...

'Every moment was now of such vital importance that ceasing my efforts to attract the attention of those who were fighting in front to their assailant in the rear, and shouting to the few who were around me, I rushed up into the salient already occupied by the enemy. This sudden impulse saved us. Those who had already penetrated were in a moment struck down on the platform where I stood and their gallant leader – as he was about to cross his sword with mine – received a ball in the centre of his forehead and fell backwards into the ditch. Seven Russian soldiers lay dead at my feet. Still the brave young volunteers who had made up the attacking column came swarming up, but the deadly and deliberate fire from within kept them in check and their bravest already lay thickly in and on the edge of the little ditch which surrounded the work.

'It was a terrible scene before the day broke; in the darkness and confusion Russians actually got inside our redoubt and three men were killed at my feet, while an officer, dashing over the parapet was shot down almost at the point of my sword.'

Teesdale saw that another large enemy column was about to mount its assault. Leaving his men, he went in search of a gun and crew and fortunately found one which had lost its way just as dawn was breaking.

'By dint of yelling and beating the gunners, I succeeded in attracting their attention to explain what I wanted. Leaving two men at the limber to supply nothing but grape, I managed with the help of four of the gunners to run the gun up into the salient. Acting as No.1, I pointed at the thickest of the mass that approached us which was but a few yards from the muzzle. Six times the iron shower tore through their ranks and left long lines of dead and wounded in their tracks. Then the attacking column in utter confusion from the rapidity of the fire broke and fled past the redoubt down the hill pursued by the infuriated Turks.'

The fighting continued unabated. 'The horrid carnage continued until, stopped by a mound of dead, and dislocated by the repeated discharges of grape, the Russians were brought to a standstill.'

Teesdale then performed an act that was the have an effect on his future experience with the Russians. During this stage of the battle, three Turkish soldiers pushed a wounded Russian officer back from the parapet and followed him over to finish him off with their bayonets. Teesdale spotted this and leapt over the breastwork and cut down the foremost Turk with his sword, calling in French to the Russian to surrender. This he did and was handed over to Dr Sandwith, who treated him so that he recovered from his wound.

While Teesdale was busy repelling the Russians at Tachmash, an equally desperate battle was taking place at the Inglis tabia on the northern side of Kars, which was eventually beaten off. Teesdale recalled:

'Incredible as it might appear, the last hour of that battle was fought with ammunition from the Russian dead. Sallies were made for no other purpose than to obtain the needful supply, and at one point, part of the garrison was employed in stripping off the pouches from the fallen on one side of the redoubt and throwing them up to their comrades who were thus able to repulse the enemy from the other side.'

Having sustained huge losses, the Russians began to fall back, but the energetic young Teesdale was not finished fighting.

'Tired of acting so long on the defensive, I mounted my horse, which had remained unhurt, and led a charge against the enemy's chasseurs and stragglers who, favoured by the ground, still kept shooting our men at leisure. This was no easy task, and on reaching the exterior of Tachmash tabia we found ourselves confronted by a regiment of the enemy – fresh men firing heavily along their front. It was the last remnant of the Russian infantry. The Turks still left alive in Tachmash tabia could no longer be restrained; seeing our plight they burst forth like a pent-up torrent from the redoubt and rushed with the blind fury of wild animals to our assistance – and the Russian regiment seemed to melt before them. In a moment the ground was thick with corpses and the survivors flying as best each one might. Our men could not be stopped until they had passed the road at the bottom of the hill – but the affair was over. A few more shots were fired at the fugitives when a band struck up and the soldiers were dancing amidst all the horrors of a battle ground.'

The casualty list was high. The defenders lost 1,096 killed or wounded, while the Russians were reported to have suffered the loss of 5,900 men and 250 officers.

This overwhelming victory proved to be a hollow one. The Russians tightened the ring around Kars and let starvation do their work. The onset of winter and lack of fuel added to the defenders misery. General Williams considered trying a breakout, but the weakened state of his men forced him to abandon such a plan. The famine cost the lives of over 2,000 soldiers and townsfolk. With no hope of outside help, Williams rode out to the Russian camp on 27 November to negotiate the surrender of Kars.

The Russian commander, General Mouravieff showed great humanity for the gallant defenders. His first act was to feed them with bread and soup before they were led off into captivity. The General sought out Christopher Teesdale and thanked him for his chivalrous act in saving the wounded officer.

The British prisoners then faced a long and arduous journey to Riazen. When they were released in the following March, they were presented to the Tsar at St Petersburg before departing for England. Soon after their arrival home, Williams was appointed KCB and, remarkably for someone so young and of junior rank, Teesdale was made a Companion of the Bath.

After a well-deserved leave, Teesdale took up his duty once more as ADC to the now promoted Major General Williams, who was made Commandant Woolwich District. In this capacity, he was in charge of the troop of horse artillery and the field batteries of foot artillery that were part of the great military parade at the first investiture of the Victoria Cross held at Hyde Park on 26 June 1857. No doubt, Lieutenant Christopher Teesdale was alongside him during this momentous occasion. It would only be another three months before Teesdale himself was gazetted for this new gallantry award. His citation that appeared on 25 September 1857 read:

'For gallant conduct, in having, while acting as Aide-de-Camp to Major-General Sir William Fenwick Williams, Bar. KCB, at Kars, volunteered to take command of the force engaged in the defence of the most advanced part of the works, – the key of the position – against the attack of the Russian Army; when, by throwing himself into the midst of the enemy, who had penetrated into the above redoubt, he encouraged the garrison to make an attack, so vigorous, as to drive out the Russians therefrom, and prevent its capture; also for having, during the hottest part of the action, when the enemy's fire had driven the Turkish Artillerymen from their guns, rallied the latter, and by his intrepid example induced them to return to their post; and further, after having led the final charge which completed the victory of the day, for having, at the greatest personal risk, saved from the fury of the Turks, a considerable number of disabled among the enemy, who were lying wounded outside the works – an action witnessed, and acknowledged gratefully before the Russian Staff by General Mouravieff.'

Later Life
On 21 November 1857, he was decorated with his Cross at a ceremony in the quadrangle of Windsor Castle by Queen Victoria. Her Majesty must have been impressed by Teesdale, for she appointed him Equerry to The Prince of Wales, a position he occupied until 1890. He also carried out his duties as ADC until 1864 to his old mentor, General Williams, who became Inspector General of Artillery.

Teesdale moved up the promotion ladder and, when he reached the rank of colonel, he was appointed ADC to the Queen. In 1887, he rose to Major General and was appointed Master of the Ceremonies by the Queen in 1890 before retiring in 1892. The following year, he suffered a minor stroke while on a lengthy visit to Germany. He returned to his estate at South Bersted in Sussex and suffered another seizure while attending church. He died the following day on 1 December 1893 at the age of sixty and was buried at St Mary Magdalene Churchyard.

General Teesdale's impressive array of medals and decorations does not include a British campaign medal. Kars was not regarded as part of the Crimean campaign, so Teesdale is one of the few men to be awarded the VC without an accompanying campaign medal.

For the 111 men who survived to receive their new gallantry medal and enjoy their moment in the sun, the aftermath was mixed. Many were able to handle the prestige and turn it to their advantage, particularly the officer-class. There were also many Other Ranks who returned to civilian life where their sacrifice was soon forgotten and they dropped back into a life of poverty, neglect and despair.

It is worth noting a rather morbid statistic regarding the awarding of these early Victoria Crosses. At a time when the average suicide rate in Britain was eight per 100,000, of the 111 men who were awarded the VC during the war against Russia, seven took their own lives. Admittedly, these tragedies took place over a period of years but they, nevertheless, point to the disturbing fact that many heroes were damaged by their experiences. Although there were to be tragedies associated with future VCs, there was never the same high proportion as these of the early recipients.

Chapter 2

Persian War, 1856–57

Number of VCs awarded	3
Number of VCs awarded to officers	3
Total awarded to British Indian Army	3

Origins of the War

The Anglo-Persian War, fought between 1 November 1856 and 4 April 1857, was a result of Persia's long-running disputed claim for the city of Herat in western Afghanistan. Several times during the nineteenth century the Persian forces had invested the city, which stands 100km inside the Afghan border, but had been forced to retreat. Since the last siege in 1847, diplomatic relations between Britain and Persia had been cordial. Britain's concern was more to do with Russian influence than the fate of a remote city. By the 1850s, it was perceived that Persia had been encouraged by Russia to once again annex Herat. A new ruler, Mohammed Yusuf Sadozai, had murdered the Shah and seized Herat causing alarm in Britain and India. Diplomatic protests from Britain brought no response, so war was declared on 1 November 1856.

The campaign was initially led by Major General Stalker but he was succeeded by Major General Sir James Outram and was fought in two locations – on the Persian Gulf and in southern Mesopotamia. It was decided to mount amphibious landings rather than march through Afghanistan and risk supply problems. Thanks to superior technology, organisation and discipline, victory was gained despite a numerically superior enemy and extended supply lines. The campaign was conducted largely by officers and men of the Indian Army and Navy and got under way on 12/13 November with a landing near the Persian Gulf port of Bushire.

Under the command of General Stalker, the first division, with the exception of HM 64th Regiment, consisted entirely of men of the Bombay Army. These included squadrons of the 3rd Cavalry and Poona Horse, the 2nd European Light Infantry, the 4th (Rifles), the 2nd Belooch Battalion and

20th Regiment. Together with units of artillery and engineers, the force had a fighting strength of 5,670 men.

The expedition slowly made its way up the Persian Gulf until it landed at Halilah Bay about twelve miles from Bushire. The few enemy soldiers that appeared on the shore were soon dispersed by naval gunfire and the British made an unopposed landing. The Old Dutch Fort of Reshire, was well defended and blocked the route to Bushire. On 9 December, the British stormed the battlements and the Indian Army's first Victoria Cross was won.

One of the three VCs that resulted from this campaign was that of John Augustus Wood:

JOHN AUGUSTUS WOOD VC (1818-1878)

Wood was born 10 June 1818, at Fort William in the Scottish Highlands. The son of an Indian Army general, he attended the HEIC College at Addiscombe and gained a commission in the 20th Bombay Native Infantry. Like most soldiers who joined the Honourable East India Company (HEIC) Army he was to spend the remainder of his life in the East.

He was promoted to lieutenant and saw his first service in the First Afghan War of 1842 and participated in Sir Charles Napier's conquest of Scinde in 1843. Promotion was slow and by the time he landed in Persia, he had only attained the rank of captain, commanding the Grenadier Company of his regiment.

VC Action

A fellow officer of the 20th, Lieutenant F.W. Brown, described the attack on Reshire: 'On the morning of Tuesday the 9th, we were again on the move, and had a very dusty march of it for about 5 miles, when we came in sight of Reshire, which is an old Dutch Fort close to the sea. It was full of men and a very strong position; the walls were nothing but heaped up sand with a deep dry ditch around the sand side.

'The ground all around it was broken, covered with loose stones and prickly hedges, to say nothing of great yawning wells without any parapets round them. The artillery were brought up and played at it for some time, but soon found it quite useless as all the balls struck harmlessly in the sand. The ships too tried too but, after killing one of the 2nd European soldiers, they thought it as well to stop.

'Out now went the Light Infantry, the 4th Rifles going off to the left, our Brigade deployed in line and advanced, covered by our Light Company and that of the 64th. The 2nd Brigade was on our left in the same order. It was dreadful walking and almost impossible to keep a proper line and presently the bullets began to pitter-patter among our ranks. Soon, Col. Stopford (64th) went on with the Light Inf. And for a time there was no one to give orders. He turned round and called for the Brigade to advance, but before we got to him he fell from his horse, shot through the heart. Still, there seemed a hesitation in going on till our Regt. gave a cheer and rushed straight to the front and, in less than no time, were through the ditch and swarming up the earthwork like ants. Luckily there were two old breaches in it, one to the right and the other to the left, and through these we rushed and were first in the place.

'Then began a most desperate fight as they (the Persians) had dug large holes behind their walls and filled them with 30-40 men each, who jumped up and fired straight at us. Captain Wood fell wounded all over, but none of them serious ones. Just before he dropped, he ran a man through with his sword …'

In fact, Wood was the first man on to the parapet, closely followed by two of his men. Although seven musket balls struck him, he was able to kill the enemy leader and inspire his men to carry the position. Captain Wood's wounds, although not life-threatening, were nevertheless painful and debilitating, which compelled him to leave the expedition for a while and returned to Bombay. At the suggestion of a friend, he paid a visit to General Sir James Outram, with the purpose of asking for the command of a regiment of Irregular Cavalry. He later recalled their conversation:

'When I called on for Sir James Outram in Bombay the 3rd or 4th January (1857) he spoke very kindly when he found that I was the officer who led the assault at Rushire and was the first in the place … I took the opportunity of saying, "I hope, Sir James, you will not consider it improper of me, if I ask you to give me command of one of the Irregular Cavalry Regt. about to be raised". He said, "The gallantry you have displayed gives you a claim upon me and I will recommend you to Major Genl. Jacob. Of course, I do not interfere with him.'

Later Life

Unfortunately for Wood his application for a command of Irregular Cavalry was turned down and the only recognition he received was to be made Brevet Brigade Major. He returned to Bushire, where he spent eight uncomfortable and dispiriting months. He began to dwell on the lack of official thanks for his exploits at Reshire and began to yearn for the newly-instituted Victoria Cross. He wrote in his diary 27 March 1857 of a picnic visit to Reshire, in a somewhat garbled fashion: 'It looks very different to what it did, where I had the men of the 20th up its Eastern face, near the tree where I was afterwards laid and where our firstline hospital was, it looks a much higher place, the ditch looks also deeper and broader that I thought then and described it. The excitement of the moment did away with the difficulties – that I was first attempted to show the contrary. That is, that they came in as soon as me and my company, however that the attempt deprived us of our right … my immediate superiors not having pushed my claim. It is a bitter pill to find one's self ever crushed, and every attempt made to depreciate one – I feel I ought to feel thankful that my life was spared, that, although I received 8 wounds, not one was fatal. Everyone says that I ought to get the Victoria Cross, but no one applies for it for me.'

By April, the war was over and the Shah had agreed peace terms. On 1 August, John Wood received the shattering news that his young son, Johnnie, had died. Finally, on 28 September, he embarked on *Melbourne* and reached Bombay on 20 October. Wood's hope for a Victoria Cross was later fulfilled through the letters written by fellow officers who had witnessed his exploit. These were sent to Sir James Outram, who forwarded the claim to London with this being the citation in *The London Gazette*:

'John Augustus Wood, Capt., 20th Bombay Native Infantry. On 9 December 1856, Capt. Wood led the Grenadier Company which formed the head of the assaulting column sent against Bushire. He was the first man on the parapet of the fort, where he was instantly attacked by a large number of the garrison, who suddenly sprang on him from a trench cut in the parapet itself. These men fired a volley at Capt. Wood and the head of the storming party, when only a yard or two distant from that officer but although Capt. Wood was struck by no less than seven musket-balls, he at once threw himself upon the enemy, passed his sword through the body of their leader, and being closely followed by the men of his company, speedily overcame all opposition, and established himself in the place. Capt. Wood's decision, energy and determined valour undoubtedly contributed in a high degree to the success of the attack. His wounds compelled him to leave the force for a time; but with the true spirit of a good soldier he rejoined his regiment, and returned to his duty at Bushire before the wounds were properly healed.'

John Wood was invested with his coveted VC in Dacca in January 1861. Wood finally retired from the Indian Army as a Brevet Colonel on 12 February 1870 and died on 23 January 1878 at Poona from 'concussion of the brain' as a result of a riding accident. After his gallant charge at Reshire, John Wood's life was never again a happy one, caused by his injuries and the death of his little boy. He was buried in St Mary's Churchyard, Poona.

When General Outram took command in January 1857, he decided to attack the Persians at Koosh-ab. The battle was the largest single engagement of the war and significant for the charge of the 3rd Bombay Light Cavalry against an infantry square. In this action, two Victoria Crosses were won; Lieutenant Arthur Thomas Moore, who broke into the square, and Captain John Grant Malcolmson who followed up and rescued him.

A peace treaty was agreed on 4 March in Paris, but the news took a month to reach Persia. During these four weeks, three river steamers carrying just 150 British soldiers pursued some 8,000 enemy to Ahwaz. There they landed and destroyed the magazines and supplies so ending the fighting and securing Herat for the future.

Chapter 3

Indian Mutiny, 1857–59

Number of VCs awarded	182
Number of VCs awarded to officers	76
Number of VCs awarded to other ranks	102
Number of VCs awarded to civilian volunteers	4
Total awarded to HEIC	66
Total awarded to Royal Navy	5
Total awarded to British Army	111

Origins of the War

The Honourable East India Company (HEIC), an English joint-stock company, was formed to trade with the East Indies but ended up trading mostly with the Indian subcontinent. The HEIC was one of the greatest commercial enterprises ever seen and, as it grew, it was allowed to organise its own armies. Over a period of a century, three quite distinct armies came into being at different times and places. In chronological order these were the armies of the Presidencies of Bombay, Madras and Bengal, formed to protect the HEIC's growing expansion throughout India's interior. The British-born officers were trained at the East India Company Military Seminary at Addiscombe, near Croydon in Surrey. It soon became colloquially known as Addiscombe College. The attraction for would-be officers was that the purchase system, prevalent in the British Army, was not used in the HEIC Army; this enabled students from a less-privileged background the chance to advance.

As the decades passed, so the quality of British administrators and officers declined. Although 'John Company's' profits slumped, there was still money to be made through corruption and nepotism. Lassitude and a growing contempt for her Indian subjects by second-rate white employers increasingly opened a void between the rulers and the ruled. Even in the 1840s there was a worry that the small number of British regiments would be overwhelmed by those of the native regiments if there was a mutiny.

Colonel Colin Campbell (later General Sir Colin Campbell) then commanding the Lahore garrison wrote in1847:

'The Sikhs might come down … any night they pleased and butcher the whole corps, officers and men, when in bed … As a precaution, I ordered a double sentry to be placed at the top of the gateway between dark and daylight, to report any stir that might be heard in the citadel, or the tread of feet in numbers, like the march or movements of troops. The precaution will prevent our actually being taken by surprise, inasmuch as we may have time to fall in.'

Another officer who urged caution was General Charles Napier:

'In India, we who take these pains are reckoned cowards. Be assured that English officers think it a fine dashing thing to be surprised – to take no precautions. Formerly it was an axiom in war that no man was fit to be a commander who permitted himself to be surprised; but things are on a more noble footing now!'

This separation between officers and men caused particular resentment amongst the native soldiers (sepoys), especially those serving in the Bengal Army. There had already been rebellious incidents amongst some of the Bengal native regiments and it was an accumulation of grievances rather than a single event that triggered the outbreak in May 1857. The Bengal Army drew its recruits from higher castes as opposed to those Bombay and Madras, who enlisted more localised and caste-neutral sepoys. The domination of higher castes in the Bengal Army was one of the factors that led to the rebellion. There was a growing irritation that the Bengal Army was receiving special treatment as they were the only part of the Company's army that refused to serve overseas.

The General Service Enlistment Act of 1856 was passed to take soldiers out of India to places like Persia, Burma and China. As a concession to the Bengal Army, this only applied to new recruits who had to accept this commitment. The serving high-caste sepoys, however, saw this as the thin end of the wedge and added this to their list of grievances.

The Bengal Army further divided itself, with the infantry being Brahmins, high-caste Hindus, and Rajputs, while the cavalry, who lived apart, were for the most part, Muslims. Promotion was extremely slow and based purely on time-served rather than talent. Another fear was the increasing presence of British missionaries and chaplains, which was interpreted as threat to their beliefs and there was a real fear of mass conversions to Christianity.

There were many other factors which caused the rebellion. For the feudal nobility it was the Company's refusal to recognise the adopted children of princes as legal heirs, which prompted rebel leaders such as Nana Sahib and the Rani of Jhansi to take up arms. Also, the land reforms which sought to improve the lot of the peasant only inflamed animosity not only with the land-owners but with the peasants themselves.

Sir Charles Napier afterwards repeated the prediction that: 'When nothing else was left to conquer in India we should have to conquer our native Army.'

The spark that finally ignited this powder keg of resentment was the new Enfield rifle and its ammunition; greased cartridges. Before loading the new percussion rifle, the sepoys had to bite off the end of the paper cartridge and ram it down the barrel. The rumour soon spread that the paper cartridge was impregnated with animal fat – an anathema to both Hindu and Muslim. Too late the cartridge was withdrawn and concessions were made including allowing the sepoys to grease the cartridges themselves. But to no avail – the British were still seen as attempting to defile the sepoys' religion. At the beginning of 1857, there were several refusals to obey orders to use the new cartridge leading to one regiment being disbanded and a sepoy firing on his officer. Unfortunately, the senior officers responded with harsh and humiliating punishments culminating in the bloody mutiny at Meerut on 10 May.

After an orgy of blood-letting and with no clear purpose in mind, the mutinous native troops left Meerut for the seat of the Moghul ruler at Delhi. Soon the rebellion spread throughout the northern states with isolated British communities being slaughtered or put under siege. With few British regiments to call upon, it took a while for the authorities to react. Initially, outnumbered columns were sent to rescue those who were besieged after having dealt with the main objective – the ejection of the rebels from Delhi.

The recapture of Delhi had become a priority for the British. The hastily-raised force of 4,000 men had successfully occupied the Delhi Ridge but was far too weak to attempt to retake the city itself. Faced by over 30,000 mutineers they were hard-pressed to keep hold of this tenuous foothold so close to the city. As reinforcements gradually arrived from the Punjab, including a siege train of thirty-two guns and 2,000 men under the command of Brigadier General John Nicholson, it was now thought possible that Delhi could be taken, despite the barely improved disparity of numbers.

To prepare for the attack, the mutineers had to be pushed back from their positions between the city and the Ridge. Comparatively few in number, the British attack was focused on the north face of the Delhi defences between the Water Bastion, by the River Jumna, and the Moree (Mori) Bastion a mile away to the west, with the Kashmir Gate in between as the prime target.

For just over a week, the sappers worked under heavy fire from the city to build emplacements for the fifty-four guns and mortars. The most distant battery was 700 yards away, with the closest only 140 yards. As they were completed, the artillerymen brought up their cannons and mortars and began bombarding the twelve-feet-thick walls. Concentrating their fire, the artillery made two substantial breaches between the Water Bastion and

Kashmir Gate. The reconnaissance on the night of 13 September persuaded General Wilson and Brigadier Nicholson that the attack should proceed the following morning – 14 September.

Probably the VC feat most associated with the assault on Delhi was the blowing up of the huge double doors that blocked the entrance to the Kashmir Gate. The whole operation was reliant on this near-suicidal attempt, which was accurately termed a 'forlorn hope.' Lieutenant Colonel Richard Baird-Hope, commander of the Bengal Sappers and Miners, selected Lieutenant Duncan Home to lead the 'explosion party' made up of three other men carrying canvas bags containing twenty-five pounds of black powder. The bags would be laid against the doors with fuses exposed ready for firing. Following right behind was the 'firing party' of six men led by Lieutenant Philip Salkeld. They carried a slow match and small sacks of sand to hold the explosive bags firmly against the doors. Once the fuse had been lit, the party would join Home's party and take cover in the ditch or moat beneath the Kashmir Gate.

DUNCAN HOME VC (1828-1857)

Born in Jubbulpore, Central Provinces on 10 June 1828, Duncan Charles Home was the son of Major General Richard Home of the Bengal Army. As with many sons of serving Indian officers, he was sent to England at the early age of eight for his education. As planned, he progressed to the HEIC Seminary at Addiscombe and passed out head of his class in July 1846. After further instruction with the Royal Engineers at Chatham, he returned to India as a subaltern in the 3rd Company, Bengal Engineers. He arrived in time to take part in the final battle at Goojerat in the Punjab Campaign (Second Sikh War) in 1849.

Home spent five years working more as a civil engineer that a military man, supervising the construction of canals in the Punjab. By taking on civilian projects, junior officers could supplement their income. It also meant that he spent even less time with his men, something that further discontented the native sepoys. In 1854, at the end of his civilian work, he was promoted to lieutenant.

When news of the Meerut mutiny reached the Punjab, Lieutenant Home was delegated to select 160 of his best men, now named the Punjab Sappers, and take them to the British Camp at Delhi. Home and his canal diggers arrived on 20 August and were immediately assigned to preparing gun emplacements for the forthcoming assault. On 13 September, Duncan Home had been with one of the reconnaissance parties that had crept forward to examine the breaches in the walls. When he returned at midnight, he learned that he had been selected to lead the 'explosion party'.

VC Action

Soon after dawn the two parties led by Home and Salkeld made their way from the ruined Ludlow Castle, about half a mile north of the Kashmir

Gate, and taking advantage of any remaining cover reached the open ground leading to the gate. Moving as fast as their twenty-five-pound loads would allow, they made it to the deserted outer gate and were joined by skirmishers from the 60th Rifles. Now they had to negotiate the timber bridge that crossed the ditch, which had been made more hazardous by the removal of much of the cross planking.

Braving a hail of fire, Home was first across the bridge. Quickly dumping his canvas powder bag hard against the right leaf of the door, he jumped for cover in the ditch. Although Lieutenant Home wrote a report, it was Sergeant Smith's account that has the authentic feel for the danger and noise of the action:

'I went on, and only Lieut. Salkeld and Sergt. Burgess were there; Lieut. Home and the bugler had jumped into the ditch, and Sergeant Carmichael was killed as he went up with his powder on his shoulder, evidently having been shot from the wicket while crossing the broken part of the bridge along one of the beams. I placed my bag, and then, at great risk, reached Carmichael's bag from in front of the wicket, placed it, arranged the fuse for the explosion and reported all ready for Lieut. Salkeld, who held the slow match. In stooping down to light the quick match, he put out his foot, and was shot through the thigh from the wicket, and in falling had the presence of mind to hold out the slow match, and told me to fire the charge. Burgess was next to him and took it. I told him to fire the charge and keep cool. He turned round and said, "It won't go off, sir; it has gone out, sir." I gave him a box of lucifers, and as he took them, he let them fall into my hand, he being shot through the body at the wicket also, and fell over after Lieut. Salkeld. I was then left alone, and keeping close to the charge, seeing where the others were shot, I struck a light, when the port-fire in my fuse went off in my face, the light not having gone out as we thought.

'I took my gun and jumped into the ditch, but before I had reached the ground the charge went off, and filled the ditch with smoke so I saw no one. I turned while in the act of jumping, so that my back would come to the wall to save me from falling. I stuck close to the wall, and by that I escaped being smashed to pieces, only getting a severe bruise on the leg, the leather helmet saving my head.'

As soon as the door was blown off, Home ordered Bugler Robert Hawthorne of the 52nd Regt to sound the 'advance' for Colonel Campbell's column to come on and take the Gate. Despite the dust, Hawthorne stood in the centre of the ditch, moistened his lips and sounded the agreed signal. About fifty yards to the rear, Campbell strained to hear the bugle call above the tumult of battle. Sending his orderly bugler forward to listen, he received a wave of acknowledgement, and drawing his sword, led his column forward.

Colonel Baird-Smith was unstinting in his praise for this operation while Major General Archdale Wilson went even further. As he was General

Officer Commanding, he felt empowered to recommend the Victoria Cross to Home, Salkeld, Smith and Hawthorne. Salkeld, who was mortally wounded, evidently learned of this before he died on 10 October. Strictly speaking, Home, Salkeld and Smith were not eligible to receive the VC as they were not members of Her Majesty's Army. This problem was rectified by a new Warrant dated 29 October 1857, which included members of the HEIC. It did not get around the fact that Home and Salkeld both died before the Queen had approved of their awards and the original VC Warrant made no provision for posthumous awards.

It is one of the anomalies of the Victoria Cross that Home and Salkeld were regarded as special cases and their Crosses awarded and sent their families. Carmichael and Burgess would probably also have been rewarded, but they had the misfortune to die before Archdale Wilson could confer the award. All the Indian sappers received the Indian Order of Merit, promotion and grants of land.

Once the door had been blown, Home remained in the ditch while Campbell's No.3 column dashed across the bridge and through the Gate. Pausing to make sure the wounded were taken care of, he climbed out of the ditch and followed Campbell's men into the city. He caught up with them locked in a savage hand-to-hand battle amongst the narrow streets. Unable to join in the fighting, he found a sheltered corner and fell asleep, having been awake for over thirty-six hours.

When he awoke, he re-joined the advance and was slightly wounded. For the next few days, Home was with the troops as they closed in of the Royal Palace. Repeating his feat at the Kashmir Gate, Home dashed forward, placed an explosive charge and blew in the doors. By 20 September, the city was in British hands and the surviving mutineers streamed away to the south and east.

Last Days

Home joined one of the columns that went in pursuit of mutineers. He was appointed Chief Field Engineer in Colonel Greathed's column which left Delhi on 24 September. On 28th, they caught up with a strong force of rebels at Bolandshahr and, after a sharp fight, captured the town. From there, cavalry patrols were sent out to scour the surrounding countryside and one reported that a small, deserted fort at Malagarh had been used as an arsenal. They also reported that it was in a dangerous condition with large quantities of munitions scattered all about.

Duncan Home was given the task of blowing up the fortifications and making the area safe. For the next three days he worked with his sappers and some men of the 9th Lancers sorting through what could be safely saved and what should be destroyed. On the third day, with his work nearly completed, he was killed. In a letter to Home's brother, fellow-Bengal Engineer, Lieutenant Arthur Lang described what happened:

'I saw him run up to the slow-match with his port-fire in his hand. Heaven only knows how, but instantaneously the mine sprung, to our horror! We rushed down and called all men to dig, but after a moment I looked round to see if I could see him anywhere near, and in a hollow some fifteen yards off I found your poor brother's body. He must have been killed instantly…Fancy escaping from the blowing of the Cashmere Gate, where he and Salkeld earned the Victoria Cross, to meet his end in exploding mines before a deserted fort. It is not now half an hour since the accident occurred.'

Duncan Home's VC was sent to his parents. Sometime in the 1920s it was lost when the son of the owner took the VC outside the house to play soldiers with it in a field. After intensive searches, then and later, it has never been found.

With the conclusion of the Persian War, the commander of the 2nd Division, Brigadier General Henry Havelock, returned to Calcutta where he learned that he was to command a Moveable Column in place of General Anson, who had died. The column was to march to give support to Sir Hugh Wheeler at Cawnpore and Sir Henry Lawrence at Lucknow.

There were many problems to overcome before Havelock could begin marching up the Great Trunk Road, amongst which was lack of transport; a shortage of gunners to man the six-gun battery; too few cavalry and the worse season of the year to embark on a campaign, with its debilitating heat interspersed with torrential rain. One redeeming note was that Havelock would have the 64th (Staffordshire) Regiment and the 78th (Ross-shire) Highlanders who had served him well in Persia.

The transport problem was sorted out and the shortage of gunners was resolved with the transfer of infantrymen who had some knowledge of working the guns. Besides the thirty Sikh irregular cavalry, another eighteen former officers of mutinied regiments, a couple of infantrymen and a few civilians who volunteered as horsemen. The only thing he had no control of was the extreme conditions in which his men had to march.

Finally, on 25 June, Havelock's Moveable Column left Calcutta on a march to Cawnpore that would see them fight a series of battles and defeating an enemy many times larger. This scratch column consisted of about 600 men each of 64th Regiment and 78th Highlanders, a six-gun battery, thirty Sikh Irregulars and eighteen Mounted European Volunteers. Passing first through Benares and then on to Allahabad, Havelock's men were marching in the wake of Colonel James Neill's avenging force. Along the route was evidence of the terrible indiscriminate retribution Neill and his men had wreaked on the mutineers and the largely innocent villagers. The route was lined with trees and hastily-made gallows which still displayed their grisly human remains. Finally, the column caught up with

Neill at Allahabad on 30 June and the two forces were combined under Havelock.

On 3 July news was received of the terrible massacre at Cawnpore where the male survivors of General Wheeler's defence had been tricked and slaughtered at Satichaura Ghat. This spurred on the Moveable Column which left Allahabad and forced marched its way to towards Cawnpore, fighting a series of battles as they approached their destination.

On the 16 July, the Column reached the village of Aherwa about four miles from Cawnpore. Here they were confronted with the large force commanded by Nana Sahib, one of the prominent rebel leaders, but far from their most skilful. In a fierce fight lasting several hours, Havelock's exhausted command managed to drive the enemy from the field. In doing so, the first of several Victoria Crosses was won in highly controversial circumstances.

HENRY MARSHMAN HAVELOCK VC (1830-1897)

Brigadier General Henry Havelock had employed his son, also named Henry but familiarly called Harry, as an aide of his staff in the Persian War and did so again in the current conflict. Harry was born of 6 August 1830 at Cawnpore. When he was just fifteen, he was commissioned as Ensign with the 39th (Dorset) Regiment before becoming a lieutenant by purchase with 86th (Royal Ulster) Regiment. He then transferred to the 10th Regiment as Adjutant in 1852 and was appointed to his father's staff for the Persian War and the Indian Mutiny.

Towards the end of the battle at Aherwa, which is more commonly referred to as the First Battle of Cawnpore, Nana's force had pulled back to a position where they were supported by a 24-pounder. The British attack began to falter as casualties mounted from this well-sited gun. With the 64th and 78th taking cover after their huge efforts in pushing back the enemy, General Havelock called for one last charge to take the 24-pounder which stood between them and Cawnpore.

VC Action

Accounts of what happened next widely differ. The 64th was chosen to head the attack led on foot by their commander, Major Thomas Stirling, whose horse had been shot. Harry Havelock, the General's ADC, also placed himself in the front of the regiment on horseback and at walking pace, headed directly for the enemy's cannon. All the time the regiment was under heavy fire but when they got within range, they charged with the bayonet and soon captured the gun putting Nana's men to flight.

For his prominent involvement in the advance, Harry Havelock was provisionally recommended for the Victoria Cross by his father. This was later endorsed by General James Outram, who arrived in Cawnpore on 16 September to take overall command.

Lieutenant Havelock's citation published in *The London Gazette* on 15 January 1858 reads: 'In the combat at Cawnpore, Lieutenant Havelock was my Aide-de-camp. The 64th Regiment had been under much artillery fire, from which it severely suffered. The whole of the infantry were lying down in line, when, perceiving that the enemy had brought out the last reserved gun, a 24-pounder, and were rallying around it, I called up the regiment to rise and advance. Without another word from me, Lieutenant Havelock placed himself on his horse, in front of the centre of the 64th, opposite the muzzle of the gun. Major Stirling, commanding the regiment, was in front, dismounted, but the Lieutenant continued to move steadily on in front of the regiment at foot pace, on his horse. The gun discharged shot until the troops were within a short distance, when they fire grape. In went the corps, led by the Lieutenant, who still steered steadily on the gun's muzzle until it was mastered by a rush of the 64th.'

Lieutenant Harry Havelock later recalled the battle and his part in it: 'Eager to get ahead of the Highlanders, the 64th had got a little in advance of their front lines when all at once a shrapnel shell from the 24-pounder in their front struck their No. 5 Company, burst, and knocked over six men, one of whom was killed and the other five awfully mutilated. At this, someone shouted out that they were to lie down. They got into confusion. Many broke their ranks and ran back into the village for shelter, and it looked as if they were going to break into a general rout …

'I rode up, dismounted, and got the men out of the village by abuse and entreaties. I then got them to lie down in the front line. There the wounded men were left groaning a few paces in advance of the line; and Major Stirling, the commander, instead of sending a few men to remove them, kept beckoning and calling out to me, in the presence of his regiment, 'For God's sake, get some help for these poor fellows …

'I at last went over and quietly spoke to him about it, and he left off his whining and the men were removed as I suggested. I had noticed earlier in the day that his nerves were badly shaken, and now the thing was critical enough in itself without his making it worse. And I confess that I thought it was all up with us … I must confess that I felt absolutely sick with apprehension; and if I looked calm, I never was before and hope never to be gain in such a funk in my life …

'Just then, the General rode bareheaded to the front. He was the only man who dared raise his head, so close and thick was the fire that rained down upon us; but he had a charmed life, and had come out of some thirty actions without a scratch, though he had lost many a mount. He pulled up with his back to the fire; and smiling, he said clearly and calmly, "The longer you look at it, men, the less you will like it. We must silence those noisy guns. Rise up! The brigade will extend in skirmishing order to the left, in battalion echelon from the left."

'I think I was the first on my feet, shouting, "Get up, men, and take those damned guns!"

'I rode on the right flank of the 64th ... However, contrary to the General's wishes and the rules of the Service, these same officers dismounted and were advancing on foot so as to be less exposed. They were hardly visible to their men and consequently lost in the ranks as far as example or leadership was concerned.

'Major Stirling later claimed that he was on foot because his pony was rendered unrideable by a shell bursting close by. If this was the same animal he was riding the day before, I can understand its excitability. For I saw it on the loose and advancing on its hind legs, determined to bite some other horse if possible, and I had to draw my sword to defend my own mount if necessary. But it doesn't explain the Major's allowing his subordinates to dismount. And worst of all, he was merely grazed on the left shoulder and immediately went to the rear. I then asked each of the three other senior officers of the regiment to take his place; but they all declined, saying it was not their duty to do so. This was poppycock, of course, and they knew it; but there was no time to argue the matter; so I rode forward at once and led the regiment myself, shaming and ridiculing then into steadiness over those twelve hundred yards of level ground, with the enemy blazing shot and shell into us the whole way ...

'To say nothing of the other officers, this action of mine was in itself highly irregular; and I got criticised for it afterwards, especially as I did it without orders; but I had no regrets, considering the irregular conduct of the other officers, and the General thought it was an action worthy of the Victoria Cross; for if it didn't save India, at least it saved the day.'

There is little dispute that Harry Havelock performed an act of gallantry, something he was to often repeat. In response to the accusations of nepotism, his father issued a disclaimer stating that, 'On this spontaneous statement of the Major-General [Sir James Outram] the Brigadier General [Havelock] consents to award the Cross to this officer which, if originating from himself, might from the near relationship Lieutenant Havelock bears to him, assume the appearance of undue partiality.'

It certainly did reek of nepotism and caused much resentment among other officers, particularly those of the 64th. When the wording of the citation reached India, the officers of the 64th felt that it badly reflected on them and wrote to Sir Colin Campbell, the new Commander-in-Chief. Never an advocate of the Victoria Cross, he sent the officer's letter to the Adjutant-General with his own pithy comments:

'This instance is one of many in which, since the institution of the Victoria Cross, advantage has been taken by young Aides-de-Camp and other staff officers to place themselves in prominent positions for the purpose of attracting attention. To them life is of little value, as with the gain of a public honour, but they do not reflect, and the General to whom they belong do not reflect, on the cruel injustice thus done to gallant office, who beside the excitement of the moment in, have all the responsibility attendant on the situation. By such despatches as the one above alluded to, it is made to appear to the world that a regiment would prove wanting in courage, except for an accidental … ; such a reflection is most galling to British soldiers, indeed it is almost intolerable, and the fact is remembered against it by all the other corps in Her Majesty's service. Soldiers feel such things very keenly. I would, therefore, again beg leave to dwell on the injustice sometimes done by General officers when the give a public preference to those attached to them over the officers who are charged with the most difficult and responsible duties.'

Later Action

The troops nearly dropping from exhaustion pursued the enemy to the edge of Cawnpore before Havelock called a halt. At the beginning of the battle, Brigadier Havelock passed his watch to his orderly to time the duration of the fight. At its conclusion, the orderly announced that that victory was achieved in two hours and forty-five minutes. In nine days from 7 to 16 July, the Column had marched 126 miles and fought four actions all in the heat of an Indian midsummer. They were, however, twenty-four hours too late to avert the cruel fate of the 120 women and children slaughtered and dismembered at the Bibighar.

Promoted to Captain, Harry Havelock took part in the First Relief at Lucknow. On 25 September, he joined the Volunteer Cavalry in their charge to take the Charbagh Bridge, but a shower of grapeshot left only Havelock alive although badly wounded.

This may be the incident that led General Henry Havelock to again recommend his son for a bar to his Victoria Cross.

In must have been with some consternation that the War Office received this new recommendation in May 1858, coming just four months after Harry Havelock's citation appeared in *The London Gazette*. Anxious not to stir up the resentment expressed with the first award, the Board of Field Officers managed to fudge the issue with a not very convincing technicality. Edward Pennington, the Clerk at the War Office, wrote to Sir Henry Storks, the Permanent Secretary, on 12 November 1858 and put into words what the military establishment believed:

'I confess I do not see the force of this reason; because the fact of the Cross having been conferred for the first act … even it if had been known at the time he [General Havelock] recommended for the second act, might not have precluded the last recommendation being made if the claim was really established. It seems like saying; you are not entitled to it for the first act, but you got it, and you must consider that as your reward for the second act.'

During the intense street fighting suffered by Havelock's men as they slowly made their way to the Residency, part of the 78th who had been instructed to wait for the heavy guns, found they were forming the rearguard. As night fell, General Outram ordered that the force should hold the ground they had won until first light the following day. The halt would allow the wounded and the heavy guns to close up with the main column. The wounded were helpless in their covered stretchers (*dhooly*) and men of the 78th were assigned to protect them. Private Henry Ward stood guard over the wounded Lieutenant Harry Havelock through the night. In the morning, he rounded up four *dhooly*-bearers to carry Havelock and another wounded private to the Residency. An officer of the 78th wrote:

'Lieutenant Harry Havelock, with his left arm shattered at the elbow, and a wounded Highlander lying beside him, was in the leading litter and would have suffered the same fate had it not been for Private Ward of the 78th, who forced the bearers to go on at bayonet point. For that he was awarded the Victoria Cross.'

Harry Havelock appointed Ward as his personal servant. He was recommended for the VC by General Outram and received his Cross in late 1858 without a presentation. Later he was promoted to Quartermaster Sergeant, before leaving the Army in 1865. He did not survive civilian life long and died on 12 September 1867 at Malvern, Worcestershire. He was buried in a pauper's grave but when Harry Havelock learned of this, he had a handsome gravestone erected.

Moving on and taking terrible casualties, the Column finally reached the Residency and Lieutenant Havelock and his father thus joined the defenders until Campbell's Relief Column reached them in November. Once relieved, Harry Havelock continued campaigning and commanded the 1st Hodson's Horse and, by the end of the Mutiny, had been brevetted lieutenant colonel at the age of thirty.

Havelock received his Victoria Cross from the Queen on 8 June 1859. He also succeeded to the baronetcy bestowed on his father, who died of dysentery at Lucknow within hours of the Residency being relieved by Campbell's force. Parliament also awarded annual pensions of £1,000 to both Harry and his mother.

Later Life

Havelock went on to serve in the New Zealand War, Canada and Dublin. He had a gift for writing and took a leave of absence to act as a war correspondent in the Franco-Prussian War 1870-71 and the Russo-Turkish War 1877. Ill health forced his retirement in 1881 but when the Anglo-Egyptian War broke out in 1882, he made his way to the British Headquarters in Ismailia, telling a war correspondent he knew: 'Don't for goodness sake mention me in your despatches, for my wife thinks I'm somewhere on the Riviera, but I could not resist coming here to see the fun!'

He petitioned the British commander, Sir Garnet Wolseley for a role on the staff, but the General refused. Publicly, Wolseley had described Havelock in the Mutiny as the bravest man in India but was his usual waspish self when he wrote in private to his wife:

'Havelock is still here as mad as ever; I received a letter from him yesterday, begging to have it sent home as it was a request to be re-employed, etc., etc., in his usual strain. I am extremely sorry for him, and I feel for him very much, but still feel that he can never be employed again: he is not sane enough to argue with.'

Despite this rejection, Havelock somehow managed to take part in the Battle of Tel-el-Kebir, following the Highland Brigade and riding into the Egyptian defences armed with just a riding crop. He is also said to have joined the Cavalry Brigade in their ride into Cairo.

He became a Liberal Unionist MP in South East Durham and championed the local coal miners. He inherited the estates near Darlington from his cousin, Robert Allan, a condition of which he changed his name to Havelock-Allan.

At the age of sixty-seven, Havelock, now created Colonel of his old regiment, the 18th (Royal Irish) Regiment, visited them on the North-West Frontier. They were part of the Malakand Expedition under General Sir William Lockhart, who provided an escort for his visitor. Promising not to take any unnecessary risks, but unable to resist the thrill of danger, Havelock rode on ahead of his escort and was shot dead by Afridi tribesmen on 30 December 1897 and later buried at Rawalpindi.

With increasing numbers of British troops arriving it was now possible to mount a viable force to relieve Lucknow. The new Army Commander, General Sir Colin Campbell, recognised that General Havelock had been hurried into marching on Lucknow with an inadequate force and terrible logistical problems. Campbell was not going to make the same mistake. With the prospect of receiving some 30,000 troops from garrisons around the Empire he set about organizing an adequate transport and supply system.

Instead of the weeks that many had hoped for, it was to be late October before Sir Colin was able move his column to Cawnpore and then Lucknow. On 3 November 1857, unable to wait for the large reinforcements promised, he reached Cawnpore with a force of only 4,500. This included HM 23rd, 82nd, 93rd, 53rd, 8th, and 75th Foot, with EIC 2nd and 4th Punjab Infantry. The mounted troops were mainly Punjab Cavalry, HM 9th Lancers, along with a contingent of artillery and 200 men of the Naval Brigade from HMS *Shannon*.

A steady supply of reinforcements increased Campbell's force to about 8,000 by the time he reached Lucknow.

Practically all men who are confronted with danger are driven by different motivations to perform an act of outstanding gallantry. Usually it is for altruistic motives like pride in the regiment, comradeship or pure bloody mindedness. Very few actually plan their moves so their bravery will show them in a good light and enable them to advance their station in life.

One such VC recipient, from the fighting at Lucknow, was not even a serving soldier but a member of the Bengal Civil Service who saw an opportunity to escape from his impoverished and humdrum circumstances.

THOMAS KAVANAGH VC (1821-1882)

Thomas Henry Kavanagh was born in Mullingar, County Westmeath on 15 July 1821, the third son of the bandmaster of the 3rd foot. The Kavanagh family moved to India in 1834 when his father was transferred with his regiment. In 1839, Thomas was employed as a clerk in the office of the Commissioner for Meerut, before working in a Counting House for a merchant at Mussoree until 1843. He then advanced to Head Clerk to the Government Treasury at Ambala. Another move found him appointed Head Clerk at the Board of Administration at Lahore and then Assistant Magistrate at Jullindur. Despite being constantly in employment and gradually moving up the Civil Service ladder, Kavanagh was experiencing financial hardship. It was when he transferred to Mooltan that he narrowly escaped dismissal for his increasing debts. It took the intervention of Lord Dalhousie to save Kavanagh and to secure him a position of Superintendent of the Office of the Chief Commissioner in Lucknow. This was a small demotion but more lucrative. He was working here when it was learned that the Mutiny had broken out.

His family was staying with friends in Cawnpore but Kavanagh's wife had fallen out with her hosts and returned with the children to Lucknow. Fortuitously so, for shortly after their departure the rebels laid siege on Cawnpore, culminating in the infamous massacre of the women and children captives at the Bibigarh.

Besieged

Sir Henry Lawrence was the commanding officer at Lucknow and he decided that the most suitable defensive position was inside the British Residency compound, so he organised for the gathering of British families from the small military stations in the surrounding region. On 30 May, the sepoys at Lucknow mutinied, though some, along with the Sikhs, remained loyal. Unexpectedly the natives did not try to press home their advantage giving Sir Henry the precious time he needed to organise the defences.

Thomas Kavanagh was put in charge of the civilians and he set about organising them into a fighting unit. He arranged accommodation and issued them with arms, which some felt was a foolish move as they were a bigger threat to themselves than the enemy. Thomas tried to ensure these new civilian units behaved with as much military discipline as was possible given the circumstances, but many of his charges found his methods overbearing and some questioned his authority.

By the end of July there was another threat to the defenders in the form of constant heat and unsanitary conditions which were perfect conditions for cholera, fever and small pox. Kavanagh lost his eldest child, Cecil, to sickness and was haunted by the fear that a similar fate awaited the rest of his children. It was almost impossible to keep the healthy completely separate from the sick.

Throughout August there were constant rumours of imminent relief. Time and again it was imagined the sound of British artillery could be heard on the outskirts of the city, but on each occasion excitement gave way to despair. The situation inside was getting more desperate. The heat was stifling, food was low, rats swarmed everywhere and disease continued to extend its grip.

Kavanagh began to explore other ways of involving himself in the action. One of these was to engage in what he called 'man shooting' Kavanagh would climb onto one of the defence batteries and from a range of 100 yards take pot shots at the enemy. During one of these episodes he had a narrow escape when an enemy shell brushed past his head badly burning the side of his face.

September brought some relief from the scorching sun in the form of rain showers. Cool and refreshing, they helped revive the spirits and also had the more practical effect of cleansing the compound of dirt, blood and decaying flesh. Soon their hopes were raised when then learned that the column under the joint command of Sir Henry Havelock and Sir James Outram, was fighting its way towards Lucknow from Cawnpore. On 25 September, it had reached the edge of the city and was about to make the final push. Inside the Residency word spread that salvation was at hand and many climbed onto the rooftops to glimpse their saviours. As the relief force advanced, it came under close fire from doors, windows and rooftops. When the battling soldiers came into view of the Residency the defenders on the roof erupted with cries of joy and support to those who had come to their aid. When the gates were, at last, opened and the ragged troops poured through, men and women alike were reduced to tears of gratitude. Over 200 of the 1,000 that attempted the perilous journey were lost. Almost as soon as the gates were closed and the cheers subsided, spirits sank a little. Welcome as the relief force was, it was not large enough to turn the tide. The new combined force numbered around 1,500 and there were still around 10,000 sepoys on the other side of the defences and they were still prisoners but now with even more mouths to feed.

At the end of October, Kavanagh was made Assistant Field Engineer, which he felt was in recognition of his endeavours, and his focus now moved below ground level. The sepoys were digging tunnels beneath the compound through which they hoped to plant explosive charges. Kavanagh was responsible for the discovery of these mines and their destruction through countermining. Whenever he discovered a tunnel about to open he would wait in the shadows for a sepoy to emerge and then step forward and fire. The Sikh soldiers who had remained loyal in the Residency nicknamed Thomas 'Burra Surungwalla' – the Great Miner.

On 29 November, Thomas learned that Kunoujee Lal, an Indian messenger, had managed to get inside the Residency. He carried with him a dispatch from Sir Colin Campbell, at Cawnpore, who hoped to break the siege within a week. In the preceding few days officers at the Residency had drawn up a plan to assist such a force, outlining the best route through the city.

VC Action

It occurred to Thomas that the plan was of little use without someone to explain it. He became convinced that with his knowledge of the city and of the enemy's positions he should act as a guide. The Residency could not afford the luxury of a third attempt – the food was almost exhausted and the sick and wounded were dying for want of medical supplies. He met with Kunoujee Lal and outlined his plan to accompany him on his return journey. The messenger refused point blank due to the added risk of having to care for an accomplice, especially a European one. In the end Thomas convinced him by hinting at the chance of a great reward for such a service.

Having convinced the messenger he now faced the more difficult task of convincing his superiors. How would any European manage to slip undetected though the many enemy patrols and checkpoints, never mind one who was over six feet tall and had blue eyes, a shock of red hair and freckles! He donned a native dress, lamp-blacked his face and entered the room. After the initial shock of an Indian daring to enter they were convinced by Kavanagh's appearance to sanction his offer.

At 18.00 hours on 9 November, Kavanagh kissed Agnes and his children, giving the impression he was heading for mine duty as usual. In a small deserted room, and with the aid of a colleague, he put on his disguise of native clothing including a small shield and a tulwar. He then applied lamp black to his face and hands and to be sure the disguise was convincing, he entered the quarters of Sir James and took a seat where he sat in silence. All of the staff on duty knew Kavanagh well but it seemed none of them recognised him. Indeed the atmosphere was one of agitation that a native would be so impudent. When Sir James entered he also failed to recognise Kavanagh immediately and, having passed this simple test, the messenger and officers felt more confident that the seemingly hopeless mission might succeed. Sir James and the other officers present made some final adjustments and alterations to complete the disguise.

At 20.00 hours, bidding farewell, Kavanagh and Kanoujee Lal left the Residency from the north side overlooking the river and their first obstacle was to cross the Gomti. Kavanagh removed his clothes, gathered them into a bundle on his head, and slipped into the icy cold water. As the cold took hold of Thomas' body he began to have serious doubts and he was about to call to the guide and abandon the journey when he realised that the distance between them was too great. Lal was almost at the other bank and to call out loudly might attract the attention of the enemy, so Kavanagh completed the crossing and joined up with his companion.

Dry and in warm clothes again, Kavanagh felt a little better so they made their way a hundred yards or so inland. Encountering a sentry, Kavanagh exchanged pleasantries before moving to the Iron Bridge leading back into the city. Kanoujee Lal explained to the guard that they were returning to the city and were allowed to pass.

Their journey now took them into the heart of city and although Kanoujee Lal wished to use the small side streets, Kavanagh thought it best to stay on the main street with the crowds where they were less likely to stand out. This proved the correct choice for they were stopped and questioned only once as they made their way to the eastern suburbs. Eventually, they found themselves in open country. The pair continued on for five miles until Kanoujee Lal realised his mistake for they had wandered into the rebel-held Dilkusha Park. With the guidance from an old lady they met, the pair were pointed in the right direction.

After a couple of hours they came across a man singing at the top of his voice. Despite the noise he was making the man heard them as they approached and immediately sounded the alarm. A party of sepoys came rushing out of a hut and began to ask questions. Kavanagh stepped forward and assumed control of the situation, explaining that the excited behaviour of the soldiers was frightening his poor companion for they were to deliver bad news to a close friend. The British at Lucknow had just shot his brother and they were worried about how to break the news to him. Accepting the explanation the sepoys allowed them to proceed and even advised them on the best route.

Another obstacle to overcome was a marsh which they had to cross. The cold water was dirty and heavy mud sucked off Kavanagh's footwear. Progress was slow and it took almost two hours to traverse the marsh by which time Kavanagh was so exhausted he had to rest. Staggering on, Thomas succumbed once more to fatigue and decided to lie down and rest for an hour. Kanoujee Lal , who seems to have been the fitter of the pair, went to find out where they were. He had only walked a few yards before a challenge of 'Who comes there?' rang out. Kavanagh was immediately alerted and heard his companion in conversation with some native soldiers, attempting to determine where their loyalties lay. It soon became apparent that the soldiers were under the command of the British and within minutes Kavanagh and his companion were being escorted to meet with the commander-in-chief.

Lucknow Relief

By 05.00 hours, they were standing in front of Sir Colin Campbell. At first the commander had difficulty believing the pair had come from the Residency until Kavanagh removed his turban and from it took a piece of paper which he then handed to Campbell. The message, written in Greek to fool the enemy, was from Sir James Outram and addressed to Campbell personally. Thomas was physically and mentally drained and begged that he be allowed to sleep. Later that morning over breakfast with Sir Colin, Kavanagh rediscovered the simple and delightful pleasures of bread and butter. It had been months since he had tasted coffee with sugar and the flavour of it too was wonderful. He recounted his adventures to Sir Colin and the other commanding officers, who were full of admiration for him. When the officers had left, some time later, Sir Colin outlined his impressions of the plan contained in the message from Outram.

On 14 November the second attempt to break the siege of Lucknow began. Arriving on the outskirts of the city, Campbell's force came under sporadic fire from the sepoys. Their progress was checked when they came to a canal that was crossed by a stone bridge. The following morning Kavanagh found Campbell on high ground surveying the city for weaknesses and potential trouble spots, and confessed to him that he was unhappy with the route chosen by Sir James Outram. It was the same route taken by Havelock and he was sure it would be heavily defended. Thomas Kavanagh proposed an alternative route that was more likely to offer the opportunity of surprise.

News of the British advance and their successes quickly spread throughout the city. The result was an exodus of civilian and sepoy alike. Three key buildings were targeted en route to the Residency and were soon occupied and with relative ease. The Residency was now in sight and Kavanagh decided to try and reach it alone. Running haphazardly through the streets he managed to dodge the enemy's fire until he met with a soldier from the Residency. Together they ran at full tilt until they reached the 'Steam Engine House' where some officers from the Residency were taking cover. Only when Thomas was upon them did they recognise him.

Kavanagh was quickly shown to Sir James and he escorted the Lucknow commander back through enemy fire to Sir Colin Campbell's command post. Kavanagh was able to announce, 'Sir James Outram is waiting, sir, to see you'.

Bitterness

Thomas Kavanagh had achieved the fame he sought but was less satisfied with the cash award. In return for his services during the relief of Lucknow the Indian government awarded him £2,000 which Kavanagh felt to be a miserly sum considering that his actions had also saved the public treasure, which he estimated at around £300,000. This was to be a sore point that stayed with him until the day he died. Other criticisms he harboured included the lack of a statue raised in memory of his outstanding act or a public subscription to ensure him a comfortable old age.

When Thomas was first nominated for the Victoria Cross the application was refused. There were two issues that weighed against him. First, the board in charge of examining submissions responded that Thomas would in all likelihood receive a special medal that the Queen would award to the garrison and relief force of Lucknow. Second the Royal Warrant, which outlined those eligible to receive the Victoria Cross, stated that it could only be conferred on military personnel. A second civilian, Ross Lewis Mangles, had also been nominated for distinguished conduct during the Indian mutiny and many thought that they both fully deserved the award. A tribute from Sir Colin Campbell must also have contributed significantly;

'This escape at a time when the entrenchment was closely invested by a large army, and when communication, even through the medium of natives, was almost impossible, is in Sir Colin Campbell's opinion, one of the most daring feats ever attempted.'

After much lobbying the Royal Warrant was amended to allow nominations for anyone who 'was serving under the orders of a General or other officer in command of troops in the field'. Thomas was presented with his medal by Queen Victoria on 4 January 1860. He also received the Indian Mutiny Medal with clasps for the Relief and Defence of Lucknow. Thomas returned to India with the impression that the VC had only been awarded grudgingly and wrote:

'I shall probably be on my way back (to India), reluctantly to resume my duty under a Government that thinks me undeserving of the honour, and to labour hard in a climate from which I cannot hope to escape again to Europe.'

The £2,000 Kavanagh received is worth approximately £175,600 in today's money. This was obviously not enough because Kavanagh again went into debt in 1876 and was compulsorily retired from the Indian Civil Service with a pension of £500 (£44,000) per year.

Kavanagh still courted controversy after the Mutiny with the publication of his book *How I Won the Victoria Cross*. He was castigated in some quarters for both profiting from his deed and self-aggrandisement. There were some who felt that, as Kanoujee Lal was the only witness and did not leave a memoir, Kavanagh exaggerated his account. Certainly there were those who met him found him conceited and one recalled seeing the VC emblem on his slippers. Probably, if he had entitled his account differently, then there would not have been such vilification. Despite the bitterness, Kavanagh may have felt about the dismissive attitude of his detractors, the British public and media regarded him as one of the greatest heroes of the Victorian age.

Last Days

In later life, Thomas did return to his native Ireland. At the invitation of the Governor of Gibraltar, Kavanagh sailed in the P&O ship *Khedive* and was taken ill on board. On arrival, Thomas was taken to hospital where he died on 11 November 1882. An indication of the esteem in which he was held, he was given a full military funeral and his coffin was conveyed to the North Front Cemetery by 200 soldiers of the Loyal North Lancashire Regiment. There is no doubt that he was a man of great personal courage, but the wrangling involved securing the Victoria Cross mutually soured attitudes between the British government and Kavanagh.

On 14 November, Sir Colin Campbell had made up his mind regarding the route the column should take based on the information supplied by Thomas Kavanagh. Rather than cross the Charbagh Bridge and following Havelock's example of fighting his way through the narrow and dangerous streets of Lucknow, Campbell opted for wide flanking attack to the east with Dilkushka Park as his first objective.

The city of Lucknow was bordered by the canal which ran north-east to south-west, and the area in which Campbell's column was advancing was countryside with some farms, jungle, marshes and a few sumptuous palaces and pavilions. After the Dilkusha and La Martiniere were taken largely without a fight, the next obstacle to overcome was the Secundra Bagh, a far tougher objective which saw some of the fiercest fighting of the campaign.

In fact two battles were to be fought on 16 November, one leading into the other, which saw a record number of seventeen Victoria Crosses being awarded. These included:

WILLIAM GEORGE DRUMMOND STEUART VC (1831-1868)

Born 11 February 1831 in Edinburgh, George was the only son of William Drummond Steuart (not Stewart as it is sometimes incorrectly spelt) and Christine Mary. He was brought up on the Steuart family estate of Murthly Castle, Grandtully (pronounced 'Grantly'), Perthshire. Despite being born into one of Scotland's leading families, young George was to have an unsettled childhood.

His father, William, born in 1795, had purchased a commission into the 15th (King's) Hussars and took part in the Battle of Waterloo in 1815. Five years later, he retired as a captain on half-pay. When George's grandfather, Sir George Steuart, died, the estate and title were passed to his eldest son, John Archibald Steuart, who assumed the title of 6th Baronet of Grandtully and Murthly. In 1832, the year after George's birth, the new laird and George's father had a violent quarrel, resulting in the latter leaving his wife and son in Scotland and sailing for America.

Reaching St. Louis, which at that time was on the US frontier, William joined the pack train led by Robert Campbell which was going to the 1833 Rendezvous of Mountain Men on the Green River, Wyoming. Here, Steuart met famed frontier men like Jim Bridger, Tom Fitzpatrick and others. For the next two years, William travelled throughout the Rockies until, in 1835, his income from Scotland declined and he was forced back into civilisation once more. He spent the winter of 1836-37 in New Orleans, speculating in cotton to recover his finances. He also spent a few months in Cuba before he joined Tom Fitzpatrick's train to the Rockies and another rendezvous in Wyoming. Later in the year, he again returned to New Orleans to learn that his brother was dying of cancer. This meant that he would succeed to the baronetcy and that he would no longer have to struggle with his finances.

He took one more trip to the Rockies and, on the death of his brother, returned home as the 7th Baronet

When he returned, he brought with him, not only his hunting guide and two Native Americans, but also a vast array of artefacts, plants and animals. He planted buffalo grass and released several bison and a bear onto the estate. This caused quite a stir, not least to Queen Victoria. In 1840, venturing north for the first time, a honeymooning Queen Victoria was startled to see these impressive beasts, noting in her diary that she and her husband had encountered 'those strange hump-backed creatures from America'.

William's late brother had run up debts of £250,000, which were cleared by the sale of his wife's family estates. When he had left his family in 1832, William had sworn that he would never sleep under the roof of Murthly again, so he hit upon the idea of building a new wing with a private bedroom and marble bathroom. He took his oath so seriously that he ordered that if he was seen to doze off in his chair while in the old part of the castle, he was to be awoken at once.

Homesick for the American West, William returned in late 1842 and attended the very last Mountain Men rendezvous in 1843 in the area that was to become Yellowstone Park. He then returned to his estate at Grandtully for good.

There appears to have been little time for any sort of bonding between William and his son, for the young George was sent off to board at the Jesuit-run Oscott College, near Birmingham. Although it was a seminary for priests, it also accepted lay pupils. At the age of seventeen, young George was appointed Ensign by purchase into the 93rd Sutherland Highland Regiment and, after four years of home service at Glasgow, Portsmouth and Plymouth, was promoted to lieutenant.

It was in 1853, while he was stationed at Portsmouth, that he had an affair with a girl named Mary, the daughter of a Southampton merchant. She died giving birth to twin boys, who were named George William Drummond and Herbert John.

With the outbreak of war with Russia in the spring of 1854, the 93rd were part of the Highland Brigade sent to the Crimea. George left with his regiment and it would appear that his mother, Christine, and his uncle, Archibald Douglas Steuart, took responsibility for his sons. In fact, although he was named as the father, George was not present at the twins' baptism and their certificates were signed by Christine and Archibald. It is probable that William, the adventurer, remained unaware of the existence of his two illegitimate grandsons.

Overseas Service

The 93rd were to gain immortality two months later when just four companies, including Steuart's, stood between the Russians and the British supply port of Balaklava. William Howard Russell, *The Times'* special correspondent, viewed the action from a distant vantage point on the Sapoune Heights. Below him he could see the Cavalry camp sited amongst some vineyards at the base of the Causeway Heights. As mentioned in the earlier chapter, the only infantry he could make out were the 93rd Regiment of Highlanders, drawn up under the heights above Balaklava and supported by some Royal Marine artillery. Russell arrived just as the Russians overwhelmed Number 1 Redoubt, the furthermost earthwork, and put the Turks to flight. The next two redoubts quickly fell and the plain leading to Balaklava was filled with Turks running for their lives and being pursued by Russian cavalry. As they came within range, the two ranks of the 93rd, under the command of Sir Colin Campbell, fired a volley. This, together with the Marines' artillery fire, caused the Russians to turn about and return to the Causeway Heights.

Russell immortalised this action in a phrase, now misquoted and beloved of headline writers. He wrote, 'The ground flies beneath their horses' feet; gathering speed at every stride, they dash towards that thin red streak topped with a line of steel.' This was later shortened to 'the thin red line' and taken into the English language to mean any last-ditch defence against overwhelming odds.

With winter beginning to bite, sickness thinned the British ranks as much as enemy action. On 29 December, George Steuart was promoted to captain at the young age of twenty-three and suffered with his men the terrible first winter above Sebastopol. He wrote often to his mother and enquired about the health of 'my two dear boys'.

For the rest of the war, the 93rd endured the rigours of trench duty as the siege dragged on. The two abortive assaults on the Great Redan led to the fall of Sebastopol in September 1855, but Steuart and his regiment remained in the Crimea until July 1856.

The 93rd returned home but only until the following spring. News of the outbreak of mutiny amongst the sepoys of the Bengal Army hastened the sending of reinforcements to the seat of this new conflict. Arriving at Calcutta in September 1857, the 93rd were in time to join their old commander, Sir Colin Campbell, in his advance to lift the siege of Lucknow.

VC Action

The first major obstacle for Campbell's men to overcome was the Secunderbagh (Garden of Alexander the Great). This palace had been built by a former king as an animal and bird sanctuary and was a formidable looking place, about 130 yards' square with double thick walls about twenty feet high. Campbell ordered up his artillery to pound the walls but heavy fire from three different directions caused heavy casualties.

An eyewitness, Surgeon William Munro of the 93rd, recalled: 'The 53rd skirmishers advanced steadily and, supported by the 93rd, drove the enemy out of the village. While following them in rapid pursuit, the 93rd came unexpectedly out on to an open space, on the opposite side of which stood a large, square-turreted building with loopholed walls – the famous Secunderbagh – from which a tremendous, but not effective, musketry fire was poured on the regiment as, on emerging from the village, it formed into line in the open. To avoid the storm of fire, and to be under cover until artillery could be brought up to breach the wall, Colonel Leith Hay was ordered to move the regiment to the shelter of a long low embankment which ran parallel to the south face of the building and at a distance of about one hundred yards from the wall.

'There, under shelter, the regiment remained until two of Travers' heavy guns having been brought up – a nine-pounder having proved useless – succeeded in breaching the tower at the south-west corner of the building, while our men by a steady rifle fire kept back the enemy from their loopholes, and from showing themselves above the parapet on the top of the walls…

'While the two heavy guns were battering the base of the tower, Colonel Hay, with two companies of the regiment, drove the enemy out of a large square enclosure (the Serai) opposite the western face of Secunderbagh. Captains Cornwall and Stewart [*sic*], with Nos.2 & 3 companies and sections from 4 & 8 companies, were sent out to the left front to keep down a flank fire from two guns, which the enemy had brought forward and with which they were raking the road … and interfering with the breaching operations.

'But Stewart [*sic*], perceiving the annoyance which these two guns were causing, called upon his company, and at the head of it … dashed forward in a most gallant style, captured the guns at the point of the bayonet, turned them on the flying rebels.'

George Steuart had charged up a long, level road, straight towards the fearsome gun muzzles as they were manoeuvred towards him. Narrowly, his company managed to win the race and his exploit was acknowledged many years later by Lord Roberts in his book, *Forty-one Years in India*. Lord Roberts recalled that this action; 'was as serviceable as it was heroic, for it silenced the fire most destructive to the attacking force'.

The nearby large fortified barracks, built in the form of a cross, was then captured and Steuart was later joined by Major Ewart and three companies. They remained there to secure the column's rear until the final evacuation of the Residency two days later. After intense fighting, the Secundrabagh fell with no prisoners taken. After another day of fighting, contact was made with a party of men sent out from the Residency and on 19 November, the evacuation began – Lucknow was relieved.

George Steuart and his comrades were again under Sir Colin Campbell's command when Lucknow was finally captured in March 1858. He again distinguished himself in the attack on the Begum Kothee, a key enemy position. As the rebels began to waver, he led a small party in pursuit and chased them out of the buildings.

Steuart was involved in the fighting in Rohilkund and the general pacification of Oude. As the campaign drew to a close, so the C-in-C's attention turned to rewards and decorations. The Mutiny had involved several large battles in which there were many outstanding acts of gallantry. The awarding of a Victoria Cross for this eventuality had been included in the First Warrant (Clause 13) which provided for a ballot to be taken for the regiments to select their choice. Thus, one officer was chosen by the officers, one non-commissioned officer by the NCOs and two privates by the privates.

In the ballot amongst the officers of the 93rd, George Steuart was voted to receive the Cross, which was gazetted on 24 December 1858. The citation was a masterpiece of brevity: '16 Nov.1857. In leading an attack upon and capturing two guns by which the Mess House was secured. Elected by the officers of the regiment'. He was highly thought of by his brother officers and was described as' an officer of remarkable coolness in action.'

Steuart actually received his Cross before the official announcement in London. On 6 December 1858 at a special ceremony at Ambeyla, Major-General Sir Robert Garrett pinned the VC to Steuart's tunic.

On his return from India, Captain Steuart was invited by the tenantry of his father's estates to a dinner at Birnam and presented with a handsome sword of honour from the hands of his friend and mentor, Lord Panmure, the former Secretary for War. On being promoted to a majority, for which there was no opening in the 93rd, George elected to go on half pay and retired from active service.

After Service

There is something of a mystery about George's activities after he left the army. He did serve for a short time as Assistant Inspector of Volunteers, but the actual dates are unknown. Handwritten notes in the margin of the copy of *History of 93rd Sutherland Highlanders* held by the regimental museum hint of a man who was something of a rake. To quote the notes:

'Drummond had a child by a Miss Wilson, I think, daughter of a fishing tackle maker in Edinburgh. Miss Wilson tried to force a marriage but this failed and the child died and saved complications for the heir.'

The final, reference to Steuart's post-service activities happened at Fawley near Southampton. On 18 October 1868, George attempted a trick that he would have seen during his service in India. Amongst the entertainers that frequented the camps or bazaars were snake charmers, magicians and sword swallowers. In an attempt to emulate what he had seen ten years before, it would appear that Steuart thrust a stick down his throat but the trick went horribly and fatally wrong. At the inquest held on 20 October, Robert Harfield, the Deputy Coroner stated that the cause of death was inflammation of the lungs.

The verdict was not death by misadventure but whilst in an unsound state of mind. This suggests that he committed suicide and that the sword swallowing story was a cover up. It seems inconceivable that anyone would choose such a painful and lingering form of suicide. On the other hand, the location is significant and one that could have made him despondent. His twin boys were educated at a Catholic boarding school near Southampton, paid for by Archibald Steuart. It would appear that a condition was placed on George not to reveal himself to them as their father and they went through their lives never knowing who their father was. It could be that George observed them from afar and, in a fit of depression, deliberately killed himself.

William's body was brought back to Scotland and deposited in the small Roman Catholic Chapel attached to the castle. Three days later, it was carried in procession and laid to rest in the same vault as his beloved mother in the church of St Mary, Grandtully. His father had an impressive arch built on the estate in his memory which was named The Malakoff Arch, after the Russian strongpoint at Sebastopol.

The widowed and heirless Sir William died three years later in April 1871 and the title and estate passed to his youngest brother, Archibald, the twin's secret benefactor. When he died childless in 1890, the estate and castle passed out of the family. Through George's illegitimate twins, however, the line has survived.

VALENTINE BAMBRICK VC (1837-1864)

On April Fools' Day 1864, a prisoner was found hanged in his cell in Pentonville Prison, North London. Sadly, prison suicides were not uncommon, but what separated this tragedy from others was that the victim had belonged to that elite band of heroes, a recipient of the Victoria Cross.

Valentine Bambrick was born on 13 April 1837 in Cawnpore, India to a father who was stationed there with the 11th Light Dragoons. Both his father and his uncle, after whom he was named, were Troop Sergeant Majors in the 11th and had seen service from Waterloo to Bhurtpore. His older brother, John, would later join the 11th Hussars, as the 11th Light Dragoons became, and was one of the Gallant Six Hundred who charged down the North Valley at Balaklava.

When Valentine was just sixteen, he enlisted in the 1/60th Rifles, which were stationed in India. When the Mutiny broke out in 1857, the Regiment was heavily involved at the Siege of Delhi and the hard campaigning that followed as the mutineers were hunted down.

VC Action

It was during the assault on the city of Bareilly, 140 miles east of Delhi, that the twenty-one-year-old Bambrick displayed outstanding courage as the British troops charged through the narrow streets and alleyways. A party of fanatical Ghazis cornered Bambrick and his Company Commander Lieutenant Cromer Ashburnham. Bambrick's citation dated 24 December

1858 is brief and does not convey the desperation of the contest: 'For conspicuous bravery at Bareilly, on the 6th of May 1858, when in a serai, he was attacked by three Ghazees, one of whom he cut down. He was wounded twice on this occasion.'

A more detailed account is written in the Regimental History: 'On the north side Bareilly is covered by the Dhuranea River, the bridge over which was commanded by some of the enemy's guns. Upon these our heavy guns, escorted by the Riflemen who were thrown into the gardens through which the road led, opened fire with great effect. The enemy's artillery being silenced, the Riflemen advanced …

'In the street fighting that followed, D Company under Lieutenant Cromer Ashburnham once more distinguished itself. A party posted on the roof of a house were warned of the approach of a body of Ghazis or desperadoes. The men dropped from the roof; Colour Sergeant Henry Bailey fell, covered with sword cuts, and Lieutenant Ashburnham barely escaped the same fate. A stroke from a tulwar hardly missed his head, and his own sword too blunt to cut. A point therewith, however, finished the career of the assailant.'

It would appear that Bambrick's intervention helped save Ashburnham's life.

He received his Cross in 1859 but there is no record of an investiture. When the 60th returned to England, Bambrick preferred to stay in India and transferred to the 87th (Royal Irish) Fusiliers. When they returned to Ireland, Bambrick took his discharge at Aldershot on 16 November 1863 and celebrated his introduction to civilian life with a night out on the town.

Tragic End

While he was relaxing in an establishment, he heard the cries of a woman from upstairs. Going to her assistance, he found a Commissariat Sergeant named Russell beating a woman. Bambrick waded in and got the better of the NCO.

Later Russell brought a charge of assault and theft of his medals against Bambrick and was backed up by some of his cronies. Bambrick, at his own expense, paid for the female victim to stay in a hotel until the trial. When the trial began at Winchester Assizes on 3 December 1863, Bambrick's only defence witness had disappeared. Russell was able to call one of his soldiers as a prosecution witness and his word seems to have been accepted without much of a challenge. Bambrick does not appear to have done his cause much good by verbally abusing the judge, who handed down a guilty verdict and sentenced the prisoner to three years in Pentonville Prison.

This was harsh indeed, but worse was soon to follow. Under the rules of the Royal Warrant dated 4 September 1861, Bambrick was forced to forfeit his Cross – not for going to prison – but for the offence, 'theft of a comrade's medals.' Both governors of Winchester and Pentonville prisons considered Bambrick an innocent man and lobbied for his release. Expecting their petition to be successful, their efforts were tragically pre-empted. Bambrick could bear the injustice of the prison sentence, but the confiscation of his hard-won Cross was too much to bear and he made this clear in the letter he wrote before he hanged himself in his cell on 1 April 1864. Bambrick's body was taken and buried in the St Pancras & Islington Cemetery, in an unmarked grave.

Bambrick's case was taken up by the editor of the *United Services Gazette* who called upon the Queen to restore his Cross, but to no avail. Belatedly in 2002, a plaque was unveiled in the Islington Chapel at the Cemetery to honour this wronged soldier.

Chapter 4

Third China War, 1860

Number of VCs awarded	7
Number of VCs awarded to officers	4
Number of VCs awarded to other ranks	3
Total awarded to British Army	7

Origins of the War

The origins of the Anglo-Chinese Opium Wars were the direct result of China's refusal to redress the imbalance of trade between the two countries. The Manchu-led Qing dynasty's refusal to allow in pernicious foreign ideas and goods from the West resulted in a highly restricted and unbalanced trade. The Chinese had what the West wanted; silk, porcelain and tea. Prior to 1830, Canton was the only port open to British and American merchants and there only one commodity the Chinese would accept; silver. Anxious to correct the trade imbalance with something other than silver, which was at that time in short supply, the merchants began to push for the importation of opium. It had been banned by an Imperial edict in 1729 as an illegal drug but was allowed in small quantities for its medicinal properties. It was one product the Chinese did not grow but one that an ever-increasing number of them wanted. The Honourable East India Company enjoyed a monopoly in the supply of Indian-produced opium but in 1833 her hold was ended by the British Government which opened the trade for cheap opium by dozens of British companies.

During the 1830s, opium flooded the black market in China and by 1837 opium represented fifty-seven per cent of Chinese imports. The habit of opium smoking spread until ninety per cent of all Chinese males under the age of forty in the country's coastal regions were addicted. The effect was shocking. Business activity was badly reduced, the civil service ground to a halt resulting in fall of the standard of living. Thanks to corrupt Chinese customs officials and ruthless merchants, who defied the Imperial instructions, the importation continued unabated. With estimated numbers suffering from opium addiction approaching 12,000,000, Emperor Dai guang's special anti-opium commissioner, Lin Ze-xu took drastic action. He ordered the confiscation of some 20,000 chests of opium from English ships and refused to pay compensation to the British traders. Lin closed the channel to Canton, effectively holding the British merchants hostage in the city. As well as seizing opium supplies in Canton's thirteen hongs or factories, he ordered troops to board British ships in international waters and destroyed their cargoes of opium.

Lin then demanded that all merchants sign a bond promising not to deal in opium under pain of death. This threat sparked the 1840 First Opium War. Lord Palmerston, the British Foreign Secretary, justified it on the grounds of the principle of free trade. Others saw it as Britain's need to uphold its reputation and not bow to the arrogance of China and her opposition to global free trade. There were others who were appalled by the immorality that Britain was going to war over an addictive drug against the wishes of the host country. William Ewart Gladstone denounced the war as 'unjust and iniquitous'.

In a war that lasted from June 1841 to August 1842 largely fought along China's coastline from Canton in the south to the Taku Forts guarding the approaches to Pekin in the north. The Treaty of Nanking or, as the Chinese called it, the Unequal Treaty, gave Britain extraterritorial privileges in the treaty ports of Canton, Xiamen, Fuzhou, Ningbo and Shanghai. The British seized Hong Kong (Fragrant Harbour) island, which was to become one of its most important colonies. The ease with which the 19,000 British troops overcame China's 200,000-strong army was later regarded as the start of the 'Century of Humiliation'.

For Britain and the West, it opened the lucrative Chinese market to global commerce – and the opium trade. Another plus for the British were the travels of a Scottish botanist named Robert Fortune to China. He was able to bring back to Britain many exotic and beautiful flowers and plants including azaleas, chrysanthemums and peonies. In 1848, his most far-reaching accomplishment was the successful smuggling of tea plants, forbidden by the Chinese government, to northern India, so starting the flourishing Indian tea industry.

To give Chinese merchant vessels operating the treaty ports the same privileges accorded to British ships by the Treaty of Nanking, the British authorities granted these vessels British registration in Hong Kong. One of these vessels had been a pirate ship that had been captured by the Chinese government and then sold and registered as a Chinese-owned ship. Now British-registered and renamed *Arrow,* she flew the British flag, even though the crew were Chinese. Her English captain was not on board at the time but claimed he witnessed the incident. When the *Arrow* was off Canton on 8 October 1856, she was seized by Chinese marines, who pulled down the British flag and arrested the crew on a rumour that the *Arrow* was still involved in piracy. Demands for the release of the Chinese crew were met, but claims the Chinese soldiers had insulted the British flag was ignored. The fact was the beleaguered Qing dynasty was too embroiled in the Taiping Rebellion to devote any time or attention on this minor infringement. (See next chapter).

This incident heralded what was called the Arrow War or more accurately, the Second Opium War. Without consulting his superiors in London, the Hong Kong Governor, Sir John Bowring, ordered Admiral Sir Michael Seymour to bombard Canton. The British navy easily destroyed the Barrier Forts on the Canton River, captured or destroyed twenty-three Chinese junks and bombarded the city. The French also had a motive in reacting to Chinese aggression. In February 1856, a French Catholic missionary, Auguste Chapdelaine was arrested, imprisoned and severely beaten. He was then locked in a small cage and hung at the gate of the prison. Mercifully, he was already dead when he was beheaded.

With the British making all the running in China, France decided the Chapdelaine incident gave them a good excuse to declare war on China, even though they had never reacted to the deaths of previous missionaries. Lord Elgin, the British High Commissioner for China, acknowledged the French ultimatum presented by the French ambassador. 'The fact is, that he has had a much better case of quarrel than we; at least one that lends itself much better to rhetoric.'

In March 1857, the Anglo-French force attacked from the Pearl River and occupied Canton. This was fortuitous as, with the outbreak of the Indian Mutiny in May, most British troops were diverted to India. Despite this, a weakened Chinese government was unable to put up much resistance. The result was another humiliation for the Quing regime with the signing of the Treaty of Tientsin in June 1858 which allowed not only Britain but France, Russia and the United States to establish embassies in Pekin, a previously closed city, but also permitted all foreign ships access to the Yangtze River, and the opening up another eleven ports to foreign traders.

Almost immediately, the more hawkish ministers around the Emperor sought to prevent the encroachment on Pekin. The Xianfeng Emperor ordered that the Taku Forts should be reinforced with additional artillery and obstacles lain across the mouth of the Hai River. On 24 June, the British blew up the cables and iron stakes placed in the river. The following day Admiral Sir James Hope endeavoured to force a passage but low tide and soft mud prevented their landing. An amphibious attempt to capture the forts by landing marines and sailors from small gun-boats ended in failure. Unable to manoeuvre freely, the ships made easy targets and the gunboat *Plover* was sunk with thirty-one men lost, including her captain. Hope's ships managed to retreat, thanks to covering fire from the American ship carrying their envoy. Her launch helped collect the wounded and is probably the first occasion on which British and American servicemen fought side by side. The failure to take the Taku Forts led directly to the Third China War and the awarding of seven Victoria Crosses.

In 1860, an Anglo-French expedition was sent to China to compel the Chinese government to honour the trade treaty agreed at Tientsin. Lieutenant General Sir James Hope Grant KCB (a veteran of the First Opium War, First Sikh War and the Indian Mutiny) was in command of the British forces and General Charles de Montauban commanded the French forces.

On 1 August 1860, 10,000 British troops and 7,000 French troops landed at Pei Tang Ho, at the mouth of the Peh-Tang River, approximately eight miles up the coast from the Taku Forts. Heavy rain made the country almost impassable and it was not until 12 August that the Allied Army was able to leave Pei Tang Ho. That morning, General Hope Grant's column marched round the huge expanse of marshes between them and the forts and at Sinho met and defeated a Chinese army. After capturing the town of Tangku on the Pei-Ho River, two days later, the combined force was approximately three miles from the Taku Forts – on the land side. Meanwhile, British and French warships waited at the entrance of the Pei-Ho River for the attack to begin. General Hope Grant decided to attack the Small North Fort, further upriver rather than the Great North Fort, on 21 August. In the days before the attack began, he brought up a battery of guns and mortars close to the fort in preparation for the bombardment and to protect the troops making roads and bridges over the many ditches and canals. Fortunately, most of the Chinese guns were on the other side of the forts, facing the river mouth.

Because of the marshes and the narrow causeway across them, the attacking force, commanded by Major General Sir Robert Napier, was restricted to about 2,500 British troops and 400 Frenchmen. The British troops were mainly the 44th (Essex) Regiment and the 67th (South Hampshire) Regiment, plus a detachment of Royal Marines, with the French on the right flank. At 05.00 hours on 21 August 1860, the attack began. The Allies advanced under constant musket fire and crossed several water-filled ditches, with rows of sharp bamboo stakes planted between the ditches, to reach the wall of the fort. British artillery fire soon put the guns of the fort out of action and at about 07.00 the bombardment blew up the fort's magazine. British ships at the mouth of the river shelled the Great North Fort and Great South Fort to keep them under pressure.

Reaching the wall of the North Fort, the French placed their scaling-ladders against the ramparts but these were pushed away as the defenders shot those who attempted to climb them. With the Allies reaching the walls of the fort, the Chinese could no longer fire their muskets at the troops directly below them. Instead they bombarded them with jars of quicklime and stink-pots (primitive grenades which produced clouds of sulphurous smoke).

Lieutenant Nathaniel Burslem and Private Thomas Lane, of the 67th Regiment, were among the first to reach the main gate of the fort and they climbed up to a small embrasure which they proceeded to widen. Lieutenant Robert Rogers and Private John McDougall of the 44th Regiment, together with Lieutenant Edmund Lenon, 67th Regiment, swam the water-filled ditches and reached the fort. They were followed by Ensign John Chaplin, also of the 67th Regiment, who carried the Queen's Colour of the Regiment.

Lieutenant Rogers scaled the wall of the fort with the help of Lenon, who thrust his sabre into the mud wall to act as a ladder. Rogers was able to enter through an embrasure, to be was followed by Private McDougall and Lieutenant Lenon. Lieutenant Burslem and Lane broke through their embrasure at about the same time and both were seriously wounded; Burslem received a severe gunshot wound to his shoulder. Rogers, McDougall and Lenon were the first men to reach the top of the walls of the fort and in doing so, most of them were wounded. Lenon was wounded in the arm, although not seriously, but Rogers was severely wounded on his right side by gunshot. Ensign Chaplin, though wounded several times, planted the colours of the 67th Regiment on the summit of the fort.

This opened the way for the British and French infantry to clamber up the walls through the widened embrasures. Fierce hand-to-hand fighting ensued, in which 400 of the Chinese holding the garrison were killed. Sir Robert Napier's column captured the other forts later the same day, while Royal Navy gunboats cleared away the obstacles which had been blocking access to the Pei-Ho River. In total British casualties were seventeen killed and 184 wounded.

Lieutenant-General Hope Grant wrote to the Military Secretary at the War Office on 15 November 1860, recommending Lieutenant Edmund Henry Lenon together with Lieutenants Nathaniel Burslem and Robert Montresor Rogers, Ensign John Chaplin and Privates Thomas Lane and John McDougall for the Victoria Cross. The War Office decided 'not to entertain' the recommendations on the basis that, 'what had been done in each case appeared to have been done in the course of duty'. General Hope Grant wrote again on 22 June 1861 explaining that he had made promises under clause seven of the Royal Warrant which he felt were binding on himself and the Government. HRH The Duke of Cambridge, the Commander-in-Chief of the Army, decided that under the circumstances the War Office could not recommend Chaplin and Lane for the VC without also putting forward recommendations for the other four men named by General Hope Grant. Consequently, recommendations for VCs for all six men were accepted.

Separately, an honours board sat at Tientsin in 1861 to investigate the claim of Hospital Apprentice Andrew Fitzgibbon, attached to the 67th Regiment, who received his Cross in 1862. He is recognised as being the youngest Victoria Cross recipient at the age of fifteen years and 100 days. Drummer Thomas Flinn, the Indian Mutiny VC, was also born in May 1845 but, to date, his actual birthday has not been confirmed.

The following are amongst those individuals awarded the VC during the Third China War:

THOMAS LANE VC (1836-1889)

In the church of St Mary and St Anne, Cork, on the 6 May 1837, the Rev John Holland baptised Thomas Lane, son of Thomas Lane and Jony Lane (Desmond). There is a long gap until the first confirmed documentary evidence of the life of Thomas Lane is contained in the muster rolls of the 47th (Loyal Lancashire) Regt. He enlisted into the regiment at Cork on 21 February 1853. He was described as a labourer, 5ft 5ins tall and sixteen years nine months old. This would indicate a birthday in May 1836. He was given six months training at the Regimental Depot at Limerick and during this time, he went Absent Without Leave (AWOL) for two days, thus setting a pattern of his future military career. The following year, he served two months in the civil prison in Tipperary for an affray.

Private Lane was released early so he could join his regiment as they sailed in the SS *Kangaroo* for Varna in Bulgaria. Fortunate to avoid the cholera that had taken the lives of so many soldiers in the Varna camps, he sailed for the Crimean Peninsula and landed at Calamita Bay on 14 September 1854. On the 20 September, the regiment fought in the Battle of Alma as part of General Sir George de Lacy Evans's 2nd Division. On the 5 November, Lane was present at the Battle of Inkerman, in which the regiment had nineteen soldiers killed and two officers, two sergeants and forty-three men wounded. Private John McDermond was awarded the VC for saving the life of the 47th's Commanding officer, who lay wounded and surrounded by a party of Russians.

A grim winter was spent in the trenches before Sebastopol which reduced the British Army to the extent that the French army took over much of the British line.

In 1855, Lane went AWOL on two occasions and was hospitalised for fifteen days at the hospital at Scutari. Following the abortive assaults on the Great Redan, after which the Russians abandoned the city, the regiment remained on the plateau above Sebastopol until peace was declared on the 30 March 1856.

On the 9 October 1857, Thomas Lane deserted from his regiment, which was by then in barracks in Portsmouth. He was apprehended on the 4 November and kept in the guardroom until the 19 November, on which date he appeared before a court-martial, charged with 'desertion and losing necessaries.' He was found guilty and sentenced to eighty-four days' hard labour and forfeited all past service. He was released from confinement on 6 February 1858, but was obviously not a reformed soldier for he continued to be AWOL on several occasions. On 13 September, probably to the relief of the 47th Regiment, Thomas Lane transferred to the 67th (South Hampshire) Regiment, then on the point of embarking for India. After a long and slow voyage, Calcutta was reached on 14 December 1858, too late to qualify for the Indian Mutiny campaign medal as it was presented only to all troops who had borne arms or had been under fire. There is no evidence that anyone in the 67th qualified for the medal but this did not deter Lane from wearing the ribbon on his police tunic in his only known picture.

China

The regiment left India on the 21 September 1859 for China, landing in Canton a month later. In March 1860, they sailed up the coast to Northern China. It appears the regiment stayed aboard ship until 13 July, when it landed at Talien Wan Bay. It is of note that the following day Marine John Dallinger was hanged at the yardarm of HMS *Leven* for attempted murder and this seems to have been the last time such a punishment occurred in the Royal Navy.

On 21 August, the 67th were in the forefront of the assault upon the Taku forts. Thomas Lane was one of four winners of the Victoria Cross from the regiment on that day. To this can be added the unique award to Hospital Apprentice Fitzgibbon, who was attached to the regiment and is recognised as being the youngest ever recipient. Lane, together with Lieutenant Nathanial Burslem, swam the ditches of the North Taku forts and, 'persevering in attempting during the assault and before the entrance of the fort had been effected by anyone, to enlarge an opening in the wall through which they eventually entered and, in doing so, were both severely wounded'.

Burslem is shown on the casualty list as being seriously wounded with a gunshot wound to the shoulder whereas Lane seems to have had a slight gunshot wound to the left side of the face. Lane was also mentioned in the citation of fellow VC recipient Lieutenant John Chaplin; 'who was carrying the Queen's Colours of the Regiment, and first planted the Colours on the breach made by the storming party, assisted by Private Lane.'

After the battle, Lane accompanied the regiment to Peking and was present at the surrender of the city and probably witnessed the burning of the Imperial Palace. When most of the victors departed with their spoils, the 67th remained behind. Lane's company remained at Taku until mid-1863. During this time, he spent several periods in hospital and was in the cells for six days in July 1862. In November 1862 Lane was presented with his VC by Brigadier General Stavely at a parade in Shanghai, to which location his company moved in the second quarter of the following year. During this time the British Army was assisting the Imperial Government in its struggle with the Tai-Ping rebels and other insurgents. Several members of the 67th received awards from the Chinese Government for their efforts during this period. Colonel Gordon (later of Khartoum) was commanding a band of mercenaries known as 'the Ever-Victorious Army' in Shanghai at the time and the 67th certainly assisted this organisation.

Lane remained in Shanghai until July 1865 during which time he continued his pattern of sickness, AWOL and cells. On the 18 July, Lane embarked upon HMS *Adventurer* for passage to Hong Kong, arriving there a week later. On the 26 July, his company went on board *Tamar* for the journey to South Africa, where they arrived on 12 September. During the voyage, Lane was in the cells for two days. He remained in Africa until 21 April 1866 at King Williamstown. At this time regiments returning from the Far East often spent some time in South Africa in order to regain their strength after service in unhealthy areas of the tropics.

He sailed for England on 21 April 1866 and during the voyage he again spent two weeks in the cells on board ship. His patchy service in the British Army was coming to a close for he was discharged as being time expired on 25 June 1866 at the then regimental depot in Belfast.

Later Service

Thomas Lane now slips out of sight until he next appears in New Zealand in 1874. He had added to his spurious Mutiny ribbon by wearing the ribbon of the Maoris Wars of the 1860s, for which he was not entitled. He next appears in South Africa for the beginning of the Anglo-Zulu War of 1879. Although his military record was abysmal and he never attained non-commissioned status, his soldering experience elevated him to the rank of sergeant in one of the battalions of the Natal Native Contingent (NNC). Poorly led and suffering from low morale, these short-lived regiments were manned by rival Zulu bands opposed to the Zulu king, Cetswayo. At the disbandment of the NNC, the white NCOs were transferred to the Natal Horse, sometimes referred to as Bettington's Horse.

With the conclusion of the war in December 1879, Lane is next heard of in 1881 as a member of a unit called Landrey's Light Horse. This was raised to fight against dissident chiefs in Basutoland and Transkei. Lane joined C Troop, made up of three officers and sixty-five men. The troops were of low calibre, recruited mostly from the gold-fields, and evidence reveals that Landrey's Light Horse was a far from efficient unit. There was widespread venereal disease amongst new recruits and outbreaks of fighting between the recruits resulted in the death of a trooper which led to the resignation of a troop commander.

Desertion was a constant problem and, on 7 April 1881, Sergeant Thomas Lane, who was no stranger to going AWOL, slipped away from the unit near Ladybrand in the Orange Free State. Believing he was entitled to back pay, which was well in arrears, he took with him his horse, carbine, revolver, bandolier, spurs, mackintosh, blankets (two), nose bag, curry comb and brush, waterproof sheet, knee band, saddle, valise, haversack, saddle bags and water bottle, all valued at £59-1-6d. He had overestimated what he was owed for back pay, for March/April only amounted to £13-6-0d, he was £45-15-6d in debt as well as being a deserter.

The unpopular Landrey wrote to the Colonial Secretary from Basutoland on the 18 May 1881 informing him that: 'A man named Thomas Lane, VC, formerly a private in the 67th Regiment who joined Landrey's Light Horse ... deserted from my Corps while on the line of march through the Orange Free State on 8 April, taking with him a horse etc. My object in writing to you is to request that steps may be taken to stop his pension, even if nothing further could be done.

'Description of Thomas Lane VC – an Irishman – about 5 feet 8 inches tall – age about 47 years – hair turning grey – much addicted to drink.'

Landrey lost twenty-eight men as deserters between February and May and one must wonder if he troubled the Colonial Secretary about any of the others.

Eventually the report ended up on 12 July 1882 at Horse Guards and they realised that a Victoria Cross holder had seemingly disgraced himself. The fifteenth clause of the Victoria Cross warrant made provision for the erasure from the list of holders and cessation of pension in the event of conviction for a felony and other more serious offences. Thus, wheels were set in motion to carry out the provisions of clause 15 in the case of Thomas Lane.

Lane in the meantime was languishing in the Pretoria gaol, having been sentenced to six months' imprisonment for pulling down the Republican flag in front of the public offices in Pretoria, whilst possibly serving in the King Williamstown police force. The military authorities were also seeking the return of Lane's Victoria Cross although the warrant makes no provision for forfeiture. It is possible that Lane was aware of this because he apparently gave his medal to Captain J. Tennant, the commanding officer of the Cape Town Volunteer Engineers. It has been suggested that Tennant was a fellow member of Landrey's Light Horse.

Thanks to Henning Pretorius, an officer in the Transvaal States Artillery, Lane was released early from the Pretoria gaol. Henning wanted experienced soldiers for his mounted commando in the campaign against Chiefs Nyabela and Manpuru in what was called the Mapoch War. Once again Lane could not resist getting into trouble. He was sentenced to two years' hard labour for placing the decapitated head of an African on a pole outside General Joubert's tent. Thanks to the support of Henning Pretorius and other Boers in the laager, Lane's sentence was rescinded.

At the end of the short campaign, Lane was released from his role with Pretorius's commando and is next heard from in Pretoria gaol again, but this time in an unlikely capacity. In September 1884, less than two years after being released as a convict, Lane was appointed a warder at the gaol. Somewhere along the line, he had acquired a wife and she was appointed as a matron. Typically, all was not well in his new career and, by 18 December, Lane was jobless and on his way to Kimberley. It seems that

Lane did not get on with the Chief Warder and on the 14 December his superior had him locked in a cell and discharged him following day.

Lane immediately went onto the attack and wrote to the State President and members of the Executive Council protesting that: 'He was locked in prison by the Chief Warden and discharged in a suspicious way. The reason was that I caught him in a criminal connection with my wife and although I told the magistrate everything about the intimateness and meanness of the Chief Warden, he took no notice of it.'

Two days later he swore a statement before a Justice of the Peace: 'I bumped into the Chief Warden, Van Reenan, coming round the corner of the house. I entered the room, I went out and saw her (his wife) coming from the same direction. Because it looked suspicious I spoke to Van Reenan. He said he had given her a glass of gin. … Last Saturday, when my wife was busy locking up the female prisoners, the cook of the Chief Warden came along and just when she turned her back, he started doing rude indecent things with her.'

Mrs Elizabeth Lane was well advanced in pregnancy at this time which makes the behaviour in the warder's quarters at Pretoria gaol even more extraordinary. After this setback, the Lanes set off for Kimberley. There on 29 April 1885, Mrs Elizabeth Lane gave birth to a girl, baptised on 20 March 1886 as Anne Elizabeth Lane at St Mary's Church. Thomas Lane joined the Cape Police (District 7, Griqualand West) in Kimberley in August 1885 under the command of Commissioner Ewan Christian, consisting of seventeen Sergeants and 100 policemen.

Lane died in the Carnarvon Hospital, Kimberley on 13 April 1889 of 'inflammation of the lungs' and was buried the next day in the Catholic section of the Gladstone cemetery. He died a fairly prosperous man as he owned two properties in Kimberley. He was obviously well-known in the town for his funeral is recorded in the *Daily Independent* and the *Diamond Fields Advertiser* under the headline, 'Death of a Victoria Cross hero'. The fulsome obituary notice describes a military funeral procession wending its way from the hospital to the cemetery consisting of contingents from the Victoria Rifles, the Diamond Field Horse, the local police force and the members of the Municipal Fire Brigade. Three hundred civilians on foot and in carriages followed the cortege. His obituary goes on to mention his war service and gives an optimistic account of his medals, awarding him a clasp for Balaclava and medals for the Indian Mutiny and is very specific that he was entitled to the Maori War medal. It is ironic that large crowds assembled to witness the procession of a man who served eighty-four days in a military prison and at least sixty days in military cells, as well as spells in Nenagh, Pretoria and Kimberley gaols, and that he should qualify for a funeral with military honours.

Lane represents the sort of Irish soldier recorded by Kipling. He was a rogue but even in his last years at Kimberley he was reported as saying; 'I would be the first to volunteer again to fight for the honour of the British flag'. He was a hard-drinking hell raiser, who was just the kind of soldier to have in a tight spot, but a regimental nightmare in peacetime.

ANDREW FITZGIBBON VC (1845-1883)

Born on 13 May 1845 at Petoragurh, Gujerat in north-west India, Andrew was the son of William Fitzgibbon and his wife, Elizabeth, both from Tipperary. William had enlisted in the Bengal Artillery in 1826 and, at the time of Andrew's birth, was Quartermaster Sergeant of the Kumaon Battalion, later the 3rd Gurkha Rifles.

On 5 July 1859, Andrew passed his exams and joined the Bengal Subordinate Medical Service as a Hospital Apprentice. He was sent to Barrackpore where he was attached to the newly-arrived 67th (South Hampshire) Regiment and sailed with them from Calcutta on 21 September 1859 bound for Canton, China.

Relations with China had been strained since 1856 but, with their involvement in the Indian Mutiny, the British had not given much attention to the problem that was brewing in the Far East. With the conclusion of her Indian problem, Britain, through her Plenipotentiary to China, tried to deliver a treaty to the Emperor but found his way was blocked at the mouth of the Pei-ho River by the guns of the formidable Taku forts. In order to advance on Pekin, the Taku Forts needed to be silenced and the 67th was part of the 3,500-strong Anglo-French force sent to assault the forts on 21 August 1860.

VC Action

Hospital Apprentice Fitzgibbon accompanied a wing of the 67th as it took up a position about 500 yards from the Northern Fort. During the initial artillery fire from the fort, a *dhoolie* bearer (stretcher bearer) was badly wounded. Andrew Fitzgibbon was instructed by the Assistant Surgeon to attend to him despite the heavy fire. He then re-joined the regiment as it advanced across the flat open ground. Seeing a wounded artilleryman, Fitzgibbon ran to him and bound up the soldier's wounds. As he was returning his bandages to his haversack, he was hit in the right forearm and the ball lodged at his elbow.

The following year, a board was convened at Tientsin to investigate the claims for awarding the Victoria Cross. Seven VCs were awarded to Lieutenants Nathanial Burslem, Robert Rogers and Edmund Lenon, Ensign John Chaplin, Privates Thomas Lane and John McDougall, and Hospital Apprentice Andrew Fitzgibbon. All seven were gazetted in *The London Gazette* on 13August 1861. Fitzgibbon's citation stated:

'For having behaved with great coolness and courage at the capture of the North Taku Fort on the 21st August 1860. On the morning of that day he accompanied a wing of the 67th Regiment when it took up a position with 500 yards of the Fort. Having quitted cover, he proceeded under a very heavy fire, to attend to a *dhoolie*-bearer, whose wound he had been directed to bind up; and while the regiment was advancing under the enemy's fire, he ran across the open to another wounded man; in doing so he was himself severely wounded.'

Later Service

Fitzgibbon's forename was incorrectly published as 'Arthur' instead of Andrew. All seven Crosses were presented the following year, but there are no details about where or when Fitzgibbon received his Cross. Back in India he served at the Depot Hospital, Raneegunge and in 1863 was with B Battery, 5th Royal Horse Artillery Brigade. There were postings to Peshawar and the 20th Hussars in 1866. On 2 January 1867, he was appointed Assistant Apothecary 2nd Class and, ten years later, promoted to Apothecary 1st Class. On 3 May 1869, he married Mary Amelia Coleman in Peshawar and fathered two children.

From 1870 to 1872 he was at the Civil Dispensary at Mussoorie and promoted Assistant Apothecary 1st Class. In 1878, he was upgraded to Uncovenanted and Subordinate Medical Officer in the Civil Medical Department but around this time his conduct was being questioned. On 12 September 1879, the Adjutant General wrote that, although not found drunk on duty, Fitzgibbon was ascertained to have drunk sufficiently to render him unfit to perform his duties. The letter was accompanied by two statements by senior surgeons that Fitzgibbon was addicted to drink and unsafe to care for sick soldiers.

Andrew Fitzgibbon was given the opportunity to change his ways but does not seem to have heeded the warning. On 30 January 1880, Bengal General Orders announced that he had been struck off the Medical Service list. Although he was not entitled to a pension, he was awarded a monthly Special Compassionate Allowance of twenty-five rupees in recognition of his previous gallant service. It would appear that the authorities did not want the publicity of the youngest VC recipient appearing before a court.

Andrew Fitzgibbon did not survive for long as a civilian and died of a stroke in Delhi on 7 March, 1883, aged just thirty-seven years. He was buried in the Old Military Cemetery, Delhi in an unmarked grave and reported to be wearing his VC.

Having captured the Taku Forts, the Allies advanced on the Chinese capital, from where the Emperor had fled. After the fall of Tsientsin, the Chinese made overtures of peace. A treaty party of diplomats, accompanied by a small escort of Indian troops and *The Times* correspondent, Thomas Bowlby, rode towards Peking under a flag of truce. En route, they were detained and tortured. The diplomats were soon released but most of the rest of the group suffered appalling treatment, including two Britons who were decapitated. Bowlby was beaten, starved and left to die. As the Allies pushed forward his captors sought to hide their crime. The British found his body by the gates of Peking, greatly disfigured by the quicklime. As a punishment for Bowlby's death and the maltreatment of the rest of the party, the Summer Palace, which had been looted by the French, was burnt as a reprisal.

The Allies began preparations to storm the enormous walls of the city but after a few days the gates were opened and the British and French entered unopposed. They occupied the city until a treaty was signed on 24 October bringing to an end a war that, to many, was unjustified. One was twenty-two-year-old Redvers Buller, an officer in the 60th Rifles, who would rise to command the army in South Africa. Unlike most of his contemporaries, he had a conscience, believing that the war was unjust and annoying his fellow officers for many years by refusing to wear the campaign medal.

Chapter 5

The Taiping Rebellion, 1851–64

Number of VCs awarded	1
Number of VCs awarded to other ranks	1
Total awarded to Royal Navy	1

Origins of the War

The Taiping Rebellion took place in southern China from 1850 to 1864 between the Taiping Heavenly Kingdom and Manchu-led Qing dynasty. This was not just another rebellion but one that cost the lives of an estimated twenty to thirty million people; one of the deadliest military conflicts in history.

It was started in the 1840s by a convert named Hong Xiuquan who had his own view on Christianity. Several times he had sat for the Imperial Examination in the hope of joining the ranks of scholar-officials, but was rejected each time. It may have been because he was a Hakka, a subgroup of the Han community, which was looked down on by the Manchus. Shortly after, he fell sick and was laid low with fever. Having previously read a pamphlet from a Christian missionary, he imagined that he was the younger brother of Jesus who had been sent to rid China of the corrupt Manchu Quin dynasty, who had denied him access to the civil service, and their Confucian teachings.

It says something of the Hong's charismatic character that he was able to spread his ideas and attract a huge following. The Quin government, led by ethnic Manchus, was seen by many of the Han Chinese population as an ineffective and corrupt regime. Amongst Hong's close associates was an American Baptist missionary named Issachar Jacox Roberts, who acted as his teacher and adviser. Another close member was Yang Xiuquin, who claimed to be able to act as the voice of God.

The revolt began in early January 1851 with the Taiping forces overcoming the Imperial army. As the Taiping revolt spread, Hong withdrew to Nanking from where he issued written religious proclamations. Reclusive and increasingly unhinged he began to see plots everywhere, including his close associate Yang Xiuquin. Suspected of treason, Yang and his family were put to death in 1856, followed by the killing of those loyal to Yang.

Baptist minister Roberts was becoming alarmed by Hong's eccentric behaviour and the way the beliefs of the Taipings departed widely from his own Christianity. When a dispute with Hong resulted in him being accused of murder, Roberts saw the light and managed to escape on a British gunboat.

The Taipings tried to persuade the British, French and Americans to support them, but they decided to remain neutral, which in light of the recent war with the Quin dynasty, was more of a business decision than a moral one. As the war dragged on, it was clear that the Quin government would win in the end so the Western Allies threw in their lot with the Manchus and allowed military leaders like the American soldier of fortune, Frederick Townsend Ward, to lead the Ever-Victorious Army to a series of victories. When Ward was killed in 1862, his place was taken by General Charles Gordon, who, with the help of foreign navy brigades, went on the finish the job by 1864.

By early 1864, Hong Xiuquan declared that God would defend Nanking which was besieged by the Ever-Victorious Army. With supplies running low, Hong ate some tainted vegetables and died of food poisoning. A few days after his death, Nanking was taken with the subsequent blood-letting reprisals. This marked the end of the rebellion although there were still pockets of resistance that held out until 1871.

In the fighting that followed the introduction of Western support in 1862, there was one action in which the Victoria Cross was won. It was to be the first of several VCs awarded without the support of a campaign medal.

GEORGE HINCKLEY VC (1819-1904)

George Hinckley was born in Liverpool on 22 June 1819, the son of Joseph Hinckley, a butcher. Nothing is known of his early life, but it is likely that he went to sea at an early age. The first official record of Hinckley to be documented was on 22 February 1842 when he joined the Royal Navy. He was described as five feet eleven inches tall, with dark complexion, hazel eyes and brown hair. His first ship was the old fifth rate frigate, HMS *Tortoise,* built in 1784 as the merchantman *Sir Edward Hughes* until purchased by the Royal Navy in 1804. Since 1840 she had been used as a store ship. Still regarded as seaworthy, she made the long voyage to the naval station at Hobart, Tasmania carrying supplies. In an eighteen-month round trip, *Tortoise* returned with a cargo of Kauri conifer timber from New Zealand. Growing tall and straight, the Kauri conifer was used by the navy for masts and spars.

Eight days after his return, Hinckley transferred to HMS *Penelope* on 19 December 1843, the first British naval vessel converted from sail to steam, with the addition of boilers and side paddles. With little prospect of naval action, Hinckley transferred to HMS *Linnet*. She was part of the West Africa Squadron tasked with interception the slave ships that made the run from Sierra Leone, the centre of this illegal and evil trade. In the four years of patrolling this unhealthy coast, any hope of gaining some prize money disappeared when the only vessel the *Linnet* captured was released without charge.

On his return to England he was transferred to the newly-built wooden screw gunboat, HMS *Partridge.* He was promoted to quartermaster but his time on *Partridge* lasted just six months. He was charged with 'assault and affray' by a civil court and sentenced to three years in a civilian prison. Significantly, his naval record is blank but on his release in October 1859 he was reinstated in the Royal Navy on full pay and his old rank of quartermaster. The suggestion is that the crime he committed was an affair of naval honour and the naval authorities did not frown upon it.

VC Action

His new ship was 232-ton gunboat *Snap,* which took up station in the South China Sea on 28 May 1860. Hinckley was immediately transferred to the First Class paddle sloop, HMS *Sphinx,* commanded by George Fiott Day, winner of the Victoria Cross in the Crimea. She had an impressive service record having served in the India Squadron, the Second Burma War, the Crimean War and now the China Squadron. Unfortunately, Hinckley allowed his fists to do the talking and was sentenced to just under a year in confinement in Hong Kong. In May 1862, he re-joined *Sphinx* as she became involved in the long-running Taiping Rebellion. Coincidentally, he joined the same time that Colonel Charles Gordon volunteered and took command of the Quin's Ever-Victorious Army at Shanghai.

The rebels threatened another attempt to take Shanghai from their fortified town of Fung-wha, about ten miles distant. The 3,000-strong Ever-Victorious Army supported by 500 men of a French-Chinese naval force marched on Fung-wha. They were joined by a Royal Naval brigade of 300 men from HM Ships *Encounter, Flamer, Hardy* and *Sphinx,* who landed on the coast thirty-five miles from Fung-wha and set out to march there overnight. They marched in torrential rain which made the terrible Chinese roads almost impossible to travel. Hinckley recalled that, 'the only dry thing about us was our ammunition – the seventy rounds of ball in our pouches'. About 04.00 hours, they made camp and ate a meagre breakfast of biscuit and half a gill of rum.

At 08.00 hours on the morning of 9 October the Naval Brigade, supported by Ward's force, attacked the east gate of the fortified town but found it blocked and were unable to break through. They met fierce opposition and suffered heavy losses, forcing them to withdraw under a hail of musket and gingall (a type of large musket) fire. The enemy's ammunition consisted of jagged lumps of iron, screws, nails and stinkpots, which created choking sulphurous smoke.

Regrouping, it was noticed that Lieutenant Richard Croker, Master's Assistant of HMS *Sphinx*, was not with them and was lying wounded in front of the east gate. They could hear the mud and gravel ploughed up around the wounded officer and it was considered of the greatest importance that no British fighters should fall into the hands of the Taiping rebels. Knowing the wounded officer would be subjected to barbaric treatment, Hinckley volunteered to go back to bring him to safety. Running and dodging the rebel fire, Hinckley reached Croker and lifted the officer's dead-weight on to his back before making the return journey through the enemy fire. Staggering under the weight, Hinckley managed to carry Croker to the cover of a joss house (a Chinese temple), approximately 150 yards away.

After handing the wounded man over to the surgeon, Hinckley then ventured out into the open again to rescue a second wounded man who was seen to be lying close to where Lieutenant Croker had fallen. Still under a deadly fusillade, Hinckley reached the man, Captain Bremen, an American officer of the Ever-Victorious Army and brought him back to the joss house. Both officers Hinckley rescued survived their wounds

The attack on Fung-wha continued for several days ending with its capture and sparing Shanghai another attack. The forty-three-year old Hinckley finally moved up the promotion ladder when he was rated 1st class on 15 October 1862 and further elevated to leading seaman on 1 January 1863 and reinstated as quartermaster on 1 July. Hinckley was recommended for the VC by Commander Theodore Morton Jones, the Captain of HMS *Sphinx*, on 15 October 1862 in a despatch to Vice Admiral Sir James Hope KCB. This was received at the War Office, via the Admiralty in London, on 15 January 1863. It was noted at the War Office that:

'The acts of bravery in the present instance were not performed under orders, in the course of duty, but were voluntary, and on that account come within the scope and intention of the institution of the Cross.'

The recommendation was submitted to Queen Victoria on 29 January 1863 and duly approved. The award was announced in *The London Gazette* dated 6 February 1863. Hinckley was invested with the VC by Admiral Sir Houston Stewart KCB, Commander-in-Chief Plymouth, at Mount Wise, Devonport, on 7 July 1863.

After the storming of Fung-wha, Hinckley did not see active service again. He had returned to England for his VC investiture and three days later, on 10 July 1863, he was transferred, retaining the rank of quartermaster, to HMS *Indus*, a guard ship at Devonport. From this shore posting, Hinckley joined HMS *Royalist* on 13 November. He was then transferred to HMS *Aboukir* on 19 November 1864 and remained there until 24 February 1865, when he was transferred to HMS *Shannon* on the West Indies Station. He returned to England in April 1865 and served on HMS *Scorpion* until 1 January 1866. HMS *Scorpion* was an iron-hulled turret ship which had been built in a British shipyard for the Confederate Navy during the American Civil War but was confiscated after pressure from the American Union Government.

On 9 July 1865, Hinckley married Jane Oliver, a farmer's daughter from Landewednack, near Lizard, Cornwall, at Stoke Damerel Parish Church, Devon. It is likely that Hinckley could not read or write as he made his mark instead of a signature on the marriage certificate. They had three children: two girls and a boy.

On 2 January 1866 he returned to land-based duties on HMS *Britannia*, a cadet training ship at Dartmouth and remained there until 29 June 1867, when he was discharged to shore. On 29 October 1867, his second daughter, Rosina Fanny Oliver Hinckley, was born deaf and dumb and was initially schooled at home before being placed at the Deaf and Dumb Institution at St Leonard's, Exeter in 1877.

George Hinckley's last posting was a return to the guard ship HMS *Indus* on 6 December 1867, after a shore break of over five months. *Indus* already had its full complement of quartermasters, so he had to accept demotion to able seaman – the rank he held when he joined the Royal Navy twenty-three years earlier.

His third child, George Richard Hinckley, was born in March 1869 and, like his sister Rosina, he was born deaf and dumb and was also placed at the Deaf and Dumb Institution at St Leonard's, Exeter in 1877. Two months later, Hinckley applied for retirement and was discharged from HMS *Indus* on 29 May 1869. He retired from the Royal Navy on 1 June 1869, three weeks before his fiftieth birthday, having served twenty-three years and 123 days. His two disabled children were taught trades to help them earn a living; Rosina became a milliner and George Richard became a tailor.

In addition to the VC, Hinckley received the Second China War Medal 1857-1860 but he did not qualify for the Naval Long Service and Good Conduct Medal.

George Hinckley VC died at his home at 44 North Street, Plymouth on 31 December 1904, aged eighty-five. His cause of death was recorded as senile decay and cardiac failure. He was buried at Ford Park Cemetery, Plymouth and buried with him are his wife Jane, who died in 1917 aged eighty-eight, and their son George Richard, who died in 1914.

VC Mystery

Hinckley lost his VC at a funeral in Plymouth in November 1863 and the War Office informed the Admiralty that the Cross would be replaced, subject to the Admiralty being satisfied that the conditions for replacement were complied with. A replacement was forwarded to Hinckley on 12 December 1863, at a cost to him of twenty-four shillings.

After his death, several VCs said to be his found their way on to the market. The first was sold at auction for £43 in 1925 and was held in the Ward Room at the Royal Naval Barracks at Portsmouth.

A second Hinckley VC was offered for sale at Glendining's for £440 in July 1962. At this point the Royal Naval Barracks at Portsmouth announced that they held the official replacement VC, raising questions about the authenticity of both Crosses. A spokesman for the makers, Hancocks, did not rule out the possibility that both decorations were genuine, but after examination ruled that the Glendining's VC was the official replacement. It was bought by Messrs A.H. Baldwin and later resold to a Colonel Gaynor. He sold it at auction at Sotheby's for £3,200 in November 1988 as 'the official replacement Second China War Victoria Cross'.

To confuse matters, a third Hinckley VC was taken to Glendining's and found to be a copy. It was later advertised as a 'Victorian Replacement Victoria Cross to Able Seaman George Hinckley'. It has been reported that a fourth Hinckley replacement VC was sold by Smith & Wilde, auctioneers, for £800 in March 2008 but no further details are known.

The whereabouts of George Hinckley's original VC remains a mystery.

Chapter 6

Second New Zealand or Maori Wars, 1860–66

Number of VCs awarded	15
Number of VCs awarded to officers	10
Number of VCs awarded to other ranks	5
Total awarded to Royal Navy	2
Total awarded to British Army	12
Total awarded to Militia	1

Origins of the War

In the early nineteenth century, the New Zealand Crown Colony was neither an essential nor even desirable possession of the British authorities. It was a six-month-long voyage; too distant to control and seemingly without trading possibilities. Britain was concentrating her resources on the defeat Napoleon Bonaparte and had little time for two large islands the other side of the world. Despite this lack of interest, New Zealand did attract settlers, traders and missionaries termed *Pakeha* (of European descent) by the indigenous population, the Maoris. Largely left unmolested, the British were horrified by the violent and bloody battles the Maoris fought against each other; from 1818 to 1821 it was estimated that around 500 engagements were fought. The Maoris not only slaughtered each other, they also practised torture and cannibalism. Despite this, the British saw the Maori as a noble warrior let down by their appalling habit of eating each other.

The establishing of the New Zealand Company in 1837 changed the balance between Maori and British settler. Founded by Edward Gibbon Wakefield, who had been imprisoned for three years for eloping with a fifteen-year-old heiress, saw great possibilities for the profitable exploitation of the new country. Wakefield envisaged a neo-feudal arcadia, 'a perfect English society' in the southern hemisphere. Its opponents were not so much the Maoris but the British Colonial Office, the Church Missionary Society and successive governors sent by London, who saw the New Zealand Company's aims as an inevitable conquest with the extermination of the present inhabitants. The Company was successful, however, in attracting thousands of settlers and went about purchasing enormous tracts of land from the Maori tribes, who had little idea of the conception of selling land.

With the increased influx of new settlers, the British declared sovereignty over New Zealand and, in the Treaty of Waitangi, declared that the Maori were prohibited from selling land to anyone but the Government. This seemingly altruistic treaty soon turned sour and soon there were outbreaks of violence between Maori and settler as the demand for land grew.

The First Taranaki War

In 1859, the minor Atiawa chief, Te Teira Manuka, offered to sell land to the Crown at Waitara on the North Island. Surrounded by a large Maori population, this 600-acre block would enable settlers in New Plymouth to expand their enclave around the settlement. This did not go down well with the 2,000 indigenous Te Atiawa Maoris who declared that, although they did not want war, they would obstruct all attempts to survey the area. Finally, they constructed a fortified village or *pah* at Te Kohia, just inside the disputed territory. Although the British authorities knew it would lead to an armed conflict, they also saw it as an opportunity to impose their sovereignty over the country.

On 28 March 1860, a force of 335 men commanded by Lieutenant Colonel G.F. Murray, including twenty-eight Bluejackets from the screw corvette HMS *Niger*, eighty-eight from the 65th Regiment and 103 members of the Taranaki Rifle Volunteers, landed at New Plymouth and advanced towards the Maori *pah* at Omata. As they neared the *pah*, they came under fire from the Maoris hidden in the surrounding bush. After sustaining a few casualties, Murray ordered a retreat to New Plymouth.

Reinforcements were called for from *Niger*, and forty-eight marines and sailors, commanded by Captain Peter Cracroft, were landed. Marching towards Omata, they met up with the retreating troops. Murray ordered an about-turn and they returned to attack Omata. Armed with 24-pound rockets *Niger's* sailors fired into the *pah* and stormed it as darkness fell. According to the gung-ho account in James Cowan's book *The New Zealand Wars:*

'Three flags bearing Maori war-devices were seen waving above the smoke-hazed palisades. "Ten pounds to the man who pulls down those flags!" shouted Cracroft. Yelling, shooting, slashing, the Navy lads were over the stockade in a few moments "like a pack of schoolboys", in the phrase of a survivor of Waireka. The first man in was William Odgers, the Captain's coxswain. He charges to the flagstaff and hauled down the Maori ensigns.'

This symbolic act was deemed worthy of a Victoria Cross and reflected the rash of 'first in' VC actions during the 1860s. In fact, Captain Cracroft recommended a further three sailors for much the same action although he mentioned Odgers as 'being the most daring'. Sir Edward Lugard, the Permanent Under Secretary, jealously guarded the awarding of the Victoria Cross and wrote to Secretary of State for War, Sydney Herbert:

'I do not see sufficient grounds for granting this distinction – indeed the practice of giving it on every paltry occasion lowers the character of the distinction.'

In reality, the assault was not so fraught with danger. Cracroft was lauded as a hero and in his report he claimed that the number of Maoris killed ranged from seventy to 150, while European losses were fourteen killed and wounded. In fact, the *pah* was little more than a camp and all but empty for the Maoris had slipped away. Cracroft's estimation of the enemy's casualties was also exaggerated as the total Maori casualties amounting to just one. Even the settlers who were who were supposedly under threat were dismissive, saying that they did not want an armed force as they were perfectly safe. Faces had to be saved and the attack was hailed as a great victory. One of the losers was Colonel Murray who was condemned for retreating and subject to a court of inquiry.

On 27 June 1860, the British suffered their heaviest defeat in the campaign. Led by Major Thomas Nelson, 350 men left their camp at Waitara to attack the Puketakauere *Pah.* In a frontal attack, Nelson did not take into account that the Maoris occupied flanking rifle pits and lost thirty men killed and thirty-four wounded. Once again, Maori losses were exaggerated; five to eight became 'between 130 and 150 killed.'

New Plymouth's population, crowded with hundreds of settlers from outlying farms, was hit with outbreaks of disease, including scarlet fever, which killed 121. After a year of inconclusive fighting, the war petered out with an uneasy truce. The resulting fighting had left the area devastated and the local economy in tatters.

The Second Taranaki War

Military activity flared up again in March 1863 and the Governor, George Grey, asked the Colonial Office in London for three additional regiments. In a skirmish on 2 October at Allan's Hill near Omata, two Victoria Crosses were awarded to Ensign John Down and Drummer Dudley Stagpoole of the 57th Regiment. Under heavy fire from the bush, they volunteered to collect a wounded soldier from the hillside.

The VCs of the New Zealand wars seem to been something of a *bête noire* for Sir Edward Lugard. He felt that the Cross was becoming cheapened and being awarded for acts that should be rewarded with the Humane Society Medal. He particularly singled out the recommendations for Downs, Stagpoole, Lieutenant Pickard and Assistant Surgeon Manley – all men who had attended wounded under fire. There may have been another reason for his reluctance to accept these recommendations which sprang from the fact that the campaign was not of sufficient military significance and more to do with helping the New Zealand settlers in their quest for more land.

The Waikato War

The Taranaki wars had ended in stalemate with no clear victory for the Imperial forces. Now attention focused on the Waikato, near Auckland, which appeared to be the centre of Maori unrest. In July 1863, six HM Regiments, Royal Artillery, a Naval brigade and the Auckland Militia commanded by Lieutenant General Duncan Cameron, launched a massive invasion with the intention of expelling all Maoris from the area. Pushing south, a number of assaults against the *pahs* gradually forced the Maoris back. Finally, the British military might overcame the dogged resistance of the Maoris. At the conclusion of the war, the British withdrew their troops leaving the New Zealand volunteer regiments to enforce the peace.

Some thirteen Victoria Crosses were awarded from 1863 to 1865, including the first to a member of the New Zealand Militia.

CHARLES HEAPHY VC (1821-1881)

Charles Heaphy was born in 1821 in St John's Wood, northwest London. He was the youngest child of Thomas Heaphy, a professional artist, who painted society portraits. In 1812, he had accompanied the Duke of Wellington as staff artist during the Peninsular War. As a child, Charles received tuition from his father and, in 1837, entered the Royal Academy's school of painting. After eighteen months, Heaphy joined the newly-established New Zealand Company with a view of creating paintings of the new country to be used for advertising the Company.

Charles Heaphy made the six-month long voyage with the brother of the Company's founder, William Wakefield. For over two years he travelled extensively around the country, living out of a tent or staying with friendly Maori. His landscapes were well received, but by 1841 his services were no longer required. Nevertheless, he returned to London to deliver his report to the directors of the Company. Despite his success with the New Zealand Company, he could not get any further work from them, so he decided to return to New Zealand. He had already bought a property near Nelson, which he farmed not very successfully.

Once again, Heaphy was taken on by the New Zealand Company to look for land suitable for settlement. He undertook one expedition along the West Coast of South Island that lasted six months. It was tough going, the weather was poor and it convinced Heaphy that the West Coast was not suitable for settlement. With little prospect of work around Nelson, he accepted a job with the Auckland Survey Office in 1848. As chief draughtsman, he spent the following years surveying and mapping and augmenting his income with painting commissions.

Heaphy married in 1851 and in November 1853, accompanied Sir George Grey, the New Zealand Governor, in his trip to the islands of New Caledonia. Several of the paintings he made there are now exhibited at the British Museum. In 1856, Heaphy joined the Auckland Rifle Volunteers as a private but in August 1863 he was commissioned and made captain of his local unit, Parnell Company.

General Cameron initially employed Heaphy as his military surveyor and guide who helped build the main road into the Waikato. He then was attached as a guide to the staff of Lieutenant Colonel Henry Havelock VC of the 18th Regiment. As the Maoris withdrew to their fortified positions at Paterangi they mounted raids on small groups of soldiers.

VC Act

On 11 February 1864, some soldiers of the 40th Regiment were bathing in the Mangapiko Stream near Paterangi when they were ambushed by a raiding party. Reinforcements from the 50th Regiment rushed forward, including Heaphy and a party of the Auckland Militia. Heaphy managed to fall on the enemy reserve guarding the route back to Paterangi. He then led his men to the ambush site to help the soldiers of the 40th. Despite being outnumbered, the British beat off the Maoris who retreated into the bush. Private Cussan followed them into the undergrowth but was shot. Heaphy and the three remaining men went to Cusson's aid but soon found themselves in trouble. Three, including Heaphy, were shot at close range by the enemy hidden in the bush.

Unable to extricate themselves, Heaphy and the remaining unwounded soldier, Private Cooney, sheltered in a shallow gully and provided cover to prevent the wounded men being axed by the Maoris. Conserving their ammunition, they were able to hold off the Maoris until Havelock arrived. Two of the wounded died as they were rescued. Charles Heaphy had been wounded in the arm, hip and ribs but refused Havelock's orders to have them treated. He remained in the field guiding the stretcher parties and firing at the Maoris, who were still a threat in the bush. Finally, more reinforcements arrived and finally drove off the Maoris.

Now began the convoluted attempt to have the Victoria Cross awarded to Charles Heaphy. As it stood, he was not eligible because he was a member of a colonial militia, but as three civilians had been awarded the VC in the Indian Mutiny, it seemed almost logical that a serving colonial soldier under British command should also be included. It started with a letter dated 24 December 1864 from Governor Grey to the Colonial Secretary, Lord Cardwell. It was supported by General Cameron, the British Commander in Chief New Zealand and Lieutenant Colonel Henry Havelock. So began a round of meetings and memos beloved of Whitehall. Having heard that he had been recommended for the Cross, Charles

Heaphy joined in the paper-chase with his own letter of appeal. Finally, Queen Victoria put her signature on Appendix VIII of the Warrant was published on 1 January 1867: 'Extended the Victoria Cross to the Local Forces in New Zealand and in the Colonies and their Dependencies Generally.'

Charles Heaphy's citation appeared in *The London Gazette* of 8 January 1867. He became the first member of a colonial unit and the last of the New Zealand Wars to receive the Victoria Cross. He was invested with his Cross by Major General Sir Trevor Chute, GOC New Zealand, at a parade in Auckland on 11 May 1867. This was to be the high point of his career as a public official for two years later he was expressing disappointment with his life in New Zealand.

Although he was in constant demand for his surveying skills, he was bedevilled with financial troubles brought about by poor investments. Overwork and poor health hastened his end. He moved to Queensland with his wife seeking a drier climate for his tuberculosis but with a few months, he died in Brisbane on 3 August 1881.

Chapter 7

The Umbeyla Expedition, 1863–64

Number of VCs awarded	2
Number of VCs awarded to officers	2
Total awarded to HEIC	2

Origins of the War

With the HEIC rule abolished in India, its army was reorganised. The Madras and Bombay armies, which were almost entirely unaffected by the Mutiny, remained much the same. The major change was to the Bengal Army which was completely overhauled. Although the regiments continued to bear the title 'Bengal', its soldiers were rarely from that Presidency. No longer were Hindus from Oudh and Rohilkand recruited but were replaced by the martial classes from the north; Sikhs, Jats, Dogras, Pathans, Baluchi, Punjabi and Gurkhas. The period of peace after the Indian Mutiny did not last long and these new units were soon to be tested in the rugged mountainous terrain of the North-West Frontier.

For years, a fanatical Pashtun sect known as the Warriors of God – 'Mujhaddin' – dwelt in the Black Mountains in what is now known as the Tribal Areas in northern Pakistan. Their numbers had been swollen by the sepoys of the mutinous 55th Bengal Native Infantry at the beginning of the Mutiny and other Muslims from Bengal. In 1860, from their new base at the village of Malka, they began raiding and plundering across the Indus River east into Hazara. Driven by their fanatical belief, they set out to wage war against non-believers. Their call to exterminate the infidels increasingly attracted more Moslems to their cause and by 1863 the British decided to mount a major campaign to root them out. This was against the wishes and advice of the Army Commander-in-Chief, General Sir Hugh Rose. He thought that with winter approaching and the small number of available troops, the expedition should wait until the following spring. His opinion proved prescient.

Led by the experienced commander, Brigadier General Neville Chamberlain, 5,000 men set out on 18 October 1863. It was the largest force yet to undertake an expedition in the northwest, consisting of the 11th Bengal Cavalry, the Guides, HM 71st Highland Regiment, 101st Bengal Fusiliers, the Punjab Irregular Frontier Force, 5th Gurkhas, Pioneers and Artillery. The plan was to prevent the Pashtuns from escaping north into the hills, so the advance would approach behind their base at Malka through the Umbeyla (Ambela) Pass into the Chalma Valley and then drive the enemy south towards the Indus where there would be confronted by another force.

To keep this plan secret, the local Bunerwal tribe were not informed of the force's passage through their territory until the day before the pass was entered. By that time, the Pashtun had persuaded the Bunerwals to oppose any incursion of their land. Chamberlain entered the Umbeyla Pass on 22 October and found the going harder than expected. The Bunerwals were affronted by the British failing to ask permission to march through their territory and had prepared for battle. Massing on Chamberlain's left flank, the Bunerwals had called for other tribes to join them. Chamberlain realised that he could be confronted by overwhelming numbers of hostile tribesmen and it was suggested to him that he should retire rather than face defeat. With the frontier tribes watching this stalemate, Chamberlain chose not to lose face and deciding to stay put and hold out until reinforcement arrived. He set about fortifying his position, which was not particularly favourable. Lieutenant Fosbery described the British defences:

'The small portion of the pass occupied by the force (about 200 yards in width at that point), and filled with huge rocks in every direction, was dominated on both sides by almost precipitous hills; 1,500 feet up, the distance between them was only 800 yards, which gives a fair idea of their sharp angle of ascent. From below, the ridges immediately commanding the camp were plainly visible, and on these it was proposed at first to establish out-posts, but on reaching these points, it was discovered that they in their turn were dominated by strong positions further up in the hills, and it thus became necessary to push post after post, into the mountains one either hand until the process was only stopped at the Eagle's Nest, on the left flank, and the Crag picket on the right by the impossibility of adequately relieving or supporting the troops at greater distances. As it was, no relief from below could reach the Crag picket in less than 45 minutes, nor the Eagle's Nest in less than one hour from the time of leaving the camp below, and as these posts were invisible from thence, assistance when required must be sent for, which practically doubled the distance.'

The two rocky outcrops, Eagle's Nest and Crag Piquet, could only hold a few men on their summits and both became scenes of fierce hand-to-hand fighting, changing hands several times. On 30 October, Crag Piquet was attacked and taken by the Pathans but a strong counter-attack by the British saw two Victoria Crosses awarded to lieutenants Fosbery and Pitcher.

On 11 November, a six-hour-long night attack on the Crag by 2,000 tribesmen was beaten off with bayonets and rocks. On 18 November, Chamberlain abandoned his position on the north of the pass and concentrated his troops in a new camp on the south. In the process, he lost 118 men killed and wounded. For weeks Chamberlain's force held out, defending against constant attack. On 20 November, the Crag was lost for the third time and so important was it to be re-taken that Chamberlain led the successful attacking party but was severely wounded.

When General Rose and his staff had reached Lahore he sent his young ADC, Frederick Roberts VC and another officer to assess the situation. Arriving on 25 November they were encouraged by the spirit of the embattled force, which was daily being reinforced. The Bunerwal tribesmen had become somewhat discouraged and many had drifted away. Chamberlain was replaced by Major General John Garvock, who led a two-column attack on 15 December, which after a hard day's fighting, dislodged the enemy from their lofty positions. As a result, the Bunerwals came into camp and made terms. During this long stand-off, the British sustained 1,000 casualties

On 19 December, seven staff officers, including Roberts, set out in heavy rain with four companies of Guides. By 21 December, they reached Malka where, despite hostile posturing by angry tribesmen, they set alight the village. It was a very tense situation as more hostile natives arrived until the column was outnumbered by a hundred to one. Just when things looked like they would get out of hand, one of the Bunawal elders intervened, saying that he had given his word and protection. These brave words diffused the tension and the British were able to withdraw safely.

Roberts was reprimanded by Rose for risking his life but nevertheless recommended him for a brevet lieutenant colonelcy. This was turned down by the Viceroy on the grounds that Roberts, at the age of thirty-two, was too young!

The two VCs from the Umbeyla Expedition were those awarded to the following:

GEORGE VINCENT FOSBERY VC (1833-1907)

George Vincent Fosbery was born at the family seat of Fosbery near Devizes, Wiltshire, on 11 April 1832 to the Reverend T.V. Fosbery. He was educated at Eton and attended Addiscombe College before being commissioned into the Bengal Army on 20 January 1852. He was appointed to 48th Bengal Native Infantry and then 3rd BNI in 18 July 1856. Promoted to lieutenant on 1 July 1857, he arrived just as the events of the Indian

Mutiny were unfolding. For some reason, he was granted a leave back to England, which lasted until 1861, so missing taking part in the Mutiny. The 3rd BNI mutinied and Fosbery, although absent, was placed on the roll of the 4th Bengal European Regiment.

When he returned to India, the 4th had been disbanded and Fosbery was attached to the newly named British Regiment, 104th Regiment (Bengal Fusiliers), formally the 2nd Bengal Fusiliers. Fosbery's uneven service career threw up an unusual remark; in the Bengal Army List he was shown as 'Instructor of Music.'

He would appear to have had an innovative bent more suited to the Ordnance Department. This was evidenced when, as a volunteer during the Umbeyla Campaign, he commanded thirty marksmen drawn from HM's 71st Regiment and 101st Fusiliers who were armed with one of his inventions; the explosive bullet. This was developed as a means of ascertaining range distances for the Mountain Artillery and infantry.

VC Act

In a lecture he delivered about the Umbeyla Campaign on 12 April 1867 at the Royal United Services Institute, Forbery described the events of 30 October:

'The Crag picket … had hitherto been only occupied by Colonel Keyes as a post of observation, and on the night of the 29th was occupied by twelve men only. The enemy, however, seeing its importance and the command which its possession would give them, approached it towards morning, overpowered and drove out the feeble garrison, and occupied the summit of the rocks with some 250 men, the remainder waiting on the ridges in the neighbourhood to take advantage of the confusion which their fire must produce at daylight in the posts below.

'The nine survivors of the picket, however, retreated only as far as the rocks at the base of the Crag itself, and, opening fire on the enemy above, who were busy strengthening their position, called loudly for support. Colonel Keyes at once answered this appeal. Taking with him an officer and ten of his own men, he proceeded to join them, directing his adjutant, Lieutenant Pitcher, to bring up more men as fast as they could be got together.

'By dawn he had with him some seventy-five men at the foot of the rocks, on whom the enemy poured a continuous and heavy fire, hurling down at the same time huge stones, which caused several severe hurts. As soon as it was light enough to distinguish friend from foe, and his left flank was covered by Colonel Brownlow's corps, who moved out into the ravine below, he divided his force into two parties, gave the order to fix swords, and sounded the charge. The Pathans gave a wild shout of 'Allah! Allah!' (in the name of God) and rushed at the Crag, scrambling like cats from rock to rock, by ways through which but one man could pass at a time, in the face of hot fire and heavy shower of rocks and stones.

'Stragglers now and then arrived; and one man, a private of the 71st, who had been stunned by a heavy fall amongst the rocks, by ways through which but one man could pass at a time, in the face of a hot fire and heavy shower of rocks and stones. This daunted some of the men and Lieutenant Pitcher who was leading at the time being stunned by a heavy stone, but two officers, Colonel Keyes and another, and about twenty-five men, arrived at the summit where they became engaged in an exciting hand-to-hand conflict. Colonel Keyes was severely wounded, but the place was won. The nature of the struggle may be judged of from the fact that sixty of the enemy's killed and wounded were left on the ground, three standards captured, and the rest of their force was so much discouraged by the action as to retire from that flank altogether. Meantime an attack had been made on the front of the camp, which was repulsed by the 71st and 101st regiments, aided by the fire of the guns in position, and a dashing charge made by the Goorkahs [*sic*], in which, however, the latter suffered severely. Their dead, when brought in, were found to have did not arrive until dawn on the following morning, having escaped, by what seems almost a miracle, the parties of the enemy who patrolled the sides of the hills.'

In an act of frustrating modesty, Fosbery completely omits his part in the fighting for the Crag Picquet. Fortunately, his actions are described in the citation which appeared in *The London Gazette* dated 7 July 1865:

'For the daring and gallant manner in which, on 30 October, 1863, acting as volunteer at the time, he led a party of his regiment to recapture the Crag Piquet, after the garrison had been driven in by the enemy, on which occasion 60 of them were killed in desperate hand to hand fighting. From the nature of the approach to the top of the Crag, amongst large rocks, one or two men only could advance at one time. "Whilst ascending one path", relates Lieutenant Colonel Keyes CB., commanding the 1st Punjab Infantry, "I directed Lieutenant Fosbery, of the late 4th European Regiment, to push up another at the head of a few men. He led this party with great coolness and intrepidity, and was the first man to gain the top of the Crag on his side of the attack." Subsequently Lieutenant Colonel Keyes was wounded, Lieut. Fosbery assembled a party, with which he pursued the routed enemy in the direction of Lalloo Ridge, inflicting further loss and confirming possession of the post.'

George Fosbery was promoted to captain in 1864 and served with several Indian regiments, none for very long. He took a leave of absence from 1866 to 1869, and retired from the Indian Army as a lieutenant colonel in 1877. On returning to England, his firearm skills were recognised and he concentrated on his passion for invention. With the advent of the machine-gun into the British Army he helped perfect its development.

Invention

His main claim to fame was the 'Paradox Gun', an automatic revolver that bears his name. When the first shot was fired, the recoil drove the top section back and by means of a lug engaging in the zigzag cut into the cylinder, rotating it and cocked the hammer before moving back under spring pressure to the firing position. On pulling the trigger again, the process was repeated. Invented in 1895, it was taken up by the Webley & Scott Revolver and Arms Company. The Webley–Fosbery Automatic Revolver was subsequently produced as a six-shot .455 and an eight-shot .38 calibres. About 4,000 were issued in the First World War but, although effective in normal conditions, the mud and muck of the trenches rendered the gun unreliable.

Fosbery married in 1858 to Emmeline Hall, the daughter of a Royal Naval officer and fathered ten children. He died on 8 May 1907 in Bath and is buried in a neglected grave in the town's Smallcombe Cemetery. His medals are displayed in the Lord Ashcroft Gallery, Imperial War Museum.

HENRY PITCHER VC (1841-1875)

Henry William Pitcher was born on 20 December 1841 at Kamptee on the North-West Frontier of India, the second son of Vincent Pitcher, an officer in the 6th Madras Light Cavalry. Sadly, his father died when Henry was in infancy and his mother returned to her home in Jersey and remarried. Henry was educated at Victoria College, Jersey, and studied at Addiscombe College before being commissioned ensign in the Indian Army.

This happened as at the height of the Mutiny, so Pitcher was attached to HM's 79th (Cameron) Highlanders and took part in the capture of Lucknow and subsequent battles that followed throughout Oude. At the end of the campaign, he joined the 1st Punjab Irregular Infantry, otherwise known as 55th Coke's Rifles (Frontier Force) in the winter campaign of 1859 against the Kabul Khel Wazir tribes, for which he received the Indian Service Medal, clasp 'North-West Frontier'. He then served as adjutant and took part in the Umbeyla Campaign.

VC Action

He was recommended for the Victoria Cross for two acts of gallantry to do with the fighting on Crag Piquet. The citation reads the same as Fosbery's with further additions by Major Keyes:

'Lieutenant Pitcher, equally cool and daring, led a party of men up to the last rock, until he was knocked down and stunned by a large stone thrown from above, with a few yards of him.

'Lieutenant Pitcher also displayed great gallantry in leading on a party of his regiment to endeavour to recover Crag Picquet, when it again fell into the enemy's hands on the 13th November, as related in the following extract from Major Keyes's report of the 16th of that month. "The duty of leading the first charge devolved upon Lieutenant Pitcher, and I beg to bring to the special notice of the Brigadier-General commanding, the admirable manner in which he performed this important duty. He was many yards the foremost of his party, and the gallant bearing of this excellent young officer was the admiration of all spectators. It is impossible to say too much or to overrate his services on this occasion. Lieutenant Pitcher was severely wounded and was obliged to be carried back."'

The awarding of a Victoria Cross did not necessarily mean swift promotion. For Pitcher, promotion came slowly and it was not until 1869 that he was promoted to captain. He was still serving in this rank with the 1st Punjab when he died from sunstroke on 5 July 1875 at Dera Ghazi Khan.

Henry Pitcher's VC group was sold at auction in 2008 and later presented to the island of Jersey.

Chapter 8

Shimonoseki Expedition, 1863–64

Number of VCs awarded	3
Number of VCs awarded to officers	1
Number of VCs awarded to other ranks	2
Total awarded to Royal Navy	3

Origins of the War

The Tokugawa Shogunate was the last feudal Japanese military government which existed between 1603 and 1868. Seeking to have an open-door to foreign trade, the Shogunate stirred up resentment amongst many of the feudal daimyos (clan lords) who, although subordinate to the shoguns, ruled most of Japan. In 1863, things came to head when the Emperor Komei, breaking with imperial protocol, issued his order to expel all barbarians (foreigners). Defying the Shogunate, the Chusan clan leader, Takachika, ordered his forces to open fire on all foreign ships crossing the Shimonoseki Strait, the 122-meter wide waterway separating the islands of Honchu and Kyushu.

The first recipients of this aggressive act were on ships belonging to the Americans, soon to be followed by the French. Within a short time, the Chusan war-lord had fired on most of the ships with consulates in Japan. A period of negotiating the re-opening of the Shimonoseki Strait by the Americans, British, French and Dutch met with procrastination. By May 1864, the anti-foreigner faction had destroyed foreign properties and shipping following which the British suggested that a joint military force should confront Takachika. With America fighting her Civil War and the French mired in keeping Emperor Maximillian on the Mexican throne, the burden fell to Britain as the main protagonist.

A naval force of nine ships of the Royal Navy, supported by four Dutch vessels and three French, prepared to sail into the Shimonoseki Strait. On 5 September, the naval guns soon silenced the Chusan emplacements, but not before having two of its ships severely damaged and losing seventy-two killed or wounded. The following day, the Naval Brigades landed and stormed the main stockade. In what came to exemplify their gunboat diplomacy, the European colonists used this means as a way of resolving small outbreaks of unrest throughout the world.

This brief conflict ultimately opened up Japan to Western influence, particularly industrial, and within forty years she was technically strong enough to inflict defeat on one of the world's strongest countries – Russia. Although no campaign medals were issued, three Victoria Crosses were awarded, including William Seeley, an American serving as an Ordinary Seaman, Captain of the After Guard, Thomas Pride and a seventeen-year old midshipman, Duncan Boyes.

DUNCAN GORDON BOYES VC (1846-1869)

Duncan Gordon Boyes was born at 3 Paragon Buildings, Cheltenham on 5 November 1846, and was educated at Cheltenham College. In 1860, his sister Louise married Thomas Young, HMS *Shannon*'s gunnery lieutenant, who had been awarded the VC for gallantry at the Second Relief of Lucknow. Perhaps this inspired the young Boyes to pursue a naval career for he became a cadet, qualified and joined his first ship, the fifty-one-gun frigate HMS *Euryalus*. Almost immediately he was to be involved in combat.

HMS *Euryalus* also formed part of the force sent to open up the Shimonoseki Straits which, on 6 September, landed a Naval Brigade to destroy the enemy's guns and ammunition.

VC Action

As the Naval Brigade assembled on the shore, a large force of Japanese advanced on the troops and began firing. They were met by a determined charge by the bluejackets, with seventeen-year-old Duncan Boyes holding aloft the Queen's Colour in the leading company. He kept the flag aloft despite one of his colour-sergeants being killed and the other, Thomas Pride, wounded. Afterwards, the standard was found to have six bullet holes. He was recommended for the Victoria Cross which was gazetted on 21 April 1865 and read:

'For the conspicuous gallantry, which according to the testimony of Capt. Alexander C.B., at the time Flag Captain to Vice-Admiral Sir Augustus Kuper K.C.B., Mr. Boyes displayed in the capture of the enemy's stockade. He carried a Colour with the leading company, kept it in advance of all, in the face of the thickest fire, his colour-sergeants having fallen, one mortally, the other dangerously wounded, and he was only detained from proceeding yet further by the orders of his superior officer. The Colour he carried was six times pierced by musket balls.'

When *Euryalus* returned to England, Midshipman Boyes, Captain of the After Guard Thomas Pride and the Ordinary Seaman William Seeley were awarded the Victoria Cross at a special ceremony on Southsea Common on 22 September 1865. Queen Victoria was so impressed by the action of the

Colour party that she commanded that the large parade should include other naval Cross holders, including John Commerell, William Hewitt and Hugh Burgoyne. The ceremony was watched by many thousands of spectators and HMS *Victory* fired a salute. For Duncan Boyes, this was to be the high point in his short life.

Disgrace

Six months later, Boyes was serving in HMS *Cadmus* on the North American Station when his world fell apart. He and another midshipman were caught trying to break into the Naval Yard at Bermuda, presumably after overstaying their shore leave. They had previously been refused admittance by the Warder at the main gate who was enforcing the Standing Order of not allowing entry without a pass after 23.00 hours. Both admitted the offence and pleaded guilty.

The extraordinarily harsh sentence of dismissal from the service was passed for what appears to have been a fairly minor offence. There may, therefore, be more to this misdemeanour than it appears on the surface. Perhaps Boyes had previously fallen foul of the naval base's authorities or flaunted his award too publicly? The Royal Navy was very sensitive to any scandal for it had only been five years earlier that another young naval VC, Edward Daniels, had been dismissed from the service. Officially it was for desertion but the real reason was for persistent drunkenness and sodomy. At least Boyes did not have his Cross forfeited like Daniels. Perhaps, with the Daniel's experience still fresh in their minds, the Navy decided to get rid of a potential problem.

Young Boyes was devastated by this decision and became increasingly depressed. In an effort to help lift him out of his misery, he was sent out to New Zealand to join his elder brothers, who had a sheep station in Otago Province. Coincidentally, Edward Daniels also went to New Zealand. The change obviously did not work for Boyes.

Still crushed by the fall from grace he suffered a nervous breakdown. It would appear he had tried to drink his way out of his depressed state and, in a fit of dark despair, he jumped out of an upper-floor window on 26 January 1869 in Dunedin. The death certificate, however, stated that he died of 'delirium tremens'. His death was recorded in a diary kept by Midshipman Marcus McCausland serving on board HMS *Liffey*. He wrote:

'I heard here of the death of poor Duncan Gordon Boyes. He jumped from the window of a house in Dunedin in a state of DT's and smashed on the spot.'

This was to be half of a double blow to his sister, for Boyes's brother-in-law, Thomas Young VC, died two months later in Caen on 20 March 1860 aged just forty-two. Duncan Boyes bequeathed his Cross to Cheltenham College, who in turn sold it to the Lord Ashcroft collection. Boyes was buried in Dunedin, but his grave fell into disrepair. His remains were reinterred at the service's cemetery at Anderson's Bay in 1954.

Chapter 9

Bhutan War, 1864–65

Number of VCs awarded	2
Number of VCs awarded to officers	2
Total awarded to British Indian Army	2

Origins of the War

Every year during Queen Victoria's reign there was military activity of one sort or another. An area that was in almost constant turmoil was the fringes of Britain's Indian Empire. Most trouble came from the tribes on the North-West Frontier but there were also lesser known conflicts to the northeast in the foothills of the Himalayas.

Bhutan is bordered to the north and east by Tibet and to the west by the Darjeeling District of Bengal. There had been border disputes and incursions since 1841 when the British occupied Assam to the south. A diplomatic mission was sent to Bhutan in the autumn of 1864 to negotiate a settlement. Instead, the diplomats found themselves imprisoned until forced to sign, under duress, a document relinquishing British control of Assam. A demand of an apology by the British was rejected, so a punitive expedition was mounted

This force quickly and successfully occupied the important fortresses that lay along a 180-mile line some twenty to thirty miles inside the Bhutanese border. On 25 January 1865, just as the British-led force was about to hand over control to the Bengal police, it was surprised by a series of attacks that forced its withdrawal. At the most significant of these forts at Dewangari, which dominated the main routes in the area, the garrison was forced to withdraw when their water supply was cut off. The retreat almost became a rout and some of the wounded and much equipment was abandoned.

The commanding general was sacked and replaced by Brigadier General Henry Tombs VC. His plan was to advance in two columns, one to the west and the other, which he accompanied, to the east with Dewangari as the main objective. Given that the Bhutanese were armed with sling-shots, swords and ancient blunderbusses, and the British force comprised of five batteries of artillery, two British regiments, the 55th and 80th, and four native regiments; a veritable nut-cracking sledgehammer! Also accompanying the Tombs' force was No.7 Company, Bengal Sappers and Miners, which included Captain William Trevor and Lieutenant James Dundas.

After the debacle of the first occupation of Bhutan, the column led by Henry Tombs, advanced on Dewangiri, a fortified settlement that occupied a commanding position on the easternmost route into Bhutan. The terrain was most difficult, being steeply rising tracks surrounded by thick jungle and ideal for ambush. The Sappers were employed hacking their way through the dense jungle in advance of the column but sickness took its toll and progress was slow.

Tombs decided on a feint and sent a strong party along a route to the west of the objective. This successfully drew most of the enemy and left Tomb's with his chosen route which he completed unopposed. On 2 April, his force stood just half a mile from the high ridge at Dewangiri without suffering a single casualty. The sudden appearance of Tombs's force caused most of the Bhutanese to flee, but about 200 barricaded themselves in a blockhouse.

The onset of night obliged Tombs to mount a frontal attack the following day. Using the 12th Native Infantry and the Sikhs of the 29th Punjabis for the main assault up the steep approaches, he sent the 55th (Border) Regiment on a secondary assault on a smaller blockhouse to the left. The Bhutanese advanced to meet the 55th, but were soon put to flight by the redcoats' accurate musketry.

The main assault had become bogged down because the covering artillery fire had proved ineffectual and the Indian infantry found itself exposed. Tombs needed swift action to prevent any chance of the Bhutanese from returning and reinforcing the main position. He called upon the two officers of the Bengal Engineers, whose subsequent action led them being awarded the Victoria Cross.

WILLIAM SPOTTISWOOD TREVOR VC (1831-1907)

William Spottiswood Trevor was born on 9 October 1831 at Sultanpore, the second son of a Bengal cavalryman, Captain R.S. Trevor. When he was only ten, he was involved in the events of the disastrous First Afghan War. His father was a Political Officer who took his family to Kabul when the British occupied that city in August 1839. They had deposed the unfriendly ruler, Dost Mohammed, and replaced him with their preferred but unpopular candidate.

Despite the simmering discontent, the occupying force had been greatly reduced. By the end of 1841, a popular insurrection broke out demanding the deposed ruler be reinstated. The insensitive British Envoy, Sir William Macnaghton, accompanied by three of his political officers, including Captain Trevor, was invited to a meeting by the rebels. This turned out to be a trap and Macnaghton was taken away and murdered. The political officers were released but on their way back to the British cantonment, Trevor's father was set upon by a crowd and hacked to death.

Young William, his mother and five siblings were taken in to captivity by Akhbar Khan, the son of Dost Mohammed and were thus spared the appalling retreat of the British garrison through the mid-winter snows of the Afghan mountain passes. Harried all the way by tribesmen and suffering from the freezing temperatures, some 16,000 perished. It was the worst military disaster of Queen Victoria's reign. During the nine months of captivity, young Trevor learned Hindustani and Persian. Akhbar Khan tried to use him, with little success, to translate letters from India as well as finding out what was being talked about by the prisoners. A favourite amusement of Akbar's was encouraging fights between Trevor and the Afghan boys, offering as prizes legs of mutton.

It was not until October 1842, that Kabul fell to General Pollack's 'Avenging Army' and the prisoners released. The Trevor family returned to Britain and stayed with their maternal grandfather, William Spottiswoode, Laird of Glenfernet in Perthshire. When he was old enough, William Trevor attended the Scottish Naval and Military Academy in Edinburgh, which was run by the East India Company on the same lines as the more famous Addiscombe College, to which he later attended. He was an exemplary cadet and passed-out third in his year. On 11 December 1849, he was commissioned as second lieutenant in the Bengal Engineers and sent to the Royal Engineers Establishment at Chatham for further training. While there, he was selected for special duty under the Commissioners of the Great Exhibition of 1851.

Finally, he was sent to India, arriving on 5 February 1852 and was immediately detailed for active service with General Godwin's 'Army of Ava'. He served through the Second Burma War and was twice Mentioned in Despatches for his conduct in leading a storming party up one of the ladders in the attack on the White House Picket Stockade and leading the way into the stronghold at Donabew.

William Trevor remained in Burma on various engineering projects until October 1857 and missed the main conflicts of the Indian Mutiny. On 19 June 1858, he married Eliza Fisher who gave him two daughters. Sadly, Eliza died in 1863.

Promoted to Captain, Trevor was then involved in the constructing of barracks at Darjeeling when he accompanied the Darjeeling Field Force to prevent mutineers from Dacca from joining their comrades at Nilfigorie. They intercepted the mutineers on the Bhutan border at Cherabunda and in a sharp engagement, put them to flight. Afterwards, Trevor was employed on the construction of the Ganges to Darjeeling Road and in 1861, was Garrison Engineer at Fort William, Calcutta.

In February 1862, he was appointed Superintending Engineer of the Northern Circle and began to criticise the wasteful methods of the Public Works Accounts Department. As a result of his vociferous criticism, he was appointed Controller of Public Works Accounts and reformed the system.

VC Action

With the outbreak of hostilities in Bhutan, he was made Commanding Officer of the Bengal Sappers & Miners and joined General Tombs' Bhutan Field Force. En route, he had received an arrow through his trousers and near misses from other missiles. As the force approached the Dewangiri blockhouse, Trevor, who was suffering from a severe fever, heard Tombs make an appeal for officers to take the lead and show the troops the way into the blockhouse. Trevor later recalled that, 'it struck me as a reproachful appeal to those within hearing'.

Answering Tomb's appeal, Trevor charged forward, followed by Dundas and Tombs's Brigade Major, Major Sankey. Tombs could not spare Sankey, and called him back. To gain entry into the blockhouse, the only apparent access was through a two-foot space between the top of the fourteen-foot-high walls and the roof. Both engineers managed to scale the wall and squeezed head-first through the gap. Incredibly, neither was badly injured. Perhaps the narrowness of the gap prevented the defenders from using their swords effectively. Trevor was able to fire his revolver to good effect and keep the occupants at bay until joined by the storming party of Sikhs.

In a frenzy of bloodletting reminiscent of the taking of the Secundra Bagh at Lucknow, the Bhutanese were slaughtered and it was only the presence of the British officers that allowed forty-five prisoners to be taken. This, and other reports of prisoners being killed, led to a bitter controversy which Tombs felt denigrated his expedition's success in defeating a numerically stronger foe.

A further controversy arose when Tombs publicly stated that both Trevor and Dundas deserved the Victoria Cross. Trevor wrote to the Commander-in-Chief, General Sir William Mansfield, who rejected it on the grounds that, as Trevor later wrote:

'In his opinion Dundas and I as Engineer officers had acted officiously and altogether out of order in entering at all into the struggle … In fact he considered we had been guilty of an irregularity which if repeated might prove seriously detrimental to the discipline of the army and which he was determined not to encourage.

In other words, Sir William Mansfield wanted to discourage the participation in infantry battles by those whose business lay elsewhere. A similar example occurred during the Zulu War of 1879. Captain Duck of the Veterinary Corps had been recommended a VC by Colonel Redvers

Buller for his gallantry in the retreat from Hlobane Mountain. This was rejected on the grounds that he had no right in being there!

Trevor refused to accept what he saw as a rebuff and a slight on his honour. He lobbied support from Tombs and Sir Henry Durand, the distinguished political officer and military member of the Governor-General's Council. Finally, despite Mansfield offering a brevet majority, Trevor managed to have the C-in-C's decision reversed and the Queen approved of the award. On 23 March 1868, nearly three years after the event, both Trevor and Dundas received their Crosses from Major-General Fordyce at Fort William, Calcutta.

Later Life

William Trevor must have wondered if his persistence in seeking the VC was worth it for he received scant recognition for his considerable service to India. He did receive his majority in 1872 and was Chief Engineer in Central India in 1873. He returned to Burma 1875-1880 as Chief Engineer of the Public Works Department. Further prestigious appointments followed, for he was a talented engineer and administrator.

When lesser men were receiving their KCBs, William Trevor retired on 19 February 1887 as a major general. His health never recovered from his service in Bhutan. The gash on his forehead continued to torment him for the rest of his life as did the reoccurring attacks of jungle fever. He lived out his retirement in England and died at his home at 11, Queen's Mansions, Victoria Street London., where he died on 1 November 1907 aged seventy-six. He was buried at Kensal Green Cemetery.

JAMES DUNDAS VC (1842-1879)

James Dundas was born on 12 September 1842 at 28 Abercrombie Place, Edinburgh, the second, and twin with brother Colin, of nine children of George Dundas, a judge, and Elizabeth MacKenzie. When he was ten, he was sent to Edinburgh Academy and was in the same class as another future VC recipient, John Cook.

He later attended Trinity College and Glenalmond. In 1859, he studied at Addiscombe College and on 6 June 1860 was commissioned into the Bengal Engineers. He carried out his basic training with the Royal Engineers at Brompton Barracks, Chatham before sailing to India in March 1862, where he was posted to the headquarters of the Sappers & Miners at Rurki. He obviously showed talent for he was soon promoted to Executive Officer to the Public Works Department in Bengal.

Gallant Actions

His first experience of active service came when he was chosen to take part in the operations against Bhutan in 1865 and came under the command of Captain William Trevor. James Dundas seems to have been the passive partner in Trevor's quest for the Victoria Cross. When his partner in the action was successful in securing the award, it would have been impossible to exclude Dundas. After the war, he re-joined the Bengal Public Works and, after a leave in Britain in 1870, he was appointed personal assistant to General Sir Alexander Taylor.

In 1878, he again performed a heroic act. A house in the Simla bazaar had caught alight and the roof had partly fallen in, trapping the occupant. Dundas was passing and attempted to enter the blazing building but was driven back by smoke and falling rubbish. He called for a volunteer to help him and a Royal Artillery officer responded. This time Dundas reached the trapped native and carried him to safety, sustaining badly burned hands.

In the summer of 1879, he opted for active service and joined General Frederick Roberts as Commanding Royal Engineer in the advance on Kabul. With the onset of winter, Roberts's Field Force retired into the Sherpur Cantonment until the spring. On the afternoon of 23 December 1879, Captain Dundas and Lieutenant Charles Nugent were ordered to blow up a line of enemy forts to the south of the cantonment. Finding one of the fuses was defective they improvised a home-made device which caused a premature explosion, killing them both.

James Dundas was buried in the Seah Sang Cemetery near Sherpur. He is also commemorated in five places including St Mary's Cathedral, Edinburgh, Glenalmond School and a stained-glass window in Rochester Cathedral, Kent. As recently as 2002, he received another memorial in the shape of a replacement bridge on the road between Kabul and Bagram. Built by the Royal Engineers, it is called the Dundas Bridge.

Chapter 10

Fenian Raids – Canada, 1866

Number of VCs awarded	1
Number of VCs awarded to other ranks	1
Total awarded to British Army	1

Origins of the War

After the American Civil War, the Fenian Brotherhood, an Irish Republican organisation founded in 1858 in the United States, began agitating again for Irish independence. The Brotherhood raised money by the issue of bonds which were bought by the faithful in the expectation of them being honoured when Ireland became independent.

Large quantities of arms were purchased and preparations to send raids into Canada were openly made. Its membership comprised mostly of recently discharged soldiers of Irish descent, who now had military experience. As John Black Atkins wrote, 'Again and again, the United States Government had alarmed Great Britain by language which displayed a provocative sympathy with the Irish and seemed to threaten Canada'. The American Government initially did turn a blind eye to the Fenian's activities mainly because of Britain and Canada's support for the Confederate States in the Civil War.

In 1866, the Fenians began to cross the Canadian border in large numbers with the intention of seizing the transportation network of Quebec and Ontario. This was expected to force the British Government into a trade-off to grant independence to Ireland. Although there were British regiments stationed in Canada, these incursions in April and June were easily dealt with by the local Canadian militias. Nevertheless, the threat was still there and the border area was kept on high alert.

In early June, a sergeant and three riflemen of the Rifle Brigade, were delegated to escort a boxcar loaded with munitions and blankets to supply the militia on the border at Lake Erie. In order that it should be unnoticed by Fenian spies, the boxcar was attached midway to a four-carriage passenger train carrying German immigrants. As the train moved in to the station of the small town of Danville, about seventy miles from the Vermont border, an alert engineer spotted smoke and fire coming from the ammunition car. It was here that a Victoria Cross was awarded despite not being in the presence of the enemy and causing an inconvenient precedent.

TIMOTHY O'HEA VC (1846-1874?)

Timothy O'Hea was born at Schull, County Cork on 11 June 1843. Like many of his countrymen, poverty forced him to join the British Army.

On 6 November 1863, he enlisted in Dublin with the 1st Battalion Rifle Brigade. He was immediately posted to Canada, where the regiment had been sent in 1862. The American Civil War, which had started in 1861, posed a real threat that it could spill over in to Canada. With the cessation of that conflict, the regiment pulled back from the border and was garrisoned at Quebec.

VC Action

The regiment was not involved in the raids by the Fenians except for guard and escort duties. One such was accompanying the munitions boxcar to the border. On 9 July, as the train approached the small town of Danville in Quebec, the munitions wagon was seen to be on fire. It seems probable that sparks from the engine had set alight the dry timbers of the boxcar. The brakeman, Albert Marquette, had the presence of mind to disconnect the smouldering car from the rest of the train and to have the engine move the front two passenger cars away from the station while the rear cars were moved by some railway workers. Also in the station at the time were two full passenger trains.

The burning car contained over 2,000 rounds of ammunition and ninety-five barrels of gunpowder, which was unknown to the many onlookers enjoying the spectacle. When word was received of its contents, the crowd quickly dispersed. The four-man escort responsible for the munitions wagon gingerly approached the isolated car. Sergeant Hill, who held the key to the car, was uncertain what to do and stood dithering for a few minutes. Finally, O'Hea passed his rifle to a comrade, grabbed the key from Hill and ran to the burning car.

Fortunately for the immigrants, they were unaware of the terrible danger they were in and cheered on the lone soldier. O'Hea unlocked the door and slid it open. The flames were licking on the back wall and sparks and splinters were falling and threatening the gunpowder barrels. O'Hea called for water and a ladder. The only person to respond was Marquette, the brakeman, who climbed into the wagon and joined O'Hea as he tried to beat out the flames with a blanket.

There are several versions of what happened during the next hour. Some state that O'Hea acted entirely alone, even making nineteen trips to fill buckets from a nearby creek. It seems more likely that O'Hea's example galvanized some into action. A bucket chain was organised and water was passed from the station's rainwater tubs to douse the flames. O'Hea and Marquette began to unload the munitions for one spark would have set off such an explosion that a large part of Danville would have been destroyed.

At length, the fire was extinguished and a blackened and exhausted O'Hea emerged from the smoke-filled wagon. The German immigrants cheered and a hat was passed around among the onlookers, to reward the private who had risked his life to save Danville. Another wagon was found and the munitions were loaded. The train was then re-coupled and completed its journey.

One of the witnesses to O'Hea's efforts was Captain Henry Hanning of the Danville Volunteer Rifles who wrote to Lord Alexander Russell, the Colonel of the Rifles praising O'Hea's gallantry. This, together with other eye-witness accounts, prompted Colonel Lord Russell to send a report to the General Officer Commanding Troops in Canada who in turn forwarded it to Horse Guards without recommendation or suggestion of bestowing the Victoria Cross.

Quandry

Once received in Whitehall, O'Hea's case became a political football. To understand this, one must go back to the Indian Ocean about 800 miles off Mauritius.

On 11 November 1857, the troopship *Sarah Sands* carrying a detachment of the 54th (Dorsetshire) Regiment bound for India caught fire. Most of the crew took to the boats, but the soldiers remained and, after eighteen hours, managed to put out the fire and bring the ship safely to Mauritius.

There was much lobbying for this outstanding act of collective bravery to be rewarded with the Victoria Cross. One of its chief supporters was the Secretary of State, Major General Jonathan Peel. As there was no provision in the existing Warrant to reward gallantry performed *not* before the enemy, it was proposed that the statutes of the VC be amended to include acts of gallantry as performed by the men on board the *Sarah Sands*. On 10 August 1858, Queen Victoria signed the Warrant Extending the Victoria Cross to Cases of Conspicuous Courage and Bravery Displayed under Circumstances of Danger but not before the Enemy.

This new Warrant was not popular with the civil servants and the Clerk at the War Office, Edward Pennington, commented that it 'would be making the Victoria Cross too cheap to grant it'. In fact, it was never published in *The London Gazette* and was something of a guilty secret. In the event, it was not implemented in the case of the *Sarah Sands*. With the fall of the Derby-Disraeli Government in June 1859, General Peel ceased to be the Secretary of State and the contentious Warrant was quietly shelved.

In July 1866, it was reactivated in the case of Timothy O'Hea. Another change of government saw General Peel back at the War Office as Secretary of State. As the 1858 Warrant had been drawn up under his direction, the recommendation for O'Hea's Cross was implemented despite the lingering feeling by many that it set an inconvenient precedent. On New Year's Day 1867, *The London Gazette* published O'Hea's citation:

'For his courageous conduct on the occasion of a fire which occurred in a railway car containing ammunition, between Quebec and Montreal, on the 9 June last. The sergeant in charge of the escort states that, when at Danville Station, on the Grand Trunk Railway, the alarm was given that a car was on fire; it was immediately disconnected, and, whilst considering what was to be done, Private O'Hea took the keys from his hand, rushed to the car, opened it, and called out for water and ladder. It was stated that it was due to his example that the fire was suppressed.'

It is significant that O'Hea's VC is the only one in which the Warrant of 1858 was mentioned in the citation. On 25 April 1867, Private Timothy O'Hea was invested with his Cross by Colonel Thomas Pakenham in a ceremony on the parade ground at the Quebec Garrison. O'Hea's moment of glory was brief. His health had started to cause concern. Smoke inhalation and unhealthy conditions in the barracks probably contributed to O'Hea contracting tuberculosis. Just five months after the VC was pinned to his chest, O'Hea was invalided back to England and the Netley Hospital near Southampton.

By 17 March 1868, his condition had deteriorated to the point where he was medically discharged from the Army. He would receive seven pence a day for one year to augment his £10 annuity for receiving the Victoria Cross. His fare was paid so he could return to his home in Ireland, where it was expected he would soon succumb to his terminal sickness.

Mystery

The following four years are frustratingly blank. Based on what was to follow in the Antipodes, educated guesswork must be applied. Timothy's date of death is so far unknown but probably occurred 1869-70. His younger brother, John, appears to have been an active nationalist and known to the British authorities. It seems probable that the dying Timothy passed on his VC and pension to John, who planned to travel to the other side of the world.

This he did and in 1873, John O'Hea assuming Timothy's identity, enlisted firstly in the Otago Police and then in the New Zealand Armed Constabulary. The late Elizabeth Reid wrote a book entitled *The Singular Journey of O'Hea's Cross* and compared Timothy's army enlistment documents with those in New Zealand and noted some compelling differences. Although there is only a difference of half an inch in height, the eye colour is different, as is the occupations, 'labourer' instead of 'clerk'. The clincher is the baptismal date; Timothy was on 11 June 1843, whilst John's was 10 January 1846. The latter is shown on the New Zealand document. With his brother's VC Warrant, John was able to draw the pension from the local District Office. The two images show a family likeness but are not the same man. The VC Timothy wore in his photograph looks identical to John's image in Australia as it has the same buckle fixing.

The records show that O'Hea left the New Zealand Constabulary on 30 May 1874 and next appears in Sydney, Australia. Here, he comes to the attention of Frederick Du Faur of the Occupation of Crown Lands Office and member of the Royal Society of New South Wales. As a patron of exploration, Du Faur persuaded O'Hea to join an expedition to discover the fate of Ludwig Leichhardt's trans-continental expedition of 1848, which had disappeared after moving inland from the Darling Downs.

O'Hea left some belongings with Du Faur, including his photo. He entrusted his VC to Du Faur's brother-in-law, Major Henry Crummer. The expedition appears to have been badly led and by November 1874, O'Hea disappeared in the bush near Noccundra Station, Graham's Creek, Sturt's Desert, Queensland. His body was never found. Knowing no better, the Australian newspapers reported the death as that of the Irish VC winner, Timothy O'Hea and this became his accepted fate. The mystery, however, had not run its course.

Unable to trace O'Hea's relatives, Major Crummer kept the Cross for thirty years before donating it to the National Art Gallery of NSW, of which Du Faur was the president. On 29 June 1900, another O'Hea Cross was sold at Debenhams in London for £57. It was bought by an American collector, who later gave his collection to the American Numismatic Society in New York.

Frederick Du Fau learned of this sale and was convinced that the American Cross was a fake. To prove this, he sent his VC to London in 1907 where it was authenticated by Hancocks. The Americans declined to submit theirs. This case prompted the War Office to ask Hancocks to include some secret and inconspicuous mark to be incorporated on all future Crosses they made.

The genuine Cross was returned to Australia and eventually removed from public display and placed in storage. It was re-discovered in 1950 and on 29 May 1951, presented to the Rifle Brigade. In 1953, the American Numismatic Society questioned the authenticity of this Cross. This time Hancocks examined both Crosses and declared the one held by the Rifle Brigade to be the original.

Chapter 11

Gambia Expedition, 1866

Number of VCs awarded	1
Number of VCs awarded to other ranks	1
Total awarded to British Army	1

Origins of the War

The West African coastline had been an important source and departure point for slaves bound for the West Indies and the southern states of America. The decline in the slave trade was thanks to Britain abolishing of this awful practise and policing the coast with a Royal Navy anti-slavery squadron. Based in Sierra Leone, with a military presence at the mouth of the River Gambia, the Royal Navy gradually overcame the slavers.

Having established a garrison and founded the town of Bathurst on the south side of the Gambia estuary, Britain laid claim to the navigable stretch of the river which extended into French Senegal. By the end of the nineteenth century, a border had been established with the French, whose colony surrounded the new British territory, which was little more than the downstream half of the river and its two banks. Named 'The Gambia', it was one of the smallest African countries to be established by the nineteenth century colonists, being just 48km wide at its greatest width and about 100km in length to the border with Senegal.

The British presence was not welcomed by all of the native tribes, in particular the Muslim slavers. In the 1850s, Islamic fundamentalist warriors, referred to as Marabouts, began infiltrating Gambia from Senegal and other parts of the interior. The local rulers, as well as the British, were alarmed by these warlike intruders and there was stiff fight in 1853 in which the Marabouts were beaten by the British. The defeated Marabouts were so fanatical that many committed suicide rather than surrender. There were two more fierce encounters before some of the Marabout leaders agreed to a treaty.

One leader who did not was Amar Faal, who created severe problems for the tribal headsmen who relied on British protection. Finally, Lieutenant-Colonel George Abbas Koolie D'Arcy, the Governor of the Gambia, decided to assault Amar Faal's stockaded town of Tubabekolong (also known as Tubab Kolon) on the north side of the river. D'Arcy was also commander of the West India Regiment stationed at Bathurst. In earlier days' it was the British-based regiments who were sent to the Gambia, which was like a death sentence for they were so prone to tropical diseases that their numbers soon dwindled and they ceased to be effective units. It was concluded that the West India Regiments, recruited and stationed in the British colonies of the Caribbean, would be better adapted to tropical service.

On 26 July 1866, the Bathurst garrison of the 270 men and officers of 4th West India Regiment led by Colonel D'Arcy made their way upriver in two ships. Landing at Albreda, the West Indian troops were joined by some 500 Soninke warriors, and the expanded force set off through the jungle towards the enemy's stronghold at Tubabekolong.

SAMUEL HODGE VC (1840-1868)

On 30 July, Tubabakolong was reached. The West Indian soldiers began a bombardment with their light guns and rockets, neither of which proved effective against the wooden stockade walls. Colonel D'Arcy called for volunteers to join him in hacking a breach in the stockade wall. Lieutenant Jenkins and Ensign Kelly with fifteen men, including Hodge, seized pioneer's axes and followed him. By the time the party reached the stockade, both officers were dead and only Privates Hodge and Boswell were unwounded.

As Hodge and Boswell began chopping at the vines that bound the stockade posts together, the latter was killed. Finally, a breach was made and Hodge and Colonel D'Arcy forced their way through the gap. Amar Faal, the Marabout chief, came forward and fired almost point blank at Colonel D'Arcy but miraculously missed him. D'Arcy's aim was true and the chief was killed. Hodge remained with D'Arcy, handing him loaded muskets. With the rest of the regiment coming up, Hodge made for the main gate to his right. Still brandishing his axe, he put the defenders to flight, before hacking open the two gates from inside, allowing the rest of the force to stream through into the town. As he completed his task, Hodge was shot and badly wounded. In the fierce fighting that followed, several hundred Marabouts were killed and the stockade was burned to the ground. The British casualties amounted to two officers and four men killed, and nearly sixty others wounded.

Early Life

Samuel Hodge was about twenty-six-years-old and was born in Tortola in the British Virgin Islands. He enlisted in the West India Regiment as a

Pioneer and sent to the Gambia. Colonel D'Arcy recommended Private Hodge for the Victoria Cross, which appeared in the January 1867 edition of *The London Gazette.*

Promoted to lance corporal and still suffering the effects of his wounds, Hodge received his Victoria Cross on 24 June 1867 in British Honduras (now Belize) from Brigadier General Robert Harley. Sadly, Hodge succumbed to his wounds on 14 January 1868 and was buried in Belize Military Cemetery.

Chapter 12

Andaman Expedition, 1867

Number of VCs awarded	5
Number of VCs awarded to officers	1
Number of VCs awarded to other ranks	4
Total awarded to British Army	5

Origins of the War

In 1789, the government of Bengal established a naval base and penal colony on Chatham Island off Great Andaman Island in the Bay of Bengal. After two years' it moved to Great Andaman but by 1796 disease and death forced the colony to be abandoned. The islands gained a sinister reputation for any unfortunate shipwrecked sailors who were washed up and often attacked by the cannibalistic natives. The instances of these outrages forced the British government to once again occupy Great Andaman and establish a convict colony. In much the same way that Alcatraz Prison was established in San Francisco Bay, so the Andaman Islands, in the Bay of Bengal and hundreds of miles from a mainland, were regarded as escape proof.

The Indian Mutiny saw many rebel prisoners condemned to this convict establishment and it was through their labours that a prison was constructed at Port Blair away from the malarial swamps of the previous colony. For some time, the sickness and mortality rate were high, but swamp reclamation and forest clearance lowered the incidence of death.

It is of interest that in December 1879, a Chief Commissioner and Superintendent of the Andaman and Nicobar Islands was appointed, He was the Indian Mutiny VC, Thomas Cadell, who administered the prison colony in a humane and considerate manner until his retirement in 1892.

Ships sailing between India and Burma had to pass through the Andaman chain of islands. Sailing from Rangoon, the merchant ship, *Assam Valley*, anchored off Little Andaman Island on 21 March 1867. The vessel had lost her main top-sail in a storm en route from Bombay but had been unable to replace it at Rangoon. The captain decided to stop at the island where there was plenty of timber for the ship's carpenter to fashion a replacement spar. Led by the captain, seven crew members went ashore to search for suitable timber and were seen from the ship to land and enter the thick jungle.

About an hour later about thirty natives were spotted coming from the same part of the jungle into which the ship's party had entered. Unable to land because of the heavy surf, *Assam Valley* waited a further two days without sighting their fellow crew members. Finally, they sailed back to Rangoon and reported the disappearance.

Another ship, *Sylvia,* returned to the island but without success other than finding a sailor's cap on the beach. A few days later the gunboat *Kwang Tung* from Port Blair carrying the British Officer in Charge of the Andamese, along with some local natives to show their friendly intention, landed only to be met by the hostile native Onge tribe. Driven back to their boats, the British returned to Port Blair. It was then decided to send a larger party with a military presence from Rangoon.

Arracan arrived off Little Andaman Island on 6 May, seven weeks after the disappearance of the crew of *Assam Valley.* A party from the 2/24th Regiment, sappers from the Madras Engineers and members of the Naval Brigade made up the rescue mission. Two cutters and a gig were launched. Aboard the first cutter were thirteen crew and ten soldiers of the 24th who were to act as a covering party.

In the second cutter carrying twenty-five including crew, was a young lieutenant, William Thomas Much of the 24th, who's report described their landing. Much, however, omits to mention that Assistant Surgeon Douglas was in the third vessel, the gig, which accompanied the landing, carrying fourteen including crew. As it approached the shore, it lost its rudder and Douglas and four others swam ashore to join Much's party:

'We left on the 6th or 7th at 8.30 a.m., I left the ship to land on Little Andaman in a big boat with seven Brigade men and five Sappers. I carried a rifle and revolver. The surf did not seem very bad, and so, after the sea had washed two or three times over us, we jumped out of the boat on shore in about 4½ feet of water, holding our rifles over our heads, and our revolvers and ammunition buckled around our necks. Sometimes a wave would come, and the water would be up to my neck, and I could just touch the bottom with my toes. We got on shore all right, but nearly all our powder was wet, so I made the men dry it in the sun. We then went to the spot where they said the men had been killed.

'The sands were only about twenty-five yards wide, and then there were very thick bushes and trees. We had to keep a sharp look-out, as the savages might come out of these bushes, where we could not see them and fire arrows at us. We found a European skull, one side broken, with a little brown hair knocked in, one ankle boot and parts of the boat.'

Douglas, who had joined the party by then, described the skull as having been beaten with a club or an axe.

'We found a grave where four others had been buried. They were laying full length on the beach. They had their clothes on. One had a pair of long sea boots.'

Lieutenant Much rather gilded the lily with his account of the skirmish with the natives:

'Several times the savages fired arrows at us from the bushes. We could only see them now and then. When we did, we killed them. They were generally in small pits, lying on their bellies, and only showed their heads and shoulders. My men killed a great many. I think about thirty – some say fifty – others over one hundred. It was impossible to say how many, as they did not utter a word when shot, and the bushes were too thick for us to go in and see the dead. Sometimes the arrows were flying all around me – some at my feet, others over my head. I had to bob my head to get out of the way. We were only fifteen yards from them. The arrows are five feet long, made of pointed wood, and would right through a man.

'I called to the boat that brought us on shore to come and fetch us, but in trying to come near us they were capsized, and the surf was then from ten to twelve feet high. One officer who could not swim and had only come to see what could be seen was in this boat, and he, poor fellow was drowned. I saw him in the boat, and never saw him again.'

This cutter to which Lieutenant Much refers was swamped and capsized. Only along for the ride, Lieutenant Glasford of the 9th (Gurkha Rifles) Regiment Bengal Infantry was unable to swim. Douglas saw his plight and plunged into the surf but hit his head on a rock, disorientating him for a while until he recovered enough to swim out to the gig with the covering party. Lieutenant Much continued:

'The surf was fearful for about fifteen miles around. The boat sent us a raft and I and three others got on it, and boat pulled us out very slowly. The waves were breaking on us every minute. We had to hold on the spars forming the raft. We had got about 300 yards from the shore when an enormous wave broke on us ... It washed me right off and left me struggling in the water. I had a pair of white trousers and coat, flannel shirt, and a revolver in a belt around my waist. As soon as I rose to the top, I looked around and saw the raft about ten yards from me. I knew I could never reach it, so I turned towards the beach, the waves overtaking me every now and then, and sending me right under the water. I was getting quite exhausted, and seeing the beach a long way off, I thought I would be drowned. I struggled along and got about twenty yards from the beach. When I touched the bottom, I tottered along and held up my hands to my men on shore, who came and dragged me on shore as helpless as a child.

'About 3 o'clock our doctor (Douglas), with four of our soldiers (24th) came in one of the ship's boats through the surf to try and rescue us.'

CAMPBELL MELLIS DOUGLAS VC (1840-1909)

Born on 5 August 1840 in Grosse Isle, Quebec, Campbell Mellis Douglas was the eldest son of Dr George Mellis Douglas and Charlotte, née Campbell. Dr Douglas was the Superintendent at the Gaspe Island / Grosse Isle Quarantine Station, a position he held for nearly thirty years. Campbell Mellis Douglas was educated at St John's College and Laval University, Quebec, before graduating from Edinburgh University with an Masters' degree in 1861. He joined the British Army and was commissioned in May 1863 as Assistant Surgeon attached to the 24th (2nd Warwickshire) Regiment. It was while stationed in Rangoon that the regiment received the order to investigate the disappearance of the men from *Assam Valley.*

VC Action

In what had been a mercy mission began to turn into a highly dangerous situation, as the landing party of seventeen men was soon attacked and the men retreated to an open beach but were unable to leave due to heavy surf, caused by a violent storm, swamping their boat.

The attempt by the first cutter to rescue the marooned men ended with the boat capsizing and Lieutenant Glasford being drowned. Douglas, who, as we have seen, had hit his head on a rock in an attempt to rescue Glasford, managed to swim through the breakers and reach the gig with the covering party. He prepared to return to the shore and his call for four volunteers was answered by privates Cooper, Murphy, Bell and Griffiths of the 24th.

Douglas was an accomplished boatman and had previously prepared a regatta crew in Burma. The crew that he had trained was so strong that after winning the first race, it was banned from further competition to give the other crews a chance. His crew's names were not recorded, but it is likely that it was the same crew concerned in this rescue.

Managing to keep the gig upright, the crew noticed that some men had been swept into the sea from a raft. Douglas, a strong swimmer, dived in and managed to grab Lieutenant Much and put him back on the raft, from where he was again swept away. Douglas then swam to save Chief Officer Dunn, who was floundering in the turbulent surf. With the gig filling with water Douglas and the crew were forced to retire and try again. High, rolling waves had thwarted their first attempt, but a second an hour later managed to get through the crashing surf. With Douglas in the gig's bows, he kept it on an even keel by shifting his weight from side to side and using an oar as a rudder. With night rapidly approaching, Douglas and his crew made two trips through the surf and brought all seventeen soldiers away safely.

Later Service

Having ascertained the fate of the crew of *Assam Valley*, the *Arracan* returned to Rangoon. Soon the story of the rescue reached the ears of the Commander-in-Chief in India, Sir William Mansfield. Remembering the recent example of Private Timothy O'Hea and the 1858 Warrant, Mansfield forwarded his own recommendation for the Victoria Cross to be awarded to Douglas and his four crewmen.

The War Office was still not comfortable about the 1858 Warrant which: 'Extended the Victoria Cross to Cases of Conspicuous Courage and Bravery under Circumstances of Danger but not before the Enemy'. In fact, the Warrant was short lived as there were no further VCs awarded for such a circumstance and in the 1919 Warrant under Number 3 of Rules and Ordinances it was clearly stated that: 'It is ordained that the Cross shall only be awarded for most conspicuous bravery or some pre-eminent act of valour or self-sacrifice or extreme devotion to duty in the presence of the enemy.'

On 17 December 1867, *The London Gazette* published the citation that covered all five men who had battled their through the heavy surf at Little Andaman Island. On 16 April 1868 at a special parade in Rangoon, the five men were presented with their Crosses by Major-General Faunce the GOC Pegu Division.

Thomas Murphy left the Army the following year and immigrated to Philadelphia where he died in 1900 aged sixty.

Birmingham-born James Cooper returned to his previous trade as a jeweller in the Birmingham Jewellery Quarter in the Hockley area of the city and died in Birmingham in 1882

Irishman David Bell was discharged from the 24th in 1873 and worked at the Chatham Dockyards. He died at his home in Gillingham in 1920.

Another Irish soldier was William Griffiths who was still a private in 1879. He was with the 2nd Battalion 24th Regiment that was all but wiped out at the Battle of Isandlwana on 22nd January 1879.

In addition to receiving the Victoria Cross, Surgeon Douglas was also awarded the silver medal by the Royal Humane Society, for the same rescue mission. The Society's citation read:

'While in this critical and very dangerous predicament … Dr Campbell Douglas showed all the qualities of a real hero. Being an excellent swimmer, and possessing great boldness and courage, he swam after the drowning men. Twice was Lieutenant Much, the commander of the party, washed off the raft, and while struggling in the rolling waves, Dr Douglas swam to his rescue, and brought him back safe to the raft; similarly, Mr Dunn, the chief officer of the *Arracan,* was sinking, confused and overcome by the surging waves. Here again Dr Douglas played the part of the hero, and saved the drowning man; there were others thus rescued by the brave doctor, but his efforts to save poor Lieutenant Glassford [*sic*], of the Ghoorka Regiment, were unsuccessful.'

Campbell Douglas transferred to the Royal Artillery in Nova Scotia in 1872 and was promoted to surgeon major. While stationed in Halifax, he met and fell in love with Elenore Burmester, the widow of Surgeon Valentine McMaster, the Indian Mutiny VC. The couple married on 10

August 1874 in what is probably a unique instance of a woman marrying two recipients of the Victoria Cross. The British Census of 1881 shows the family, with the addition of another son, living at 4 Burdon Terrace, Jesmond, Northumberland. On 1 October 1882, he retired from the Army with the rank of lieutenant colonel and honorary brigade surgeon.

Douglas took his family, now increased with a daughter, back to Canada and set up a private medical practice in Lakefield, Ontario. When the Riel Rebellion broke out on the prairies in 1885, Douglas was recruited to take charge of a field hospital in Saskatchewan. On arrival by rail, he found the steamer that was take him to the 1st Canadian Field Hospital at Saskatoon had run aground on a sandbar. Undeterred, he unpacked his collapsible canoe and paddled the 200 miles up the Little Saskatchewan River to Saskatoon. He used the same collapsible boat to canoe from New York to Boston in 1889 and, in 1895, he paddled across the English Channel.

After the Reil campaign, the Douglas family moved back to England. Although he had retired from the British Army, he acted as Depot Medical Officer at Berwick and Perth, before finally retiring in 1902. Campbell Douglas died on 31 December 1909 at his daughter Muriel's home in Somerset. He is buried in Wells Cemetery (grave M-20) and, when she died in 1963, Muriel was buried with her father.

Chapter 13

Abyssinian War, 1867–68

Number of VCs awarded	2
Number of VCs awarded to other ranks	2
Total awarded to British Army	2

Origins of the War

In 1818, a child named Kassa Haile Giorgis was born in the north-west of Abyssinia (Ethiopia) near the Blue Nile. Displaying intelligence, he was sent to a Coptic monastery to be educated as a scribe. Learning quickly, he became literate and well versed in Bible history, seemingly destined for a devout future.

Abyssinia was country rife with civil war and a local warlord sacked the monastery but Kassa managed to escape. Abandoning thoughts of training to be a monk, he turned to the more lucrative employment of a warlord. Soon he commanded his own army, large by local standards, and he set about subjugating his rivals. In 1852, he married Tewabech Ali, the granddaughter of the warlord who controlled the Gondar region. The marriage seems to have been a happy one, but the relationship between Kassa and his new in-laws became deadly. In 1854, he deposed his Gondar relations, had them executed and proclaimed himself Emperor Theodore II (Tewodros II).

He believed in his own version of Christianity which did not sit well with Western missionaries but, as they were treated well by the new emperor, they turned a blind eye to his excesses. Theodore sought to eliminate all Muslims from the country and was guilty of many barbaric acts. He was also astute enough to seek European technological know-how, particularly in artillery, which he saw as a sure way to conquer his enemies.

A Protestant mission sent a group lay preachers who were also skilled artisans who organised an ordnance casting works. Other missions were also sent to the country despite the Abyssinians considering their brand of Christianity superior to any other. Britain established a friendly connection with Theodore through a young diplomat named Walter Plowden. During an uprising, Plowden was captured by a band of rebels and seriously wounded. Theodore offered a large ransom and Plowden was released but succumbed to his wounds. Outraged, Theodore dealt cruelly with the rebel band and over 1,500 were slaughtered.

To add to his distress, Theodore's wife died around this time (1860) and this had the effect of tipping him over the edge. By this time, he was firmly in control of the country but decided to launch another blood-letting campaign against the Gallas with the intention of exterminating them. He became increasingly prone to bouts of uncontrollable rage exacerbated by his taste for the potent liquor arrak. This increasing addiction to drink made him ever more belligerent and unstable.

The British Foreign Office appointed Captain Charles Cameron as consul to replace Walter Plowden. He was instructed to base himself at Massawa on the Red Sea and avoid becoming involved in any factional disputes in the country. In 1862, Cameron reached Theodore's camp with a letter from Queen Victoria, a rifle and a pair of fine pistols. Theodore expressed pleasure at the gifts, though he rather dampened the feelings of goodwill by announcing he had slaughtered over a thousand men in order to demonstrate his admiration for the English Queen.

Cameron spent a month in the camp and left with a letter to Victoria expressing his thanks and calling on Britain to join the military action again the Muslims. The letter eventually reached the Foreign Secretary, Lord John Russell, in 1863 and was viewed with some alarm. Russell, elderly and frail and with a reputation for rashness untarnished by experience, did nothing. Britain could not be expected to join an obscure despot in a crusade against Islam when many millions of Muslims made up large parts of the Empire. The letter was quietly shelved in the hopes that Theodore would forget all about it.

Cameron did not return directly to Massawa but visited the Egyptian cotton-growing area bordering Abyssinia. The American Civil War was cutting supplies from the Confederacy to the Lancashire cotton mills and Cameron was tasked with looking for alternative suppliers. When Theodore found out that Cameron had visited the hated Egyptians, and also had not brought a reply from Queen Victoria, he had the consul and five other Europeans arrested. They were sent to the mountain fortress of Magdala where they were tortured and put in fetters. Cameron was especially singled out for harsh treatment. He was subjected to a primitive rack until he fainted and flogged until he bled. To add to his agony, he was rolled in dry sand. Cameron was then forced to write to London with the succinct message, 'No release until civil answer to King's letter arrives.'

This was the first of several messages Cameron sent but Gladstone's Liberal Government was loath to send a military force. Instead they pursed a diplomatic course during 1864 with the appointment of Hormuzd

Rassam, an archaeologist who undertook tasks for the British government. During 1865, the prisoners from Magdala were escorted to Kuarata on the Blue Nile and the feeling was that diplomacy had succeeded. Then suddenly Theodore's mood changed and he had his prisoners again confined. He harangued Rassam, demanding teams of European engineers to erect machinery to make arms and munitions. Theodore wrote two letters to Queen Victoria and the Secretary of State reiterating his request and demanding artillery instructors to train his men.

With Theodore's sanity in decline, the country was in a state of general discontent, although none actually opposed him. He continued his oppressive and cruel rule, adding Rassam and his companions to his other captives. In 1867, Lord Derby's minority Conservative government replaced the Liberals, who had spent the previous five years procrastinating about the Abyssinian problem. Although the incoming government accepted that to sanction a military rescue mission would be extremely expensive, public pressure now demanded that it should be launched. The first alternative was to send home-based British units, but a mixture of a hostile climate and difficult transport problems (the Suez Canal had not been completed) made the government look to India.

It was soon decided that Bombay should be the base of the expedition with the Commander-in-Chief of the Bombay Presidency Army, Lieutenant-General Sir Robert Napier as its commander. This turned out to be a wise choice, for Sir Robert was a cool and methodical soldier. He had graduated from Addiscombe and commissioned in the Bengal Engineers and became well versed in constructing roads in rugged terrains. He gathered a talented staff about him who collected detailed information about the country and its people. The force he put together included explorers, map producers, artists, linguists and, above all, engineers.

The military element was made up primarily of the Bombay Native Cavalry, Infantry, Artillery and Sappers and Miners. The British regiments who were serving in India, were the 4th (King's Own), 26th (Cameronians), the 33rd (Duke of Wellington's) and 45th (Sherwood Foresters). In addition, were the 10th Company Royal Engineers, 3rd Dragoon Guards and a contingent of the Royal Artillery. A ninety-strong Naval Brigade from HMS *Dryad* equipped with rocket tubes was invited to join the expedition. Essential for the advance into largely unknown territory were the thousands of draft animals needed to carry stores, equipment and food. According to Sir Robert's memorandum dated 6 September 1867, the round numbers were 4,000 British, 8,000 Indian, with at least an equal number of camp followers, and 25,000 head of cattle for food. In addition, the draft animals included horses, mules, camels and elephants.

A survey for a suitable landing-place decided on Zula in Annesley Bay. Even here the engineers had to overcome the long-shallow beach and build two 300-yard-long jetties to enable the ships to unload their men and supplies. Soon tents and piles of supplies lined the roadway south out of Zula. A new innovation essential for the expedition's success was the construction of a desalination plant for water supplies in the area, though supplies from these were at best fitful.

A forward base was set up sixty-five miles to the south at Senafé, a fertile area which abounded with game. It was here that the commander of the 33rd Regiment met his untimely death. One of the Army's youngest colonels, Alexander Dunn VC of Light Brigade fame, went shooting with a companion, who described the accident:

'Leaning over going uphill to take some water from his servant below him, he leant his arm, it appears, over the muzzle of his rifle, and his gaiter or something or other caught in the trigger, sending the contents of both barrels through his body, one of the barrels being loaded with slugs. He was greatly liked by his men and everybody, being a most popular man and had just got command of his Regiment for the campaign.'

It sounds as if Dunn was too easy going for Ensign Walter Wynter, who rather censoriously described him as; 'a bad Commanding Officer and not a good example to young officers and although a popular man he had gone far to destroy the Regiment.'

General Napier's caution and attention to detail paid off. The engineers, helped by gangs of road-builders, including the soldiers, had laid a road that enabled the advancing army to be constantly supplied. Finally satisfied, Sir Robert's force left Senafé in early February 1868 and began its march on Magdala, 325 miles to the south. The nearer they got to their target, the more Napier shed unnecessary personnel and reduced the baggage carried.

On 24 March the force approached Dildi from where Magdala could be seen twenty-five miles away as the crow flies. The mountainous going became evermore tough and finally some men of the 33rd Regiment had had enough. Dozens of men lay down and refused to move. Staff officers were jeered at and their own officers ignored. Although the incident was a minor one, the normally equable General Napier was incensed. He called a parade the next morning and told the 33rd that they were no longer the advance regiment and that the 4th (King's Own) was to take their place; a bitter pill to swallow as the two regiments loathed each other.

The mountainous terrain, the terrible weather and a sudden break in supplies caused the advance to halt with a few days' march of their target. As the force closed up and supplies resumes, Napier again ordered an advance and, on 10 April 1868, the long and arduous journey was nearly over as Magdala was approached through a narrow defile and onto the plateau of Arogi below the formidable mountain fortress.

From his position looking down at the plain, General Napier realised that he had been caught off balance as he had sent his pioneers, artillery and Naval Brigade via an easier route and they had arrived before his infantry. Fortunately, the 4th Regiment soon arrived, exhausted after another steep climb. As they slumped down, Theodore's artillery opened-up from the fortress and spasmodic shot landed wide of them. With the prospect of battle, the infantry men leapt up and clambered down the mountain and took a position to the right of the Naval Brigade.

Eager to take the initiative, Theodore launched some six or seven thousand foot soldiers. Down the slope they ran towards the pioneers and mountain artillery. The Naval Brigade set up their troughs and began firing the wildly inaccurate rockets. Some hit their target and gaps appeared in the charging mass. On the right the skirmishing line of the 4th and Baluchis waited until the Abyssinians came into range. To the left the mountain artillery opened fire but still the enemy came on.

The Sikh pioneers on either side of the guns, opened fire at 100 yards' range. They fired two volleys and then charged with the bayonet. In the fierce and confused fight, the Sikhs chased Theodore's men until the slope was covered with bloody corpses. Another section of the Abyssinians made for the baggage guarded by men of the 4th Regiment. Opening fire, the mob fled back towards the bayonet-wielding Sikhs. In the three-hour-long battle, some 2,000 of Theodore's army lay dead or dying below the fortress. The cost to the British was negligible, just twenty men wounded, two of whom died later.

This unexpected battle provoked by Napier's tactical error had proved decisive. The British camped for the night at Arogi without tents in pouring rain. The many dead and wounded on the slopes and in the ravines around the camp attracted the jackals and hyenas which kept the troops awake with their hideous howling.

The following day, after much debate with his advisors, Theodore relented and released his British prisoners. Apart from Cameron, they were in surprisingly good shape. A little while later, all the artisans who worked for the Emperor were also released. The total number of prisoners freed, including the British, was fifty-nine.

Theodore and about 2,000 of his followers remained in the fortress and refused to surrender. Napier then prepared to attack with his full command that had reached Magdala during the day. The advance began at 08.30 hours on 13 April. Accompanied by sappers carrying scaling ladders, the leading infantry battalion was the reinstalled 33rd Regiment. Their ascent was unopposed despite being forced to crawl on all fours up the steep slopes. At this point, hundreds of warriors, women and children came scrambling down the hill to surrender.

The fortress still had to be taken and it was going to be a difficult task. The bastion of Magdala rose some 300 feet sheer above the surrounding area. After an artillery barrage, the infantry assault began. Carrying their colours into action for the last time, the 33rd Regiment advanced up the narrow path to the main gate. From here they returned the fire from the forts loopholes. When it was revealed that the engineers had forgotten to bring the powder bags to blow the main gate, another way in had to be found. Three companies of the 33rd followed the wall to the right of the gateway. The wall was further protected by a barrier of thorn bushes and it was here that two VC acts were performed.

JAMES BERGIN VC (1845-1880)
MICHAEL MAGNER VC (1840-1897)

James Bergin was born on 29 June 1845 at Killbriken, Queens County, Ireland. He enlisted in the 10th Regiment in 1862 and the following year transferred to the 108th Regiment with whom he sailed for India in 1863. An exceptionally tall and powerful man, he volunteered for the 33rd Regiment which was departing for Abyssinia.

Michael Magner Barry was born in Fermanagh, Ireland on 21 June 1840 to Edward Barry and Margaret Magner. It would appear that his father was killed fighting a duel in Paris and his mother and Michael returned to Cork to live with his uncle. Sent to a boarding school, which he obviously hated, he ran away and enlisted in the British Army as a fourteen-year-old drummer. He used his mother's maiden name Magner when he signed up with the 33rd Regiment.

VC Action

Private Bergin was one of the soldiers who sought a way through the thorn bushes fronting the wall at the Magdala fortress. Spotting a slight gap, he pushed his way through, followed by Drummer Magner. Climbing on Bergin's shoulders, Magner stretched to reach the top of the wall but was a few inches too short. Bergin reversed his rifle and put the butt under Magner's buttocks and gave a heave until his smaller companion was on top of the wall. With help from other comrades, Bergin was hoisted up and together the pair started firing at some of the defenders who rushed to confront them. Soon they were joined by their comrades, who ran to the main gate and opened it from the inside allowing the rest of the 33rd to rush the inner gate brushing all opposition aside.

Once inside, they discovered a body covered by a white cloak which was identified as that of Emperor Theodore. Realising that all resistance was useless and fearing punishment, Theodore had placed one of Queen Victoria's gifts against his head and shot himself, which effectively ended all resistance. It is of note that the pistol was returned to the British monarch. During the 1920s, it reappeared when a young Haile Sallisse visited Britain on a mission for technical support of his country. He was entertained by King George V, who presented him with the same firearm that had been sent to Theodore.

With Magdala captured and resistance scattered. Napier blew up the fortress and returned to the coast. Despite the 33rd's temporary fall from grace, Napier recommended Bergin and Magner for the Victoria Cross as the first men to enter the fortress. Their joint citation appeared in *The London Gazette* on 28 July 1868.

James Bergin returned to India where he received his Cross from Brigadier General James Domville at Belgaum in April 1869. He later transferred to the 78th (Ross-shire Buffs) Regiment but died at the early age of thirty-five in Poona, India.

Michael Magner left the army soon after his investiture by Lieutenant General G. Buller at Portsmouth on 4 November 1868. He married Margaret Carroll in 1873 and immigrated to Tasmania in 1886. Because of his declining health, he later moved to Melbourne where he died of tuberculosis on 6 February 1897.

It is of interest to note that the Abyssinia Medal was the only British campaign medal to have the name of the recipient embossed. This meant making separate casts for all 14,000 medals issued, thus making it the most expensive ever medal-issue.

Chapter 14

Lushai Expedition, 1872

Number of VCs awarded	1
Number of VCs awarded to officers	1
Total awarded to British Indian Army	1

Origins of the War

The next serious outbreak occurred in one of the Raj's most inhospitable regions on India's Eastern Frontier. With Manipur to the north, the Chin Hills to the east and the Arakan to the south, it was still virtually untamed. During the First Anglo-Burmese War in 1824, the Bengal Government of the HEIC attempted to administer this wild and mountainous border area which had been claimed from Burma. This turned out to be an impossible task and only stirred up problems which lasted for the rest of the century. The main thorn in India's side was the warlike Lushai tribes who enjoyed nothing so much as plundering villages and taking the heads of the inhabitants.

When the Chinese tea plant was introduced to the border region and grafted with the wild local version, the result was the successful Assam tea bush. By the early 1860s, tea gardens or plantations began to multiply and by 1874 there 113 plantations in the lowlands of Assam and Dajeeling. This was too tempting for the Lushai tribes who raided at will until several British-led expeditions restored a temporary peace.

On 23 January 1871, the Lushias went too far when they attacked the Alexandreapur tea plantation in the Cachar area and killed the manager, James Winchester. Furthermore, they abducted his illegitimate six-year-old daughter, Mary, which was enough to stir the British into launching a punitive expedition.

Colonel Frederick Roberts VC, the Assistant-Quartermaster General, was appointed chief staff officer and instructed to proceed to Calcutta to arrange a rescue expedition. It was decided that the expedition should be made in two columns; the right advancing from Chittagong and the left from

Cachar. Roberts attached himself with the latter under the command of General Bouchier. It was not until 23 November that the Cacher column started out and immediately entered dense jungle. The column had to make its own roads and by the end of January had completed only 110 miles. Conditions were very arduous; steaming heat, steep mountains, deep gorges and virtually impenetrable bamboo forest. To add to their troubles, cholera broke out amongst the Nepalese *sherpas* and over 250 died.

On 25 January 1872, the Lushais attacked the column in a narrow ravine but were driven off by a determined rush by the Bengal Light Infantry. General Bouchier was wounded in the attack and instructed Roberts to take a small party and burn the village belonging to the natives who had attacked the column. This he managed to do in the face of heavy opposition.

Word reached Bouchier's column that Brigadier General Brownlow's column had reached the Lushai's main village and rescued the child. The tribe also released 115 British subjects including Christian missionaries and Indian workers that they had captured during the raids. Although the expedition had been practically bloodless, it had been successful and resulted in a treaty that the Lushai's should cease their raiding, which they managed to do for another twenty years. During the campaign, one Victoria Cross was awarded.

DONALD MACINTYRE VC (1831-1903)

Donald Macintyre was born on 12 September 1831 at Kincraig House, Ross-shire and educated at private schools in England and abroad. In 1848, he attended Addiscombe Seminary and received his commission into the Bengal army on 14 June 1850. He joined the 66th Gurkha Regiment which had just replaced the 66th Bengal Native Infantry.

The Native Infantry had been paid extra for taking part in the Sikh Wars of the 1840s but now these were ended, the HEIC wished to return to the previous lower scale. Unwilling to return to lower wages, some sepoy regiments revolted and refused to accept their pay. The new commander-in-chief in India, General Sir Charles Napier, nipped the revolt in the bud by disbanding the 66th BNI and replacing it with a Gurkha regiment.

It was with his new regiment that Ensign Macintyre took part in the 1852/3 campaign led by Sir Colin Campbell against the marauding Ranizi tribe on the North-West Frontier. No sooner had this tribe been subdued when the Mohmunds rose against the British. Emboldened, the Ranizi's tore up their treaty and joined the Mohmunds in attacking Campbell's column. The expeditions resulted in the destruction of the fortified village of Prangghur and the action at Ishkahot. Macintyre also took part in the expedition against the Boree Afridis in November 1853. After a year's marching and skirmishing in the dangerous mountains along the Frontier, an uneasy peace was restored.

In 1856, he was promoted to lieutenant and took part in the Kurram Valley expedition. During 1857 and 1858, when engaged in raising an extra Gurkha regiment, which became the 4th Gurkhas, he took part in protecting the hill passes on the Kale Kumaon frontier from the Rohilkund rebels. In November 1858, he transferred to the Sirmoor Rifle Regiment (2nd Gurkhas) and was appointed second in command six months later. He took part in various expeditions against the hostile tribes along the North-West Frontier.

VC Action

In 1871-72, his regiment was moved from the north-west to the north-east of India and he accompanied the Chittagong Column under Brigadier General Brownlow. After weeks of hacking their way through thick jungle and fighting two heavy skirmishes, they reached Chief Lal Gnura's fortified stockade on 4 January 1872. The 2nd Gurkhas charged up the steep and rugged hillside, with Captain Macintyre urging his men on. Macintyre was the first to reach the bamboo stockade, which stood nine feet high. All the time the enemy fired on him with a hail of musket balls, spears and poisoned arrows, but Macintyre and a Gurkha called Inderjit Thapa climbed over the spiked fence and hacked a gap for the rest of the regiment to follow. After a stiff fight, the village was captured.

The Gurkhas' commanding officer, Colonel Macpherson VC, was so impressed he recommended Macintyre for the Victoria Cross. Riflemen Inderjit Thapa received the Indian Order of Merit 3rd Class. In addition, Macintyre was promoted to lieutenant colonel and, in 1876, given command of the 2nd (Prince of Wales's Own) Gurkha Regiment.

Two weeks later, Mary Winchester was rescued alive, well and quite happy. She had adopted the ways of the tribe and had already lost her native tongue. She was found wearing a blue rag around her loins, smoking a pipe and ordering some small boys about. The Lushai seemed to regard her as if she were some sort of royalty. Mary Winchester returned to her grandparents in Elgin, Scotland eventually marrying and working as a headmistress in London. She died in 1955 at the age of ninety.

In 1878, Donald Macintyre's 2nd Gurkhas were part of Sir Garnet Wolseley's force at the occupation of Cyprus. During the 2nd Afghan War, he commanded his regiment at the Bazar Valley, Khyber Column and Pershawar Valley Field Force.

Major General Donald Macintyre retired in 1880 and wrote about his life as a soldier, traveller and big game hunter. He became a Justice of the Peace for Ross-shire and died at his home at Fortrose on 15 April 1903. He was buried in the church at Rosemarkie alongside his brother-in-law, Doctor William Brydon, famous for reportedly being the only surviving member of the disastrous retreat from Kabul in 1842. He was the subject of one of Lady Butler's most famous paintings entitled *Remnants of an Army*, showing the weary doctor and his equally exhausted horse approaching the fort at Jellalabad.

Chapter 15

First Ashanti War, 1873–74

Number of VCs awarded	4
Number of VCs awarded to officers	3
Number of VCs awarded to other ranks	1
Total awarded to British Army	3
Total awarded to the British Indian Army	1

Origins of the War

Further down the West Coast of Africa there was trouble brewing from another bellicose tribe called the Ashanti (Ashante) ruled by the barbarous King Kofi Karikari, whose name was soon anglicised to King Coffee.

In a complicated arrangement, Britain held several fortified trading posts on the coast of an unhealthy spot called the Gold Coast. It was probably the least regarded of all Britain's possessions, producing little in the way of a trading return and having a deadly climate that was the original 'white man's grave'. Britain used the local coastal tribe, the Fantee, to act as their go-betweens in their dealings with the Ashanti, who traded in gold. When the Ashanti attacked the Fantes, the local authorities organised a defence force formed from the local tribes, the West Indian Regiment and the crews of Royal Navy ships in the area.

For nearly a year, there were continuous skirmishes with the 12,000 strong Ashanti army which dominated the country, leaving the heavily outnumbered British barely able to keep their finger-hold on their coastal settlements. Belatedly, and with some reluctance, the Government finally sent out the 23rd Royal Welsh Fusiliers, the 42nd Highland Regiment and a battalion of the Rifle Brigade under the command of thirty-eight-year-old Garnet Wolseley.

Major General Sir Garnet Wolseley was the most famous soldier of his day. Unlike many of his contemporaries, he was energetic, innovative and successful. Taking on this seemingly minor and inglorious task, he emerged with his reputation further enhanced. Amongst the forward-thinking decisions Wolseley made was for the British soldiers to be kept on board their transports some miles from the coast so as to cut the risk of tropical diseases and to clothe the men in a lighter-weight grey material instead of the familiar heavy serge red tunics. They also received a daily dose of quinine and a list of 'do's and don'ts' for the tropics.

During the voyage from England, officers were required to acquaint themselves thoroughly with the area of operations by reading all available accounts and studying the latest maps. This ran counter to the usual expectation of the English officer who took a pride in his lack of professional knowledge, preferring to limit his conversation to hunting and society gossip.

Wolseley planned a swift direct thrust north to take and destroy the Ashanti capital, Kumasi. Approaching from the east was a column led by a former Royal Navy officer, John Hawley Glover, the administrator of Lagos Colony in Nigeria. Glover had formed the nucleus of the Nigerian Army and Police and had spent much time in repelling the incursions of the Ashanti so welcomed the opportunity to join Wolseley's expedition.

The advance was as arduous as any experienced by the British army and the Ashantis proved to be a very tough nut to crack. Struggling through the curious half-light of the thick jungle, Wolseley's men were frequently ambushed and everyone suffered from the high temperatures and humidity. The men were constantly tormented by mosquitoes, ticks and leeches. There was also the ever-present threat of snakes and crocodiles as they waded through swamps and streams.

As they neared the capital, they approached through pools of stagnant water strongly smelling of blood. It was later found to be the blood of human sacrifices that had run into the water. There was one more encounter with the Ashanti before all opposition evaporated and the victorious soldiers entered a deserted Kumasi (Coomassie) in the evening. The exhausted and feverish soldiers gave three weary cheers but the light-hearted mood soon turned sombre. There was a tangible atmosphere of evil about the place. The *Daily Telegraph* reporter graphically described Kumasi as 'A town over which the smell of death hangs everywhere, and pulsates on each sickly breath of wind – a town where, here and there, a vulture hops at one's feet, too gorged to join the filthy flock preening itself on the gaunt dead trunks that line the road; where blood is plastered, like a pitch coating over trees and floors and stools.'

The victors explored the town and its surroundings and what they found was the stuff of nightmares. In a grove behind the main street they came upon the King's slaughter place where the remains of the victims of human sacrifice were deposited. There were thousands of piled-up skulls amongst the trees and the ground was thick with whitened bones. Several decapitated bodies were in various stages of putrefaction and the stench was sickening. The troops found a dungeon full of intended sacrificial prisoners who refused their freedom because they had accepted their fate as offerings to their deity. Before leaving, King Kofi's two-storey stone-built palace was searched. The interior was less than imposing, being furnished in trade cloths and cheap European furniture. Leaning against the bed was a British sword bearing the inscription 'From Queen Victoria to the King of Ashanti', which had been presented to the king two years earlier.

On 17 March 1874, the Treaty of Fomena brought the war to a close, with the Ashanti having to pay an indemnity of 50,000 ounces of gold and renounce the practice of human sacrifice. Thus, the Gold Coast was added to Britain's expanding Empire. In the advance, there were significant fights at Amoaful, Becquah, Ordashu and Abogu for which four VCs were awarded to Lieutenant Lord Edrick Gifford, Lance Corporal Samuel McGaw, Lieutenant Mark Bell and Major Reginald Sartorius.

REGINALD WILLIAM SARTORIUS VC (1841-1907)

Reginald William Sartorius was born on 8 May 1841 in Cintra, Portugal, the second of three sons born to Admiral Sir George Rose Sartorius, commander of the Portuguese Navy. His father had fought at Trafalgar and was present when Napoleon surrendered to his captain, Frederick Maitland, on HMS *Bellerophon*. Reggie Sartorius and his brother Euston were sent to board at Victoria College, Jersey in 1855.

In January 1858, Reggie entered the Indian Army through Addiscombe and was on the unattached roll of the 72nd Bengal Native Infantry. He arrived in India in time participate in the final pursuit of the rebels and joined Brigadier General Lugard's Azimghur Field Force in the fighting at Gorakhpur. He took leave in 1862-64 returning to join the 5th Bengal Cavalry which took part in the Bhutan Expedition. His career at this point was unsettled as he was again attached to another regiment, the 14th Bengal Cavalry, in 1866, before finally settling on the 6th Bengal Cavalry on 20 August 1867, where he received promotion to captain.

He took leave in 1873 and was attached as a Special Service Officer in the Ashanti Campaign. He was sent to Accra to serve with the nascent Gold Coast Constabulary, made up of the Hausa, a largely Muslim group recruited from Nigeria. They were commanded by Captain John Glover RN, who had been appointed administrator and colonial secretary of Lagos Colony until 1872. In September 1873, he marched from Cape Coast to Accra and built up a considerable force of local natives who had a strong hatred of the Ashantis. Unfortunately, this hatred disappeared when it came to confronting their formidable enemy, so Glover had to rely on his well-trained Hausas to take on the Ashantis.

VC Action

On 16 January 1874, Glover's 3,000-strong force crossed the Volta River and made its first advance into Ashanti territory. The first fight was at the village of Abugu (Abogu), which was taken at a rush. In a stiff fight, Glover lost three killed and several wounded. Separated by miles of jungle, communication with Wolseley's column was virtually impossible. Guessing that Wolseley had reached Kumasi some forty-five miles away, Glover pressed on deeper into Ashanti territory and captured Konomo after another fierce fight.

Glover was forced to pause and wait for the ammunition supply to catch up but was loath to delay the chance of meeting up with Wolseley's column. By now they were only twenty-five miles from Kumasi, a distance that could be accomplished by a few men in a forced march. Contact with the main column was essential and Glover chose Captain Sartorius and 130 men to make this dangerous journey. Very soon Sartorius found he had been completely cut off from Glover. Deciding to minimise his force even further to speed up his advance on Kumasi, Sartorius sent forty of his force back to Glover. Coming upon two villages, Sartorius's small unit fought their way through with just one man injured.

With his flank being menaced by Glover, the King had detached part of his army to confront the eastern column. Unknown to Glover, King Kofi had accepted part of the British demands. Sartorius paused about six miles from Kumasi and waited for Glover. When Glover arrived, he sent Sartorius with twenty Haussas to deliver a letter to Wolseley at Kumasi asking for orders and to return the next day.

Glover became alarmed when Sartorius did not return the following day and ordered the column forward to Kumasi. When he entered, he found the place partially burned and deserted. Wolseley had already departed. Glover decided to follow Wolseley's trail and catch up with him. Soon he came upon a white man who had been decapitated and he feared it was Sartorius. Nearby, he found one of his wounded Haussa propped under a tree with provisions left by Sartorius two days previous.

It became apparent that Sartorius' small band had passed through Kumasi two days before and after a perilous thirty-five-mile journey through territory teeming with Ashanti, reached Wolseley on 12 February. Later Glover recalled Sartorius's endurance and leadership in leading his small band through enemy jungle:

'They heard the rustling of invisible movement in the bush dogging them all the way; in the evening the enemy openly menaced them, and they had to halt in a slightly defensible position, and nothing but Sartorius personal forwardness induced the Haussas to move in the morning.'

Sartorius finally caught up with Wolseley's camp just outside Kumasi just as King Kofi accepted terms. Wolseley was full of praise for Sartorius feat:

'A most remarkable march of 53 miles through the heart of the enemy's country, often surrounded or threatened, without provisions, and without having fired a single shot or lost a man of his small escort.'

A VC was suggested and was brought to the attention of the War Office on 11 July 1874. Although Wolseley and the Colonial Secretary, Lord Carnarvon, were keen for Sartorius to receive the Cross, his perilous trek did not seem to be covered by the terms of the Warrant. Also, as the only white man in the command there was no one to give adequate testimony as to his conduct.

After much thought and exchanges of correspondence, a solution was found. In the first confrontation with the Ashanti at the village of Abugo on 17 January, and under the command of Captain Glover, Reginald Sartorius performed an act of bravery. This was reflected in the citation that appeared in *The London Gazette* dated 27 October 1874: 'For having during the attack on Abogoo, on 17th January last, removed under a heavy fire Sergeant Major Braimah Doctor, a Houssa Non-Commissioned Officer, who was mortally wounded, and placed him under cover.'

This bending of the rules satisfied the civil servants but Sartorius never believed his award was for his deed at Abugo but was for his journey through the jungles of the Ashanti. Reginald Sartorius was invested with his Victoria Cross by Queen Victoria at Windsor on 30 March 1875.

Reginald Sartorius was promoted to major and awarded the CMG (Order of St Michael and St George). In 1875-76, he was on the Staff of the Prince of Wales when he toured India. By September 1878, he was appointed lieutenant colonel in the 6th Bengal Cavalry and took part in the Second and Third Afghan Wars 1878-80.

It was during the Second Afghan War that his younger brother, Captain Euston Henry Sartorius, was awarded the Victoria Cross for gallantry at Shahjui on 24 October 1879. This made them one of four instances of brothers winning the Victoria Cross. Reginald Sartorius retired from the Indian Army as a major general in 1895 and died on 8th August 1907 at Cowes on the Isle of Wight.

Chapter 16

Perak Expedition, 1875–76

Number of VCs awarded	1
Number of VCs awarded to officers	1
Total awarded to British Indian Army	1

Origins of the War

Britain's imperial obligations in India caused her to lose focus on her Crown Colony of The Straits Settlements consisting of Penang, Malacca and Singapore. A rash of lawlessness and piracy along the coast alerted the British to the stability Straits Settlements and a treaty was sought with Sultan Abdullah of Perak, which lay between Penang and Malacca. Perak, which means 'silver' in Malay, was a state that stretched about 160 kilometres along the coast and ran inland about eighty kilometres.

The 'silver' was in fact tin, for the area was rich in the ore which was in great demand by the industrialised British. The Malay administrators imported experienced Chinese miners to work the mines that also brought inter-clan friction. Fighting amongst the Chinese extended to the local Malays and so another small state turned red on the map with its annexation by the British.

The first British Resident in Perak was James Birch, a brusque intolerant man with no experience of Malaya. Resentment built and Birch gained unpopularity at a rapid rate to the extent that the local leaders decided to kill him in the hope that the British would go away.

On 2 November 1875, a year after his appointment, Birch landed at Pasir Salak on the lower Perak River. Despite spear wielding Malays, Birch ordered the posting of notices about the new administration. He then bathed in the river in a small screened-off floating bath house. His unfortunate interpreter who posted the notices was attacked and mortally wounded.

He managed to reach to the river and was rescued by one of Birch's craft but died soon after.

At the same time, another group of armed locals surrounded Birch's bath house and speared him through the screen. The badly wounded Resident staggered into the river where he was finally killed with sword blow. His body was later recovered displaying ten wounds. The commander of his twelve-man escort, a naval sub-lieutenant had been shooting game on the other side of the river and his Sikh sepoys refused to do anything without his orders.

Very quickly the forces of retribution were assembled with about 1,500 troops sent from India, Burma and Singapore. On 7 November, a small force arrived and they were led by Assistant Special Commissioner Frank Swettenham up the Penang River to attack the stockade at Pasir Salak. In a poorly led shambolic attack, men of the 10th Regiment were fired upon by the Penang Police, who refused to leave the shelter of the trees they were hiding behind.

On 27 November, a column from India arrived and soon restored order to Upper Perak. It was followed in early December by Major General Francis Colborne who arrived from Hong Kong to command the Perak Field Force. On 17 December, this force advanced and captured the main rebel stockade at Kuta. The country was now entirely under British control except for continued resistance at Sungei Ujong near Malacca in the south and it was here that a Victoria Cross was awarded.

GEORGE NICHOLAS CHANNER VC (1843-1905)

Born on 7 January 1843 in Allahabad to Colonel George Girdwood Channer of the Royal Artillery and his wife Susan née Kendall, George Channer was the eldest son of eight children. He was educated at Truro Grammar School and Cheltenham College before entering Addiscombe Seminary.

Channer was commissioned into the Bengal Infantry on 4 September 1859 as an unattached Ensign. In August 1861, he was promoted to lieutenant and served in the Umbeyla Campaign with the 89th and 95th Regiments. After taking leave, he returned as Quarter Master, 35th (Manipur) Regiment in 1867 and took part in the Lushai Campaign in 1870 with the 2nd Bengal Light Infantry. Promoted to captain, he joined 1st Gurkha Regiment in 1873. It was while serving with his regiment that he became the third Gurkha to be awarded the Victoria Cross.

While the Perak River and Larut River columns had successfully pacified most of the state, the Malacca Column under the command of Lieutenant Colonel Bertie Clay were sent to destroy the stockades of the rebel chief, Tunka Antah, who held the strategic Bukit Putas Pass. Clay formed two columns; one led by himself would approach the Pass while the other, commanded by Lieutenant Colonel R. Sale Hill (1st Gurkhas), would march on the rear of the Bukit Putas Pass before Clay attacked. Unfortunately, the latter was delayed by obstacles set by the rebels, dense jungle and the unforgiving terrain.

VC Action

Captain Channer was with Clay's column and commanded a detachment of 1st Gurkhas. After reaching the approaches to the Pass on 20 December 1875, Channer was sent with fifty Gurkhas to reconnoitre the enemy stockade that controlled passage through the Pass. Three hours later, Channer sent a message to say the jungle was so thick that reconnaissance was impossible from a safe distance. Clay returned his message telling Channer to get as close as he could to estimate ranges for the guns and rockets.

Changing direction, Channer managed to creep to the rear of the fort and discovered that all twenty-five or more defenders including the sentries were eating a communal meal. Beckoning his men to join him, Channer clambered over the bamboo palisade and into the stockade. There he saw a log house, with trees laid latitudinally to the thickness of two feet, loop-holed, with two narrow entrances. Dashing in, he shot dead one of the rebels with his revolver. He was quickly followed by Riflemen Balbir Gharti and Jitman Thapa, who shot and killed two more of the enemy. (They were later awarded the Indian Army Order of Merit). The rest of the Gurkhas poured in, killing six and chasing off the rest. On hearing the firing, Clay pushed on up the Pass but had to deal with deadly obstacles put in his way. Despite some sepoys firing at the Gurkhas in mistake for the enemy, the operation was a success. Channer lost two Gurkhas killed and two were wounded by enemy *ranjons* (caltrops of sharpened sticks tied together with at least one spike point up). This campaign was the first overseas deployment of the Gurkhas and saw the first VC awarded.

Colonel Clay recommended Channer for an award stating that if Channer had not taken the fort: 'Then a great loss of life must have occurred, as from the fact of my being unable to bring my guns to bear on it, from the steepness of the hill and the density of the jungle, it must have been taken at the point of a bayonet.'

Captain Channer was duly awarded the Victoria Cross, which was gazetted on 12 April 1876 and later that year received his Cross in India. He was also promoted to major and saw service in 1877 serving with the 29th Punjab Regiment in the Jowaki Afridi Expedition.

Later Service

During the 2nd Afghan War, Channer took part in General Robert's successful assault at Peiwar Kotal but suffered the humiliation of having his regiment withdrawn from the front. Roberts had chosen the 29th Punjab Infantry to lead the way because of its high reputation. Consisting of a mixture of Sikh and Pathan companies, its slow progress aroused Robert's suspicions as to the reliability of Muslim Pathans. This was further confirmed when two shots rang out in the echoing darkness of the ravine intended, no doubt to alert the enemy, but these appear to have gone unnoticed for there was no response.

Changing the formation, Roberts brought up a company each of the 5th Gurkhas and 72nd Highlanders to lead the advance. After the victory, Roberts still had to deal with the treacherous soldiers of the 29th. A court martial was convened and the guilty men received lengthy prison sentences.

In 1879, Channer became second in command of the 32nd Punjab Regiment and then commanded the 14th Ferozepore Regiment in the Black Mountain Expedition of 1888. He retired as lieutenant general in 1896 and made full general in 1899. He was an excellent revolver shot and keen explorer of Tibet and other remote parts of the Himalayas. Like many Indian-born officers, on retirement he left India and died on 13 December 1905 at Westward Ho, Devon.

Chapter 17

Quetta Incident, 1877

Number of VCs awarded	1
Number of VCs awarded to officers	1
Total awarded to British Indian Army	1

Origins of the War

Quetta in Baluchistan was a small dusty settlement situated in a highly strategic position. The surrounding district was very mountainous bounded to the north-west by Afghanistan and on the south by the Bolan Pass. It was temporarily held by the British during the First Afghan War 1839-42 but then all but forgotten for the next decade or so.

On the chance that it might be used again, a treaty was made with the ruler or Khan of Kalat in 1854 granting a lease to occupy Quetta if strategically necessary. It was not felt at the time that it would ever be implemented as its strategic importance was overridden by the fact that it was surrounded by hostile tribes and cut off from its nearest British base by 400 kilometres.

The British held off until the threat of Russia getting ever closer to the northern Afghan border prompted the occupation of Quetta despite its isolated and precarious position. It was the result of the Russo-Turkish War of 1876-77 that alerted Britain. Thwarted in their plans to occupy Turkish territory around the Black Sea, the Russians diverted their efforts to conquer and occupy the countries bordering Persia and, alarmingly, Afghanistan.

In 1876 the British renewed their agreement with the Khan of Khalat by increasing his subsidy and permitting the garrisoning of troops, the building of railways and installation of telegraph lines through his territory. The country was riven with unrest and the Khan was happy for a British presence to bring some stability to his Khanate. For the British, the region was widely regarded as the mountain bastion which strengthened the outer defences of India. The occupation of Quetta, however, was seen in many quarters as an aggressive move, even in British political circles.

Early in 1877, men of the Indian Army marched into Quetta and set up a cantonment in the face of intense hostility from the largely Muslim Pathans. Building operations supervised by the Royal Engineers started, and a Residence for the Administrator, houses for political and military officers and barracks for the troops were all built. The Quetta fort, known as the Miri, was retained in possession of the Khan's troops. At this time the Khan's regular army consisted of 3,500 mercenary troops with thirty guns and 500 cavalry. With such simmering resentment, it was not long before there was a fanatical outbreak which led to the British occupation of the Miri and the eventual creation of the Baluchistan Province.

ANDREW SCOTT VC (1840-1882)

Early Other Rank Victoria Cross recipients are often difficult to research due to inadequate birth and service records. Also, once discharged the former soldier disappeared from view and was only heard again when he died, often in a workhouse. This state was almost unheard of when it came to the mid-Victorian officer whose life was well-documented and generally followed a predictable route.

One exception was the case of Andrew Scott who, despite attaining the position of brigade major in the 2nd Afghan War, remains one of the least known VCs of that period.

Early Life

Andrew Scott was born in Devon on 22 August 1840. To whom and exactly where is unknown. He joined the Indian Army as an unattached ensign on 4 March 1860 at a time when the Indian Army was going through a radical reorganisation. He was promoted to lieutenant in 1862 and was finally appointed to the 4th Sikh Infantry, Punjab Frontier Force on 6 June 1865 and sent to serve on the turbulent North-West Frontier region. He was promoted to captain on 4 March 1872 and was in this rank when his regiment was sent to Quetta in early 1877.

This garrison embarked on a building program in anticipation of housing a force that could be used against the Afghan ruler, Sher Ali. Despite the undercurrent of resentment from the local inhabitants, the British employed many Pathans as labourers. On the evening of 26 July 1877, three local Kakar Pathans attacked Royal Engineer lieutenants Hewson and Kunhardt who were overseeing building operations of the new Residency. In a frenzied knife attack, Hewson was killed and Kunhardt badly wounded. A soldier of the 4th Sikhs rushed up and defended the stricken Kunhardt but in doing so, lost his life.

VC Action

Captain Scott, who was drilling his men nearby, heard the commotion and dashed to the scene followed by some of his men. Grabbing a rifle with fixed bayonet from one of his men, Scott killed two of the murderers. He then got into a tussle with the third man who managed to wound

Scott, but his men arrived close behind and made short work of the assailant.

The cause of this attack was the imprisonment of some Pathans who displayed their resentment of the British presence by deliberately maiming some Army-owned camels. The Pathans were imprisoned in the Miri or fortress where the attack had been planned. This was occupied by the Khan of Khaled and his 3,500-strong army and Richard Bruce, the political agent, suspected some sort of collusion and ordered the seizure of the fort. This was swiftly carried out by Captain Charles, commanding troops at Quetta, peacefully without opposition. The fort was then used as the arsenal by the occupying troops.

For his gallantry in coming to Lieutenant Kunhardt's rescue, Captain Scott was recommended for the Victoria Cross, the last time one was awarded for gallantry not in the face of the enemy. There is a lack of documentary evidence about his VC, which while timely, seems hardly to merit the highest award. On 18 January 1878, his citation was published in *The London Gazette* and he received his Cross on 15 April that year, although there is no record of an investiture.

At the outbreak of the long-anticipated Afghan War in 1878, Andrew Scott was attached to the Bengal Staff and served as brigade major with the 1st Infantry Brigade, under the command of Brigadier General Alexander Cobbe, a future VC recipient. The Kuram Valley Field Force was placed under the command of Major Frederick Roberts who was given the local rank of major general. Scott was present in the frontal attack at Peiwar Kotal on 1 December 1878 and the subsequent operations in the Khost Valley including the victory at Matun, for which he was Mentioned in Despatches.

Scott began to suffer stomach problems and was invalided out in June 1879. On 4 March 1880, he was confirmed as major but appears to have been continually dogged by ill health. He finally died of peritonitis at the age of forty-two years on 5 September 1882 at Srinagar, Kashmir.

Chapter 18

The Ninth Cape Frontier War, 1877–78

Number of VCs awarded	1
Number of VCs awarded to officers	1
Total awarded to British Army	1

Origins of the War

The Cape Frontier Wars or, as they were formally referred to, the Kaffir Wars, were a series of nine wars or uprisings that spanned the years between 1779 to 1879. The early conflicts were fought between the Xhosa, the collective tribes of south-east South Africa and the Dutch Boer settlers with the British not getting involved until the Fourth War in 1811. The area in which these conflicts occurred was the Eastern Cape in South Africa. By 1872, the Cape Colony had its own elected government under Prime Minister John Molteno, having achieved partial independence from Britain. It had little interest in territorial expansion and had created a period of peace along the border with the native Xhosa of Galekaland or Eastern Cape. The border was patrolled by the Frontier Armed and Mounted Police, a locally recruited multiracial force which maintained peace along the colony's frontier.

In September 1877, the Galeka tribe crossed the Krei River in an attempt to join forces with their allies, the Gaikas, and challenge the British colonists, who occupied their tribal grazing lands. Separating them was the territory occupied by the Fingo (Mafengus) tribe who were friendly towards the British. A quarrel flared up between the Gaikas and Fingos at a wedding party which sparked the Ninth and last Frontier War. This seemingly minor disagreement was just the excuse for British involvement. The British High Commissioner, Sir Bartle Frere, decided that Galekaland should become part of a South African Confederation and be settled by whites. As Imperial Commander-in-Chief he took charge of the war, dismissing the Molteno cabinet who opposed the British intervention. In its place, Frere appointed a new and more amenable ministry. He also insisted that Imperial troops, under the command of sixty-five-year-old General Sir Arthur Cunynghame, should be involved in defeating the recalcitrant tribes. The campaign started with Cunynghame deploying troops along the Krei River in an attempt to keep the Galekas and Gaikas divided.

More men arrived including local volunteers and two or three thousand Fingoes, anxious to pay off old scores. Having held back the Galekas, the British raided their territory, burning kraals and bringing away some 13,000 head of cattle. All this happened during a severe drought, which added hardship to the dismal campaign. General Cunynghame's desultory handling of the campaign resulted in his dismissal and General Frederic Thesiger, later Lord Chelmsford, taking over. He brought with him the more active colonels, Redvers Buller and Evelyn Wood.

Reinforced with men of the 24th (Warwickshire), the 90th Cameronians) and Royal Artillery, the tempo of the campaign increased. Sending his men into the bush to flush out the enemy which resulted in a few skirmishes but not the full-scale battle Chelmsford sought. Finally, the Xhosa was worn down by being constantly on the move. The death of the Gaikas king, Sandili, in a skirmish and the continuing famine brought this frustrating campaign to a conclusion in May 1878. Galekaland was then administered by the Cape until it was finally annexed in 1894.

There was one controversial Victoria Cross awarded in this shapeless and stumbling campaign.

HANS GARRETT MOORE VC (1834-1889)

Hans Garrett Moore was born to be a soldier. Hans, or Garry as he was familiarly called, saw the light of day in Richmond Barracks, Dublin on 31 March 1834, the son of Captain Garrett Moore of the 88th Connaught Rangers and Charlotte Butler of Tipperary. He was educated at the Royal School, Banagher and when he was sixteen, went to Trinity College, Dublin. When he was twenty-one, he obtained a commission without purchase due to his father's lengthy and distinguished service.

His first appointment on 7 June 1855 was as an ensign in 59th Regiment but, on 13 July, he was transferred to his father's regiment, the 88th. Due to the loss of many officers in the Crimea, it was not long before he was promoted to lieutenant on 26 October and joined his regiment at Aldershot on their return from the war.

The 88th's home posting did not last long before they were again sent overseas. In July 1857, the regiment sailed for India to help suppress the Indian Mutiny. Arriving in Calcutta in early November, the 88th was immediately sent to reinforce Sir Colin Campbell's force, which was marching to relieve the Lucknow Residency. When they reached Cawnpore, however, they found that Major General Charles Ashe Windham had gained permission from Campbell to retain the reinforcements to help defend the town and the vital river crossing. The defences had been considerably strengthened but the numbers of defenders were still inadequate in the face of the approaching rebel Gwalior contingent under the command of Tanti Topi.

On 26 November, leaving 300 men to guard the entrenchment, Windham led forward his small force of 1,300 to meet what he thought was about 3,000 rebels. Under the command of their Colonel, George Maxwell, the 88th crossed the dry river bed of the Pandu Nadi and assaulted the rebel's position. In a brief but sharp fight, Windham's force drove the enemy back in confusion and captured three of the rebel's guns. Faced by an increasing number of the enemy, Windham retreated back to Cawnpore and managed to hold the all-important bridge until the arrival of Sir Colin Campbell's force. On 6 December, Sir Colin Campbell launched his attack on the Gwalior army of Tantia Topi and Rao Sahib and routed it in the decisive Battle of Cawnpore.

For Lieutenant Garrett Moore it had been a tough baptism of fire which was just a prelude to the campaigning of the following year. In January 1858, the 88th joined Sir Hugh Rose's army in the hard-fought Central India campaign. The main enemy, from which there was no escape, was the heat. Marching in temperatures of 120° in the shade, men dropped from heat exhaustion and sun-stroke. Despite this, they successfully assaulted the formidable rebel position at Kalpi on 23 May. At a fight at Selipore on 23 September, Garry Moore was slightly wounded by a musket ball to the abdomen and had the 'eights' shot off his cap.

During this lesser-known campaign, numerous fights took place against pockets of rebels who refused to surrender. One such was the storming of the fortified village of Birwah on 21 October, which resulted in the 88th's largest list of casualties. The fight lasted eight hours, with the 88th bearing the brunt of the fighting. Moore was again in the thick of the fighting during which his revolver was broken at his side. Armed only with his sword, he later entered a house and killed three sepoys. His conduct was noted and he was Mentioned in Despatches.

He ended the campaign with a reputation of being a fearless officer and a tough campaigner. Later, he showed another side to his character when, on a shooting expedition in Oudh, he dived fully clothed into the fast flowing Goomti River to save a native beater who had fallen in. Garry was a strong swimmer and superb horseman, winning many steeple-chases. He also became Master of the Connaught Ranger's pack of hounds during their long posting in India.

On 18 August 1863, Moore was appointed Adjutant, a post he held for nearly ten years. On 17 November 1870, the 88th sailed from Bombay, having served in India for thirteen years.

Gold Coast

On 19 June 1872, Garry was promoted to captain but, tiring of being garrisoned in Gosport, applied to join Major General Sir Garnet Wolseley's expedition to punish the Ashanti tribe who had invaded the British processions of Cape Coast. Moore, along with many other ambitious middle ranking officers, saw this as an opportunity 'to be seen' while on campaign. Wolseley was limited to the selection of thirty-six staff and special service officers. In making his choice from among the many volunteers, he looked for thinking soldiers with proven courage. It was little surprise that he included in his selection fellow Irishman Captain Hans Garrett Moore, who joined that elite band of officers nicknamed the 'Ashanti Club'.

The Government's first intention was to raise local native volunteers, but this was always an over-optimistic hope. Eventually Wolseley got his way and three battalions of British soldiers were sent out to march on the Ashanti capital and defeat the enemy in a short-lived campaign.

Garry Moore was employed in enlisting reluctant natives from the western Wassaw tribe to fight the Ashanti. When this recruitment drive failed and British troops arrived, so the employment need for natives changed. Thousands of bearers to carry supplies to support the advance became a priority. Using unashamedly strong-arm methods, the special service officers employed in the Transport Department managed to coerce the recruits required. On the successful completion of this short punitive expedition, Moore was rewarded with a brevet majority.

The next overseas posting for the 88th was to South Africa where they arrived in July 1877. Almost immediately they were sent further up the coast to the Transkei in Eastern Cape, where another of the Frontier Wars had erupted. The local colonial troops were too few in number and not well regarded by the British authorities, including the Commander of Imperial Forces, General Sir Arthur Cunynghame. The 88th arrived in East London on 28 August and a detachment commanded by Garry Moore was sent first to Fort Cunynghame and then to Komgha, the seat of the unrest.

VC Action

On 29 December, mail riders carrying post to the Kei Road Station had been fired on and forced to return to Komgha. The Gaikas now commanded several miles of the road between King William's Town and Komgha and Major Moore was ordered to take thirty-two men of the Frontier Armed and Mounted Police (F.A.M.P) to Draaibosch, the scene of the attack, and investigate.

After some skirmishes with the enemy, the patrol arrived at the burning remains of the Draaibosch Hotel where they were confronted by about 300 Gaikas. Four police scouts were just ahead of the main body and Moore ordered them to fall back. Dismounted, the police fired a few shots before remounting to retire. One of the scouts, Private Giese, was unable to mount his panicked horse and was in immediate danger of being overwhelmed. Seeing this, Garry Moore spurred his horse forward and joined the other three scouts in riding to the stricken policeman's rescue. Fighting his way through the mob of spear-wielding natives, Moore reached Giese too late to save him. The latter had been repeatedly stabbed. Now Moore fought to extricate himself from the clutching hands and was hit by a thrown assegai, which stuck in his upper arm.

Reaching the rest of the patrol, he ordered them in to cover but the Gaikas retreated. Moore then calmly sat on a tree stump, smoking his pipe while the patrol's doctor extricated the assegai blade. When the doctor attempted to cut away the sleeve of his patrol jacket, Moore objected, saying; 'Hold on, this is my only coat. Rip it up the seam.'

As the only Imperial officer present, Moore's version of events was the only report sent forward to General Cunynghame. It would seem that an award of a Victoria Cross may have been mentioned for, some seventeen months later, Moore wrote to Cunynghame again to press his case for the award. He stated that he had been quite alone with Giese when the latter died and had killed two natives, Also, he and his horse had had been wounded by assegais and it was only then that the other three police came up.

This appeal resulted in a quick response. Just six weeks later *The London Gazette* of 27 June 1879 announced: 'Hans Garret Moore, 88th Foot. For his gallant conduct in risking his own life in endeavouring to save the life of Private Giese of the Frontier Armed Mounted Police, on the occasion of the action with the Gaikas, near Kohgha on the 29th December 1877.

'It is reported that when a small body of Mounted Police were forced to retire before overwhelming numbers of the enemy, Major Moore observed Private Giese was unable to mount his horse, and was thereby left at the mercy of the Kaffirs. Perceiving the man's danger, Major Moore rode back alone into the midst of the enemy and did not desist in his endeavour to save the man until the latter was killed. Major Moore having shot two Kaffirs and received an assegai wound in the arm during his gallant attempt.'

This version of what happened certainly did not square with the members of the F.A.M.P. The scouts who were nearest to Private Giese were Sergeant Dan Harber, Corporal John Court and Private Martindale. Major Moore joined them as they tried to save Giese. Private Martindale's horse was shot from under him and he was rescued by Sergeant Harber, who carried him to safety.

As a result of their action, both Harber and Court were promoted. Another disgruntled policeman stated that: 'I could not recall the particular deed of heroism the he (Moore) had performed for which he himself recommended that he should be adorned with the VC.'

By the time of the announcement of Moore's VC, the Anglo-Zulu War had been fought amongst great controversy. One of the bones of contention was the dismissive attitude of the British authorities, in particular the Army officers, towards the colonial volunteers. Belatedly, efforts were made to smooth the ruffled colonial feathers and the awarding of the Victoria Cross was extended to include non-Imperial personnel.

As for Garry Moore, there was no suggestion that he was anything but extremely brave, as witness what happened the day after his VC exploit. Despite his painful wound, Moore led a force of thirty F.A.M.P and fifty men of the 88th out from Komgha to Draaibosch. Lining his small force along the crest of a hill overlooking the burnt-out Draaibosch Hotel, Moore faced the advancing Gaikas, who numbered 1,000, with 600 on horseback. Twelve years later, an eye-witness account was published in *The Times*:

'Suddenly, and when they were within about 350 yards of us, they deployed, one half sweeping round our left flank, and the remainder to our right, whilst the horse went at a canter to our rear… the force of the enemy flanking our position in that direction were nearest, and were then charging up the hill with loud cries. Before the movement could be completed the enemy were upon us – some of the FAM Police flung themselves on their horses and rode hard away (I may here mention that others of that force remained and did gallant service afterwards), and the young soldiers of the Rangers, mere boys for the most part, showed no sign of wavering. What at this moment was Colonel Moore doing? He was sitting immovably, calm, on his horse, facing the hordes of the enemy, and issuing the words of command to his forces as if he had been on parade.'

Although the firing of his young soldiers was wayward, Moore maintained order and put on such a brave front that the Gaikas did not take advantage of their numerical superiority and retreated after about ninety minutes. The casualties were light; two men killed and three wounded. Garry Moore's horse was hit three times and died the following day. The narrow victory, however, did little to improve relations between the Imperial and Colonial participants. The latter resented being made scapegoats by Moore and even suggested that it was the soldiers who had wavered.

Moore was Mentioned in Despatches and promoted to brevet colonel. On 6 June 1878, he was placed on half pay and the following day took up a new appointment. In the reorganisation that came with the end of the Ninth Frontier War, the F.A.M.P were reorganised into a regular unit of mounted riflemen and designated the Cape Mounted Rifles. Somewhat surprisingly, Garry Moore was appointed their first Commanding Officer. It is not clear whether this was a popular appointment for both parties but, after just over six months, Moore resigned and returned to England.

Later Service

On 15 March, he transferred to the 1st Battalion 93rd Argyll and Sutherland Highlanders which had just been stationed at Gibraltar. On 6 September 1879, the garrison paraded on the Alameda for the presentation of the

Victoria Cross to Major Moore by the Acting Governor, Major-General Anderson. 1879 was a good year for the Moore family; his brother's son, Garrett Moore, won the Grand National on his horse *Liberator*.

In July 1882, an announcement that Sir Garnet Wolseley was to head an expedition to Egypt prompted Major Moore to apply for a position on the staff. Sir Garnet favoured his faithful and talented 'Ashanti Club' and Moore was appointed Provost Marshal and Acting Assistant Quartermaster General. He was present at the battle of Kassassin on 28 August and the night attack at Tel El Kebir on 13 September. For his service, he was Mentioned in Despatches and made Companion of the Bath.

On 1 July 1887, Garry Moore succeeded Colonel Nightingale as Commanding Officer of the 2nd Battalion. Six months later, on 10 January 1888, after thirty-three years' active service, mostly abroad, Hans Garrett Moore retired but refused the offer of the rank of major general. Returning to Ireland, Garry was able to indulge his passion for sailing and bought a steam yacht named *Foam*.

It was while sailing up the River Shannon and on to Lough Derg in Tipperary that he met with his untimely death. On the night of 6 October 1889, after going ashore to dine with an Army friend, Moore and his stoker returned to the *Foam*. A storm broke and whipped up the lake's waters. Fearing they would drift, Moore rowed the skiff to secure the mooring rope to a buoy. The wind was so strong that he was unable to row back to the yacht and he was blown into the darkness of Dromineer Bay, where the skiff capsized. Moore's body was later recovered and he was buried at Mount Jerome Cemetery, Dublin.

Chapter 19

Second Afghan War, 1878–80

Number of VCs awarded	16
Number of VCs awarded to officers	11
Number of VCs awarded to other ranks	4
Number of VCs awarded to Civilians	1
Total awarded to British Army	9
Total awarded to British Indian Army	6

Origins of the War

By the end of the 1870s, Britain's domination of India was all but complete with the defence of the sub-continent assured with impassable mountains to the north and north-east. It was to the north-west and Afghanistan that caused the Raj her major worry, not so much of an invasion by the Afghans, for the emir Dost Mahomed took no advantage of Britain's difficulties during the Indian Mutiny, but the threat posed by Russia.

Since the 1840s when Russia annexed the Trans-Caspian region, she had moved steadily eastwards. By 1868, Russia had occupied Samarkand and Bokhara and in 1873, she occupied Khiva, just 400 miles from India. In response to Britain's annexation of Quetta in 1877 and a move to rob the Tsar of his triumph over Turkey in the war of 1877-78, Russia massed 15,000 troops just north of the Afghan border.

The British had little stomach for occupying such an ungovernable country but wished to keep Afghanistan as a buffer state against any encroachment by the Russians. The new Indian Viceroy, Lord Lytton, decided on a generous policy toward Afghanistan in the hope that she would rebuff any Russian attempt to subjugate the country. Offering money and the recognition of Shere Ali's dynasty, but with the proviso that there should be British agent at Kabul, met with failure.

Shere Ali was caught between two powerful nations and did not wish to choose between them. Having refused the Russians a mission in Kabul,

Shere Ali's hand was forced when one was sent against his wishes. When the British learned of this, they demanded the Emir receive a British Mission as well and sent Sir Neville Chamberlain and the French-born Major Pierre Louis Napoleon Cavagnari as representatives. Entering the Khyber Pass, they were turned back at the fort at Ali Masjid, the narrowest part of the Pass. Lytton demanded an apology and the installation of a permanent British Mission. When no response was received, Britain was determined to have her own way and declared war on 20 November 1878.

The invasion was carried out by three columns; in the south, the Kandahar Field Force, then the Kuram Valley Field Force and the main thrust through the Khyber by the Peshawar Valley Field Force. Due to the distances between them they were unable to communicate and so acted independently. On 21 November 1878, the Peshawar Valley Field Force under General Sir Sam Browne traced the route taken by Chamberlain and Cavagnari up the Khyber Pass and were again confronted by the fort of Ali Masjid, perched 500 feet above the gorge. Afghan regulars with artillery occupied fortifications on both side and tribesmen waited in the surrounding hills.

Browne had anticipated being held up here and had already sent part of his force on a wide flanking march to cut in across the enemy rear. A second force was detached to attack the Afghan left, while the remainder of the force advanced frontally. The flanking columns met with huge problems which considerably delayed their progress. In the event, their presence was enough for the defenders to abandon the fort leaving Browne to advance to Jalalabad, which he reached on 20 December. Here the Pershawar Valley Field Force remained for the winter. It was about this time that Shere Ali fled north to seek asylum with the Russians, leaving his son Yakub Khan as the new Emir. On 21 February 1879, it was learned that Shere Ali was dead.

Having wintered in Jalalabad, Browne pressed on to Kabul on 28 March. He detached three columns, one of which was under his direct command, with the others being led by Brigadier Generals Charles Gough VC, and Herbert Macpherson VC. Tragically, the latter's squadron of 10th Hussars misread the location of a ford crossing the Kabul River and forty-seven officers and men were swept away and drowned.

Brigadier Gough's column consisted of horsemen of the Corps of Guides, 10th Hussars and infantry of 45th Rattray's Sikhs and the 17th (Leicestershire) Regiment, with a battery of the Horse Artillery. About fifteen miles along the Kabul Road near Futtehabad they were confronted by a strong well-entrenched force of 5,000 Afghans.

It was there that one the best-known Victoria Cross recipients of the Victorian period gained recognition. Curiously, he is more famed for his death than the action for which he was awarded his Cross

WALTER RICHARD POLLOCK HAMILTON VC (1856-1879)

Born on 18 August 1856 at Inistioge, County Kilkenny, Ireland, Walter Richard Pollock was one of seven sons born to Alexander Hamilton JP and Emma, (née Pollock). He was the nephew of General Sir George Pollock who led the Army of Retribution after the disastrous retreat in the First Afghan War. When he was old enough, he was sent to England for his education; first to Eagle House Preparatory School, Wimbledon and then to Felstead School, near Dunmow, Essex.

As was the norm in those times, there was a pecking order for sons of the landed gentry and, being fourth in line, Walter's options were somewhat restricted. Being an active youth, he chose the life of a soldier, possibly influenced by his famous great-uncle. A commission was obtained and 2nd Lieutenant Walter Hamilton joined the 70th (Surrey) Regiment on 28 February 1874.

After six months of depot duty, Hamilton and the regiment sailed for India. Here he was posted to the regimental headquarters at Rawalpindi and soon promoted to full lieutenant. He was then offered a transfer to the elite Queen's Own Corps of Guides, recognised as the finest regiment in the Indian Army. Within three months, after intensive study, Walter Hamilton passed the higher standard examination in languages, presumably those spoken on the North-West Frontier.

On October 1877, Brigadier General Keyes led a punitive expedition against one of the Afghan tribes which was a constant thorn in Britain's side – the Jawaki Afridis. Hamilton was appointed ADC to Keyes and it was his first taste of campaigning in the harsh terrain of the Frontier. Advancing steadily through the narrow passes and under harassing fire, the Anglo-Indian force destroyed villages, crops and fortified towers. The Jawaki's principal stronghold of Jummu was taken in a surprise night attack. A final defeat on 15 February 1878 brought the operation to a close.

There soon followed another small expedition involving the Guides, this time against the Utman Khels. Under the command of Captain Wigram Battye, the Guides were accompanied by Captain Pierre Louis Napoleon Cavagnari, of the Bengal Staff Corps who was the political officer for the area. Cavagnari was to play a large part in Hamilton's short life.

The accomplishment of this small force was impressive. They made a night ride of thirty-two miles, dismounted and marched a further two miles over heavy ground and then four miles along a river bank. They then climbed for a mile up a steep and narrow path to reach the village of Sapir at daylight. Before the sleeping tribesmen knew what was happening, the Guides rushed in and took the village.

A similar expedition in the Swat Valley a month later saw the Guides use the same successful tactics, having marched fifty miles in just twenty-four hours. Under the leadership of Captain Wigram Battye, Walter Hamilton was quickly developing in to a highly experienced and valuable Frontier soldier. As such, he and the Guides, formed part of Browne's expedition to Afghanistan.

VC Actions

On 2 April 1879, Gough's column of 1,200 men was confronted by 5,000 tribesmen drawn up behind strong stone works. Their flanks were protected by steep bluffs and from their position the ground sloped down towards Gough's position. There seemed no alternative but to attack head-on. He sent forward his cavalry and guns to within a mile of the enemy with orders to fire a few rounds before retiring. He hoped to lure the tribesmen out of their position, giving his cavalry and infantry a chance to get at them. The trick worked.

The tribesmen rushed forward to pursue the retiring cavalry and guns and were charged in the right flank by the hidden infantry. In the fierce hand-to-hand struggle the tribesmen were slowly pushed back. At this point, the cavalry was released onto the enemy's left flank and shattered it. During the mêlée, Captain Battye was shot in the hip early on and forced to walk his horse as the rest of the cavalry charged on. A little while later, he was shot again in the chest and killed.

The command devolved on Walter Hamilton who, cheering his men on to avenge his beloved commander's death, reached the enemy line. Here they were confronted with a nine-foot-deep *nullah* just in front of them but the Guides were going too fast to avoid it. They plunged down the steep drop and up towards the tribesmen firing at them from the top of the other bank. The enemy were unnerved and fell back as Hamilton and his screaming *sowars* stormed up the slope and cut through them. Hamilton spotted Sowar Dowlut Ram pinned helpless under his dead horse and in immediate danger of being hacked to pieces by three of the enemy. Spurring his horse forward Hamilton cut down all three assailants and helped extricate the trapped man.

The rest of Gough's force soon arrived and the guns opened fire on the fleeing enemy. Their losses were estimated at 400 dead, while the British had six dead and forty wounded. Gough's victory was emphatic and he recognised the decisive part played by the Guides Cavalry and their young leader, Lieutenant Hamilton, whom he recommended for the Victoria Cross.

On 15 May, the Government of India forwarded this recommendation to the India Office in London who, in turn, forwarded it to Horse Guards on 22 July. A further delay followed while the Duke of Cambridge considered the claim. To the disappointment of the India Office, they were informed that Hamilton's act did not come within the regulations of the VC and was, therefore, declined.

Meanwhile, the Treaty of Gandamak was signed between the new Amir, Yakub Khan, and the British, which brought the Second Afghan War to a close, or so it seemed. Part of the agreement was that a British envoy should be resident in Kabul and the British forces withdraw, but keep control of the strategic passes on the Frontier. The envoy appointed was Major Cavagnari, who was allowed to bring a small escort with him. To fill this role, he selected Lieutenant Walter Hamilton with twenty-five Guides Cavalry and fifty-two Guides Infantry. The number had been kept small for Cavagnari believed that a large escort would inflame Afghan resentment.

They arrived in Kabul on 24 July 1879 and were given quarters in the Bala Hissar fortress. It was a compound containing a cluster of bungalows and huts situated only 250 yards from the Amir's own residence. From the start, the atmosphere was tense. Cavagnari put on an outward show of confidence but was well aware of the surrounding hostility. The Afghans saw him as a symbol of their national humiliation and it was only a matter of time before a spark would set off the powder keg.

This came in the form of members of the Afghan army who had been stationed at Herat in the west of the country and had not been involved in the recent fighting. They had not been paid for months and had arrived in Kabul demanding their arrears in back pay. They also turned their discontent on the small British presence and demanded to know why they had been allowed to remain in Kabul. A partial payment of their arrears pacified them temporarily and they returned to their cantonment. With all the self-confidence of inexperience, the Herat soldiers started going about the city with drawn swords and inciting the population against the Amir and the British.

Early on the morning of 3 September, the Herat troops again marched on the Bala Hissar demanding the remainder of their back pay. They rejected a further partial payment and decided to go to Cavagnari at the Residency and demand payment from him. This he firmly rejected and resulted in some stone throwing and an attempt at looting. After one of the Guides was fatally struck by a rock, Hamilton's escort fired a few shots over the heads of the rioters. This was a signal for the Afghans to rush off and arm themselves. Cavagnari sent an urgent message to the nearby Amir asking for protection, but there was to be no response.

Hero's Death

Within an hour, the soldiers returned fully armed and were joined by a citizen mob. The Residency was wholly unsuitable for defence, being surrounded on three sides by buildings from which the Afghans could pour in a constant fire, causing casualties and forcing Hamilton to pull back his men to the main building. By mid-afternoon, two cannon were brought up and Hamilton led charges against the gun crews but, without the means to spike them, these forays were futile.

Two more attempts were made to capture the guns and pull them into the Residency, but the effort of pulling them and defending themselves was too much for the Guides. Finally, the Residency was set on fire and the survivors retreated and prepared to make a last stand. One of the guns blew down a wall behind which a wounded Cavagnari was being tended by Dr Kelly. The mob swarmed through the breach, butchering the two men to death. Hamilton either made one last attempt to silence the gun or decided to take as many of the attackers as he could with him. Leading a few Guides, he charged amongst the enemy, shooting three with his revolver and cutting down two more with his sword. Finally, he was overwhelmed and hacked to death.

The twelve remaining *sowars* were offered the chance to surrender, which they rejected and continued fighting until all were killed. This ended the unequal fight which came to represent all that was both gallant and noble about the Victorian officer in the face of overwhelming odds. The defence had lasted twelve hours and an estimated six hundred Afghans lay dead around the Residency. All the defenders were dead except for seven members of the escort, who were spared. This epic resistance was later recognised with the whole native escort being awarded the Indian Order of Merit and the Corps of Guides was authorised to wear the battle honour 'Residency, Kabul' on its colours and appointments.

Hamilton's death put the Horse Guards in something of a quandary. Having had the recommendation for a VC turned down, the India Office made another approach pointing out that Hamilton's action was very similar to those of Captain John Cook and Lieutenant Reginald Hart, both of whom had received Crosses after charging against overwhelming numbers of enemy natives. The Duke of Cambridge was persuaded and agreed that Hamilton's action merited the VC. Unfortunately, this acceptance was dated 16 September and Hamilton had been killed on the third. As there was no provision to grant a VC to anyone who had died before a submission was put before the Queen, Hamilton should have been disqualified.

With the story of the Residency defence in every newspaper and the lionising of young Walter Hamilton, it was decided to bend the rules. In Michael Crook's book *The Evolution of the Victoria Cross,* he refers to a note accompanying the submission to the Queen which had been predated 1 September, two days before Hamilton's death 'so as to avoid creating an awkward precedent in giving the decoration after death'.

The award was announced in *The London Gazette* on 7 October and the Cross sent to Hamilton's father on 25 October. Walter Hamilton has no known grave as he was buried in a garden close to the Residency. He is remembered with several memorials and a statue in Dublin. A copy of this statue is now on display at the National Army Museum. Also, the great Imperial poet, Sir Henry Newbolt, wrote *The Guides at Cabul* to commemorate his death. In the 1970s, M. M. Kaye wrote a best-selling novel, *The Far Pavilions* which was later made in to a TV mini-series, in which one of the main characters is based on Hamilton.

In 1998, the Ashcroft Trust Collection purchased Hamilton's VC group, which is displayed in the Ashcroft Gallery at the Imperial War Museum.

The death of Cavagnari and the rest of the British Mission caught the British unprepared. The Pershawar Valley Field Force had been reduced and the remaining troops were occupying positions to keep the Khyber Pass open. The Kandahar Field Force was isolated at that southern city. With only Roberts' force still intact in the Kurram Valley, it was arranged that it should advance at once on Kabul. It was reinforced with units from the Khyber, including the 92nd (Gordon Highlanders). The newly-knighted General Sir Frederick Roberts returned to take up his 6,000-strong command, now named the Kabul Field Force and on 30 September, Roberts' forty-seventh birthday, the advance began heralding the Second Campaign. There are those who consider this was a separate conflict and refer to it as the Third Afghan War.

By 5 October, the Kabul Field Force had reached the village of Char Asyab (Charasia), having left Brigadier Macpherson's First Infantry Brigade a march away to act as a rearguard. Here he was faced with the last major geographical obstacle before Kabul. A crescent range of hills reaching heights between 220 to 500 metres dominated the road and were defended by approximately 10,000 Afghans.

The following day, Roberts split his outnumbered force of 3,500 as he had done at the Battle of Peiwar Kotal on 28-9 November 1878. He sent Brigadier Thomas Baker with the Second Infantry Brigade to attack the Afghan positions on the west of the range and roll them up along the hilltop ridges. Meanwhile a smaller force under the command of Major George White of the 92nd would hold the enemy to the east and prevent them from sweeping down from the hills.

Baker's command made successful progress and after two and a half hours had cleared the first ridge. On the eastern flank, White realised that the only way to dislodge the Afghans was to launch an infantry attack despite being heavily outnumbered. With four companies of the Gordons, White led a charge up the steep hill and encountered stiff resistance. Taking a rifle from one of his men, he moved forward on his own. Advancing from one rocky outcrop to another, he got within range and shot dead the Afghan leader. At this, the Afghans lost heart and fled, leaving White's men in command of the position. By 17.00 hours, Baker's men had taken the rest of the heights and the battle was won. For his gallant part in the battle, George White was awarded the Victoria Cross.

Once again, Roberts's tactic of flanking attacks against a vastly superior enemy had succeeded and the way to Kabul was clear. On 13 October, he made his formal entry into the city with the cavalry brigade and five battalions of infantry. Roberts prepared to spend the winter at Kabul but found the huge Bala Hissar fortress ramshackle and unsuitable. After a couple of accidental explosions which killed a number of Gurkhas, Roberts ordered that the fortress be destroyed. He then moved his command to Sherpur, the cantonment that Sher Ali was building north of the city. Parts of the defences were incomplete, but these were soon strengthened and Robert's command could feel secure within its walls. It was a strong defensive position being one-and-a-half-miles long and three-quarters-of-a-mile broad with a good supply of water and stores.

Roberts then turned his attention to rounding up those guilty of storming the British residency and murdering Cavignari and his escort. Fifty-three were hanged, including the mayor of Kabul, creating considerable unrest amongst the Afghan population. With the British holed up, the Afghans smelled blood and declared a *jihad* calling on the tribes to converge on Kabul. Roberts learned of this and vowed to strike before they could amalgamate into one unifying force.

Towards the end of November, reports were received of the gathering of considerable numbers of tribesmen. Roberts sent two forces into the area of the Chardeh Plain under the commands of Baker and Macpherson intended to catch the Afghans in a pincer movement. Roberts was alerted by the heavy firing and hurried to the scene. He then made a series of decisions that extricated the cavalry and ensured the Afghans kept their distance. He was helped when Macpherson's command made contact with the enemy's rearguard, causing their advance to stall.

At a crucial stage in the action, Roberts was to witness a VC act that necessitated the drawing up of a unique new Warrant to enable the recipient to be rewarded.

JAMES WILLIAM ADAMS VC (1839-1903)

James William Adams was born in County Cork, Ireland on 24 November 1839, the only son of James O'Brien Adams, a brewer and local Justice of the Peace, and his mother, Elizabeth Williams. His father died in 1854. Young James proved to be an exceptional scholar and in early November 1856, the sixteen-year-old secured a place at Trinity College, Dublin.

Although he studied hard, he still found time to indulge in numerous sports. Powerfully built, he was known to be a first class horseman and regarded by contemporaries and opponents alike as one of the strongest men in Ireland. Adams often competed against his friend, Frederick Burnaby, in gymnastics. Burnaby of the Royal Horse Guards was also toted as the strongest man in the British Army but regarded as a loose cannon as far as the military hierarchy was concerned. In the Egyptian War, he served as a Special Service officer and was killed at Abu Klea on 17 January 1885.

James Adams studied a variety of subjects and developed an interest in religion. After graduating with a Bachelor of Arts Degree in 1861, he decided to enter the Church and sat the Divinity Testimonium gaining a second-class pass the following year. In 1863, Adams became a deacon, which was quickly followed with his ordination in 1864 by the Bishop of Winchester. After moving to England, his first appointment was curate of a church in Hyde, Hampshire and then, in 1866, a year at Shottesbrooke,

Berkshire. As a naturally active man he sought a more challenging ministry and, in 1868, he accepted a position of chaplain in India with the Bengal Ecclesiastical Establishment.

India

On arrival in India, Adams was struck down with a bout of scarlet fever. When he had recovered, he was sent to Peshawar in northern Punjab and set about his chosen task with great energy. He had time to indulge his passion for sports and was appointed as honorary secretary of the Peshawar Vale Hunt. In 1874, he was sent on special duty to Kashmir and finding no church, built one from pine logs. He travelled from one harsh place to another, enjoying little comfort but administrating spiritual help and comforting the victims of an outbreak of cholera.

In 1876, he was appointed Head of Chaplaincy Services at the cavalry and artillery camp at Meerut, which coincided with the Prince of Wales' visit. Further brief appointments to Chakartad in 1877 and Jabbalpore in 1878 led to his attachment to the Kabul Field Force. Unlike the shambles of 1842, the occupation of Kabul was well conducted thanks to the leadership of General Roberts. Accompanying Roberts was James Adams, who could be relied upon to contribute more than spiritual succour. In a letter from his wife some years later, she wrote: 'I have heard Lord Roberts speak of the invaluable help rendered to him in December 1878 at the Peiwar Kotal action by my husband, acting as an ADC, in recovering a large body of troops, who had gone astray in a forest at a very critical time.'

With the winter weather closing in, Roberts had unfinished business to attend. The abdication of Yakub Khan had created a vacuum and a successor had to be found. Unable to return to the border, Roberts had little alternative but to accumulate supplies and spend the winter at Sherpur.

Learning that the insurgents were again on the offensive and advancing on his position, Roberts split his command sending the brigades of Generals Macpherson and Baker in a pincer movement. On the 10th, Macpherson took a route west and occupied a position on the edge of the Chargeh plain. Baker headed south and then west to where the Kabul River joined the Nirikh. He was then to sweep northwards while Macpherson moved south-westwards with the intention of striking the insurgents between them.

Such manoeuvres were risky and reliant on timing as the two columns would be out of contact with each other. Roberts gravely miscalculated the numbers of insurgents and, instead of the expected 2,000, there were more than five times that number.

VC Action

Roberts then sent Brigadier General Dunham Massy with a small column of cavalry consisting of squadrons of 9th Lancers, 14th Bengal Lancers and 'A' Battery Royal Horse Artillery, with instructions to delay his advance until he had met Macpherson's command. Massy ignored his explicit order and moved through the village of Killi Kazi and entered the Chardeh valley.

As Massy topped a rise, he was confronted with about 10,000 Afghan tribesmen heading towards Kabul. With only 350 men, Massy made a forlorn attempt to stem the advance.

Lieutenant Colonel MacKenzie described the scene: 'The enemy advanced over the hills in dense masses like a swarm of bees … and crowning the heights on our right front … they were in numbers of say 12,000, some say 15,000. Our fire had little or no effect on them. The bullets were now coming in like hail and knocking the horses down in both [the] squadron and the RHA horses. The ground was intersected with *nullahs* (ditches) and watercourses … Awful ground for cavalry. The enemy were scattered all over the place in small bodies, some behind hillocks, some on horses, but all firing like the devil into us. The mounted enemy kept following us, riding round and round and firing and cutting at us with their swords, shouting 'Allah! Allah!'

Roberts and his staff, including James Adams, had moved forward alerted by the firing. He later recalled in his memoirs: 'I galloped across the Chardeh Valley as fast as my horse would carry me, and on gaining the open ground beyond Bhagwana, an extraordinary spectacle was presented to my view. An unbroken line, extending for about two miles, and formed of not less than … 10,000 men, was moving rapidly towards me … To meet this formidable array, instead of Macpherson and Massy's forces, which I hoped I should have found combined, there were but four guns, 198 men of the 9th Lancers, 40 of the 14th Bengal Lancers, and at some distance Gough's troop of 9th Lancers, who were engaged watching the enemy's cavalry.'

Roberts's first action was to secure a line of retreat and to order Macpherson to push on with all speed. He then ordered a fighting retreat to the village of Bhagwana across terrain that was totally unsuited for cavalry and horse artillery. Two of the guns had to be spiked and abandoned. The retreat to the village was chaotic and not helped by the inhabitants opening fire from their rooftops. Roberts was even attacked by the headman and was only saved by a *sowar* of the Bengal Cavalry.

It was during this passage of the fighting that James Adams performed his VC action. Roberts described it thus: 'Our Chaplain who had accompanied me throughout the day, behaved in this particular place with conspicuous gallantry. Seeing a wounded man of the 9th Lancers staggering towards him, Adams dismounted, and tried to lift the man to his own charger. Unfortunately, the mare broke loose and was never seen again. Adams, however, managed to support the Lancer until he was able to make him over to some of his own comrades.

'Adams rejoined me in time to assist two more of the 9th who were struggling under their horses at the bottom of a ditch. He was an unusually powerful man, and by sheer strength dragged the Lancers clear of their horses. The Afghans, meanwhile, had reached Bhagwana and were so close to the ditch that I thought my friend, the padre, could not possibly escape.

I called out to him to look after himself, but he paid no attention to my warnings until he had pulled the almost exhausted Lancers to the top of the slippery bank.'

Just as Roberts was reorganising his troops to make a planned withdrawal, the tardy Macpherson turned up and attacked the Afghans' rear. With this, the picture changed and, with the infantry increasing their pressure, the Afghans turned and fled.

Adams remained on Roberts' staff during the winter at Kabul and took part in the epic Kabul to Kandahar march in August. The final victory on 1 September 1880 at Kandahar brought to an end the Second Afghan War.

Special Warrant Change

Roberts wrote to the Adjutant General in India on 29 January 1880, recommending James Adams for the Victoria Cross in the full knowledge that there was no precedent for a clergyman winning the award.

On the 11 May, this recommendation went before the Military Department of the Government of India, who responded: 'In the opinion of the Government of India the precedents established in 1857 when the VC was conferred on Messrs Mangles and McDonell [*sic*] … and Mr. Kavanagh … would be applicable to the case of Mr Adams … The circumstance of that gentleman's position as a non-combatant and a clergyman do, in the opinion of the Government, mark the character of his gallantry in a special and remarkable manner.'

On receipt at the War Office of the fulsome recommendation from India, the Military Secretary, Lieutenant General Sir Edmund Whitmore tersely rejected it.

'The Revd J.W. Adams is not eligible for the decoration in question as it appears that he holds no Military Commission. The cases of Kavanagh, Mangles & McDonnell do not constitute a precedent in as much as the decoration was conferred on these gentlemen by a special Warrant.'

Frederick Roberts' star was in the ascendancy after his own successful Afghan exploits. The weight of British public opinion was with him as well as the favour of Queen Victoria so that Whitmore had little alternative but to accede to Roberts' determination to see his respected chaplain's gallantry rewarded.

He wrote stating that if the present Warrant did not allow Adams to receive the VC, why not draw up a new warrant? This was readily endorsed by the India Office and, although it had never been suggested before, had the desired effect. On 6 August 1881, Queen Victoria approved a new category – Appendix XI – *Warrant Extending for the Victoria Cross to the Indian Ecclesiastical Establishments.* For the first and only time was a Warrant specifically made for one individual and the odds of anyone else being eligible was nil. On 26 August 1881, *The London Gazette* published the Adams citation:

'During the action at Killa Kazi, on 11th December 1879, some men of the 9th Lancers, having fallen with their horses, into a wide and deep *nullah* (or ditch), and the enemy being close upon them, the Rev J.W. Adams rushed into the water (which filled the ditch), dragged the horses from off the men, upon whom they were lying, and extricated them, he being at the time under a heavy fire and up to his waist in water. At this time, the Afghans were pressing on very rapidly, the leading men getting within a few yards of Mr Adams who, having let go his horse in order to render more effectual assistance had eventually to escape on foot.'

The award was not without its detractors who questioned the idea of a forty-year-old man pulling struggling horses off trapped men in waist-deep water. Undoubtedly Robert's version of events prevailed and his friend was presented with his Cross by Queen Victoria at Windsor Castle on 1 December 1881. The year was also memorable for, on 16 August, he married Alice Mary, the eldest daughter of General Sir Thomas Willshire. Adams and his new wife returned to India to take up his pastoral duties once more. Between 1882 and 1885 he was sent to Lucknow, Naini Tal and finally Meerut.

This relative tranquillity was interrupted in 1886 when he was asked by his friend Roberts to join his staff once more as part of the Burma Field Force. In a short but uncomfortable campaign described by one commentator as 'not a war at all –merely a street row', the victorious British annexed Upper Burma.

This was to be Adams' final military involvement and, having served for twenty years in India, he decided to return to England. In 1887, Lord Roseberry nominated Adams for the post of rector of Postwich near Norwich. Here he stayed until 1893 when ill health forced him to spend two years convalescing in Jersey. When he was fit enough, he took up the post of Rector of Wimbotsham and vicar of Stow Bardolph near Downham Market. Although he was nearly sixty, his desire to continue God's work was undiminished with two churches and a school under his auspices. After his death, a stained-glass window was dedicated to his memory at Stow Bardolph.

In 1900, Adams was appointed Honorary Chaplain to Queen Victoria and he continued after her death as Chaplain-in-Ordinary to Edward VII. As a member of the Chapel Royal, he took part in the King's Coronation in 1902.

In the same year, illness forced him to take a less strenuous role and he took the appointment of Rector of Ashwell Church near Oakham in Rutland. Here he died of acute neuritis (inflammation of the nerves) and advancing paralysis on 20 October 1903, one month short of his sixty-fourth birthday. He was buried in Ashwell Churchyard and his funeral was attended by his old friend and comrade, Lord Roberts.

Retreating to the Sherpur cantonment, Roberts prepared to face an enemy buoyed up by their apparent victory in the Chardeh Valley. Despite being forced from the field, the British casualties were light, with thirty killed and thirty-five wounded.

Part of his preparations included the occupation of the nearby Bimaru (Asmai) heights to the south west of the cantonment. This later proved to be a shrewd move. In the attack of 14 December 1879, Victoria Crosses were awarded to Captain Arthur Hammond of the Corps of Guides, Captain William Vousden of 5th Punjab Cavalry and Lance Corporal George Sellar of 72nd Regiment. On 23 December, the Afghans were fired up by their mullahs into a militant frenzy, and about 100,000 Afghans advanced to attack the southern and eastern faces of the cantonment.

The infantry held its fire until the last moment and then unleashed devastating volleys against the leaderless mob. The artillery on the Bimaru heights fired into the flank of the attackers, causing terrible slaughter. This had the desired effect and the tribesmen wavered before retreating. The cavalry was then unleashed and the rout was complete.

Roberts had good cause to be pleased with his defence which had numbered just 7,000 troops. He had out-generalled and out-fought a huge fanatical Afghan mob. The force spent the rest of the winter in the cantonment until relived on 2 May 1880. A treaty was signed with the new Emir, Abdur Rahman, and the war was over. Just as the Roberts prepared to depart, news reached them that a British force of 2,500 had been overwhelmed at Maiwand about fifty miles north-west of Kandahar. The survivors had retreated to Kandahar closely followed by an army of 25,000 Afghans. Two VCs were awarded for gallantry during the retreat, one of which became highly contentious.

EDWARD JAMES COLLIS VC (1856-1918)

Edward James Collis is probably the best known of the forfeited VCs, if only for the offence he committed. Born in Cambridge on 13 April 1860, Collis joined the Army in 1872 and was enlisted in the 32nd (DCLI) Regiment and later transferred to the Royal Horse Artillery. In 1880, he was serving with 'E' Battery, 'B' Brigade, which was part of General Burrow's 3,000 strong force which had been sent from Kandahar to counter the advance of Ayub Khan's army. Inadequate intelligence meant that Burrow did not know where Ayub's main force was located.

On 27 July, the British reached the village of Maiwand expecting to find only a small number of the enemy; instead, he ran into the whole of Ayub's force, now swollen to about 20,000. Burrow's men attempted to make a stand but were hopelessly outnumbered and outflanked. To their credit, the small force held off this superior force from 09.00 to about 16.00 hours. At a crucial moment, the Indian sepoys panicked and gave way, leaving the men of the 66th (Berkshire) Regiment to hold the hordes of tribesmen at bay. Supported by the RHA, the 66th fought to the last man. The last eleven men left alive charged to their deaths rather than be taken alive.

VC Action

The men of 'E' Battery waited until the last moment before they were forced to limber up and retreat. Gunner Collis was later interviewed and his graphic account appeared in 1891 in the popular magazine, *The Strand*: 'Major Henry Blackwood, commanding my battery, gave the order "Action front". I was a limber gunner that day. We began firing with common shell from the right of the battery. After we had fired a few rounds, their artillery replied. The first shot struck the near wheel of my gun, killing a gunner, wounding another and Lieutenant Fowler. The limber box upon my gun was smashed by a shell, which also killed the wheel horses, but did not touch the driver. Several riding horses of my battery were killed and a good deal of damage done to guns and carriages. Four gunners and Sergeant Wood the No.1 of my gun were killed, leaving only three men to work the gun. I took Sergeant Wood's place.'

As the day wore on, the enemy moved closer.

'About 4 pm a large body of the enemy's infantry charged the left of the battery, the men of the left division, 5 and 6 being compelled to use their handspikes and charge staves to keep them off. Major Blackwood, on this, ordered the battery to limber up and retire. When Lieutenant Maclaine heard this order he said, "Limber up be damned! Give them another round". We limbered up and retired at a gallop about 2000 yards.

'In the meantime, Major Blackwood remained behind with Lieutenant Maclaine's guns and was killed … We then limbered up and went off. Just then a shell burst open our treasure chest. Many of the troops and camp followers stopped to pick up the money and were overtaken and killed. Just after that some of the enemy's cavalry caught up the guns. One of them wounded me on the left eyebrow as he passed. He wheeled round and came at me again; I took my carbine, waited until he was within four or five yards, and let drive, hitting him on the chest and knocking him off his horse.'

Collis further distinguished himself by picking up exhausted and wounded men and putting them on the gun and limber. About 16.00 hours the following afternoon, they reached Kokeran, a village seven miles from Kandahar and Collis went in search of water. A dozen enemy horsemen appeared and made for the wounded on Collis's gun. Collis took a rifle and ran into a *nullah* from where he opened fire, killing two of the enemy. Firing off more than thirty rounds, the enemy thought that there was more than a single rifleman and were driven off. A senior officer saw this act and noted Gunner Collis in his notebook.

The exhausted survivors reached Kandahar that evening with the enemy still hot on their tail. During the siege that followed, Collis once more came to the attention of senior officers, when he volunteered to carry a message beyond the ramparts of the fort to an outpost 200 yards distant. Climbing down the forty-foot rope, Collis ran through heavy fire and delivered the note. He then returned, pulling himself up the rope with bullets striking the wall beside him. One shot actually cut off the heel of his boot.

James Collis received his well-earned VC on 11 July 1881 from Lieutenant-General Roberts at a ceremony held on the Poona Racecourse.

Bigamy and Abuse

Taking his discharge, Collis enlisted in the Bombay Police until he re-joined the Army in 1888. During this period, he married Adela Grace, by whom he had three sons. His health began to suffer and he returned to England without his wife. He was formally discharged on medical grounds after examination at the Netley Military Hospital.

In 1893, he was further hospitalised for three months suffering from rheumatic fever, the blight of many a serviceman. In that year, he married Mary Goddard, a cook, and Collis was employed by the London County Council as a garden constable (park keeper).

In 1895, his past caught up with him when it was disclosed that he had committed bigamy. When confronted with this by his second wife, he told her to clear out as he had another girl to take her place. The aggrieved Mary went to the police and Collis felt the full weight of the law. When he was arrested, Collis told the police that he had not seen his wife for years and thought that he was free to marry again. He also gave his profession as 'groom'.

At his trial, which was reported in *The Times* on 27 November 1895, it emerged that the VC hero had seduced three women. At the time of his arrest, he was courting another young woman, who had consented to marry him. In another case, he had set up home with a woman and after an argument, had turned her out and sold the house. She bore him a crippled child, which he failed to maintain; damning evidence that the prosecution used to great effect. The prosecution rested its case with the statement that Collis had treated all his women with the greatest cruelty. His lawyer used his VC exploit at Maiwand in his defence, which did reduce his punishment somewhat, but he was sentenced to eighteen months with hard labour.

The prosecution also raised an issue which illustrated just how tough life could be for the poor at that time. Because Mary Goddard had to attend the trial as the main prosecution witness, she was fired from her job at a Woolwich public house. The judge said that unless she was reinstated, he would ensure that the landlord lost his licence.

Collis served his sentence but soon appeared before another court facing a more serious charge of paedophilia. In the *Illustrated Police News* dated 20 November 1897, it was reported: 'James Collis VC, thirty-six, labourer, was indicted for indecently assaulting Kathleen Emily Smith, aged twelve, and Mary Evelyn Oxley, aged thirteen, whose parents he was in the habit of visiting.

'Mr A. Hutton, who prosecuted, said that Detective Sergeant Lennox, M Division, had made enquiries into the prisoner's past which had proved to be of a most remarkable nature. Collis served in India as an artilleryman, and at the Battle of Maiwand saved a gun [*sic*], for which brave deed he received the Victoria Cross. He left the Army after that, for what reason the police have been unable to discover, and then joined the Indian Police, but at the expiration of twelve months he gave up his position. Several crimes which he ought to have elucidated remained undetected, and it was suggested that he received money to keep them quiet. He was called upon to explain his conduct, but failed to do so.

'He then came over to England and joined the Corps of Commissionaires, but was dismissed because he had so many "sisters" visiting him. He was next appointed a constable (park keeper) by the London County Council, but soon complaints were made with respect to the park under his care. It was alleged that it was the prisoner's practice to allow couples to act indecently in the park, receiving entrance money from them. This was proved by a detective visiting the park one night, accompanied by his sister.

'The prisoner at this stage in his extraordinary career was arrested for bigamy, and the Old Bailey it was proved that he had married three women, was engaged to a fourth and seduced a fifth. It was the worst case of bigamy ever to come before the court. He obtained £50 from one of the women, and when she complained he threw her out of the window. Numerous assaults had been committed by him upon children. When asked to address the jury the prisoner said in a wild manner, 'They are putting an iron band round my head, and keep screwing it tighter'.

'Mr Hutton said the prisoner was only feigning insanity. He did the same thing at the Old Bailey, and boasted that he would "kid" the judge and jury to think he was mad. Dr Scott of Holloway Prison said that the man was of a low type of intellect, but he was not insane. The jury found the prisoner guilty.

'Mr. McConnel (to the prisoner): This is an extremely bad case. Your career, except the time you behaved with bravery in battle, has been disgraceful. I am sorry to say that what you earned in bravery you have since lost by your shocking conduct. Your actions towards unprotected children are unworthy of the brave soldier you proved yourself to be in the better part of your career. Your attempt to get out of this on the ground of insanity is simply shamming. The law does not allow me to have you whipped or to send you to penal servitude, but I sentence you to two year's hard labour. The prisoner preserved a callous demeanour as he left the dock.'

Collis further suffered the humiliation of forfeiting his VC. He was no longer in possession of it, as he had pawned it, possibly for safe-keeping while he served out his sentence. The War Office redeemed it in 1908 but had exceeded its legal authority in taking back the Cross. The War Office responded with ill-graced offialdom by petulantly stating: 'It was not to be returned to Colliss [*sic*) unless he asks for it.'

As Collis was never informed that he could have his VC back, so he never asked for it. If he had, it would have caused some embarrassment for his Cross was sold by Sotheby's in 1910 for £50. When it again surfaced at auction in 1979, it was withdrawn on the grounds that it had been taken illegally from the War Office. Eighteen months later, it was again submitted for auction and sold for £7,200.

Having served his sentence, Collis was employed as a carman (a driver of horse-drawn delivery carts), until 1907. When the First World War broke out, James Collis volunteered and enlisted in the Suffolk Regiment at the advanced age of fifty-eight. By 1917, he was again medically discharged and on 28 June 1918, he died in a London hospital of heart disease. His sister sent a petition to George V requesting that his name should be restored to the register of VCs. The King stated that:

'Even were a VC to be sentenced to be hanged for murder, he should be allowed to wear the VC on the scaffold.'

The restoring of forfeited Crosses was included as Item 12 in Appendix XIII of the Warrant dated 22 May 1920. He further ordered that Collis's name should be included on the tablets of the Royal Artillery Victoria Cross memorial. Collis had been buried in an unmarked grave in Wandsworth Cemetery. On 22 May 1998, a white Commonwealth War Graves Commission-style headstone, bearing the emblems of The Suffolk Regiment and the Victoria Cross, was erected for this most-flawed of VCs.

A mission to rescue the survivors trapped in Kandahar was quickly formulated. General Roberts selected the best regiments who could withstand the rigours of forced marches through harsh mid-summer terrain. Meanwhile, General Donald Stewart, who had arrived at Sherpur three months earlier, would oversee the rest of the Kabul garrison back to India in accordance with instructions from the government for the withdrawal of all British forces from Afghanistan.

Roberts' force consisted of 9,986 fighting men made up of 2,562 British and 7,151 Native troops. In addition, there were 8,000 camp followers. Each soldier had to pare his kit to 20-30lbs and no wheeled transport was taken. All artillery was mule-carried mountain guns. On 7 August, the relieving army moved out of the Sherpur cantonments and began its epic march. To start with, Roberts restricted the length of the daily marches to enable the troops to build up their stamina for the more severe conditions that were to come.

For some, the march was unbearable. About twenty camp-followers just laid down exhausted and refused to move. The tribesmen, who hovered around the rear, made short work of them. Three soldiers actually took their own lives, one of the 72nd Highlanders and two *sepoys* from the Native Infantry.

On 27th, Roberts was prostrated with fever and had to be conveyed by *dhoolie*. The column reached Kandahar on the 31st and for dignity's sake, Roberts forced himself upon a horse when within sight of the city. Hardly pausing to rest, Roberts ordered a reconnaissance of Ayub Khan's position and decided to attack the following day.

To reach the enemy's camp and main position, the Babawali Pass had to be forced, and the fortified villages of Gundi Mulla Sahibdad and Gundigan had to be cleared. The battle for the former was particularly hard-fought with the 92nd Highlanders and 2nd Gurkhas finally taking it with the bayonet. The infantry brigades made steady progress despite a determined defence. Finally, Ayub Khan's camp was taken intact and its leader made a speedy retreat. Roberts lost about 100 men killed while the Afghan losses were over 1,000 killed and 4,000 wounded.

The Battle of Kandahar brought to a close the Anglo-Afghan War. Roberts left Kandahar on 9 September and on 15 October he resigned his command. Still suffering from fever, he took sick leave and returned to England, where he was feted for his famous march and final battle. He was created K.C.B and G.C.B and a baronet and recognised with the thanks of both Houses of Parliament.

Chapter 20

The Anglo-Zulu War, 1879

Number of VCs awarded	23
Number of VCs awarded to officers	11
Number of VCs awarded to other ranks	12
Total awarded to British Army	20
Total awarded to Colonial Regiments	3

Origins of the War

After the brief and frustrating campaign against the Xhosas in the Eastern Cape, Britain turned her attention to Zululand to the north. The British High Commissioner in South Africa, Sir Bartle Frere, and his Secretary for Native Affairs, Sir Theophilus Shepstone, shared the opinion that safe frontiers could be gained only by aggressive forward thrusts followed by annexation. The comparative ease with which the Eastern Cape had been subjugated led them to believe that Zululand would soon follow.

The impoverished Boer republic of Transvaal had suffered a defeat by an African tribe called the Pedi under King Sekukuni and was in jeopardy. The Boers misfortune led to Britain sending troops to guard against the Pedi incursions, something for which the Boers were temporarily grateful. Zululand was now virtually surrounded from the Transvaal in the north and the British colony of Natal on its west and southern borders.

Frere and Shepstone portrayed King Cetshwayo's Zululand as a savage militaristic nation anxious for war. In fact, there was no standing army; the Zulu warrior was trained to fight but only called to arms when Cetshwayo deemed it necessary to fight other tribes or for cattle raiding.

When Chelmsford arrived to assess Natal's defences, he was appalled at the porous state of the border. There was over 100 miles of river border across which a Zulu army could pass with ease and was patrolled by just a small number of native border guards. In the build-up to the anticipated invasion, the few locally-stationed British troops arrived from the Eastern Cape. By portraying the Zulus as a threat to Natal the desired effect was achieved, with a rush to volunteer in the locally-raised regiments. An excuse, however, had to be manufactured to justify the invasion.

In July 1878, two Zulu women, one the wife of Chief Sihayo, started affairs with younger lovers and escaped across the border into Natal. The brothers of the women went after them and took them back into Zululand where they were put to death. Such incidents had occurred before without causing problems between the two countries. This time it was seized upon as an excuse to portray the Zulus as a merciless race but this alone was not enough of an excuse to force an invasion. The announcement of a boundary decision gave Frere the opportunity to confront Cetshwayo with an impossible ultimatum.

On 11 December 1878, dressed up as a ceremonial meeting under the shade of two large fig trees on the bank of the Tugela River, Shepstone presented Cetshwayo with thirteen demands which had to be answered in twenty days. Amongst these included the disbandment of the Zulu army, something both sides knew would not happen. It says something for Cetshwayo's determination not to play Frere's game that he accepted much of the ultimatum, while other demands were put before the Zulu council. Feigning surprise, Frere described this response as 'a pitiful evasion', and set in motion the invasion of Zululand.

Chelmsford had had plenty of time to prepare since the previous August. He had 6,600 British troops, including artillery, engineers and HM Regiments of the 3rd, 13th, 24th, 80th and 90th Foot Local volunteers constituted all the mounted troops, while 9,000 natives were employed in short-lived regiments like the Natal Native Contingent or as labourers. Detail was paid to logistics with ample ammunition and stores held in the depots. To transport the invasion, 725 carts and wagons and 7,626 draft animals were aquired. Facing the invading columns would be an estimated 35,000 Zulus. At the last minute, he decided to reduce the number of invading columns from five to three with one crossing the Lower Tugela in the south and another column covering the north. Chelmsford took command of the main Centre Column comprising of some 7,800 men which assembled on the bank of the Buffalo River by the forward base at Rorke's Drift.

For his part, Cetshwayo's strenuous attempt to avoid war with the British limited the Zulus' scope. He directed his warriors to defend their country only if attacked and not carry the war beyond its borders. He also ordered his warriors to defend their country, ordering them to avoid killing any invaders other than the regular red-coated British soldiers. In the event, his orders were not obeyed.

On the mist-shrouded morning of 11 January 1879, Chelmsford's column crossed the swollen Buffalo River unopposed. After ten days of slowly moving through swampy and rugged terrain, interrupted by a brief skirmish at Sihayo's stronghold, the column reached a broad valley dominated by an impressive rocky outcrop roughly in the shape of the sphinx badge of the 24th Regiment. The Zulus called this Isandlwana, which has a variety of meanings including 'Little Hut' and 'Little Hand'. Either way, it was about to become one of the most recognisable mesas in military history.

During the desperate battle that took place the following day, the only Isandlwana VC was awarded, but only after a tortuous process.

SAMUEL WASSALL VC (1856-1927)

Samuel Wassall was born on 28 July 1856 in No.11 Court, Alcester Street, Aston in Birmingham, the son of Thomas Wassall, a wire-maker, and his wife Elizabeth (née Silk). He worked as an apprentice dyer before enlisting at Dudley on 28 November 1874 in the local 80th (Staffordshire Volunteers) Regiment. Within eighteen months of joining, Wassall was on the way to South Africa with his regiment on the troop ship *Orontes* arriving at the Cape in May 1876.

From there, the regiment was transported to the Eastern Cape and took part in the Galeka War of 1877. Moving to Natal, the regiment marched from Newcastle to Utrecht on the border with the Transvaal where they built an earthwork fort. Their first taste of campaigning was against Sekukuni's Pedi tribe in a remote mountain area of eastern Transvaal. In an abortive march to attack what was called 'Sekukuni's Town' the column, commanded by Colonel Hugh Rowlands VC, was defeated not by the Pedi but by high temperatures and scarcity of water, forcing them to turn back.

Sometime during the summer of 1878, the Mounted Infantry had been increased to squadron strength of 120 men, drawing on recruits from the 3rd, 13th and 80th Regiments. Amongst these recruits was Private Samuel Wassall who, along with some of his comrades, volunteered for the 1st Squadron Imperial Mounted Infantry. On 11 January 1879, they were part of the main invading Centre Column under the command of Lord Chelmsford that crossed the Buffalo River at Rorke's Drift and into Zululand.

The Mounted Infantry was under the command of Lieutenant Colonel John Russell a Special Service officer of the 12th Lancers, scouted ahead of the huge column. Apart from a short skirmish against a kraal in the Batshe valley, their progress was unopposed. The route, however, was difficult and tortuous; first heading north-east, then moving south and then east, until Chelmsford set up camp in a wide valley beneath a prominent rock outcrop called Isandlwana. Given the length of time it had taken, Isandlwana was only nine miles from Rorke's Drift as the crow flies.

Learning from his scouts that Zulu activity had been spotted to the south-east, Chelmsford departed that night with half his command, including the bulk of the Mounted Infantry under Russell, leaving the rest to break camp and follow. The twenty men of the Mounted Infantry who remained in the camp fully expected to re-join Chelmsford column later that day with the hope of joining in a deciding battle against the main Zulu army. It transpired that the Zulus had cleverly posted decoys to draw the British away from where their main force was hidden in a valley five miles from Isandlwana. In what turned out to be a fruitless pursuit, the elusive decoys drew Chelmsford's men further from the camp.

On the morning of 22 January, the main Zulu army was discovered bivouacked in the Ngwebeni Valley by a patrol of the Natal Native Horse. This provoked the Zulus to prematurely launch their attack on the British camp that was preparing to re-join their commander, some twelve miles away. Scrambling over the Inyonoi Heights and into the valley before Isandlwana, the 20,000 Zulus assumed their traditional form of attack with a centre body and flanking horns, a formation well suited to open, flat country. After staunchly repelling the Zulu attack, the thinly spread infantry were soon outflanked and overwhelmed.

Unable to retreat down the track they had travelled from Rorke's Drift, the survivors were pushed and funnelled into a rock-strewn valley which was later referred to as Fugitive's Drift. This six-mile long trail led to the cliffs above the fast-flowing Buffalo River and the border with Natal. Those survivors on foot stood little chance against the pursuing Zulus and even those who rode horses were vulnerable as they gingerly picked their way at walking pace through the rocky terrain. Among the mounted survivors who did reach the river was Private Samuel Wassall.

At the Buffalo River, a reception committee of Zulu warriors awaited the fugitives. Pressed from behind, the survivors descended the steep path down the cliff to an area of flat grassland at the edge of the rushing torrent. Here the Zulus were slaughtering the remnants of the fleeing British troops as they tried to plunge into the swiftly-running river.

VC Action

One of the horsemen to reach the river was Captain William Barton of the Natal Native Horse. Despite the carnage going on around him, he was so taken by the coolness and courage of one man that he later tried to trace this anonymous hero.

Eventually, twenty days later, Barton was able to compose a statement which read in part: 'As I approached the river, a man in the Mounted Infantry was riding in front of me, and I also saw at the same time another man of the Mounted Infantry struggling in the river and he called out his comrade's name; he was apparently drowning. The Zulus were at that time firing at our people from above us, others were down on the bank of the river stabbing others of our people on both sides of where I was. The man of the Mounted Infantry, who rode down in front of me, dismounted, left his horse on the Zulu side and sprang into the river to save his comrade.

'I consider this man to have performed a most gallant and courageous act, in trying to save his comrade at the almost certain risk of his own life.

I crossed the river myself, about the same time and did not think it possible that either of these two men could have escaped alive; indeed I spoke some days afterwards to Lieutenant Walsh [Adjutant] of the Mounted Infantry of the circumstances which I had witnessed and I spoke of it to him as evidence of my having seen two of his men lost at the Buffalo River.'

Barton believed that he was merely reporting the certain deaths of two of Walsh's men. A few days later Barton was visiting the makeshift hospital at Helpmekaar, when one of the patients, Private Westwood, overhead Barton recount the gallant conduct of the unknown soldier. Westwood immediately cried out, identifying himself as the one who had been rescued and Wassall as his saviour. It was then that Barton decided to report the matter in writing.

On 12 February, the day following Barton's written statement, Walsh visited Westwood in hospital, noting that he was still very ill. Despite this, Westwood was able to dictate his statement: 'I wish to bring to the notice of the Commanding Officer, the gallant conduct of Pte Wassall, 80th Regiment, who saved my life and nearly lost his own in doing so.

'In attempting to cross the river, I got exhausted and cried out for help. I saw Pte Wassall on the bank of the river on the Zulu side. On seeing me, he jumped from his horse and getting into the river seized me and dragged me back to the bank on the Zulu side, advising me to cross by the upper ford, which I did. The enemy at the time Pte Wassall got in the river were keeping up a heavy fire on us, the bullets striking all around. Others were stabbing wounded men. Had it not been for Pte Wassall I must have lost my life, and in saving it, he was placing his own in very grave danger.'

The written statements of Barton, Westwood and Walsh were then submitted to Captain Edward Browne, 1/24th Regiment, the officer commanding the Mounted Infantry left in camp. Browne immediately wrote to his commanding officer, Russell: 'Sir, I have the honour to forward the accompanying reports for submission to HE The Lieutenant General Commanding (Chelmsford) … As the identity of the man mentioned, viz. Pte Wassall 80th Regiment, 1st Squadron Mounted Infantry, has now in my opinion been fully established, I now respectively submit for the consideration of HE The Lieutenant General Commanding, the circumstances of the case and hope that he may deem the gallant action performed by Pte Wassall worthy of being rewarded with the decoration of the Victoria Cross.'

Russell, following correct procedure, in turn wrote to Colonel Richard Glyn, the Commander of No.3 Column, who was still entrenched in appalling conditions at Rorke's Drift with what was left of his shattered command: 'Sir, I have the honour to forward to you a letter and correspondence I have received from Captain Browne, commanding 1st Squadron Mounted Infantry, with reference to the gallant conduct of the man mentioned in the margin. This man appears to have behaved in an exceptionally brave manner, in saving the life of his comrade, and I trust that it may be considered right to bring his name forward for a special mark of distinction.'

With the loss of so many officers and men of his regiment at Isandlwana, Colonel Glyn was a depressed man with much on his mind. On 18 February and without comment, he merely sent the statements off to Lord Chelmsford's military secretary at Pietermaritzburg. The Commanding Officer, if anything, was even more preoccupied with the Isandlwana disaster than Glyn, who he had tried to blame for the debacle.

In a reflection of the animosity existing between them, Chelmsford did not send a letter but scrawled an abrupt rebuke across the bottom of Russell's letter: 'In cases like the one under reference, it is absolutely necessary that you should yourself enquire into the matter and express an opinion as to the accuracy of the statements made'. Chelmsford's secretary then added, 'Please return without delay.'

The Mounted Infantry squadron was no longer attached to Glyn's command and had been transferred north to No.4 Column, commanded by Colonel Evelyn Wood VC. Without further ado, Glyn passed on the bundle to Wood, scrawling under Chelmsford's comments, 'Officer Commanding No.4 Column. Passed onto you as the Mounted Infantry is under your command.'

On receipt of the papers, Wood read between the lines and decided to pass part of the ball back to Glyn to whom he wrote on 9 March: 'It would appear that Pte Westwood is still serving under your command – perhaps you will enquire to his statement, and forward your remarks direct to the Military Secretary. I have ordered the attendance of Lieutenant Walsh and Pte Wassall at this camp, and will forward the result of my enquiries to the Military Secretary.'

Taking his time to reply, Glyn wrote to Wood on 28 March: 'Full enquiries have been made about Pte Westwood but he cannot be traced in connection with any corps in this command.'

Westwood, it seems, had disappeared and the ball was back in Wood's court. The possible award of the Victoria Cross to a brave and deserving man was in danger of being lost due to indifference and pettiness. Wood then instructed his staff officer, Captain Maude, to return the bundle back to Colonel Russell, with a note: 'For further enquiry and report.' There was now another conflict between senior officers which added to the tortuous journey of Wassall's award.

Colonel Russell had either been misinformed or deliberately misread his instructions for the part the Mounted Infantry was to play in the abortive attack on Hlobane Mountain on 28 March. Subsequent knowledge would point to Colonel Wood sending Russell to the wrong location, although the latter should have realised that it was a mistake. In consequence, there was a great deal of animosity between the two colonels.

Russell, fuming and disinterested, replied to the effect that it was no longer his responsibility. Although Westwood had been sick in Helpmekaar, it was now believed that he had been taken to Pietermaritzburg. To his credit, Wood, again wasted no time in writing a letter dated 5 April to the Officer Commanding Troops, Pietermaritzburg, requesting him to track down Westwood. It was now almost two months since Barton had written his first statement and probably Wassall was aware of the stir he was causing in high circles.

At length, Westwood was found in hospital and brought before the Pietermaritzburg District Magistrate to make another statement. This time Westwood's account was recorded verbatim and not transposed into a formal style as had obviously been the case in his initial evidence taken down by Walsh.

The spontaneous simplicity of Westwood's new statement would underline his honesty: 'I was in the camp at Isandlwana on the 22 January last with some more men of the squadron of Mounted Infantry to which I belong. At about 1.30pm we found the Zulus surrounding us and I and my comrades thought we could do no more, and we had better get away. So about four of us got on our horses and made towards the river as we thought. Pte Wassall was one of the party and was with me all the way from the camp to the river. He was generally a little behind but I know he was one of the party.

'When we got to the river we had to cross by a narrow causeway of big stones, only one man could go properly at one time. Some men had crossed before me and the Zulus were firing at them when we crossed the river. While I was crossing the river, and was almost in the middle of it, a stone gave way and the stream took my horse off its legs and turned him right over, and carried him down the stream and me too. I had to let go my horse and rifle and tried to swim across the river.

'The stream was carrying me down the river, and I was getting tired, when I saw Wassall on the bank. I called out to him as much as I could when I saw him. He was then on his horse on the Zulu side and there were some Zulus on the right of him firing at the men trying to cross the stream. There were lots of men of all sorts trying to cross the river. As soon as Wassall saw me, he jumped off his horse and pulled his bandage out of his pocket (probably an equestrian tail bandage) and threw the end to me, which I caught and he dragged me to the Zulu side, the stream had brought me near it.

'After I got out, he got on his horse and rode him into the river and told me to catch hold of the horse's tail and so he dragged me across the river. His horse was swimming most of the time, and the Zulus were firing at us all the time. When we got across, we went up the other side together for about a mile and then I told him to go on as I thought I could get on by myself. I lost my way and did not get to Helpmekaar until the morning of 24th (two days later)

'I am quite sure I should have been either drowned or shot if it had not been for Pte Wassall, for when he got off his horse to help me, the Zulus were twenty five yards from us, it was as much as ever, and I am sure that Pte Wassall might have got across the river much quicker, but that he stopped for me.'

It was a simple but most convincing declaration and the following day the Officer Commanding Troops, Pietermaritzburg, sent the statement to Lord Chelmsford, accompanied by the following note:

'I have had the statement of Pte Westwood, 80th Regiment, who is at present in Pietermaritzburg, taken down and I now forward it to you as directed. As near as possible, the man's own words were taken down, and he made the statement clearly and without hesitation, and without any leading questions being put to him. From the way in which the man made his statement, I should say that he was in no way exaggerating the circumstances.'

From then on, events moved quickly and on 17 June, Samuel Wassall's citation appeared in *The London Gazette*. It was not until after the Zulu War was officially over on 1 September that Wassall finally received his VC. General Garnet Wolseley, who succeeded Chelmsford, travelled from the defeated Zulu capital, Ulundi, to Pretoria in the Transvaal. On the way, he stopped at Utrecht to perform one more duty. On the morning of 12 September, two parades were held. The earlier one consisted of the 2/24th Regiment drawn up on the garrison parade ground as Wolseley presented Crosses to Rorke's Drift defenders, Gonville Bromhead and Robert Jones.

A little while later, the 80th Regiment assembled and watched as Samuel Wassall received his well-merited VC. The odyssey of Wassall's recommendation had been protracted one and, but for the perseverance of men like Barton, Browne and Wood, a brave man would have gone unknown and unrewarded.

Lieutenant Melvill and Lieutenant Coghill

Samuel Wassall remained the sole Isandlwana Victoria Cross winner for twenty-seven years, until two officers of the 24th Regiment were amongst six to receive posthumous awards in 1906, when the Warrant was amended to include such cases. Of all the many images that the Zulu War produced, the one that epitomised self-sacrifice and valour for the late-Victorian public was that of Lieutenants Melvill and Coghill, riding together through the Zulu hordes to carry the colours to safety. The reality, although dramatic enough, was somewhat more prosaic. It has never been confirmed that Teinmouth Melvill received any such orders to save the colours but he did leave with the colours encased in a cumbersome black leather tube just before the camp was overrun.

Neville Coghill had departed a little earlier and at no time were the two men seen together during the six-mile retreat along the Fugitive's Trail to the Buffalo River. Here, Coghill managed to coax his mount across to the Natal bank. When he looked back, he saw Melvill clinging to a rock midstream. Coghill bravely attempted to urge his horse, which had been severely wounded by stab wounds, back into the stream until it was shot dead. Swimming to the rock, Coghill found the exhausted Melvill had lost both his horse and the colours. Somehow, they both managed to swim to the shore and begin to climb the steep sides of the canyon. Finally, they could go no further and were surrounded and killed by allies of the Zulus living nearby.

An emotional Colonel Glyn stated that if they had lived they should have received the Victoria Cross. General Sir Garnet Wolseley, ever critical of officers who he considered to have deserted their men, wrote: 'I am sorry that both of these men were not killed with their men at Isandlwana instead of where they were. I don't like the idea of officers escaping on horseback when their men on foot are killed. Heroes have been made of men like Melvill and Coghill, who, taking advantage of their horses bolted from the scene of the action to save their lives, it is monstrous making heroes of those who saved or attempted to save their lives by bolting.'

Wolseley's views did not prevail and Melvill and Coghill remain amongst the most heroic figures of the Victorian era.

Soon after, Wassall left the Army and married in 1882, settling down in Barrow-in-Furnace where he worked in the electrical department of the Barrow Shipyard. Together, he and his wife had four sons and three daughters. In 1917, he met King George V and Queen Mary during their visit to Barrow. Wassell was among the 324 VC holders who were guests of the royal couple at the celebrated garden party in June 1920. On 31 January 1927, at the age of seventy, Samuel Wassell died and was buried at the Barrow-in-Furness Cemetery in Section 3.B, plot 1952, He medals are held by the Staffordshire Regiment Museum in Lichfield.

As the battle unfolded at Isandlwana, the post at Rorke's Drift learned some details from mounted survivors who rode past to the relative safety of Helpmekaar about fifteen miles away. The buildings at Rorke's Drift were used as a Swedish missionary station until requisitioned by the British Army as their supply base for the invasion by the Centre Column.

The Mission consisted of a bungalow that was used as a hospital and the nearby church was used as a store. Apart from the patients and hospital staff, the base was occupied by the Commissariat, some Royal Engineers and guarded by eighty-five men of 'B' Company of 2nd/24th (Warwickshire) Regiment. The latter were disappointed that they had been given this mundane duty while their comrades had crossed into Zululand looking for an expected victory against Cetshwayo's army. Also present was a company of the Natal Native Contingent (NNC), an ill-trained regiment regarded with contempt by the British and consequently of dubious reliability.

The sound of firing could be heard from the direction of the British camp at Isandlwana some nine miles distant and those officers who climbed the nearby Oscarburg Hill saw through their telescopes that a big battle was in progress. Later this was confirmed by the arrival of some fugitives from the battle with the shocking news that the camp had been overrun. Barely breaking their progress, the survivors made their war towards Helpmekaar yelling advice that the men at Rorke's Drift should follow their example. This was enough for the NNC, who departed en-masse.

Urged by a couple of Natal Native Horse officers who stopped, 'B' Company's commanding officer, Lieutenant Gonville Bromhead, ordered preparations to be made to evacuate the post. It was at this point that a middle-aged veteran soldier, now employed in the Commissariat, intervened. He pointed out that burdened with the sick, a slow-moving convoy could not hope to outrun the Zulus and that it was more sensible to stay and fortify their post. This was good advice for some 4,000 Zulus, who had formed the extreme right flank of the attack at Isandlwana and subsequently not taken part in the fight, were already approaching.

Disappointed that they had missed out on the subsequent looting and 'washing of spears', they were determined to plunder and capture Natal cattle, despite Cetshwayo's orders not to cross the border. The Zulus crossed the Buffalo about four miles from Rorke's Drift where it narrowed enough to be leap over. At that point, there had been no intention of investing the British store base.

Bromhead later acknowledged the advice to stay and fight given by Acting Assistant Commissary James Dalton, the last of eleven Victoria Crosses awarded for the celebrated Battle of Rorke's Drift.

JAMES LANGLEY DALTON VC (1832-1887)

The early life of James Langley Dalton is something of a mystery. He may have been born in the London district of Holborn in December 1832, possibly to Charles Dalton and Hannah Langley, but searches of the Roman Catholic parish registers have not revealed his baptism. It is possible that he was taken to Ireland to be shown to his grandparents and was baptised there.

James Langley Dalton would appear to have had some education for he was both literate and numerate and briefly, when he left school, he was employed as an assistant in a stationery shop. He was living in Ireland when he enlisted in the Army on 20 November 1849 and assigned to the 85th Regiment in Waterford. If it was adventure he was seeking then he had chosen the wrong regiment for he was posted to Preston, Hull and Portsmouth. In March 1853, the regiment sailed on TS *Marion* for a three-year posting to Mauritius, thus missing being involved in the Crimean War. Dalton, despite his youth, was promoted to sergeant in 1855.

Canada

In 1856, promoted to the rank of sergeant-major, he and the 85th were sent to South Africa to take part in the 8th Frontier War. Returning to England, he transferred to the Commissariat and Transport Department in 1862 and in 1866, he was again promoted to master sergeant and then to Staff Sergeant First Class before he was sent to Quebec, Canada in 1868. There was an anti-British feeling in the states of north-east America, arising from the perception of British government support for the Confederacy in the Civil War which encouraged the Fenians to carry out raids in to Canada in 1866 and again in 1870.

These raids were dealt with by locally-raised Canadian militias supported by the British Commissariat. Dalton would also have been involved in another flashpoint that occurred in remote Manitoba when a rebellion broke out led by self-styled 'General' Louis Riel. In early 1870, he and his supporters occupied Fort Garry and declared their own provincial government. The Canadian government sent an expedition to restore law and order to the Red River area.

Led by Colonel Garnet Wolseley, a force of 1,200 took three months of incredible effort to overcome natural obstacles to reach Fort Garry. Riel and his supporters believed they were unreachable by a large force. As Wolseley's men approached, Riel and his men took to their heels and fled. A bloodless victory had been gained without loss of a single man. The expedition has been used as an example of how a well organised and adequately-supplied force can succeed in the face of nature at its most obstructive.

James Dalton's part in the Red River Expedition is not clear. It would appear that he had some supporting role and was not amongst Wolseley's command for his name does not appear on the Red River medal roll. In 1871, he returned to England and, after twenty-two-years' service, he retired from the Army with a well merited Long Service and Good Conduct medal.

South Africa

As a bachelor with few ties in England, it is possible that he soon went to Cape Province, South Africa; a place he liked and where he had connections. With the outbreak of the 9th Frontier War in 1877 in the Eastern Cape, Dalton volunteered to serve with the Commissariat. His excellent service record and long experience elevated him to the commissioned rank of Acting Assistant Commissary (equivalent to lieutenant). He was in charge of stores at Ibeka, which was in the forefront of the fighting and at one point was cut off by the Xhosa. For his part in the campaign he was Mentioned in Despatches. At the end of this confusing and frustrating campaign, Dalton resigned his appointment only to take it up again with the outbreak of the Zulu War of 1879.

Dalton rode into Fort Helpmekaar in pouring rain on New Year's Day 1879. He had been ordered to join No.3 (Centre) Column of the invasion force that was assembling near the Natal / Zululand border prior to seeking a decisive battle against the recalcitrant Zulus.

Soon, the entire force moved down from the heights of Helpmekaar to the small missionary station of Rorke's Drift on the banks of the Buffalo River. This was the stepping off point for the invasion and the supply depot for the force. The missionary station had been a trading post consisting of a small bungalow and a store house which had been converted to a church. It again reverted to its former function and was filled with supplies. The bungalow was converted into a hospital and at the time of the battle housed about seventeen patients.

James Dalton had two fellow commissaries. His senior was Assistant Commissary Walter Dunne and a twenty-two-year-old civilian clerk named Louis Byrne. The days before the invasion began on 11 January were spent stock piling the large amount of stores, including bags of mealies for the native auxiliaries and boxes of hard tack (biscuits) for the soldiers. Left to guard the crossing was Bromhead's company of the 2 / 24th, and a company of the 2 / 3rd Natal Native Contingent numbering about 300. Advancing on this tiny force was the Zulu army.

VC Action

Having decided against retreat, the officers, Chard, Bromhead, Surgeon Reynolds and James Dalton, gathered to discuss the best means of defending the small station. They had just the right sort of stores to erect breastworks; heavy sacks of grain, boxes of biscuit, barrels of lime juice and ox-wagons. Supervised by Chard, Bromhead and Dalton, a solid barricade was erected encompassing the hospital and storehouse, which were about forty yards apart. It was fortunate that the 300 natives of the NNC were present as the work would not have been accomplished in time.

A succession of fugitives came past the Drift and all urged the garrison of the futility of trying to defend the post. This finally got to the natives of the NNC, who suddenly leapt over the barricades and fled. This left fewer than 140 men to defend the perimeter, so an adjustment to the defences was made. This was a new barricade running from the corner of the store to the front barricade. This effectively isolated the hospital, which had been loop-holed and manned by riflemen, including some of the patients.

When the 4,000-strong Zulus force appeared, they quickly surrounded the post and began to probe the defences for a weakness. All attempts to climb the barricades were beaten back. James Dalton was in the thick of the fighting and his conduct was recorded by Chaplain George Smith: 'Mr Dalton, who is a tall man, was continually going about the barricades, fearlessly exposing himself, and cheering the men, and using his own rifle most effectively. A Zulu ran up near the barricade. Mr Dalton called out, "Pot that fellow!" and he himself aimed over the parapet at another, when his rifle dropped and he turned round, quite pale, and said he had been shot. The doctor was at his side at once, and found that a bullet had passed quite through above the right shoulder. Unable any longer to use his rifle (although he did not cease to direct the fire of the men who were near him) he handed it to Mr Byrne who used it well.'

Dalton was carried to the mealie sack redoubt and placed inside – his role in the battle effectively over. Around him, the outnumbered defenders fought desperately to keep the waves of Zulus at bay. The hospital was set alight and the defenders heroically fought off the Zulus while the sick were evacuated to comparative safety.

With nightfall, the attacks began to peter out. With daybreak, the Zulus were gone, leaving some 400 dead littering the ground around the small post. Just fifteen defenders were killed and fifteen wounded in this remarkable defence which has entered the nation's psyche. Its significance, however, has been somewhat exaggerated mainly by those seeking to deflect attention away from the appalling defeat at Isandlwana

There was a lavish awarding of Victoria Crosses. *The London Gazette* of 2 May 1879, published eight names and citations of the Rorke's Drift defenders. John Chard, Royal Engineers and seven members of 'B' Coy 24th Regiment; Gonville Bromhead, John Williams, Henry Hook, William Jones, Robert Jones, William Allen and Frederick Hitch. There followed some furious lobbying which saw Surgeon James Reynolds also being awarded the VC.

Praise for Dalton

As more became learned about the action from the letters and comments by the defenders, so the public heard of the role that James Dalton had played. Badly wounded and spending six months convalescing, Dalton was probably unaware of the lobby pressing for recognition of his role in the fight at Rorke's Drift.

Ordinary soldiers like Private Henry Hook recorded that before the battle: 'Orders were given to strike the camp and make ready to go, and we actually loaded two wagons. Then Mr Dalton, of the Commissariat Department, came up and said that if we left the drift every man was certain to be killed. He had formally been a sergeant-major in a line regiment and was one of the bravest men that ever lived.'

In his account, Private William Jones praised Dalton: 'I remember seeing between the party bearing the wounded from the hospital and the defenders at the mealie bags the central group, consisting of Surgeon Reynolds, his bull-terrier and a wounded man, the gallant Dalton, who played a prominent part in the defence. Dalton was a man of towering structure and he had been foremost in the defence, exposing himself fearlessly above the low barricade, using his rifle with deadly aim and his bayonet with Herculean strength. He was shot down in the act of taking aim and passed his rifle to another Commissariat officer, Mr Byrne, who was himself shot almost immediately in the head as he was bringing water to a wounded man of the Natal contingent. Dalton's rifle was passed to Lieutenant Chard at the barricade and a wounded man handed him the cartridges. Surgeon Reynolds applied a hasty bandage to Dalton's wound and he remained to cheer on the defenders.'

Even General Sir Garnet Wolseley, who took over from Lord Chelmsford, added his usual astringent comment: 'I presented Major Chard RE with his Victoria Cross: a more uninteresting and more stupid fellow I never saw. Wood (Sir Evelyn) tells me he is a most useless officer, fit for nothing. I hear in the camp that the man who worked hardest at Rorke's Drift was the Commissariat Officer (Dalton) who has not been rewarded at all.'

The Commissary General, Sir Edward Strickland, orchestrated a campaign for both Dalton and Dunne to be recognised and received a letter of support from John Chard.

When the appeal finally reached the Duke of Cambridge, the Commander-in-Chief commented: 'We are giving the VC too freely, I think, but probably Mr Dalton has as good a claim as the others who have got the Cross for Rorke's Drift Defence'.

In October, when the invading force was broken up and the troops sent new postings, 'B' Coy 2/24th was marching through Pietermaritzberg when James Dalton was spotted amongst the cheering crowd by one of the soldiers, who cried out, 'Why there's Mr Dalton cheering us! We ought to be cheering him! He was the best man there!' Dalton was hauled out of the crowd and made to march with 'B' Company to thunderous cheers.

Belatedly the name of James Dalton was acknowledged as the man who persuaded Chard and Bromhead to stay and defend the hospital and stores base and to oversee its defence. Finally, James Dalton received his just reward.

On 17 November 1879, *The London Gazette* published his citation: 'James Langley Dalton, Acting Assistant Commissary (now Sub-Assistant) Commissariat and Transport Corps. For his conspicuous gallantry during the attack on Rorke's Drift Post by the Zulus on the night of the 22nd Jan.1879, when he actively superintended the work of defence, and was amongst the foremost of those who received the first attack at the corner of the hospital, where the deadliness of his fire did great execution, and the mad rush of the Zulus met with its first check, and where, by his cool courage, he saved the life of a man of the Army Hospital Corps, by shooting the Zulu who, having seized the muzzle of the man's rifle, was in the act of assegaing him. This officer, to whose energy much of the defence of the place was due, was severely wounded during the contest, but still continued to give the same example of cool courage.'

A glowing citation, indeed, and one that contains information not mentioned in other accounts. On 16 January, 1880, James Dalton was presented with his Cross by Major-General Hon. Henry Clifford VC in a ceremony held on the parade ground of Fort Napier, Pietermaritzberg. He was also promoted but put on half pay.

In his obituary, the *Port Elizabeth Telegraph* says that he was offered a post in the Egyptian Campaign of 1884 and served as a captain, but there is no record of this. He did return to England in February 1880, but the lure of South Africa soon pulled him back. He took part shares in the Little Bess Gold Mine at Barbeton in the eastern Transvaal. He spent Christmas 1886 at the Grosvenor Hotel in Port Elizabeth, run by his old friend, ex-Sergeant John Sherwood Williams. He was taken ill and spent the 7 January in bed. That night he died, aged just fifty-three. He was buried in Russell Road Roman Catholic Cemetery, Port Elizabeth (Plot E) and a handsome headstone erected. He is the only Rorke's Drift VC to be buried in South Africa.

The first invasion of Zululand had been a disaster. Full of confidence, Lord Chelmsford's only concern was that he might not draw the Zulus into battle. Instead, he had been out-thought by an enemy he despised. The casualties at Isandlwana numbered about 1,300, including the entire 1st Battalion of the 24th Regiment and a good many of the 2nd Battalion.

Stunned by the suddenness and violence of the Zulu attack, Chelmsford retreated into Natal. There he learned of the successful defence of Rorke's Drift. Pausing only to congratulate this gallant band, Chelmsford left for Pietermaritzburg to compose his explanation of the defeat for his political masters and leaving the remnants of his invasion force on the border. Besides shifting responsibility to others, Chelmsford sought to divert attention by playing-up the role of the defenders of Rorke's Drift.

In his report, Bromhead put forward the names of six members of his of company for the award. Without consulting the regiment's commanding officer, Colonel Glyn, Chelmsford added the names of Bromhead and Chard. Though Chard was the nominal ranking officer during the defence he was not consulted about the distribution of the VCs.

A bandwagon began to roll. In May, Doctor Ward MP, asked the Secretary State for War why Surgeon Reynolds had been overlooked for an award. In fact Reynolds had been rewarded for his sterling efforts during the fight by being promoted over the heads of sixty-four other medical officers to surgeon major.

More pressure from the medical lobby saw Reynold's name added to the list of VC recipients. Those who had actually taken part in the battle recognised that it was Acting Assistant Commissary James Dalton who had been mainly responsible for organising the successful defence and he belatedly joined the ranks of the eleven Rorke's Drift VCs.

Colonel Evelyn Wood VC, commanding No.4 Column in northern Zululand, was urged by Lord Chelmsford to make some diversion in order to take pressure away from the south, where an expedition was to be launched to relieve the besieged mission at Eshowe.

Urged on by his second in command, Redvers Buller, Wood decided to attack a flat-topped mountain called Hlobane, home to an aggressive Zulu clan. Another motive was that the clan grazed their 4,000-strong cattle herd on the mountaintop. Capturing cattle was a lucrative side-line and the prize-money was a great incentive for the mounted troops under Buller's command.

The attack was ill conceived from the start. The Hlobane Mountain towered 1,500 feet above the surrounding plain; some four and a half miles long and a mile wide and, with the exception of two or three precipitous pathways, was inaccessible. The mounted force made a pincer attack from the east and west ends of the mountain during the early hours of the morning of 28 March, but the surprise element was lost and the Zulus put up stiff opposition.

The main thrust of the attack began to unravel on the rolling plateau above. Fierce resistance had delayed progress and as the colonials drove some captured cattle towards the western end of the plateau, Buller's attention was drawn to distant black shadow to the south that spelled trouble – it was the main 20,000 strong Zulu impi which was fast approaching and threatening to encircle the mountain. The only possible route of escape was down the Devil's Pass, a precipitous rock fall at the western end; a difficult enough route on foot but almost impossible for mounted troops.

Buller's men were channelled to the edge of this unappealing escape route, and forced to either abandon their horses or try to coax their mounts down the boulder-strewn slope. As the men scrambled over the rocks, closely pressed by the more mobile Zulus, so another series of heroic acts led to more Victoria Crosses being awarded. Major Leet, despite a badly damaged knee, pulled a colonial officer to safety, as did Lieutenant Browne of the Mounted Infantry. It was Redvers Buller, seemingly to relish the danger, who repeatedly returned to the fray to carry unmounted men to safety. One of these was Captain Cecil D'Arcy of the Frontier Light Horse, who having been rescued, caught a loose horse and returned to bring away a wounded trooper.

There were so many such acts that the War Office was forced to prune the number of recommendations for the Cross. One such was the appropriately named Veterinary Surgeon Francis Duck, but this was rejected on the grounds that he had no business being on Hlobane in the first place: a novel criterion for rewarding gallantry.

Buller and Leet were duly rewarded but D'Arcy was rejected, which caused uproar amongst the colonials. This was later redressed when D'Arcy made an abortive attempt to rescue a soldier in a skirmish the day before the final battle at Ulundi in June. It was felt by some that it was a belated award for Hlobane.

HENRY CECIL DUDGEON D'ARCY VC (1850-1881)

Henry Cecil Dudgeon D'Arcy was the first colonially-born individual to be gazetted VC. He was born on 11 August 1850 at Wanganui, the son of Major Oliver D'Arcy of the 65th Regiment stationed in New Zealand. At an early age, Cecil moved with his family to the Cape and, after his education, joined the civil service. With the outbreak of the Ninth Frontier War, Cecil volunteered for the Frontier Light Horse (FLH). By the time the Zulu War started, he had been commissioned and joined Evelyn Wood's column on the rugged northern border.

Under the command of Redvers Buller, the combined volunteer units were moulded into an effective mounted force and were constantly in the saddle, scouting and cattle rustling. Their run of success came to an abrupt end at Hlobane. D'Arcy wrote to his father, who had retired to King William's Town, describing his narrow escape and the battle of Kambula the following day:

'I sent a telegram on the 30th of last month, telling you I had pulled through two hard fights, in which the Frontier Light Horse suffered severely. Poor Barton [Captain the Honorable Robert], the Baron [Lieutenant von Stietencron] and another officer called Williams [Lieutenant George) were killed, whom you did not know.

'Now to give you a short account of the two events. 350 of the mounted men had to take a very strong position, a hill called Zlobane [Hlobane]. We got up there, driving the natives back at every point, although they fought very well. Williams was killed as we charged up the hill, the Baron on the top when he was in command of his troop. A Zulu spotted him from a hole, and shot him right through his head. Barton was sent down a hill with some of C troop, and just got down when we saw about twenty thousand Zulus below us, trying to get between us and the camp; we at once crossed the hill [plateau] to come down a most fearfully steep place [Devil's Pass]; the Dutchmen got to the place, rushed down and bolted as hard as they could go. My troop was leading and Blaine, myself and Hutton got them to go quietly down the hill, as we were retreating; the Zulus at this time giving us awful pepper from the Martini rifles. I saw, I thought, all our men down, and then considered I had to think of myself.

'I got half way down when a stone about the size of a small piano came bounding down; I heard a shout above, "look out below", and down the beastly thing came right on my horse's leg, cutting it right off. I at the same time got knocked down the hill by another horse, and was nearly squeezed to death. I had taken the bridle off, and was about to take the saddle (I mean I was going up the hill to take it off my horse) when I heard a scream; I looked up and saw the Zulus right in amongst the white men stabbing horses and men. I made a jump for it and got down somehow or other, and ran as hard as I could with 70 rounds of ball cartridge, a carbine, revolver, field-glasses and heavy boots.

'I went some 300 yards when a fellow called Francis got a horse for me, but no saddle or bridle, a riem [*sic*] did for both, when one of the Frontier Light Horse got wounded through the leg, and I had to jump off, put him on my horse, and run again.

'Colonel Buller saved my life by taking me up behind him on his horse, then Blaine, who was keeping the natives off in the rear, saw me (as after I got my breath, I got off the Colonel's horse) and he nearly cried when he met me, all the fellows thinking I had been killed on top of the hill. He behaved as he always does and stuck to me, and pulled me through a second time. A third time, a major in the Artillery, Remlett [Major E. Tremlett] by name, took me up behind. Our men and officers all behaved well, but the other volunteers were what Major Robinson would call a big rabble. We lost 93 white men and a number of natives. The Frontier Light Horses lost 3 officers and 24 non-commissioned officers and men, and 66 horses. Our men arrived in camp with another man behind him.

'The next day our coloured brothers came on and attacked the camp [Kambula] in numbers from 20,000 to 23,000 and, after six hours hard fighting, they bolted. We killed a little over 2,300, and when once they retired all the horsemen in camp followed them for eight miles butchering the brutes all over the place. I told the men, "no quarter boys and remember yesterday", and they did knock them about, killing them all over the place.

'On the line where I followed them there were 157 dead bodies counted the next day. We have buried 800 of them that were killed close to the camp, but there are hundreds and hundreds of men some miles off, that are being eaten by dogs and vultures. We got about twenty or thirty of the 24th rifles, some carbines belonging to the men we lost the day before, and a number of little things taken from the General's camp [Isandlwana], besides 500 odd rifles of various descriptions. Poor old Sweep was shot through his leg, but is doing well, and Bob, who went through the Zulus like a buck, had lost an eye, otherwise the horses are fit.

'We are all in high feather at having had such a good fight with the Zulus. I never saw such a lot of blacks together in my life, as came on the day of attack. They fought well and kept rushing in the most plucky way, but I knew what the result must be …

'I am sure you will be sorry to hear my Dutch friend, Piet Uys, commandant of the Dutch, was one of the killed at the place where I nearly came to grief; his two sons pulled through. He was as plucky as possible.'

It was thanks to a rearguard, which included Cecil D'arcy, that so many managed to escape down the precipitous slope. Finally, Buller's defeated horsemen travelled the twenty miles to the main camp. Although the official casualty list puts the number of dead as ninety-one, subsequent research puts the number as nearer 130. In addition, some 200-300 native auxiliaries were slain. After Isandlwana, it was the most costly engagement of the Zulu War.

Buller was lavish in his recommendations for awards and included D'Arcy for his steadiness in the rearguard. Despite the fact that it was almost entirely a colonial force, the two VCs awarded for the Devil's Pass fight went to Redvers Buller and Major William Leet of the 13th Regiment, both Imperial officers.

VC Act

When this was learned, there was a considerable outcry from the Natal Government and Press that no volunteer had been so honoured. It may have been with this in mind that Cecil D'Arcy did receive his Cross for a later action in which he failed in his attempt to save the life of a fallen trooper. During a reconnaissance on 3 July 1879, D'Arcy attempted to lift a wounded FLH trooper named Raubenstein onto his horse and carry him to safety. Unfortunately, the horse threw them both and D'Arcy put out his back. Unable to lift the unconscious man, D'Arcy just managed to haul himself onto his mount and make his escape. The abortive rescue hardly seemed to warrant the awarding of the Victoria Cross, especially as D'Arcy had been forced to abandon his comrade to his grisly fate. In the same action, Lord William Beresford and Sergeant Edmund O'Toole were awarded their Crosses for successfully rescuing a Mounted Infantryman.

As if to make up for its failure to honour the first colonial officer for his gallantry at Hlobane, the VC was bestowed on D'Arcy for his abortive attempt to save a stricken comrade. The ever-critical Sir Garnett Wolseley noted in his diary: 'I gave away the VC to Captain D'Arcy today on parade. I don't think he was a good case for the citation, as he did not succeed in saving the life of the man he dismounted to assist.'

Tragic End

The satisfaction of being awarded the VC was short-lived for D'Arcy. The years of living and campaigning in South Africa had taken their toll.

After the Zulu War, he took part in General Wolseley's campaign against Sekukuni in the Transvaal and, when the Frontier Light Horse was disbanded, he joined the Cape Mounted Rifles. He then went on to serve with distinction in the Basuto War of 1880, but a combination of malaria, bilharzia, asthma and fluke worm caused his resignation in April 1881.

It is likely that his deteriorating state of health led to bouts of drunkenness and he was asked to resign his commission. D'Arcy accepted an invitation to stay with his friend Reverend Taberer, who lived in the mountains of Cape Province, suggesting the clear air would improve his condition. Ill, depressed and drinking too much, Cecil retired to his room after dinner on 3 August 1881. He was never seen again.

Extensive searches yielded nothing until, on 28 December, a native found a skeleton in a gully bearing a signet ring, scraps of clothing and a pocket watch, which identified the remains as those of the missing hero. The remains were buried on 3 January 1882 in a family plot in the Eastern Cape Cemetery, King William's Town.

Many years later, an intriguing possibility came to light when a note was discovered in the Killie Campbell Africana Library suggesting that D'Arcy changed clothes with a dead man that he found lying in the snow. The mystery of D'Arcy's fate again surfaced fifty-six years later when a spectator was recognised from a photograph by a cricketer in Newcastle, Natal. When confronted, the man is said to have begged the cricketer not to make his identity known, wishing to remain dead to the world.

Up in the north on the remote border where Natal meets the Transvaal and Zululand, the 80th Regiment was occupied with the unglamorous routine of escort duty and protecting the scattered Boer settlements from marauding allies of the Zulus. It was here that the next disaster occurred. Incessant March rains had swollen the Intombi River so that when a twenty-strong wagon train reached Meyer's (Intombi) Drift, they had great difficulty in crossing.

Major Tucker, the commanding officer at nearby Luneburg, sent about one hundred men to help with the crossing of the floundering wagons and to offer protection. Struggling in the rain, they managed to get two wagons across to the Luneburg bank before evening, when it was decided to laarger the remaining wagons and camp within its protection for the night. A small detachment stayed with the two wagons that had crossed and it was a member of this detachment who was belatedly recognised as a worthy VC hero.

ANTHONY CLARKE BOOTH VC (1846-1899)

Anthony Clarke Booth was born on 21 April 1846 at Club Row, Bulwell Lane (now called Hucknall Road), Carrington, a village about two miles from the centre of Nottingham. He was one of five children born to William and Sarah (née Clarke) who worked as lace makers.

Club Row was a large three story building that housed a floor of lace machines which meant that the whole family lived and worked in their workplace. Conditions were unhealthy, the pay minimal and the hours long. Anthony did receive an education at the National School, but like other children employed in the lace trade, attendance was sporadic at best, depending on the lace work to be done.

For many young men brought up in similar conditions, the armed forces offered an escape from the remorseless misery of Victorian industry. When he was eighteen, Anthony received his father's consent and enlisted in the Royal Marines at Nottingham and was sent to Derby for a medical examination. Much to his disappointment, he was rejected for heart palpitations. Thinking himself perfectly fit, he tried again a few months later when he was visiting Sheffield and was accepted into the 80th Staffordshire Volunteers and joined the regiment at Cork on 10 November 1864.

Malaya

On 20 April 1869, he was promoted to corporal and on 1 January 1872 raised to sergeant. Eleven days later, he and the regiment embarked on the troopship *Orantes* for overseas duty at the Straits Settlement, Malaya. A further promotion later in the year found him Acting Barrack-Sergeant in the Commissariat Department on Hong Kong Island before returning to Singapore on 15 February 1876. In November 1875, part of the 80th Regiment was ordered to Perak, where there was an outbreak of violence from native tribesmen. When the remainder of his regiment were ordered to Perak, Booth resigned from the Commissariat and joined his company in sailing for Malacca on HM gunboat *Ringdove*.

A brief campaign followed in which a unit of the 80th Regiment rowed upstream through a steaming jungle under a broiling sun. Although elements of the 80th took part in attacking and capturing an enemy stockade, Booth was not involved in any fighting. He was entitled to wear the Indian Service Medal with the 'Perak' clasp but he never applied for it as he felt that he had not earned it.

South Africa

The Regiment returned to Malacca and Booth was promoted to Colour Sergeant on 3 April 1876. After leaving Singapore for a new station in Mauritius, the regiment was diverted to the Cape. In 1877, it sailed for Natal and marched to its new station at Pietermaritzburg.

When the Pedi tribe began raiding the newly British annexed Boer territory of the Transvaal, the Commandant of the Transvaal, Colonel Hugh Rowlands VC, was ordered to lead a punitive expedition against their recalcitrant chief, Sekhukhune. The 80th marched to Pretoria, where they formed part of Rowland's 1,800-strong force. This force was considerably reduced when many of the 600 volunteer horsemen exercised their right not to go. Hard marching and drought conditions took their toll until Rowlands was forced to order a return to Pretoria, even though they were in sight of the enemy's stronghold.

After the Isandlwana massacre, Rowlands was replaced by Colonel Evelyn Wood who moved the bulk of his command to Khambula, just inside Zululand. He ordered the 80th Regiment under Major Charles Tucker to garrison Luneburg and, by March, Luneburg was occupied by five companies of the 80th Regiment. Their aim was to keep an eye on the Swazi chief, Mblini, who it was felt would support the Zulus. Supplies for this garrison were sent from Derby, the road from which crossed a drift or ford on the Intombi River.

On 7 March, a company of the regiment under the command of Captain David Harry Moriarty left Luneburg to meet the Derby convoy and to bring it in. When they reached the drift, it was found impossible for the convoy to cross as heavy rains had swollen the river. For two days, the escort and waggoneers laboured and managed to get two of the wagons across the river to the south bank, but the continuous heavy rain meant that there was no alternative other than to wait until the river subsided.

On 11 March, Major Tucker accompanied by Lieutenant Henry Harward rode to the drift to assess the situation. He saw that there were still sixteen wagons on the north bank and he expressed his concern that they were not laagered correctly. They were formed into an inverted 'V' from the river and the gap between the wagons was too far apart. Moriarty acknowledged this but the adverse conditions dictated the formation and nothing was done to improve the defence of the encampment. Tucker returned to Luneburg, leaving Harward to assist Moriarty.

Booth later recalled that Captain Moriarty had told him that the inhabitants in this part of the country were all friendly. In fact, Mblini, the Swazi leader and Zulu ally, had his stronghold in the caves of the nearby Tafelberg Hills. He was spotted by Booth entering the camp to sell mealies with several local natives. When Booth pointed this out to Moriarty, the latter again assured him they were friendly and jokingly added; 'You are as bad as your pals said of you. You would shoot your own brother.'

VC Action

After two days of heavy work, Moriarty's men were tired and wet. Stripping off their wet clothes, they were at last allowed to sleep under shelter for the first time in days. At about 04.00 hours, Harward was awakened by the sound of a distant shot. He ordered Booth to alert the other bank, as no one had stirred, not even the sentries. After some yelling, Booth managed to arouse someone, who spread the warning, but most of the exhausted men continued to sleep.

Booth, however, felt uneasy and remembered Mblini's visit. Dressing and buckling on his ammunition belt, he climbed into one of the wagons for a smoke. Unbeknown to the sleeping soldiers, Mblini and about 800 warriors were closing in on the laager through the early morning mist. They were stripped naked, each carrying only a stabbing spear and a knobkerrie club. A few were armed with pillaged Martini-Henry rifles. Expecting little resistance, they had left their shields behind.

At about 04.45 hours another shot rang out close by. Booth jumped from the wagon to see the Zulus emerge from the mist and fire a volley into Moriarty's tent before rushing in with a chilling cry of '*Usutho!*'

In seconds they overwhelmed the sleeping camp. Moriarty dashed from his tent firing his revolver before an assegai was plunged into his back and he was shot in the chest. As naked and partially clothed soldiers struggled from their tents, they were clubbed and stabbed to death in the hellish melee of frightened cattle and terrified men. Some men plunged into the river but few reached the safety of the far bank. Those that did took shelter behind the flimsy barrier of the two wagons.

Booth and his comrades scrambled beneath the wagons and started firing at the mass of Zulus. In jostling to take cover, Booth had his helmet knocked off, which rolled towards the river. He put his arm on the rear wheel to steady his aim and fired as fast as he could. He noticed that he was next to Lieutenant Harward's pony, which was tied to the wagon. Harward emerged from his tent and saw that the Zulus, attracted by the fire from Booth and his men, were crossing the river further upstream. Maybe gripped by a vision of another Isandlwana, Harward blurted out: 'Fire away, lads. I'll be ready in a minute'. He then pulled himself onto his unsaddled pony and rode off up the road to Luneburg, followed by most of his men and a few escapees.

Booth was shocked by this the abandonment by his officer, Booth gathered the remaining eight men of his company who were joined by some of the men who crossed the river. They donned whatever clothing was available and armed themselves. Seeing his position was hopeless, Sergeant Booth, assisted by Lance Corporal Burgess, formed the remaining men into a square and began to retire towards Luneburg. Booth was later complimented for choosing this formation instead of an extended line. Each time the Zulus threatened the small band, they were kept at a distance by the group's volley fire.

Most of the Zulus were more interested in plundering the two wagons than pursuing Booth's men so that, by the time they reached a deserted farmhouse a mile short of Luneburg, the attacks had ceased. Apart from four men who decided to break away and take a short cut only to run into the Zulus, Booth managed to bring his men to safety.

While Sergeant Booth was calmly extricating his men from almost certain death, his superior officer, Lieutenant Harward, had galloped to Luneburg, arriving at 06.30 hours. He roused Major Tucker with the following words: 'The camp is in the hands of the enemy; they are all slaughtered and I have galloped in for my life'. According to Tucker, Harward then fell on the bed in a dead faint. After being revived, Harward told to story of the attack on the camp. Tucker ordered 150 men to march to the drift and recalled:

'About a mile from the scene we were on high ground and could see from there and from miles away to our right, dense masses of Zulus extending for at least two miles under the hills, and the last Zulus were then leaving the laager for the hills eastward.'

Cover-up

Tucker wrote a long and detailed letter to his father, including the fact that they found one survivor in the river. Inexplicably, he made no mention of Sergeant Booth's commendable exploit even though he came upon the party at the farmhouse. Booth volunteered to accompany Tucker's command, but was told that he had done enough. In the aftermath of the disaster, there was a considerable amount of covering up of what was an embarrassing episode for the regiment. Backed by Major Tucker, Lieutenant Harward's report stated that:

'The enemy were now assegaing [*sic*] our men in the water, and also ascending the banks of the river close to us; for fear therefore, of my men being stabbed under the wagons, and to enable them to retire before their ammunition should be exhausted, I ordered them to retire steadily, and only just in time to avoid a rush of Zulus to our late position. The Zulus came on in dense masses and fell upon our men, who being already broken, gave way, and a hand to hand fight ensued. I endeavoured to rally my men, but they were too much scattered, and finding re-formation impossible, I mounted my horse and galloped into Luneburg at utmost speed, and reported all that had taken place.'

Inaccurate as his account was, Harward did have the good grace to acknowledge his sergeant's sterling behaviour. In his report, Major Tucker made no mention that he felt that the camp had been inadequately laagered. Furthermore, he praised Harward's efforts in giving covering fire to enable some men to escape across the river. These two reports were the basis of Lord Chelmsford's report to the War Office, which was not received in London until 21 April. As reports from NCOs were not required, the truth would appear to have been contained within the regiment.

As Colour Sergeant Fredericks had perished in the camp, Booth was promoted to Colour Sergeant on 13 March. Over the following weeks, the regiment moved to Utrecht and joined Wood's Flying Column in its advance on the Zulu capital at Ulundi. Significantly, Lieutenant Harward was left behind.

The 80th formed part of the massive square that finally broke the Zulu fighting machine. The regiment sustained two dead and five wounded. Sergeant Booth, himself, was slightly wounded in a freakish way. While instructing a soldier building an entrenchment, a bullet struck his mess tin and he received some metal splinters to his face, his only wound in a long military career.

With the Zulus defeated, the 80th were involved in much of the mopping-up operations under the new commander in chief, General Sir Garnet Wolseley. In November, they took part in the attack on Sekhukune's stronghold and were the first troops to reach the summit, gaining high praise from Wolseley. Indeed, the 80th had been closely associated with the Commander since his arrival, as they supplied his personal escort.

By the middle of December, the regiment was concentrated at Pretoria and it was here that months of resentment and shame came to the boil. Three survivors of the Intombi River massacre wrote to Wolseley on 20 December 1879 to set the record straight and 'to be of good service to Colour Sergeant Booth'. This was followed by a belated recommendation from the newly-promoted Lieutenant Colonel Tucker for the Distinguished

Conduct Medal to be awarded to Booth. As this was the result of Wolseley's enquiry in response to the three survivors' testimony, Tucker was asked why he had not previously recommended his sergeant for a medal. Tucker was then forced to explain that to do so would have brought to light the far different conduct of Lieutenant Harward.

On 26 December, the whole regiment was paraded prior to leaving for England. Sir Garnet Wolseley took the salute and, in a most unusual ceremony, presented Colour Sergeant Booth with a revolver, holster, belt and a knife, which were donated by European settlers. On the same day, Wolseley forwarded his personal recommendation that Booth should be awarded the Victoria Cross, something the general was usually loath to do.

On 14 February 1880, as a result of Wolseley's investigations, Lieutenant Harward was arrested and taken to Pietermaritzburg where he was charged with misbehaviour before the enemy. Much to Wolseley's disgust, the court-martial accepted Harward's version of events and he was acquitted and allowed to return to his regiment.

Wolseley could not alter the verdict of the court but he did add his own trenchant view. When the court's finding and Wolseley's comments reached London, the Duke of Cambridge, the Commander in Chief of the Army, instructed them to be read out as a General Order to every regiment. With his army career in tatters, Harward had little option but to resign his commission.

Colour Sergeant Anthony Booth was summoned from his station in Ireland to Windsor Castle, where Queen Victoria presented him with the Victoria Cross on 26 June 1880. His citation reads:

'For his gallant conduct on 12th March 1879, during the Zulu attack on the Intombi River, in having when considerably outnumbered by the enemy, rallied a few men on the south bank of the river, and covered the retreat of fifty soldiers and others for a distance of three miles. The officer commanding the 80th Regiment reports that, had it not been for the coolness displayed by this non-commissioned officer, not one man would have escaped.'

Later Life

Curiously, Booth reverted to the rank of sergeant on 19 October 1880 but was again elevated to colour sergeant on 15 March 1884. On 1 October 1883, he gave notice of his desire to continue in service. By 1885, he had served over twenty-three years. His health was also reflecting his age and from 1885 to 1888 he suffered from pneumonia, dyspepsia and bronchitis.

He and his wife, Lucy, produced eight children in sixteen years and their places of birth trace the many postings in which Booth served; Dorset, Fleetwood, Belfast, Hong Kong, Natal, Dublin and Tralee. On 7 May 1888, Anthony Booth was posted to 1st Volunteer Battalion South Staffordshire Regiment as Sergeant Instructor until his retirement on 30 April 1898. His total service was an astonishing thirty-three years and 182 days. Sadly, his retirement did not last long for he died eighteen months later, on 8 December 1899. He was given a full military funeral and many thousands lined the route to his final resting place at St Michael's Church, Brierly Hill – a truly great and gallant soldier.

The second invasion of Zululand culminated in the destruction of the Zulu army and their capital Ulundi on 4 July 1879. Thus ended a campaign that destroyed or tarnished many reputations with few emerging with much credit. Among those who did were such worthy recipients as James Dalton, Samuel Wassall, Cecil D'Arcy and Anthony Booth.

Chapter 21

Sekukuni Campaign, 1879

Number of VCs awarded	2
Number of VCs awarded to other ranks	2
Total awarded to British Army	2

Origins of the War

Although the events of 1879 in South Africa had been focused on Zululand, there was an ever-present threat on the Transvaal border in the shape of Sekukuni and his Bapedi tribe. Even before the first invasion against the Zulus, the British Commander, Lord Chelmsford sought to neutralise this potential danger to his northern flank. To remove this threat, he ordered an expedition to be mounted under the command of one of his most experienced senior officers.

Colonel Hugh Rowlands, a Crimea War VC, had been appointed Commandant of the Transvaal in July 1878. Within a month, Lord Chelmsford had issued instructions for Rowlands to seek out and destroy Sekukuni's belligerent Bapedi tribe situated in the mountains of northeast Transvaal. As early as late summer, Chelmsford was already planning on an invasion of Zululand and wanted to be sure that allied tribes like the Bapedi would be neutralised beforehand. Previous attempts had been made and failed and Rowlands was not at all sanguine about success.

He set out from Pretoria on 28 August with a mixed force of Imperial infantry, the 13th (Somerset Light Infantry), volunteer cavalry and artillery, numbering about 1,800. The terrain they were invading was rugged and gripped by a long drought. Progress was slow and uncomfortable. When they camped at the foot of the Lulu Mountains, which harboured the almost impregnable Sekukuni's 'Town', horse sickness caused heavy losses to the horses and cattle. Rowlands did lead a party into the mountains but, with no sign of a water supply, decided to abandon the advance. He brought together all his unit commanders, including Major Redvers Buller of the Frontier Light Horse, and informed them of his decision. There was only one dissenting voice raised – Buller's – but the general feeling was that it would have been folly to have continued.

By 7 October, Rowland's force returned to base camp at Fort Burghers, defeated by thirst. For Rowlands, it was a bitter blow and his otherwise impeccable reputation suffered, especially at the hands of men like Redvers Buller.

When Cetshwayo was captured on 28 August, the Zulus were finally subjugated and they no longer posed a to Imperialist plans. The old Zulu kingdom was broken up and a commission was quickly appointed to settle the boundaries of thirteen independent kinglets. General Sir Garnet Wolseley was only too pleased to be rid of this problem which had brought him little glory. Instead, as the newly appointed High Commissioner, he turned his attention to the simmering problem of the Transvaal.

If the Boers thought their claim for independence would be viewed more sympathetically by Sir Garnet, then they were in for a big disappointment. Annexation is irrevocable was his message and he backed this up with a strong military presence: unfortunately this military presence brought its own problems. The veteran war correspondent, William Russell, reported that bored and unruly British troops were not just getting fighting drunk but actually housebreaking and robbing with violence. Russell referred to; 'an increase of convicts wearing the Queen's uniform'. In the town of Heidelberg, soldiers had even stolen the town hall clock. Although these disagreeable occurrences were distressing, the disgruntled Boers remained largely passive in their resistance. Of more serious concern was the unresolved problem of Sekukuni.

The defiant chief of the Bapedi still controlled a triangular–shaped territory in the north-east corner of the Transvaal and his remote base was in the Lulu mountain range. From here, his tribe was able to raid with impunity. Hugh Rowland's abortive expedition had only reinforced Sekukuni's belief in his invincibility. The Bapedi had continued to give trouble to the British during the Zulu War but few men could be spared to do more than occupy the dreary forts in the area and send out the occasional patrol. Wolseley wanted to avoid another war and made diplomatic approaches to Sekukuni, which were firmly rebuffed. Wolseley also recognised that a successful campaign would restore British prestige in the Transvaal and a forceful display of military power would impress the Boers. Failure, on the other hand, could spark the rebellion that lay just below the surface.

For all his faults and vanities, Wolseley was an excellent organiser and field commander. He gathered as much intelligence as could about the Bapedi and their base of Sekukuni's Town, sometimes called the 'Gibraltar of the Transvaal'. The Lulu Mountains rose from the flat plain like an enormous termite hill. Sekukuni's Town was in the centre of these steep and rugged mountains where many caves in the slopes offered excellent defensive positions. Close by was a 150 feet-high rocky outcrop named 'Fighting Kopje', which was defended by 4,000 natives armed with muskets and rifles. The entire area was protected by thick stone walls, thorn bush *zaribas* and even bee-hives strategically placed so they could be upset in case of attack. Both strongholds were honeycombed with caves and crevices. The Bapedi, unlike the Zulus, were experts in defence.

Having delivered an ultimatum, which Wolseley knew Sekukuni would reject, he assembled the Transvaal Field Force at Middelburg. It was made up of 1,400 British infantry from the 21st (Royal Scots Fusiliers), the 94th (2nd Connaught Rangers) and detachments of 80th Regiment. They were supported by men from the Royal Engineers, four guns of the Transvaal Artillery, 400 colonial horse and nearly 10,000 natives, of whom 8,000 Swazis were of the greatest value, as they were sworn enemies of the Bapedi. As an added incentive, they were promised that they keep the cattle they might take and to share in whatever fine was levied against the Bapedi. Unlike Rowlands, Wolseley was able to secure stockpiles of supplies to avoid the logistical issues that had bedevilled Rowlands' expedition.

The advancing force faced days of long hot marches and nights of freezing temperatures interspersed with violent thunder storms with several men being killed by lightening. Instead of taking the more direct route across the arid mountains from the west, the main column marched up the valley of the Oliphants river. On 23 November, the main force reached the Lulu Mountains from the north and prepared to traverse south down a valley some twenty miles long. A smaller force was to approach from the west and the two converge at Sekukuni's Town. Men of the 21st and 94th Regiments were reduced to marching in sodden rags as they stumbled through dense bush and soaked by remorseless rain and hail. Once Wolseley was satisfied that his supplies were sufficient and secure, he reconnoitred the enemy stronghold.

Just before daybreak on 28 November, Wolseley's men began their advance. The mountain or Town was to be attacked first by the colonials and Swazis, while the artillery bombarded the Fighting Kopje and the British troops took up positions around the base to contain the defenders. The centre position was given to Lieutenant Colonel John Murray with six companies each of 2/21st and 94th Regiments and detachments of 80th Regiment, the Royal Engineers and the Colonial Artillery. This formidable hill, about 300 feet long and 200 feet wide, was honeycombed with caves and massive caverns created by the great splits in the huge granite boulders and formed an ideal fortification for the Bapedi who had laid in supplies of grain and also limited supplies of water.

The Town was built partly in the valley and partly up the slopes of the mountain in the western range. It consisted of about 3,000 huts which stretched for about two miles along the foot of the mountain and its lower slopes. Above were many caves to which the Bapedi could flee if driven from the Town. Unbeknown to the attackers, Sekukuni and his retinue had already retreated to one of these caves above the Town from where he could watch the battle. Captain Ferreira with his dismounted commandos and native contingent advanced from the right. The left attack was entrusted to Major Frederick Carrington with the rest of the colonials. Major Bushman and the Swazis were to ascend the mountain from the eastern or rear side during the night, so as to reach the summit and begin the assaulting descent upon the Town in the morning, thereby co-operating with Ferreira and Carrington from above. It was during the attack on this formidable position that two Victoria Crosses were awarded.

FRANCIS FITZPATRICK VC (1859-1933)
THOMAS FLAWN VC (1857-1925)

Thomas Flawn was born in the village of Finedon in Northamptonshire on 22 December 1857. According to the 1871 Census, he was an agricultural labourer at the age of thirteen. He enlisted in October 1876 in the 25th (King's Own Scottish Borderers), then transferred to the Cameronians before finally settling in the 94th Regiment. He and Fitzpatrick received their Crosses from Lieutenant Colonel P.R. Anstruther at Lydenburg on 17 September 1880. The regiment was heavily involved in the First Boer War and he was most likely one of those besieged at Lydenburg. As soon as his time expired, he left the Army in 1882. In the 1891 Census, Flawn is listed as married and employed as a stoker. He died at his home in Plumstead, Kent (now South East London) on 19 January 1925.

Francis Fitzpatrick was born in 1859 in County Mayo, Ireland, and is one of the many Irish soldiers who leave few clues about their lives. Shortly after he was awarded his Cross in September, he lost it during fighting against the Boers on 20 December 1880 at Bronkers Spruit. A replacement was sent to him in June 1881 but, when the original was found, it was returned to the War Office. At some stage, Fitzpatrick sold his original VC and had a copy made for his own use. After his service with the 94th, he transferred to the Duke of Cornwall's Light Infantry until he was discharged in 1888.

He re-enlisted in the Argyll and Sutherland Highlanders and took part in the Second Anglo-Boer War and was entitled to the Queen's South Africa Medal with the clasps 'Cape Colony' and 'South Africa 1902'. His civilian life is unknown and he died in Glasgow on 10 July 1933 aged seventy-three. He was buried in an unmarked grave.

A company of the Mounted Infantry from the 94th was detached from the centre column to give support. During the advance up the slope, Lieutenant James Cumming Dewar of the King's Dragoon Guards, was shot and severely wounded. As a cavalry officer during the Zulu War, he had been attached to the Mounted Infantry.

With him were privates Thomas Flawn and Francis Fitzpatrick, who gathered six native allies to carry Dewar to safety. Suddenly, about thirty Bapedi appeared and rushed towards them. The natives quickly dropped their burden and fled leaving the helpless officer on the ground with his escort. Picking up Dewar, the pair alternately carried him while the other fired at the Bapedi and kept them at a distance. In this way, they brought the wounded officer to safety. For this gallant act, both men were recommended for the Victoria Cross.

After three hours of fierce fighting, both Sekukuni's Town and the Fighting Kopje were captured. The slaughter was horrendous, with the Swazis inflicting punishment on their hated enemy and all-but exterminated the Bapedi tribe. The Swazis lost some 400-500 killed, which indicates that the Swazis played an overwhelming part in the battle. The British, on the other hand, had just thirteen dead.

Somehow, Sekukuni managed to slip away and it was not until a few days later that he was captured and brought to Wolseley's camp. Rather like a victorious Roman general entering Rome, so Wolseley returned to Pretoria with his infamous prisoner to be greeted by the whole population. As a sequel, Sekhukuni was released the following year only to be murdered by his brother. Sir Garnet could not wait to be clear of South Africa and its problems and departed in May 1880. The Sekukuni expedition had been a text book campaign and he had kept the Boers quiet if not reconciled.

Chapter 22

Basuto War, 1879–82

Number of VCs awarded	4
Number of VCs awarded to officers	2
Number of VCs awarded to other ranks	2
Total awarded to Imperial forces	4

Origins of the War

While Britain's attention was concentrated on the events in Zululand, an all-colonial war was taking place in Natal's western neighbour, Basutoland. Owing to their involvement with the Zulus and the Sekukuni uprising, the Imperial authorities had warned the Cape Government that it would not be able to help in Basutoland.

In 1871 this mountainous and largely arid protectorate (later Lesotho) had been annexed by the Cape Colony. In 1879 a revolt flared after the Cape Government had become concerned with the amount of gun-running taking place on the Basuto border.

Fearing a combined inter-tribal uprising, the authorities attempted the removal of firearms from the tribes and met violent opposition. Three fierce and difficult mountain engagements were fought between one of these tribes, the Baphuti, under Chief Morosi and men of the Cape Mounted Rifles (CMR) and the Cape Mounted Yeomanry (CMY). Ensconced in a highly precipitous and well defended mountain stronghold named after Morosi, the Baphuti proved to be a particularly hard nut to crack. Morosi's Mountain rose to a height of 1100 feet in a series of tiers and sheer cliffs. Thick stone walls added to the formidable obstacles that confronted the Cape forces and their two 7-pounders proved ineffectual.

On 8 April 1879, Captain Grant led a force of thirty-nine CMR and 100 CMY in the first assault during which two Victoria Crosses were won.

PETER BROWN VC (1837-1894)

Little is known of this Swedish-born recipient of the Victoria Cross other than he was born in 1837 and that Peter Brown was not his real name. Brown, who had served with the Frontier Armed Mounted Police under Hans Garrett Moore VC during the 1878 Xhosa Campaign, transferred to the newly-formed Cape Mounted Rifles.

Led by Captain Grant, a storming party of 140 led the first assault and were met by heavy fire and showers of rocks, which forced the troops to take cover. Three wounded men managed to crawl behind an isolated small rock within 200 yards of the defenders. Pinned down for several hours, the troops were unable to go to the aid of their wounded comrades, who were suffering terribly from thirst.

Captain Grant later wrote of Peter Brown: 'He was a rough, ignorant, but excessively manly and kind-hearted man … I am certain that Brown did not know of such a decoration as the VC when he performed his signal act of bravery. He was one of the advanced party of stormers in the assault made on Morosi's Mountain stronghold on 8th April 1879. As I rushed up to the assault several men fell killed or wounded. Three wounded crept to the shelter of a small rock that lay in the middle of a perfectly open space not 200 yards from the lower tier of the *schanzes* [breastwork of stones].

'The stormers had passed on to the left of this open space and were trying to scale the defences on the flank of the position, when these three men began to cry piteously for water. It appeared certain death to go to them as the open space where this sheltering stone lay was completely swept by the fire of all the *schanzes* on that part of the mountain. Their screams, however, became quite heart-rending; and after a minute or two, Brown said with an oath, "I can't stand this any longer; has anyone any water?" He was handed a tin canteen half-full of water, and he coolly walked across the open space, knelt down beside the rock and, without making the slightest attempt to shelter himself, began to pour water into the mouth of one of the wounded men. While doing this a bullet broke his arm; he quietly picked up the canteen and went on pouring the water into the man's mouth with his other hand, and almost immediately a second bullet struck him in the leg, and he fell over among the men to whose help he had gone.

'It is hard to imagine an act of more deliberate self-sacrifice, coupled with absolute dauntless bravery, than that performed by poor Peter Brown. No one who saw it will soon forget it.'

A fellow Mounted Rifleman later added his observation: 'Early in the attack … Sergeant Edwards and Trooper Paskie of the CMR were wounded … About 10 a.m. they were again wounded and wanted water badly … Paskie and Edwards lay under fire from 8 a.m. to 8 p.m. until rescued after nightfall.'

Brown did manage to find better cover where he was later attended by Surgeon Edmund Hartley, who treated many of the wounded during the abortive attack. It was not until darkness fell, that a retreat could be made and the wounded removed.

Captain Grant belatedly recommended Brown for the VC only because he did not believe colonial forces were eligible. He finally received his VC from General Wolseley at King Williams Town in May 1880. After the investiture, Brown confided that:

'I often ran greater risks, and if I hadn't been so badly wounded it would have escaped notice.' He retired due to his wounds and died of Bright 's disease in Cape Town on 11 September 1894.

After the wounding of Peter Brown and several others, volunteers were called for to use the 7-pounder time shells as hand grenades. The two artillery pieces had been unable to inflict much damage on the strongly constructed defences so a more effective way of delivering the shells was called for.

ROBERT GEORGE SCOTT VC (1857-1918)

Robert George Scott was born on 22 April 1857 at Whittlesey near Peterborough, Cambridgeshire, the son of a Royal Navy surgeon and educated at Aberdeen Grammar School and Epsom College.

Scott was posted to South Africa with a batch of recruits but on 26 September 1876 joined the Cape Mounted Rifles, serving in the Ninth Frontier War and the Zulu War. He was soon promoted to sergeant and, along with three men, volunteered to use the 7-pounder time-fused shells as hand grenades against the well-entrenched defenders.

VC Action

Scott ordered his men to take cover while he went forward alone. Despite a withering fire, he climbed a steep wall of rock to within feet of the sheltering Basutos. He lit the fuse of the first shell timed for nine seconds, waited to the last moment and then flung it over the wall. It was almost immediately thrown back but failed to explode.

The second bomb had a defective fuse and exploded as soon as he lit it, shattering his hand, wounding his left leg and severely burning himself. Scott's men immediately rushed forward to help but he ordered them back. Instead, he rolled to the edge of the wall and dropped twenty-five feet, which miraculously did not kill him. Re-joining his men, he refused to be taken back to camp as it would have exposed others to the heavy fire.

No further attempt was made to assail the impregnable defences and it was not until darkness fell that soldiers were able to withdraw. The attack had been costly, the CMR having suffered twenty-five per cent casualties. Scott, whose damaged arm was amputated, was recommended for the Cross but it was not gazetted until 1 October 1880. By that time, he had been promoted to lieutenant and returned to England. He was presented with his Cross at Windsor Castle by the Queen on 17 December 1880.

During the Anglo-Boer War, the one-armed Scott served with the Kimberley Light Horse during the Siege of Kimberley. After the siege was lifted, he raised a couple of units called 'Scott's Railway Guards' and 'Cape Railway Sharpshooters' to patrol and protect the Orange River-Kimberly line. They were involved in many skirmishes with roving bands of Boers, who were attempting to sabotage the line.

At the end of hostilities, Scott was awarded the DSO. Even in the First World War, and despite poor health, Scott raised and commanded the Kimberley Central Commando and fought on the German South West Africa border. He died just before the end of the war on 3 October 1918 and was buried in Plumstead Cemetery, Wynberg.

EDMUND BARRON HARTLEY VC (1847-1919)

The third man to be awarded the VC for this unsuccessful assault was Surgeon Edmund Barron Hartley. Born at Ivybridge, Devon on 6 May 1847, he was the son of a doctor and followed his father into the profession. Once he had qualified in London, he took up the post of district surgeon in British Basutoland. With the outbreak of the 1877 Frontier War, he volunteered his services to the Frontier Armed and Mounted Police.

In 1878, Hartley was appointed principal medical officer to the Cape Colonial Forces, a post he held until his retirement. He was prominent during the first attack on Morosi's Mountain but it was during the second and equally unsuccessful assault that he was recommended for the Victoria Cross. At dawn on 5 June, another advance was made but was soon pinned down among the rocks below the Baphuti position.

VC Action

One witness later wrote as part of the recommendation for an award for Hartley: 'Dr Hartley, while the storming party was waiting to advance from under the ledge, went out under heavy fire from the *schanzes* to a flat place where lay Corporal A. Jones, No.1 Troop, CMR, who was wounded a short time before. You attended his wound in the head, carried him off the exposed flat place and ran with him in your arms about 150 yards back to where the stretcher bearers were in waiting. Corporal Jones received a second wound from the enemy while being carried. That afterwards you returned under the full and severe fire of the enemy from the *schanzes* to the storming party at the ledge where we had halted, and dressed all the other wounded men, one of whom was in imminent danger of bleeding to death from a bullet wound in the arm.'

Although his bravery was acknowledged by all who had witnessed it, no recommendation was submitted for the Cross on the grounds that the commander, Colonel Brabant was unaware that members of the colonial forces were eligible for the award. As with the case of Peter Brown, it was not until the awards to the colonial recipients of the Zulu War were gazetted that Brabant was able belatedly to forward his recommendation for Hartley. Finally, on 3 December 1881 that he received the medal from Brigadier General Charles Clark.

A third assault on Morosi's Mountain was made by the CMR on 20 November, and this time they took the defenders by surprise and routed the

Baphuti, killing Morosi. Hartley served on many minor campaigns over the following years and was wounded during the Bechuanaland-Langeberg Campaign of 1897. He was promoted to colonel and became Principal Medical Officer to the Colonial Forces during the Boer War. He founded what was to become the South African Medical Corps and after his retirement in 1903, returned to England. He died on 20 March 1919 at Ash, near Aldershot, which is the home of the Army Medical Services and where his VC group of medals is held. He was buried at Brookwood Cemetery, Surrey.

The Basuto Gun War continued into 1881, dragging the Cape Colony towards bankruptcy. The well-armed Basotho forces relied primarily on ambushes against the numerically inferior colonial units. In an attempt to relieve 200 Cape Mounted Riflemen under the command of their commanding officer, Colonel Frederick Carrington, besieged at Mafeteng just across the Orange Free State border, the Cape Mounted Yeomanry was attacked near Kalibani and lost forty men.

This prompted Colonel Carrington, who had previously raised the Mounted Infantry in the East Cape and Zululand, to increase the colonial force to 2,000 men. In early January 1881, Colonel Brabant of the CMY led a large patrol of 180 infantry and 380 mounted troops towards a mountain stronghold about ten miles from Mafeteng. It was in the ambush that followed that the fourth VC was awarded.

JOHN FREDERICK McCREA VC (1854-1894)

John Frederick McCrea was born on 1 April 1854 at Fort George, Madras, India, to Captain Herbert Taylor McCrea of 43rd Regiment and his wife Elizabeth (née Carey). Tragically, both his parents died the following year; Captain McCrea in Cape Town on 8 April and his wife in Madras on 6 July from complications while giving birth to a daughter. Both infants and a four-year-old brother were taken in and raised by their Aunt Charlotte in Guernsey.

John was educated at Elizabeth College and went on to study medicine at Guy's Hospital, qualifying as a member of the Royal College of Surgeons of England and Edinburgh.

With the outbreak of the Zulu War in 1879, he volunteered to go to South Africa and worked as a Civilian Surgeon with the British Army in Cape Town. A year later he moved to Fort Beaufort in the Eastern Cape but decided to join the newly formed 1st Regiment Cape Mounted Yeomanry as a surgeon.

Very quickly he became involved in the Basuto War and narrowly escaped death during an ambush at Kalibani in October 1880. His batman, who rode beside him was shot and killed along with forty-nine others. The Basuto commander, Lerothodi, had 23,000 mounted men generally armed with the most modern rifles which outranged the colonial horsemen's old Snider carbines. The Cape government was unable to persuade Lerothodi and his men to join forces to defeat Chief Morosi; instead they joined the rebellion.

VC Action

On a misty and rainy 14 January 1881, Colonel Brabant's 1,000-strong patrol entered a wide, marshy valley surrounded by high ridges near Tweefontein. The 400 Burghers in the patrol were ordered to burn a nearby village, which they did, but disobeyed an order not to try the same thing at Sepechele, which lay on a plateau on the right flank. Suddenly 3,000 mounted Basutos charged out of the misty rain forcing a hasty retreat by the Burghers back to the main body. The CMR's 110 men dismounted and opened fire and split the Basuto charge which retired several hundred yards away. Now surrounded on three sides, Lerothodi's force subjected the colonials to a heavy fire.

Surgeon McCrea had gone with the Burghers to help with the wounded. In the attack, sixteen were killed and twenty-one wounded. McCrea and another officer went forward to rescue one of the wounded and treated him behind a giant ant-hill. As McCrea went to fetch a stretcher, he was hit in the breast-bone by a bullet. Despite the pain, McCrea plugged the hole in his chest with gauze and completed his ministrations.

Reaching the CMR skirmish line, a sergeant in the CMY rode up with an assegai protruding from his back. With the help of two others, McCrea eased the spear from the sergeant's back and treated him. The action lasted another five hours until the Basutos mounted up and retired. There was another fight on 15 February in which heavy losses were inflicted on the Basutos, which persuaded them to sign an armistice on 18 April, so ending this tough and little-known conflict.

On learning of Surgeon McCrea's role in the battle, Colonel Carrington forwarded his recommendation for the Victoria Cross. This posed a problem at the War Office in London, for although the Warrant dated 1 January 1867 allowed for a member of the colonial forces to receive the Victoria Cross if under the command of a British commander, the Basuto War involved no Imperial Forces. Pressed by the Colonial Office, the recommendation was accepted and John McCrea received his VC from Brigadier General Charles Clark at King William's Town on 25 October 1881.

McCrea was promoted to surgeon major and transferred to the Cape Infantry Regiment until its disbandment in 1882. He then joined the Cape Mounted Rifles and joined the regiment at Kokstad, where he married Elizabeth Watermeyer. Surgeon Major John McCrea died in service at Kokstad on 16 July 1894 from a lung inflammation.

It took the authorities until 1900 to issue a 'Basutoland' clasp to the Cape of Good Hope Service Medal, so John McCrea became one of the few recipients to be solely awarded the Victoria Cross, which is in the Lord Ashcroft Collection at the Imperial War Museum.

Chapter 23

Naga Expedition, 1879–80

Number of VCs awarded	1
Number of VCs awarded to officers	1
Total awarded to British Indian Army	1

Origins of the War

The Naga Hills in the far remote North-East India were inhabited by six tribal groups, prominent of who were the Bhutias, Abors, Garos and the Angamis Nagas. The British had tried to install a Resident as far back as 1847 but the effort was abandoned in 1854 when he was murdered.

The Lieutenant Governor of Bengal decided to try again rather than appear to give ground to these wild tribes. He wrote to the Government of India pointing out that the policy towards the Nagas had been a mistake and that the installation of a Political Officer, Lieutenant Gregory, supported by a force of 150 police, all well-armed hill-men was the only way to impose peace on that turbulent frontier. It would appear that Gregory and his successor, Captain Butler, were partially successful in influencing the tribes. The only thing they could not control was the intertribal feuds and the resultant bloody warfare.

In 1873-74, survey operations extended into the Naga Hills which upset the Nagas. One of the parties under Lieutenant Holcombe was attacked and had eighty men killed and another fifty wounded. A punitive expedition carried out by the 44th (Sylhet) Bengal Native Infantry destroyed the villages of the perpetrators of the attack and a certain peace returned to the area. The death of Captain Butler during an ambush resulted in another punitive expedition until an uneasy calm was re-established.

In November 1878, it was decided to build a stockade near the village of Kohima, which was a less feverish position than the village used by the Political Officer and his military force. Mr Damant had taken over as Deputy Commissioner and Political Agent and was cautious in his dealings with the local tribes.

One of these tribes, the Angamis Nagas, whose main home was the village of Konoma, was the strongest and most warlike of the local communities and resented the British presence. They particularly disliked the suppression of blood-feuds and head-hunting, pursuits most dear to the Naga mind, but also the payment of tribute and the frequent supply of labour to the British authorities. The fear was that their influence with weaker tribes would destabilise the present situation.

Mr Damant came to the conclusion that Konoma should be destroyed and the Angamis Nagas subdued. Unfortunately he chose to march on Konoma when he was at his weakest. The 44th (Sylhet) BNI had received orders to reinforce the army in Afghanistan and had already begun its long westward journey. The situation in Afghanistan changed and the order was given to return to Kohima, but too late to join the Damant column. The column was far too weak, consisting of just twenty men of the 43rd Assam Light Infantry and sixty-six frontier police. After an overnight stop, they proceeded to Konomo.

An Angamis Naga fortress known as the Theboma Khel was situated on the crest of a steep spur which rises to about 1,200 feet above a valley, strongly fortified with terraces of stone walls and towers. When Damant column arrived at the foot of the heights, the baggage was left in a meadow guarded by about half the escort while remainder accompanied Damant in the climb up to the Theboma Khel.

A survivor later recalled: 'We approached the village by a lower road and passed along the outside of the Somama Khel to the entrance to the Theboma Khel. The gate was found closed. Almost immediately on arrival of the party at the gate, two shots were fired, killing two men of the Frontier Police. The Nagas then opened a heavy fire and four men and the Political Agent [Damant] were killed.'

The path into the Theboma Khel was narrow; one side a precipice and the other a loop-holed wall of stone from which the Nagas fired. Those that reached the meadow found themselves surrounded but they managed to put up a defence until forced to retire. Utterly dispersed, it took about seven days before all the survivors made it back to Kohima. In total, there were thirty-nine killed and nineteen wounded.

On 19 October, the Nagas followed up their victory with an attack on Kohima, Samaguting and a small stockade at Piphima, which was burnt to the ground and 4,000 rounds of ammunition seized. Very quickly an expedition was mounted destroy the Theboma Khel once and for all and restore order in the Naga territory. It was during the assault that the Victoria Cross was awarded.

RICHARD KIRBY RIDGEWAY VC (1848-1924)

Richard Kirby Ridgeway was the second son of a surgeon, Richard Ridgeway and his wife Annette (née Adams). Born 18 August 1848 in

Oldcastle, Co. Meath, Ireland, he entered Royal Military College Sandhurst and commissioned into the 96th (Manchester) Regiment on 8 January 1868.

Ridgeway was promoted to lieutenant on 14 February 1870 and, on 6 January 1872 he was transferred to the Bengal Staff Corps. He was appointed to the 43rd (Assam) Regiment, Bengal Native (Light) Infantry and, two years later, transferred to the 44th (Sylhet) Regiment BNI, and served as Adjutant until 1880. He was with the regiment throughout the troubles with the Naga tribes during the 1870s and was mentioned in despatches in the attack on Lieutenant Holcombe's survey party.

The 44th, having had their orders to travel to Afghanistan cancelled, arrived back on 1 November and joined the expedition under the command of Brigadier General J.L. Nation. Gathering at Kohima, Nation's force numbered 1,135 with two mountain guns.

By 22 November, a full month after Damant's death, the column was positioned below Konoma, which reported held some 3 to 4,000 Nagas. Nation made his dispositions and sent about 300 of the 44th under Colonel Nuttall to lead the main attack. Although the Theboma Khel was found abandoned, it was soon apparent that the strength of the Konoma defences was much greater than had been supposed. The series of terraces, their scarps revetted with stone and topped by walls were perfectly bulletproof and well loop-holed. Each terrace formed a separate fortification defensible from either side. The whole place was a mass of redoubts and retrenchments within retrenchments and, as the area the attackers could move was so restricted, progress was difficult and slow as they laboured up the narrow paths.

The Gurkhas of the 44th managed to capture a portion of the entrenchment at the north end of the village but were held up by a stone stockade. Brigadier Nation went forward and called up the two 7-pounder mountain guns, to blast a way through the gate. The effect was not encouraging and the obstacle remained. In a final effort to take the stockade, Nation split the dwindling numbers into three groups and, led by their officers, the Gurkhas rushed forward. Every attempt to surmount the high scarp and barricade failed with evermore casualties.

VC Action

It was during this final assault that Lieutenant Ridgeway performed his VC exploit. Reaching the gateway, he attempted to tear down the planking surrounding it but an almost point-blank rifle shot hit his left shoulder and he had to fall back. In this final assault, the 44th suffered twenty dead. With the coming of darkness and having fought since 11.00 hours, Nation was determined to remain on the ground that had been captured.

The force prepared for another assault on the following day but daylight found that the Nagas had evacuated their positions and retreated to deeper into the hills. Further expeditions were made until the Nagas sued for peace in March 1880.

Lieutenant Ridgeway was hospitalised and sent back to England to recover from his wound. On 8 January, he was promoted to captain and on 11 May 1880 was gazetted for the Victoria Cross. His wound prevented him from attending an investiture and his Cross was sent to him in Ireland.

When he had recovered, Richard Ridgeway returned to India, passed the Staff College entrance exam and was appointed Deputy Adjutant and Quartermaster General Bengal Army in August 1884. He took up a position with the Boundary Commission in Afghanistan and spent six months travelling hundreds of miles throughout that country.

Promoted to major as Adjutant and Quartermaster General at Army Headquarters, he re-joined his old regiment as commander in 1889. During his tenure, it became the 44th Gurkha (Rifle) Regiment. They took part the Manipur expedition where Ridgeway was Mentioned in Despatches. Promoted to colonel, he served in the Tirah campaign as Assistant Adjutant General, and in similar posts at Peshawar until 1900. He was created C.B. in 1905 and retired in 1906.

Ridgeway attended the Garden Party for Victoria Cross recipients at Buckingham Palace in 1920. He died at Harrogate on 11 October 1924.

Chapter 24

First Anglo-Boer War, 1880–81

Number of VCs awarded	6
Number of VCs awarded to officers	1
Number of VCs awarded to other ranks	5
Total awarded to British Army	5
Total awarded to Imperial forces	1

Origins of the War

It was not only the black indigenous inhabitants of southern Africa that Britain sought to overcome. A small European community mostly of Dutch extraction also stood in the way of plans for a federation along the lines of Canada under British supremacy.

Unable to accept the British policy of outlawing slavery, coupled with a desire to escape control from a central government, the Boers voted with their feet. Between 1835 and 1845, about 15,000 Boer *Voortrekkers* left the British Cape Colony and journeyed north to the open plains beyond the Orange and Vaal Rivers. Here they declared their own independent republics – the Transvaal (more correctly the South African Republic) and the Orange Free State, which were recognised by Britain at the Sand River (1852) and Bloemfontein (1854) Conventions.

Boer is the Dutch and Afrikaans word for farmer, but they were not strictly speaking sons of the soil. They made a subsistence living as livestock herders living a semi-nomadic existence by moving their flocks and herds from one pasture to another. Dour, tough and resourceful, they followed a Calvinist culture and, through necessity, developed into skilful horsemen and excellent shots. They became an opponent which the British Army had not before encountered.

For decades, the Boers enjoyed relative peace but became increasingly alarmed as the British pressed steadily north and east by annexing areas close to the Boer borders. The desperate state of the near-bankrupt South African Republic, caused by the Boers not paying their taxes, was exacerbated by the war they were fighting against the belligerent tribes to the east. The Boers were defeated by the Pedi under Sekekuni, and for a while were forced to accept British military protection. In 1877, the British Secretary for Native Affairs, Sir Theophilius Shepstone, annexed the Transvaal using a special warrant but, as the Boers found themselves between a rock and a hard place, they accepted this until both the Zulus and the Pedi had been defeated.

Fighting the common enemy of the Zulus, had only delayed the Boer's determination to recover their independence from the British. Friction was exacerbated by the bleak choice of Colonel Sir William Owen as the new Administrator of the Transvaal. This arrogant martinet with a hatred of the Boers was just about the worst appointment the British could have made.

The imposition of taxes led to the first confrontation which was the catalyst for war. In November 1880, a Boer farmer refused to pay a tax on his wagon and it was confiscated by the bailiff. On the 18th, a crowd of 100 irate Boers seized it back from the bailiff. Armed with a new sense of strength, around 8,000 to 10,000 Boers gathered at Paardekraal on 8 December and declared the restoration of the Transvaal Republic, so precipitating a war the British wished to avoid. With most of the British Army departing South Africa for other stations around the Empire, their presence had been pared down to a minimum. About 1,800 soldiers were left to garrison six small isolated forts spread across the Transvaal.

The first declaration of war took place at Bronkhorstspruit on 20 December 1880. A 250-strong column of the Connaught Rangers was on its way to the fort at Lydenburg when it was ambushed by about the same number of Boers. The horses and oxen pulling the wagons at the front and rear of the column were killed thus trapping the column. In an action that lasted just fifteen minutes, 156 British were killed or wounded and the survivors forced to surrender.

The Boers followed this up by surrounding the garrisons at Lydenburg, Wakkerstroom, Standerton, Marabastad, Rustenburg and Potchefstroom with the object of starving them into surrender. In an early skirmish at Elandsfontein on 16 January, 1881, the first of six Victoria Crosses were awarded for this conflict that the under-prepared British did not want.

JOHN DANAHER VC (1860-1919)
JAMES MURRAY VC (1859-1942)

James Murray was born in February 1859 (some sources state 1857) in St Michaels, Cork, Ireland. He joined the 2nd Battalion Connaught Rangers, the 94th Regiment, and took part in the Zulu and Basuto Wars as trooper in the Mounted Infantry.

John Danaher, another Irishman, was born on 25 June 1860 at Limerick. At the age of seventeen, he left school and travelled to South Africa to seek his fortune. He was possibly lured by the discovery of diamonds at

Kimberly on the Transvaal border. Obviously, he had not made his fortune, for he was one of sixty men who enlisted in a locally-raised unit called Nourse's Horse in Pretoria. Raised by Captain Henry Nourse in late 1880, this small mounted unit augmented the garrison's mounted arm at Pretoria which consisted of about 170 horsemen and 300 infantry, made up of 120 Royal Scots Fusiliers, thirty from the Connaught Rangers and 150 Pretoria Rifles.

On 11 January 1881, a hay cutting party had gone too far from the garrison and been attacked by the Boers. They managed to escape with the loss of a wagon and mules but, more critically, the precious mowing machine. It was thought that the machine was held at a laager on Elandsfontein Farm, about ten miles west of Pretoria. At 04.00 hours on 16 January, a column of 290 under the command of Lieutenant Colonel George Gildea left Pretoria to attack the Elandsfontein laager and retrieve the hay mower.

A separate party of Royal Engineers had left to create a diversion by exploding some dynamite to draw the Boers away from their laager. This was only partially successful as the defences were found to be stronger than expected, consisting of a stone blockhouse, a loop-holed wall and *schanzes* on a nearby ridge. At one point, it seemed the laager would be taken, but the artillery piece that had been brought could not be wheeled into action. With Boer reinforcements arriving, Gildea decided to pull back.

VC Action

As the withdrawal was taking place, it was noticed that two Scots Fusiliers who had been on the extreme left of the skirmish line were lying injured and under fire from the Boers. Two mounted men, James Murray, Mounted Infantry and John Danaher of Nourse's Horse, galloped to the stricken men who were well within range of the Boer's rifles. On the way, Murray's horse was killed by the gunfire and he made the rest of the way on foot.

A French war correspondent, Charles Duval witnessed the rescue and recalled: 'Murray and Danaher advanced for fully five hundred yards to where their wounded comrades were lying, exposed all the time to the fire of the Boers, until they reached the wounded men, to find that one was beyond human aid. They then carried the other man between them until Lance Corporal Murray was shot in the back and fell alongside his comrade for whom he had risked his life. Murray then ordered Danaher to retire, and as the latter realised that he could not save Murray under such heavy fire, he fired a few shots over his prostrate companions, gathered up their rifles and marched back to receive the praise of all who witnessed his plucky adventure.'

Murray, and Davis, the wounded man of the 2/21st Royal Scots Fusiliers, together with the body of Private Charles Byrne of the same regiment, were returned the following day under a flag of truce. Unfortunately, Private Davis died five days later.

Murray later paid tribute to the way he had been treated by the Boers and for the granting of permission to return to Pretoria the following day.

Both men were recommended for the Victoria Cross by Lieutenant Colonel Gildea and it is interesting that before the recommendation went forward to the War Office, a questionnaire was administered by General Evelyn Wood's Chief of Staff, Colonel Redvers Buller, asking for details of Murray and Danaher's gallant act.

Lieutenant O'Grady of the 94th, who commanded the Mounted Infantry, provided the answers. One of the queries was how close were the enemy to Murray and Danahar? It transpired that there were about sixty Boers firing at the pair from about 100 yards and that the nearest British troops were 500 yards away. Satisfied with the answer, the recommendation went forward. Both men were gazetted on 14 March 1882. It does, however, beg the question as how so many Boers managed to miss such easy targets from such close range.

John Murray received his Cross from Queen Victoria on 15 May 1882 at Windsor Castle. His subsequent life is not known, although he did marry and have a daughter, who, in 1960, erected a handsome headstone over his unmarked grave. He died in Dublin on 19 July 1942 and his medal group is displayed at the Lord Ashcroft Gallery, in London's Imperial War Museum.

John Danaher received his VC from the Viceroy at a parade held at the Curragh in Dublin on 23 August 1882. He left Nourse's Horse when it was disbanded and joined the Connaught Rangers, returning to Ireland with them in 1882. Maybe this was a means to return home after his abortive attempt to make his fortune. Nevertheless, he attained the rank of sergeant and retired from the Army in 1908. He became the publican of the Dog and Duck Public House in Portsmouth from 1913 to his death on 9 January 1919.

When word of the Boer uprising reached Major General Sir George Pomeroy Colley, the British High Commissioner for South East Africa, he set about gathering a relief column. Instead of waiting for the reinforcements on the way from India, he decided to make haste and take what troops he could to relieve the besieged Transvaal garrisons.

Colley gathered his force of about 1500 men at Newcastle and, after his ultimatum issued to the Boers and its rejection, he advanced towards the Transvaal border. On the morning of 28 January 1881, Colley decided to attack the strong Boer defences at Laing's Nek, a ridge that blocked his progress into the Transvaal. Where the road climbed up to Laing's Nek, the hills on either flank were occupied by the Boers. An abortive charge by mounted troops was easily repelled with some loss. A 1st Dragoon Guardsman, John Doogan, was awarded the Victoria Cross for giving up his horse to his wounded major.

Colley then ordered the five companies of the 58th (Northamptonshire) Regiment to attack the Boer's left flank. With their colours flying and in their bright red tunics, the regiment made an easy target for the Boer marksmen as they laboured up the open hillside. Only a few managed to reach the Boer's trenches until driven back by a devastating fire. The 58th suffered 173 casualties which included most of the officers. Lieutenant Alan Hill (later Hill-Walker) made an abortive attempt to save a brother officer and later rescued a wounded soldier. For this, he was awarded the Victoria Cross.

Six weeks later, Private James Osborn of the 58th, attached to the Mounted Infantry, rescued a wounded comrade under heavy fire at Wesselstroom on 22 February.

General Colley followed up his ill-fated attack at Laing's Nek with another disastrous decision. On 7 February and with only 350 men of the 60th Rifles, he attacked a smaller Boer force at the Ingogo River and managed to get pinned down, resulting in over 150 casualties.

Brigadier General Sir Evelyn Wood, the vastly experienced soldier and one of the few successful commanders of the recent Zulu War, arrived with more reinforcements. After a meeting between the two men, Colley agreed to wait until all the reinforcements had arrived before embarking on any further advance. When Wood returned to Natal, Colley ignored the compact and, thinking that the Boers were becoming weaker, decided to take a strong-point commanding Laing's Nek. This prominent feature was called Majuba (the Hill of Doves) – a 2,500 feet high flat-topped, steep-sided hill.

Leaving most of his force of 4,000 men in camp, Colley took twenty-two officers and 627 men and began the steep ascent at 22.00 hours on 26 February. A few medical orderlies accompanied the soldiers. The climb in darkness was exhausting with the men carrying full packs and heavy equipment. Slowly the troops hauled themselves over tufted grass and projecting rocks until they reached the summit at 03.40 hours. On the way up, Colley had dropped off men to dig in on the side of the hill so that when the top was reached, his force had shrunk to 354 men.

Thinking his position was impregnable, no orders were given to the men to prepare defensive positions. Colley commented that 'we could stay here forever'. Indeed, the occupation of the summit was a complete surprise to the Boers when they became aware of the British on the morning of 27 February. Sporadic rifle fire aimed at the Boers below prompted Commandant General Joubert to send parties of volunteers up the hill. The scaling of Majuba may have been an exhausting and lengthy experience for the British redcoats but not so for the Boers, who used a zigzag technique, to cover the hillside with the older marksmen covering the younger men. In this way, 4 to 500 Boers made their way to the summit by keeping the British troop's heads down with accurate fire.

Firing continued throughout the morning until noon, when the hundreds of Boers swarmed on to the summit. Many of the British, including Colley himself, had only just awoken. Lieutenant Ian Hamilton asked Colley for permission to attack but was told that: 'We will wait until the Boers advance on us, then give them a volley and charge'. By then it was too late. In one of the worst disasters of British arms, one VC was awarded to a medical orderly who managed to keep calm amongst the chaos around him.

JOSEPH JOHN FARMER VC (1854-1930)

Joseph John Farmer was born 5 May 1854 in Clerkenwell, London. His education at the local National School was scant for he left before his teens to learn a trade. He was apprenticed in the building trade but, finding the life unappealing, he went to sea as a ship's boy at the age of thirteen.

For the next eight years, he sailed around the world serving on several vessels and experienced the hazards of life at sea. In 1875, his ship was wrecked off the Isle of Wight and the following year, his next ship was disabled by a hurricane off Hong Kong. By 1878, Farmer had had his fill of sea life and returned to England, where he contracted smallpox. Whilst still undergoing treatment in a hospital at Hampstead Heath, Farmer became involved in preventing a delirious patient from jumping out of a window. Perhaps this act inspired him to try medical care as a profession for it led him to apply for a job when he recovered as Hospital Porter at the same hospital.

The only way for an unqualified man to learn about medical care was to enlist in the Army Hospital Corps and this Farmer did on 27 February 1879. He was sent to the AHC establishment at Aldershot where he learned about anatomy and ambulance work in the field. While he was undergoing his training, the Anglo-Zulu War was being fought out during the first six months of 1879. Anticipating a swift victory over the Zulus, the British army in South Africa was both small and unprepared for a longer campaign. The shocking defeat at Isandlwana and the reverses at Intombi Drift and Hlobane forced Lord Chelmsford to withdraw his troops back across the Zululand border to Natal and wait for reinforcements to arrive before attempting a second invasion.

A shortage of medical personnel led to female nurses being sent to a war zone for the first time since the Crimean War. This was vehemently opposed by the military, in particular the AHC, who rushed all available male nurses to South Africa. Private Joseph Farmer was amongst the reinforcements who took the long and slow journey to Durban, arriving when the war was all but over. There was, however, plenty for the medics to do as the war provided lots of casualties. There were relatively few wounded from fighting the Zulus but there were many suffering from tropical sicknesses and heat-related ailments. Farmer probably attended patients at the base hospitals set up at Pietermaritzburg and Durban.

VC Action

It was on Majuba in 1881 that Joseph Farmer first experienced coming under fire. With the British taking casualties from the rapid and accurate fire, many troops panicked and fled down the steep slope. All order was gone as officers shouted conflicting orders. Colley stood and sought to rally his command and was struck in the forehead by a bullet. Unable to make a stand as there were no prepared defences, the redcoats were easy targets for the Boer marksmen. Soon dead and wounded covered the summit.

The small hospital area was full of stricken soldiers, including Sir Arthur Landon of the Army Medical Directorate, who had been paralysed with a bullet to the spine. He instructed Private Farmer to wave a triangular bandage over his head to alert the Boers that they were firing on a hospital area. Standing up, Farmer held aloft the white cloth until a bullet hit him in the right wrist. Dropping the bandage, he picked it up with his left hand and continued to wave until he was shot through the left elbow.

In later years, Farmer recalled: 'When the Boers closed in with the British troops near the hills, another man and myself were helping Sir Arthur Landon … to tend the wounded, who were falling thick and fast. Both cried out that they were hit, and the soldier I was bandaging was, I believe, killed at the same moment. Sir Arthur Landon, I ought to say, was one of the best and bravest men who ever lived or died. Well, as soon as I saw what the Boers were about, I jumped up waved the bandage I was using – which might have served the purpose of a white flag – and shouted that they were shooting wounded men. The enemy either did not know the usages of civilised warfare or, in their blind fury, they did not heed what they were about …

'Anyhow, a Boer took a pot-shot at me and the bullet went through my right wrist. Here is the mark [he said] that has affected free use of my hand ever since, though not disabled it. As the report of the affair by Major Elliott says, I, on being hit in the right arm called out "I have another!" and transferred the white flag to the left hand and continued to wave it.

'My Boer friend, however, was a persistent beggar, for he had another try, and this time he shot me through the left elbow joint. His endeavours rather convinced me, notwithstanding opinion to the contrary, that the Boers are not such remarkably good shots as they are said to be. I was, however, placed hors de combat; but the surgeon, though himself mortally wounded, injected morphia to deaden the pain, and so the limbs were saved to me. The left arm is, however, a good deal wasted and crippled.'

In all probability, Farmer had not been specifically targeted but had been hit by the many bullets that were flying about in the British area. Indeed, the Boers behaved with chivalry, allowing the wounded to return to the British camp.

Joseph Farmer was hospitalised and learned that he had been recommended for the Victoria Cross, which was announced in *The London*

Gazette on 17 May 1881, where it was noted; 'he showed a spirit of self-abnegation and an example of cool courage which cannot be too highly commended'. Farmer was the only VC to be awarded on a disastrous day that claimed ninety-three dead, 133 wounded and fifty-eight taken prisoner. By contrast, the Boers suffered the loss of only one dead and five wounded.

Farmer's VC is one of that small number of duplicate issues arising from the slowness of communications at that time. A Cross was prepared and sent out on 27 May for presentation by the General Officer Commanding, Sir Evelyn Wood. This coincided with Farmer's departure from South Africa en route to England. A second Cross was prepared and Provisional Lance Corporal Joseph Farmer travelled to Osborne House on the Isle of Wight to receive it from the Queen on 9 August 1881.

Later Life

As a result of his wounds, Farmer was medically discharged. His latter years were largely uneventful, though he did join the Corps of Commissionaires and met up with Rorke's Drift VC, Frederick Hitch, who also lived in the Fulham area.

As a commissionaire, Farmer spent the next forty years working for a manufacturer in Fulham before retiring at the age of seventy-four. On 26 June 1920, he was one of the 310 VC heroes who attended the Royal Garden Party at Buckingham Palace.

On 30 June 1930, aged seventy-six, Joseph Farmer died in Northwood, Middlesex. Such was the high regard in which he was held that his coffin was carried on a gun carriage through the streets of Fulham, lined with hundreds of onlookers, to his final resting place in Brompton Cemetery. Placed on his grave is a granite boulder with the inscription: 'This rock was sent from the scene of the Battle of Majuba Hill … erected by his family, old comrades in the Durban Light Infantry, together with comrades of his corps and Fulham citizens. Rest in Peace.'

This demoralising defeat inflicted on the British Army resulted in an armistice and peace negotiations took place on 2 March. This led to the Boers being given self-government under an overall British suzerainty.

Chapter 25

Anglo-Egyptian War, 1882

Number of VCs awarded	3
Number of VCs awarded to officers	1
Number of VCs awarded to other ranks	2
Total awarded to Royal Navy	1
Total awarded to British Army	2

Origins of the War

Throughout the 1870s Egypt was in a financial and political crisis. Tewfiq Pasha, the new Khedive of Egypt and Sudan, had replaced the former incumbent, Ismail Pasha, who for many years been mismanaging his country's affairs and reducing the country to bankruptcy. It had been this urgent need for money which led Ismail to sell his shares in the Suez Canal in 1875 to Britain, a move which was very unpopular in Egypt. To protect their interests in the Canal, Britain and France (the canal was a join France-Egypt venture) took control of Egypt's finances, appointing their own officials to run key ministries.

These actions were regarded by many Egyptians as unwarranted interference in their own country's affairs. In June 1879, the British replaced Ismail with his eldest son, Tewfiq, who found himself between a rock and a hard place. In September 1881, the Egyptian Army led by Colonel Ahmed Urabi (Arabi) Pasha, staged a nationalist revolt against the new Khedive and forced him to dismiss the prime minister, Urabi Pasha, who had been appointed Minister of War, and demanded an end to foreign domination – Turkish and European. This anti-foreign movement began to prepare for war.

In May 1882, Britain and France sent a combined fleet to the Egyptian port of Alexandria to protect the large European community living there and to demonstrate support for the Khedive against his own Minister of War. An anti-Christian riot broke out in Alexandria on 11 June, in which several hundred people including fifty Europeans were killed. Urabi did attempt to quell the riot and at the same time prepared the city for the retaliation he knew would follow. Large scale defensive works included the mounting of new heavy gun batteries in the forts overlooking the harbour where the assault from the Anglo-French fleet was expected.

On 10 July, Admiral Sir Beauchamp Seymour sent an ultimatum demanding that the forts surrender within twenty-four hours or they would be bombarded. The French were furious that Seymour had taken it upon himself to issue the ultimatum. They emphasised their displeasure by withdrawing their fleet, although much of this attitude had to do with the political turmoil in France and the French Navy expected to be recalled home. Instead, the French retreated to Port Said to wait until the bombardment was over.

As anticipated, the ultimatum was rejected. All merchant vessels and foreign ships left Alexandria as the British Fleet prepared for action. Admiral Seymour's fleet consisted of sixteen warships including of eight battleships, five gunboats and various support vessels. In an act reminiscent of Charles Lucas' exploit in the Baltic in 1854, a single Victoria Cross was awarded to the Royal Navy during the subsequent bombardment.

ISRAEL HARDING VC (1833-1917)

Israel Harding was born in Portsmouth on Trafalgar Day, 21 October, 1833. His parents were John Harding, a Queen's Pilot at Portsmouth for many years, and Sophia (née Martin). Israel Harding, like many of his generation, came from a large family; the 1841 Census shows him living with his mother and seven siblings at 11 White Hart Row, Portsmouth. He was educated at the Royal Victoria School and Bethel School, Old Portsmouth and then a private school where he learnt navigation. Aged fourteen, he became a cabin boy and pilot's apprentice in his father's ship, HMS *Echo*.

Harding enlisted in the Royal Navy in 1849 and served as an ordinary seaman in HMS *Arrogant*, on home service, from 1849 to 1853. In 1853 he attended a gunnery course on board HMS *Excellent*, the Naval Gunnery School at Portsmouth. One part of the course was particularly fraught with danger. With other naval students, he was given the task of testing a newly-invented rifled bore gun mounted in HMS *Skylark*. The gun was fired with a long lanyard reaching to the boat next to *Skylark*. Harding and three other hand-spikemen just had time to drop down the fore-hatch before the gun was fired. It was fortunate that they were all below deck at the time for after a firing a few rounds, the gun burst.

Harding described the scene: 'The muzzle and chase went over the side, and one half of the cascabel flew over the bow, cutting the foremast in two, and bringing it crashing down above our heads; the other half passed through the funnel, crashing through the mainmast, and bringing that down too; then it passed over the stern. It was a remarkable and unexpected accident, and, but for the fact that we were all below, the loss of life would have been very heavy.'

Crimean War

Whilst serving at HMS *Excellent*, Israel Harding married Harriett Ellis, aged nineteen at St Mary's Church, Portsea on 10 January 1853. Harding transferred to HMS *Cressy* as Gunner's Mate and served in the Baltic Sea in naval operations against Russia, 1854-1855. The Russian Fleet declined to sail from the safety of its heavily-fortified base at Kronstadt, leaving the British and French Fleets to operate a blockade of the port and seek other targets. Harding took part in the Anglo-French bombardment of the Russian fortifications at Sveaborg in August 1855 and was awarded the Baltic Medal.

He was later promoted to Captain of the Foretop in HMS *Cressy*, stationed with the Channel Squadron and was promoted to Gunner (a warrant officer rank) in March 1860. In 1861, he was drafted to HMS *Barracouta*, paddle sloop, which was sent to the North America and West Indies Station in 1860, remaining there until 1870.

Harding served as Gunner on an expedition to Mexico and later took part in the occupation of Vera Cruz, Mexico's main Gulf port. British, Spanish and French Fleets arrived at Vera Cruz in January 1862 in order to pressure the Mexican Government into settling its international debts but Britain and Spain withdrew when it became clear that France intended to invade Mexico. Harding is said to have assisted in the rescue of the gunboat HMS *Plover*, for which he was recommended for promotion to lieutenant – the promotion was not approved.

In 1871, Harding joined HMS *Gladiator* on the South American Station and is shown in the 1871 Census as being on board the ship in Montevideo Harbour. He led a Royal Naval party ashore to fight a fire in a munitions factory in Rio de Janeiro and for his services in this action he received a Brazilian award and a testimonial letter from the Princess Imperial of Brazil.

When he returned to England, he divorced his wife, Harriett, on the grounds of her adultery and in 1873 married Emma Annette Nunn, the daughter of an inspector in the Storekeeper's Department in Woolwich Dockyard. In 1874, Harding joined HMS *Victor Emmanuel*, a ninety-one-gun warship launched in 1855, which served off the African coast as a hospital ship during the Ashanti War of 1873-74. For the next few years, Harding was given command of HMS *Castor*, a drill ship for naval reservists on the Tyne.

Israel Harding's next posting was as Gunner to HMS *Alexandra*, the battleship in which he won the Victoria Cross. HMS *Alexandra*, launched in 1875, was one of the new ironclad battleships and, with her ten and eleven-inch guns, was one of the most powerful ships in the Royal Navy. She was the last British battleship to carry her main armaments below decks. She was originally to be named HMS *Superb* but this was changed when Princess Alexandra launched her. When Harding joined the *Alexandra*, it was the flag-ship of the British Mediterranean Fleet commanded by Admiral Sir Frederick Beauchamp Seymour GCB.

VC Action

At 07.00 hours on 11 July 1882, two hours after the ultimatum had expired, HMS *Alexandra* fired the first salvo, directing her fire at Fort Adda. This was the signal for the bombardment to begin and soon the other ships joined in, firing at their own targets.

As Harding noted: 'Each ship fired independently, each captain of a gun aimed for a certain mark, each gun's crew set hard to work in this contest of pounding to see who could pound the hardest, and each ship's company strove to score a first place in marksmanship.'

The gunboats, meanwhile, moved close to the shore to fire their small cannons and Gatling guns at the rebel gunners. After the return fire from Fort Mex had ceased, landing parties from HMS *Invincible* destroyed three guns and spiked six others. Landing parties from other ships put out of action any guns which had survived the naval shelling. The bombardment of Alexandria lasted until late afternoon. By 16.00 hours, all the shore batteries had been silenced and most of their magazines blown up but the bombardment continued until 17.30 – ten and a half hours after it had begun. Urabi Pasha paid a high price for his defiance; it was estimated that at least 2,000 of his Egyptian followers were killed in the bombardment. Rioting broke out in Alexandria and continued for days, until a Naval Brigade landed to restore order.

The return fire of the shore batteries, which had as many guns as the British Fleet, caused some damage to the battleships but none were sunk. Casualties were light with ten men killed and twenty-seven wounded. Although the Egyptian guns were mostly smaller than those on the British battleships, the action took place at fairly close range. The firing of the shore batteries was at first erratic but it improved as more direct hits were made on the ships. HMS *Alexandra,* the lead ship in the bombardment was hit sixty times, with one man killed and three wounded.

Israel Harding was in a good position to observe the damage inflicted by the shelling from the shore batteries: 'The shot and shell which crashed against our armour broke up; but those which struck the weaker portions of the ship penetrated and did a lot of mischief. Our own practice, as we could see from time to time when the smoke cleared, was deadly and demoralising. Every shot seemed to strike home, and forts were shattered and gunners destroyed in a way that showed the utter hopelessness of resistance. But the Egyptians had warmed to their work, and their fire was becoming very accurate.

'The *Alexandra* was naturally a special target, and there was plenty of her to hit. The excitement began early. A shell came through the port side forward, and bursting close to the sheep-pen, killed the only occupant;

another cut away a stout iron stanchion, and, narrowly missed the captain and the staff-commander, carried off a piece of the fore funnel casing. Another shell struck the steam launch, and exploding in her smashed her to atoms, killing one man and wounding two others. Again the captain had a very narrow escape – there were many close shaves that day.'

With the Gunnery Lieutenant sick, the gunnery duties devolved on Harding, who was constantly on the move between decks, checking ammunition supplies and helping to lay the guns. About two hours after the bombardment began, a shell crashed through the port bulwarks and exploded in one of the officers' cabins.

'I was recovering from the shock of that explosion and was starting to descend the hatchway on the next deck leading to the after-magazine, when a shell penetrated the ship's side, passing through the torpedo lieutenant's cabin. Then it struck against the iron coamings of the engine-room [hatch], rebounded round the rifle-racks, and lodged close to a large tub of water which had been placed in readiness to put out any fire that might occur.'

Mr James Maxwell, Assistant Paymaster, was walking on the main deck at the time with Mr William Horniman, a clerk, and witnessed the landing of the ten-inch spherical shell, with its fuse still burning. In his VC recommendation eyewitness statement he said: '[It] then rolled over to the starboard side of deck, right under our feet (we having walked aft as far as the hatchway just outside [the] ward room door, where they were handing up powder). I, imagining it to be simply a solid shot, kicked it, causing it to turn over, when I saw it was a live shell, which fact I shouted out, to prevent the powder men and others from coming up the ladder.'

The hatchway which Mr Maxwell mentioned led to the magazine which contained approximately twenty-five tons of gunpowder. Hearing the cry that there is a live shell just above the hatchway, Harding came rushing up the ladder from the deck below. He saw the shell, with its short fuse burning, and without hesitation took some water from the tub and threw it over the shell. He then picked it up, burning his fingers on the fuse as he did so, and dropped the shell into the nearby tub of water. The shell contained approximately twelve pounds of gunpowder and if it had exploded would have caused considerable damage and loss of life. Harding had, undoubtedly, saved a great many lives but was typically modest about his actions:

'I turned round swiftly and saw the awful missile at my feet. At such a time a man does not stop to think, and I stooped and picked up the shell and instinctively placed it in the tub of water, although the chances are even that a fuse will not be extinguished by such means as that. Yet what I wished for happened – the water did its work, the fuse ceased to burn, and the projectile became a harmless object … every possible circumstance contributed to the chances of destruction, and yet they were circumvented on the spur of the moment because of the more or less chance presence of a tub of water, and because of that early training in a hard school.'

Harding was given immediate promotion to Chief Gunner. Captain Charles Hotham, commanding *Alexandra*, reported Harding's brave action to his Commander-in-Chief, Admiral Seymour, who mentioned it in his despatch to the Admiralty on 20 July 1882. Admiral Seymour wrote: 'Captain Hotham of the *Alexandra* has specially brought to my notice a deed of valour performed by Mr Israel Harding, the Gunner of that ship, who probably saved many lives by lifting and placing in a tub of water a 10-inch shell with burning fuse, which had passed through the ship's side and lodged on the main deck.'

Admiral Seymour recommended him for the Victoria Cross on 15 August and enclosed a report from Captain Hotham and eyewitness accounts of Harding's bravery signed by James Maxwell and William Horniman. The VC recommendation was forwarded by the Admiralty to the War Office and was approved by Queen Victoria.

The award was notified in *The London Gazette* of 15 September 1882 on the same day British forces occupied Cairo and Urabi Pasha was captured. Israel Harding received his VC at Malta on 14 November 1882, from his commander, Admiral Seymour. The shell which Harding extinguished was mounted on a wooden stand and presented to HRH The Prince of Wales as a souvenir of the bombardment. It is now on display at the Lord Ashcroft Gallery, IWM London.

Later Life

Harding joined his final ship, HMS *Duke of Wellington*, at Portsmouth in December 1883. His last posting was as officer in charge of Naval Recruiting at Portsea and he was discharged from the Royal Navy as Chief Gunner in 1885. After retirement, he lived in his home town of Portsmouth and later received a Greenwich Hospital pension of £35 per year. In retirement, Harding was the Honorary Agent and Receiving Officer for the Portsmouth Branch of the Shipwrecked Fishermen and Mariners' Royal Benevolent Society. In this capacity, he attended the funerals of two local VC recipients: William Hewett VC and John Robarts VC. Both men were buried in Highland Road Cemetery, Portsmouth.

During the First World War, Harding served on minesweepers, even though he was then in his eighties. Contemporary newspaper reports state that three minesweeping ships in which he served were blown up. In one explosion, he sustained a broken leg. For his wartime service, he was promoted to honorary lieutenant on the 1917 Navy Retired List, although he does not appear to have received any of the First World War medals.

Israel Harding VC died on 22 May 1917, aged eighty-three, while he was visiting his eldest daughter Sophia Williams at Silkstead House, Billingshurst, Sussex. His body was brought back to Portsmouth and he joined other VC comrades in the Highland Road Cemetery.

With Alexandria in flames and mobs roaming the streets wreaking revenge on any European they could find, Admiral Seymore landed a force of sailors and marines to restore order. Also landed were the men of 1/South Staffordshire and 3/ King's Royal Rifle Corps who had been sent from Cyprus to secure the Suez Canal. When it was learned of the confrontation in Alexandria, they were diverted to help. Meanwhile, Colonel Ahmed Urabi had withdrawn his army about forty miles south to prepare a defensive position at Kafr-ed-Dauar. Not only was he appointed Commander-in-Chief, but became the effective leader of Egypt.

The Egyptian Campaign was the first in which infantry battalions fought under their new designations, but old habits die hard, and it took a while before the use of the old numerals were finally dropped. Thus, the South Staffs and the KRRC were still referred to as the 38th and 60th respectively. It was a member of the latter regiment who performed the second VC act of gallantry.

FREDERICK CORBETT VC (1856-1904)

Frederick Corbett was born David Embleton on 19 September 1853, the eleventh of twelve children born to William Embleton, a baker in Maldon, Essex, and his wife, Jane. Little is known of his early life other than as a teenager he joined the 2nd Essex Rifle Volunteers. The lack of opportunity locally and his taste of soldiering persuaded him to enlist in the regular Army at Colchester. In 1873 he signed under the assumed name of Frederick Corbett and enlisted with the 3rd Battalion 60th Regiment.

In 1879, the regiment was amongst the first reinforcements sent out to South Africa after the disastrous defeat at Isandlwana in January 1879. For some reason, his name does not appear in the medal rolls or pay lists for this campaign but he was definitely in Cape Town in 1882 when the regiment boarded the troopship *Orantes* on 22 February and, sent to Cyprus via Malta. The regiment was soon called upon to take part in the Egyptian Campaign and the newly-designated KRRC was landed on 14 July from the troopship *Agincourt.*

Captain Hutton selected those riflemen who could ride to form a Mounted Infantry unit as there were no cavalry amongst the first units landed. Corbett was one to be selected and he and his comrades were soon in action under the command of Major Henry Hallam Parr of the Somerset Light Infantry. Having secured Alexandria, the British army occupied nearby Ramleh and exchanged artillery fire with Arabi's army. Corbett had been appointed as batman to Lieutenant Henry Granville Lindsay Howard-Vyse and, on 22 July, accompanied him on a patrol to protect an armoured train which had been sent to blow up the railway line at Mallaha Junction. In their first action, the Mounted Infantry blocked the enemy cavalry trying to attack the train.

On 9 August, an advance was ordered towards Urabi's position at Kafr-el-Duar. Half the force followed the railway line, while the other on the left, including the KRRC, followed the line of the Mahmudiyeh Canal. This force was split as they patrolled either side of the canal, with the Rifles on the right bank and the others on the left.

VC Action

Very soon, those on the left bank made contact with the enemy, who fled into the bush pursued by the British. This left the Rifles unsupported on the right, so Parr, Lieutenant Vyse and another officer, together with six men, including Corbett, moved forward to cover any enemy movement. They had not ridden far when they ran into a large enemy force, which opened fire. Dismounting, the patrol returned fire, expecting the rest of the Rifles to join them. Instead, an order to retire had been given, leaving the nine men isolated and facing hundreds of enemy infantry.

Casualties were soon suffered, including Lieutenant Vyse who was shot in the thigh and mortally wounded. Corbett tried to staunch the flow of blood, but the femoral artery had been severed and Vyse bled to death in a few minutes. Corbett refused to leave the stricken officer despite being exposed to enemy fire. He asked permission to stay with his officer and Parr recalled that, 'he sat down quite contentedly with the poor boy's head on his lap and I found him there when I was ordered to retire'. As the patrol pulled back, Corbett assisted in carrying Vyse away. The other fatality was Private J. House, whilst Private S. Howes was severely wounded. The British forces, by this time, had regained their composure and attacked along both sides of the canal, forcing the enemy to retreat.

The following day, Vyse and House were buried at Ramlah Station. Private F. Wilson of 'B' Coy 3rd KRRC wrote; 'The Officer's horse is dressed and his boots turned round with the toes to the rear of the horse.' For both the dead men; 'coffins of deal wood taken off a shed in the barraks [*sic*].'

Major Parr was on the staff of the force commander Lieutenant General Sir Garnet Wolseley and on 7 October was appointed commander of the Military Foot Police. He wasted little time in having Corbett transferred as his servant into the police. Their station was Cairo and Parr recommended Corbett to be awarded the Distinguished Conduct Medal. He wrote; 'a soldier of whose steadiness and gallantry under fire I have been frequently a witness.' Promotion to corporal followed on 14 November and his Mentioned in Despatches appeared in *The London Gazette* of 2 November 1882.

Sir Garnet Wolseley annotated the citation for the DCM, which was transmitted to the War Office on 4 January 1883, and suggested that a Victoria Cross was more apposite. This was submitted to the Queen, who gave her assent on 9 February.

The London Gazette of 16 February 1883 published the following: 'During the reconnaissance upon Kafr Dowar, on 5 August 1882, the Mounted Infantry with which Private Corbett was serving, came under a hot fire from the enemy and suffered some loss, including Lieutenant Howard Vyse, mortally wounded. This officer fell in the open, and there being no time to move him, Private Corbett asked and obtained permission to remain with him, and though under a constant fire, he sat down and endeavoured to stop the bleeding of this officer's wounds, until the Mounted Infantry received orders to retire, when he rendered valuable assistance in carrying him off the field.'

Major Parr noted in his memoirs the pleasure he felt that his servant was to receive the DCM, but did not mention him getting the more prestigious Cross. On 2 March 1883, Field Marshal Lord Napier of Magdala officiated at an investiture on Abdin Square in Cairo. Corporal Frederick Corbett in the uniform of the Military Foot Police received his VC from the famous victor of the Abyssinian War. The only known photograph of Corbett was probably taken at this time for it shows him wearing solely the Victoria Cross pinned to the breast of his police tunic. It was at that period standard protocol for the recipient not to wear other medals for an investiture.

The Egyptian War was over by October 1882 and Corbett returned to England with his old regiment. Increasing problems with his leg led to his medical discharge on 18 June 1883. He was found to have a large varix (a permanent abnormal dilation of a vein or artery) in his thigh. In addition to his Cross, he was also awarded the Egypt Medal with clasp *Tel el Kebir* and the Khedive's Star.

Changed Character

It is from family oral history that his younger brother was said to have recounted: 'Dave came back to Maldon and was feted by everyone, including strangers, who just wanted to buy him a drink, but he was teetotal. In the end, he got tired of saying he didn't drink and began to accept these. He got embarrassed that he didn't have any money and couldn't stand his corner, so he sold the Cross to a London dealer for fifteen guineas. That began a rift with his elder brother, John.' So, having fallen into bad company, David Embledon's character changed.

Unable to adjust to civilian life, he applied to re-join the army. On 19 December 1883, the Medical Board passed him fit and he enlisted as a driver in the Royal Horse Artillery. He again joined under the name Frederick Corbett and gave his place of birth as Camberwell, South London and that his father was deceased, when, in fact, both parents were still alive. It is not known quite why he went to such lengths to disguise his background, especially as he was the holder to the Queen's highest award for gallantry.

On 24 February 1884, Corbett was on his way back to Egypt to take part in the Expedition against the Mahdi and was involved in operations around the Red Sea port of Suakin. When this three-month long conflict ended, Corbett was able to add the bar 'Suakin' to his Egypt Medal. Corbett seems to have undergone a personality change, for he went from being a steady soldier, well regarded by his officers, to one who was unreliable and troublesome.

Corbett returned to England on 3 June, but went absent without leave from 12 to 23 July. On 30 July 1884, he appeared before a District Court Martial at Aldershot, charged with being absent without leave, theft and embezzlement. He was convicted and imprisoned for twenty-eight days with hard labour.

Queen Victoria then endorsed a warrant depriving him of his medals and the prison governor was directed to confiscate three medals: these appear to have been a copy VC, the Egypt Medal and the Khedive Star. Corbett is said to believe thereafter that Queen Victoria had recommended that he could have that honour restored to him after a period of rehabilitation, but that the Army had apparently decided otherwise. The War Office's erratic behaviour regarding custodial sentences on Victoria Cross recipients highlights the case of Private Edmund Fowler VC who was convicted of a similar offence in 1887, but the Queen refused to sign the forfeiture Warrant.

Having served his sentence, Corbett re-joined his regiment and was sent to India. He continued his descent from being a good soldier to one who was a trouble maker. On 28 February 1887, he was convicted by a District Court Martial of losing by neglect his equipment, clothing etc., and stealing the property of a comrade and sentenced to eighty-four days' hard labour. On 17 September 1889, he again stood before a District Martial and was given another eighty-four days' hard labour for striking an NCO.

Corbett returned home on 1 December 1890. He was constantly in trouble with the authorities and, on 16 January 1891, was finally discharged as medically unfit. He left without a pension with nine entries against his name in the Regimental Defaulters Book and seventeen in the Battery Defaulters Book. His medical records refer to periods of treatment for alcoholism and for sexually transmitted diseases, not uncommon in a soldier at that time, and would explain his insubordinate behaviour.

Corbett returned to civilian life and reassumed his true name. He tried to make a living by becoming a house-painter without success. This forced him to enter the Workhouse system, from which he could not escape.

An article in the *East London Advertiser* on 14 March 1896 reported that he had been charged with refusing to work at the Greenwich Union Workhouse. In September 1904, he was sentenced to one month's hard labour for breaking a glass panel in the door of the War Office. He probably acted out of a grievance, having learned that his Cross had come into the possession of Mr W.T. Mansfield of Kingsbury, who had tried to return it to him. The War Office had intervened, stating that under no circumstance should it be returned to Corbett. A local newspaper reported this and added that the VC had been rescinded, a fact that to this point had not been made public. An angry Corbett blamed the War Office for his troubles and made his impotent attack.

It is recorded that the fallen hero spent sixteen years at the Greenwich Union Workhouse before returning to Maldon. His final years were spent in Maldon Workhouse, where he died at the age of fifty-nine on 25 September 1912. He was buried in an unmarked pauper's grave in the London Road Cemetery in Row 4 Grave 27. In a dedication ceremony on 16 April 2004, his final resting place was marked with a King's Royal Rifle Corps memorial stone.

The Cross, or copies of it, continued to cause controversy. One was bought in Middlesex whilst Embleton was still alive. Both the Royal Artillery at Woolwich and the Museum of the King's Royal Rifle Corps (now the Royal Greenjackets Museum) once thought that they possessed the original. The inscription on these two was compared with the records of Hancock's and was as follows: VC in possession of KRRC: '3804 Pte. F. Corbett 5 Aug 1882', VC at Woolwich: 'Pte. Frederick Corbett 3rd Bn. King's Royal Rifle Corps 5 August 1882'.

The records at Hancock's show that the inscription on the original read: 'Pte. F. Corbett 60th Royal Rifles 5 Aug 1882.' As Hancock's have no records of any duplicates being made, it is assumed that Corbett had these made.

The British now had to tackle the strong defences at Kafr-ed-Dauer which blocked their advance on Cairo. Wolseley ordered Lieutenant General Hamley with his 2nd Division forward to threaten the Egyptian Army. In fact, Wolseley had no plans for attacking Kafr-ed-Dauer but concentrated his main force further east at Port Said and Ismalia with the intention of striking across the desert and attacking Urabi's army at Tel-el-Kebir. General Hamley was furious that his command had been used as a diversion and relations between the two men became decidedly frosty, despite Wolseley's promise that the 2nd Division would be needed at Tel-el-Kebir.

On 13 September 1882, Urabi's army stood in their hastily prepared defences that covered a front of four miles and prepared to meet Wolseley's 8,000-strong force. After a night march across the desert, the British surprised the enemy and, in a brief battle, the Egyptians were soon overrun and pursued by the cavalry. Cairo was defenceless and soon captured. The British had lost only fifty-seven troops while killing about 2,000 of the enemy. Although the British public rejoiced at the victory, there were many who felt queasy about what they saw as an unjust campaign.

One of Wolseley's staff, Colonel William Butler who rose to become Major General Sir William Butler, was married to the celebrated battle artist, Elizabeth Butler. He did not approve of his wife's painting, *After the Battle,* which depicted Wolseley standing up in his stirrups surrounded by his staff, including Butler, at the moment of victory at Tel-el-Kebir. The battle was neither glorious nor necessary in Butler's view, 'to beat those poor *felhaeen* (peasant) soldiers was not a matter of exultation ... and … the capture of Arabi's earthworks had been like going through brown paper … it gave the god Jingo a new start'. This painting no longer exists for it was cut up on the death of William Butler, probably as a belated gesture to his wishes. All that remains is the centre group of Wolseley and his staff.

A legacy of the victory was that it began to involve a reluctant Britain in the inherited thorn in Egypt's side, the Sudan.

Chapter 26

Sudan War, 1883–85

Number of VCs awarded	5
Number of VCs awarded to officers	2
Number of VCs awarded to other ranks	3
Total awarded to Royal Navy	1
Total awarded to British Army	4

Origins of the War

Rather like Abyssinia, Sudan was cut off from the outside world by deserts, equatorial forests and feuding Arab tribes. She shared one thing in common with her northern neighbour Egypt – the River Nile. The rise of the Egyptian ruler, Mohammed Ali Pasha, in the 1820s and his defeat of the Ottomans alarmed the European powers, especially Britain who relied on the Isthmus of Suez for its route to India. In a brief invasion in which a primarily British force defeated the Egyptians in Syria in 1840, the Convention of London did not remove Mohammed Ali from power but used him as a block to Ottoman expansion. Thus the period of the Khedive, or the governor of Egypt and Sudan, came dominate Egyptian affairs.

For the next four decades, Egypt extended her domination of the Sudan until by 1870, she had secured an enormous region extending 800 miles south of Khartoum. Hand in hand with the domination came the usual sins of oppression, corruption and exploitation. Although she paid lip service to the abolition of slavery, the corrupt Egyptian officials turned a blind eye to the Arab slavers who flourished in this huge country. To disarm European suspicions of Egypt's ambivalent attitude to the slave trade, the Khedive Tewfik Ali appointed Colonel Charles George Gordon of the Royal Engineers as Governor of Sudan's Equatorial Province. He had been a highly successful commander of an irregular Chinese army which helped defeat the Taiping uprising.

He was a man of intense religious faith and fervently anti-slavery. During his tenure, he struck at the roots of slavery and, in 1877, he was appointed Governor-General for the whole of Sudan until ill health forced his return to England.

After the short-lived war against Egypt, Britain took on the role of occupier, mainly to protect their improved route to India made possible by the newly-opened Suez Canal. She also inherited an area she did not want – the Sudan.

The Khedive, who had relied on Britain to keep him power, had to contend with an uprising in the Sudan of Sufi Muslim 'Dervishes' led by Muhammed Ahmad – the Mahdi. He appointed Colonel William Hicks, a retired Indian Army officer looking for employment. He was given the title of major general in the Egyptian Army and tasked with defeating the Mahdi and his followers. On 9 September 1883, he led a reluctant and ill-disciplined force into the Kordofan desert looking to defeat the Dervishes. A month later, word came back that Hicks Pasha's rag-tag army of badly-trained and ill-equipped Egyptian *felhaeen* soldiers had been annihilated at the hands of the followers of the Mahdi.

In February 1884, Major-General Charles Gordon returned to Khartoum with instructions to evacuate Egyptian forces and officials. Instead he chose to stay and defend the city trusting, no doubt, that the British government would send a strong relief force to defeat the Mahdi. William Gladstone's Government was firmly against the involvement of British arms but the threat of a hostile-held shore posing a threat to the sea lane to India belatedly persuaded him to send a force to help the Egyptian Army in Eastern Sudan along the Red Sea littoral.

Before an expeditionary force of some 4,000 men assembled at Port Said could reach the war zone, another British-led Egyptian force had been completely routed at El Teb on 4 February 1884. The expeditionary force, under the command of Major General Gerald Graham VC, sailed to Suakin on the Red Sea coast and then on to Trinkatat, where Rear Admiral William Hewett VC was in overall command of naval forces.

ARTHUR KNYVET WILSON VC (1842-1921)

It was almost inevitable that young Arthur Wilson would become a Victorian hero. Born on 4 March, 1842 at Swaffham, Norfolk, Arthur Knyvet Wilson was the third child of six to Rear Admiral George Knyvet Wilson and Agnes Mary (née Younger).

Young Arthur had several naval officers as relatives and ancestors – including Henry Keppel and Horatio Nelson. His uncle was Major General Sir Archdale Wilson, who commanded the Delhi Field Force during the Indian Mutiny.

After just two years education at Eton, the thirteen-year old sat the examination for the Navy and joined the *Victory* as Naval Cadet on 29 June 1855. Within three months, he was serving aboard the ninety-gun *Algiers* at the bombardment of the Kinburn forts in the Crimea. He briefly served under his father, who was captain of HMS *Rodney*, before transferring to *Colossus* under another relative, Captain Keppel. While berthed at Balaclava, young Arthur was sent ashore to look for a dog lost by an Army officer. When he got back to port, he found that *Colossus* had sailed without him.

Wilson's next ship was the frigate *Raleigh* with Keppel again his commander. On 15 March 1857, during the voyage to join the China Station, the ship struck a submerged rock and became a total loss. The crew were rescued safely and Arthur joined the flagship *Calcutta,* serving on her during the Second China War. Although he was barely sixteen and still a cadet, he had campaign medals for the Crimea (bar *Sebastopol)* and China (bars *Canton 1857, Taku Forts 1858*). In addition, after the capture of the Taku Forts, Arthur was Mentioned in Despatches.

He passed his professional exams and was appointed lieutenant in 1861. He showed a technical bent which was recognised early on. In 1867, Wilson was part of a small party of officers and senior ratings that was sent to Japan to set up a new school in Tokyo to train young naval cadets. The project lasted less than a year as internal troubles forced the school to close. In later years, however, no Japanese naval officer ever failed to pay his respects to Wilson as one of his Navy's earliest instructors. Wilson went directly from one instructional post to another when he was appointed to the training ship *Britannia* at Dartmouth.

In 1870, he joined a committee to investigate a new type of torpedo, thus starting his considerable expertise on the subject. After serving on several ships, he was promoted to Commander and executive officer on the newly-built steam frigate *Raleigh* under the command of a rising star in the Navy, Captain George Tryon.

In 1876, the torpedo school *Vernon* was formed and Wilson was appointed Commander. He stayed for four years producing the *Torpedo Manual*, which drew from his knowledge of this increasingly important weapon. In 1881, in recognition of this, Wilson was promoted to captain and given his first command, the new torpedo depot ship *Hecla*. The following year Wilson saw action for the first time in nearly twenty-five years, when *Hecla* was part of the fleet that bombarded into submission the defences of the Egyptian port of Alexandria on 12th July 1882. Once Alexandria fell, the Navy landed and occupied the city. Captain Wilson was given the task of destroying the guns in Fort Mex and neutralising about 100 guns in the seaward defences.

After the short-lived war against Egypt, Wilson and *Hecla* resumed their duties in the Mediterranean, which involved frequent visits to the Adriatic port of Fiume. It was here that the favoured torpedo at that time, the Whitehead, was produced at the inventor's factory in Fiume. During one of the frequent visits to the area, *Hecla* received orders to collect the marine detachments from the ships of the Mediterranean Fleet and sail for the latest flashpoint – Sudan.

VC Action

On 29 February 1884, General Graham's force advanced inland towards El Teb. Adopting a large square formation, the Naval Brigade, with their machine-guns, was at the two leading corners. *Hecla* had contributed two officers, twenty-five sailors and a Gardner machine-gun but Wilson, who had no role, went along simply as a spectator.

The march carried Graham's men over the battlefield of 4 February and the barren, sandy soil was littered with the black, decaying corpses of slain Egyptians. A further three miles brought the square within sight of earthworks thrown up by the Dervishes on which were planted the captured Krupp guns and tribal banners.

After an exchange of artillery fire, the square advanced towards the enemy, estimated to be about 10,000 strong. As they neared the earthwork, the British were peppered with musket fire. Lieutenant Royds of the Naval Brigade was mortally wounded, so Arthur Wilson volunteered to take his place.

The tribesmen attacked in dense masses and were repelled with great difficulty, leaving many dead and wounded before the square. Wilson attached himself to the right-hand battery of machine-guns which was next to men of the York and Lancaster Regiment. Some of these soldiers, thinking that the Krupp battery was abandoned, charged into the earthworks, only to re-emerged almost immediately chased by Dervish spearmen. At the same moment of confusion, the enemy rushed the corner where the sailors were dragging one of the Gardener machine-guns and threatened to overwhelm the detachment. Captain Wilson rushed forward with drawn sword to try and protect a Marine who was hard pressed.

Wilson later recalled: 'One fellow got in close to me and made a dig with his spear at the soldier on my left. He failed to reach him, and left his whole side exposed, so I had a cool prod at him. He seemed to be beastly hard, and my sword broke against his ribs.'

Despite being unarmed, Wilson continued to fight with his fists and sword-hilt. He received a slashing blow to the head, but his pith helmet took the brunt resulting in a superficial cut. Blood streamed down his face and into his beard presenting a terrifying sight. Later he attributed his VC to his appearance: 'If only I could have got a basin of water and washed my face I should have escaped notoriety.'

In danger of being blinded by his blood and weaponless, he was protected by the bayonets of the men of the York and Lancaster. After about three hours desperate fighting, the Dervishes retreated, leaving behind over 2,000 dead. British casualties amounted to thirty-five dead and 155 wounded.

Another VC, who was present, was the commander of the infantry, Major General Redvers Buller, who witnessed Wilson's action and recommended him for the Cross. This was duly gazetted on 20 May 1884. His Cross was presented to him in a special ceremony on Southsea Common witnessed by thousands. With seeming indifference, Wilson noted in his diary: '6th June. Docked ship. Received the VC.'

Fatal Error

Wilson's rise through the naval hierarchy was inexorable and he became one of the leading sailors of his day. He saw no more action but was a close witness to one of the Navy's most bizarre disasters. In 1893, while he was captain of the new battleship *Sans Pareil,* he took part in manoeuvres with the fleet off Tripoli, Lebanon. The fleet commander was Admiral Tryon, Wilson's old captain, and one of the most respected sailors of that period.

Tryon wanted to attempt a new formation that involved two lines of ships sailing parallel to each other and, at a given signal, turning inwards and sailing back the way they had come. Despite it being apparent that the distance between the two lines was too narrow, no one felt that they should question such a great seaman's order. Arthur Wilson was second in line behind *Camperdown* when she collided with Tryon's ship, *Victoria.* Tryon, together with 365 officers and men, perished. Wilson later observed that Tryon made an extraordinary stupid bungle by mixing up the radius with the diameter of the ship's turning circles.

Despite being the foremost authority and champion of the torpedo, Wilson was dead set against its perfect platform – the submarine. In fact, he called it 'a damned un-English weapon' and recommended that captured submarine crews should be hung as pirates. Arthur Wilson retired, a lifelong bachelor, as Admiral of the Fleet and First Sea Lord on 4 March 1912 after fifty-seven years in the Service.

Wilson was recalled to the Admiralty at the beginning of the First World War until he finally retired in 1918, his service adding up to more than sixty years. He attended the Royal Garden Party for VCs at Buckingham Palace in June 1920 before returning to his birthplace at Swaffham where he died a few months later, on 25 May 1921 aged seventy-nine.

ALFRED SMITH VC (1861-1932)

Alfred Smith was born in 1860 in Barking, Essex, the son of a fisherman, who died soon after his son was born. He joined his local regiment, the Royal Artillery, at nearby Woolwich across the Thames and was posted to 1st Battery, 1st Brigade, Southern Division and sent to Egypt. Here they joined the Nile Expeditionary Force sent to relieve General Gordon at Khartoum. They were equipped with the 2.5 inch RML Mountain Gun more commonly referred to as the 'Screw Gun'. They also had to get used to using camels for transport.

As the journey down the Nile progressed, information was received from Khartoum urging the Expeditionary Force to come urgently. Gordon was certain that just the appearance of a force of British soldiers would be enough for the Mahdi to call off his siege. Although the Nile provided water, the desert either side yielded few resources, which restricted the options open to General Wolseley. The Expeditionary Force reached Korti on the great southern bend in the river. If the Force continued on the river, it would be confronted with the 4th and 5th cataracts, both time-consuming obstacles to overcome.

Wolseley decided to send his Chief of Staff, Herbert Stewart, with a force of 1,400 men he dubbed the Desert Column, to cross the shortest stretch of desert to Metemmeh just above the 6th cataract and 100 miles from Khartoum, thereby cutting out the long bend of the river.

Setting out on 30 December 1884, the column consisted of four regiments of camel-mounted troops, detachments of infantry and cavalry, and the Naval Brigade manning a Gardner machine-gun. Loaded on nine camels were the Royal Artillery's three 7-pounder screw guns and 300 rounds of ammunition.

VC Action

On the afternoon of 16 January 1885, the column was approaching the wells at the rocky gorge of Abu Klea when large numbers of the enemy were spotted in the hills surrounding the wells. Stewart decided to camp and make his attack the following day. An uncomfortable night was spent behind a *zariba* (thorn barrier) with the enemy continually sniping at the camp and inflicting a number of casualties.

On the morning of 17th, the small column prepared to confront the Mahdi's force of about 10,000. Stewart formed his men into a square and started to move slowly towards Abu Klea. Gunner Smith and his comrades were on the front face with the three screw guns and the Naval Brigade's Gardner machine-gun on the left corner on the rear face. Skirmishers led the way towards the pass to the wells but the sudden appearance of the main body of the enemy from a ravine to the left front caused them to quickly retreat to the square. Their retirement masked the fire from the front of the square so that when the defenders had a clear field of fire, the Dervishes were only 200 yards away and rapidly closing.

As the screaming Dervishes charged the left front of the square, the Mounted Infantry fired a withering fusillade which diverted their charge to the left rear of the square. Instead of keeping the square intact, Captain Lord Charles Beresford ordered the Navy's Gardiner gun to be run about twenty yards outside the square so it could be operated effectively. Unfortunately, not only did the gun jam after a few rounds had been fired, but a gap had opened which the Dervishes swiftly exploited. All the Gardiner gun crew were killed, with the exception of Beresford, as the Dervishes poured through the seventy-yard gap causing great confusion amongst the dismounted heavy cavalry who manned the rear of the square.

The Scots and Grenadier Guards on the right flank of the square about turned and began firing at the Dervishes who had penetrated the square. The Dervishes found they could not advance far because of the tethered camels in the centre of the square. Although the Guards inflicted some casualties on their own side, they managed to bring down those Dervishes who had got inside the square.

In the meantime, on the leading side of the square, Gunner Alfred Smith was performing his act of gallantry. His role in the gun team was that of a striker, whose job it was to tighten the junction nut by hammering on the trunnion.

A fellow gunner, Acting Bombardier Watts, recorded Smith's action: 'Owing to a casualty occurring, I was promoted to Acting Bombardier and put in charge of the first line of ammunition camels and Gunner Smith, also a striker, took my place. When the face of the square began to crumble up it was a case of "officers to the front" and Mr Guthrie was stabbed and when Gunner Smith saw this he picked up the traversing handspike and hit the Arab who had done it over the head. The little locking stud on the handspike split his head right open and then Smith stood astride Mr Guthrie and kept the Arabs off with his handspike until the square reformed a few minutes later. I was standing within a few yards of the place and saw everything.'

Despite Smith's effort in defending Lieutenant Guthrie, the wounded Dervish managed to stab the officer in the thigh causing a mortal wound. Alfred Smith was recommended for the Victoria Cross, which was gazetted on 12 May 1865: 'At the action of Abu Klea on 17 January 188, when the enemy charged, the square fell back a short distance, leaving Lieutenant Guthrie, Royal Artillery, with his gun in a comparatively unprotected position. At this moment a native rushed at Lieutenant Guthrie with a spear, and would have in all probability have killed that officer, who had no weapon in his hand at the time (being engaged in superintending the working of his gun), when Gunner Smith, with a handspike, warded off the thrust, thus giving Lieutenant Guthrie time to draw his sword, and with a blow bring the assailant to his knees, but as the latter fell he made a wild thrust at the officer with a long knife, which Gunner Smith again warded off, not, however, before the native had managed to inflict a wound in Lieutenant Guthrie's thigh. Before the Soudani could repeat the thrust, Gunner Smith killed him with the handspike, and thus for a time saved the life of his officer, though the latter unfortunately died some days afterwards of his wound.'

Gunner Smith received his Cross from GOC Egypt, General Sir F.C.A. Stephenson, on 3 August 1885.

The fierce action lasted no more than ten minutes. Despite its brevity, 1,100 Dervish bodies were counted in or near the square. The British lost nine officers and sixty-five men killed, and nine officers and eighty-five men wounded. Two officers later died, including Lieutenant Guthrie.

Alfred Smith was discharged on 4 December 1889 and the 1891 Census shows that he was working as a furnace stoker and labourer, probably at the

Woolwich Arsenal for a later census shows him as a works driver at the Gun Factory. He had married Elizabeth after his discharge and fathered four children. He died at his home in Plumstead on 6 January 1932 and was buried at Wych Hill Cemetery, Plumstead. His gravestone contains the lines written by W. Stubbs about Colonel Bunaby, who was killed at Abu Klea:

Come listen to my story lads
There's news from overseas
The Camel Corps have held their own
And gained a victory
Weep not my boys for those who fell
They did not flinch or fear
They stood their ground like Englishmen
And died at Abu Klea

Having secured the water at the Abu Klea wells, the Desert Column moved on. Its progress was hampered by constant sniping, which caused several casualties including the mortal wounding of Lieutenant Colonel Herbert Stewart who was forced to hand over command to Major General Sir Charles Wilson. After another battle at the village of Abu Kru, the column reached the Nile. Selecting two steamers, Wilson prepared to sail to Khartoum in the hope that Charles Gordon had managed to hold out.

On the morning of 28 January 1885, Khartoum was sighted but it soon became apparent that the city was in the hands of the Mahdists and Gordon's long defence had been ended. When the news reached Britain, it was received with great dismay and much of the blame was heaped on Prime Minister Gladstone, whose administration was defeated in the June 1885 election. Ironically, the Mahdi died of typhus in June that year.

Chapter 27

Third Burma War, 1885–93

Number of VCs awarded	3
Number of VCs awarded to officers	3
Total awarded to British Army	2
Total awarded to British Indian Army	1

Origins of the War

The Third Burma War was the result of secret negotiations between King Thibaw and the French. The British reaction was similar to that which precipitated the Third Afghan War when the Russians made overtures to the Afghan king. Ultimatums were sent to Thibaw demanding that a permanent British Resident should be installed and have control of Burmese affairs. This may appear to be the height of arrogance but it was the way the great powers strove to outbid each other to safeguard their interests. In Britain's case, it was India that required neutral neighbours.

King Thibaw attempted to gain support and aid from France, whose forces were stationed in adjoining Indochina, in the hope that this would deter the British from invading his country. But by the time the Franco-Burmese Convention was ratified in November 1885, the British had already assembled an intervention force of some 10,000 men in India.

The Burmese were entirely unprepared when the force commanded by General Sir Harry Prendergast VC landed at Rangoon between 5 and 14 November and advanced to Mandalay. King Thibaw, who had most of his family put to death, was made a prisoner and exiled to India. With no effective government, the population resorted to banditry and acts of anti-British violence.

The British Government, preoccupied with the 'Irish Question', failed to provide Prendergast with the resources he needed to pacify the whole of Burma, and his men were occupied as policemen in suppressing the bands of dacoits (armed robbers) that roamed the country. Some of these bands were like small armies hiding out in the jungle and difficult to engage. The situation gradually improved with the recruitment of locals into the Burma Police and system of constant flying columns and patrols which pushed the dacoits further north deeper into the jungle-covered mountains of the Shan States and the Chin Hills.

It was during these expeditions that two Victoria Crosses were awarded, both to medical men; Ferdinand Simeon Le Quesne of the Army Medical Service and John Crimmin of the Bombay Medical Service.

JOHN CRIMMIN VC (1859-1945)

John Crimmin was born 19 March 1859 in Dublin and trained to be a doctor, gaining his LRPC, LRCS and DPH (Ireland). He joined the Indian Medical Service in 1882 and was appointed Regimental Surgeon to the 4th Bombay Infantry. In 1885, he transferred to 26th (1st Belooch Battalion) Bombay Light Infantry and sent to Burma.

Crimmin was Senior Medical Officer with the Northern Column of the Karene Field Force operating against the warring Chief of Eastern Karenni, one of the Shan States, who had refused to submit. The 400-strong Northern Column consisted of two mountain guns and a mixture of mounted infantry and infantry drawn from the Rifle Brigade and the 27th Bombay Light Infantry.

VC Action

The column set off on 29 December 1888 and engaged the Karens on New Year's Day at the village of Ngakyaing, near Lwekaw. When the column's scouts were fired upon, Lieutenant Tighe of the 27th Bombay Light Infantry led a charge with the Mounted Infantry despite the ground being unsuitable for cavalry. Crimmin's citation appeared in *The London Gazette* on 17 September 1889 and describes the action that followed:

'Lieutenant Tighe, 27th Bombay Infantry, (to the mounted infantry of which corps Surgeon Crimmin was attached), states that in the action near Lwekaw, Eastern Karenni, on the 1st January, 1889, four men charged with him into the midst of a large body of the enemy who were moving off from the Karen left flank, and two men fell to the ground wounded. He saw Surgeon Crimmin attending to one of the men about 200 yards to the rear. Karens were round the party in every direction, and he saw several fire at Surgeon Crimmin and the wounded man.

'A Sepoy then galloped up to Surgeon Crimmin, and the latter joined in the fighting line, which then came up. Lieutenant Tighe further states that very shortly afterwards they were engaged in driving the enemy from small clumps of trees and bamboo, in which the Karens took shelter. Near one of these he saw Surgeon Crimmin attending a wounded man. Several Karens rushed out at him. Surgeon Crimmin thrust his sword through one of them and attacked a second; a third Karen then dropped from the fire of a Sepoy, upon which the remaining Karens fled.'

The column inflicted at least 150 casualties for the loss of four killed and eight wounded. Surgeon Crimmin received his VC from the Duke of Connaught, the Commander in Chief Bombay, later in 1889.

On his return to India, he acted as both a civil and military surgeon at various postings. He rose to become the Health Officer of the Port of Bombay in 1900 and was promoted to colonel on 1 October 1913. On 18 February 1916, he became Honorary Physician to King George V and retired in 1919. He returned to England and died at his home in Wells, Somerset on 2 February 1945.

By 1892, Britain's sheer weight of numbers and superior firepower brought the fighting to a close. There were still occasional flare ups but this involved mostly banditry by the Kachin tribe who attacked and plundered caravans travelling through the region and preying upon travellers.

A final Victoria Cross was awarded for this long campaign fought in some of the remotest parts of the Empire. On 6 January 1893, Surgeon Owen Pennefather Lloyd of the Army Medical Service performed his act of gallantry during an attack on a military police post in the Kachin Hills.

Chapter 28

Manipur Expedition, 1891

Number of VCs awarded	1
Number of VCs awarded to officers	1
Total awarded to British Indian Army	1

Origins of the War

The small hill state of Manipur situated between Burma and Assam was cut off from India by steep jungle-clad mountains and fast flowing rivers. After the death of Maharaja Chandrakirti Singh, his eldest son Surchandra succeeded as Raja of Manipur in 1886. With his succession, the royal family became divided into two factions with Surchandra's brothers continuing a festering resentment which manifested itself in a palace revolt on 21 September 1890.

The ousted Raja travelled to Calcutta and appealed for help from the British Government. Seeing an opportunity to control Manipur and secure the Indian border with Burma, the British threw their support behind Surchandra.

The usurper was Jubaraj Kullachandra, but the brain behind the coup was Senapati Tikendrajit. Lord Lansdowne, the Viceroy instructed James Wallace Quinton, the Chief Commissioner of Assam, to travel to Manipur and demand the reinstatement of Surchandra, the natural successor. Accompanied by an escort of Gurkhas under the command of Lieutenant Colonel Charles Skene, Quinton travelled to the Imphal, the capital and arrived on 24 March 1891. After being welcomed with guard of honour by the royal troops, Quinton attempted to arrest Tikendrajit but Skene's small force was driven off by the Manipur army and retired to the British Residency. After several hours, it was clear that the Residency could not be held much longer. Quinton then sent a letter requesting a meeting to arrange an armistice.

James Quinton, his Assistant Secretary, Lieutenant Cossine, Frank St Clair Grimwood, the political agent in Manipur, Colonel Skene and a bugler were accompanied to the palace, where they met with Tikendrajit and his general for a parley. After an exchange of pleasantries, the mood changed and the British were seized. On the orders of Tikendrajit and General Thangal, the men were dragged outside and publicly beheaded by the public executioner in front of the two dragon statues which stood outside the palace. This was a signal to attack all British outposts in Manipur resulting in more British deaths.

Frank Grimwood's wife, Ethel, was staying in the Residency, which was little more than a thatched bungalow, when it was attacked. With the help of several Gurkhas, she managed to escape through the surrounding jungle and reached Assam.

On 27 March, news of the executions reached the Burmese station of Tammu close to the border, and a junior officer took it upon himself to launch a relief expedition for which he was awarded the Victoria Cross.

CHARLES JAMES WILLIAM GRANT VC (1861-1932)

Charles James William Grant was born on 14 October 1861 at Bourtie, Aberdeenshire, the son of Lieutenant General P.C.S. St. J. Grant and Helen (née Birset). He was privately educated and entered the Royal Military College Sandhurst from where he was commissioned in the Suffolk Regiment on 10 May 1882 before being appointed to the Madras Staff Corps on 21 May 1885.

Grant took part in the Burma War and was appointed Wing Officer in the 12th Madras Regiment, which was later re-titled the 2nd Burma Battalion. It was in this capacity that he was serving on the Indian border at Tammu with a detachment of fifty troops when he learned of the dreadful events at Manipur. He telegraphed for permission to attempt a rescue the besieged British party at Imphal. Just before he left, he was joined by thirty-two Gurkhas who had escaped from near Imphal and joined Grant in his rescue bid.

VC Action

Grant and his mixed command left early the following morning to cover the forty miles. They were soon confronted by the Manipur army, which they forced to retreat. On the 30th, they reached Thobal about fifteen miles from the capital. Here they found the river bank occupied with about 800-1,000 enemy troops stretched in a front about one and half miles wide. The attack was made more difficult as Grant's men had to cross the Thorbal River under fire. Fixing bayonets, Grant led his men in a charge which dislodged the Manipuris who retreated into the jungle. Grant was slightly wounded and decided to remain in a nearby village, which he set about building a stout defensive position.

The first attack began on the 31 March and continued until 9 April. Grant and his men held off all attempts to take the town despite the Manipur army swelling its ranks to 2,000 and bringing in artillery. Finally, he was ordered to withdraw, which was successfully done and he returned to Tammu. This minor against-the-odds defence earned all fifty men of the 2nd Burma Battalion and the thirty-one Gurkhas the Indian Order of Merit, 3rd Class; the largest number ever awarded for a single action. The Gurkha officer received the Order of British India.

Lieutenant Grant was recommended for the Victoria Cross, which was gazetted on 26 May 1891. He received the medal from Lord Wenlock, the Governor of Madras on 6 July 1891. He was also promoted to captain on 10 May 1891 and made up to brevet major the following day. The following month he was appointed ADC to the C-in-C Madras. He was granted a four-year leave and returned to command a Wing (half battalion) of 32nd Burma Infantry. He was promoted to Commandant of 89th Punjabis in 1906, and finished his career as Colonel of the 92nd Punjabis in 1911. With the outbreak of the Great War, he joined the 3rd Royal Scots.

Grant retired at the end of the war. He died at Sidmouth on 23 November 1932.

It was clear that a much larger force would be needed to defeat the Manipuris and at the end of April, three columns led by Brigadier General Thomas Graham set out separately at different start dates to arrive at Imphal on the same day. The only column to meet with opposition was Graham's Tammu Column. In a fierce hand-to-hand fight at Bapam, the Manipuris finally gave way for the loss of two Gurkhas and another thirteen wounded. The three columns met up at Imphal on the 27th and the brief conflict was over.

The men involved in the brutal executions were rounded up and put of trial. A Special Court which included Major Richard Ridgeway VC, found the men guilty. Jubraj Tikendrajit and General Thangal were publicly hanged and three other hanged in prison. Twenty-two others, including Jubaraj Kullachandra, were transported for life. The result was that Manipur was absorbed into the British Raj

Chapter 29

Hunza-Nagar Expedition, 1891

Number of VCs awarded	3
Number of VCs awarded to officers	3
Total awarded to British Army	1
Total awarded to British India Army	2

Origins of the War

The Hunza River runs ninety miles east and then south from the Karakorum Mountains to Gilgit where it joins the 150-mile-long Gilgit River which flows into the 1,900-mile-long River Indus. In 1891 the area was sensitive for it was where Afghanistan met the British, Russian and Chinese empires.

Hunza is on the River Hunza's west bank, with Nagar on its east bank. In 1891 Hunza was ruled by its Thum, Safdar Ali Khan, who had taken power in 1886 by killing his father and two brothers. The father had some years earlier taken power by killing his own father. Though Nagar was officially ruled by Thum Zafar Khan, it was, in reality, governed by his son, Rajah Uzr Khan, who had murdered two of his brothers to usurp power early in 1891.

The Hunzas and Nagaris, who together were often called Kanjutis, lived by agriculture, caravan raiding and kidnapping people to be sold as slaves in Chinese Turkestan or Kyrgyzstan. They often fought each other but would unite against foreign invaders. A small annual tribute was paid to the Maharajah of Kashmir, who had nominal control.

The British found the high mountains flanking the Hunza Valley practically impassable not least because the height caused altitude sickness. The only feasible invasion route was from Gilgit up the Hunza Valley. This was only practical at certain seasons, for melting summer snow turned the river into a raging torrent and the thick snow and cold of a Karakorum winter rendered campaigning nigh impossible. Historically any invading force faced a daunting task; a Sikh invasion force had been wiped out in 1848 and a Kashmiri Dogra invasion force heavily defeated in 1866.

Colonel Algernon George Arnold Durand, the British Agent at Gilgit, backed up by his brother Sir Henry Mortimer Durand, the Foreign Secretary of the Indian Government, had forced the Hunza-Nagar Thums to sign a treaty giving up caravan and slave raiding in 1889. This was soon broken and in 1891 it was decided to annex them. An ultimatum demanding surrender was rejected by the Thum of Hunza who threatened to cut Colonel Durand's head off and send it to the Indian government. The British had also become alarmed at the increasing Russian influence in the area which was part of the shadowy Great Game played out by both countries in the border lands.

Colonel Durand and fifteen other British officers assembled a force at Chalt on the lower Hunza River near Gilgit in November 1891. It contained 188 Gurkhas, twenty-eight Punjabi Infantry, a mountain battery, eight Bengal Sappers, 661 Kashmiri Imperial Service troops, 200 armed Pathan navvies, and some Puniali levies, about 1,000 fighting men in all. They had two 7-pound artillery pieces and a Gatling gun. Two thousand Balti coolies carried supplies. The all-native rank and file was almost entirely acclimatised to the thin mountain air.

Colonel Durand's force marched out of Chalt up the Hunza Valley on 1 December 1891. This was late in the year for such a march but it had taken longer than expected to gather troops and supplies. At first the only obstacles were natural and were quickly overcome by the Sappers who built a temporary road up the valley and temporary bridges across the Hunza. On 2 December 1891, having marched thirty miles the force reached the fortress at Nilt, some 7,500 feet above sea level. The short, sharp campaign that followed was sometimes called the War on the Roof of the World and saw the awarding of three Victoria Crosses.

Edward Frederick Knight, *The Times*' war correspondent, accompanied the force, having been emergency commissioned an Indian Army officer to regularise his status. In a report in *The Times* of 21 April 1892, Knight graphically described the attack on Nilt Fort:

'The strip of cultivated land along which we had been advancing narrowed considerably as we reached Nilt. This fortress was a very formidable place indeed. As is the case in all Kanjut villages, the villagers live within the fort itself, which is a very rabbit warren of strongly built stone houses two or three storeys high in places with narrow alleys between, the whole enclosed within a great wall carefully built of stones and strengthened with massive timbers. This wall is 15 feet to 20 feet in height and is 12 feet thick in most places, with large square towers at intervals. The flat roofs of this fortified village are covered with stones, and are so well constructed that they were proof against our shell when dropped upon them, while guns of very much heavier calibre than ours would have failed to make any impression on the great wall, the loopholes of which, again, are very small and offered little mark to our riflemen. The garrison of Nilt was, indeed, practically secure from any ordinary mode of attack.

'Another wall about 8 feet high and also loop-holed for musketry surrounds the main wall, and from here the ground falls away precipitously on all sides, save at one point where there is the narrow approach to the chief gate. A steep watercourse serves as a trench to that side of the fort which faced us as we approached, and here the enemy had placed a strong abattis of branches to oppose us. In all their preparations, the Kanjutis exhibited considerable foresight and skill, and there can be no doubt that they had with them leaders of no mean military ability.

'And now it will be understood that our men had no light task before them, for it was absolutely necessary to capture this strongly defended place – which the Thum had flattered himself he could hold against us for a year and more – in the course of a few hours. We had to effect this or retire, for it was discovered that the enemy had cut off the water source which irrigates the cultivated terraces, while the bed or the river was an absolutely untenable position. In short, Nilt had to be captured before our men could satisfy their thirst.

'Admirably had Colonel Durand made his arrangements for this attack, which was well considered, wisely bold, and well calculated to inspire a wholesome terror in an enemy who are stubborn enough behind stone walls, but to whom the style of fighting they were to witness this afternoon was an entirely new experience. The difficulties of the road had delayed us a good deal so that it was not until one o'clock in the afternoon that we came in front of the fort. So strategically situated is it, covered by a projecting spur of the mountain, that it is impossible to open fire on it until one is almost right under it, at a distance of 200 yards or so. It was consequently necessary to bring the guns into position at this distance from the fort, an almost unexampled proceeding; but it would have occupied the best part of six months to seize such a place as Nilt had our officers felt bound to follow the hard and fast rules of warfare. At this short range and quite exposed to the musketry fire of the enemy, which was at once directed on this spot, Lieutenant Gorton, with his two guns, opened fire on the fort with shrapnel and shell.

'The 5th Gurkhas, under Lieutenants Boisragon and Badcock, led the attack. In consequence of the broken nature of the ground they had to advance section after section, and, availing themselves of what cover there was, opened a brisk fire at short range on the loop-holes of the fort and on the defenders whenever they showed themselves above the parapet, which was not often. The Kanjuts had judiciously cut down the fruit trees in the vicinity of the fort so that these should not afford us cover. In the meanwhile, the Punialis under Lieutenant Manners Smith had swarmed up a height overlooking the fort, and were firing into it from above.

'The enemy's fire was very well directed, and it is certain that they had excellent marksmen amongst them, – even at long ranges – as we afterwards discovered. They had many arms of precision – Russian Berdan rifles, Martini-Henrys, Sniders, Winchesters and Spencers, in addition to their long home-made matchlocks, and they knew how to use them. Our loss in the course of this assault would have been exceedingly heavy had it not been for one fortunate circumstance. The Kanjuts had erred on the side of caution and had made their loopholes so small that though they effectually protected their bodies they hampered their fire considerably, and indeed, from some of the loop-holes a musket could only be directed on a certain spot, the range of which had, no doubt, been previously ascertained. The loop-holes again were limited in number and thus the enemy's fire was luckily of a somewhat intermittent nature.

'We were thus engaged for nearly an hour, the men within the fort being so well sheltered that it is doubtful whether more than two or three of them had been hit, whereas on our side there had been numerous casualties. Our two guns appeared to produce no practical effect, even when brought to bear on the towers, which are not nearly so strongly constructed as the wall. However, some of the more timid of the garrison soon began to escape from the fort at the back of it, one man at a time scrambling down the river bed from rock to rock. Many of these were picked off by our men, and also by the Gatling Gun which had been brought into position by Lieutenant Moloney, while the handful of 20th Punjab Infantry men, led by Captains Colin Mackenzie and Twigg, having accompanied the Punialis over the hill, descended to the trench of the fort itself on its further side, where they not only fired into the loop-holes at a few yards' range, but did great execution among the Kanjuts who were escaping into the *nullah* behind.

'The best marksmen among the enemy had been told off to fire at the British officers, of whom there could not have been one who did not have some narrow escape on that day. Lieutenant Moloney, for instance, while in the act of stooping to lay his Gatling, had his helmet shot through by a bullet which just grazed the top of his head. Unfortunately three of our officers were severely wounded, Colonel Durand himself receiving a very serious wound in the groin with a jezail bullet – a garnet enclosed in lead – and his command now devolved on Captain Bradshaw.

'Just before he was hit Colonel Durand had given the order that the fort should be taken by assault. How this was done will be long remembered as one of the most gallant things recorded in Indian warfare. It being impossible to break through in any other fashion, it was now the business of our engineer, Captain Aylmer, to blow up the gates of the fort so as to admit the storming party. First our guns and rifles opened a very heavy fire upon the fort under cover of which 100 of the 5th Gurkhas, led by Lieutenants Boisragon and Badcock, made a rush at the outer wall and began to cut their way through the abattis with their kukris, the garrison the while firing steadily into them.

'A small opening having been thus made, the three officers, closely followed by about half a dozen men, pushed their way through it. They then made for the wooden gate of the outer wall which they soon hacked to pieces. They now found themselves in front of the main wall, and while his companions fired into the loop-holes – the officers using their revolvers – Captain Aylmer, accompanied by his Pathan orderly, rushed forward to the foot of the main gate, which was strongly built and had been barricaded within with stones, in anticipation of our coming.

'The enemy now concentrated their fire upon this gallant little band, and it is marvellous that any escaped death. Captain Aylmer placed his slabs of guncotton at the foot of the gate, packed them with stones and ignited the fuse, all the while being exposed to the fire from the towers which flanked the gate, as well as from some loop-holes in the gate itself. He and his orderly then followed the wall of the fort to a safe distance and stood there awaiting the explosion. But there came no explosion, for the fuse was a faulty one, so Captain Aylmer had once more to face an almost certain death. He returned to the gate, readjusted the fuse, cut it with his knife, lit a match and re-ignited the fuse.

'This time a terrific explosion followed, and at once, before even the dust had cleared, or the stones had ceased dropping from the crumbling wall, the three British officers, with the six men at their back, clambered through the breach and were within Nilt Fort. Enveloped in dense smoke and dust, their comrades, who had been cutting their way through the abattis, could not find the breach; indeed they did not realise that one had been effected and that their officers were within the gates; so for many minutes that little handful of gallant Englishmen and Gurkhas was engaged in a hand to hand fight with the garrison in the narrow alley leading from the gate. Having gained this position, they held it resolutely, but it was obvious that not one of them would be left alive unless they were soon supported.

'Accordingly Lieutenant Boisragon went outside the gate once more to find his men, and thus exposed himself to the fire of both friend and foe. In a very short time he was back again at the head of a number of little Gurkhas eager to avenge the comrades they had lost. The Gurkhas poured into the narrow alleys of the fort and fought as they always do fight. The Kanjuts defended themselves like fanatical dervishes at first, but soon lost heart before the fierce attack.

'While this was going on a fire was still kept up from the loop-holes on our supports, the detachment of the Raghu Partab Regiment (Imperial Service) which now came up led by Lieutenant Townshend. The fort was soon swarming with our men, who hunted the Kanjuts through the intricate alleys and holes. The Wazir of Nagar himself was killed, but the principal leaders escaped, as did most of the garrison, who, availing themselves of their knowledge of the maze which was their home, found their way to a small gate opening on to a steep *nullah* behind the fort.

'Thus was Nilt Fort taken after a daring rush which perhaps has not had its equal since Umbeyla. As is so often the case, the boldest course of action here proved to be the safest; our total loss was only 24 wounded and five killed – a number of which would have been much exceeded had what some might consider a more prudent course of action been adopted. The loss of the enemy was uncertain. At least 50 must have been killed. Of the gallant handful of men who followed the three officers through the trench, two were killed and nearly all were wounded. Captain Badcock was severely wounded, and Captain Aylmer received no fewer than three severe wounds while blowing up the gate, which may be considered as a very lucky escape when one remembers what he did. These three officers were all recommended for the Victoria Cross, which they so well deserved. Captain Aylmer has obtained it.'

FENTON JOHN AYLMER VC (1862-1935)

Fenton John Aylmer was born at Hastings on 5 April 1862, the third son of Captain Fenton John Aylmer of the Northumberland Light Infantry Militia. His father had fought in the Crimea War in the 97th Regiment and contracted a sickness that killed him in 1862 when his third son was just four days' old. His mother brought him up and he was educated privately before attending the Royal Military Academy at Woolwich. He was an outstanding cadet and attained second place in his exams. He was commissioned in the Royal Engineers on 27 July 1880 and saw his first active service in Burma in 1886.

Promoted to captain, Aylmer was attached to the Bengal Sapper and Miners for the Black Mountain Campaign of March 1891 and it was during this time that he became acclimatised to the high Himalayan altitudes. It was during the attack on the fort at Nilt on 2 December 1891 that Aylmer performed his act of gallantry in blowing the main gate. Recommended for the Victoria Cross, his citation appeared in *The London Gazette* of 12 July 1892 and he was invested on 28 October by the GOC Rawlpindi.

The 12 July 1892 *Gazette* citation to Aylmer reads: 'For his conspicuous bravery in the assault and capture of the Nilt Fort on 2 December 1891. This officer accompanied the storming party, burst open the inner gate with gun-cotton, which he placed and ignited, and though severely wounded, once in the leg and twice in the right hand, fired nineteen shots with his revolver, killing several of the enemy, and remained fighting, until fainting from loss of blood he was carried out of action.'

Captain Aylmer remained on the North-West Frontier and took part in the Isazai Campaign in 1892 and the Relief of Chitral in 1895. During the latter campaign, Aylmer distinguished himself by constructing a suspension bridge over the swollen Ranjkora River. The original bridge had been swept away by debris washed down by the floodwaters leaving the Guides Infantry stranded and under fire from the Chitalis on the far bank. Aylmer and his men built the bridge in record time between 14 and 16 April and relieve the stranded Sikhs.

He gradually climbed the promotion ladder until he was promoted to major general in 1909, and from 1912 to 1915, he acted as Adjutant General in India until promoted to lieutenant general in 1916. He was given command of the Tigris Corps for the relief of Kut from 6 January to April 1916. He received the KCB the same year and commanded the Mhow Division from 4 May 1916 to 1 June 1917. He retired on 24 February 1919 and died at his home in Wimbledon on 3 September 1935.

Colonel Durand and the other wounded returned to Gilgit and Captain (later Major General) Laurence Julius Elliott Bradshaw of the Indian Staff Corps took command. On 3 December, he resumed the advance up the Hunza Valley but this was quickly checked by fierce resistance from breastworks and Thol fort behind the Nilt Nullah – a gorge that carries a tributary of the Hunza River. The enemy's flanks were covered by the river and the mountains. On the other side of the river another tributary flowed through another deep gorge and it was defended by a strong fort at Mauin.

Several attacks on the Nilt Nullah failed. Eventually Nagdu, a Kashmiri Dogra in the British service, climbed the mountain flanking the enemy positions and discovered a weak point in the defences. Captain Bradshaw had returned to Gilgit to consult with Colonel Durand but Captain Colin John Mackenzie took command and made another attempt to take this most difficult stronghold. In doing so, another Victoria Cross was won.

JOHN MANNERS SMITH VC (1864-1920)

On 30 August 1864, a fifth son was born in Lahore to Surgeon General (I.M.S.) Charles Manners Smith. Named just plain John Smith he was given his father's middle name and in some sources he is referred to as 'Manners-Smith'. He was sent to be educated in England, and attended Trinity College, Stratford-upon-Avon, King Edward VI School, Norwich, and the RMC Sandhurst. Smith was commissioned in the Norfolk Regiment on 10 March 1883 and appointed to the Indian Staff Corps on 25 March 1885 as a lieutenant in 3rd Sikh Infantry and later the 5th Gurkhas. In 1887, he joined the Political Department of the Indian Foreign Office and accompanied Sir Mortimer Durand on his missions to Sikkim and Afghanistan.

VC Action

During the second phase of the Hunza-Nagar Expedition, Lieutenant Smith performed his daring feat in the attack on the precipitous fortress of Thol.

On the night of 19/20 December 1891, Smith, with fifty Gurkhas and a reserve of fifty Dogras from the 2nd Kashmir Rifles, left the camp at 22.00

hours. They stealthily crossed the valley and sheltered in the dead ground under the cliffs beneath the fort. A second detachment divided into four sections, manoeuvred to the high ground overlooking the enemy's position. By the time this was achieved, dawn was breaking. This detachment started putting the defenders under fire to keep their attention away from Smith's command as they began the perilous ascent of the 1,200-foot cliff.

At first attempt, they were forced to return to the base of the cliff as there was no practical way up. The second attempt was successful and the assault got to within sixty yards of the summit before it was discovered. The defenders, largely pinned down by the fire from the second detachment, resorted to dropping rocks and boulders on the attackers. Fortunately, an overhang protected the climbers from being hit. After four hours of climbing, Smith was the first to reach the top and with his Gurkhas, charged the sangars and entered the fort. In his citation, it mentions that Smith shot the first rebel they met. The action was over very quickly and the rebels evacuated the fort. Ten men were awarded the Indian Order of Merit and Lieutenant Smith was recommended for the Victoria Cross. There is no record of any investiture, so he may have received it through the post.

Smith continued as a 'Political' and from 1906 to 1916, was the British Resident in Nepal. He was awarded the CVO (Commander of the Victorian Order), which was bestowed on him by King George V on his visit to Nepal in 1911. His final appointment was Agent to the Governor General in Rajputana and Chief Commissioner in Ajmer-Mewara from 1917 to 1919. This was brought to a premature close when he became sick and returned to England, where he died in London on 6 January 1920.

Having driven the defenders from the fort an immediate pursuit followed. Nagar town was captured on 21 December and Hunza town the next day. The Hunza Thum, Safdar Ali Khan, fled across the mountains to China, successfully evading a pursuit force. Hunza and Nagar were declared under British protection. Nazim Khan, a half-brother of Safdar Ali Khan, was installed as the new Hunza Thum. The aged Zafar Khan was reinstated as Nagar Thum. His son Rajah Uzr Khan also escaped to China but was arrested and handed over to the British authorities and imprisoned.

Chapter 30

Chitral, 1895

Number of VCs awarded	1
Number of VCs awarded to officers	1
Total awarded to British Indian Army	1

Origins of the War

While not in strict chronological order, the following events relate to the previous campaign. The British occupation of Hunza north of Gilgit during 1891 was to prevent Russia from laying any claim to the mountainous border area which was thought to be a possible route for the invasion of India. The Great Game between the two imperial powers proceeded like a game of chess leaving the last unclaimed area of Chitral to be fought over. The Russians had already reached Hunza and Chitral territory in 1889 but had been thwarted by the British in the Hunza-Nagar Expedition.

Chitral was a small and remote mountainous area on the Russo-Chinese border and although ruled by a tribal leader, was under the protection of the Maharaja of Kashmir. In early 1895, the Chitrali leader was murdered by his uncle in what was succession of internecine killings. One of the old ruler's sons, Nizam-ul-Mulk, fled to the British at Gilgit. A small British force advanced towards Chitral which was enough to deter the usurper, Sher Afzul Khan, who retreated to Kabul. With Britain's blessing, Nizam took the throne and Lieutenant B.E.M. Gurdon, a British political agent, was installed. Nizam's reign lasted just a year when he was assassinated. Another tribal leader, Umra Khan, joined forces with Sher Afzul Khan, who had re-entered the contest, with the plan that Sher would take the throne and Umra Khan a slice of Chitral territory.

This aggressive arrangement did not suit the British and in early February 1895, Surgeon Major George Scott Robertson, the senior British officer in Gilgit, gathered a small force of native troops and marched west to Chitral to install a more acceptable ruler on the throne. As Robertson's small force moved into Chitral territory known as 'the Roof of the World', they were met by increasing hostility and took refuge in Chitral fort on the bank of the River Chitral. The fort was a stone, mud and timber structure, eighty-yards square with walls twenty-five feet high walls and eight feet thick. Some 543 people, including 343 fighting men commanded by five British officers, crammed into the small fort. The units were made up of the 14th Sikhs and a detachment of the Kashmiri infantry. Two 7-pounder mountain guns with eighty rounds of ammunition gave some support. There were only 300 rounds per man and supplies for only a month. The numbers of the Chitrali besiegers varies between 2,000 to 5,000 who had the advantage of firing into the fort from the surrounding mountains and the many trees that grew nearby.

The siege did not take place immediately which enabled the British to send out reconnaissance patrols to gauge the strength of the enemy. On 3 March, Sher's men occupied villages about two miles from the fort. Led by Captains Campbell and Baird, about 200 men of the Kashmiri Rifles, including Gurkhas and Dogras, rashly confronted this superior force and had great trouble in extricating themselves. It was during this fight that the only Victoria Cross for the campaign was awarded.

HARRY FREDERICK WHITCHURCH VC (1866-1907)

Harry Frederick Whitchurch was born on 26 September 1866. Accounts vary as to whether he was born in Kensington or Sandown on the Isle of Wight, his father's residence. He was educated in England, France and Germany but, choosing a medical career, he entered St Bartholomew's Hospital in 1883 and emerged fully qualified.

In 1888, he joined the Indian Army as a surgeon in the Bengal Medical Service and that same year served in the Looshai Expedition. He went on to act as surgeon in the relief of Aijal, Changsil and the Defence of Malakand in 1897, and the relief of Chakdara in 1897-98. His most notable service on the North-West Frontier was performed during the Siege of Chitral Fort.

The centre of the government in the area was the collection of hamlets called Chitral with the main structure being the Chitral Fort. Surgeon Major Robertson decided that the only defensible position was the fort on the Chitral River and his force entered it on 3 March 1895.

VC Action

That same day, Captains Campbell and Baird led a sortie of 200 men against the rebel Chitralis who occupied villages about two miles away. This was despite a warning from Lieutenant Gurdon, the British Political Officer in Chitral that they had underestimated the strength of the opposition. Many of the tribesmen were armed with breech-loading rifles and were skilled mountain fighters. Unfortunately, Campbell and Baird overestimated the competence of their own soldiers, most of who were not fully trained in the use of their firearms and fired too high.

Early in the fighting, Captain Baird was mortally wounded and Surgeon Whitchurch went to his assistance. The enemy succeeded in overrunning the British fighting-line and it was only the coming of night that saved the British from annihilation. With only a handful of Gurkhas and Kashmiris, Whitchurch found himself completely isolated. Placing Baird on a *dhoolie,* Whitchurch's small group attempted to return to the fort. Three of the four Gurkhas carrying the *dhoolie* were killed and the other severely wounded. Whitchurch then hoisted the wounded Baird on his back and continued the retreat. Unable to take a direct route, the group were forced to take a circuitous route of three miles and were exposed to enfilading fire from the enemy posted on the surrounding hills and cliffs.

Frequently, Whitchurch had to lay his burden down and to force a way over some walls held by groups of the enemy. Eventually the group reached the fort with seven surviving troops. Just as Whitchurch reached safety, a third bullet struck Baird in the head and he died the following day. Before he died he was able to tell of Whitchurch's heroic behaviour.

George Robertson later wrote in his report to the Government: 'Characteristically the dying Captain Baird urged me not to forget Whitchurch and has told me how Whitchurch had to charge walls and small *sangers* on the road. On one occasion the party was surrounded, and must have been cut to pieces, Baird says, but for splendid charge by Whitchurch who lost four of his own men in hand-to-hand fighting, but inflicted such loss on the enemy that they did not come within range of the bayonets. It is difficult to write intemperately about Whitchurch, and men who have themselves won the Victoria Cross have said that never has it been more gallantly earned than on this occasion.'

Harry Whitchurch's citation appeared in *The London Gazette* on 16 July 1895 and he received his Cross eleven days later from the Queen at Osborne House, Isle of Wight, on 27 July 1895. He was promoted to surgeon major in 1900 and in 1901 was sent to China with Admiral Seymour's Expedition to relieve the embattled Legation in Peking. He took part in the actions at Yangstan and Pertsang and was Mentioned in Despatches.

In 1907, Whitchurch was serving with the 1st Gurkha Rifles at Dharmsala in the Punjab when he contracted and died of enteric fever on 16 August.

Chitral Fort was invested on 4 March 1895. With Baird dead and Campbell badly wounded, the only officers left to Robertson were Lieutenant Gurdon, Captain Charles Townsend who became senior military officer, Lieutenant Harley of the 14th Sikhs and Surgeon Captain Whitchurch. The Kashmiri Rifles had suffered heavy casualties and the burden of the defence fell upon Harley's Sikhs.

The besiegers were able to occupy positions as close as twenty-five yards from the walls of the fort and even construct a mine under one of the towers. It was only a bayonet charge by the Sikhs that thwarted this attempt. Another boost to morale was Robertson's request that a Sikh tailor make a large Union Jack flag from scraps he found in the fort. This was flown from one of the towers as a defiant gesture to the besiegers.

Finally, on 19 April, a message was received that the Chitrali besiegers had gone. Two British columns had set out independently to relieve the Fort. Major General Robert Low's considerable column with some 15,000 men set out from Peshawar on 30 March. The first to arrive, however, was the 1,400-strong 32nd Punjab Pioneers from Gilgit commanded by Colonel James Kelly, who had left a week earlier. They had crossed 150 miles of mountains in late winter, including the 12,000-foot Shandur Pass, and had taken the Chitrali rebels by surprise. Umra Khan gave up and returned to Afghanistan while Sher Ali was captured and went into exile in India. Besides Surgeon Whitchurch's VC, George Robertson was knighted, Colonel Kelly was made ADC to the Queen and given the CB, and eleven DSOs were awarded. It was later learned that the Russians had planned to occupy Chitral if the British abandoned it.

Chapter 31

Gambia, 1892

Number of VCs awarded	1
Number of VCs awarded to other ranks	1
Total awarded to British Army	1

Origins of the War

For the British, the Gambia River in West Africa had been an unresolved irritation for some thirty years. Thirty miles wide and 200 miles long, this tiny British territory was surrounded by French Senegal. Finally, the two countries formed a Boundary Commission to agree on a definite border. This agreement did not sit well with a local chief named Fodeh Cabbah who objected to this foreign division of his tribal land.

Early in 1891, a party of the Boundary Commission was attacked by Fodeh Cabbah followers, resulting in several casualties. In July, an insufficient combined force of the Naval Brigade and the 2nd Battalion West India Regiment advanced into Fodeh Cabbah's territory. It was not enough to prevent Fodeh Cabbah and his followers escaping to French territory.

In early February 1892, the 1st Battalion West India Regiment replaced the 2nd battalion at Bathurst. The village chief of Toniataba, Suleman Santu, sent a message that he wanted to come to Bathurst to acknowledge British authority. This seemed a little unlikely as Suleman was a henchman of Fodi Cabbah. Instead, Major George Madden with a detachment of twelve soldiers travelled to Suleman's village where a Victoria Cross was won.

WILLIAM JAMES GORDON VC (1864-1922)

William James Gordon was born in Jamaica on 18 May 1864. He enlisted in the 1st Battalion West India Regiment on 9 July 1885 and was promoted to lance corporal.

In 1892, he was one of a detachment of twelve who accompanied the commanding officer, Major George Madden, eighty miles up the Gambia River to escort Suleman Santu back to Bathurst. The West Indians arrived at the stockaded village of Toniataba, where there appeared to be no armed Africans in sight. The entrance gates were barred and the soldiers found a beam that they used as a battering ram.

Lance Corporal Gordon's action was well described in his citation dated 9 December 1892: 'During the attack on the town of Toniataba, Major G.C. Madden, West India Regiment, who was in command of the troops, was superintending a party of twelve men who were endeavouring with a heavy beam to break down the south gate of the town, when suddenly a number of musket muzzles were projected through a double row of loop-holes which had been masked. Some of these were within two or three yards of that Officer's back, and before he realised what had happened Lance Corporal Gordon threw himself between Major Madden and the muskets, pushing the officer out of the way, and exclaiming "Look out, Sir!" At the same moment Lance Corporal Gordon was shot through the lungs.'

Major Madden and his men withdrew to Bathurst with their badly wounded comrade. Gordon was recommended for the Victoria Cross, which was presented to him in late 1892. Unfortunately, it was stolen soon after and Gordon was sent a replacement. He attained the rank of sergeant until his wound forced his retirement from the Army in 1902.

Gordon returned to Jamaica and joined the Kingston Militia. He was re-employed by his old regiment at their recruiting depot and spent his final years in charge of an army firing range, where he lived in a grace and favour house. He died on 15 August 1922.

Toniataba was attacked by a much larger British force and burnt to the ground but unrest continued for another ten years. Finally, Fodi Cabbah and his followers were caught in the town of Madina in French Senegal. After a three-hour bombardment, the French stormed the town and killed Fodeh Cabbah and 150 of his men.

Chapter 32

Rhodesia, 1896

Number of VCs awarded	3
Number of VCs awarded to officers	1
Number of VCs awarded to other ranks	2
Total awarded to Imperial forces	3

Origins of the War

Queen Victoria signed a royal charter in 1889 which gave its blessing for the British South Africa Company (BSAC) to administer the territory stretching from the rivers Limpopo to the Zambezi.

This organisation was modelled on the lines of the old British East India Company and its driving force was Cecil Rhodes, Prime Minister of the Cape Colony, who planned that the BSAC would promote colonisation and economic exploitation across what soon became known as Rhodesia. He also hoped that Portugal could be persuaded by money or force to hand-over Portuguese East Africa and that the Transvaal would return to British control. Like the HEIC, the BSAC formed a paramilitary, mounted infantry force which evolved into the British South African Company Police.

In 1890, the famous scout and big game hunter Frederick Selous led the first group of settlers through Matabeleland and into Shona territory to establish Fort Salisbury. The Matabele chieftain, Lobengula, wished to avoid clashing with the white settlers, being aware of their superior weaponry and rifle skills. The British were also happy to avoid conflict with the natives.

Having kept the peace with the British, the Matabele felt no similar compunction regarding the Shona. In late 1893, Lobengula sent a raiding party of several thousand warriors to punish a recalcitrant vassal, resulting in the destruction of many villages and many deaths. The British demanded that Lobengula withdraw immediately, which he refused to do.

A mounted force of about 700 men supported by a similar number of Bechuanas, who were allies of the British, marched on Lobengula's capital,

Bulawayo. Attacked by 3,500 warriors, the settlers responded with their Maxim guns and, according to a witness: 'mowed them down literally like grass'. Another confrontation a week later resulted in more deaths. Lobengula quitted Bulawayo, leaving it for the British to establish a new Company-run city on the ashes of the Matebele capital.

What became known as the Second Matabele War started in March 1896 and soon spread to involve the Shona tribe to the east. The Matabele spiritual leader began fomenting unrest by spreading the claim that the settlers were responsible for the drought, locust plagues and the cattle and horse disease rinderpest that was ravaging the country at that time. The timing for this call to arms was fortuitous for the Matabele as it followed the disastrous Jameson Raid on the Transvaal. The BSAC's Administrator General, Dr Leander Starr Jameson, had led most of his men and arms in the ill-fated raid in January 1896, so stripping the country of its military strength.

The rebellion soon spread with hundreds of settlers murdered and farms and mines burnt. About half of the Native Police defected to the rebels bringing with them the latest Martini-Henry and Winchester rifles. At Bulwayo, with few troops to support them, the settlers formed a laager of sandbagged wagons and spread the surrounding position with broken glass and barbed wire. Frederick Selous arrived with his wife and set about organising a mounted force of thirty-six men, the most that could be armed and horsed, and forming the nucleus of what was to be known as H Troop, Bulawayo Field Force. It was a member of this troop who was awarded the first of three Victoria Crosses for an outstandingly selfless act.

HERBERT STEPHEN HENDERSON VC (1870-1942)

Herbert Stephen Henderson was born at Hillhead, Glasgow on 30 March 1870. He came from a long-line of engineers; his grandfather was a shipbuilder and his father, William, ran the Bishop Street Engineering Works. He was educated at Kelvinside Academy and served an apprenticeship with J and J Thomson Engineers before moving to Belfast where he worked for Harland and Wolff.

Taking his engineering skills with him, Henderson left Scotland in 1892 and headed for the Rand in South Africa, working at the Langlaagte, Primrose, Croesus and the George and May Gold Mines.

In 1894, he moved to Rhodesia where he became the engineer at the Queen's Reef Mine. When the Matabele rebellion broke out, he rode from the Mine to Bulawayo armed only with a revolver and one bullet. There he joined the Bulawayo Field Force as a scout and was soon to see action. On 27 March 1896, news was received that seven settlers were besieged at Inyati Post some fifty miles north-east of Bulawayo.

A detachment of eleven rode out to try and rescue the trapped men. Picking up four more settlers on the way, the detachment came under attack and took cover at Campbell's Stores. Here they learned that the seven men at Inyati had been overwhelmed and killed. Deciding they could withstand an attack, two men were sent back to Bulawayo for reinforcements. On receipt of the request, a thirty-strong patrol immediately rode out, including Trooper Henderson.

VC Action

Riding through the night, they headed for the Queen's Reef Mine where they briefly halted. From there, Henderson and Trooper Celliers rode ahead as scouts. In the early hours of 29 March, the patrol was attacked in dense bush about five miles from Campbell's Store. The Matabele opened fire at close range and although the darkness and thick bush favoured the natives, the accurate return of fire from the patrol enabled them to fight their way out of the ambush. Finally emerging from the bush at dawn, the patrol rode across the open veldt and reached the store to the cheers of the defenders. It was only then that it was realised that Troopers Henderson and Celliers were missing.

Henderson and Celliers had been well ahead of the main body when the Matabele sprang their ambush. In the first fusillade of firing, Celliers was shot through the knee and his horse sustained five hits. Cut off from the rest of the patrol, the two troopers swung off the trail and into the dense bush, putting as much distance they could from the Matabele. After their wild gallop, Celliers' horse collapsed and died. Henderson dismounted and put his comrade on his horse and led him away from the sounds of the ambush.

In great pain from his wound and loss of blood, Celliers pleaded for Henderson to leave him. Henderson refused to listen and began the thirty-five-mile trek back to Bulawayo through rough country swarming with Matabele. For two days and nights, Henderson led his horse carrying his painfully wounded companion. They had no food except some plums Henderson found along the way. They had a narrow escape when they hid up for the night close to a Matabele camp. Finally, on the morning of 31 March, an exhausted Henderson led his horse and comrade into Bulawayo and safety. Celliers survived the ordeal until 16 May when he succumbed to blood poisoning when his leg was amputated.

The patrol's commander, Captain MacFarlane, and ex-officer of the 9th Queens Royal Lancers, wrote a letter recommending Henderson for the Victoria Cross. The award was granted and gazetted on 7 May 1897, the first to a Rhodesian VC and one not under British military command. Trooper Herbert Henderson received his Cross from Lord Milner at the opening of the Bulawayo Railway on 4 November 1897.

Henderson returned to the mining industry and became a timber contractor for the Globe and Phoenix goldmines. He later prospected for the German Administration in South West Africa. At the start of the First World War, Henderson volunteered for service but was refused as his engineering skills were regarded as essential for the country's gold mining industry. After the war, he married and had two sons. On 10 August 1942, he died of a duodenal ulcer and buried in Bulawayo Cemetery. His Victoria Cross is displayed by the National Army Museum in London.

By mid-summer, the war in Matabeleland was effectively over and the Bulawayo Field Force was disbanded on 4 July 1896. However, in neighbouring Mashonaland, the territory of the Shona people, a new war was just beginning.

In June, the Shona rebelled and killed more than 120 settlers. Egged on by their spiritual leaders, they were persuaded that they would be impervious to the white-man's bullets. The district was alarmingly under-protected, as its police had been lost on the Jameson Raid and most of the available fighting men were still absent, having been involved in the Matebeleland uprising.

In one of the first actions of this short conflict a Victoria Cross was awarded for a most thrilling rescue that was reminiscent of an American Western.

RANDOLPH COSBY NESBITT VC (1867-1956)

Born at Queenstown, Cape Colony on 20 September 1867, Randolph Cosby Nesbitt was educated at Dale College, King William's Town and then sent to England where he completed his studies at St Paul's School in London. His father, grandfather, grandmother and uncle had journeyed to South Africa on the ill-fated *Birkenhead,* and survived when the ship founded on rocks off Danger Point in Simon's Bay in 1852. His father was Major Charles Nesbitt and Randolph and his brother, Charles, followed him into the service when they joined the Cape Mounted Rifles.

Both brothers then joined the British South Africa Company Police, moving north to what became Rhodesia. They took part in the Occupation of Mashonaland Expedition of 1890. Randolph was commissioned later that year but resigned to take up the position of Chief Constable at Fort Pedie in the Cape. When the Matebele War of 1893 broke out, Randoph returned to Mashonaland and tried, without success, to become involved in the conflict. He was appointed a Sub-Inspector (Lieutenant) in the Mashonaland Mounted Police and sent as Acting Commandant to command the Umtali District. On 1 June 1895, he was promoted to Inspector (captain) and was stationed at Salisbury in June the following year when the natives of Mashonaland rebelled.

On 17 June, hearing that Norton's Farm was being attacked, Nesbitt took seven men but arrived only to bury the dead. Two days later began a series of events that were to win him the Victoria Cross.

VC Action

On 17th, the surviving residents of the Mazoe Valley assembled at the Alice Mine for protection. The mine manager, J.W. Salthouse, managed to send a telegraph message to Salisbury asking for help as the rebellious Mashona had cut off any hope of retreat.

The message was received by Dan Judson, the Inspector of Telegraphs. He immediately organised a seven-strong party to ride to the mine. This they managed to do after encountering much opposition. Unable to bring away the Alice Mine civilians, Judson and his band were themselves besieged. Unable to use the telegraph, Judson wrote a message and gave it to Native Constable Hendricks to try to reach Salisbury to get help.

The letter read: 'Sir, I beg to inform you that I arrived here about 1.30pm, having literally fought our way through nearly whole of Mazoe Valley. Lost two horses killed and Trooper Niebuhr badly wounded and Pollett slightly (both these men's horses were shot and they consequently rode behind riders of two other horses). In this respect I would mention Trooper C. Hendricks, who picked up Pollett and carried him nearly five miles. I sent back early in the day Troopers Finch, Guyon, King and Mullaney with three horses (knocked up).

'Mr Salthouse in charge here reports Messs. Blakiston, Routledge, Dickinson, Cass and Faull killed. Since my arrival, we have had natives firing at us from distances varying from 200 to 1500 yards, and there is no doubt we are all in a critical position as ammunition is rapidly running out. We have also absolutely no shelter for ladies and they have to crouch behind rocks; provisions also running out.

'It is imperative that a force of at least 40 men with a Maxim should come to our relief at once, as I am afraid all the Mashonas here will rise if present rebels (number estimated about 1000 – mostly Mashonas and easily licked) are not vigorously dealt with. Mesdames Salthouse, Cass and Dickinson are with us and bearing up bravely.

'When relief column enters Mazoe Valley, let them watch closely the dense patches of grass along roadside, as small parties of rebels lie in ambush. Send some Martini Henry ammunition and we can then give our help. Men in laager, in addition to my patrol, are Darling, Spreckley, Zimmermann, Pascoe, Burton, Fairburn, Goddard and Salthouse. Mr Stamford Brown met us on the road and accompanied us here. I may mention that we sent most of the rebels – who shot horses and wounded our men – to the happy hunting grounds. Am sending this by despatch rider (Cape boy Hendricks), who has been promised £100 if he delivers it safely. Send out 12 spare horses. We have two mules and wagonette.'

In the meantime, Judge Vintcent had received reports of just how widespread the rebellion was and decided to send out a stronger patrol to the Mazoe Valley. He called upon the newly-returned Inspector Nesbitt to lead twelve men the thirty-five miles to the relief of Alice Mine. This number included Sergeant Charles Nesbitt, Randolph's brother.

They left the Salisbury laager at 22.30 hours on the 19th. Riding at walking pace to save their horses, they met the despatch rider, Trooper

Hendricks, who handed Nesbitt Judson's note. Aware of the dire plight of the Alice Mine defenders, Nesbitt decided to press on. Hendricks's horse was completely exhausted, so he joined Nesbitt's force as a guide. (Hendricks was later murdered). With guns cocked and smoking forbidden, Nesbitt's patrol rode in complete silence.

At 04.20 hours, they entered the Mazoe Valley. In the surrounding hills were numerous fires burning and the patrol proceeded cautiously with guns at the ready. It was not until they were just a half a mile from the mine that they encountered the Shona.

In the half light of dawn, they rode through a narrow pass with high rocks on each side; a perfect spot for an ambush. A volley rang out and Sergeant Nesbitt's horse was wounded. Returning a volley, the patrol dug in their spurs and galloped out of the ambush. Half an hour later they sighted the small kopje where Salthouse had formed a defensive laager. To their relief, they heard the cheers from the defenders as they approached.

Nesbitt quickly summed up the situation. To have stayed and swelled the numbers of defenders would have only prolonged their ultimate defeat, for there was no one left at Salisbury who could come to their rescue. A brief council was held with Salthouse and Judson and it was decided to ride for Salisbury as soon as possible before the natives could concentrate. With so many dismounted men and the three women, the wagonette became central in their plans to escape.

To make the wagonette bullet proof, iron sheets were nailed to the sides. Nesbitt then organised his force. There were twelve mounted men, eighteen dismounted and three women. All the mules had been scattered, so six horses had to be used to pull the wagon. Volunteers were called to act as the advanced guard and Troopers Harbord, Ogilvie, Van Staaden and Arnott stepped forward. As they set off, 150 yards behind came the dismounted men and the wagon carrying the women and wounded. A short distance behind came the rear guard. The route taken was up the Tatagura Valley, which followed the course of the Tatagura River.

After a mile, as they passed the old Vesuvius Mine camp, the advanced guard were fired on. Dismounting, they returned fire from behind their horses and, with the whole party arriving, soon drove off the enemy. This was not for long, for the natives kept up an almost continuous fire from the many vantage points along the route. Lieutenant McGeer and two horses were killed as the party was constantly harassed. Nesbitt ordered the advanced guard forward to secure all the higher ground on the line of march to cover the party's advance.

Trooper R.A. Harbord later wrote: 'Presently, in going round a sharp corner with high rocks to one side, we ran into a regular ambuscade; I heard a lot of firing, and coming quickly round the corner, I almost rode over Van Staaden, who was lying in the open with the side of his head shot away and his horse dead under him. Just at that moment, two Cape boys, well dressed and armed with rifles, jumped up out of the grass in front of me.

'For half a second I thought they must be our boys, having no idea that the Mashonas had any Cape boys with them, and it was decidedly surprising to see men in khaki coats, breeches and boots and armed with rifles, instead of raw kafirs with assegais and blunderbusses. I jammed my spurs into my horse and galloped for all I was worth, killing, as I passed, one of the Cape boys, who had just fired at and missed me. The bush, or grass, about six feet high and very thick, was alive with niggers. I raced for about three hundred yards and luckily was not hit.

'Then I pulled up and looked round for the wagon. It was still out of sight round the corner, and of the others in the advanced guard only one, Ogilvie, was to be seen, on some rising ground about a quarter of a mile ahead; two were lying dead in the road; Arnott, the fourth, had given it up as a bad job and cleared for Salisbury … taking with him Hendrikz [*sic*], who was shot through both jaws.

'I halloed to Ogilvie, who rode back to me, his face spattered all over with blood from Hendricks' wound, and we decided that we had better ride back to the wagon and see the end of it there; I had given up all hope of coming out of it alive. All this time, without seeing the natives, I kept blazing away into the long grass just to keep them quiet, and I had ridden back to see if anything could be done for Van Staaden, but he was stone dead.

'The wagon came on and Ogilvie and I, still keeping in advance, galloped up every kopje and bit of rising ground in front of us and fired over the top of the wagon and the heads of the dismounted men at the niggers, who by this time had become so confident of getting us that they were running along the road behind us and along the hills each side of the path to take up fresh positions ahead … we were fighting for over three and a half hours before we finally fought our way through. I fired two hundred rounds, and my rifle was so hot that it blistered my hands.'

It was during the dangerous crossing of the Tatagura River that the wagon was brought to a standstill when most of the horses were killed. Keeping up a heavy fire into the long grass and reeds that hid the natives, the party managed to replace the dead horses and continue the crossing. Another equine casualty was Nesbitt's own mount, but its rider escaped unscathed.

The fighting retreat went on for another four miles until Mount Hampden and more open country was reached. Here the natives withdrew and Nesbitt's battered party travelled the ten miles to Salisbury, which they reached at 21.30 hours. Given up for dead, Nesbitt's party was greeted with great enthusiasm. Given the intensity of fighting during the rescue, the casualties were light; just three killed and five wounded, which spoke volumes to the accuracy of the enemy. Of the twenty horses that went out, all but five were either killed or wounded.

In his report to Judge Vintcent dated 22 June, Captain Nesbitt concluded: 'I estimated the enemy's strength to be at least 1500, many of them being armed with Lee-Metford, Martini and Winchester rifles, and appearing well supplied with ammunition. I have every reason to believe that Cape boys and Matabele were the leaders of this attacking party. I compute that the enemy's loss must have been about one hundred.

'The men of the patrol behaved splendidly all through; many of them had never been under fire before. I would especially mention the good services rendered by Messrs Ogilvie, Pascoe and Harbord.'

There was little time to recover from the ordeal. Reinforcements began to arrive and Nesbitt was active in leading a series of patrols and raids against the rebels and their food sources until the main Mashonaland Rebellion was suppressed.

On 1 October 1896, the various police forces were amalgamated under the name of the British South Africa Police and Nesbitt was appointed Inspector. He was given command of Fort Martin, about forty miles south of Salisbury, which had been established to guard against Chief Matshayangombi and his followers, who were still active. On the morning of 17 March 1897, Nesbitt's garrison was attacked by between 300 to 400 natives. After three hours' heavy fighting, the rebels were repulsed. It was not until 26 July that a combined force of BSAP and 7th Hussars finally killed Matshayangombi and ended all resistance.

On 7 May 1897, *The London Gazette* announced: 'Randolph Cosby Nesbitt, Capt. Mashonaland Mounted Police. This officer, on 19 June 1896, led the Mazoe rescue patrol, consisting of only thirteen men, fought their way through the rebels to get to Salthouse's party, and succeeded in bringing them back to Salisbury, with heavy fighting, in which three of his small force were killed and five wounded, and fifteen horses killed or wounded.'

In a special parade in Salisbury on 11 November 1897, Randolph Nesbitt was presented with his Victoria Cross by Lord Milner. He was suffering from fever and was barely able to stand, so a chair was provided and from which he received his Cross.

Later Life

During the Boer War, Nesbitt served with the Mashonaland Division of the BSAP and was part of Colonel Plumer's column that fought its way to raise the siege of Mafeking. On 31 March, when they were just six miles from the town, a portion of his force consisting of 200 mounted men came into collision with the Boers. In a three-hour-long battle, Plumer was wounded and he lost ten killed and twenty-five wounded and forced to retire. Plumer's column finally marched into Mafeking on 17 May.

After the war, Nesbitt served in various districts of Rhodesia until he suddenly resigned in 1909. He had been promised that he would succeed as Commissioner of Police, but he was passed over. Instead, he acted as Native Commissioner at Goromonzi, a position he filled until his retirement in 1927 at the age of sixty. After his wife died, he moved to Muizenberg and later remarried.

In 1947, Nesbitt was presented to King George VI during the Royal Tour of 1947. He was to have travelled to London in June 1956 to take part in the celebration of the Centenary of the Victoria Cross, of which he was then the oldest living holder. Sadly, his health prevented him from attending and after a short illness he died at his home on 23 July 1956 at the age of eighty-nine. He was cremated and his ashes interred at Anglian Cathedral, Salisbury, now Harare.

Chapter 33

North-West Frontier War, 1897–98

Number of VCs awarded	11
Number of VCs awarded to officers	7
Number of VCs awarded to other ranks	4
Total awarded to British Army	8
Total awarded to British Indian Army	3

Origins of the War

After decades of fighting three wars and mounting punitive campaigns against the various troublesome tribes on the North-West Frontier, a final agreement was reached between the British Government and Abdur Rahman Khan, the Afghan Amir, to fix the limit of their respective spheres of influence and improve diplomatic relations and trade. Named after the diplomat, Sir Mortimer Durand, the Durand Line drew a 1,400-mile long border between Afghanistan and what is now the Tribal Area of Pakistan. Even today, despite the border being regarded internationally as the western frontier of Pakistan, it remains unrecognised by Afghanistan.

Although the Amir initially agreed to the pact, he soon had second thoughts. News of the Mahdi's defeat of Generals Hicks and Gordon in the Sudan and the Ottoman's defeat of the Greeks encouraged the Border Pathans to mount a jihad to expel the hated British from their lands. The Sultan of Turkey also saw a way of taking revenge of Britain for supporting Greek independence against by sending emissaries to Afghanistan to fan the flames of insurrection.

In the summer of 1896, an Indian clerk was murdered at a levy post in northern Waziristan and the killer escaped undetected. The British authorities imposed a collective fine on the area and sent the Tochi Political Agent with a large escort of over 300 Indian troops to meet with the tribal leaders at Maizar in the Tochi Valley.

After an apparently amicable meeting, the mood suddenly changed when the tribesmen opened fire. Quickly, all the British officers were either killed or badly wounded and the command devolved on Havildar-Major Muhammed Ismail who managed to extricate the command to a more defensible position. The arrival of some reinforcements gave them the opportunity with withdraw to the British camp at Datta Khel.

When news of the attack reached Kohat, a punitive column was formed and named the Tochi Field Force. After an arduous journey, during which many of the troops fell sick or were affected by sun-stroke, the village of Maizar was reached and found to be abandoned. With no enemy to fight, the villages in the area were destroyed. This almost bloodless expedition was just a foretaste of what evolved into the greatest Indian frontier war ever fought by the British Raj. Egged on by their spiritual leaders, nearly all the Pathan tribes rose up and in eight months intense fighting, very nearly drove the British from the region.

The next action began 200 miles north of Tochi at Malakand. On 26 July 1897, news was received that thousands of Afridi tribesmen led by one of their spiritual priests, were on their way to attack the scattered posts along the Nowshera to Chitral road. One of these was the fort and camps at the Malakand Pass.

The British position was not an ideal one as the camps were isolated from each other and overlooked by the towering mountains. The thousands of fanatical natives began their attack at dusk and soon got among the camps and piquets. The ferocious fighting went on for over six hours in darkness, occasionally illuminated by star-shells, until about 03.30 hours. In one of the near-run attacks, a Victoria Cross was won by Lieutenant Edmond William Costello of the 24th Punjab Infantry when he braved heavy enemy fire and saved the life of a wounded lance havildar.

The following evening, the tribesmen recommenced their attack but the defenders survived another night of intense fighting. The defences were strengthened and bonfires lit in front so the defenders could see the attackers more clearly. Lieutenant Colonel Robert Adams led the Guides Cavalry and Infantry to reinforce the defence and arrived the following day after a night march of thirty-two miles from Mardan. The Guides occupied the Lower Camp and were involved in fierce fighting during which Adjutant Lieutenant Hector MacLean received a painful facial wound.

After a week of heavy fighting, the attacks were beaten off and the tribesmen turned their attention to the Chakdara Fort, ten miles distant, which also managed to hold out against huge odds. It was not until the Guides Cavalry appeared that the Afridis melted away. During the exchange of fire, Adams had his horse shot under him. The forgotten defence of Chakdara by six British officers and 240 Indian soldiers against the sustained attack by 14,000 Pathan tribesmen was every bit as gallant as the over-awarded defence of Rorke's Drift.

Disheartened, the tribesmen pulled away giving the British breathing space to organise the Malakand Field Force under the command of General Sir Bindon Blood. It consisted of 6,800 infantry, 700 cavalry and twenty-four guns. It was necessary to drive the enemy away from the lush lands of the Swat Valley. Heavy rains delayed the advance, but on 16 August, scouts located about 5,000 enemy tribesmen holding a long, flat ridge near Landakai overlooking the Swat River.

Supported by artillery, the 1/Royal West Kents skirmished to engage the tribesmen's attention. Up into the hills to the right climbed the 24th and 31st Punjab Infantry and 45th Sikhs, supported by a Mountain Battery. This appearance above the enemy's left flank took the Afridis by surprise and they began to fall back. The West Kents then advanced rapidly to clear the ridge and link up with the flank attack.

Now the opportunity arose for the Guide Cavalry to ride in pursuit and finish the task. The retreating Pathans were close to the village of Kotah as the Guides rode through heavy rice paddies, always tiring for the horses. The Cavalry needed to intercept the retreating forces before a group of hills was reached and two of the better-mounted horsemen broke away ahead of their colleagues. They were Captain H.T.E. Palmer, who commanded one of the squadrons, and Lieutenant R.T. Greaves, who was on leave from the Lancashire Fusiliers and who had been given permission to go to the front as a War Correspondent for several Indian papers.

They were now near to the village of Kawa Kila. They suddenly came under ambushing fire from 500 tribesmen at the side of the hills, and Greaves horse panicked and carried him right among the enemy. Palmer was still close behind and wounded as they were directly attacked by the Ghazis bearing swords. Greaves was shot from his saddle and was hacked as he lay on the ground. It was at this point that three more Victoria Crosses were earned.

ROBERT BELLEW ADAMS VC (1856-1928)
HECTOR LACHLAN STEWART MACLEAN VC (1870-1897)
ALEXANDER EDWARD MURRAY VC (1871-1962)

Three officers, Lieutenant Colonel Adams, Lieutenant Alexander Murray (Viscount Fincastle), ADC to Viceroy of India and in the field as a War Correspondent of *The Times*, and Lieutenant MacLean who with a party of *sowars* had ridden to a slightly different location by a clump of trees from which Adams had thought effective dismounted fire could be used against the bulk of the fleeing tribesmen. When Adams and Fincastle noticed the plight of Palmer and Greaves they immediately galloped to the rescue, whilst MacLean momentarily stayed behind to organise his men into good fire positions.

Along with five *sowars*, MacLean rode to support his fellow officers. With the appearance of Adams and Fincastle, the tribesmen fell back a little but then opened fire killing Fincastle's horse. MacLean arrived soon after and, as he helped to lift the mortally-wounded Greaves onto his horse, he was shot through both thighs, severing his femoral arteries. Carrying him back to his lines, there was nothing that could be done for him and he bled to death.

In the rather breathless style of writers of Victorian military actions, the following account was witnessed by H. Woosnam Hills and appeared in the *Civil and Military Gazette* in October 1897: 'The two British were now facing a determined enemy at close quarters and unless help came quickly their fate was assured. Twenty yards away were any number of rifles and the chances of escape were nil.

'Then it was that gallant MacLean rode up with his few sowars, and threw himself and his men right into the thick of the fray. The struggle was short and bloody. Around the bodies of their comrades these British officers and Indian sowars fought grimly with the host of fanatical Ghazis. Desperate as the struggle was, it seemed at first as if it was going to be successful. The gallant band recovered the lifeless body of poor Greaves whilst Colonel Adams's placed it on one of the sowars' horses.

'Then they dashed in again at the foe and gallant MacLean was shot through both thighs. He fell into the midst of the bloody arena, and bled to death almost immediately. Colonel Adams had his horse shot but gathering his little party together once more they nobly dashed in, and after a hard struggle brought away the bodies of their brother officers ...

'Those watching from the heights speak of the ride of the Guides as magnificent, whilst the conduct of officers and men when they fell into ambush was worthy of the high reputation of the famous veterans of the Punjab Frontier Force.

'There is something peculiarly sad in the deaths of Lieutenants Greaves and MacLean, and nothing throughout the present operations on the frontier caused more general and widespread sorrow.

'MacLean of the Guides was a well known figure He was one of the best and most dashing officers of the Guides, popular with all good soldiers, and at the time he met with his death he was acting adjutant of the Regiment. Only a little time before he had been at Malakand, fighting gallantly with the defending forces against the same foe, by whom he was shot through the cheek and it was only his keenness for the battle field which carried him into the second affair almost direct from hospital. Poor MacLean's body was carried to Mardan and buried where most, if not all, of the gallant dead of the Guides repose.'

Early Lives

Robert Bellew Adams was born in Muree in the Punjab on 26 July 1856, the son of Lieutenant Colonel Robert Roy Adams and his wife Frances Charlotte née Bellew. His father had been assassinated by Muslim fanatics in 1864 while serving as District Commissioner of Peshawar. Robert was educated privately by tutors and also at the Forest School, Walthamstowe. He attended the RMC Sandhurst and was commissioned in the 12th (Suffolk) Regiment and served with them in India. In 1879, he transferred to the Bengal Staff Corps and was appointed to his father's regiment, the Corps of Guides, in the Second Afghan War. He took part in the Chitral Relief Expedition and during the operations on the North-West Frontier he was Mentioned in Despatches four times. At the time of the Malakand fighting, he was Brevet Lieutenant Colonel of the Guides Cavalry that rode from Mardan to reinforce the beleaguered camp at Malakand.

During the abortive attempt to save Lieutenant Greaves, Adam's horse was wounded in the close-range fire. After the war, Adams was promoted to Commandant of the Corps of Guides and received the CB. He was also appointed ADC to the newly-crowned Edward VII. In 1904, he was promoted to brigadier general and destined for a higher rank, but in 1908 he suffered a bad fall from his horse. This affected his mobility to the point where he was forced to resign from the Army in 1910. The following year he received a knighthood. At this time, he was living in St Albans, Hertfordshire but later moved to Scotland where he died on 13 February 1928 at Reay House, Inverness.

Alexander Edward Murray, Viscount Fincastle and 8th Earl of Dunmore, was born on 22 April 1872 at Portland Place, London. He was educated privately and at Eton before joining the Army. On 30 May 1892, he was commissioned in the 16th Lancers and sent to India. During the Malakand operation, he was on leave from his own unit and accompanying the expedition as a special correspondent for *The Times*. One of the conditions for being a neutral correspondent was he should in no way serve with the Field Force nor be eligible for any medal or gratuity. Fortunately, these points were side-stepped and Sir Bindon Blood led the way to that recognition by attaching the Viscount to the Guides Calvary.

Fincastle served in the Anglo-Boer War in 6th Dragoons and 16th Lancers and was present at the Relief of Kimberley. In September 1901, he raised his own Fincastle's Horse, (31st Battalion Imperial Yeomanry). In 1907, Fincastle inherited the title of Earl of Dunmore. At the outbreak of the First World War I he was recalled to the 16th Lancers. He served on the Staff and was wounded during the Battle of the Somme. A DSO was added to his VC before he left the Army at the end of the war. Between the wars, he served as government whip in the House of Lords. He died at his home in London on 29 January 1962, at the age of eighty-nine.

Hector Lachlan Stewart MacLean was born in a tent on the hill of Sheikh Bannu on the North-West Frontier on 13 September 1870, the eldest son of Major General Charles Smith MacLean. He was sent to Scotland and received his education at Fettes College, Edinburgh. He was commissioned in the Northumberland Fusiliers in 1889 before joining the Indian Staff Corps on 17 February 1891. This was but a stepping stone to transferring six weeks later to his father's old regiment, the Corps of Guides at Mardan.

He was immediately sent on the Black Mountain Punitive Expedition on 18 March 1891 against the Hazara tribe. During the Relief of Chitral in 1895, MacLean distinguished himself by swimming across a river to join and encourage a detachment that had been cut off by the rapid rising of the water (see entry for Fenton John Aylmer VC in Hunza-Nagar Expedition 1891).

In 1896, he was appointed Adjutant of the Guides Cavalry. A popular officer, he was a very keen huntsman and captain of the Guides' Polo Team.

In 1907, King Edward VII yielded to pressure to allow posthumous awards to those servicemen who had been recommended retrospectively for the Victoria Cross but who had died before they could be awarded. A short list of six was announced in *The London Gazette* on 15 January 1907: 'The King has been graciously pleased to approve of the Decoration of the Victoria Cross being delivered to the representatives of the under-mentioned officers and men who fell in the performance of acts of valour, and with reference to whom it was notified in the London Gazette that they would have been recommended to Her late Majesty for the Victoria Cross had they survived:

'Lieutenant Hector Lachlan Stewart MacLean, Indian Staff Corps, on account of his gallant conduct, would have been recommended to Her Majesty for the Victoria Cross had he survived. During the fighting at Nawa Kili, in Upper Swat, on 17th August, 1897, Lieutenant-Colonel Adams proceeded with Lieutenants H.L.S. MacLean and Viscount Fincastle, and five men of the Guides, under a very heavy and close fire, to the rescue of Lieutenant R. T. Greaves, Lancashire Fusiliers, who was lying disabled by a bullet wound and surrounded by the enemy's swordsmen. In bringing him under cover he (Lieutenant Greaves) was struck by a bullet and killed. Lieutenant MacLean was mortally wounded, whilst the horses of Lieutenant-Colonel Adams and Lieutenant Viscount Fincastle were shot, as well as two troop horses.'

Two weeks after the relief of Chakdara and Malakand, the Afridi-Orakzai tribes of the Mohmand region, to the north of the Kabul River and Khyber Pass, attacked a fort about fifteen miles from Pershawar. Now the British had to deal with a general outbreak covering hundreds of miles along the border west of Pershawar.

The Mohmand Field Force under the command of Brigadier General Edmond Elles left Persawar on 6 September with the object of linking up with Major General Bindon Blood's division. The latter had fewer miles to cover and reached Nawagi on 14 September. Blood detached a brigade under Brigadier Jeffries to advance up the Mahmund Valley.

Establishing a camp at Inayat Killa at the head of the valley, Jeffries split his command into three columns, sending one to attack the village of Domodoloh to the right, another to take Badalai at the head of the valley and the third to destroy villages to the west. In the day-long advance on these targets, the individual columns came under great opposition from superior numbers of tribesmen and at the end of the fourteen hours' hard marching and fighting, the columns withdrew to their camp in a violent thunderstorm. It was then that it was discovered that some of the brigade was missing, including their commander, Brigadier Jeffries.

During the retirement that evening, Jeffries was with about 100 men including some Sikhs, thirty Bengal Sappers, four guns of No.8 Battery and eleven soldiers of the Buffs. When the storm broke, Jeffries ordered a stop at the village of Bilot.

As they approached, they came under a hail of fire. Quickly, they took cover in ditches and behind low walls. Both Jeffries and the battery commander were hit. All around the casualties were mounting and it was two Royal Engineer officers and a Buff's corporal who led a charge that kept the Afridis at a distance. Finally, at midnight, the search party found them and drove the tribesmen from the village. No further attacks occurred and the survivors made their way back to camp. The casualties of this action numbered 149. For their gallant and timely action, Lieutenants Thomas Watson and James Colvin with Corporal James Smith of the Buffs were awarded the Victoria Cross.

There were more outbreaks by the Afridis in late August on outposts along the Kohat-Kurram road and the Khyber Pass. On 23 August, the fort at Ali Masjid fell and it was months before the Khyber Pass was reopened. It became imperative that the British quickly re-establish themselves and attack the natives in their homeland. Faced with an estimated 50,000 Afridis and Orakzais, a large field force was organised under the command of Lieutenant General Sir William Lockhart. Lockhart saw his first action with the 5th (Northumberland) Fusiliers during the Indian Mutiny and had campaigned in many of the North-West Frontier campaigns since. He took the field with largest force ever employed on the Frontier: 11,900 officers and men with a further 19,900 non-combatants.

Named the Tirah Field Force, Lockhart's aim was to quickly establish his command in the heart of the Afridi-Orakzai homeland by taking a direct approach rather than a more cautious advance. The railhead at Kohat was the stepping-off point for the Field Force, who had to march across the mountains and passes to Shinawari Fort. Once assembled and organised, the advance was made on 18 October with the village of Karappa as its target. To protect his left flank, Lockhart ordered that the village of Dargai should be cleared as it dominated their route. It was here that four more VCs were won.

HENRY SINGLETON PENNELL VC (1874-1907)

Henry Singleton Pennell was born on 18 June 1874 in Dawlish, Devon, to Edwin Francis and Henrietta (née) Copeland. The family moved to Clifton,

Bristol and later to Eastbourne. Between 1887 and 1892, Henry attended Eastbourne College before entering RMC Sandhurst in 1892. On passing out, he was commissioned 2nd Lieutenant into the 1st Battalion Sherwood Foresters (Derbyshire Regiment) on 21 October 1893, then garrisoned in Ireland. Promoted to lieutenant, he was sent to join the 2nd Battalion stationed in India on 18 July 1896. The battalion had been overseas since the early 1880s and had taken part in the Sikkim Campaign of 1888.

In September 1897, the battalion was put on alert for active service in response to uprising on the North-West Frontier and joined Lockhart's Tirah Field Force. This comprised of two Divisions and the Derbyshires formed part of the 1st Brigade of the 1st Division along with the 1st Battalion the Devonshire Regiment, 30th Punjab Regiment and the 2/1st Gurkha Rifles. While the battalion was being mobilised, Henry was away on a course at the School of Musketry in India. He re-joined his colleagues at Rawalpindi on 27 September during the move to the concentration area at Kohat. By mid-October the general advance north into Tirah commenced.

The Derbyshires prepared for the campaign by dulling their mess tins, washing the pipe clay out of their belts, straps and pouches and staining them with tea. What they were not prepared for was the toll the march took. In fact, the general unfitness of most British regiments was commented upon, the exceptions being the King's Own Scottish Borderers and the Gordon Highlanders, both of whom had taken part in the recent Frontier campaigns.

A day's march ahead of the 1st Division was the 2nd Division, which reached a pass dominated by the Dargai Heights, from where the Afridi and Orakzais tribesmen could harass the British with long-range firing. To remove this irritant, troops of the 2nd Division were deployed in a frontal and flanking attack. Captain Shadwell described this feature in his book *Lockhart's Advance through Tirah*: 'The village of Dargai lies on the northern side of a small plateau. The eastern edge of this tableland breaks off, at first, in an almost abrupt cliff; but some distance lower down, though steep, shelves away almost precipitously. The slope is thrown out from the bottom of the cliff in the form of a narrow razor-like spur, with a path or track lying along its northern side, well within view and range of the cliff-head …

'Connecting the crest of the spur, however, and the foot of the cliff, there is a narrow neck or saddle 100 yards long by 30 broad, whose sides are too precipitous to allow any movement along them. Though devoid of all cover and completely exposed to the heights above, this ridge had to be crossed to reach the path ascending to the summit.'

Supported by mountain guns, the 1/3rd Gurkhas, the KOSB and the Northampton Regiment, managed to reach the 1,100-foot summit and put the tribesmen to flight at the cost of seven dead and thirty-five wounded.

Having spent most of the day in capturing Dargai, it was decided to abandon the position partly through lack of water in the vicinity but also to press on with the main objective of reaching the Tirah Maidan. The sound of the gunfire had attracted thousands of Afridis from the nearby Khanki Valley. As they hurried towards Dargai, their numbers increased as they rallied their Orakzais brothers. They reached Dargai as the last British troops were retiring and heavy firing hastened them on their way.

VC Action

When word reached General Sir William Lockhart, he ordered that the Dargai Heights should be retaken as there was no alternative route. He then detached from the 1st Division, the Derbyshires, 3rd Sikhs and a mountain battery, who set off in the early hours of 20 October. At 10.00 hours, the artillery opened fire at the summit, with little effect. The tribesmen had built strong sangars and the huge rocks offered secure cover. The infantry was sent into the attack, with the Gurkhas in the lead followed by 1/Dorsetshire Regiment, with the Derbyshires in reserve. Further back, the Gordon Highlanders provided long-range covering fire. Henry Pennell was second in command to Captain William Smith of 'D' Company. A Regimental eyewitness described the ascent:

'The path towards Dargai was only a narrow track, along which it was impossible to advance except in single file, so that a battalion was spread over a good half-mile. The Gurkhas and most of the Dorsets were out of sight before the head of our Battalion started upon it. After winding along this for about a mile, more or less on the level and fairly good going, we reached the village of Mamu Khan.

'A short distance beyond it the path ran along a level bit exposed to the enemy's fire, but too distant to matter. Then the track, which could scarcely be recognised as a path, took a sharp turn to the right directly towards the position, and a stiff climb of about half a mile began, zigzagging up a watercourse to the top of the ridge immediately beneath the position, so steeply that the men were obliged to make constant halts to recover their breath before going on. This very steepness, however, had the immense advantage of affording complete protection from the enemy's fire.

'When within some 200 yards of the top we were halted. Anything like regular formation on such ground was out of the question. Companies sat or lay down at intervals, the men of each section grouped around their commander. What was going on above we could not tell, nor why we were halted. The slope of the ground lessened for the last fifty yards or so below the gap at the top of the ridge, so that from the spot where we lay nothing whatever could be seen, either of our own fighting line or the enemy's position. The sound of continuous heavy firing, however, told us that there was warm work ahead.

'It was now about 11 am, the sun was just hot enough to make the shade of a single large ilex worth going a few yards out of the way to lie under. We sat there for what seemed like an interminable length of time, though it cannot have been much over an hour. Presently, wounded men, chiefly

Gurkhas at first, began to come down past us. It was not for some days afterwards that we heard what had been going on above us; how two companies of the Gurkhas first had charged across the deadly space from the gap, losing 67 men in ten minutes; how the survivors established themselves under scrawny cover beneath the cliff; how the second rush of the Gurkhas, was hurled back over the gap, how their CO signalled back to the rest of his men to remain where they were until reinforced; now the Dorsets in their turn made gallant and repeated efforts to support the Gurkhas, and had section after section swept away as soon as they rushed across the gap, losing more men than any other British regiment that day.'

The open slope which was swept by deadly and accurate fire was the only way to reach the final cliff, on top of which the Afghans were firmly entrenched. In many ways, the battlefield resembled a condensed version of the assault on the Great Redan at Sebastopol in 1855: a bare steep slope in front of a formidable fortress, which had become a killing ground. The Derbyshires' eyewitness continued:

'Shortly after this, A and C Companies were ordered up to relieve the Dorsets in the firing line, covering the advance, or attempted advance, through the gap. Next, B, D and E Companies were ordered up to the gap, and as these Companies scrambled up to reach the point where the slope lessened, 50 yards or so beneath the gap, they came within view for the first time at close quarters of the enemy's position and of the state of things at the gap. Right opposite, only 350 yards away, rose a line of almost sheer cliffs, 400 feet above, lined for length of some 400 yards by an invisible enemy, whose rifles and jezails were all levelled at the gap. Away to our right out of sight from this spot, the cliff took a sharp turn backwards and became less precipitous, and it was round this turn that the track led to the top.

'At the gap, there was a terrible block, some 400 men and several wounded being all tightly packed there, and fresh troops could only elbow their way through one at a time, so that it was impossible to direct the continuous stream of men needed to rush the place with any real hope of success.

'Nevertheless, Captain Smith, who commanded D Company, the first of ours to come up, forced his way through the mass and, followed by his subaltern, Pennell, and three or four men of the Company who managed to struggle through at short intervals, made a dash across the gap into the open under a continuous hail of bullets. Before he had gone more than a few yards, Smith fell, shot through the head, and the men immediately behind him were mown down.'

It was at this point that young Henry Pennell performed his heroic but unsuccessful act. Seeing that his captain was no longer with him, he ran back through the fire to try and get him into cover. Smith was a big man and a dead weight for Pennell to lift.

Calling to some Dorsets who were lying around, he asked them to help and one replied: 'We're all wounded, sir, except those that are dead'. Despite his acute danger, Pennell continued to drag Smith back until he realised that Smith was dead. Placing Smith's helmet over his dead comrade's head, Pennell scrambled back to the cover of the ledge.

Lieutenant Tillard of the 3rd Gurkhas, who was one of those stranded at the base of the cliff, recalled that, 'It was hard to understand how he (Pennell) escaped untouched as at the time he was the only man moving on the dangerous zone and all the Afridi rifles directed at him!'

There was now a hiatus. The sheltering Derbyshires, Dorsets and Gurkhas remained below the ledge as it was obvious that any attempt to cross the slope would bring down a curtain of fire. Disheartened and helpless the intermingled troops waited for direction from below.

Four hours after the attack began saw the arrival of the Gordon Highlanders. The three stranded battalions were to move aside and follow in support. All twenty-four mountain guns put down a three-minute concerted barrage and when this was lifted, the Gordons poured over the ledge and rushed up the open slope, closely followed by the 3rd Sikhs, the Gurkhas, Dorsets and the Derbys.

Although there was heavy firing and casualties, the British reached a point of comparative safety at the foot of the cliff. Immediately, the Gordons began ascending the narrow path to the summit, but when they reached it, they found that the tribesmen were disappearing into the distance. So the battle of Dargai Heights was won, but at a heavy cost – 197 casualties including thirty-nine dead.

Four Victoria Crosses were awarded for this battle, the most celebrated being Piper George Findlater of the Gordons, who, despite being shot through both feet, sat up under heavy fire and continued playing the regimental march to encourage his comrades. Another Gordon, Private Edward Lawson, received his for carrying a wounded officer to safety. The Dorsets, who had the highest casualties, had Private Samuel Vickery so recognised for also rescuing a wounded comrade.

Later Service

The fourth was Lieutenant Henry Pennell, who, along with the other three, was gazetted on 20 May 1898. He received his Cross from his Commanding Officer, Colonel Edward Dowse, at a ceremony at Bareilly on 2 September 1898. The campaign against the warring tribes lasted until April 1898, but the 2nd Battalion remained on the North-West Frontier. Pennell was in England on leave at the outbreak of the Anglo-Boer War in October 1899. He volunteered for attachment to one of the participating regiments and on 20 October, he embarked on *Rosin Castle* with the West Yorkshire Regiment.

Rosin Castle was the first ship to arrive in Cape Town on 9 November, which also carried Major General Hilyard and his staff. The West Yorkshire

Regiment formed part of Hilyard's 2nd Brigade, which was sent across country to Port Elizabeth and thence by sea to Durban. From here, the brigade was sent north to become part of General Buller's Ladysmith Relief Force. It was expected to take two weeks but took nearly three months.

Henry Pennell took part in all the major battles as the British tried to force their way across the Tugela River, the major obstacle to the relief of Ladysmith. When the Colenso battle ended in disaster, Buller moved his force to the west, only to suffer a devastating blow at Spion Kop. Eventually, the Tugela was crossed but there were still fierce fights to follow to take the important positions at Vaal Krantz and Pieter's Hill. It was during the fight for the latter, that Pennell was severely wounded. On 30 May 1900, he was promoted to captain and company commander, before returning to England that November. He received the Queen's South Africa Medal with the clasps for *Relief of Ladysmith, Tugela Heights, Laing's Nek* and *Transvaal*. He was also twice Mentioned in Despatches.

Recognised as an outstanding officer, Pennell was admitted to Staff College, 1902-1903, where he distinguished himself. When Edward VII visited the Staff College, he was struck by the number of officers wearing decorations, for amongst them were five VCs and twenty DSOs.

In 1905, Pennell was appointed Staff-Captain at the Headquarters of Administration, Southern Command at Salisbury. He was remembered as being very sociable and an enthusiastic sportsman, being particularly fond of fox hunting, rarely refusing a jump. Rather surprisingly for such a man of action, he was also a keen gardener, and cultivated a piece of land adjacent to the headquarters.

Tragic End

Just after Christmas 1906, Henry took some leave and went to the Swiss Alps for a holiday with a party of fellow officers.

During his stay at the Kulm Hotel, St Moritz, he was introduced to the pleasures of alpine sports. At that time, British tourists dominated the mountain slopes and are still known as the instigators of the famous Cresta toboggan run. Built first in 1885, this three-quarter mile long run of packed and banked ice has ten testing corners. Face forward on skeleton toboggans, the riders travelled at speeds of about 50mph, finishing at about 80mph. This would have been something that would have appealed to a natural thrill-seeker such as Henry Pennell.

On 19 January 1907, Henry became an unsought first. During a descent, he lost control and went into the difficult bend known as Shuttlecock, where he was hurled over the bank at high speed. It was his wretched luck that instead of landing in soft snow, which the organisers went to great pains to maintain, he landed on a hard and solid mass. The violence of the fall ruptured vital organs and internal haemorrhaging resulted. The unusual occurrence that caused Pennell's death was a fall over Shuttlecock by the previous rider, Captain C. C. Grieve, one of Pennell's travelling companions. Grieve lay in the soft snow behind the bank and was hit by his toboggan. A crowd of spectators clambered over the barrier which protected the precious snow and clustered around the fallen Grieve, trampling the area to hard ice. It was onto this unforgiving surface that poor Pennell landed

Barely conscious, he was carried back to the hotel, where he died from his injuries shortly before midnight. He was the first rider to be killed on the Cresta. Before his body was conveyed to England, a service was held in the Kulm Chapel.

Pennell's body was taken by train from Switzerland to Dawlish. On 25 January, the cortege left the station, the coffin covered with a Union Jack and carried by a detachment of the Royal Field Artillery to St Gregory's Churchyard, where he was laid to rest.

The taking of Dagai Heights and the VCs awarded lulled the British public into thinking that the Tirah campaign was over. In fact, two more months of hard marching in appalling weather followed.

The Afridis had suffered heavy casualties and did not attempt any more massed charges. They did, however, resort to a perpetual guerrilla warfare selecting small parties to ambush and snipe at. With most of the tribes submitting to the British who had denied them access to their winter quarters, Lockhart prepared to withdraw on 9 December in bitterly cold weather. Although the 1st Division achieved the withdrawal unopposed, the 2nd Division was harried for four days and nights as it pulled back along the Bara Valley.

With the threat of another punitive force being sent against them, the Afridis agreed to pay the fines and surrender their rifles. Finally, the Tirah Field Force was broken up in April 1898. Although there was to be more campaigns launched in the coming years, never again would so many Frontier tribes combine to take on the British Raj.

Chapter 34

Sudan Campaign, 1898–99

Number of VCs awarded	5
Number of VCs awarded to officers	4
Number of VCs awarded to other ranks	1
Total awarded to British Army	5

Origins of the War

The Mahdist War between Egypt and the Sudan had been fought off and on from 1881 to 1899. Direct British involvement occurred in 1882 to 1885 to put down the Urabi Uprising and the death of General Gordon. In the intervening years, Tewfik Pasha was still the Khedive but it was the British who largely took control of Egypt's affairs.

One of Britain's most important roles was to organise and train the new Egyptian Army by using British officers and NCOs. The British instructors treated the troops in their care firmly but justly, making sure they were fed, clothed and paid. Within a few years, the Egyptian Army bore little resemblance to the previous ill-trained and reluctant shambles it had been under the corrupt regime. In particular, the Soudanese battalions of the Egyptian Army were regarded as brave but wild. There was still a question mark, nevertheless, whether the Egyptian *fallahin* (peasant) conscripts would stand firm against a determined Dervish attack.

One of the first and most influential British officers to be appointed to the Egyptian Army was Major Herbert Kitchener. He swiftly rose in rank to become Adjutant General and oversaw his reformed Egyptian Army in its defeat of the Mahdi's successor, Abdallahi ibn Muhammed – the Khalifa – in his attempt to invade Egypt. Kitchener, who had taken part in the abortive attempt to save Charles Gordon, regarded this failure as England's disgrace and looked for an opportunity to invade the Sudan and drive out the Khalifa's fanatical followers.

During his leadership, Abdallahi had dismantled the administrative systems and weakened the Sudanese tribal unities. From 1885 to 1898, the population of Sudan collapsed from eight to three million due to war, persecution, disease and famine. If ever there was an opportunity to overthrow this cruel theocracy, then the moment had come.

The invasion of Sudan was not one campaign but several. In 1896, the battles of Firket and Dongola fought by the Egyptian Army forced the Khalifa back towards his capital, Omdurman. A push to finally defeat the Dervishes would involve British troops. Initially the British government was reluctant to pay the enormous cost of funding an invasion, but public opinion was becoming aware of the achievements that Egypt had achieved under British stewardship. A more political reason for securing the Sudan was the French plans to occupy the southern provinces for which there was no legal authority. As these territories contained the Upper Nile, Britain's attitude to this lawless and desolate land went through a sudden change of heart and she supported a campaign of reoccupation. France's goal was to have an uninterrupted link between the Niger River and the Nile thus controlling all trade from the Sahel region. With her small colony of French Somaliland (Djibouti), at the mouth of the Red Sea, the proposed French territory would extend in an east-west belt across the continent.

The British, on the other hand, saw their colonial aspirations as a north-south link between Southern Africa, Kenya, Uganda to the Nile basin. The Prime Minister of the Cape Colony, Cecil Rhodes, had ambitions to build a Cape to Cairo Railway, which would have intersected the French line near the town of Fashoda on the White Nile in eastern South Sudan. It was at Fashoda where a small French force led by Major Marchand was confronted by General Kitchener, backed by a powerful British flotilla of gunboats, that a stand-off took place. Kitchener had just defeated the Khalifa at Omdurman and had the man-power and weaponry to persuade Marchand that confrontation was not an option. After a couple of months of bitter wrangling by the British and French governments, the latter pulled back and the crises passed. In March 1899, the French and British agreed that the source of the Nile and the Congo rivers should mark the frontier between their spheres of influence.

Herbert Kitchener had been elevated to Sirdar, Commander in Chief of the Egyptian Army, but was nagged by the prospect that he would be subservient to a British Army general. On 4 January 1898, this was solved when he was appointed overall commander of the British and Egyptian troops. He had already overseen the building of a railway to carry his troops from Wadi Halfa, through Abu Hamed to the recently abandoned Berber. Learning from the earlier 1880's campaigns, water was brought by train in 1,500 gallon tanks so obviating the need to rely on remote wells and their questionable water.

As the British reinforcements arrived in Cairo, Kitchener led an Anglo-Egyptian force and defeated the Dervishes at Atbara on 8 April 1898. This put Kitchener just 200 miles north of Khartoum.

On 28 August, Kitchener's 25,800-man force consisting of a British Division, an Egyptian Division and supported by cavalry, artillery and gun-boats began its final approach to Omdurman. During the course of the coming battle, four Victoria Crosses were awarded.

NEVILL MASKELYNE SMYTH VC (1868-1941)

Nevill Maskelyne Smyth was born on 14 August 1868 in Westminster, London, to the noted geologist Sir Warington Wilkinson Smyth and his wife, Anna Maria Antonia, née Story-Maskelyne. Educated at Westminster School, he graduated from RMC Sandhurst in 1888 and was commissioned in the Queen's Bays (2nd Dragoon Guards) in India as a second lieutenant. In 1890, he was attached as escort to the Royal Engineers who were surveying a railway during the Zhob Valley expedition on the North-West Frontier.

From 1895 to 1897, the Bays were transferred to Egypt. Lieutenant Smyth was seconded to Kitchener's command and helped chart some of the Nile cataracts prior to the invasion of Sudan for which he received a Mentioned in Despatches He was also awarded the Order of the Medjidie and promoted to captain in 1897. He was appointed to the staff and employed as Intelligence and Orderly Officer to Major General Sir Archibald Hunter, commander of the Egyptian Division.

On 1 September 1898, the Anglo-Egyptian army had disembarked on the left bank of the Nile above the Khalifa's capital, Omdurman. Five of the six infantry brigades were arranged in an arc some 2,000 yards from end to end facing west. The gun-boats returned from bombarding Omdurman and moored to the bank behind the army with a clear field of fire. A rather flimsy *zariba* was built in front of the infantry, who spent a nervy night expecting to be attacked. Searchlights from the gun-boats constantly swept the ground in front of the *zariba* and patrols were sent out to give warning of any approach.

After this lengthy build-up, the two armies finally faced one another at dawn on 2 September. The 20,000 strong Anglo-Egyptian army faced west with its backs to the Nile. Supporting them were six gunboats, with all guns pointing towards the advancing army of the Khalifa. George Steevens, reporting for the *Daily Mail*, wrote;

'The noise of something began to creep in upon us; it cleared and divided into the tap of drums and the far-away surf of raucous war-cries. A shiver of expectancy thrilled our army, and then a sigh of content. They were coming on. Allah help them! They were coming on.

'It was now half-past six. The flags seemed very distant, the roar very faint, and the thud of our first gun was almost startling. It may have startled them too, but it startled them into life. The line of flags swung forward, and a mass of white flying linen swung forward with it too. They came very fast, and they came very straight; and then presently they came no farther.

With a crash the bullets leaped out of the British rifles. It began with the Guards and Warwicks – section volleys at 2000 yards; then, as the Dervishes edged rightward, it ran along to the Highlanders, the Lincolns, and to Maxwell's Brigade. The British stood up in double rank behind their *zariba;* the blacks lay down in their shelter-trench; both poured out death as fast as they could load and press trigger. Shrapnel whistled and Maxims growled savagely. From all the line came perpetual fire, fire, fire, and shrieked forth in great gusts of destruction.'

What an extraordinary sight they made and something that would never again be witnessed. Like some vast medieval horde, 50,000 banner waving foot soldiers and horsemen advanced like a storm-cloud towards the waiting invaders in a suicidal mass frontal attack. The first phase of the battle was really a one-sided affair. Concentrated artillery and machine-gun fire ensured that the Dervishes got nowhere close to Kitchener's men. Through the dust and gun-smoke could be seen the plain covered with the dead and dying. Steevens reported: 'It was the last day of Mahdism and the greatest. They could never get near, and they refused to hold back. By now the ground before us was all white with dead men's drapery. Rifles grew red-hot; the soldiers seized them by the slings and dragged them back to the reserve to change for cool ones. It was not a battle but an execution.'

VC Action

Two war correspondents, Bennet Burleigh and Bennett Stamford, rode out onto the corpse-covered plain to explore the scene of the recent carnage. Suddenly, they were confronted by a grizzled warrior, who pulled himself up and came at them with a spear. Stamford fired his pistol then turned and galloped back to the safety of the column.

The *Daily Telegraph*'s special reporter, Bennet Burleigh, had problems turning his horse and had to draw his revolver. In his excitement, he managed to empty his weapon, hitting everything except his adversary. Spotting that the reporters were in danger, Captain Nevill Smyth, spurred his horse and galloped out of the column. He put himself between the reporter and his assailant and received a spear thrust in the arm. Burleigh made himself scarce and hurriedly returned to the British lines. Drawing his revolver, Smyth shot and killed the Dervish. For this act, Smyth was awarded the Victoria Cross and in the citation dated 15 November 1898, he was described as saving 'a camp follower', a description which must have wounded the collective pride of the Fourth Estate and Burleigh's in particular.

Nevill Smyth returned to England where he received the Victoria Cross from the Queen on 6 January 1899 at Osbourne House, Isle of Wight. When he had recovered from his wound, he returned to the Sudan and was appointed assistant to General Wingate, Kitchener's Intelligence chief. Learning that the Khalifa was still active and leading at least 10,000 followers, Kitchener sent Wingate to find and capture this troublesome leader.

Sir Luke O'Connor, VC, KCB.

Alexander Roberts Dunn VC.

Joseph Malone VC.

Sir Christopher Charles Teesdale VC, KCMG, CB

John Augustus Wood VC.

Sir Henry Marshman Havelock-Allan 1st Baronet VC, GCB, DL.

Thomas Henry Kavanagh VC.

George Hinckley VC.

Charles Heaphy VC.

Henry William Pitcher VC.

Duncan Gordan Boyes VC.

Caption: Timothy O'Hea VC

Samuel Wassall VC.

Robert Scott VC.

Richard Kirby Ridgeway VC, CB.

John Danaher VC.

Joseph John Farmer VC.

Israel Harding VC.

Frederick Corbett VC.

Sir Arthur Knyvet Wilson,
3rd Baronet VC, GCB, OM, GCVO.

John Crimmin VC, CB, CIE, VD.

Charles James William Grant VC.

Sir Fenton John Aylmer, 13th Baronet of Donadea, VC KCB.

John Manners Smith VC, CIE, CVO.

Harry Frederick Whitchurch VC.

William James Gordon VC.

Herbert Stephen Henderson VC.

Randolph Cosby Nesbitt VC.

Sir Robert Bellew Adams VC, KCB.

Henry Singleton Pennell VC.

Sir Nevill Maskelyne Smyth VC, KCB.

Thomas Byrne VC.

William Job Maillard VC.

Matthew Fontaine Maury Meiklejohn VC.

Arthur Herbert Lindsay Richardson VC.

William House VC.

Sir John Edmond Gough VC, KCB, CMG.

John Duncan Grant VC, CB, DSO.

Charles Allix Lavington Yate.

Alfred John Shout VC, MC.

Sir Adrian Paul Ghislain Carton de Wiart VC KBE, CB, CMG, DSO.

Frederick McNess VC.

Lionel Wilmot Brabazon Rees VC, OBE, MC, AFC.

William Edward Sanders VC, DSO.

Cecil John Kinross VC.

John William Sayer VC.

Edward Benn Smith VC, DCM.

Ferdinand Maurice Felix West VC, CBE, MC.

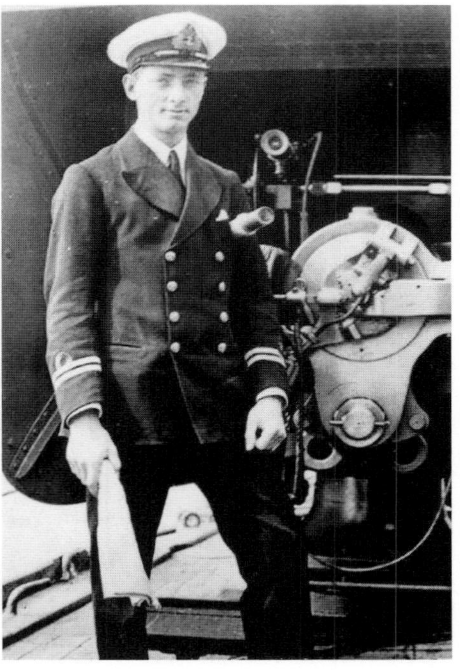

Augustus Willington Shelton Agar VC, DSO, RN.

Eustace Jotham VC.

Gerard Broadmead Roope VC.

Alfred Clive Hulme VC.

Augustus Charles Newman VC, OBE, TD, DL.

John Kenneally VC.

John Pennington Harman VC.

Francis Arthur Jefferson VC.

John Alexander Cruickshank VC.

Ian Oswald Liddell VC.

Rambahadur Limbu VC, MVO.

Rayene Stewart Simpson, VC, DCM.

Joshua Leakey VC.

Johnson Gideon Beharry VC.

On 25 November 1899, Wingate led an attack at Umm Diwaykarat in what was to be the final battle of the protracted war. At dawn the Mahdists began their attack but were driven back by sustained fire from Wingate's Maxim machine-guns. Accepting that he was defeated, Abdallahi and his Emirs went into a huddle, with the Khalifa seated on his *furwa* or sheepskin – as was the custom of Arab chiefs who refused to surrender. A Soudanese regiment soon made short work of the Khalifa and his faithful lieutenants.

Later Service

After the battle, Captain Smyth was appointed temporary governor and military commander of the Blue Nile district. He was awarded the Order of Osmanieh and, despite Kitchener' s request that he join him in the Boer War, was active in charting the Nile Cataracts from Wadi Halfa to Abyssinia. Before he left the Sudan, he was employed on establishing a fixed border with Abyssinia. He finally joined his old commander in South Africa in 1902 and re-joined his regiment.

On 1 April, three squadrons of the Queen's Bays were sent to attack what was thought to be a small force of Boers camped at a farm called Holspruit. Arriving in the dark, it was discovered that some 600 men Boers were camped at the farm and outnumbered the British three to one. In the fierce fire-fight, the Bays retreated to higher ground. Smyth's horse was killed and he, along with some troopers whose horses had also been shot, covered the retreat of their comrades. As dawn broke the Bays found themselves surrounded on their small *kopji* (hill) but the timely arrival of the 7th Hussars and some horse artillery forced the Boers to pull back. The casualty list made sad reading – the Bays had lost eighty killed or wounded, with the Boers losing a similar number of men

After the war, Smyth was promoted to major and transferred to the Carabiniers (6th Dragoon Guards) which was serving in India but moved to South Africa in 1908. He was promoted to colonel and returned to England in 1912. Smyth was an enthusiast for the new craze of flying and achieved his Aviators Certificate in 1913. Although he could have joined the newly-formed Royal Flying Corps, he chose to return to Egypt and was appointed Commandant of the Khartoum District in 1913-14. Like his predecessors, he was active in combating the slave-trade, which still flourished.

Australian Command

With the outbreak of the First World War, Colonel Smyth was among several officers recalled by Lord Kitchener to command troops in the Gallipoli Campaign of 1915. He was given command of 1st Australian Infantry Brigade and in May, supervised the truce of 24th to allow the Turks to bury their dead.

Smyth was present at the battle of Lone Pine in August and won the trust and admiration of his men. A superior officer described Smyth as, 'sphinx-like, silent and imperturbable'. Another said: 'Among the soldiers he was recognised as an officer of wise moderation and calm courage, a strict disciplinarian'. At the evacuation of Gallipoli, Colonel Smyth was one of the last officers to leave the peninsula.

Smyth led his Australians in the severe fighting for Pozières and Mouquet Farm during the Battle of the Somme. At the end of 1916, he was promoted to major general and given command of the 2nd Australian Division. In the spring of 1917, he led his division in the attacks at Bapaume, Bullecourt and the dreadful battle of Passchendaele. When he transferred back to the British Army in May 1918, he told the Australian commander, Lieutenant General Sir John Monash: 'The fortune of war has indeed treated me kindly in enabling me to have the honour of being associated with your historic force.'

For the final months of the war, he commanded first the 58th British Division and then the 59th Division. He also indulged his love of flying by borrowing an aeroplane to do his own 'spotting' of the enemy trenches. After the war, he was GOC Channel Ports and in 1919 was given command of the 47th Territorial Division. He was knighted in 1919 and awarded the Belgian Croix de Guerre and the French *Légion d'honneur*. In all, he had been Mentioned in Despatches eleven times.

In 1924, General Sir Nevill Smyth retired from the British Army. The following year, he and his family immigrated to Australia. He said that he regarded the Australians as the finest troops with whom he had ever served and he wanted to live among them in their country. He settled in Victoria and in 1931 was an unsuccessful National Party candidate for the Victoria Senate.

Smyth died at his home at Balmoral on 21 July 1941. He was buried in the local cemetery.

Eventually, there was a lull as the attacks of the Dervishes grew weaker and the firing petered out. Kitchener then ordered an advance parallel with the river towards nearby Omdurman.

The Dervish army of some 50,000 had been defeated by an Anglo-Egyptian force of 25,000. They had also suffered some 23,000 killed or wounded compared with 330 from the British-led force. Such a horrendous casualty list spelt the end of the Khalifa's regime although there was still more fighting to be done before the flame of fanaticism was extinguished.

There was one more action during the mopping up after the battle that established Omdurman in the British psyche – the Charge of the 21st Lancers. Rather in the vein of the Balaklava Charge, it was a gallant but pointless gesture by a regiment eager for any sort of action that would earn them a battle honour. It also produced three Victoria crosses.

THOMAS BYRNE VC (1866-1944)

Thomas 'Paddy' Byrne was born at 46 Bride Street, Dublin on 9 December 1866 to Thomas and Eliza (née Devitt). 'Paddy' Byrne enlisted in the 8th

Hussars in 1886 but a year later transferred to the 21st Hussars just as it was being sent to its overseas posting in India, first to Bangalore and then Secunderabad. During this time, Paddy was appointed batman to Major Crole-Martin.

After nine undemanding years in India, the 21st Hussars was ordered to Egypt in late 1896. In April 1897, there came the order for the regiment to convert from Hussars to Lancers of the Line. This change was wholly unexpected and purely an administrative one. The Army had decided to 'twin' existing lancer regiments – while one was posted abroad, its twin would serve at home. As there were an odd number of Lancer regiments, it was decided to convert the 21st Hussars.

There was very little time to train the soldiers in the use of their new weapon, the nine-foot long lance, before they embarked for the Sudan as part of the Kitchener's Anglo-Egyptian force. As we have seen, the prime aim was to invade and occupy the Sudan before the French did. The newspapers preferred to announce it as 'Avenging the death of General Gordon!'

There were eight attached officers who joined the regiment for the campaign including a 4th Hussar lieutenant named Winston Churchill. Unwanted by both Kitchener and the 21st, Churchill used his mother's influence to join the expedition and, through letters to her, reported the war's progress for the *Morning Post*. The press coverage of the regiment was not universally glowing and its relationship with Churchill became strained.

Eager to prove themselves and to shake off the ribbing they received from other cavalry regiments about their lack of battle honours – the lancers were mock-awarded the motto *Thou Shall Not Kill* – they, frustratingly, had to sit and watch the Dervish attacks being repelled at the Battle of Omdurman. But their chance for glory was soon to be realised.

As the Dervishes withdrew, Kitchener knew that he would have to occupy Omdurman before the Dervish army if he wanted to avoid any costly street fighting. Kitchener sent Lieutenant The Honourable R.F. Molyneaux of the Royal Horse Guards with an order for the 21st to ride to Jebel Surgham, a ridge from where it was expected to observe the Dervish army on the other side. They were also ordered to clear the enemy from Kitchener's march south and protect the right flank. This changed their principle task from reconnaissance to engagement.

VC Action

As they moved south, the 21st spotted about 200 of the enemy formed across the line of their advance to the city. Unseen by the lancers were another 2,600 concealed behind in a dried water course (*khor*). Confident that they could sweep away the enemy with a charge, the four squadrons of 440 lances formed up about 300 yards from the line of Dervishes. Presenting a front of over 400 yards, the 21st immediately spurred their mounts and followed Colonel Martin into a charge up the slope.

During the charge that lasted just thirty seconds, Paddy Byrne, in 'B' Squadron on the rear rank of the right centre, was hit by a bullet in the lower end of his right bicep, which caused him to drop his lance and he was forced to slow down.

Meanwhile, the charge was pressed home and the awful realisation that the enemy were in far greater numbers hit the lancers just as they reached the rim of the *khor.* Too late to stop, the lancers plunged into the mass of enemy, who were armed with fearsome short spears and heavy swords. The shock of the charge took the lancers into the centre of the mass and desperate and vicious hand to hand fighting ensued.

Paddy Byrne, with great difficulty due to his badly wounded sword arm, managed to draw his weapon and follow his comrades. He was the last man to enter the *khor.* It was here that the *khor* was at its widest point and held the greater number of enemy making it the hardest passage of all.

As the horses tumbled into the river bed they were stabbed by the spears waiting to receive them. Riders were thrown only to be hacked to death by the fearsome tribesmen. The bed became so densely packed that Byrne was unable to find a way in. Turning his horse to the left, he rode along to where 'C' Company had entered on the left flank.

Swinging his sword caused him great pain and he saw a route to ride clear of the mêlée. As he urged his horse forward, he heard an officer cry out for help. Turning, he saw the unseated and disarmed Lieutenant Molyneaux surrounded by four Dervishes who were closing in for the kill. Kitchener's galloper had decided to stay and take part in the charge but was now facing a horrible death at the hands of a merciless enemy.

Wheeling his horse around, Paddy rode straight at the four tribesmen, battering them aside with his horse. This gave the wounded Molyneaux the breathing space to run to safety. Recovering quickly, the Dervishes attacked Byrne, knocking his sword from his weak grasp and stabbing him in the chest with a spear. A sword slash caught him in the back but fortunately it was deflected by his bandolier. Seeing that his officer had managed to climb out of the *khor,* Paddy spurred his horse and scrambled to safety.

Twice wounded and dizzy from loss of blood, Byrne found his way back to 'B' Squadron. Here, he re-joined his troop and found that only Lieutenant Raymond de Montmorency and six men had survived the charge. Byrne was covered in blood but with his adrenaline pumping he called for another charge until Montmorency order him to be taken to the medics at the rear.

The 21st regrouped 150 yards south of the *khor,* for the Dervishes still numbered 2,000 and were preparing to attack. Unsheathing their carbines, the lancers put down an accurate fire that eventually drove off the enemy, who withdrew to the north-west.

Paddy Byrne's chest wound had to be dressed four times that night, so great was the inflammation. When he was set upon a camel, slung side by side with a man whose arm had been severed at the shoulder, every jolt pitched him forward and struck his wound against the front of the pannier. Byrne was amongst the many wounded who were taken to one of the hospital barges moored at the captured city. Paddy casually mentioned that he had saved an officer but this was not traced to him until Winston Churchill visited the hospital steamer, which was transporting the wounded down the Nile.

Churchill told him, 'I believe you are the man we have been looking for all the while'. The wounded Lieutenant Molyneaux was also on the hospital steamer and was called to identify his saviour.

Byrne did recover from his wounds but the fingers of his right hand were slightly withered and he never recovered their full use. The casualty list was grim – five officers and sixty-five men killed or wounded. The estimates of the Dervish dead varied from twenty to seventy, which demonstrated how costly had been the charge and beggared the question, 'was the charge necessary?'

Very quickly, controversy over the charge broke out with Colonel Martin being accused of recklessness. The newspapers soon took up the theme that the charge was a gross blunder on the lines of Balaklava. Two weeks after the regiment returned home, Martin was removed from his command.

One thing that everyone agreed was the outstanding bravery shown by the officers and men of the 21st Lancers in taking on such a numerically superior enemy. In his despatch, Winston Churchill wrote of Paddy's exploit, 'it was the bravest act I have ever seen performed'.

Amongst the many awards bestowed on the Lancers were three Victoria Crosses – those to Captain Paul Kenna, Lieutenant de Montmorency and Private Thomas Byrne. All three were gazetted on 15 November 1898 and returned home for a special investiture.

On 6 January 1899, they were received by Queen Victoria at her favourite home, Osborne House on the Isle of Wight, and presented with their Crosses. That is as far as the democratic process went, for the two officers were brought from Cowes in a royal carriage and later dined with the Queen. Paddy Byrne travelled by a hackney carriage and shared his dinner below stairs with the servants.

Later Service

The 21st Lancers returned for home duty in Ireland just as the Anglo-Boer War began. Having just completed their long stint of service abroad, there was little prospect of being sent to South Africa. A number of officers and men, however, managed to volunteer for special service or get transferred to an outgoing regiment.

Amongst these were Captain Kenna, who transferred to the staff of the Cavalry Division and Captain de Montmorency, who raised a mounted force named Montmorency's Scouts. Byrne, who was now Montmorency's servant, accompanied his master. De Montmorency, Byrne and the newly-formed Scouts, joined General Gateacre's force, which had suffered a reverse at Stormberg on 19 December 1899. The Scouts saw their first action in a sharp skirmish on 31 December in which they drove off the Boers.

Gateacre's force was gradually pushing the Boers back out of the north-east Cape Colony and into the Orange Free State. Sadly, de Montmorency did not live to see this for he was shot dead on 24 February 1900 and a distraught Paddy Byrne had to be restrained from trying to recover the body. The Scouts went on to take part in operations around Pretoria and some severe fighting at Wepener. When he returned home, Paddy brought back Montmorency's mount – a grey polo pony that had carried him at Omdurman – and handed it over to his father, General Viscount de Montmorency.

Paddy re-joined his regiment, which was still stationed in Dublin. It was here that he met Bridget, the twenty-year-old daughter of John Pender, a green grocer who had a contract to supply the Army with its fruit and vegetables. Soon they were married, and when the regiment was transferred to Canterbury, she came to the town which was to remain their life-long home.

Retirement

On 19 September 1910, after nearly twenty years' service, Paddy retired from the Army. He and Bridget lived at several addresses in Canterbury. They had eight children, Edward, Norah Thomas, Lilian, William, Thresa and Margaret. The eighth was four-year old Brian, who was knocked down and killed by an Army lorry.

When the First World War broke out in August 1914, the forty-nine-year-old Paddy Byrne immediately re-joined the Army. He was employed in his old station, the Canterbury Cavalry Depot, as a garrison policeman. At the end of the war, he remained at the Depot working as a messenger at the Cavalry Pay and Records Office until his retirement in 1931 having served the Crown for forty-six years. As a VC, he also attended both the King's Garden Party in 1920 and the 1929 House of Lords Dinner.

The next two years saw his health failing until he died at the age of seventy-seven at the Municipal Hospital on 15 March 1944. Paddy was afforded a full military funeral and his flag-draped coffin was carried on a gun carriage through the crowded city streets to the West Gate Cemetery.

Chapter 35

Crete, 1898

Number of VCs awarded	1
Number of VCs awarded to officers	1
Total awarded to Royal Navy	1

Origins of the War

The island of Crete was an Ottoman possession which was inhabited by a mostly Greek-speaking Christian population. During the Greek War of Independence (1821-1829), the Cretans rebelled and sought union with Greece. The outbreaks over the following decades were brutally put down and in 1878, after European pressure, a pact was signed establishing the island as an autonomous state under Ottoman suzerainty. This lasted only ten years before the Ottomans reneged on the agreement. This led to further unrest and there was another rebellion in 1895 to 1897, which led to the Greeks sending military forces to the island, thus provoking a war with Turkey.

In an unequal contest, the Turks crushed the weak Greek army which prompted the Great Powers of Great Britain, France, Italy and Russia to intervene. The conditions imposed by this intervention were that the Greek army withdrew from Crete and the Turks halted their advance. The Great Powers decided to restore order by appointing a committee of four admirals who would remain in charge until the arrival of Prince George of Greece who was appointed the High Commissioner. This decision effectively separated Crete from the Ottoman Empire and set up the short-lived Cretan State.

In 1908, Crete declared unilateral union with Greece but still discontent rumbled on. It was not until 1913, at the end of the Balkan War, that the Ottoman Sultan relinquished his formal right to the island.

An unusual Victoria Cross was awarded during this conflict in which Britain was not at war. Surgeon William Maillard's VC is unique in that was for gallantry under fire from a civilian mob in a United Nations-style intervention.

WILLIAM JOB MAILLARD VC (1863-1903)

William Job Maillard was born in Barwell, Somerset on 10 March 1863 to a Methodist minister, Daniel Gallard Maillard and his wife Winifred Elizabeth née Dawkins. William attended school at Dunheved College, Launceston and Kingswood School, Bath, before going to Guy's Hospital to study medicine (1882-89). He qualified as MRCS and LRCP and was awarded a Gold Medal for Medicine.

Maillard joined the Navy on 22 August 1889 and obtained his MD. He served on several ships before joining the torpedo gunboat, HMS *Hazard* in Malta in 1897. Almost immediately, the ship was sent to patrol the seas around Crete. The situation was rapidly deteriorating with the Greeks holding the countryside and the Turks occupying the towns, aided by their notorious and brutal Bashi Bazouks (irregular militia). In the British zone was the capital of Candia (now Heraklion), where the Highland Light Infantry was stationed.

The decision of the four Great Powers' admirals to collect export customs duties inflamed an already volatile atmosphere and was just the excuse a mob needed to attack Christians, including the hated British. On 6 September 1898, they slaughtered 500 Christians and besieged about 130 soldiers of the HLI in the Customs House by the waterfront. The British Vice-Consul perished when his house was burned down when the mob set the town on fire.

VC Action

The Turkish mob of several thousand began to inflict casualties on the soldiers in the Customs House. *Hazard* was lying just offshore and received a message for help. Two parties of about fifty men were sent ashore and relayed back a message for medical help, as the HLI had suffered many wounded. Surgeon Maillard and two officers were rowed ashore by a crew of five.

As they approached the quay, they came under fire from the mob. Leaving the boat, two were killed and three wounded as they made a dash for the shelter of the Custom House. When Maillard reached the Custom House, he looked back and saw that badly wounded Ordinary Seaman Arthur Stroud had fallen back in the boat. Without considering the almost certain chance of being killed, Maillard turned and sprinted back through the hail of bullets to the boat. His efforts to lift the mortally wounded seaman failed as the boat began to drift away and Maillard was forced to abandon Stroud, who was close to death. He made another dash back through the curtain of fire and when he reached the shelter of the Customs House, it was found that his clothes were riddled with bullet holes but miraculously, he had not been wounded.

The Times published an eyewitness account a few days later: 'Instantly, the whole of the houses round the harbour opened fire on the Customs House and English patrol. Every window held two or three riflemen, and the fire is described as something appalling. The patrol immediately got into the Customs House and started to return the fire.

'There was a guard of forty-five Highlanders near the telegraph office and forty of these were brought down to reinforce, but they came via the tunnel and archway through the town wall just behind the Custom House, losing several men ... The *Hazard*'s men behaved magnificently, and I hope they get something out of it. Their doctor should get the VC. His clothes were shot through in at least a dozen places whilst he was helping the wounded, and he escaped marvellously without a scratch.'

William Maillard was indeed recommended for the Victoria Cross and it was announced in *The London Gazette* on 2 December 1898. He was presented with it by the Queen at Windsor Castle on the 15th. Maillard later stated that he should have been reprimanded for exposing himself to also certain death when he was the only doctor present able to treat the wounded.

The sequel to the events at Candia was that the town was bombarded by the Royal Navy and the ringleaders were captured and hanged. Sadly, Surgeon William Maillard did not enjoy his fame for long. He was promoted to Staff Surgeon and served for a further four years until ill health forced his premature retirement.

Maillard died in Bournemouth, possibly of a brain tumour on 10 September 1903 and was buried in the town's Wimbourne Road Cemetery. He was one of those rare recipients who had no accompanying campaign medal with his Cross.

Chapter 36

Second Anglo-Boer War, 1899–1902

Number of VCs awarded	78
Number of VCs awarded to officers	37
Number of VCs awarded to other ranks	41
Total awarded to British Army	55
Total awarded to Imperial forces	23

Origins of the War

The complex origin of the animosity between the British and the Boers goes back to the Napoleonic Wars. The Cape Colony belonged to Napoleon's vassal, the Batavian Republic (Holland). Because the sea route around the Cape was important for Britain and her Indian possessions, a force was sent to seize the colony and prevent it coming under French control.

In January 1806, the almost bloodless victory saw the British establish their foothold in southern Africa and later encourage the immigration of British settlers who were at odds with the Boer settlers. In particular, the Boers objected to Britain's anti-slavery laws which led to a mass eastward and north-eastward emigration away from the British-controlled Cape Colony. Those Boer Trekkers who went east, once again journeyed northward into the interior to avoid the British who annexed Natal in 1843. Here they established two independent countries in the 1850s; the Transvaal and the Orange Free State.

For twenty-five years, there was peaceful coexistence between the Boers and the British, until the latter provoked a war with the Zulu nation. The Transvaal was vulnerable to attack from the Zulus and their allies and was virtually bankrupt. The British stepped in to help defend the country, but at the end of the war decided to annex the republic.

The First Boer War (1880-81) ended in an ignoble defeat for the British and the restoration of the two Boer republics. Relations between the Boers and the British, however, remained uneasy and were exacerbated by the discovery of diamonds at Kimberley in West Griqualand and gold in the Transvaal. Although the Orange Free State laid claim to the diamond fields of Kimberley, a ruling favoured West Griqualand, which opted to become a Crown Colony in 1877.

There was little the British could do to claim the gold discovered in the Transvaal, which made the republic the richest and potentially the most powerful nation in southern Africa. The only drawback for the Boers was that they had neither the manpower nor industrial know-how to develop this resource. Reluctantly, the Transvaal was forced to allow the immigration of thousands of *Uitlanders,* mostly British, to work the goldfields. Soon it became apparent to the Transvaal that the *Uitlanders* would quickly outnumber the Boer settlers. A refusal to allow the newcomers a vote or equal rights led to an abortive attempted coup in 1895 by Cecil Rhodes and Leander Jameson.

It was now clear that the British wanted to incorporate the two Boer Republics, now named the South African Republic, into a federation under British control. The Boers recognised that the granting of voting rights to the *Uitlanders* would result in the loss of Boer control in the Republic with the probability of annexation. Despite negotiations between the Republic's President, Paul Kruger and the British Colonial Secretary, Joseph Chamberlain, war looked inevitable. Kruger demanded Britain remove her troops from the borders of the Transvaal and the Orange Free State, but ordered his own commandos to advance on the Natal border. Finally, on 11 October 1899, war was declared.

It was the Boers who mounted the pre-emptive strikes on Kimberley, Mafeking and Ladysmith. One of the rare early victories for the British Army was at the Battle of Elandslaagte, during which four Victoria Crosses were awarded.

MATTHEW FONTAINE MAURY MEIKLEJOHN VC (1870-1913)

Matthew Fontaine Maury Meiklejohn was born in Clapham, London on 27 November 1870, to Professor John and Jane Meiklejohn, their first son was christened in a singular way. He was named after the American pioneering oceanographer, Matthew Fontaine Maury and it seems likely that Matthew's parents attended one of Maury's London lectures and were impressed enough to want to favour their offspring with such a lengthy name.

Professor Meiklejohn of St Andrew's University was from Edinburgh and when Matthew was old enough, he was sent to one of Scotland's finest schools, Fettes College. Although he did not come from a military family, upon completing his education, young Meiklejohn was sent to the Royal

Military College, Sandhurst in February 1890. He is recorded as being 5ft-5in tall and his conduct 'exemplary'.

On 17 June 1891, he was commissioned and posted to India to join 1st Battalion Gordon Highlanders. He took part in the relief of Chitral with General Low's force and later was one of the Dargai heroes who crossed the fire-swept plateau to eject the Afridis from the heights. He was transferred to the 2nd Battalion when the 1st Battalion returned to Scotland.

Anticipating war with the Boers, the 2nd Battalion was sent to South Africa, disembarking at Durban on 9 October, two days before the declaration of war. They were immediately sent by rail to Ladysmith, the Aldershot of South Africa. Here they were brigaded under Colonel Ian Hamilton, along with 1st Devons, with whom they had sailed from India, and 1st Manchesters.

The Boer's central aim was to cut railway communication with the coast and prevent the British moving their troops to the main theatre of operations. Three towns were singled out as key targets; Kimberley, Mafeking and Ladysmith. Of the three, Ladysmith was the central point of the whole Boer plan.

On 11 October 1899, the Boers crossed the Natal / Transvaal border, and nine days later confronted the small British garrison at Dundee, forty miles northeast of Ladysmith. The Boers had taken up a position on top of a steep ridge called Talana Hill about two miles from the camp. A Creusot 75-mm shell landed near the line of tents and the first battle of the Boer War began.

The British advanced in close order, a formation General Penn Symons insisted upon, resulting in many dead and wounded. Amongst them was Symons, who was mortally wounded. Gradually, the British inched their way up the steep flanks of Talana until they forced the Boers to retreat. It was a British victory but, at best, a Pyrrhic one.

The Boer invasion force had been split in two. Generals Erasmus and Meyer had marched on the rich coal-mining town of Dundee, while General Koch was to hold a defensive line on Mkhupe Pass over the Biggarsberg Mountains in case the British counter-attacked. Three days after the Battle of Talana, the Boers succeeded in dislodging the British from Dundee, who withdrew to join the main body of the army at Ladysmith.

Koch's commando exceeded its instructions and advanced on the mining town of Elandslaagte, which lay on the Ladysmith–Dundee railway line. A cavalry reconnaissance was sent out from Ladysmith and reported that the Boers had occupied the horseshoe-shaped ridge to the south-east that commanded the railway and the Dundee road. Unbeknown to both sides, the depleted British garrison from Dundee was withdrawing down this road to Ladysmith.

Early on 21 October, Lieutenant General Sir George White VC, Officer Commanding, Natal Field Force, ordered Major General John French to take five squadrons of the Imperial Light Horse, a battery of the Natal

Volunteer Artillery and four companies of the Manchester Regiment and eject the Boers from Elandslaagte. On arriving and exchanging artillery fire, French saw that his guns were hopelessly outranged and started to pull back. He telegraphed General White for reinforcements, which were swiftly despatched, the cavalry and artillery by road and the infantry by train

It was around 13.00 hours on a thundery and sultry afternoon that the off-duty Gordons and Devons were ordered to prepare to embark on cattle trucks that were to take them the dozen or so miles to Boer-held Elandslaagte. This came as a shock for those who thought the Boers had been repulsed at Talana, forty miles away, and yet here were the enemy within reach of Ladysmith.

About five miles short of Elandslaagte, the trains clanged to a halt and the troops disembarked. General French was in overall command but in command of the infantry was Colonel Ian Hamilton, a former Gordon Highlander. He was known to Matthew Micklejohn as he had commanded a brigade during the Tirah campaign. The British then faced the Boer position some 5,000 yards across a rolling veldt without much cover. They were entrenched along a range running at right angles to the railway with the highest point about 800 feet. The range itself was a succession of kopjes, each one commanding another so they resembled the teeth of a saw.

Hamilton then began his attack with the Devons advancing across the open ground, closely supported by the artillery. When they were about 800 yards from the enemy's position, the Devons took cover behind termite hills and boulders while they waited for the right flank attack to develop. This was performed by the Manchesters and Gordons, who were joined by the Imperial Light Horse. It was about 17.00 hours when the Gordons reached the shelter of a rocky ridge on the southern end of the horseshoe. Along the crest ran a barbed wire fence which impeded their progress. Men began to fall as they attempted to pull down the fence. At last, a gap was made and the Highlanders surged through. Colonel Dick-Cunningham VC was felled with a bullet through the arm and fainted. The light was fading and not helped by the black storm clouds that had gathered over the ridge which threw into relief the flashes of gunfire and exploding shells. Suddenly, the clouds burst and a deluge of rain covered the battlefield.

VC Action

Still the Gordons advanced, taking the series of kopjes (rocky hills that rises abruptly from virtually level ground) until they leapt over the final barricade to capture the Boer guns on the main kopje.

Meiklejohn later wrote a report of the battle and described this moment: 'The end was coming. The whole line surged forward in an indistinguishable mass – except for the kilts of the Highlanders – of Gordons, Manchesters and Imperial Light Horse. Every rifle was in the firing line. The excitement among the men of the Imperial Light Horse was delirious and, I believe, contagious ... I saw one man throw his rifle in the air with a shout and catch it again. Another I noticed bring down a flying enemy with a pretty shot which struck him between the shoulders. An officer of the same regiment let off his revolver within two inches of my ear and, on turning round to remonstrate, begged pardon but remarked that he had "shot a Boer". All were infected with the lust of the fight.

'Nothing could stand before this irresistible rush. The wounded lay where they fell. Presently, a confused heterogeneous mass, breathless but victory within their grasp, our troops had topped the last ridge and were looking down on the Boer camp, which lay in a hollow just below.

'In the fading light, Boers were jumping up like startled hares and scurrying away ... Two of the enemy's guns were in our hands. The honour of their capture seems to lie between the Devons and the Gordons. Impartially speaking, I think the latter.'

Another newsman, Henry Nevinson, was with the Gordons and wrote: 'Wildly cheering, raising their helmets on their bayonets ... line after line of khaki figures, like hounds through a gap, came pouring into position, shouting fiercely: Majuba, Majuba.' It was a particularly poignant moment for Colonel Hamilton to savour as he had been badly wounded in the British defeat at Majuba Hill in the First Boer War of 1881.

A white flag was waved and Hamilton ordered a cease fire. Meiklejohn continued: 'The men, some sitting down, some standing up, were talking or cleaning their rifles, when suddenly, from both flanks, a fire as heavy as, perhaps heavier, than that which we had already experienced struck our unprepared lines. They imagined, with justice, that nothing now remained but to collect the wounded.'

Hamilton had been wrong in assuming that the battle was over, when in fact General Koch and some of his men had retreated to another position and were able to pour a deadly crossfire on the British. Having advanced through heavy enemy fire and survived, the British troops, their adrenaline spent, were reluctant to start fighting again. The Gordons had lost most of their officers and were leaderless. Nevertheless, Captain Meiklejohn stood up and called for his company to follow as he charged the second enemy position. Aided by Sergeant Major William Robertson, his men responded and the final Boer position was taken. Unfortunately, Meiklejohn was hit four times, his right arm shattered.

The Boers were put to flight and they attempted to mount up and ride away. They took the full impact of a charge by the 5th Lancers and 5th Dragoons which completed the rout as night fell. The victory, however, was the only one the British would enjoy for many months. The Gordons suffered the greatest losses, 123 casualties, including thirty-one dead. Only three officers emerged unscathed.

For those wounded scattered over the battlefield, the next few hours were terrible. Pitch darkness and cold, torrential rain added to their wretched state. One of these unfortunates was Matthew Micklejohn who was eventually found and conveyed to the Elandslaagte station and put in a truck with the other wounded. He was then carried to Ladysmith and treated in the base hospital.

Wounded

One unfortunate fatality was that of Colonel Dick-Cunningham, who having recovered from his wounds, was killed by a stray bullet. In his weakened state, it was a minor miracle that Meiklejohn emerged from the siege with his health intact and was recovering from the shock of losing a limb despite the ravages of disease and starvation

Meiklejohn spent the next six months convalescing. His recovery was aided when he learned that he and Sergeant Major Robertson had been recommended for the Victoria Cross. Both were gazetted on 20 July 1900. The latter received his Cross from the Queen at Windsor Castle on 25 August whereas Meiklejohn was not able to return to England until 26 October.

On 15 December 1900, along with John Milbanke, Horace Glascock and Henry Engleheart, Captain Matthew Meiklejohn was presented with the Victoria Cross at Windsor Castle. He had the distinction of being the last officer invested by Queen Victoria before her death on 22 January 1901.

Although he had lost his right arm, Meiklejohn was a natural left hander and this enabled him to continue his Army career. He was still able to participate in the Boer War, albeit from a distance, when he was appointed Garrison Adjutant at the remote South Atlantic island of St Helena. This small volcanic island is famous for being Napoleon's final prison. Now it was being used to incarcerate some 5,000 Boer prisoners of war, the most prominent being General Piet Cronje, who stayed in a hillside cottage. Boredom was the greatest threat, although some 200 prisoners died of disease.

At the end of the war in 1902, Meiklejohn sailed for home and returned for a while to Edinburgh. Here, life as a regimental officer was now out of the question so his only option was to enter Staff College. Upon completing the course, he became an instructor at the Royal Military College, Sandhurst. He met and fell in love with Vera Josephine, the daughter of Lieutenant Colonel Lionel Marshall. They married in 1904 and set up home at Hartland House, King's Road, Richmond, Surrey. Together they produced two daughters and one son.

On 22 November 1911, Meiklejohn was promoted to major and seconded to the General Staff at Army HQ, London. It was in this rank that he met with an untimely death just days after being thrown by his horse while on duty as a mounted staff officer to an Inspecting General. This happened during a review of the London University Officer Training Corps in Hyde Park on 26 June 1913, when the sound of gunfire during the General Salute startled his rather frisky mount.

Fatal Accident
Two days later, while exercising this horse along Rotten Row, Hyde Park, it again became unmanageable and bolted. Handicapped by the loss of his right arm, Meiklejohn fought to control the horse.

A letter appeared in *The Times* dated 7 July 1913, which described the fatal incident: 'As my nurse was the only eye-witness of the tragic accident which led to Major Meiklejohn's death. I think it right to acquaint the public with her story. She and my children were in Hyde Park on Saturday afternoon, 28 June. They had reached a spot opposite to Knightsbridge Barracks, and, as they were walking along the path, Major Meiklejohn on his runaway horse suddenly came upon them between the trees.

'In order to avoid danger to the children, he turned his horse against the railings of Rotten Row, which he must have known he could not clear. He thus gave his life for theirs, and added one more to the long roll of his brave and unselfish deeds.'

Meiklejohn was badly injured and taken to Middlesex Hospital. After lingering for a week, he died on 4 July. He was buried in St Jude's Avenue, Brookwood Cemetery, Surrey (Plot 3, Grave 172317). A memorial plaque was later raised near the entrance gates of Hyde Park Cavalry Barracks but this has since been relegated to a wall within the building.

ARTHUR HENRY LINDSAY RICHARDSON VC (1872-1932)
Arthur Henry Lindsay Richardson was born in Southport, Lancashire, on 23 September 1872 to William and Caroline (née Richardson). He was one of nine children brought up in a comfortable middle-class home. William died when Arthur was only eight and it was Carrie, as Caroline was known in the family, who imposed her formidable will on her children. She saw to it that all her children were well educated and went into good occupations.

Arthur was educated at the Liverpool Institute and School of Art and left to become an apprentice to a firm of dentists. This seemingly conventional and straightforward career path was suddenly shattered when Arthur was nearly nineteen. His relationship with Carrie irredeemably broke down, possibly rebelling against his mother's complete control over his life. In 1891, he packed his bags and caught a boat bound for Canada.

Canada
Not lingering in the populated provinces in the east, Arthur continued travelling west until he reached Manitoba, where he found work on a horse ranch. Three years later he moved west to Saskatchewan and on 7 May 1894, he joined the North West Mounted Police. It was just the life that suited him and he thrived. He moved further north to the town of Prince Albert and was promoted to corporal. There were even hints that he would soon gain a commission. When he was posted to Regina, he met his future wife, Florence Hughes.

When the Anglo-Boer War started in 1899, an entrepreneur named Donald Alexander Smith, 1st Baron Strathcona and Mount Royal, recruited and equipped a cavalry regiment at his own expense for service in South Africa. Lord Strathcona's Horse, as it was named, drew its skilled recruits mainly from cowboys and members of the NWMP. He put up £150,000, a colossal figure, to pay and equip 546 officers and men and 599 horses. One of the first men to enlist was Arthur Richardson, who carried his police rank of corporal with him.

Boer War

The Strathcona's Horse embarked at Halifax, Nova Scotia, on 17 March 1900 and arrived at Cape Town on 11 April, having endured a terrible journey. The weather was stormy and the seas rough, causing the deaths of 120 horses. Arthur also suffered a broken leg from a fall due to the high seas and was carried to Cape Town hospital to recover.

After six week's recuperating, Arthur re-joined his regiment, which was operating in the Transvaal. It formed part of General Sir Redvers Buller's cavalry, the 3rd Mounted Brigade, which was attempting to drive General Botha's army from the Transvaal following the capture of Johannesburg and Pretoria. Strathcona's Horse scouted ahead of Buller's main force and it was in the early hours of 5 July that Arthur Richardson performed his act that gained him the Victoria Cross.

VC Action

Richardson was part of a thirty-eight man patrol commanded by Captain Cartwright that was scouting an area about fifteen miles west of Standerton. As dawn broke, they approached the hamlet of Wolve Spruit where there were signs of enemy activity. The Canadians cautiously approached the area when suddenly about eighty Boers concealed in a dried-up water-course opened fire. Cartwright ordered a withdrawal as two men were hit and wounded. As they fell back, Private Alex McArthur was shot in the arm and leg and his horse was mortally wounded. Collapsing, the horse pinned his rider underneath and as he struggled to free himself, he became a target for the Boers.

Reining in, Arthur looked back and saw his helpless comrade. Turning, he spurred his horse through the Boer fire and reached McArthur. Ignoring the bullets, Richardson dismounted, dragged the wounded man from beneath the dead horse, lifted him and threw him across his saddle. Arthur managed to climb up behind the wounded man and gallop back to safety without injury although a Boer bullet went through his hat and two others pierced his tunic.

An eye-witness account described the escape more dramatically: 'His horse, a small one, could only go slowly. Sergeant Buchanan and six men covered his retreat, among them George Sparks, who though shot in the neck at the time, dismounted and covered the retreat. Just when the escape seemed possible fate intervened in the form of a wire fence which

Richardson's horse, now covered with foam and thoroughly exhausted, refused to jump.

'The Boers closed on Richardson, demanding his surrender, when a Boer bullet struck the horse's shoulder causing it to plunge over the fence and gallop madly towards the camp and safety. The faithful animal, however, died one hour later from its wounds and the exhaustion of the chase.'

Richardson was recommended for the Victoria Cross which was gazetted on 14 September 1900. He was the first member of the Canadian forces under British command to be awarded the VC. The citation mistakenly showed Richardson as a sergeant, but when the news reached the regiment, he was duly given the promotion.

The men of the Strathcona's Horse continued scouting and patrolling for the rest of 1900, being involved in many skirmishes across the Transvaal and Orange Free State. Sergeant Richardson fought his last engagement at Clocolan on 23 December before the regiment was withdrawn, having served its requisite time in the field. The regiment sailed from Cape Town at the end of February 1901 and on arrival in England attended a reception at Liverpool's St George's Hall. Arthur Richardson travelled to London to receive his Cross from the new king, Edward VIII, at St James's Palace on 12 March 1901. While he was in Liverpool he visited his sister Mabel, but there was no reconciliation with his mother.

Later Life

Richardson then returned to Canada and was officially discharged from the Strathcona's Horse at Ottawa. He was re-engaged by the Mounties at Battleford for a further three years. He took up again with Florence Hughes and they were married in 1901 and were blessed with a daughter, Dorothy, the following year.

In June 1902, Arthur was nominated by the Canadian Government to act as one of the mounted guard of honour of four Victoria Cross holders (one each from England, Canada, New Zealand and South Africa). They were to accompany the state coach to and from Westminster for the coronation of Edward VIII. When he arrived, he found that the enthronement had been delayed due to the king's emergency appendectomy. Arthur spent two months living with his sister, Maude, in Peterborough. Unfortunately, during the stay relationships soured with Maud and his other sister Mabel and they never spoke again.

Misfortune

The delayed coronation took place on 9 August and was filmed by Pathé newsreel. It was not until 1924, that Arthur got to see it and recognised himself as part of the guard. Sadly, on his return to Canada Richardson suffered a series of misfortunes that would dictate the rest of his life.

Florence's health went into a decline after their daughter's birth and she was diagnosed with tuberculosis, which spread to her spine. She was unable to care for Dorothy, and the burden of looking after his family began to take its toll on Arthur. He had been promoted to sergeant major in 1903, with the prospect of being commissioned.

The psychological and financial strain of looking after his sick wife and a baby meant he was getting into debt to pay for medical bills and increasingly absent from his post. His health began to suffer and he was finally declared unfit for his duties as a sergeant major. Although the NWMP refused him a commission, they did offer him a less onerous appointment as quarter-master.

On 12 November 1907, disillusioned and sick, he decided to buy his discharge and took the post of town constable at the town of Indian Head, thirty miles east of Regina. Life continued to be hard to the point that a letter from the town council to the Commissioner of the NWMP described Richardson as being in 'destitute circumstances'. The letter went on to say that the council had extended charity to him but were unable to retain him as constable. The council asked whether the NWMP could help him, but they declined and made the following comment that Richardson, 'was ruined by being awarded the Victoria Cross as he expected everything to come his way after he had been decorated'. The NWMP concluded that he had been a good constable and corporal before the award but deteriorated thereafter, 'being a victim of drink'.

In the autumn of 1908, Arthur and his wife returned to England. Florence could no longer stand the cruel Canadian winters, and Arthur was unable to get employment. Despite moving to Liverpool, Arthur made no contact with his wealthy family, who were oblivious of his return. For two years, the family lived on welfare in dire poverty. Finally, poor Florence died on 24 May 1910. When she was old enough, his daughter moved to Ireland to become a companion of Dr Hamilton and his family at Queen's College, Belfast.

Released from his obligations, Arthur was able to seek employment as a maintenance labourer with the Liverpool Corporation Tramways. For the next fourteen years, he worked anonymously on the streets of Liverpool, rising to the foreman of his gang, repairing the tram lines and replacing damaged track. No one had any idea that he was one of that elite band of VC holders.

VC Impersonator

Richardson's desire to remain anonymous opened the door to one of the most blatant examples of criminal impersonation of a Victoria Cross recipient which fooled a distinguished regiment and a whole community.

Seemingly, Arthur Henry Leonard Richardson VC died in March 1924. He was buried with full military honours and his passing was widely reported in the national newspapers.

One who read the reports with mounting disbelief was Richardson's mother, Carrie Richardson. The insurmountable breakup of her relationship with her son and the false report that he had died in a Montreal hospital in 1914 spurred her to mount an investigation. Several more versions of

Richardson's fate came to light. A cousin said that he had died in 1904, while another was sure he had died in London in 1913. Yet another reported that he had passed away in Toronto in 1923. What became increasingly clear was that the recently deceased Arthur Richardson was an imposter.

The fake Richardson had enlisted in the Gordon Highlanders in London at the outbreak of the First World War and submitted a typewritten declaration that he had been awarded the Victoria Cross during the Boer War. It is likely the sheer numbers of volunteers to join the Army in 1914 made the vetting of this flimsy evidence difficult to check. In any event, the Gordons used their new and welcome volunteer in their recruitment campaigns.

'Richardson' had served throughout the war, was wounded and promoted to corporal. After the Armistice, he moved to Aberdeen where he was feted as a hero and even invited to attend the Royal Garden Party at Buckingham Palace on 26 June 1920 (he was forty-fifth out of 310 attending to be presented to the King). He returned to Aberdeen and was employed as a cinema commissionaire, proudly wearing the crimson ribbon on his uniform, but at the time of his death he had fallen on hard times.

With the unmasking of the bogus VC in Aberdeen, the real Arthur Richardson felt he had to put himself forward. He became the focus of attention and the newspapers tried to talk up the sensational side of his past. There was a fleeting reunion with his mother and older brother which led to no permanent resumption of relationship. Within weeks, he was invited to attend a review of the 55th (West Lancashire) Division (Territorial Force) by King George V on 26 June 1924.

Arthur then resumed the life that he had chosen working as a foreman labourer. He did surface once more when he attended the Victoria Cross Dinner hosted by the Prince of Wales at the House of Lords on 9 November 1929. By this time, his daughter, Dorothy, had returned and was looking after him.

On 13 December 1932, Arthur returned from work complaining of severe stomach pains and was rushed to hospital, where he was diagnosed with acute appendicitis. It was too late to save his life and he died on 15 December aged 60, with his daughter by his side.

The real Arthur Richardson was buried alongside his wife in St James Mount Cemetery, which was closed four years later. In 1994, the Commonwealth War Graves Commission erected a new headstone by the path leading to Liverpool Cathedral and a wreath of poppies is laid there every year to honour 'the shy VC'.

ERNEST BEACHCROFT BECKWITH TOWSE VC (1864-1948)

Ernest Beachcroft Beckwith Towse was born on 23 April 1864 in London to Robert and Julia Ann. It had been intended that he would make the Royal

Navy his career and he was sent to Stubbington House School in Hampshire which was a preparatory school which coached pupils for naval cadetship. Later it was decided that he should be prepared for the Army instead and he was transferred to Wellington College.

In 1881, he entered Royal Military College Sandhurst and, in 1883, he was commissioned and joined the 3rd Seaforth Highlanders. On 16 December 1885 Towse was gazetted lieutenant into the Wiltshire Regiment. This was but a step, for on 2 January 1886 he was transferred into the Gordon Highlanders and joined the 1st Battalion in Malta.

The regiment was then sent to Ceylon in December 1888 and it was here that Ernest Towse displayed his courage and powers of endurance. On one occasion when he went elephant shooting in the dense jungle, he became separated from his tracker. He had made a kill and cut off the tail as proof. As it turned out, this was providential for Towse was lost for three days but managed to keep his nerve before he reached safety. The only food he had was the elephant's tail, which he gnawed.

In January 1892, the regiment was moved to India and Towse returned to England on leave. He used his return to marry Gertrude, the daughter of John Christie, a stockbroker. Tragically, their only child, a boy, died in infancy.

The rather pleasant routine regimental life, including polo and big game hunting, that a British officer in India enjoyed ended when the Gordons were moved to the North-West Frontier in 1895 as part of a 15,000-strong Chitral relief force was assembled under the command of Major General Robert Low. Campaign-fit, the Gordons were at the forefront of the attack on Dargai Heights in 1897, for which two VCs were awarded to the regiment.

Boer War

With an uneasy peace settling on the Frontier, the 1st Gordons had concluded their long overseas posting and were ordered back to Scotland, where they garrisoned Edinburgh Castle. This was but a brief interlude, for war broke out against the Boers in October 1899 and the battalion was ordered to South Africa. It embarked on SS *Cheshire* on 9 November and arrived at the Cape on 28th. On that same day, hundreds of miles to the north, the Battle of Modder River was being fought and, within ten days, the Gordons were thrown into the bloody field of Magersfontein.

One of the priorities for the British was to lift the siege of the important mining town of Kimberley in the North Cape. Lieutenant General Lord Methuen, with a field force of 8,500 had marched 120kms from Orange River Station to relieve Kimberley. He had fought battles at Belmont (23 November) and Graspan (25 November) until he confronted the Boer line at the Modder River just 34kms from his goal.

Methuen was used to encountering the Boers in the hills and was unaware that they had positioned themselves in trenches along the river bank. As a consequence, the British walked into an ambush and were pinned down for ten hours. Eventually a flank attack dislodged the Boers but the cost had been high, with seventy dead and 413 wounded, including Lord Methuen.

There was little alternative but to call a temporary halt while reinforcements arrived and to rest the exhausted troops, who had fought three battles in a row. It was almost two weeks before Methuen's army, increased to 13,000 with the arrival of a brigade of Highlanders, was ready to take the field again.

With the exception of Spionkop, there are few battles of the Anglo-Boer War that have provoked more embittered controversy than Magersfontein. Methuen began his attack on the Boer defences at Magersfontein Hill with an artillery bombardment which concentrated its fire on the kopje itself. This alerted the Boers of the impending attack. It was also completely ineffective as the Boers had not occupied the heights, but dug in at its base in an arc whose left flank rested on the Modder River.

The Highland Brigade, under Major General Andrew Wauchope, led the night advance in heavy rain and a bitter wind. Keeping in formation in the pitch dark was an impossibility and when dawn broke on 12 December, Wauchope's brigade found itself in the open and just 400 yards from the enemy trenches.

The Boers opened fire with devastating effect causing the Highlanders heavy casualties, including General Wauchope, who was one of the first to be killed. Pinned down with little cover, the troops began to suffer from the relentless sun which had succeeded the rain. At 14.00 hours, an order to ease back slightly was taken as an order to retire. Hundreds of Highlanders rose and began to run back, presenting the Boer marksmen with easy targets. The unattributed order to retire, which had tragically led to the bloody rout, left the Gordons with no alternative but to fall back as well.

VC Action

The Gordons, who were not part of the Highland Brigade but were with the supply column, had been ordered up to help their hard-pressed comrades. They had to cross some 3,000 yards of open plain to reinforce the Highland Brigade but as they got to within 300 yards of the Boer positions, they were enfiladed on their right flank. Their commander, Colonel Downman, waved forward his left and pulled back his right flanks, the only effective way of meeting the flanking fire. In doing so he was mortally wounded.

Captain Towse attempted to carry Colonel Downman on his back but found this physically impossible. He stayed behind scant shelter under heavy fire until he was joined by Colour Sergeant Nelson and Lance Corporal Hodgson. When the firing died down, together they were able to bring their mortally wounded colonel to safety, but it was to no avail as Downman died the following day. The two NCOs were mentioned in Lord

Methuen's despatch and Towse's action was the first of two acts for which he was recommended for the Victoria Cross.

The British losses were considerable; upward of 1,000 men killed, wounded or taken prisoner. Along with Stormberg and Colenso, Magersfontein made up the trio of costly defeats that was dubbed 'Black Week'. Captain Towse and his fellow Gordons were later involved in the battles of Paardeberg (18 February 1900) and the taking of Bloemfontein.

The Gordons became part of General Ian Hamilton's division as he advanced against General Philip Botha's and General De Wet's forces holding positions astride Hout Nek north of Thaba Nchu, fifty miles east of Bloemfontein. For two days, the Boers had beaten off the British. Carefully studying the situation, Hamilton saw that a large plateau-like hill known as Mount Thaba was not held in strength by the Boers and if the British could seize it, the Boer defences astride Hout Nek would not only be overlooked but could be outflanked. Major General Horace Smith-Dorrien's 19th Brigade was ordered to capture it.

On 30 April, Captain Towse performed his second act of gallantry which Winston Churchill witnessed: 'At first the troops made good progress, but as the enemy received continual reinforcements their resistance became more severe, until presently, far from gaining ground, they began to lose it. Finally, some 150 of the German Corps of the Boer force advanced from the Northern part of Thoda [*sic*]. Artillery opened on them, but in spite of accurate shell fire they continued to advance boldly against the highest part of the hill. Meanwhile, cloaked by a swell of the ground, Captain Towse, of the Gordon Highlanders, with 12 of his own Regiment and 10 of Kitchener's Horse, was steadily moving towards them. The scene on the broad stage of the Thoba plateau was intensely dramatic. The whole army were the witnesses.

'The two forces, strangely disproportionate, drew near to each other. Neither was visible to the other. The unexpected collision impended. From every point field glasses were turned on the spectacle, and even hardened soldiers held their breath. At last, with suddenness, both parties came face to face at 50 yards' distance. The Germans, who had already made 6 prisoners, called loudly on Captain Towse and his little band to surrender. What answer was returned is not recorded, but a furious splutter of musketry broke out at once, and in less than a minute the long lines of the enemy recoiled in confusion, and the top of the hill was secured to the British.

'Captain Towse, for his conspicuous gallantry and for the extraordinary results which attended it has been recommended for the Victoria Cross; but in gaining what is above all things precious to a soldier, he lost what is necessary to a happy life, for in the moment when his military career was assured by a brilliant feat of arms, it was terminated by a bullet which striking him sideways, blinded him in both eyes. Thus do misery and joy walk hand in hand on the field of war.'

Another eye-witness was Major General Smith-Dorrien, the CO of the 19th Brigade. He later wrote: 'It was evident to us below that they were unaware that working towards them southwards was an overwhelming force of Boers – some 150 strong. This force we had seen for some time, and so unlike Boers and so like our own troops were their movements that they were within a few hundred yards of Towse's party before we realised that they were Boers … We saw the forces, only about 100 yards apart, suddenly discover each other … It looked as if our small party must be annihilated, when these few men of the Gordons and Kitchener's rushed forward and appeared to pour a terrible fire before which the Boer line recoiled and fled back. This gallant act saved us the hill.'

The Gordon Highlanders Regimental History further adds: 'Both the Official and *Times* histories state that the Boer counter-attack was composed of foreigners, adventurers who had served in their own national armies. It was commanded by Colonel Maximoff, a Russian, who called on Towse to surrender. Regimental versions credit Towse with the most forcible possible language of refusal.'

The War Diary states that his men fixed bayonets as they charged: seven of the little band – just half– were killed or wounded; Towse himself, after wounding Maximoff with a shot from his carbine, was struck by a bullet which destroyed his sight.

General Smith-Dorrien recommended him for the Victoria Cross and later recalled: 'I shall never forget the pathetic sight of the stricken Towse, shot through both eyes; certain that he would never see again, not a thought for himself, but plenty for his men, hoping that he had done his duty, and with it all so cheerful and apparently happy. He spoke as quietly and as lucidly as if he was in the best of health. He spoke most highly of the behaviour of Kitchener's Horse.'

Blinded

The award of the Victoria Cross was announced in *The London Gazette* on 6 July 1900. The citation covered both his acts of gallantry. On 18 July, Towse and his wife travelled to Windsor Castle and, in a private audience, he was invested with his VC by a visibly affected Queen Victoria.

Later that year, the Queen appointed him as a Sergeant-at-Arms in Ordinary. From 1903 to 1939, he served as a member of the Honourable Corps of Gentlemen-at-Arms and as such was on guard at the lying in state of Queen Victoria, King Edward VII, Queen Alexander and King George V.

Life's Work

With the same determination and application he had shown as a serving soldier, he would not let blindness daunt him. 'Blindness' he said 'can either master a man or a man can master blindness'. In 1901, he joined the National Institute for the Blind and for the next fourteen years, he taught himself to touch type and read Braille and soon became expert in both arts. So began his great life's work.

In 1914 he made an approach to King George V to be permitted to go to the Front in France and Belgium to help wounded soldiers in Base Hospitals, the following year this was granted by the War Office. He was appointed as a staff captain without pay or allowances on 11 September 1915.

Towse made brief notes in Braille concerning his patient's wounds and the addresses of next of kin. His memory was exceptional and he remembered each individual case and wrote home to parents, wives and friends telling them all about their men. He would work far into the night at his typewriter and he rarely snatched more than a few hours' sleep. He received many letters of gratitude from relatives and comrades of the servicemen. For his service during the First World War he received the 1914-15 Star, 1914-1920 War Medal and the Victory Medal. He was also Mentioned in Despatches in June 1916 by General Sir Douglas Haig.

In 1921, he was appointed Chairman of the National Institute for the Blind, a post he held until ill health forced his resignation in 1944. Following his initial suggestion, St Dunstan's Hospital for the Blind was established in 1915 to care for ex-servicemen blinded through enemy action. He also became a Vice President of the British Legion.

In 1920, he was created a Commander of the Order of the British Empire and in 1927, he was knighted. His wife, who had been such a great help to him, died in 1935. His niece made a home with him and looked after him for the rest of his life. During the Second World War, his home at Goring on Thames, Oxfordshire, was used by civilians recuperating from being blinded in air raids.

After a long illness, this exceptional man died on 21 June 1948 and was buried in the churchyard of St Thomas of Canterbury, Goring on Thames. His decorations and medals are held at the Gordons Museum at Aberdeen.

In the early stages of the war, the Boers outnumbered the British and their pre-emptive incursions should have resulted in victory. Instead they chose to invest Mafeking, the northernmost town in Cape Colony and surround Kimberley, which cost them momentum.

Lieutenant George White VC commander of forces in Natal ignored orders not to try and defend Ladysmith stating that: 'I hold Ladysmith for the Queen'. All three towns held out for four months or more, tying up the Boer besiegers and the British relief columns. After the raising of the three sieges, weight of numbers began to tell on the skilful but undisciplined Boer fighters. The British and Colonial forces would eventually muster about 500,000, while the Boers numbered 88,000 at the beginning of the war, being considerably reduced by 1901.

By June 1900, Britain had overrun the Orange Free State and annexed the gold-rich Transvaal. Despite the apparent series of victories, the war was not at an end and the Boers resorted to what they were expert in – hit-and-run guerrilla tactics, which prolonged the war until 31 May 1902.

In the interim, there were many incidents where the Victoria Cross was won, mostly for saving lives. One such was the tragic case of a private in the Berkshire Regiment.

WILLIAM HOUSE VC (1879-1912)

The wounds that some soldiers carried could have a delayed effect years after they had sustained them. Years of nagging pain, with no prospect of ever being free, drove some to end their own lives. Others, who had been badly wounded, appeared to recover and pick up their lives once more, only to suffer sudden relapses that made their suicides so shocking. One such soldier was the Boer War VC hero, William House.

Early Life

Born into rural poverty on 7 October 1879, William John was the only son born to farm labourer Thomas House and his wife Sally. He grew up at Hatch Gate, Cold Ash, Thatcham in Berkshire and seemed destined to follow his father onto the land; a prospect he obviously did not relish.

After a rudimentary education, the seventeen-year-old William enlisted in to the 2nd Battalion, Royal Berkshire Regiment on 3 November 1896. After training, the country boy who had probably been no further than the nearby market town of Newbury, found himself on the way to the battalion's new posting in the Cape Colony.

Disembarking from the long sea voyage, the Berkshires were sent by train to the remote north-east of the colony, where they were based in Queenstown. It was thought prudent to protect the all-important railway system and a detachment of the Berkshires were sent to Stormberg Junction where they constructed a series of redoubts.

When the Boers invaded Cape Colony, these troops were withdrawn to Queenstown to be consolidated with the Northumberland Fusiliers and the Royal Irish Rifles under the command of General Gatacre. On 9 December 1899, Gatacre took his small force to retake Stormberg, which had been occupied by the Boers. Instead of taking the Berkshires, who were familiar with the area, he left them to guard the lines of communication. As a result, Gatacre's men lost their way during the night march, lost all element of surprise and were forced to retreat. Stormberg was the first of the three British defeats in a week that the newspapers labelled 'Black Week'.

It seemed to be the Berkshires' lot to act as guards rather than be involved in any fighting and it was not until July 1900 that this changed. The battalion joined a 7,600-strong force under the command of Major General Sir Ian Hamilton and were sent to secure the mountain passes in the Magaliesberg range to the west of Pretoria. In charge of the infantry was Brigadier General G.C. Cunningham.

VC Action

On 2 August, Cunningham's force of 1st King's Own Scottish Borderers, 1st Border Regiment, 1st Argyll & Sutherland Highlanders and the 2nd

Royal Berkshire Regiment, approached Zilikat's Nek, which was found to be strongly held by the Boers. While the main part of the brigade exchanged fire, Cunningham sent two companies of the Berkshires to scale a steep position on the east flank. 'A' (House's) and 'B' Companies commanded by Major McCracken were to lead off with the rest of the battalion in support.

After a couple of hours of climbing, the leading companies managed to scale the steep cliffs on the eastern buttress under a heavy crossfire. Having gained the summit, Sergeant Gibbs was sent forward to reconnoitre. Before he could re-join his comrades, he was spotted by the Boers, who opened fire. Gibbs was hit and lay severely wounded in full view of the enemy, who continued to lay down a heavy fire.

Private House, immediately volunteered to go forward to try and rescue the helpless sergeant, despite the lack of cover and being cautioned not to do so. Running forward under some covering fire from his comrades, he reached the wounded man and attempted to carry him to safety. The Boer fire was both heavy and accurate and House was hit in the neck and the head and fell severely wounded beside the man he had attempted to rescue. Calling out to his comrades, he told them not to try and rescue him. Shortly afterwards, the British advanced and forced the Boers to flee. The Berkshire lost five killed, including Sergeant Gibbs and thirty wounded. The wounds were found to be serious and captured Boers admitted that they had used soft-nosed bullets.

The great majority of Boer War VCs were awarded for humanitarian acts such as that performed by William House in going to the rescue of a fallen comrade. This led to a school of thought that said that such acts performed against a 'civilised' enemy like the Boers should not be regarded as worthy of VC but should be awarded the lesser DCM. The Boers were not barbaric like some of Britain's enemies, who would routinely torture and mutilate both wounded and prisoners.

The Commander in Chief, Lord Kitchener expressed this opinion in a letter dated 26 June 1901, in which he wrote: 'I think that some steps should be taken to discourage recommendations for the Victoria Cross in civilised warfare in cases of mere bringing in of wounded and dismounted men.'

General Cunningham overrode the battalion's recommendation for the Victoria Cross and House was awarded the DCM, gazetted on 27 September 1901. There the matter would have ended but for the determination of the officers of the battalion.

A letter dated 20 August 1902, was sent to the Commander-in-Chief, Lord Roberts asking him to intercede on House's behalf and pointing out that: 'There have been many cases where the Victoria Cross has been awarded for a less daring deed. The letter concluded with a rather over-the-top plea. I beg of you to do your utmost in the matter as the private's health is greatly undermined and as he has a widowed mother and young children, it will be extremely hard if he gets invalided out through doing one of the most daring deeds for a boy of 20 years in the late war.'

This letter did generate some debate and it was generally felt that the DCM should be changed to a VC. Sir Ian Hamilton shared this view in his recommendation for a VC to Private House. 'I have usually objected to VCs being awarded for "rescuing" wounded men in civilised war when, if they lay quite still, were probably safer than being rescued. But the particular coolness of this man as evinced by his warning to the others not to follow his example is very commendable and I would gladly see him get his decoration.'

William House was gazetted on 7 October 1902, his twenty-third birthday, and received his Cross from King Edward VII on the 24 October. He became the regiment's only living VC.

In 1904, his service expired and he was placed on the reserve. Unable to settle in civilian life, he soon re-enlisted and re-joined his old battalion. Because of his Cross, he was regarded as rather special. When his battalion was serving in the Sudan, he was selected to be one of the guards of honour to Lord Cromer at the opening of Port Sudan on the Red Sea in 1906. The 2nd Battalion was then posted to India. At the inspection of the regiment at Meerut in 1911, the Commander in Chief in India, Sir O'Moore Creagh VC, sought out and had a personal meeting with his fellow VC, Private House.

Personality Change

Soon after, House was promoted to Lance Corporal and was cross-posted to the 1st Battalion, then stationed at Dover. It was during this period that it was noticeable that House had undergone a personality change, becoming withdrawn and listless.

Just before 08.00 hours on 28 February 1912, House was dressed for parade and due to drill some new recruits, a duty he disliked. He was joined by six comrades in their room at the Grand Shaft Barracks, which sat on the cliffs overlooking the Western Docks. While the six soldiers were looking out of the window watching the daily parade, House was at the other end of the room.

Suddenly a shot rang out. The shocked soldiers found House dead, with half his head blown away. He had tied his pull-through lanyard to his bed frame and attached the other end to the trigger of his rifle. Standing up, he pointed the muzzle at his head and tugged with fatal results.

The cry 'Bill House has blown his brains out!' quickly spread throughout the barracks. This sudden death profoundly shocked the regiment and there was much speculation as to why he did it. Was it because of his promotion, albeit to the lowest NCO rank, and his dislike in drilling recruits? It may have been the transfer from the 2nd Battalion, which had been his home for over fifteen years and being separated from his old friends. Or it could have been something to do with his recent posting to India. His head wounds he had received during his VC exploit were thought to be the main reason, although it is possible that all these factors may have combined to lower his spirits enough to cause severe depression.

The other question was where he had obtained the bullet, for it was forbidden to have ammunition other than on the shooting range. It was generally felt that this is where he picked up the round. At the Coroner's Court, Lance Sergeant Stroud gave evidence: 'I had known the deceased before he volunteered to go abroad with a draft to India. He came home November last. He seemed altered altogether from when he went out. There was a terrible change in him. Before he went out he always had plenty to say and was lively, but on coming home he would hardly speak to anybody … Last Saturday afternoon, the deceased was in bed and jumped up two or three times in a rather startled fashion … He used to mope around his cot a good deal since he had been home and seemed strange.'

The coroner in his summing up concluded the following: 'Considering all he [House] had gone through, and the wound, it was probable that there was some brain trouble.' He thought if they looked at it in that light, they would satisfy their own consciences and do justice to the man. In his opinion, the wound and the hot climate of India and the evidence that had been heard showed that the deceased must have been strange at the time he committed the act and that his mind must have gone. The verdict of suicide through temporary insanity was then recorded.

It is of note that the suicide of Charles Wooden VC, who had ridden in the charge of the Light Brigade at Balaklava, also took place in the barracks at Dover and he was buried at the same cemetery as House.

As befitting a hero, William House was given a funeral with full military honours at St James' Cemetery, Dover. His mother, brother and two sisters as well as the regiment's senior officers were at the graveside as a firing party fired three volleys over the flag-draped coffin. It was not until 1994, however, that a headstone was finally erected, in this case by his regiment.

Chapter 37

China, 1900

Number of VCs awarded	2
Number of VCs awarded to officers	2
Total awarded to Royal Navy	2

Origins of the War

The Society of Righteous Harmonious Fists, abbreviated by westerners to Boxers, was the name given to a religious, fanatical uprising of the Chinese people who believed that all western foreigners were bent on destroying their traditional Chinese culture. Chief among their targets were the Christian missionaries who were particularly active at that time.

These resentments had risen in one of the West's most lucrative trading places – China. Throughout Victoria's reign this vast country had experienced major European powers almost compelling the Chinese Government to trade with them. This can be seen in the case of opium, which was deemed desirous to the Chinese.

During the opium wars of the 1860s the Chinese were all but forced to trade with the West to gain the drug they needed. This had caused the number of trading posts to mushroom. The French, British, Germans and Americans had carved up Shanghai into personal trading spheres. The rapidity of European expansion in China can be seen in the acquisition of Kiachow by Germany in 1897, Port Arthur by Russia and Wei-hai-wei by Britain in 1898. Resistance by the Chinese to this alien intrusion was weak. The Chinese Government saw its sovereignty eroded, but retaliation was rarely an option. Foreign forces had modern weaponry and organised regiments that could easily crush any rebellion by Chinese imperialist armies.

Although the province of Shandong saw the emergence of the Boxers in 1898 it was not until the summer of 1899 that the full force of the Boxers was felt. Missionaries were particularly abhorred ever since the 1899 edict allowing exemption for missionaries from local laws.

The Boxers had tacit support from the Dowager Empress, T'Zu His. By giving her approval to the uprising, she gained wide support from the population believing that the destruction of the Foreign Legations would end the European, American and Japanese influence over China and its trade. The Dowager walked a tightrope. On the one hand provoking the West could cause a backlash and militarily they would win in any battle. On the other she could not deny the anti-Western sentiments felt by her subjects – and her authority would only hold out if she had their endorsement.

This is further supported by the banners and slogans that the Boxers adopted: 'Support the Ch'ing, destroy the foreigner.'

The Boxers original target was to overthrow the Government but the Empress engineered it to look like they were supporting it. Edicts were passed declaring that secret societies were part of the fabric of China's history and were not criminal. This further angered the West who saw this as evidence of official backing of the Boxer movement.

The Boxers had no named leaders or recognised direction except to destroy and expel all foreigners. By the spring of 1900, the poorly organised Boxer uprising gathered momentum with the burning of foreign-owned property, the killing of Christian converts and the murder of western missionaries.

As the rebellion reached Peking with the destruction of the racecourse, the first of the many Boxer attacks against foreign property in the capital, the British Ambassador, Sir Claude McDonald sent word to the British Naval C-in-C, Admiral Sir Edward Seymour, to send troops to protect the legations from further bloodshed. In an alliance with other nations who were keen to protect lucrative trading posts, they anchored a number of vessels at Taku Bar, at the mouth of the Peiho River – the closest the military could get to Peking.

Amongst the small group sent ahead to guard the British embassy was an officer who was awarded the Victoria Cross on the first day of the besieging of the Legation Quarter.

LEWIS STRATFORD TOLLEMACHE HALLIDAY VC (1870-1966)

Lewis Stratford Tollemache Halliday was born on 14 May 1870 at Medstead House, Hampshire, and eldest son of Lieutenant Colonel Stratford Charles Halliday of the Royal Artillery. His grandfather had served in the Royal Marine Artillery in the 1830s and it was inevitable that young Lewis would follow the family tradition of joining the Royal Artillery.

Although he was regarded as a delicate child, he grew to be constitutionally tough. He was educated at Elizabeth College, Guernsey, but before his entry exam, he broke his leg and failed to obtain enough marks to enter the Royal Military Academy at Woolwich.

In 1888, he managed to pass the Sandhurst exam and was commissioned into the Royal Marine Light Infantry on 1 September 1889. He was then sent to the Royal Naval College at Dartmouth and emerged as a lieutenant on 27 October 1890. For the next eight years, he served on ships in the Channel Squadron until he was transferred in February 1899 to HMS *Orlando* bound for China.

After about a year on the China Station, news of the Boxer uprising spread and *Orlando* joined Admiral Seymore's flotilla at Taku at the mouth of the Peiho River. In response to Sir Claude McDonald's request for some men to guard the Peking Embassy, Captain Lewis Halliday left with fifty men. On 31 May, they embarked on a shallow-draft steamer which took them the Tientsin. Here an additional twenty-five men, who had just returned from the capital, joined them to catch a train to take them to Peking. They arrived shortly before both the railway and telegraph were cut by the Boxers. In spite of the deteriorating situation, the British managed to arrange a cricket match between the Royal Marines and the 'Rest of the World'! To his chagrin, Halliday dropped a catch and was still lamenting this later as he lay in hospital. The slack fielding had cost the Marines the match. The 'Rest of the World' was the military guards of the USA, France, Germany, Austria, Russia, Italy and Japan.

VC Action

For several days, the British Legation and compound was filled with a steady stream of refugees, mostly Christian Chinese and missionaries. Although the Legations were being sniped at, the Boxers did not attack and this gave time for the buildings to be sandbagged and fortified.

On 14 June, Halliday noted in his diary: 'They were waving their torches and shouting in a silly way. I thought they might be a religious procession but they answered 'sha! sha! (kill! kill!) and came on. I fired a volley which stopped them.'

In another entry, he wrote: 'Led a party of twenty of own men and twenty Germans to the Roman Catholic cathedral. Found the whole place a smouldering ruin. Horrible scenes. Rescued 290 Christians (Chinese). Shot a few Boxers and looters.'

On the 23rd, the Boxers set fire to the nearby Han-lin or Great Library of China, which contained many priceless works of literature, including the great Chinese encyclopaedia of nearly a million pages. With the smoke threatening the Legations, Captain Halliday, Dr Poole and George Morrison, *The Times*' correspondent, along with a detail of marines, breached the Han-lin wall to enable parties of volunteers to get in and tackle the fire and save the precious manuscripts.

Men, women and even children formed themselves into bucket chains to douse the flames while under fire from the Boxers. Eventually the fire was put out. Dazed with exhaustion, the marines and sailors had been fighting almost continuously.

On 24 June, Sir Claude MacDonald's report was used by *The London Gazette* dated 1 January 1901: 'On 24th June, the enemy consisting of Boxers and Imperial troops made a fierce attack on the west wall of the British

Legation, setting fire to the west gate of the south stable quarters, and attacking cover in the buildings which adjoined the wall. The fire, which spread to part of the stables, and through which and the smoke a galling fire was kept up by the Imperial troops, was with difficulty extinguished, 1and as the presence of the enemy in the adjoining buildings was in grave danger to the Legation.

'Captain Strouts, with my sanction, organised a sortie to drive them out. A hole was made in the Legation wall, and Captain Halliday, in command of 20 Marines, led the way into the buildings and almost immediately engaged a party of the enemy. Before he could use his revolver, however, he was shot through the left shoulder at point blank range, the bullet fracturing the shoulder and carrying away part of the lung; notwithstanding the extremely severe nature of the wound, Captain Halliday killed three of his assailants and telling his men to "carry on, and not mind him", walked back unaided to the hospital, refusing escort and aid so as not to diminish the number of men engaged in the sortie. For some days, the surgeons feared the wound mortal, but I am happy to say that, though still in the convalescent hospital, Captain Halliday is out of danger.'

Just to emphasise that not all citations are accurate, Halliday's own diary records his own recollection of events: 'I was sent with six Marines and six civilians to help the Japs, who, however, said they were able to hold their own: so came back to find a bad attack on the south-west stable. Led sortie among the ruined houses. Went down a narrow alley and came upon five men with rifles round the corner of a house. One immediately plugged me in the shoulder cutting the left brace of my Sam Browne belt in half. I then began to empty my revolver into them, as they were only a yard away there was no question of missing.

'I finished four and the fifth bolted round another corner. The men had then come up and I told them to go on. I found my way back to the hole in the wall through which I was helped. [Dr] Poole helped me to the hospital and dressed me there. Had no pain to speak of. That finished my active share in the siege which was rather bad luck.

'Strouts then took out 20 or 30 men and pulled down the small building and cleared the field of fire. He told me next morning that my pistol had had a misfired round so I merely pressed the trigger at the fifth man and he had escaped. It will be seen that I was acting under orders and I think anyone must have done as I did.'

Halliday himself raised the question mark over the awarding of the Victoria Cross for such a brief and routine exchange of fire, especially as it rendered him *hors de combat* for the rest of the siege. Perhaps the desperate defence required a hero figurehead. Sir Claude MacDonald promised Halliday that he would receive a brevet if they survived. Halliday did receive his brevet – along with the Victoria Cross.

At the end of the fifty-day siege, Captain Halliday returned to England with the other wounded on the SS *Julunga.* He became a patient of Miss Agnes Kayser at her hospital for officers at Grosvenor Square. The patron of the hospital was Edward, Prince of Wales and later the hospital became known as the Edward VII Hospital. As such, he was a frequent visitor and became acquainted with Lewis Halliday. In October, the Prince unveiled a memorial in St James's Park depicting two Marines in fighting order. One of them was based on a photograph of Lewis Halliday.

Twenty-one days after his citation in *The London Gazette,* Halliday witnessed Queen Victoria's funeral procession and wrote in his diary: 'At the funeral of Queen Victoria some of us "walking cases" in a nearby London Hospital were allowed to watch the procession from a window in Piccadilly overlooking Green Park. I was proud to see that the troops lining the street below us were a fine Battalion of RMLI.'

Later Life

Captain Halliday received his Cross from the newly-crowned King Edward VII at St James's Palace on 25 July 1901. Incredibly, Halliday made a rapid and complete recovery given the damage caused by the Boxer's bullet. The only lasting effect was that he was not able to lift his left arm above his shoulder.

By the end of 1901, he was well enough to return to service and commanded the Marine detachment on HMS *Galatea.* He then progressed to HMS *Empress of India,* the flagship of the Home Fleet.

In June 1905, he joined the Staff College at Camberley and, successfully completing his exams, was appointed as Staff Officer to the Portsmouth Division of the Marines. His brevet to major was regularised and he received the CB in 1911.

Lewis Halliday married Florence Budgen in January 1906 and in 1909 she gave birth to a son. Sadly, complications caused her death a few days later.

During the First World War, Halliday was an instructor at the Naval War College at Portsmouth and was able to return to the family home at Medstead House at weekends. On 9 November 1916, he married Violet Blake and together they had a son and daughter.

By the end of the Great War, Halliday had risen to colonel and, in 1923, became Colonel Commandant. In 1927, he was promoted to the rank of lieutenant general and retired in 1930 as Adjutant General and honoured with a KCB.

After he retired, Halliday and his family lived for some years at South Brent in Devon before moving to Kingsbridge. He served as Deputy Lord Lieutenant of Devon before settling with his daughter in Dorking. It was there that General Sir Lewis Halliday died on 9 March 1966 and his ashes interred with his first wife at Medstead.

While the 'United Nations' were defending their Legations in Peking, another allied force of some 2,000 marines and sailors had been forced to turn back by the destruction of the railway. With over 230 wounded and food rapidly running out, Seymour's troops had to withstand attacks by the Boxers in an inhospitable terrain. With little choice, they retreated towards Tientsin. As luck would have it, they stumbled upon a Chinese arsenal at Hsiku on the 22 June. Here they dug in to await rescue. With the Chinese officially declaring war on all foreigners on the 21 June, allowing Boxers and Imperial troops to kill at will, thousands swarmed around and laid siege to Tientsin.

Another mixed force was sent to relieve Tientsin, which was achieved after heavy fighting on 13 July 1900. A second Victoria Cross was awarded to Midshipman Basil Guy of HMS *Barfleur* who saved a wounded sailor under heavy fire.

With the fall of Tientsin, a 20,000-strong force had been assembled which was strong enough to march on Peking. The 120km march saw minor skirmishes but the terrain and punishing temperatures (often reaching 110 degrees) caused severe heat exhaustion and was the main enemy.

The defeat of the Imperial Army and the capture of Peking on 14 August lifted the siege of the Legations. There followed uncontrolled plundering and the summary executions of all suspected of belonging to the Boxers.

The Peace Agreement or 'Boxer Protocol' was finally signed on 7 September 1901, an act which allowed foreign troops to be stationed in the capital. An even more bitter pill was swallowed when 450 million taels of silver, which was more than the Chinese Government's annual tax revenue, was to be paid as an indemnity over the next thirty-nine years to the eight nations involved.

Chapter 38

War of the Golden Stool, 1900–01

Number of VCs awarded	2
Number of VCs awarded to officers	1
Number of VCs awarded to British Army	1
Number of VCs awarded to Indian Army	1

Origins of the War

While Britain was involved in the war with the Boers in South Africa, a little-known war flared up between the British and the Ashanti of the Gold Coast. The brief campaign of 1874 (see Chapter 15) had been a punitive expedition to stop the Ashanti attacking the friendly Fanti tribes in Britain's unhealthy trading colony. Further aggression followed, and in 1895 another expedition was undertaken to remove the tyrannical King Prempehn from his capital, Kumasi. He was forced to give up all his treasures to pay for the various campaigns the British had mounted against his people. The one object they did not receive was the fabled Golden Stool of Ashanti. The Empire of Ashanti had been treated as an autonomous state but its continued aggression threatened the British and the friendly coastal tribes which led to another confrontation.

It took the high-handed action of the British Governor, Sir Frederick Hodgson, to spark a serious insurrection. Hodgson and his wife visited Kumasi in late March 1900 to meet with the Ashanti chieftains. He told them that the deposed King would never return as he had been exiled to the Seychelles. In addition, he demanded that the fabled Golden Stool, used only by Ashanti royalty, be handed over so it could be presented to Queen Victoria. When this was not forthcoming, a search was made of the nearby bush but failed to locate the Stool.

Hodgson's attitude infuriated the Ashantis, who attacked the small search party, but a sudden rain storm enabled them to retreat to the Government stockade in Kumasi. The stockade was just fifty yards' square with twelve-feet-high loop-holed stone walls with firing turrets at each corner. Now finding himself and the tiny garrison besieged, Hodgson called for reinforcements and on 18 April about 100 Gold Coast Constabulary arrived to swell the numbers in the fortified government building and stockade.

On 23 April, three small columns carried out attacks on the camps and villages occupied by the rebels. Two were successful, meeting little opposition, but the third was ambushed about ten miles from Kumasi and in a fighting retreat returned having sustained many casualties. By this time the Ashantis had amassed a large force, estimated at 12,000, which attacked the defenders on 25 April. In a day-long fight, the small garrison managed to hold off the large numbers of warriors. Because of the lack of space, they also had to push back the large number of refugees who sought sanctuary from the Ashanti. In a desperate struggle, the armed defenders had to use their rifle butts to beat back the terrified crowd. Further reinforcements arrived some 500 Nigerian Hausas with six small field guns and four Maxim machine-guns.

The Ashanti realised that the British defence was too strong to storm so they settled down to starve the defenders into submission. They also cut telegraph wires and blocked all the routes into Kumasi. Apart from the occasional sniping, they sat and waited.

On 23 June, Hodgson and an escort cut their way out of Kumasi and made for the coast leaving the garrison of about 600 to defend the British residence. Finally, on 15 July, Colonel James Willcocks led 1,000 troops and relieved Kumasi.

Sporadic fighting continued until the end of September but it was not until November that the campaign was declared to have finished. The casualty list was heavy with the British and their allies having suffered 1,007 fatalities, while it was estimated that the Ashantis lost about 2,000.

A postscript to this war included the return from exile of King Prempeh in 1924. The British never did seize the Golden Stool, which was hidden deep in the forests until it surfaced again in the 1920s.

Two Victoria Crosses were awarded for this short but deadly war, being those to Sergeant John Mackenzie of the Seaforth Highlanders and Captain Charles Melliss of the 9th Bombay Infantry, both of whom were attached to the West African Frontier Force.

CHARLES MELLISS VC (1862-1936)

The son of Lieutenant General George Julius Melliss of the Indian Staff Corps, Charles John Melliss was born on 12 September 1862 at Mhow, India.

Early Life

Melliss was sent to England for his education at Wellington College and graduated to the RMC Sandhurst, from where he was commissioned in the East Yorkshire Regiment in September 1882. He transferred to the Indian Army two years later and joined the 9th Bombay Infantry. While on leave, he was attached to the 24th Bombay Infantry (Baluchi) and took part in the operations in 1896 against one of the Arab potentates, the Mazrui family, who was giving Britain's ally, the Sultan of Zanzibar, much trouble. After much marching, enlivened by the occasional skirmish, this minor campaign ended with the death of the Sultan. Captain Melliss was awarded his first decoration; the Brilliant Star of Zanzibar.

VC Action

Returning to the 9th Bombay Infantry he took part in the Tirah Campaign in 1897-98. He was seconded to the Northern Nigeria Regiment, West Africa Frontier Force, from 1899 to 1902 and took part in the relief of Kumasi. It was during the last mopping-up operation at Obassa on 29 September that Melliss performed his VC act., which was witnessed by Colonel James Willcocks, the commander of the Frontier Force, who reported:

'I left Kumassi [*sic*] in a north-westerly direction on September 29, 1900, with 1,200 infantry and three millimeter guns (?), and we passed the night in a burnt village with the rain coming down in torrents. The Achumas must have enjoyed our plight, but at dawn we were off again for our last fight in the campaign. We found them in a strong position near the village of Obassa, and worked round both flanks; the advanced guard commander then ordered a bayonet charge; but the Achumas were not going to quit their position, which was on a well-selected crest line with the bush cleared in front; and as our men made their rush they were received with a steady fire from Martinis and Lee-Metfords, and for the first time in Ashanti were stopped. A second charge, though it slightly pushed back the enemy, did not get home, and just then I arrived on the scene

'I could hear firing going on in the rear-guard, but the front was now the only place to bother about, and so, after a good look round, I let slip the detachment of Sikhs under Captain Godfrey [later killed in Somaliland]. With him went Major Melliss and as many of his Hausas as were in the neighbourhood. Mellis, fleet of foot, and I could see him well in front leading the charge, when suddenly he rolled over severely wounded and was found soon after lying disabled at the foot of a sharp decline down which he and one of the enemy had rolled together, the latter with Melliss's sword through him and a bullet from Godfrey's revolver in his head; but the end was near, and the Achumas had to acknowledge defeat.'

Major Melliss was recommended for the Victoria Cross, which was gazetted on 15 January 1901. The citation adds a little more to Willcock's account

'The enemy were determined to have a hand-to-hand fight. One fired at Major Mellisss, who put his sword through the man, and they rolled over together. Another Ashanti shot him through the foot, the wound paralysing the limb. His wild rush had, however, caused a regular panic among the enemy, who were charged at the same time by the Sikhs and killed in large numbers.'

Charles Melliss returned home to recuperate from his wounds and was invested with his Cross at St James' Palace on 12 October 1901 by King Edward VII. In the same year, he married Kathleen, the youngest daughter of Colonel, later General, John Walter, of the Devonshire Regiment. He was also awarded a brevet rank of lieutenant colonel.

Later Service

From 1902 to 1904, he served in East Africa and took part in the Somaliland campaign where he commanded Tribal Horse and Somali Irregulars and received a Mentioned in Despatches. It was not just the Mad Mullah he had to contend with, for he was badly mauled by a lion in 1903 which added to his increasing tally of wounds.

In 1906, he became commandant of the 53rd Sikhs (Frontier Force) and was appointed ADC to the King Edward. There followed a succession of appointments until he was promoted major general in 1912. He commanded the 30th Indian Infantry Brigade in Mesopotamia in 1914 and the Poona Division in 1915, the year he received the KCB.

He was in command at the Battle of Shaiba near Basra where he defeated a Turkish Arab force of some 30,000 men with his Anglo-Indian force of 7,500. Melliss also fought at the Battle of Ctesiphon, furthest up the Tigris that the 6th Division would advance. After three days of fighting and sustaining heavy casualties (the 6th Poona Division suffered a forty per-cent casualty rate, the commander, General Townsend, ordered a withdrawal to Kut al-Imara. From 5 December 1915 to 29 April 1916, the Turks besieged the town until it surrendered.

Melliss fell ill during the siege and was in hospital when Townsend surrendered. He was transported to Baghdad and remained in hospital until he was well enough to follow his Poona Division north to Anatolia. As he was a general, Melliss was allowed a travelling party and better than average supplies. Along the route, he came upon dead and dying enlisted men. Melliss took any survivors he found with him and at each stop insisted that they be treated in hospital.

Melliss spent two years in captivity in north-western Anatolia from where he wrote a constant stream of letters to Enver Pasha demanding better treatment for his men. When he was released and returned to England, Melliss was awarded the KCMG, before retiring from the Army on 24 February 1920. He died at Brockenhurst in the New Forest on 6 June 1936 but was buried in St Peter's Churchyard, Frimley, Surrey.

Chapter 39

Somaliland, 1902–03

Number of VCs awarded	6
Number of VCs awarded to officers	6
Total awarded to British Army	2
Total awarded to British Indian Army	3
Total awarded to Imperial forces	1

Origins of the War

The Somaliland Protectorate had been established in 1884 for its strategically important position as the Horn of Africa at the entrance to the Red Sea. Britain was very sensitive to any threat to her sea routes to India and it fell to the latter to administer the country. Apart from a couple of minor uprisings, there were no civil or military problems until 1898 when a native named Haji Muhammad Abdullah Hassan, known as the 'Mad Mullah' (though he was neither mad nor a mullah), started to cause trouble.

Hassan, the son of an Ogaden father and a Dolbahanta mother, had travelled on the Haj and possibly to Egypt where he had learned of the Mahdi's successes in the Sudan. This had encouraged him to return to Somaliland, determined to rid it of the British Protectorate power. His earlier forays had been met by mainly local Somali forces with Central African and Indian support under Colonel Edward Swayne, who managed to drive him across the border into Italian territory. Building support, Hassan was able to take the field with 12-15,000 men, of which 600 were armed with rifles.

In December, Hassan's Dervishes had carried out an armed raid on Berbera. Captain Henry Cordeaux, the Consul General, had reported on the raid to the Foreign Office who took early action to restore the situation. Colonel Swayne, who had commanded the first expedition against Hassan the previous year, was invalided back to Britain. His place was taken by Brigadier W.H. Manning, Inspector General of the King's African Rifles, who immediately called for regular troops to take over from the local levies.

Somaliland at that time was one of the very few British overseas dependencies that did not require financial support, having a surplus on its budget from the sale of livestock to Arabia and the Yemen. The Foreign Office, however, at Government instigation demanded that any expedition set up to defeat Hassan should not be a drain on either fiscal or military resources

Manning, however, gladly accepted the offer of assistance from India and the 1st Bombay Grenadiers were directed to Berbera as well as 1/KAR and a Sudanese Company of 3/KAR and fifty Sikhs of the 5/KAR. The Foreign Office, liaising with the Italian Government, meanwhile sought permission to land a Field Force on the Italian Somali Coast and drive inland to evict Hassan from the Mijertein tribal area.

The strengthened force chased Hassan's Dervishes into Abyssinia, but was annihilated at the Battle of Gumburu on 17 April 1903. The Dervishes elated with their success attacked at Daratoleh. It was here on 22 April that three Victoria Crosses were won by George Roland of 1st Bombay Grenadiers, William Walker, 4th Gurkha Rifles and John Gough, Rifle Brigade.

JOHN EDMUND GOUGH VC (1871-1915)

When John Edmund Gough was awarded the Victoria Cross in 1903 it was uniquely held by father, son and uncle simultaneously – and this rare distinction is highly unlikely ever to be repeated. Not only were the three kinsmen extremely brave, they also attained high positions in the Army hierarchy. Arguably, the most talented of the three was its youngest, whose full potential was cut short by a deflected bullet.

Early Life

John Edmund Gough was the second son of Indian Mutiny VC, Colonel Charles Gough and his wife, Harriette née de la Poer. Johnnie, as he was best known, was born in Murree near Rawalpindi on 25 October 1871, but spent most of his childhood with his brother Hubert at the family home at Rathronan near Clonmel in County Tipperary. Due to his parents' frequent and long absences, mainly in India, Johnnie was brought up mostly by relatives and friends. He was educated at home until 1885, when he followed Hubert to Eton.

Like his brother, Johnnie had expressed a wish to make the Army his career. An attack of typhoid fever delayed his progress and he was sent to a special clinic in Paris. He also attended a 'crammer' which enabled him to enter the Royal Military College Sandhurst. In 1891, he qualified and was commissioned into the 2nd Battalion Rifle Brigade. He was almost immediately sent out to India where he spent the next four years living the life of a typical British officer; sport, hunting and social gatherings.

When the regiment returned to England in 1895, Johnnie volunteered for special service overseas. He was appointed to the newly acquired British Central Africa Protectorate, which is now present day Malawi. Along with other British officers on secondment, he was tasked with raising native levies and training them. In order to give the new force an experienced backbone, Sikhs from the Indian Army had been offered a bounty to volunteer. They turned out to be a mixed blessing, as Johnnie observed in a letter to his mother, the Sikhs were 'capital men when on service but in cantonments they were an abominable nuisance'. The main problems were looting and quarrelling with the local tribes that made up the levies.

The new force was given the title of British Central African Rifles but its primary function was that of armed police, arresting robbers, settling disputes and stopping raids from the neighbouring Portuguese territory. By late 1897, Johnnie felt that his career had stalled and he, with his father's backing, managed to terminate his secondment and return to the 2/Rifle Brigade as it prepared to invade the Sudan.

Now the most experienced subaltern in the regiment, Johnnie joined his unit at Malta as it prepared to embark for Egypt. Because of the shortage of fit and experienced officers, Johnnie was given command of a company even though he was only a subaltern.

Sudan

Leaving Cairo on 27 July 1898, Johnnie endured a slow journey up the Nile in daytime temperatures of 115°F. Finally, at 05.45 hours on 2 September, Kitchener's Anglo-Egyptian army stood within their defensive *zariba* waiting for the approach of the Dervish army.

Johnnie later recalled: 'We saw banners topping the low hills to our right and then the whole line came into view. It looked about 3 miles long and as thick as peas. As we were watching these men on the right, we saw some more flags on their left (about 2000 yards off). They came over the rise in great style.'

The 50,000-strong Dervish army did indeed make an impressive sight but the intense fire that greeted them kept them from closing. From Johnnie's perspective, he was disappointed that the Rifles held a position that prevented them from being in the front-line. Despite this, nine riflemen were hit and one killed.

With the Dervish army fleeing towards their nearby capital, Omdurman, Kitchener ordered a pursuit. This was a misnomer, though, as the British-led juggernaut took hours to get in formation and pick its way through the body-strewn battlefield. Many wounded Dervishes who attempted to keep on firing had to be dispatched and Johnnie remarked that it was 'necessary but nasty'. He also regretted that his battalion had not been more involved in the battle.

Crete

Johnnie's battalion remained in Omdurman for only a week before it was ordered to another international flashpoint – Crete (see the earlier chapter, Crete 1898). It was to be part of an international peace-keeping force to allow the Greek-majority autonomy on the island under Turkish suzerainty.

This solution did not suit either party and there was great unrest that threatened to turn into full-scale bloodshed.

When the 2nd Rifle Brigade arrived on 23 September, there had already been a serious outbreak involving the Highland Light Infantry. The battalion's main task was the disarming of the population and the repatriation of the Turkish garrison. They managed the latter and were only partially successful at the former.

Until the Greek Christian community assumed responsibility, it fell to the officers of the Rifles to administer the island. Johnnie was appointed District Commissioner of the Malevesi district, where he was to disarm the population and raise a local constabulary. His experience in British Central Africa helped in this difficult task and, when he left Crete in October 1899, he received a glowing parting testimonial from the British Military Commissioner, Colonel Sir Herbert Chermside.

Ladysmith

The 2nd Rifles sailed from Crete and made their way to the next crisis area – South Africa. En-route, they learned that the British had rejected a Boer ultimatum and war had been declared. Expecting to go to Cape Town to join General Sir Redvers Buller's main army, the Rifle Brigade's orders were countermanded and the regiment disembarked at Durban on 26 October. From there they made their way to Ladysmith to join the command of Lieutenant General Sir George White VC.

When they finally detrained at Ladysmith on 30 October, Johnnie found that General White had gone out to do battle with the Boers with disastrous consequences. Johnnie's battalion marched out immediately to Limit Hill to cover the retreat of White's beaten army. Johnnie was dismayed at the sight of famous regiments like the King's Royal Rifle Corps and the Gordon Highlanders retiring 'in the most awful confusion'. Even worse was the capture of the Royal Irish Fusiliers and Gloucesters, who had been forced to capitulate when White failed to support them. Johnnie considered White's conduct in abandoning them verging on the criminal.

Ladysmith was unsuited for defence, being surrounded by commanding hills and ridges, which were soon occupied by the Boers. Thus, from 30 October 1899 to 28 February 1900, 21,156 souls, including some 5,500 troops, were bottled up within an eleven-mile-long perimeter.

The Rifle Brigade was tasked with manning the north-western corner of the defence perimeter known as King's Post and Leicester Post. Along with the rest of the Ladysmith garrison, Johnnie suffered from the monotony of the siege – even the shelling became unremarkable. Hopes of an early relief by Buller's army began to recede as news of defeats reached the besieged. Johnnie had no faith in the commanders, who either put forward hare-brained schemes or, mainly, showed little leadership.

Until mid-November, the weather was cold and wet which caused morale to sink. The newly-promoted Johnnie thought the garrison needed a success to lift spirits and he got his chance on the night of 4 December. His plan was to raid Thornhill's Farm close to the railway and about one-and-a-half miles beyond the British lines. Taking 183 men, Johnnie led them to where he thought the Boers slept at night. Having surrounded a group of houses, he was disappointed to find a distinct absence of enemy and had to be content with looting armfuls of fresh vegetables.

The raid encouraged the Chief of Staff, Major General Sir Archibald Hunter, to sanction Johnnie to lead an attack on Surprise Hill, where the Boers had a 4.5-inch howitzer. On the night of 11 December, Johnnie led five companies silently up the slopes of the hill and got to within a dozen yards of the summit before they were challenged. Crying out 'Charge', Johnnie's men swept over the Boer position and held off the Boer counter-attacks while Lieutenant Digby Jones of the Royal Engineers laid charges to blow up the howitzer

As 2,000 Boers swarmed around Surprise Hill, so they started to shell the Rifles on the summit. Johnnie ordered a withdrawal and remained to the end recording that he 'was never in such a hot place in all his life'. His men fought their way through the ring of Boers and Johnnie helped bring back the wounded. The cost of the raid had been relatively heavy; of 438 men, twelve were dead, seven missing and thirty-five wounded.

The Boers had made little effort to assault the Ladysmith defences and the British attack on Surprise Hill may have prompted them to launch an attack on Wagon Hill and Caesar's Camp in the early hours of 6 January. They began by attacking Wagon Hill which was the western end of a two-mile-long ridge with Caesar's Camp at the eastern end. During the desperate fighting on Wagon Hill, Lieutenant Digby Jones, the Engineer who destroyed the howitzer on Surprise Hill, was killed. He was awarded the Victoria Cross for leading a small force that reoccupied the summit at a critical moment.

By early morning the Boers held the southern slope the ridge and were able to direct a deadly enfilading fire on Caesar's Camp, which was lightly manned by men of the Gordons and Manchesters. When the Rifle Brigade arrived at the eastern end of Caesar's Camp about 08.00 hours, they found absolute chaos.

Johnnie later wrote: 'When we got there, we could not find anyone in command and no one knew in the least what was meant to be going on.'

In the absence of anyone senior, Johnnie found himself in command. With little cover, the defenders took casualties but held their positions. At 16.00 hours, a violent thunderstorm alleviated the unbearably hot temperatures. With the Boers beginning to push reinforcements up onto the summit of Caesar's Camp, Johnnie sensed that it was the moment for decisive action. Ordering a charge, the British rushed forward and poured a tremendous fire on the Boers who ran back down the slope. This signalled a general Boer retreat and the last attempt to breach the British defences.

Johnnie and his command were sent to Wagon Point, the western extremity of the ridge, where they set about building fortifications. There they remained open to the incessant rain and enemy artillery.

At dusk on 28 February – the 118th day of the siege – Johnnie heard cheering and saw distant horsemen. About midnight he received a message to go to the Iron Bridge. There he was reunited with his brother Hubert, whose squadron had led the advance into Ladysmith.

Hubert later recalled: 'I had not expected to see him with a beard. He recognised me, however, and I said: "Hallo Hubert" … and opened our reunion by simply remarking, "How fat you have got!"'

In the immediate aftermath of the relief of Ladysmith, despatches and recommendations were submitted. The Rifle Brigade's commander, Lieutenant Colonel C.T.E. Metcalfe, intended to put Johnnie's name forward for a VC for leading the attack on Surprise Hill. Johnnie was flattered but firmly rejected it.

'I wrote to him [Metcalfe],' he recalled, 'and told him not to take my breath away, as to begin with nobody could say who was first up and also that it was no VC act, to be up first and that such a thing had never entered my head – and that I thought I had been done uncommon well as it was. I hope he will never refer to the subject again; one would naturally like to earn a VC, but as I know jolly well I have never done anything approaching a VC act in my life.'

After a period of recuperation, Johnnie's battalion joined Major General Walter Kitchener's 7th Brigade in its advance into the Transvaal. He was not involved in anymore action for in July he was appointed ADC to Major General Sir Francis Howard, who led a flying column.

After the Boer's main towns were captured, the war settled into frustrating sweeps trying to capture an elusive enemy or bring him to battle. When General Howard became seriously ill and had to return to England, Johnnie, drawing from his experience in the BCA and Crete, was appointed District Commissioner at Lyndenburg.

When the Boer's accepted peace terms on 31 May 1902, Johnnie was offered a part in the post-war civil administration. This meant another year without leave and he turned it down. After nearly seven years' almost continuous service, he was in need of a break. He also was anxious to enter Staff College, something that had been delayed by the war. Once again, his plans were frustrated.

Somaliland

In October, Johnnie was staying with his sister in London and looking forward to joining the Staff College in January 1903, when he received a telegram from the War Office. He had been selected for special service in Somaliland and ordered to leave in three days. He travelled to Marseilles to catch the ship that took him the Aden. It is an indication of the way that the smaller campaigns were run for Johnnie and the other special service officers had to purchase three months' supply of food from their own pockets in Aden and transport it to Berbera on the Somalian side of the Red Sea.

The object of the campaign was the unfinished business of bringing the forces of Muhammad Hassan to battle and destroying them. The previous year had seen an unsuccessful attempt during which Alexander Cobbe had been awarded the Victoria Cross.

The 1903 campaign was to see many long, hot and thirsty marches punctuated with fierce fighting which ultimately failed to destroy or capture Hassan. Despite the frustrations he experienced, and fractious relationships he had with many of the Indian Army officers, Johnnie emerged with his reputation enhanced.

After three months of marching through the Southern Haud region, where the thorn bushes grew to a height of twenty feet and the scrub so thick that visibility was often less than thirty yards, Johnnie's command at last tracked down Hassan's forces. He believed that another British column had made contact with the enemy and decided to move from his base at Danop and march the twenty-seven miles east to Daratoleh. He hoped to either make contact with the other column or draw off some of the enemy.

VC Action

On 22 April, Johnnie set off with units of the Somali Bikanir Camel Corps, the Somali Mounted Infantry and Camel Corps, the KAR and a dozen Sikhs; the total force numbered just 206. Johnnie's staff officer was Captain C.M. Bruce RFA and his Intelligence Officer was Captain George Rolland, 1st Bombay Grenadiers. Also accompanying them was the *Daily Graphic*'s special correspondent, Will Maud, a fellow Ladysmith veteran, with whom Johnnie enjoyed a good relationship. Crucially, the weaponry included a Maxim gun with an experienced operator, Armourer Sergeant A. Gibb.

Leaving at 04.30 hours, they were about two miles from Daratoleh by 10.20 hours, when the advance guard reported that a very large enemy force estimated at over 1,000 strong was moving towards them. Johnnie formed his men into a square and, when the enemy was sighted, began to fire into the surrounding bush and long grass. The exchange of fire was between only twenty and fifty yards' distance but Johnnie was reassured by the steady volley fire by his Somali Camel Corps.

Sergeant Gibb on the Maxim gun was proving to be most effective and moved to whichever face of the square was most threatened. Johnnie was becoming alarmed at how much ammunition was being expended (a total of 17,000 rounds were fired during the whole action). He wrote to his father that most of the command was firing 'dum-dum' bullets contrary to official orders. He was convinced that the stopping power of expanding bullets saved his square from being overrun. He later wrote by way of an excuse; 'from my experience in my fight I thought expanding bullets should be used against fanatics'.

After about three hours of firing, Johnnie went with the KAR on a 100-yard charge which scattered the tribesmen and eased the pressure on the square. He then ordered another charge and the enemy fire slackened. Taking the opportunity of this lull, Johnnie organised a withdrawal to Danop.

The medical officer, Dr Horton, began to get the wounded up on to the camels, helped by Will Maud, who had been calmly writing and sketching throughout the firing. By 14.30 hours, the enemy fire was again increasing and Johnnie ordered another charge prior to ordering the square to begin the withdrawal. He sent four mounted infantry men to gallop to Danop to meet the marching square with ammunition and reinforcements.

A thirty-strong rearguard, mostly KAR, covered the retirement. Word reached Johnnie that one of the officers in the rearguard, Captain Bruce, Gough's Staff Officer, had been wounded. Johnnie dismounted and ran back to Captain Rolland, who told him that Bruce was badly hit and needed a camel to carry him away.

George Rolland wrote of the action in a letter: 'Poor Captain Bruce and I were in the rearguard together … The bush was so dense we could hardly see a yard in it. We were left behind, with four men, so Bruce called out, "Rolland, come along with these four men," and we retired slowly firing as we went. A savage crept up close to the path along which we were marching; owing to the dense grass and bush we did not notice it. Poor Captain Bruce suddenly threw up his arms and fell on his face shot through the body …

'I ran to Captain Bruce and raised him up. He was bleeding terribly, and I saw at a glance that it was a mortal wound. I dragged him a little out of the path, which was much exposed to the enemy's fire … while the three brave men covered me with their fire and kept the enemy in check who were yelling with delight as they saw one white man dying and another close to him.

'Captain Bruce was a very heavy man, of nearly fourteen stone, and I am only nine stone, so I could not lift him. None of the men could stop firing to help me, or the enemy would have been on us, so I shouted to the disappearing column, "Halt in front!" it was then out of sight, slowly retiring along the winding path, and we were practically cut off. It was a moment of great despair, as I thought my shout had not been heard. The enemy were now pressing us very hard, so I had to stop attending poor Captain Bruce, and emptied the magazine of my carbine at them. Then I fired off my revolver and emptied that too …

'To my infinite relief I then saw Captain Walker trekking towards me. He and I tried to carry Captain Bruce but it was no use, so then I left them and ran back 400 yards or more to where the rearguard was to fetch help. It was a terribly long run, and I thought I must get hit every moment, as the bullets fell splashing around me. I seized a Bikanir camel, and was running back with it when Major Gough came up and asked me what was the matter? I told him and he rushed back to Captain Bruce. I followed slower as the led camel refused to step out, and I could not induce mine to hurry up – in fact he was frightened, and did not like to leave his friends.

'I reached the little group, and made the camel sit down, and we lifted up Captain Bruce, Major Gough at his head, and Captain Walker and I at his feet. Whilst doing so, three bullets struck the ground between us. One went through poor Captain Bruce's leg but he was too far gone to feel it. Then the Sikh, who had done his duty nobly, had his arm smashed by a fourth bullet. We had to throw Captain Bruce on the camel anyhow, and as we did so the poor fellow died. The two Yaos (Africans), the Somali, and the Sikh made up the four who helped us, and they did their work well. It is a wonder to me that out of our little group, only the Sikh was wounded.'

The hard-pressed group managed to reach the safety of the square, which continued on its way. This was about the last act of the fight at Daratoleh for, as the square reached more open country, so the enemy drifted away.

By the time Danop was reached, the column was famished and exhausted. They had covered some fifty-four miles in less than twenty-one hours and been in continuous contact with the enemy for seven hours. A total of thirteen native troops had been killed and twenty-five wounded. Two officers had died including Captain Bruce. The enemy loss was estimated at between 150 and 200.

One of Johnnie's first acts was to write to Sir Charles Bruce, the Governor of Mauritius, to break the news of his son's death. In his report, he put forward his recommendation for the Victoria Cross to be awarded to Rolland and Walker, the African Distinguished Conduct Medal to the African soldiers and the Order of Merit to the Sikh. Typically, he omitted mention of his own part in the recovery of Bruce's body. He even went so far as to censor Maud's account of the action for the *Daily Graphic*. Maud, however, later sent a telegram to the newspaper explaining that Gough had removed any mention of himself in the rescue of Bruce.

Captain William Walker, 4th Gurkha Rifles (seconded to the Birkani Camel Corps) received his Cross from the GOC, Major General W. Manning, on 29 September 1903. Captain George Rolland had to wait until he returned to India and received his Cross in a ceremony at Dehra Dun on 30 November 1903.

Johnnie was soon greatly saddened by the news that Will Maud had died of fever in Aden while on his way home to his pregnant wife. He asked his father to write to the editor of the *Daily Graphic* to suggest a public subscription to which he would contribute anonymously. Given to the general suspicion that the military held for war reporters, this was an unusual and generous gesture.

The remaining seven months of Johnnie's Somalian service were unhappy. The campaign seemed to be drifting, with the Hassan's forces still at large and the efforts to catch him ham-strung by jealousies between the Indian Army commanders and the British special service officers. Certainly, some of the important appointments seemed to confirm a bias in favour of Indian officers.

After being passed over several times in favour of less experienced Indian Army appointees, Johnnie wrote to his father, asking him, and his Uncle Hugh, to use their influence to have him released from his Somalian service so he could enter Staff College. Finally, his wish was granted and he set sail for England on 30 December 1903.

Later Service

Johnnie returned to a warm welcome from his family and the good news that he would be attending Staff College on 1 February 1904. While staying with his parents, he learned that he was to receive the Victoria Cross for his part in the Daratoleh rescue bid. Besides Maud's report of Johnnie's part in the action, William Walker had written to General Manning on 25 November 1903 that Johnnie Gough's role in Bruce's rescue was equally deserved.

Manning wrote to the War Office with his recommendation and Gough's citation was published on 15 January 1904: 'During the action at Daratoleh, on April 22nd last, Major Gough assisted Captains Walker and Rolland in carrying back the late Captain Bruce (who had been mortally wounded) and preventing that officer from falling into the hands of the enemy. Captains Walker and Rolland have already been awarded the Victoria Cross for their gallantry on this occasion, but Major Gough (who was in command of the column) made no mention of his own conduct, which has only recently been brought to notice.'

Uniquely, three Goughs, father, son and uncle, now held the Victoria Cross simultaneously. Johnnie had shown reluctance in the Boer War and Somaliland to push himself forward for a gallantry award and could never be accused of 'gong hunting'. On 29 February 1904, the three Goughs went to Buckingham Palace for Johnnie's investiture. Also present was Sir Charles Bruce, which Johnnie found 'very touching'.

Johnnie then entered the Staff College when it was undergoing reform and the Army was entering a period of significant change. Graduates who passed through the College would be of a higher calibre and qualified to be employed in an Army Council with in the War Office. There was created a General Staff with a Chief of the General Staff replacing the Commander-in-Chief, in this instance Field-Marshal Lord Roberts. There was naturally an over-subscription of ambitious candidates for the twenty-four places available but Johnnie's acceptance was assured.

Johnnie spent two years at Camberley and completed his course on 22 December 1905. The following day, he took up his first appointment as Deputy Assistant Adjutant General (DAAG) at the HQ of the Irish Command in Dublin. It was during his two year stay that he met, fell in love with and married Dorothea Keyes, who was the secretary to the Lord Lieutenant's wife, Lady Dudley. They were married on 29 June 1907 and not long after, Johnnie received his next overseas posting. He was to take over as Inspector-General of the King's African Rifles.

Taking along his new bride, Johnnie's inspecting tour took them through Kenya, Uganda, Nyasaland and Somaliland before returning to England. Dorothea now pregnant and gave birth to a girl, Diana, on 18 October 1908. The following year, Johnnie returned for another tour of inspection of the KAR. His health had been poor since his time in Somaliland and he was forced to resign his post in 1909. Thanks to the Commandant at Camberley, Brigadier General Henry Wilson, Johnnie was appointed to his staff as GSO1 with the rank of colonel. His tenure at the Staff College lasted until 1913, when he was forced to leave due to his continuing ill health.

Chief of Staff

When he had recovered sufficiently, Johnnie was promoted to Brigadier General and appointed to be Chief of Staff to Lieutenant General Sir Douglas Haig.

On 24 May 1914, Johnnie was struck by severe abdominal pains and underwent emergency surgery by Sir Berkeley Moynihan who said that his patient 'could not have lived three months'. After a period of convalescence, Johnnie returned to duties just as the world was plunged into war. He travelled to France with General Haig on 16 August and was soon involved in the fighting retreat from Mons.

In what became known as the 'Race to the Sea', the Germans pushed the British further north so the new HQ of 1 Corps moved to St Omer. The critical First Battle of Ypres was fought between 21 October and 11 November and just succeeded in holding back the German breakthrough. Hubert Gough, newly promoted to Major General, was in command of the 2nd Cavalry Corps, and responded to Johnnie's call for reinforcements at a crucial moment.

On Boxing Day 1914, it was announced that the BEF would be divided into two armies and that Haig would take over the new First Army. Johnnie became involved in the detailed planning for what was to be the first independent offensive on the Western Front; the attack on the German salient at Neuve Chapelle in 1915.

One of the battalions in the line from which the attack would be launched was Johnnie's old regiment, 2nd Rifle Brigade. On 20 February 1915, he received an invitation from its commanding officer and old friend, Colonel Reginald Stephens, to inspect their defences. That same afternoon, Johnnie took the opportunity to view the ground once more and to see an old friend. Haig had no objection but cautioned his Chief of Staff not run any unnecessary risks by going too far forward.

Killed

The Rifle Brigade HQ was in a house beside the Tilleloy Road, which ran about 250 yards behind the forward line. Because the ground was waterlogged, the front line consisted of a parapet and not a trench system. Having eaten lunch with Stephens, Johnnie expressed a wish to see his old 'A' Company and was taken along the Tilleloy Road to the Company HQ by the Fauquissart Crossroads. There was little thought of danger as it was not in direct sight of the German positions.

As they passed a ruined wooden shed, Johnnie remarked to Stephens that he could not see the German lines and leaned against the shed door to look towards Auber's Ridge. Stephens stood behind him and just inside the building. All was very quiet and still.

Suddenly the silence was broken by a faint crack as a single shot was fired from a loophole in the top floor of a factory over 1,000 yards behind the German lines. The bullet took a ricochet off the Tilleloy road and hit Johnnie in his left side. From the distance it was fired, the bullet was all but spent. There was enough velocity, however, for it to penetrate Johnnie's abdomen.

A few more shots were fired as the stricken man was carried to 'A' Company HQ, where he had to remain until darkness allowed an ambulance to be brought up to fetch him and take him to the 25th Field Ambulance at Estaires.

Fortuitously, Johnnie's surgeon, Sir Berkeley Moynihan, was paying a visit to check on his patient's progress and arrived at midday the following day. When he learned the news, he hurried to Estaires and immediately performed an operation. He removed the bullet, which had damaged the small intestine and part of the pancreas before lodging near the spine. After the operation, Moynihan felt that Johnnie would be a permanent invalid but would live.

Brother Hubert left his command and hurried to Johnnie's bedside and Dorothea was en route to be with her husband. Sadly, she was too late, for Johnnie died of heart failure at 05.00 hours on 22 February. The funeral was held at 16.00 hours that afternoon and Johnnie was buried in the Estaires Communal Cemetery with the 2/Rifle Brigade in attendance and 'A' Company providing the firing party.

King George V sent a message that 'by his death the Army had lost one of its most promising and distinguished generals'. He also approved of the unusual awarding of a posthumous KCB and a special pension for Dorothea. The military hierarchy keenly felt the premature death of Johnnie Gough which was summed up when *The London Gazette* published Field Marshal French's despatch of 5 April mourning the loss of 'one of our most promising military leaders of the future'.

Chapter 40

Kano–Sokoto Expedition, 1903

Number of VCs awarded	1
Number of VCs awarded to officers	1
Total awarded to British Army	1

Origins of the War

In 1900, Sir Frederick Lugard assumed the position of High Commissioner of the Protectorate of Northern Nigeria. This region differed enormously from the tropical and lush south both in geography, climate and religion.

The northern peoples were Muslim having more in common with the Nubians of Sudan than the coastal tribes. The region was ruled by the many emirs of the Sokoto Caliphate and whose main occupation was slavery and war. Lugard's objective was to conquer the entire region and obtain recognition of the British Protectorate by its indigenous rulers, who would still hold power but be answerable to British high commissioners. Under indirect rule, caliphate officials were transformed into salaried district heads that would collect taxes and keep the peace.

Although most of the emirs accepted this indirect rule, some of the more militant would not and continued to resist the British. In 1902, Lugard ordered a series of raids against the intransigent Fulani emirates of Solkoto, Kano, Gando and Katsina. In early February 1903, a column of 700 men was sent to take the ancient city of Kano. After a bombardment on the mud-brick walls a breach was finally made by the main gate and the city taken. Lugard then turned his attention on the Fulani capital, Sokoto, which quickly surrendered, effectively ending the insurrection. It was there that the campaign's only Victoria Cross was awarded.

WALLACE DUFFIELD WRIGHT VC (1875-1953)

Wallace Duffield Wright was the fourth child born to James Sykes Wright and his wife Mary. According to the 1881 Census, James was a Commercial Clerk who must have been involved in foreign trade, for all his five children were born abroad. Wallace was born in Gibraltar on 20 September 1875, but the family returned to London and resided at 20 Ainger Road, Hampstead.

When he was nearly thirteen, he was sent to board at Cranbrook School, Kent, where two of his elder brothers had been educated. He arrived at the school in May 1888, which was a particularly bad time in the history of Cranbrook. The exceptionally able Headmaster, Charles Crowden, had resigned after a quarrel with the school governors and moved to the headship of the then lesser known Eastbourne College.

Crowden's successor failed to maintain standards and presided over a decline in boarder numbers. In a perverse way, this allowed young Wallace to shine. The school photos of the cricket and rugby teams show a very young looking Wright with much older team mates, so small was the pool from which to select. Wallace, indeed, stood out in that dismal institution and must have retained affection for the place, for he returned in later life as inspecting officer for the Cadet Corps.

India

In 1893, Wallace left Cranbrook and joined the militia, displaying leadership talents. On 9 October 1896, he was gazetted into the 1st Battalion The Queen's (Royal West Surrey Regiment). It had just moved from Malta to India, where Wright joined it at Ambala. He arrived just in time to form part of the 3rd Brigade of Sir Bindon Blood's Malakand Field Force (see the earlier chapter on the North-West Frontier War 1897-98).

On 14 September, the 3rd Brigade reached the entrenched camp at Nawagai. There it remained, completely isolated, while the tribes gathered about them. Blood had made preparations for the attack he knew would come. On the evening of 20 September, about 3,000 fanatical Mahmunds began their attacks. The Queen's, who defended the west and south perimeter bore the brunt of the attacks but their Lee-Metford rifle fire put up an invisible wall that could not be penetrated.

Winston Churchill, who accompanied the 3rd Brigade as a war correspondent, wrote: 'Their fire was crushing, their discipline was admirable, and the terrible weapon with which they were armed, and its more terrible bullet, stopped every rush. When the enemy charged, the order to employ magazine fire was passed. The guns fired star-shell. These great rockets bursting into stars in the air slowly fell to the ground, shedding a pale and ghastly light on the swarming figures of tribesmen as they ran swiftly forward. Then the popping of musketry became one intense roar. Nothing could live in front of such fire … All were swept away.'

Sir Bindon Blood described The Queen's as 'an example of what an Infantry Battalion should be'.

When the Battalion returned to Peshawar, it was transferred from the Malakand to the Tirah Field Force and was the only regiment to fight on both sides of the Frontier in that campaign. The foe this time was the Afridi tribe, who had defended the Heights of Dargai at which four VCs were awarded. It was during this campaign that Wallace Wright was wounded. He was also promoted to lieutenant.

At the cessation of hostilities, the 1st Battalion resumed garrison duties in India and thus were not involved in the Second Boer War. As often happened, young and ambitious officers would request secondment to an area of conflict where they could be noticed and enhance their chances of promotion. Wallace made such a request and was sent to Northern Nigeria.

In late 1900 the West African Frontier Force amalgamated with the Royal Niger Constabulary to form the Northern Nigerian Regiment and it was to this new unit that Wallace Wright was attached on 30 October 1901. His first taste of campaigning in this arid, semi-desert region was the Bornu Expedition, which lasted from 1 February to 16 May 1902.

The Commanding Officer, Colonel Morland (KRRC), led thirteen officers and 515 troops against the Emir of Bauchi, one of the region's principal slave traders. He had also seized the town of Guaram and massacred or enslaved all its inhabitants. The sight of Morland's force was enough to cause the Emir to flee without a fight. In his place, an imam attempted to lead a Holy War but his followers were easily defeated. Although there was little fighting, the result of the lengthy marches was to bring peace to the area.

VC Action

In early 1903, the British Resident of the town of Keffi, Captain Maloney, was murdered by a representative of the Emir of Zaria. A punitive expedition was mounted against the formidable city of Kano, where the murderer had been given refuge. Colonel Morland's force consisted of twenty-four officers, including the newly promoted Captain Wright, and 735 troops of the NNR with four 75mm guns and four Maxim machine-guns.

Kano was a city of about 35,000 inhabitants, surrounded by eleven miles of fifty-foot-high thick walls which contained thirteen gates. Shelling had little effect on the defences but a breech was finally made on one of the gates. The British force attacked and drove the Emir's army from the city which suffered about 100 dead.

After occupying Kano on 5 February, Morland then went in search of the Emir, who had taken his force of 6,000 to Sokoto. In a hastily written and almost illegible report, Captain Wright describes the events that led to his VC award: 'The last three days (25-27 Feb) have been the experience of my life. We all started (23 Feb) for a place called Duru, south east of Kaura. The column went the main way via Kina but, I with a sub lieutenant (Lt. Wells) and 45 men were sent away by Kwoterkoshi to reconnoitre the road which was unknown. All went well until we fell in with the main body of the enemy numbering over 3000 including 1200 horsemen.

'For two days, things were in the balance as on 26th at 8 am, they attacked us in a rush. I had just time to form squares round the horses and the fight lasted 2 hours during which they charged up to the face of the squares 12 times – In short I repulsed them with heavy loss and killed 11 of their leaders. The next day, I joined hands with Porter and part of the main column sent to help me.'

On 24 February, Captain Wright was commanding a scouting detachment of forty-five Mounted Infantry of the NNR, when they ran into a huge enemy force. These Africans made a colourful spectacle, with white-robed horsemen with large turbans, some with chain mail armour, mounted on prancing ponies protected with quilted padding. Following were about 2,000 infantry armed with spears, swords, ancient guns and bows and arrows.

Wright dismounted his men and had them construct a *zareba* formed into a square, within which they stood to meet the enemy. It seemed impossible that such a small group would not be overwhelmed by the 3,000 fanatical Fulani. For two hours and twelve separate attacks, the square held firm, inspired by the conduct of Captain Wright and aided by Lieutenant Wells of the NNR. At length, the enemy began to falter and gradually retreat towards Sokoto. With great confidence, Wright had his men mount up and harried the Falani until they were in full retreat. The body count revealed sixty-five enemy dead within thirty yards of the square.

Wright re-joined Colonel Morland's main force and they advanced on Sokoto, skirmishing on the way. Outside Sokoto, they found the Falani assembled, their force numbering about 15,000. After a few artillery rounds and volley fire, the enemy fled, leaving some 100 dead. With the later capture of the Emir, this particular expedition was brought to a successful conclusion.

For his outstanding bravery, Captain Wright was recommended for the Victoria Cross, which was gazetted on 11 September 1903. He travelled back to Britain and was invested with his Cross by King Edward VII at Buckingham Palace on 5 November 1903.

Later Service

Wright returned to Nigeria until 27 May 1904. He was wounded but the records do not show where or when. Instead of returning to his regiment, he passed into Staff College emerging in 1909 as GSO3 at the War Office.

There followed an appointment to Aldershot Command until 1913 before being sent back to West Africa as GSO2 with the West Africa Frontier Force. With the outbreak of war, the British and Germans manoeuvred and fought in the bush of Nigeria's southern neighbour, Cameroon. The West Africa Frontier Force fought a series of battles and defeated the German-led enemy. Wright was singled out by Major General Sir Charles Debell, Commanding the Allied Forces in Cameroon, for special mention.

Wright was then posted to the Western Front where he was promoted to major and served in a staff capacity with, successively, 55th Division, 18th Division and 17th Army Corps. He was promoted to brevet lieutenant colonel and commanded the 89th Infantry Brigade and the 8th Infantry Brigade. He remained with the latter until after the end of the war and became a full colonel. In all, he was Mentioned in Despatches five times.

On 9 August 1919, he married Flora McDonald Bewick in Paris. On 26 June 1920, Wallace Wright attended the celebratory Royal Garden Party at Buckingham Palace and, in 1929, as Major General, he was at the House of Lords Dinner. He retired in 1927 but served throughout the Second World War in the Home Guard.

This outstanding colonial officer died at his home in Chobham, Surrey on 25 March 1953. He received a funeral with full military honours at nearby Brooklands Cemetery.

Chapter 41

Tibet Campaign, 1903–04

Number of VCs awarded	1
Number of VCs awarded to officers	1
Total awarded to British Indian Army	1

Origins of the War

Britain's 'Jewel in the Crown', India, whilst being the source of both wealth and pride, caused an almost equal amount of angst. One of the main worries for decades was Russia and its intentions towards India. Throughout Victoria's reign, Russia had advanced steadily eastwards until she was now on the border of an enfeebled China. Britain had influence but not occupation of the buffer territories of Bhutan, Nepal and Sikkim but was alarmed by rumours that Russian representatives had visited the Tibetan capital, Lhasa.

In the summer of 1903, anxious to counter any Russian influence, and to firmly fix the border with Sikkim, the British sent a frontier commission with an escort of 150 Gurkhas to negotiate with the Tibetan authorities. For months, the delegation was kept hanging about at Khamba Jong with excuses and cancellations until it became clear that the Tibetans just did not want to address Britain's concerns. Exasperated and with reluctance, the Viceroy, Lord Curzon, authorised a Diplomatic Mission, accompanied by an 1,150-strong armed escort, to march on Lhasa and bring the Dalai Lama and his ministers to the negotiating table. One of the officers in the escort is credited with winning the highest (above sea-level) VC.

From the start, the Mission looked doomed. It started out in mid-winter with snow storms and sub-zero temperatures. Steadily climbing to heights where the air was starved of oxygen, there were problems with conveying supplies and a sketchiest of knowledge of both Tibet and its army. Added to this was a conflict of personality between the two men who led the expedition; all the ingredients for disaster were present. The delicately poised relationship between military and political interests is seldom a comfortable one. In the Tibetan Campaign of 1904, this relationship was tested to breaking point.

The leader of the Tibet Mission was Lieutenant Colonel (later Sir) Francis Edward Younghusband, a vastly experienced explorer of the Himalayas, political agent and a prominent player in 'The Great Game'. The command of the escort was given to Colonel J.R.L. Macdonald of the Royal Engineers, a man who had gained the reputation of being arrogant, petty and over-cautious. His remit was purely military but he constantly sought to undermine Younghusband's overall authority. With the odds against success, the long column set out for the unknown on 11 December 1903.

The first of the many natural obstacles to be overcome was the Jelap La, the 14,390-foot pass that leads from Sikkim to Tibet. From there on, all forage had to be carried as there was little or no vegetation.

By 4 January 1904, the Mission had reached Tuna with a small guard and intended to halt for a week. Colonel Macdonald decided that he would keep the rest of the escort at the base camp at Chumbi, which was below the tree line and in relative comfort. The reason he gave was concern over supplies, an ever-present problem. Instead of just a week's rest, it was to be almost three months before Macdonald could be persuaded to join the Mission which squatted in the middle of a huge desolate plain 15,000 feet above sea level.

At last, on 28 March, the advanced towards Gyantse began. After about ten miles of marching in the teeth of a bitter wind they reached a small rocky outcrop close to the village of Guru. There a large Tibetan force had erected a loop-holed wall across the road and overlooked with sangars built on the stony slope on their right flank. This was rather a pathetic barrier as their left flank was quite open and the infantry with two sections of Maxim guns practically encircled the large mob of primitively armed Tibetans. Still no shots were fired. Younghusband persuaded Macdonald not to fire the first shot and for fifteen minutes there was a standoff as the British line reached the wall. Meanwhile, Lieutenant Grant and the 8th Gurkhas were given the task of clearing the sangars. This was done rather in the manner of police marshalling a football crowd and the occupants of the sangars drifted down the slope to join the great throng behind the wall.

Although there was a certain amount of good humour on both sides, the Tibetans still refused to budge and it took just one shot to end the impasse. Macdonald ordered that the Tibetans should be disarmed and this was greeted with anger. Stones were thrown and blows exchanged. The Tibetan general, who had been sitting on the ground in front of the wall looking totally dejected and humiliated, mounted his pony and urged his animal into the mêlée. A Sikh soldier barred his way and tried to seize the bridle. The General drew a pistol and shot the soldier in the jaw. This signalled the start of an unequal fight.

One of the news correspondents who accompanied the expedition, Edmund Candler of the *Daily Mail*, was hacked seventeen times by Tibetan swordsmen and lost his right hand. For a moment, it looked bad for the British – but then the infantry and Maxim machine-guns opened up from the plain, while the Gurkhas fired down from the escarpment. The artillery lobbed shrapnel at the Tibetan's retreat as the enemy began to break. They did not flee but slowly walked away.

Very quickly, the firing ceased; the soldiers sickened by the slaughter. The Tibetan army, estimated at 1,500, left between 600 and 700 dead on the field and 168 wounded, of whom twenty later died.

The British advance continued until it encountered another wall built across Red Idol Gorge. The Gorge was a formidable barrier with almost sheer walls rising to 3,000 feet and a raging torrent on one flank. The Gurkhas were ordered to clear the cliff-top positions and endured a three-hour climb in a violent storm of sleet and snow. In a brief exchange of fire, the Maxims and artillery won the day, inflicting a further 200 casualties.

The next day, 11 April, the formidable citadel of Gyantse was sighted. Situated on an outcrop that rose almost sheer 500 feet above the plain, it reminded some officers of Gibraltar. Around its foot was a squalid warren of a town – the third most important in Tibet.

Unopposed, the British occupied the fortress but decided not to remain because of the lack of water. Instead, they occupied Chang Lo, a cluster of buildings 1,000 yards south and supplied by a stream. The usual negotiating stalemate followed and Younghusband urged the authorities by telegram to allow the Mission to continue to Lhasa. His telegram was not answered.

At the end of April reports arrived that a large Tibetan army was concentrating at Karo La, a 17,000-foot pass forty-seven miles east of Gyantse on the road to Lhasa. With the timid Macdonald withdrawn to Chumbi with the bulk of the soldiers, Younghusband agreed to allow the energetic Colonel Brander to take two-thirds of the 500-strong escort at Chang Lo and march to disperse the Tibetan force.

With Brander's force gone, Chang Lo's garrison was reduced to 120 rifles. In the early hours of 5 May, a force of 800 Tibetans crept up to the post of Chang Lo and attacked. Completely surrounded, the mixed garrison of Sikhs and Gurkhas fought desperately and managed to repel the attack, inflicting 140 dead.

A further attempt to persuade the Dalai Lama and his ministers to agree to a negotiation took another two months and brought no result. By that time the formidable Gyantse Jong fort had been occupied by an estimated 6,000 Tibetans, who subjected the Chang Lo encampment to a desultory siege. With no sign of negotiation from Lhasa, Younghusband ordered Macdonald to assault the fort. It was the bravery of a young Gurkha officer that resulted in the single VC for the campaign.

JOHN DUNCAN GRANT VC (1877-1967)

John Duncan Grant was born at the hill station Roorkee, Uttaranchal, India on 28 December 1877 into an Army family, his father being a Royal Engineer, Colonel Suene Grant. When he was old enough, he was sent away to be educated, first at Manor House School, Hastings, and then to Cheltenham College from 1890 to 1895. From there, he entered the Royal Military College Sandhurst and was commissioned second lieutenant on 22 January 1898 but remained unattached until his appointment to 30th (Punjab) Regiment of Bengal Infantry the following year.

On 22 April 1900, Grant was promoted to lieutenant and transferred to 44th (Gurkha Rifle) Regiment, which was renamed 8th Gurkha Rifles in 1902. This regiment was part of the escort of the Tibet Mission.

A day after the attack on Chang Lo, 6 May, Brander's command managed to force the gorge at Karo Lo, fought at a greater altitude than any other battle in the history of war. Once again, the Gurkhas had shown their mettle at this altitude by scaling the sides of the pass to a height that could not have been less than 18,500 feet. From there, they dominated the enemy's sangars. The defeated Tibetans suffered another 450 casualties. As Peter Fleming wrote in his book *Bayonets to Lhasa*: 'The cheapness of the British victories in the Tibetan gorges should not be allowed to obscure the hardihood and the virtuosity which won them.'

After the abortive attack on Chang Lo, an estimated 6,000 Tibetans occupied the Gyantse Jong and conducted a desultory siege of Chang Lo. An exasperated Younghusband issued an ultimatum that if the Tibetans did not come to the negotiating table, the British would attack the fort. Macdonald was ordered to bring up the main force from Chumbi and prepare an assault.

VC Action

At 03.00 hours on 6 July 1904, three columns of infantry advanced across the open plain and soon reached the wretched town at the foot of the huge rock on which the fort stood. By sunrise, the British had cleared the enemy from the labyrinth of stone buildings and stood at the rock's base looking up at the seemingly impregnable fort. It seemed an impasse had been reached.

At 15.00 hours, the artillery's 10-pounders began a bombardment on the thick walls of the fort. At length, a breach was made in one of the walls and a little later a powder magazine was hit with a dull roar. This acted as a signal for the two assault companies, 8th Gurkhas and Royal Fusiliers, to begin their climb.

The Gurkhas, more adept at this sort of work, led the way up. They were greatly hampered by masonry dislodged by artillery fire and they suffered a few casualties. Finally, the guns were ordered to cease firing. This only brought the defenders out of cover and they began to fire their matchlocks and hurl rocks. Despite this, the Gurkhas steadily advanced up the semi-precipice until their commander, Lieutenant Grant and his havildar, Karbir Pun, reached a point about below the breach.

Further progress could only be made on hands and knees and in single file. Grant and his havildar reached the breach when the officer was hit by a bullet and they were driven back, sliding down about thirty feet. Then, with covering fire, they clambered back and disappeared into the darkness of the breach. The rest of the infantry soon followed as the Tibetan resistance melted away and the fort was in British hands.

For his gallantry and determination, despite being wounded, Lieutenant John Grant was awarded the Victoria Cross and Havildar Karbir Pun, the Indian Order of Merit. There had been a debate for some years about extending the Warrant to Native Officers and Men of the Indian Army and on 21 October 1911 it was signed by King George V. Without a doubt, if it had been in force in 1904, Karbir Pun would have been the first native Gurkha to receive the Victoria Cross.

For Grant, the campaign was over. The outcome was that after entering Lhasa, a treaty was signed and the British withdrew. On 24 January 1905, *The London Gazette* published John Grant's citation and, on 24 July that year, he received his Cross from King Edward VII at Buckingham Palace.

Later Service

On 19 January 1907, Grant married Kathleen Mary Freyer at All Saints Church, Marylebone, London before returning to India after an extended leave. Grant was promoted to captain and in 1908 he entered the Staff College, Quetta. Qualifying the following year, he was appointed Brigade Major, 22nd (Lucknow) Brigade, 8th (Lucknow) Division, which was sent to Egypt at the outbreak of war in 1914.

When General Sir Charles Townsend's Anglo-Indian force became besieged in Kut-el-Amara, Mesopotamia, Grant was appointed Brigade Major of 35th Indian Infantry Brigade, 7th (Meerut) Division which was part of the 19,000 strong Tigris Corps sent to attempt to relieve Townsend's force.

On 13 January 1916, in heavy rain, they came up against a strongly defended Turkish position where the River Wadi met the Tigris. The 35th Brigade was on the right flank and advanced on the Turkish rear. In an abortive battle, the Indians suffered 1,600 casualties, including a wounded Major Grant. He returned to India where he was appointed General Staff Officer Grade 1 at Army HQ. He then served in France and Belgium in 1917 before the Indian Divisions were dispersed and sent to Egypt in March 1918.

From there, the Gurkhas were sent to Mesopotamia and, at Baghdad on 26 May, the 11th Gurkha Rifles was raised as an ad hoc unit in with troops and officers being drawn from the 2/9th Gurkha Rifles, 1/10th Gurkha Rifles and one company each from 1/39 and 2/39 Garhwal Rifles. This proved to be an unhappy mix which initially caused some problems which were finally resolved by replacing the Garhwalis with Gurkhas from 1/7GR, 1/9GR and 1/10GR. On 4 June 1918, John Grant was appointed Acting Lieutenant Colonel and Commandant the 3rd Battalion 11th Gurkha Rifles.

In August 1918, the 1st, 2nd and 3rd Battalions left Mesopotamia for India where they were stationed at Manmad in the Bombay Presidency. Whilst at Manmad the battalions were made up to strength in British Officers, some of whom came from British battalions serving in India.

With the conclusion of the Great War in November 1918, the last thing Britain needed was another war, but this is what she got in May 1919. It came from the source of most of its colonial problems – Afghanistan. Although the North-West Frontier had remained tolerably quiet during the four years of war, the Afghans and Indian Nationalists sensed that Britain was exhausted and longed for peace. During April 1919, there was an outbreak of violence in the Punjab, with rioting, arson and the murder of Europeans. For a while it looked as if the whole of the region would go up in flames and there was real fear that the British would find themselves with another Indian Mutiny on their hands.

On 13 April, a shocking event took place at Amritsar, when, against British orders, a large political gathering took place. The local commander, Brigadier General Rex Dyer, feared for his small force and the Europeans they protected and ordered his men to open fire on the mob without warning. In less than ten minutes 379 were killed and another 1,500 wounded. In the face of such an extreme measure, the insurrection petered out.

This did not stop the Afghans from going ahead with their planned attack on the Frontier and their army occupied the village of Bagh on the British side of the Frontier near the western end of the Khyber Pass. It was a small force, including Grant's Gurkhas, that pushed the fifty miles up the Khyber and was confronted by a huge Afghan army. After two days pinned down by Afghan artillery, reinforcements arrived. Under the cover of darkness, the British advanced to a more advantageous position and in the morning were able to force the Afghans from Bagh.

In the Kurram Valley to the south, the Afghan army posed a greater threat, especially as the locally raised Waziristan force proved unreliable and was disbanded. It was the discredited General Dyer who used his vast experience to finally defeat the Afghans. With the Afghans back behind their border, it was the Wazirs who now made war on the British and a spasmodic but violent conflict continued until 1924.

For his services during the Afghan conflict, John Grant was awarded the DSO. He then assumed command of the 10th (Training) Battalion of the 13th Rajput Regiment.

From 1925/1928, Grant was appointed Assistant Adjutant General Army HQ, India and on 26 September 1926, promoted to full colonel. His last appointment was as Deputy Director, Auxiliary & Territorial Force, India, until he retired on 4 June 1929. His long service was further rewarded with a CB in the Birthday Honours list.

Grant then returned to England and resided in Brighton. That same year, he attended the VC Dinner at the House of Lords on 29 November 1929. In 1934, he was appointed honorary colonel of 10th Gurkha Rifles. During the Second World War, he served in the London District Home Guard Command.

One of his last official duties was to attend the annual dinner of the Gurkha Association at the Savoy on 31 October 1960, in the presence of the King of Nepal.

On 26 June 1956, as one of the oldest VC recipients, he attended the Centenary Parade in Hyde Park. Like many old soldiers, he retired to Tunbridge Wells, where he died in the Fraserly Nursing Home, Park Road, Tunbridge Wells on 20 February 1967 aged eighty-nine.

After the attack on the Gyantse Jong fort, the Mission completed the 200-mile journey to Lhasa and received the treaty they had for so long been seeking.

Once signed, the British withdrew back to India, never again to get involved in Tibetan affairs. Significantly, there was found to be no evidence of Russian interference.

Chapter 42

First World War, 1914

Number of VCs awarded	44
Number of VCs awarded to officers	24
Number of VCs awarded to other ranks	20
Total awarded to Royal Navy	2
Total awarded to British Army	38
Total awarded to British Indian Army	4

Origins of the War

The long-anticipated war with Germany broke out in August 1914. Colonel Charles á Court Repington, *The Times* military correspondent, wrote:

'During the first ten days of August 1914 it positively rained ultimatums and declarations of war, and very soon all the great Powers of Europe, except Italy, were at war. Though war had often been expected, it had been expected for so long, and so many crises had been successfully overcome by diplomacy, that it came in the end like a thief in the night, quite unexpectedly.'

Britain was committed to go to Belgium's aid if she was invaded, an undertaking made when that small country gained her independence from the Netherlands in 1830. When the Germans crossed the border, Britain declared war on 4 August 1914, something the Germans did not expect. The Government sent her well-trained British Expeditionary Force to cover the hard-pushed French army's left flank. This was Britain's first Continental war since Waterloo and there was a less than enthusiastic response from both newspapers and the public. Nevertheless, having kept itself aloof from the power struggles in Europe for a century, Britain could no longer be a spectator as a complexity of treaties and alliances found her tied to her old enemy, France, against the Central Powers of Germany and Austria.

The BEF advanced into Belgium and met the German Army at the mining town of Mons. In a fierce holding defence, the BEF saw they were considerably outnumbered, and when the French on their right fell back, the British had little alternative but to follow suit.

On 23 August, the first two VCs of the Great War were won at Mons for the defence by a single company of the Royal Fusiliers at the Nimy railway bridge over the Mons-Condé canal. These two men were Lieutenant Maurice Dease and Private Sidney Godley.

On the same day as the BEF started to retreat, another VC was awarded to a cavalryman; the last mounted cavalry VC:

CHARLES ERNEST GARFORTH VC (1891-1973)

By the beginning of the First World War, the horse had had its day. The animal that had rapidly delivered fighting men into close combat for hundreds of years was unable to rely on its speed to beat the accuracy and sheer volume of modern weaponry. In the early months of the war, however, the horse and its rider could still provide a necessary service by acting as the eyes for the generals as they tried to locate the enemy.

Nowhere was this more urgently required than in the retreat of the British Expeditionary Force from Mons during August and September 1914. One of the regiments involved in the constant scouting was the 15th (The King's) Hussars and one of its cavalrymen became its only VC.

Early Life

Charles Ernest Garforth was a Londoner born on 23 October 1891 at 19 Chaplin Road, Willesden Green. His father was a builder and decorator and the family moved further out to Harrow, where Charles was educated at Greenhill Council School. On leaving school, he worked at a local shoe shop and became an active member of the London Diocesan Church Lads Brigade, now the Church Cadet Brigade. His first decoration was a ribbon awarded for the best tent in camp. In 1907 he left the Church Lads and joined the 9th Territorial Battalion, The Middlesex Regiment.

In 1911, Garforth transferred to the 15th Hussars as a Trooper and was sent to Aldershot for riding lessons. Having undergone his recruit's training, he was sent to join his regiment stationed at Potchefstroom in South Africa. In 1913, the regiment returned to England and the following year, Garforth was promoted to corporal.

The 15th Hussars sailed for France with the BEF on 16 August and moved north into Belgium. Corporal Garforth, of 'A' Squadron, became involved in all the major actions of the first two months of the war.

The BEF comprised of two infantry corps numbering about 70,000 with 300 guns marching east from Boulogne and north from Le Havre to meet and face an overwhelmingly superior enemy numbering 160,000 and 600 guns. The Germans were both surprised and scathing that Britain had sent their token force to support the French, referring to it as a 'contemptible little army'. This was enough to enrage the British Army, who then took a perverse pride in calling themselves the 'Old Contemptibles'.

Covering the French Army's left flank, the British reached Mons just as the overwhelming force of the enemy arrived. On the morning of 23 August, the German First Army approached from the north. Punching above its weight, the BEF inflicted many casualties that stopped the Germans. But it was no more than a holding action for the French on their right flank was already falling back. With the BEF in danger of being outflanked, so began its epic fighting retreat to the Belgium border.

VC Action

The 15th Hussars were giving cover to the rear-guard as it fell back through the gardens and small holdings of the little mining villages surrounding Mons. It was in one of these small holdings in the village of Harmignies that the Hussars were confronted by the Germans who threatened to surround them. Unable to make their escape because of a barbed wire fence, Corporal Garforth dismounted and cut the wire which enabled his squadron the escape.

As the hard-pressed BEF wearily marched south, Garforth performed another act of bravery. At Dammartin on 2 September, he pulled Sergeant Scarterfield, whose horse had been shot, to safety. Despite the attention of a German machine-gun, he extricated his fellow NCO from under the horse. He then engaged the enemy with his carbine until the sergeant was able to escape.

The following day, 3 September, Corporal Garforth repeated this action when he saved Sergeant Lewis in similar circumstances by drawing fire on to himself and enabling his sergeant to escape.

A private of the 15th Hussars wrote to a friend in Cowes: 'Which do you think is the most brave deed of the war? There have been a lot, and it is very hard to say which is the bravest. In my opinion the best was the stand of the remainder of "L" Battery of the horse artillery. They saved thousands of men. At the finish there were only three left but they won the day for us by their bravery in sticking to their guns when it seemed almost certain death to do so.

'We have a VC Hero in our regiment. He was a great friend and a braver chum I could never have. Three times under deadly fire from the enemy he went out and saved other men's lives. I am sorry to say he is missing now, and is reported as a prisoner of war.

'We have had some very rough times during the past three months, but we have gone through them with a good heart, and every time the Germans have come off second best. They seem to be getting tired of playing second fiddle to us. Each time we had anything to do we have done it. We have lost a lot of men doing it, but the enemy have lost more trying to stop us.'

The retreat continued until a stand was made at the River Aisne where the Allies halted the German advance. The BEF then moved north to Ypres and the 15th Hussars took part in the preliminary moves before the First Battle of Ypres. It was during one of these skirmishes that Garforth was captured. For one of these, he was Mentioned in Despatches on 8 October by General Haig.

On 13 October, when moving on to the La Bassee – Ypres line, Garforth was on patrol with Captain A.E. Bradshaw near Laventie. Suddenly they ran into the enemy and were quickly surrounded. In the exchange of fire, Bradshaw and seven men were killed. Garforth held out until all his ammunition was expended and had little option but to surrender. Just four weeks later, his citation for the Victoria Cross appeared in *The London Gazette* dated 16 November.

Prisoner of War

Garforth was first sent to Hemelin-on-Weser before being transferred to Gräfteniederung Bohmte, a PoW work camp for NCOs and part of the notorious Soltau camp system. Garforth made three attempts to escape, each time reaching the German-Dutch border before being recaptured. The main problem was a lack of food and exhaustion, which made him easy prey for the frontier guards. On one occasion, he went six days without food. The punishment was always the same: three week's solitary confinement in a dark cell on bread and water.

For four long years, the prisoners endured poor rations, bitter cold winters and boredom. With food supplies becoming a problem for Germany, an exchange was arranged. On 19 March 1918, Garforth and fellow prisoners were sent to neutral Holland but not allowed to be repatriated until the Armistice.

On 18 November 1918, Garforth finally reached the UK. *The Times* reported thus: 'Two vessels landed over 2,000 repatriated prisoners of war from Holland yesterday. Among the number were 250 officers including airmen. There were enthusiastic scenes on the quayside, where the men were met by Major-General Sir Stanley von Donop, commanding the Humber garrison, who delivered the King's message of welcome. The men cheered lustily, and sang the National Anthem. Among them was Corporal Charles Ernest Garforth VC, 15th Hussars, who went to France with the original Expeditionary Force in August 1914, and was taken prisoner on 13 October the same year.'

Charles Garforth belatedly met the King when he was presented with his Victoria Cross at Buckingham Palace on 19 December 1918. That same month, Garforth received £160 worth of war saving certificates and an illuminated scroll from the people of Harrow. He finally re-joined his regiment on 4 August 1919 at Kerpen near Cologne, then part of the occupying army on the Rhine. He was only there for a few weeks as the regiment was transferred to Kilkenny in September.

In April 1919, Garforth married his childhood sweetheart, Lily, with whom he had corresponded during his captivity. Then, on 11 November 1920, he attended the Armistice Service at the Cenotaph and the burial of the Unknown Warrior in Westminster Abbey. He was present at the VC

Garden Party at Buckingham Palace on 26 June 1920 and the House of Lords Dinner on 9 November 1929. He also attended the VC Centenary Review at Hyde Park on 26 June 1956.

In 1922, Garforth left the Army with the rank of sergeant and moved to Chilwell in Nottinghamshire to take charge of a warehouse. He worked as a security policemen with the local Ordnance Depot as well as with the Plessey factory. Having retired in 1956, he died at his home in Beeston on 1 July 1973. His body was cremated and his ashes scattered in the garden of remembrance. A memorial gravestone was erected at the Wilford Hill Crematorium, Nottingham.

Garforth's medals are on display at the Ashcroft Gallery, Imperial War Museum, London.

The withdrawal of the BEF continued until it reached the River Aisne in France. On 25 August 1914, a stand was made at the village of Le Cateau which further depleted the ranks of the BEF.

In the unequal contest, five Victoria Crosses were awarded, these being to Frederick Holmes, Douglas Reynolds, Job Drain, Frederick Luke and the tragic Major Charles Yate.

CHARLES ALLIX LAVINGTON YATE VC (1872-1914)

One of the first mysteries of the Great War was the unexplained death of its eighth VC recipient, Major Charles Yate. For many years, it was thought that he died while escaping from a prisoner of war camp. It was also suggested that he had been deliberately murdered by his captors because he was a spy.

Early Life

Charles Allix Lavington Yate, known as 'Cal', was born in Mecklenburg, Germany on 14 March 1872 to the Reverend Prebendary George Edward Yate and his German-born second wife, Louise-Caroline née Petersen. Charles was the only son of his father's five children. When he was two, the family moved back to England, where his father again took up the post of Vicar of Madeley, Shropshire, a position he held from 1859 to his death in 1908.

Charles grew up being bilingual in English and German. He was sent to Weymouth College, then a public school on the Dorset coast, until he was eighteen before entering the Royal Military College at Sandhurst. He must have been an exemplary cadet as he passed out ninth of 1,100 candidates. He was commissioned in 1892 and joined the 2nd Battalion, King's Own Yorkshire Light Infantry (KOYLI) at its Bombay posting. Charles Yate saw his first action in 1897 during the Tirah Expedition.

The 2nd KOYLI did not become actively involved in the fighting until the very end of the campaign. Attempts to subdue the Afridi tribe had proved to be unsuccessful and the British pulled back from the tribal area. In a final attempt to force the Afridi to negotiate an end to the constant warring, the KOYLI and the 36th Sikhs were sent to capture the bulk of the Afridi's winter food supplies.

On 19 January 1898, the two regiments advanced along one of the passes. It was felt prudent to control the high ground on either side, but due to a misunderstanding, the Sikhs abandoned the heights. The Afridis quickly took up positions above the KOYLI, and began pouring a heavy fire at the defenceless troops below. With great difficulty, the regiment extracted itself to the mouth of the pass, where it was helped by a relief column. Unfortunately, the dead and the badly wounded had to be abandoned to mercy of the Afridi. Five officers and twenty-eight men had been killed and a further three officers and thirty-four men were wounded.

Boer War

In early 1899, Yate was promoted to captain, an exceptional advance for an officer with only seven years' service. His regiment was transferred to Mauritius and Yate began studying for the Staff College. Its stay in Mauritius was short-lived due to events unfolding in South Africa. HMS *Powerful*, en route from China to Cape Town, carried the regiment to the new war front. They were employed at strategic points in Cape Colony until General Lord Methuen was ready to begin his march to relieve Kimberley. The KOYLI formed part of the 9th Brigade along with the Northumberland Fusiliers, half of the Loyal North Lancashire Regiment and the Northamptonshire Regiment.

Methuen began his advance and met the first Boer opposition at Belmont on 23 November. Despite taking casualties, the battle was won and the British pursued the Boers to their next defensive position at Enslin, or as it is also known, Gras Plan. It was as the KOYLI advanced up the main *kopje*, to carry the Boer position that Yate was hit and wounded. The wound was serious enough for him to be hospitalised in England.

When he was well enough, he returned to Madeley for convalescence. The *Shropshire Star* reported that when his train arrived at Madeley Market Station, the local miners took the place of the horses and pulled his carriage through the streets of the town and to his home in recognition of his bravery.

Charles Yate recovered and returned to South Africa in September 1902 as Staff Officer in the Transvaal and Orange River Colony. By this time the conflict had become one of guerrilla warfare, which was all that the Boer Republic could manage while facing the inevitability of defeat. Yate's part in the war was not over as he was selected as one of the deputation that approached General Botha to arrange the start of peace negotiations.

With peace declared, Yate returned to England and, on 17 September 1903, he married Florence Helena Brigg of Greenhead Hall near Huddersfield. She had been previously married to Surgeon Lieutenant Colonel George Burroughs of the Indian Army in 1893 but had divorced.

There was little chance of settling into married bliss as he was posted to Japan two days later, on a special mission.

Further Service

Charles Yate, an outstanding linguist, was able to add Japanese to his fluency in German, French, Hindustani and Persian. He was appointed Military Attaché with the Japanese Army and was a close observer of the Russo-Japanese War. He was one of the first men to enter Port Arthur with the Japanese at the end of 1904. For this he was awarded the Japanese War Medal for Manchuria (Port Arthur) and received the Order of the Sacred Treasure, 3rd Class from the Emperor.

From Japan, he took up a position on the General Staff in Cape Colony before returning to Britain on 22 March 1906. It would appear that he took some well-earned leave until he was recalled to work on the Staff at the War Office from 1908 to 1914. During this period, he made frequent visits to Germany to visit his mother's relations and certainly would have detected that country's increasing need to flex its muscles.

In 1912, he was promoted to major and in March 1914, Major Yate re-joined his old regiment at its station in Dublin. On 13 July, he was one of ten officers selected for Air Observer training with the Royal Flying Corps at Neveravon. This last appointment lasted barely a month before he requested to return to his regiment which was part of the BEF. He had also turned down an appointment to General Joffe's Staff, preferring to take a more active role as a company commander in his regiment. The KOYLI was part of the 13th Brigade in the 5th Division, 2nd Corps. It was during the BEF's retreat from Mons that Yates made his mark on history.

VC Action

On 25 August, the regiment marched some thirty miles before reaching the town of Le Cateau. The 2nd Corps commander, General Sir Horace Smith-Dorrien planned a holding action to stall the German pursuit and allow the men of the First Corps to escape.

The following day, the British were positioned to the west of the town in a steep-sided valley. The KOYLI had dug shallow trenches to the south of the Cambrai road near the crossroads to Bavai. The Germans had occupied Le Cateau and began attacking the nearest British regiment, the Suffolks. It was not until 11.00 hours that the Germans appeared to the east of the Bavai road giving Major Yate and his company a target for his machine-gunners. From then onwards, the KOYLI was continuously involved in the fighting.

By 14.30 hours, the Suffolk Regiment was finally overwhelmed and the order was given to retire. Not all the companies heard the order and remained firing until it was too late. As the reserve battalions began to fall back to give cover to the first-line troops, Yate, in charge of the remnants of 'B' and 'D' companies, along with some companies of the King's Own Scottish Borderers, in their ignorance, fought on against overwhelming odds.

By 16.20 hours this fighting rear-guard was surrounded and out of ammunition. Refusing German calls to surrender, Yate lead a bayonet charge of nineteen survivors, which was swiftly overwhelmed. Yate, who seemingly expected to be killed, had his revolver kicked from his hand by a German officer and was captured. The KOYLI lost over 600 men, half of whom were made captive. The total casualties for the day's fighting were 7,812 men, but the Germans, too, had suffered heavily. It was enough to allow the BEF to continue their retreat without further contact with the enemy.

The prisoners were held in Le Cateau before being sent to Cambrai. Yate made a statement in his fluent German that he would never consider himself a prisoner, which made him a marked man. Yate was one of a number of officers who all testified that they received very rough treatment on their journey through Germany.

Captive

This conduct can be explained by the fact that at the outbreak of hostilities, Germany was dumfounded that Britain chose to ally herself with France and Russia and not to remain neutral as she did during the Franco-Prussian War of 1870. Consequence, British prisoners came in for particularly harsh treatment and were often forced to march through a gauntlet of howling, spitting civilians on their way to their camps.

One of Yate's fellow officers described the reception they faced as they made their way through the streets of Torgau: 'On our arrival there, a vast crowd was assembled at the station. From the station to the Brückenkopf barracks (where we were imprisoned) was a seething mass of screaming men, women and children. Their anger on their faces was terrible to see. They shook their fists, spat at us, and yelled themselves hoarse.'

For Yate, his incarceration was all the more stressful as he faced the allegation of spying. Because of his fluent German, his numerous pre-war visits to Germany and the fact that he was a GSO2 (General Staff Officer at the War Office) he was singled out for special treatment. Two officers were sent from Berlin to interrogate him but Yate vehemently denied the charges but obviously felt that the matter would not be dropped.

A fellow officer, Lieutenant Breen, with whom he shared a hut, recalled: 'He was very reticent on the subject, and he did not say definitely to me whether he had been engaged on work of this kind or not.'

Another thing Yate confided in Breen was: 'That it was while he was in Japan that he became influenced by the Japanese military tradition eschewing surrender. It worried him considerably that he had been captured unwounded. In his opinion no officer should surrender while conscious.'

Escape

In September, Yate resolved to escape from Torgau and make for Dresden. There he hoped to procure a bicycle and ride over the Swiss border. The need to escape was reinforced when he learned that he was to be interrogated again. Escape from these early prisoner of war camps was fairly easy and Yate was able to put together a disguise of workman's trousers and boots and an ill-fitting cape. He was aware that the downside of an escape was the lack of identification papers and the open hostility of the local population.

Breen continued: 'Yate was convinced that an Englishmen, speaking fluent German, would inevitably be murdered by ignorant peasantry as a spy.'

On the night of 19 September, with the help of Breen and another officer, Charles Yate clambered over the high compound wall and disappeared into the night. Yate obviously managed to put some mileage between him and the camp. Later, rumours abounded about Major Yate's death. Some accounts say he was shot and drowned trying to swim a river. Others say he was killed by a rock crushing his skull. The answer was provided by an eyewitness, a Herr Brottwitz, the manager of a sugar factory: 'I was cycling towards Kosdorf, between 10 and 11 a.m., when I met a strange looking man walking on a path under some trees. The man wore a shabby cloak much too short for him, workman's trousers and was hatless. I hailed him but got no answer.'

Calling to a group of men walking to work, he gave one of them his bike so he could overtake and stop the suspect. The others hurried in pursuit. It seemed to them that the suspect's features were 'those of a gentleman', and did not correspond with the shabbiness of his clothing.

'The workmen pointed to his hands which were small and obviously unused to hard work. I asked the man whence he came and got the answer, 'Schleswig Holstein'. I asked for papers, he said he had none. 'You know you cannot travel without papers in wartime'.

The workmen removed the man's cloak and were proceeding to unfasten rather roughly a haversack which he had fastened to his back by cross straps, when he suddenly took a razor from the inner pocket of his vest and drew it several times across his throat.

'The action was utterly unexpected; we all drew back in dismay, and nobody interfered when, dropping the razor, the stranger commenced to walk away. He walked on some forty yards when he suddenly collapsed and died at once.'

Yate's bloodstained belongings were returned to the camp with no explanation. None of the British prisoners were allowed to attend his burial, which took place near where he died. Herr Brottwitz recalled: 'The peasantry were naturally excited and handled the man roughly, asking him questions, shouting, "You are a spy".'

Asked if he thought Major Yate was liable to be ill-treated if he had not committed suicide, Brottwitz replied: 'You know the feeling of the people at the time … I cannot say with certainty but I should think he would have been roughly handled and possibly severely beaten when the men discovered the contents of his knapsack that he was not a German.'

After the war, Yate's remains were reinterred in the Berlin South Western Cemetery, Brandenburg, Plot II, Row G and Grave 8. It is marked by one of the least informative gravestones to a posthumous VC. There is no date of birth, prayer or dedication, just a stark name, rank and date of death.

He was recommended for a Victoria Cross, which was gazetted on 25 November 1914. The citation read: '[He] Commanded one of two Companies that remained to the end in the trenches at Le Cateau on 26th August, and when all other officers were killed or wounded and ammunition exhausted, led his nineteen survivors against the enemy in a charge in which he was severely wounded. He was picked up by the enemy and has subsequently died as a prisoner of war.'

Yates' VC was not invested until 2 August 1919, when it was presented to his widow. This throws up another query. His marriage was not exactly a love-match and his wife obviously was out for what she could get. When she found that she was to receive £70 widow's pension, she managed to persuade her late husband's cousin, Sir Charles Yate of Madeley Hall, to use his influence to have it increased to £140. Once she got it and once the probate of Yate's estate was cleared, she got a further £2,117. She then married for a third time; a Baronet thirty years her senior.

One wonders why it took over four years from Yate's citation to investiture. There has been a suggestion that the late Mrs Yate and her newest husband spent much of the war abroad and only on her return could the VC be invested. Major Yate's VC group is now held at the Regimental Museum in Doncaster.

The fluidity of movement which had characterised the early months of the war soon solidified into a situation that lasted for the next four years. The opposing forces then faced each other from hastily dug water-logged trenches that stretched 400 miles from the Belgian coast to the Swiss border.

The Germans, having lost their forward momentum, continued to launch assaults on the depleted lines of the British Expeditionary Force. In a close-run battle, the BEF managed to prevent the Germans from entering Ypres, the only Belgian town left in the Allies' hands. The downside was that the Germans commanded the surrounding salient, thus preventing any meaningful advance by the British. German artillery dominated the town and was able to the pound Ypres into a ruin. The Germans also inadvertently destroyed the system of dykes and ditches used by the farmers to drain the low-lying land from flooding. The consequence was that the trenches were often knee-deep in stinking mud, adding to the misery of being under almost constant fire.

Chapter 43

First World War, 1915

Number of VCs awarded	115
Number of VCs awarded to officers	56
Number of VCs awarded to other ranks	59
Total awarded to Royal Navy	14
Total awarded to Royal Naval Air Service	2
Total awarded to Royal Flying Corps	4
Total awarded to British Army	75
Total awarded to British Indian Army	5
Total awarded to Canadian Army	5
Total awarded to Australian Army	9
Total awarded to New Zealand Army	1

Origins of the War

The cry that the war would all be over by Christmas sounded hollow in the freezing, flooded trenches of the Western Front as the New Year heralded in 1915.

The BEF had been badly depleted in the campaigns of 1914 and held only thirty miles of trenches. The French Army Commander-in-Chief, Joseph Joffre, wanted Britain to take a more offensive role. With the arrival of Territorials and volunteers, the British C-in-C of the BEF, General Sir John French, proposed a series of swift attacks against a weakened German army, which had withdrawn some divisions needed to attack Russia on the Eastern Front.

During March to May, the British were involved in desperate fighting at Neuve Chapelle, Aubers Ridge, Festubert and the Second Battle of Ypres, during which thirty-four VCs were awarded.

The first VC of 1915 was to an Irishman fighting in the bitter conditions of the winter operations from 23 November 1914 to 6 February 1915. For a while he became a celebrity at a time when the country needed a hero.

MICHAEL JOHN O'LEARY VC (1888-1961)

The Germans continued to launch assaults on the depleted lines of the British Expeditionary Force. One place they attacked was the salient at Cuinchy, south of La Bassée Canal. Running alongside the canal was a sixteen-foot-high railway embankment – the only high point in a country so flat that, as Rudyard Kipling wrote, 'A bullet once started had no reason to stop'.

In late January 1915, this sector was defended by the 4th (Guards) Brigade and on the evening of the 30th, the front line which ran through a brickworks, was taken over by the Coldstream Guards with the Irish Guards in support.

The centre of their line consisted of a collection of huge dull plum-coloured brick stacks, mottled with black, which might have been originally thirty feet high. Five of these were held by the Guards and the other twenty-five by the enemy. These were connected and interlocked by saps and communication trenches

VC Action

Early in the morning of 1 February a post held by the Coldstream in a hollow near the embankment was bombed and rushed by the enemy through an old communications trench causing the Coldstream to pull back. Calling on No.4 Company Irish Guards to help, the Coldstream mounted a counter-attack. No.4 Company lost all its officers and was forced to withdraw.

Orders were issued for the position to be retaken by fifty men of the Coldstream and thirty from the Irish. After a ten-minute artillery barrage, which badly damaged the German position, the Guards began their assault. No.2 Company of the Irish Guards led by Second Lieutenant Innes gave covering fire as the Coldstream advanced. Then No.2 Company was ordered to advance. Innes's orderly, Lance Corporal Michael O'Leary, ran forward, well clear of the rest. He mounted the railway embankment and fired five times in rapid succession, wiping out the German machine-gun crew manning the first barricade.

Spotting another machine-gun positioned a further sixty yards away but with the intervening ground too marshy for a direct approach, O'Leary, in full view of the enemy, climbed the embankment again and ran towards the machine-gun nest. Before the Germans could turn the gun on him, he calmly knelt and shot three of the crew before taking the other two prisoner. Unbeknownst to surrendering prisoners, O'Leary's rifle magazine was out of ammunition. Eyewitnesses reported that he went about the attack in a leisurely manner oblivious to the heavy fire around him. In the words of one witness, O'Leary was, 'as cool as if he had been for a walk in the park'.

O'Leary's name was put forward for an award and, on 18 February, his name appeared in *The London Gazette.* Not only was he the first VC awarded on the Western Front but also the first Irish Guardsman to receive the honour.

Early Life

Michael John O'Leary was born at Kilbarry Lodge, Inchigeela, County Cork, Ireland, on 29 September 1890. He was the third of four children born to Daniel and Margaret who ran a small farm about ten miles from Macroom. When he was old enough, he was expected to help with the farm work. Seeing little prospect for his future, he joined the Royal Navy at the age of sixteen and was sent to the training ship, the old iron screw yacht, HMS *Vivid*, at Devonport. He appears to have remained there until rheumatism forced his discharge in early 1910.

Returning to the family farm, he stayed until he enlisted in the Irish Guards on 2 July 1910. Apparently, they turned a blind eye to his rheumatism for, on the completion of three years Home Service, he was placed on the Reserve and immediately applied to join the Royal North-West Mounted Police.

Canada

On 2 August 1913, he took up the post of Constable at Battleford, Saskatoon, and was soon called upon to display his courage. In a two-hour running gun-battle with two criminals, he managed to capture them and was rewarded with a gold ring, which he wore for the rest of his life. He then was transferred to Regina until 22 September 1914.

With outbreak of war, O'Leary was anxious to re-join his regiment and was granted a free discharge from the RNWMP. Returning to England he was mobilised on 22 October and joined the 1st Battalion Irish Guards in France of 23 November 1914.

The battalion had practically been wiped out during the retreat from Mons and the subsequent battles. Michael O'Leary was part of a draft of 288 men sent to help reconstruct the battalion. Midwinter was spent in the miserable water-logged trenches around Cuinchy. It was noted that the water in the trenches averaged three feet, not the sort of conditions to help O'Leary's rheumatism. O'Leary was amongst the Irish Guards inspected by King George on his first visit to the Western Front. His visit was followed a few weeks later by the Prince of Wales. On 5 January 1915, O'Leary was promoted to lance corporal and Mentioned in Despatches. After his VC exploit, he was further promoted to sergeant on 4 February. There was still much fighting around the brick works until the end of the month. The battalion took part in the Battles of Neuve Chapelle in March and Festubert in May.

On 22 June 1915, Sergeant Michael O'Leary was presented with his Cross at Buckingham Palace. This was just the start of a round of public adulation for his VC-winning action. A crowd of some 60,000 thronged Hyde Park on 10 July for a reception for the hero of the hour. Crowds at recruiting events around the country and in Ireland gave O'Leary a rapturous welcome. He also married Greta Margaret, with whom he had four children.

A poem about his exploits was performed before the King; George Bernard Shaw wrote a short play about him; the celebrated artist Lady Butler painted him; cigarette cards were produced to support Irish widows and orphans. In addition, his image was used on a propaganda poster to boost Irish recruitment extolling fellow Irishmen to follow his example. Another award was bestowed to keep his VC company, as, on 25 August 1915, he received the Russian Cross of St George. He was also commissioned as a second lieutenant in the Connaught Rangers on 23 October 1915. O'Leary was transferred to the 5th (Service) Battalion Connaught Rangers and sent to join it at the new front that had opened in the Macedonian port of Salonika. The reason British and French troops were sent to this outpost in the Balkans was in response to pleas from Serbia for the Allies to support them against the combined attacks of Austro-Hungary, Germany and Bulgaria.

Gallipoli

The 5th had served in the disastrous Gallipoli Campaign suffering 684 casualties out of an embarkation strength of 975. On 10 October, the battalion arrived at Salonika and O'Leary joined them a month later where he was put in charge of scouts and snipers. The *Daily Mail*'s official reporter with the British Salonika Force, G. Ward Price, wrote about the 10th Irish Brigade:

'These Irish brigades were still imperfectly installed on a barren inhospitable Dedli ridge; they were savagely smitten by that cruel three-day blizzard which caused suffering to our troops not only in the Balkans but at the Dardanelles. It began on 27 November with torrents of rain which soon turned to snow. Then it froze so quickly that the drenched skirts of greatcoats would stand out stiff like a ballet-dancers dress.'

During that terrible winter, the Connaught's casualties amounted to 1,219. The summers were just as unbearable, with hot and dusty conditions. The troops were plagued by swarms of malaria-carrying mosquitoes and O'Leary became a victim of this debilitating sickness which dogged him for the rest of his life. During lulls in the bad weather, O'Leary was awarded another Mentioned in Despatches. It was not until 1918 that O'Leary returned to England and served out his war with the 2nd Battalion Connaught's at Dover. In March 1921, he retired from the Army and joined the Officer's Reserve.

Canada Again

Michael O'Leary returned to Canada and joined the Ontario Provincial Police as a licence inspector for the enforcement of prohibition until 1923. He was then appointed sergeant of police on the Michigan Central Railway and stationed at the border town of Bridgeburg, Ontario. The temptations offered during prohibition proved too much for the lowly paid Sergeant

O'Leary. He told a *Daily Mail* reporter: 'Unfortunately, on the railway I came into contact with bootlegging and smuggling interests. A detective has to take bribes to keep his mouth shut or else people are out to get him.'

In 1925, he was arrested for smuggling an alien into Buffalo, New York, from Bridgeburg but was acquitted. Later that year, he was again arrested and charged with 'irregularity in a search for liquor'. He spent a week in an American jail, was acquitted but lost his job with the railway company. He was unemployed for several months before being advanced £70 by the Hamilton authorities enabling his family to return to Ireland. O'Leary worked at several jobs but suffered bouts of malaria. He finally left Canada in 1930. On his return, the British Legion learned of his impoverished state and employed him as a packer in their poppy factory.

Second World War

O'Leary managed to get a job as a commissionaire at the Mayfair Hotel on London's Park Lane. Here he remained until he was called up for the Reserve of Officers in June 1939 and sent to France with the British Expeditionary Force as a captain in the Middlesex Regiment. The reoccurrence of his malarial condition force his return to England and he was fortunate to avoid the Dunkirk evacuation.

In 1944, he was transferred to the Pioneer Corps and put in charge of a prisoner of war camp in the south of England. On 19 March 1945, he relinquished his commission on the grounds of ill health and retired as Honorary Captain. He did attend the Victory Parade in London and settled down in north London with his family.

O'Leary ran a small building contractor until he retired in 1954. He attended the 1956 VC Centenary at Hyde Park and was bemused to find that there was an impersonator in a wheelchair claiming to be Michael O'Leary VC. Continuing ill-health led to his death in Whittington Hospital, Islington on 1 August 1961 and he was laid to rest at Mill Hill Cemetery, Paddington.

By the winter of 1914-15, the war on the Western Front had become a stalemate. Turkey, which had delayed in choosing sides, decided to join the Central Powers of Germany and Austria-Hungary. As early as September 1914, Winston Churchill, then the First Lord of the Admiralty, had voiced his plans to capture the Dardanelles, the narrow strait that separated Europe and Asia. This important maritime link with Britain and her ally, Russia, was closed when Turkey sided with Germany on 31 October 1914. Britain and France responded by sending a large fleet of obsolete battleships, that could not operate against the German High Seas Fleet, to force a passage up the Dardanelles with the expectation of forcing Istanbul into surrender.

On 18 March 1915, the main attack was launched. The fleet, comprising of eighteen pre-Dreadnought battleships supported by cruisers and destroyer, sailed up the Dardanelles but, due to inefficient mine-sweeping, six ships were either sunk or badly damaged. The failure of the naval attack prompted the landing of a large allied force on the Gallipoli Peninsula. Poor intelligence and the concentration of Turkish forces blocked the Allied attempt to occupy the whole peninsula and the campaign stalled.

The British troops were landed and barely able to advance much beyond the beaches. In the eight-month campaign, some 410,000 troops endured danger and privation. A total of 43,000 were killed, died of wounds and a further 205,000 suffered sickness. This costly campaign ended in January 1916, leaving an indelible impression on the men involved. Careers amongst some high-ranking British officers were ruined but the high reputation of the soldiers of the Australian and New Zealand Army Corps (ANZAC) made them an important part of their respective country's culture and established the newly-federated countries on an international level.

The *Daily Telegraph* correspondent Ellis Ashmead-Bartlett, an archetypical Englishman, was unstinting in his admiration for the ANZACs. He found the gulf between the average pallid, small and under-nourished British soldier and his ANZAC counterpart surprisingly wide: 'They create an excellent impression with their fine physical and general bearing. A truly magnificent body of men ... The men seem to discipline themselves, and the officers have very little authority over them through holding a military rank – personality plays a much more important role.'

Out of thirty-nine VCs awarded for the campaign, ten went to men of the ANZACS.

ALFRED ALFRED SHOUT VC (1882-1915)

The man known as Captain Alfred John Shout who served with the Australian Imperial Forces on Gallipoli, was a New Zealander born in Wellington on 7 August 1881. He was one of nine children born to John Richard Shout, a cook, who was born 29 May 1856 in London and his wife Agnes Mary née Kelly born 9 May 1857. Agnes was the fourth daughter of Charles Kelly, a Royal Artilleryman and his wife Ann who had settled in Wanganui New Zealand in 1849.

Agnes and John Shout had nine children, five daughters and four sons. Their first born who was destined to become a hero on Gallipoli was Alfred John, born 7 August 1881 at Bolton Street Wellington. When he was eighteen, Alfred Shout joined the New Zealand contingent to fight the Boers in South Africa.

Under the command of Colonel Baden-Powell, he joined the Border Horse and saw plenty of action, during which Shout was twice wounded, once in the chest. He was Mentioned in Despatches (Army Orders, 23 February 1901): 'At Thabaksberg, 29 January 1901, he displayed great courage and assisted greatly in keeping men together. Under heavy fire he bought out of the firing line a wounded man of the 17th Battery, RFA, and took him to a place of safety.'

He finished the war as a Sergeant and, after returning to Australia, went back to South Africa, serving as a sergeant with the Cape Field Artillery (1903-1907). During this time, he met and married Rose Alice and they had a daughter.

In 1907, Alfred Shout and his family moved to Australia where he joined the 29th Infantry Regiment (Australian Rifles) and regularly competed in rifle club events. He was employed as a carpenter and joiner in Darlington, an inner Sydney suburb.

First World War

At the age of thirty-three, he was commissioned as a second lieutenant and posted to 'F' Company, 1st Battalion, 1st Division, Australian Imperial Force (AIF) on 27 August 1914. The departure of the battalion from Sydney was delayed due to the presence of German cruisers in the Pacific. On 18 October, his battalion embarked on A.19, HMAT (His Majesty's Australian Transport) *Afric*, for what they believed was to be a voyage to England. Sailing without escort to Princess Royal Harbour Albany, Western Australia they arrived on 25 October to find fifteen other ships already in the harbour. The first contingent of ANZAC troops to be sent overseas sailed on 1 November, in a convoy of thirty-six transports carrying 20,758 Australian troops, 7,479 horses and two New Zealand brigades. On the first day out from Albany they were joined by two vessels from Fremantle and learned that England had declared war on Turkey.

On 26 November, they received orders to disembark in Egypt and establish training camps there. This decision to train in Egypt was bought about by the shortage of accommodation and training facilities in England and the feared effects of the harsh English winter on the Australian troops. Four days later the 1st Infantry Battalion boarded a train for the 20km journey to Mena, a small village located in the shadows of the Sphinx and the Giza Pyramids where they set up a training camp. Here, Alfred Shout was promoted to lieutenant on 1 February 1915.

On 25 April 1915, the 1st Australian Division under the command of Major General Bridges made an amphibious landing at Ari Burnu Point (Anzac Cove) on the Gallipoli Peninsula. Unable to advance and capture their objectives, the men clung desperately to their positions just above the landing beaches. Shout displayed his leadership qualities during this disastrous landing in which the troops found that they had landed on the wrong beach.

VC Action

Shout again showed conspicuous courage and ability during a strong Turkish counter-attack south at Walkers Ridge near Gaba Tepe, when he organised and led to safety a section of men which had suffered fifty per cent casualties while pinned down by intense enemy machine-gun fire.

While still under heavy fire, Shout led the men through thick undergrowth to a safer position. He continually exposed himself to the enemy to establish their whereabouts. Although he was wounded several times, he then led a bayonet charge against the Turkish post.

One of his men, Private Bethel, recalled: 'He was the bravest of many brave men that revealed themselves that day. I saw him first on Tuesday morning after the landing. There were only two officers left, Lieutenants Shout and Harrison, and our position was desperate. The gallantry of both was remarkable, but Lieutenant Shout was a hero. Wounded himself several times, he kept picking up wounded men and carrying them out of the firing line. I saw him carry fully a dozen men away. Then another bullet struck him in the arm, and it fell uselessly by his side. Still he would not go to the rear. "I am with you boys to the finish", was the only reply he would make. We all thought, too, that it was to be the finish for us.

'The Turks were attacking us in thousands. We were not properly entrenched and we were hopelessly outnumbered. A little while later Lieutenant Shout was wounded again and fell down. It was cruel to see him. He struggled and struggled until he got to his feet, refusing all entreaties to go to the rear. Then he staggered and fell and tried to rise again. At last some men seized him and carried him away, still protesting.'

For his actions on 27 April 1915, Lieutenant Shout was awarded the Military Cross. The 1st Division suffered 366 casualties during their first four days on Gallipoli. Shout's wounds, the most serious of which was a bullet that had passed through his arm and entered his chest, were treated on the Hospital Ship *Gascon*.

Shout's battalion commander, Colonel Henry MacLaurin, who had been Mentioned in Despatches (and promoted posthumously to Brigadier General), was killed by a sniper's bullet the following day as he stood observing the enemy from the ridge that from then on bore his name. The troops had landed with 250 rounds of ammunition but by the third day they were short of ammunition, water and exhausted through lack of sleep. A withdrawal from the peninsula was discussed and considered by General Sir Ian Hamilton before he made the decision that the ANZACS must hold their position and dig in.

Shout returned to duty a few days later only to be wounded again on 11 May. He was again treated on board *Gascon*, before he re-joined his unit on 26 May 1915. On 29 July, Shout was promoted to captain. His dedication to duty and bravery saw him awarded a special Mention in Despatches.

After months of fighting on Gallipoli, a major offensive was planned with the New Zealand contingent attacking Chunuk Bair and the British landing in Suvla Bay. To create a diversion and draw the Turks away from the planned attacks, the untried 3rd Light Horse Brigade would attack The Nek, while the 1st Light Horse Regiment would assault Dead Man's Ridge. The 1st Infantry Brigade was assigned to take the Lone Pine trenches.

The night preceding their attack on Lone Pine, Shout, to relieve the anxiety of the members of his platoon, spoke to them at length about the coming event. He concluded his talk by saying: 'We will make a name for Australia and ourselves tomorrow'.

At midday on 6 August 1915, Captain Shout issued his men with some white calico, a strip to sew on the arms of their tunics and a square for the back. This was to indicate to the artillery the position of the Australian infantry during the battle and to help the soldiers recognise their comrades in the dim light as they attacked the Turkish trenches. At 17.40 hours, the men of the 1st Brigade were lined up ready to go over the top. Taking the Turks by surprise, the soldiers leading the charge reached the first trench quickly but found it difficult to attack as it was covered with logs. Leaving some men to infiltrate the first trench, the rest were ordered to attack the second trench. After less than an hour, they had taken Lone Pine. As anticipated, the Turks counter-attacked and the battle for Lone Pine continued for five days.

The 1st Battalion was withdrawn from the line for a short respite at midday on 7 August. Returning to the line at 15.00 they beat off heavy counter-attacks for twenty-four hours before they were relieved by the 7th Battalion. The 1st re-entered the line on the morning of 9 August at a point known as Sasse's Sap after Captain Cecil Sasse, who had captured a section of the enemy's trench on the 6 August. They discovered that the enemy had reoccupied a section of the trench overnight. Shout and Sasse, with the assistance of three volunteers' carrying sandbags to build trench blocks, advanced with Shout throwing their crude jam-jar bombs and Sasse picking off survivors with his rifle. In this way, they cleared about twenty yards of trench before making another sandbag barricade. Sasse then suggested to Shout that they extend their occupation of the enemy's trench.

Gathering eight volunteers to carry sandbags and carrying extra bombs, the two officers repeated their previous successful plan of attack. Shout and Sasse charged down the trench occupied by Turks with Shout throwing bombs and Sasse shooting, killing eight of the Turks they captured a length of the trench. The process was successfully repeated a second time, then Shout, who was reportedly revelling in the fight, went over the barricade with Sasse for what they planned to be the third and final dash for the day. Shout lit the fuses of his three remaining bombs and set off down the trench. He had successfully hurled two of his bombs and was in the process of throwing the third bomb when it exploded prematurely blowing off his right hand and severely wounding the side of his face and body.

Mortally wounded Shout continued to direct the attack, then murmuring, 'Good old First Brigade, well done!' Passing out through loss of blood, Shout was carried to the rear where he regained consciousness. He even managed a cup of tea while he waited for the stretcher bearers to take him to the beach. Three days later, Captain Alfred Shout died from his wounds on board the hospital ship *Neuralia* and was buried at sea. He was thirty-four years of age.

Casualties were high on both sides. The Australians casualties numbered eighty officers and 2,197 other ranks while the Turkish 16th Division was believed to have suffered almost 7,000 casualties. Seven Australian soldiers were awarded the Victoria Cross for their actions at Lone Pine. Captain Shout's posthumous award was announced in *The London Gazette* of 15 October 1915.

The other Australian Victoria Cross recipients at Lone Pine were; English born Lance Corporal Leonard Keysor of the 1st Battalion, Private John Hamilton a butcher from Penshurst, NSW of the 3rd Battalion, and four Victorians from the 7th Battalion; Captain Frederick Tubb, Lieutenant William Symonds, Corporal Alexander Burton and Corporal William Dunstan. Captain Sasse received a DSO for his actions in gaining substantial additions to the Australian-held position at Lone Pine; Sasse was wounded three times during these daring attacks.

Mortally Wounded

Records showed Alfred Shout died on 11 August. These records were altered on 20 August to read 'Not dead! Onboard "Themistocles", returning to Australia'. Army Records had been advised accordingly by cable from Alexandria. The Australian press published news of his return advising its readers that Captain Shout would arrive at Sydney in mid-September. At a later inquiry, the official explanation for this mistake was that Second Lieutenant Arthur John Shirt, a wounded man on board *Themistocles* had been mistaken for Arthur John Shout.

Captain Shout was the most highly decorated Australian soldier of the campaign and his VC group, with other memorabilia including a cap badge, an officer's pip, a photograph of Shout, were listed for auction by Shout's, grandson, Graham Thomas, at Bonham's & Goodman, Sydney, and were purchased on 24 July 2006 for a world record sum of AU $1,200,000 (£490,000). The successful bidder was one of Australia's richest men, Kerry Stokes, who afterwards presented it to the Australian War Memorial on Friday, 25 August 2006.

While the land invasion had quickly stalled on Gallipoli, a more successful campaign was being waged beneath the waves of the Dardanelles. The Turks had tightened up the defences of the waterway with deep mine-fields, batteries of artillery lining both banks and, beyond the Narrows at Chanak, patrol boats. Surface ships were now not an option so the Navy employed their fledgling Submarine Service. In late December 1914, Lieutenant Norman Holbrook took his old and obsolete submarine HMS *B.11* as far as the Narrows, braving strong currents, diving under five rows of mines, torpedoing and sinking the Turkish battleship *Messudiyeh* guarding the mine-field. For this outstanding feat, he was awarded the Victoria Cross, the first to be bestowed on a sub-mariner.

This was followed in April 1914 by HMS *E.14* commanded by Lieutenant-Commander Edward Boyle, who spent two weeks creating havoc in the Sea of Marmara beyond the Narrows. He succeeded in sinking two gun-boats and a military transport before bringing his craft safely back to base. For this he was awarded the Victoria Cross. It is of note that in 1918, Lieutenant-Commander Geoffrey White was awarded a posthumous VC when commanding *E.14*; the only time a submarine was commanded by two VC winners.

Learning from the experiences of Holbrook and Boyle, another submarine, HMS *E.11* commanded by Lieutenant-Commander Martin Nasmith, undertook a lengthy patrol that that panicked the population of Constantinople.

MARTIN ERIC NASMITH VC (1883-1965)

One of the most successful and famous submariners of the First World War, Martin Eric Nasmith was born on 1 April 1883 in Barnes, south-west London, to Martin Arthur Nasmith, a stockbroker, and Caroline (née Beard). The eldest of three sons, he was educated at Eastman's Royal Navy Academy, Winchester, entering *Britannia* at Dartmouth in May 1898. On qualification, he joined HMS *Renown* as a midshipman before being promoted to sub-lieutenant on 15 February 1903.

The Royal Navy created its Submarine Service in 1901, and Nasmith became one of the early officers when he joined on 4 July 1904 and went to HMS *Thames* for training. He was joined by his friend and fellow cadet, Edward Boyle, who matched his prowess as a submarine captain. In 1905, Nasmith was promoted to lieutenant and given command of the submarine HMS *A.4*, the earliest of the Navy's A-class subs.

In October, *A.4* suffered a serious accident during an underwater signalling experiment off Spithead. A bell was lowered into the water some way from *A.4* and used to signal to the submarine, which was running awash. A flag on a boat hook protruding through a ventilator was used to indicate that the signal had been heard. Unfortunately, the choppy seas broke over the submarine and flooded through the ventilator causing the boat to develop a forty-degree inclination at the bow and partially filling the craft with chlorine gas from the soaked batteries. The sub sank to ninety feet before the crew managed to blow the ballast tanks and surface, where they crammed onto the deck to escape the poisonous fumes.

There was more drama as the boat was being towed back to port when there was an explosion and she slowly sank. *A.4* was salvaged and repaired. For Nasmith, he had to endure a court martial but escaped with a reprimand in consideration of his swift reaction to what could have been the loss of his crew. As part of his punishment he spent the next two years on the cruiser *Indomitable* before returning to the Submarine Service.

He took command of the C-Class *C.7* and *C.18* and, in 1912, was captain of the new *D.4*, the first submarine to have a gun fitted to the deck. In May that year, King George V was on board the Royal Yacht in Weymouth Bay to watch Fleet manoeuvres but fog disrupted the event. Instead, the King requested a wish to dive in a submarine.

On 8 May 1912, he embarked on Lieutenant Nasmith's *D.4*. What made the occasion remarkable was that, besides the King, there were his son Prince Albert (later George VI), Winston Churchill, Captain Roger Keyes (later Director of Combined Operation in the Second World War) and former Prime Minister Arthur Balfour. The current Prime Minister, Herbert Asquith, would have also been on board but had to return to London on urgent business. Considering the early technology and reliability of the submarine, it was something of a risk to be carrying Britain's elite together in one small steel undersea container. Nasmith later wondered what would have happened to the course of twentieth century history had he sunk that day.

Martin Nasmith was promoted lieutenant commander and commanded HMS *Arrogant*, the Portsmouth submarine depot ship, and was, for a time, responsible for training future submariners. He was also something of an inventor, developing a retractable periscope and a range and distance finder.

When war broke out in August 1914, he was given command of the newly completed *E.11*. Like all submarines of that period, space was at a premium. Headroom was extremely restricted due to the curving sides and there was no room to sling hammocks. The crew slept where they could; among the machinery or on the boards of the central passageway. The clatter of the engine made it impossible to be heard and communication was through sign language.

After months of patrolling off Heligoland waiting for the German High Seas Fleet to appear, *E.11* was ordered to join the East Mediterranean Fleet at the entrance to the Dardanelles. He set sail in the company of *E.15* and his friend Edward Boyle's *E.14* led by the depot ship *Adamant*. As luck would have it, *E.11* developed mechanical problems in the Mediterranean and had to wait at Malta for repairs, while his comrades sailed on.

VC Action

Finally, the repairs were made and Nasmith sailed to Mudros Harbour where the fleet lay. Nasmith decided to reconnoitre the area he was to patrol from the air. His pilot was Lieutenant Richard Bell-Davis, soon to win the Victoria Cross for rescuing a downed pilot in Bulgaria. The flight proved invaluable for pin-pointing land marks and the small harbours in the Sea of Marmara, which was typical of Nasmith's forward planning.

With final orders from Commodore Roger Keyes to 'Go run amuck in the Marmara', Nasmith and his crew cast off at 01.10 hours on 19 May 1915.

He negotiated the Narrows with its extensive minefield and entered the Sea of Marmara. Nasmith spied two old Turkish battleships with destroyer escorts about three miles away. Unable to close the gap, he moved his boat to the western end of the Sea of Marmara and devoted his attention to disrupting the enemy's supply lines by sea to the Gallipoli Peninsula.

The Marmara is a very deep inland sea about 110 miles long and forty-six broad. The first Turkish vessel they intercepted was a sailing vessel, which they boarded, only to find it was carrying logs. Nasmith decided to use the vessel as a 'stalking-horse' which would screen his sub from enemy observers. Unfortunately, the only activity they saw during the day were a few fishing boats. As darkness fell, Nasmith told the sailing ship's captain that he was free to continue his voyage.

Frustrated at the lack of targets, Nasmith decided on a bold plan; he would attack shipping in the harbour of Constantinople. On the way, they sighted a gunboat and fired a torpedo, which struck home and the gunboat began to list. Nasmith watched through the periscope as a seaman ran to a gun and trained it in his direction. Then there was a metallic clang and the periscope lens went black. By some fluke, the Turkish gunner had put a shot through the upper part of the periscope.

The following day *E.11* intercepted a small steamer, the *Nagara,* and called for her crew to abandon ship. Then a surprising number of men appeared and were identified as Turkish marines bound for the port of Charnak near the Narrows. Most of the passengers took to the boats and Nasmith and his second in command, Lieutenant D'Oyly Hughes, boarded the vessel. Here they were greeted by an American newspaper reporter, Raymond Gram Swing of the *Chicago Daily News,* who conducted an impromptu interview. He asked how many submarines were operating in the Marmara. D'Oyly Hughes replied 'Eleven!'

Nasmith ordered explosive charges to be set on the *Nagara* and went in pursuit of another steamer that was spotted. It was heading for the safety of the harbour at Rodosto, where there was a column of soldiers lining the front. The vessel, heavily laden with explosives reached the end of the pier and the crew took off for safety. Nasmith gingerly approached until the boat grounded. Using his other periscope, he ordered a torpedo to be fired at a range of 1,000 yards. They waited in suspense until there was an enormous explosion as the munitions ship went up in flame and smoke.

As they withdrew, another vessel was spotted heading for Rodosto. It was a paddle steamer with a deck cargo of barbed wire. Nasmith tried to intercept it with rifle fire but the helmsman managed to evade all efforts of surrender. Finally, the steamer beached below some cliffs and the crew ran for cover. Nasmith carefully approached and reached the stern.

D'Oyly-Hughes was ready to lay some demolition charges when a troop of cavalry appeared along the top of the cliff and sent such a heavy fire that Nasmith was forced to abandon his destruction of the paddle steamer. With bullets rattling against the hull and conning tower, Nasmith pulled back half a mile and attempted to sink the Turkish vessel with a precious torpedo. Unfortunately, it narrowly missed. Nasmith was philosophical about the episode: 'But I never thought *E.11* would be chased off by a troop of cavalry!'

Constantinople

It was on 25 May that *E.11* entered the harbour at Constantinople and went in search of a likely target. A cruiser was spotted and Nasmith lined up to fire a torpedo. At the last moment, he saw that it was flying the American flag and the attack aborted.

Then Nasmith's crew observed a large transport ship moored near the Topkkhana Arsenal. The port bow torpedo was fired but there was something wrong with the gyro. The starboard bow torpedo was then fired and it ran true towards the transport. The first torpedo was seen to be coming towards them and Nasmith ordered a crash dive. An instant later they heard an explosion near the Galata Bridge followed by a louder report as the transport was hit.

After many anxious moments of disorientation, Nasmith worked out where the sub was without the aid of the periscope and *E.11* made her way back to the Sea of Marmara. She had left behind a city in panic with the population expecting a landing at any time. Beside the moored transport, *Stamboul*, Nasmith's rogue torpedo had demolished a part of the Customs House Quay near the Galata Bridge. After a day of relaxation and celebration, Nasmith was aroused at 01.40 hours with the news that a large ship with a destroyer escort was sailing towards the Narrows.

As it was dark and practically nothing could be seen through a periscope, Nasmith ordered *E.11* to follow on the surface. As the large ship crossed a patch of moonlight, Nasmith was able to identify her as a former German battleship sold to Turkey in 1910 and renamed *Hayreddin Barbarossa*. Nasmith waited as the ship and escort approached, positioning the submarine between the battleship and the shore to be less visible against the land. As *E.11* prepared to fire at the target, one of the destroyers spotted her and Nasmith was forced to abandon his attack.

Early in the morning of 28 May smoke was spotted on the horizon. This turned out to be a convoy escorted by destroyers. Nasmith submerged and selected the largest vessel as a target. Closing, he fired his port bow torpedo and had the satisfaction of scoring a hit. On impact, there was a huge column of smoke and flames as the vessel heeled over and sank in less than a minute.

A few hours later, a large ship was spotted with people moving around on deck. Nasmith fired a torpedo which ran true but there was no explosion. The vessel stopped and Nasmith edged closer until they saw that instead of Turkish troops on the deck, it was full of civilians including women and children.

It was with a sense of relief that the torpedo did not explode and Nasmith allowed the ship to continue on its way. When it was safe, the sub surfaced and the crew searched for the torpedo. Nasmith spotted it, stripped off and dived in. He found that the head of the torpedo was damaged by the impact on the ship but failed to explode. He carefully disarmed the torpedo and the crew hauled it aboard to be reused.

The following day he examined the port of Panderma on the east side of Marmara and spotted a large liner used as a troop transport. She was identified as one of the latest ships of the German Rickmers Line. A single torpedo was fired hitting the vessel amidships causing her to list heavily to port. Nasmith retreated and headed east back towards Constantinople.

On 2 June, a large supply ship, heavily laden, was seen and intercepted. A torpedo was fired and there was an enormous explosion confirming that she was carrying munitions. Another attack on a small vessel near the coast cost them a lost torpedo and *E.11* was now down to just one. Nasmith decided to keep it for the *Barbarossa* which he was sure he would pass on the way home. A thorough search of the area yielded no sign of the *Barbarossa*. Instead Nasmith decided to sink a large supply ship at anchor near the Narrows.

Now with all torpedoes expended and an ominous crack appearing in the starboard shaft, *E.11* headed back down the Dardanelles. As they passed through a minefield, they heard a harsh scraping noise and the sub being pulled to port. Rising to periscope depth, Nasmith peered through the lens, stifling all appearance of shock. There was a large black object trailing seaweed only twenty feet from the lens which on close examination proved to be a large horned mine caught up in the port hydroplane. They still had to contend with another minefield as they scraped past the moored mines at a depth of eighty feet still trailing their unwanted visitor.

After three tense hours, *E.11* gingerly surfaced and the ensign unfurled. Nasmith spoke in a voice they could all hear: 'We've fouled a mine forward, and we're going to get rid of it by going full astern and blowing the after tanks to keep the bows submerged.'

The stern rose and the boat trembled as the reversing screws sent a rush of water forward which swept the mine over the bows until it sank, weighted down by its sinker. Nasmith's nineteen-day patrol had been a success having sunk eleven enemy vessels.

On 25 June 1915, Martin Nasmith was gazetted the Victoria Cross and on 30 June promoted to commander. His lieutenants, Guy D'Oyly Hughes and Robert Brown received Distinguished Service Crosses and the crew, Distinguished Service Medals.

Further Patrols

The bestowing of the Cross was by no means the end of Nasmith and *E.11*'s adventures in the Sea of Marmara. Ten days later he was again on patrol and sank a transport at anchor. The next day he bagged a second transport.

Nasmith had managed to have a 12-pounder gun fitted with which he could fire on any troops he came across onshore. Then came the moment he had been waiting for when the *Hayreddin Barbarossa* was spotted. Nasmith managed to fire a torpedo, striking the battleship amidships causing her to list. Attempting to reach the shore, Nasmith saw a great flash as the magazine exploded and the giant ship sank with the loss of 250 crew.

HMS *E.11* again entered the Bosphorous and sank a steamer alongside the railway pier. Using his 12-pounder, he managed to damage the Constantinople-Baghdad railway viaduct at Ismid. He then decided to give D'Orly Hughes the chance he had been keen to try for so long – the final destruction of the viaduct. D'Orly Hughes had built a raft to carry the demolition material and, with only her conning tower showing, D'Orly Hughes slipped over the side and guided the raft to the shore.

Carrying the demolition charge, D'Orly Hughes scrambled up the cliff but found the way to the viaduct blocked by a Turkish patrol. With no alternative, he laid the charge in a culvert not far from the viaduct. The sound that he made alerted the Turks and he was chased down the line until he finally lost them. He had run quite a distance and had trouble in finding *E.11* but at daybreak he finally reached the submarine. As he was hauled aboard, the Turkish soldiers opened fire from the cliff top and *E.11* quickly submerged and escaped.

Martin Nasmith and his crew continued to cause the Turks much discomfort. Even when they had used all their torpedoes, they continued to harry the enemy for another thirteen days, including a further bombardment of the railway viaduct.

When the Gallipoli campaign ended in January 1916, the most dominant and successful submariner was Martin Nasmith and *E.11*. In three patrols, she sank twelve vessels including a battleship as well as causing much damage onshore.

When he returned from the Mediterranean, Nasmith went to Buckingham Palace on 20 January 1916 to receive his Victoria Cross. In addition, he was promoted to captain on 30 June.

Later in the war, Nasmith was in charge of the Seventh Submarine Fleet in the Baltic and in 1920, appointed a CB. That year, he married Beatrix Justina Dunbar-Dunbar-Rivers and changed his name to Dunbar-Nasmith. He was captain of HMS *Iron Duke* and appointed Commandant of the Royal Naval College, Dartmouth.

During the Second World War, he served as Flag Officer in charge of London and retired in 1946. Admiral Sir Martin Dunbar-Nasmith died on 29 June 1965 and was buried in Elgin Cemetery.

After the heavy losses at the battles of Neuve Chapelle, Aubers Ridge and Festubert, the British Army had to call upon the new inadequately trained volunteers for the next major offensive. Once again, the French C-in-C,

General Joffre, put pressure on Sir John French to be part of a joint offensive in the Champagne area. The British section was in a coal mining region dominated by slag heaps and high winding gear towers.

In a battle that lasted from 25 September to 8 October, the British lost nearly 60,000 men for the gain of just two miles. Many feats of gallantry were performed and were acknowledges with the awarding of twenty-three Victoria Crosses, including the first one to a native Gurkha soldier.

KULBIR THAPA VC (1888-1956)

The outbreak of the First World War saw a huge increase in recruitment for the Gurkhas of the Indian Army and some 114,000 were called to service. They saw action in Gallipoli, Egypt, Palestine and Mesopotamia but it was on the Western Front the gallantry of the first native Gurkha was recognised with the bestowal of the Victoria Cross.

It was the amendment of the Warrant (Appendix XI) dated 21 October 1911 that extended the award to the Native Officers, Non-Commissioned Officer and Men of the Indian Army. Until then, the highest gallantry award they could receive was The Indian Order of Merit.

Early Life

Kulbir Thapa was born into the Magar clan on 15 December 1888 at Nigalpani, Palpa, Nepal. When he enlisted, he joined the 3rd Gurkha Rifles, one of the regiments that comprised of men from the Magar and Gurung clans. In 1914, he was transferred from the 1st to the 2nd Battalion, the latter having been ordered to France as part of the Indian Corps.

The battalion arrived as the retreat from Mons reached Ypres, but it was not involved in the first battle for the town. Instead, it was based further south in the La Bassée-Armentières sector and took part in the fierce battles of Givenchy and Festubert during the bleak November weather. The following March, the 3rd Gurkhas fought in the Battle of Neuve Chapelle, the first British-initiated offensive of the war. The Garhwal Brigade, of which the Gurkhas were part, succeeded in its assault and soon the village was taken.

Unfortunately, due to a shortage of shells the artillery was unable to keep up an effective barrage and the Germans counter-attacked. This was successfully fought off but no further advance was possible. The lack of ammunition brought about 'The Shell Scandal', which saw Lloyd George become Minister for Munitions. It also led to the replacing of Sir John French with General Douglas Haig as Commander-in-Chief.

In September 1915, the British launched an offensive in the area around the mining village of Loos. This stretch of the front was open and flat, though dotted by the slag heaps that surrounded the pit-heads. Due to pressure from their French allies, the British were not really prepared for such an assault as they still suffered from a shortage of shells. Also, the Army's strength had been increased with thousands of volunteers who had answered Kitchener's call to arms. These citizen soldiers were untried in battle and were about to be thrown into one of the bloodiest battles fought on the Western Front. In order to give the attacking troops more chance of success, it was decided that gas would be released against the German trenches.

The attack was preceded by a four-day bombardment. The 3rd Gurkhas, who had donned their gas-helmets, were led by lieutenants W. G. Bagot-Chester and Wood; they waited in the forward trench until zero hour. A chance shell landed in the trench where the gas cylinders were sited and gas began to seep along the British front. When the order came to attack, the area was dense with gas and the thick smoke screen that had also been laid down.

Blindly, the Gurkhas went forward until they emerged from the gloom and toxic gas. At this point the men were met by heavy German machine-gun fire which killed and wounded most of them, including Bagot-Chester. Lieutenant Wood found himself at the German wire with only four men, including Kulbir Thapa. With difficulty, they found a gap in the wire and entered the enemy trench.

VC Action

In the desperate hand-to-hand fighting that followed, Kulbir was the only one of the five to survive. Although wounded, he managed to advance and seek shelter between the first and second enemy lines where he found a badly-wounded private of the 2nd Leicestershire Regiment. It was Bill Keightley who had cleared the final few yards of No Man's Land before a machine-gun ripped through both of his knees. Bleeding profusely and unable to walk, he faced imminent death. It is likely through blood loss and shock that Keightley's grip on what took place in those long hours between life and death was loose at best and he was probably delirious. This would explain why he could not recall a Gurkha soldier being present or being carried back to the British lines. Nevertheless, Kulbir remained with the wounded soldier throughout the night despite the opportunity to retreat and save himself.

Fortunately, the following morning dawned with a thick fog. Lifting the wounded man onto his shoulders, Kulbir cautiously made his way back through the German line unseen. He found a shell-hole in No Man's Land and lay the wounded soldier there. He then crawled back to the German wire and carried two wounded Gurkhas one after the other to safety. With the fog lifting, Kulbir went back to the shell hole and brought in the wounded Leicester soldier.

It had been a most extraordinary example of devotion and bravery to his fellow soldiers. Despite suffering wounds of his own, Kulbir had rescued three men who would otherwise have died. Certainly, the men of the Leicestershire Regiment have never forgotten his selfless act and he is remembered in a special display in their museum in Leicester. Bill Keightley survived and, after the war, married and had nine children. He lived until he was seventy-three, passing away in 1957.

Kulbir was recommended for the Victoria Cross by his commanding officer and supported by the officers of Garhwal Rifles and 2nd Leicesters. His citation duly appeared in *The London Gazette* on 18 November 1915.

When he had recovered from his wounds, Kulbir re-joined his battalion in Egypt. On 5 January 1916, he was promoted to naik (corporal) at a parade. As there appears to be no record of who, where and when he was presented with his Cross, it is a good guess that this parade probably was the venue.

After the war, he returned to India with the rank of havildar (sergeant) and was discharged from the Army in 1929. He returned to his village, where he died on 3 October 1956. His medals are on display at the Gurkha Museum, Winchester, Hampshire.

Chapter 44

First World War, 1916

Number of VCs awarded	80
Number of VCs awarded to officers	34
Number of VCs awarded to other ranks	46
Total awarded to Royal Navy	7
Total awarded to Royal Flying Corps	2
Total awarded to British Army	55
Total awarded to British Indian Army	4
Total awarded to Canadian Army	3
Total awarded to Australian Army	6
Total awarded to New Zealand Army	1
Total awarded to South African Army	2

Origin of the War

Events on the Western Front in 1916 were understandably dominated by the Battle of the Somme. Despite the careful planning and the confidence that military command had in its rejuvenated artillery, the Somme developed into a hugely costly slog which changed the public's perception of the war.

Under the command of Field Marshal Sir Douglas Haig, who had succeeded Sir John French after the Battle of Loos, there was a swing towards more aggressive, war-winning Victoria Crosses. In other words, there was less emphasis placed on humanitarian acts of rescuing fallen comrades from No Man's Land. Haig deemed some acts, though undoubtedly heroic, counter-productive to the overall war effort and thus refused to recognise them with the Victoria Cross. It also highlighted the contrast between the fates of the individuals who were awarded the Victoria Cross. It was not just the men who were awarded the Cross but the thousands of men who survived the horrors of this appalling 'industrial war'. Of the many examples that could be used to illustrate this dichotomy, the following two are good examples how badly wounded men coped with their experiences.

Adrian Carton de Wiart was an indestructible soldier who was wounded eleven times including eight times in the Great War. Wealth, connections, a huge personality and a determination not to dwell on his physical condition enabled him to continue in the profession he loved until old age.

In contrast, Frederick McNess came from humbler stock but relished the life of a soldier. He would have risen to a position of a senior NCO in the Scots Guards but for the cruel wounds he received on the same battlefield as Carton de Wiart. Both undoubtedly suffered from their wounds and tried to rise above them; de Wiart succeeded; McNess did not.

ADRIAN CARTON DE WIART VC (1880-1963)

Described as 'the unkillable soldier', Adrian Carton de Wiart's life reads like a hero out of a *Boy's Own Paper.* He was born Adrian Paul Ghislain Carton de Wiart into an aristocratic family in Brussels on 5 May 1880, the eldest son of Leon Carton de Wiart and an Irish mother. When he was six, his mother died which prompted his father to move to Egypt to practice international law. Two years later, Leon remarried an English woman who was the travelling companion of a Turkish princess.

Through his stepmother's influence, Adrian was sent to board at the Oratory School, Edgbaston, near Birmingham in 1891. He overcame his fellow pupils' suspicion of being foreign by excelling at sports and was captain of both the cricket and football elevens.

In 1897, he was sent to Balliol College Oxford where he said: 'We lived in great comfort, had indulgent fathers, ran up exorbitant bills and developed a critical appreciation for good wine.' Although his sporting prowess was acknowledged, he was scholastically a disaster. Fortunately for him, the Anglo-Boer War started in 1899 and, despite his father's disappointment that his son was not going to follow him into the law, he relented and supported his wish to join the Army.

Boer War

Adrian had already enlisted as a private with a yeomanry outfit named Paget's Horse and travelled to South Africa under a false name, Trooper Carton, and claimed to be twenty-five-years-old. Weeks of boredom ended with the receipt of his first wounds. As his unit tried to cross a river in full view of the Boers, Adrian was shot in the stomach and groin and repatriated to England.

After convalescence, and with his father's blessing, Adrian joined the Imperial Light Horse and returned to South Africa. Amongst his companions were two Irish Rugby internationals who won the Victoria Cross – Tommy Crean and Robert Johnson. After serving as a trooper, he was given a commission. Then, in late 1901, he was offered a regular commission in the 4th Dragoon Guards, then stationed in India.

Carton de Wiart arrived in Rawalpindi in March 1902 and the first impressions were not encouraging: 'It was tawdry. It emitted revolting smells and noises and its only attraction in my eyes was that I knew it was a wonderful centre for sport.' Indeed it was and Adrian enjoyed pig-sticking, polo and hunting. When orders came to go to South Africa, he wrote: 'My first impression held good. India for me was a glittering sham coated with dust and I hoped I should never see her again.'

On being transferred to South Africa, Carton de Wiart was promoted to lieutenant on 16 July 1904 and a year later, appointed aide-de camp to the Commander-in-Chief, General Sir Henry Hildyard. The next ten years he regarded as his 'heyday', but he did add to his collection of wounds when he broke his leg while playing polo. In 1907, despite serving in the British Army for eight years, he had remained a Belgian subject. On 13 September, he took the oath of allegiance to King Edward VII and became a naturalised British subject.

In 1908, Carton de Wiart married the Austrian Countess Friederike Maria Karoline Henriette Rosa Sabina Franziska Fugger von Babenhausen. Together they had two daughters, one of whom died in infancy. In 1910, he was persuaded by the colonel of the Royal Gloucestershire Hussars to transfer to that regiment as a captain. The lure of excellent hunting in Gloucestershire decided Adrian and he once again became a Yeomanry soldier.

Adrian's carefree life came to a jolting halt in January 1914 when he heard that his father had crashed financially and that he could not rely on further allowances. Selling his horses to pay his debts, Carton de Wiart prepared to campaign in Somaliland with his regiment: 'Before leaving for Somaliland I had to go up for my examination for promotion to major. I failed gloriously, achieving in obtaining 8 marks out of a possible 200 in Military Law. How lucky that wars wash out examinations and I have never been asked to do another since.'

Somaliland

Whilst he was in Malta Carton de Wiart learned that Britain had declared war on Germany. At the time, he and his men were on their way to a minor campaign and it felt like playing in a village cricket match instead of in a Test Match. On arrival, he found himself seconded to the Somaliland Camel Corps and sent to fight the Dervishes of the 'Mad Mullah'. On 18 November 1914, the Camel Corps prepared to attack a stone-built blockhouse at Shimber Berris. Dismounted, the troops ineffectually fired at the small fortress and then received the order to charge.

Adrian later recalled: 'The only entrance was a door, but to get to that we had to jump three feet to the thresh-hold which was covered in loopholes above it.

'I was in shirtsleeves and the first shot at me passed through my rolled-up sleeve and did no damage, but as the muzzle of the Dervish's rifle could not have been more than a yard from me the blast blew me backwards and I wondered what to do next. Some of our men were being hit and the wounds were bad, as the bullets were heavy and soft, but luckily the Dervish, for economy's sake, used a small charge of powder.

'By this time I was seething with excitement. I got a glancing blow in my eye, but was too wound up to stop – I had to go on trying to get in.

'The next hit was in my elbow, and I plucked a large but not too damaging splinter from it. But the following shot split my ear, and as the doctor was standing conveniently near, he stitched it up there and then, looking meanwhile at my eye which was feeling pretty painful. It seemed to be beyond immediate repair …

'Patched up, and still wound up, I tried again to storm the blockhouse, but a ricochet from a bullet went through the same damaged eye.'

For his gallantry, he received the DSO on 15 May 1915. Despite his wounds, Carton de Wiart wrote: 'It had all been the most exhilarating fun and the pace too hot for anyone to have any sensation but thrill, primitive and devouring.'

Carton de Wiart then had to endure a long and uncomfortable voyage back to England, where he had his damaged eye removed. Still eager to return to the fray, Adrian applied to the Medical Board for a posting to France. Loath to grant him his wish, the Board made a compromise; if he would appear with a glass eye then they would pass him fit. He returned with an uncomfortable glass eye and was duly passed fit for general service: 'On emerging I called a taxi, threw my glass eye out of the window, put on my black patch, and have never worn a glass eye since.'

First World War

In February 1915, Carton de Wiart re-joined the 4th Dragoons at Mont de Cats, near Ypres. He found there was little the mounted cavalry could do and when the Second Battle of Ypres began on 22 April, the 4th Dragoons left their horses behind and reached Ypres in time for the first gas attack.

Carton de Wiart was standing next to his second-in-command during an intense German bombardment when a shell landed close by and threw him to the ground. Picking himself up, he found that the remains of his second-in-command had been blown thirty or forty yards away – yet another example of Adrian's charmed life.

Fate, however, dictated that he could not take part in a battle without sustaining an injury. On his first night in Ypres, the regiment was ordered to advance up the Menin Road where a staff officer would meet them and guide them to their positions. Accompanying Colonel Horace Sewell and the Adjutant, Carton de Wiart began to feel uneasy as they passed some dead Germans and had not rendezvoused with the staff officer as arranged.

Suddenly, a German soldier called out 'Halt' and a burst of firing quickly followed. 'The next second I found myself sprawling on the ground with a damaged hand,' Carton de Wiart remembered. 'I caught hold of it but it seemed to be a gory mess. I picked myself up, and although they kept on firing at me they did not hit me again.'

Wrapping a scarf around his wrist, Adrian managed to get back to his regiment and was taken to a dressing-station.

'My hand was a ghastly sight; two of the fingers were hanging on by a bit of skin, all the palm was shot away and most of the wrist. For the first time, and certainly the last, I had been wearing a wrist watch, and it had been blown into the remains of my wrist. I asked the doctor to take my fingers off; he refused, so I pulled them off myself and felt absolutely no pain in doing it.'

Carton de Wiart endured seven months of pain and innumerable operations in hospital in London with no sign of improvement. Unable to stand it any longer, he insisted that it should be amputated. He later wrote that it was no worse than having a tooth extracted.

Despite being gradually whittled away, the Army still wanted Carton de Wiart. He managed to persuade a Medical Board that he had been hunting and fishing and would still be of use in France. Passed fit, he arrived in Boulogne in early 1916 and posted as second-in-command of the Loyal North Lancashire Regiment.

VC Action

Just before the Somme offensive, Carton de Wiart was given command of the 8th Gloucestershire Regiment in the 19th Division. He wrote that he never carried a revolver: 'Being afraid that if I lost my temper I might use it against my own people, so my only weapon was a walking-stick.'

On 1 July 1916, the 8th Gloucesters were in reserve opposite the village of La Boisselle. It was one of the strongest positions on the Somme front and the two previous attacks had been unsuccessful. On 3 July, the 57 and 58 Brigades managed to capture the village and push on another 400 yards. Colonel Carton de Wiart recalled: 'The battalion we were supporting soon advanced into a heavy German barrage and, in the noise and confusion, imagined they received the order to retire. This battalion were retiring through my men, and as retirement is the most infectious disease there was a desperate moment of chaos, when the issue hung in the balance. The officers of the Gloucesters were truly magnificent, and the men rallied and responded to them. They advanced regardless of their appalling casualties until they had fulfilled their appointed task and captured La Boiselle.

'During that engagement I was compelled to use some bombs for the first time, and found a new use for my teeth, pulling the pins out; I was thankful that my teeth were my own.

'La Boisselle was a truly bloody scene. The casualties were appalling; there were dead everywhere, not a house standing, and the ground flattened as if the very soul had been blasted out of the earth and turn into a void. At one moment I sat down on a waterproof sheet to write some orders, only to find when I got up that I had been sitting on a dead body.'

Lance Corporal L. Pitt, recalled the electrifying effect that Carton de Wiart had on his men: 'I was scared stiff and my confidence was severely shaken by the fact that the original plans had all gone awry. Just before the order to go over the top, I saw General de Wiart standing on top of the trench in full view of the enemy and he was carrying a stick … the very sight of this very real soldier standing up there gave me new courage and I feel sure that it had the same effect on the rest of us. When the order came, I went over the top with all sense of fear gone.'

De Wiart did not mention that he was awarded the Victoria Cross in his biography saying that: 'It had been won by the 8th Gloucesters, for every man has done as much as I have.' His citation appeared in *The London Gazette* dated 9 September 1916. It stated: 'For most conspicuous bravery, coolness and determination during severe operations of a prolonged nature. It was owing in a great measure to his dauntless courage and inspiring example that a serious reverse was averted. He displayed the utmost energy and courage in forcing our attack home. After three battalion Commanders had become casualties, he controlled their commands, and ensured that the ground won was maintained at all costs. He frequently exposed himself in the organisation of positions and of supplies, passing unflinchingly through fire barrage of the most intense nature. His gallantry was inspiring to all.'

De Wiart received his Cross from the King at Buckingham Place on 29 November 1916.

After the battle, the 8th Gloucesters was moved to Bazentine le Petit to take part in the innumerable attacks on High Wood. In a night time assault, de Wiart was suddenly flung to the ground with the sensation that the whole of the back of his head had been blown off. After spending hours in a shell hole into which his batman had pulled him, de Wiart was taken to a dressing station. Here he learned the news that the attack had failed and the battalion had sustained terrible casualties. More than that, he was told that the eight new officers received the day before had all been killed. Such was the life expectancy of an infantry officer in the Great War.

De Wiart was sent back to his hospital in London (they now kept his pyjamas there as he was such a frequent patient). His skull was examined by the surgeon who pronounced it intact and ordered his patient a bottle of champagne. In fact Adrian had enjoyed a miraculous escape; a machine-gun bullet had gone straight through the back of his head without touching a vital part.

After three weeks convalescing, de Wiart was back with the 8th Gloucesters near High Wood. Out of curiosity, he went search for the spot where he had been wounded. He not only located the site, but also his walking stick which he had dropped when he was shot.

A little while later while serving in the front at Grandcourt, he received a shell fragment in his ankle and was soon back again at his hospital in London.

When he returned to France, de Wiart was given command of the 8th Battalion North Staffordshires at Hébuterne. While he was in the line he was promoted and given a brigade, the 12th of the 4th Division. In one year he had risen from captain to brigadier general.

In time, the 12th took part in the Battle of Arras in April 1917. The day before it was due to start, Brigadier Carton de Wiart had gone up the line and sustained yet another injury when a bit of German shell split his ear. Determined not to miss the battle, he had it sewn up quickly and returned to the front.

Passchendaele

In October, Carton de Wiart's brigade was sent to Passchendaele at the height of its appalling conditions; a vast sea of malignant mud and water. Due to heavy casualties, he was commanding a composite brigade, including men from the King's Own Regiment.

During fighting near Poelcappelle on 12 October, Private Albert Halton won the Victoria Cross for capturing a machine-gun and capturing some twelve prisoners. Brigadier Carton de Wiart recalled: 'In the middle of the battle one of my men charged a machine-gun which was holding us up, and upon reaching it killed every man who was serving it. Having recommended him for the VC which he was awarded, and richly deserved, I asked him about his action. To my amazement, I found that he remembered nothing whatsoever about it!'

The 12th Brigade was sent back to Arras front with instructions to divert the enemy's attention away from the next offensive at Cambrai. Unfortunately, the Germans retaliated with fierce bombardments and Adrian was again wounded, this time in the hip. Unfortunately, part of the uniform material had been blown into his hip which turned septic. Yet another lengthy spell back in hospital in London ended with the Medical Board, under pressure from above, permitting Carton de Wiart to return to France in March 1918. He was given command of the Bantam Brigade (men under the regulation height) but his stay was curtailed by his wounded hip flaring up again. For a while there was a possibility that his leg would be amputated, but another lengthy stay in hospital restored his health.

In October 1918, de Wiart returned to take command of a brigade in the 61st Division, but there was to be no more fighting for this much-wounded officer – in this conflict at least. After the Armistice, he must have been one of the few First World War veterans to declare: 'Frankly, I enjoyed the war; it had given me many bad moments, lots of good ones, plenty of excitement and with everything found for us.'

Brigadier Carton Wiart was made a Companion of the Order of the Bath in the King's Birthday Honour's List of 1919.

Poland

Summoned to the War Office, Carton de Wiart was offered the second-in-command of the British-Poland Military Mission under General Louis

Botha. Within a week, Botha became one of the victims of the Spanish Flu and died on 27 August 1919, leaving de Wiart in command.

Poland was fighting five wars – against the Germans, the Bolsheviks, the Ukrainians, the Lithuanians and the Czechs. It was a very confusing time and de Wiart was to confess at the end of his time in Poland that it was his complete ignorance of the country and her relationships with her neighbours that enabled him to have an entirely neutral opinion on the tangled political situation. The only really serious war was against the Bolsheviks and, to a lesser extent, the Lithuanians. Carton de Wiart did come under fire, especially when the Bolshevik Cossacks attacked the train on which he was travelling.

By 1924, the five wars were over and Carton de Wiart duties as part of the British Military Mission were over. With little prospect of anything interesting happening, de Wiart resigned from the Army. His last ADC in Poland was Prince Charles Radziwill, who owned some half a million acres in north-east Poland in the Prypet Marshes bordering Russia. On a visit with the Prince, Carton de Wiart fell in love with the country with its forest and lakes. He then took a free tenancy of a property on the estate and spent the next twenty years living and hunting there for nine months of the year.

The Nazis' annexing of German-speaking regions of Czechoslovakia alerted Carton de Wiart to the possibility that Poland could be next on the list. In 1938 he wrote to General Lord Gort, the Chief of the Imperial General Staff, to offer his services, but was disappointed to be turned down. The following July, however, he was offered his old job back as head of the British Military Mission to Poland.

It did not take de WIart long to realise that the Poles would not be able to stand up to an invasion from Germany. Then, on 1 September 1939, the Germans crossed the border, sweeping all before them. With Russia joining in the invasion from the east, de Wiart and his staff were forced south and crossed the border into Romania, despite that country's sympathies with the Nazis.

Norway

Returning to London, de Wiart underwent another series of operations and, when he had recovered, he was given command of the 61st Division, a Midland Territorial Division. This lasted until April 1940, when he was ordered to go to Norway to command the Central Norwegian Expeditionary Force. Ill-equipped and badly planned, the British and French intervention was a disaster. Carton de Wiart's command retreated to the port of Namsos, where they had landed just a fortnight before. The Royal Navy carried out the evacuation under constant attack from the Luftwaffe and managed to bring most of the Force safely back to Scapa Flow. Carton de Wiart had suffered two retreats in nine months but was hopeful of being asked to become involved in another theatre.

A brief period commanding the 61st Division in Northern Ireland was cut short when de Wiart was offered another British Military Mission – this time to Yugoslavia. In April 1941, he took-off from the UK in a Vickers Wellington. After refuelling in Malta, he continued to Cairo to receive his final orders from General Wavell.

Air Crash and Captivity

Taking off from Malta in the evening, the aircraft droned its way off the North African coast until engine failure forced the pilot to ditch in the sea about two miles from Libya. The 'plane managed to stay afloat while it was blown towards the shore until it sank about half a mile from the beach.

As they dragged themselves out of the water, the occupants were arrested by some Italian police and de Wiart found himself in the position of being a prisoner of war without having fired a shot. As a senior officer, he joined other generals in a comfortable villa in Italy at Sulmona in the Abruzzi. His fellow prisoners included Generals Philip Neame VC, Richard O'Connor, Michael Gambier-Parry and assorted brigadiers and colonels.

For four months, the prisoners were allowed privileges which included shopping in the local market and going for walks. This all changed when they were transferred to a castello-like villa with more guards and fewer comforts at Fiesole. This was to be their prison for another two years. During that time, there were several attempts to escape. Their Italian captors treated them generally very well but as the war dragged on, they were replaced with far less amenable guards.

Giving up trying to escape over the wall, Carton de Wiart and his companions decided to dig their way out. Helped by Philip Neame's engineering expertise and Gambier-Parry's gift for forging identity papers, the middle-aged prisoners managed to dig a tunnel and escape en-masse on the night of 29 March 1943. Splitting into small groups, the escapees headed for the Swiss border, some 250 miles away.

Dick O'Connor and Carton de Wiart moved north by tracks and paths through the Apennine Mountains. It was when they reached the flat Po Valley with its many towns and villages, that movement became increasingly difficult. Finally, after walking 150 miles, they were captured by a carabinieri patrol and returned to Vincigliata. Most of the other fugitive senior officers were caught in Milan and Como. One reached the Swiss frontier but was captured. Two of them, Brigadiers James Hargest and Reginald Miles, did reach Switzerland but had to sit out the rest of the war.

Typically, Carton de Wiart was pragmatic about his own capture: 'Though it was disappointing to have been caught, I felt so invigorated and exhilarated after our eight days of liberty that it saved me from any feelings of depression. Dick (O'Connor) and I covered 150 miles with good loads on our backs, and with our united ages making one hundred and sixteen (mine took sixty-three of them) we had nothing to be ashamed of … we were twice the men we had been when we started. I personally never felt fitter in my life.'

The captured escapees all suffered the regulation punishment of one month's solitary confinement. In August 1943, Carton de Wiart received instructions from the prison commandant that he was to travel to Rome. It transpired that the Italians wanted to sue for peace and discuss how to handle the hundreds of PoWs held in Italy. After a protracted journey through Spain and Portugal, Carton de Wiart landed in Britain and carefully interrogated by the Secret Service.

China

Finally, Carton de Wiart was free to enjoy a long round of social gatherings. In October 1943, he received a message to visit Winston Churchill at Chequers. Churchill wanted Carton de Wiart to be his personal representative to Generalissimo Chiang Kai-shek, the leader of the Chinese Nationalists, whose provisional headquarters was in the town of Chungking in southwest China. Despite having no knowledge of China, Carton de Wiart relished being back in the game and readily accepted.

De Wiart found the Generalissimo and his wife very charming but the organisation chaotic. The Americans were propping up Chiang Kai-shek's forces and were familiar with the supply route from India and Burma. They offered a pilot and aircraft to fly Carton de Wiart and his staff but this was politely rejected in favour of an RAF 'plane and crew.

To Carton de Wiart's consternation, the aircraft chosen was another Wellington. Taking off from India with stores including a precious cargo of Scotch, the Wellington made it safely over the high mountains nicknamed 'The Hump' only to crash-land at Chungking. Fortunately, no bottles were broken. A replacement Wellington suffered a burst tyre on landing and was a total wreck from which the indestructible Carton de Wiart emerged unscathed.

Carton de Wiart had to report personally to Churchill and later, Clement Atlee, which involved interminable and uncomfortable fights. He was present at the Cairo Conference in late 1943, which Chiang Kai-shek also attended.

De Wiart reported on the increasing power of the Communists, which he despised. He met Mao Zedong, who he described as a 'fanatic', and interrupted his propaganda speech by accusing the Communists from holding back fighting the Japanese for political reasons. Carton de Wiart advised the new British cabinet to support Chiang Kai-shek as leader of China.

Retirement

In October 1947, Lieutenant-General Carton de Wiart retired at the age of sixty-six, despite the offer of a job by Chiang. There was yet one more injury he was to suffer. On the way home in Rangoon de Wiart slipped on coconut matting and fell. He was knocked unconscious and broke several vertebrae. Encased in a body cast, he was brought back to Britain and began a lengthy period of convalescence.

While he was in hospital, the surgeons took the opportunity to remove large amounts of shrapnel (or shell or bomb fragments) from his old wounds. His wife, who does not get a mention in his biography, died in 1949.

In 1951, he married Joan Sutherland, a divorcee, some twenty-three years his junior. Together they lived at Killinardish, Co.Cork, pursuing salmon and snipe, until Carton de Wiart died at the age of eighty-three on 5 June 1963.

FREDERICK McNESS VC (1892-1956)

The other side of the coin was the tragic story of Lance Sergeant Fred McNess of the Scots Guards. He was born in Bramley, Leeds, on 22 January 1892, the son of an ex-Royal Engineer, John, and his wife, Mary. Fred grew to be a strapping and healthy youth who enjoyed rambling through the Yorkshire Dales. When he left school, he became a carter with a local carrier before enlisting in the Scots Guards in London on 10 January 1915. He was promoted twice in a year and was made up to lance sergeant, the Guard's equivalent of corporal on 25 August 1916.

On 16 September 1916, the third stage of the Battle of the Somme began. At 06.00 hours, on a misty morning, the three-day long bombardment changed to one of a creeping barrage. Twenty minutes later all along the front from Thiepval to Ginchy, the British climbed out of their trenches and headed out into No Man's Land towards the German line.

On the left and centre the attack was successful. Only around the village of Ginchy was the task incomplete. Nearly half a mile due east of Ginchy, where the Mozval Road passed through a deep ravine, the advance was held up by the German strongpoint, christened the Quadrilateral. The stronghold held and when the Guards marched out of Ginchy towards Les Bouefs they were met with a vicious machine-gun fire from both flanks and from the sunken road in front. In the attack, three VCs were awarded, including one to Lieutenant Colonel John Campbell, who led his Coldstream Guards forward to the strains of his hunting horn.

VC Action

Lance Sergeant McNess had entered the German first line of trenches at the head of his platoon but the Germans still held the left flank, from where they opened a heavy fire. McNess described what happened in a letter that was printed in the *Yorkshire Post*:

'After getting through the small opening in the barbed wire in front of the German trench, I took a party up the communication trench and for an hour and a half a corporal and I slowly but surely drove the enemy back.

The remainder of the boys passed bombs to us, we being the only two who could use them. Then we ran short, but finding large quantities of German bombs we experimented with them until we found how to use them. Then we fought them with their own bombs. It was a case of hand-to-hand fighting all the way up. Then I got wounded.

'It was like this. One of the men was shot through the lungs. I was just preparing another bomb when a German threw a bomb which burst right in front of my dial … I had to walk two miles to the first field dressing station. Here I received a rough dressing, and then German prisoners carried me three miles to the ambulance. I underwent an operation at the first hospital I came to, then another one at Rouen.'

McNess later recalled his wounding by the German bomb in more detail: 'I was just preparing another bomb, with the upper part of my head and chest well over the parapet, when a German bomb burst near my neck, blowing away the left side of same and part of jaw, lower teeth and upper teeth. Left arm was blown round my neck, and the biceps muscle was contracted like a ball on the top of left shoulder. Jugular vein, windpipe and ceratoid artery were fully exposed, and shoulder blade badly out of place. My head lay helplessly on my arm, and sometimes almost rolled on my back.

'For a moment I was dazed, as I had already been hit three times with shrapnel in the early part of the morning while organising men of some other unit, who had lost their officers and NCOs but I was soon clear again; still, what with loss of blood and almost blinded with it, I had to leave the boys, but I did not go far, only to the first line, where I lay in a shell-hole and watched how things progressed.'

Finally, weak from loss of blood and almost blinded he set off to find a medic.

'I had not gone far when I met the remnants of a carrying party. I wrote on a piece of paper asking directions for a dressing station and they asked for the direction the boys had advanced. They were carrying bombs and the boys wanted them, so, staggering away, I took them up through the barrage. Five parties I led back, but the last one never got there, for a shell came over, killed three of them, and broke my jaw in another two places, so almost blinded with blood and falling at every three or four steps, I left the field.

'I had to walk about two miles to the first field dressing station. Here I received a rough dressing. The German prisoners carried me three miles to the ambulance (at one stage he was treated by double VC recipient Captain Noel Chavasse). I underwent an operation at the first hospital I came to, then another at the 9th General Hospital, Rouen.'

Fred McNess's wounds were indeed terrible. His lower jaw had been smashed and was partially repaired by surgeons who grafted part of a rib in an effort to rebuild his face. He also lost part of his cranium and neck and was wounded in the side. A lengthy stay in King George's Hospital in London followed, a period that involved yet more operations.

McNess was, however, deemed well enough to attend his investiture at Buckingham Palace on 9 December 1916; the Cross was presented to him by King George V. McNess had been driven to the Palace accompanied by a RAMC Sergeant and would spend twenty minutes in a private meeting with the King.

More hospitalisation followed until McNess was discharged in 1918 as medically unfit. While in hospital he met and married Dorothy, the nurse that had looked after him. The town of Bramley welcomed him home and presented him with £400 to start a shoe repair shop in Leeds. Later he worked as a filing clerk for Leeds City Engineers Department until he retired in 1956.

The couple moved to Boscombe near Bournmouth in January 1956. For nearly forty years, Fred McNess had endured great pain from his wounds sinking into bouts of deep depression. He began to suffer from prostate problems and a disfiguring ulcer on his face. On 4 May 1956, while Dorothy was out of the house, Fred McNess slashed his throat to end his joyless and painful life. He was cremated at Bournemouth Crematorium and his ashes scattered.

It was not only the Army that was involved in the offensive on the Somme in 1916. High above the battlefield on 1 July, for example, a desperate fight was fought between ten German two-seaters and one single-seater 'Gunbus'. Witnessed by soldiers in the anti-aircraft batteries, the unfolding action resulted in the only aerial Somme VC.

LIONEL WILMOT BRABAZON REES VC (1884-1955)

Lionel Wilmot Brabazon Rees was born in Caernarvon on 31 July 1884 to Lieutenant Colonel Charles and Leonora Rees. His father was a solicitor and newspaper proprietor as well as the commanding officer of the 3rd Battalion, Royal Welsh Fusiliers. After attending Eastbourne College, Lionel entered the Royal Military Academy at Woolwich. In 1903, he emerged with a commission in the Royal Garrison Artillery and served during the 1900s in Gibraltar, Sierra Leone and Nigeria. During this period, he distinguished himself as an exceptional marksman. He could hit a card held by a trusting colleague with his service revolver at a range of twenty-five yards with either right or left hands.

In 1912, he learned how to fly at Larkhill and gained his Royal Aero Club certificate in January 1913, thus becoming one of the few qualified officers trained in aerial tactics. At the outbreak of the war, he completed the five-week course at the Central Flying School and joined the Royal Flying Corps as a captain. After a brief posting to No.7 Squadron, he was ordered to set up an Aircraft Acceptance Park at Bruges. This was where the various manufacturers sent their disassembled aircraft to be assembled and fully tested before being allotted to a squadron. The AAPs were also used to store the flight-tested machines until they were required in the field.

With Belgium defeated, Rees was ordered back to England where he joined No.11 Squadron. This was equipped with one of the first fighters, the Vickers FB5 Gunbus, a pusher-type of aircraft carrying an observer/gunner. In the summer of 1915, the squadron moved to an airfield near Amiens and became engaged with the German *Luftstreitkräfte.*

Lionel Rees' first taste of combat was the day after No.11 arrived. On a lone patrol over the Front, he spotted a Fokker monoplane and battle was joined. Circling around each other, shots were exchanged. The Gunbus was hit in the lower port wing, but Rees managed to get in a burst of fire which downed the Fokker behind enemy lines. He thus became the first designated fighter pilot to take part in an aerial combat.

This was one of several combats involving Rees.

On 31 August 1915, he and his observer/gunner were flying at about 7,000 feet between Bucquoy and Bapaume when they came upon a two-seater LVG, a much faster machine. Rees closed to about 200 yards and his gunner, Sergeant James Hargreaves, replied to the enemy's initial burst of firing. The German plane had the speed to pull away but seemed to relish the challenge. After forty-five minutes of manoeuvring and firing at each other, Hargreaves reported that all his ammunition had been expended. Rees then broke away and headed for his airfield. With his engine running and shouting for more ammunition, Rees took off once more and headed back to where he had fought the German.

Near the same spot, he saw the enemy about 1,000 feet below him. Immediately diving, Hargreaves fired off a drum of forty-seven rounds at the LVG. The German reacted by diving into a cloud bank and Rees was unable to follow as the steep angle of the dive caused the petrol in the Gunbus to run to the top of the tank causing the engine to stop. Disappointed, Rees headed for home. Fortunately, this second combat had been witnessed by another aircraft from No 11, who reported that the LVG had been badly hit and was spinning towards the ground. Later reports of wreckage confirmed that Rees had downed his opponent.

The Rees/Hargreaves team had another success on 21 September when they were photographing the German lines prior to the start of the Battle of Loos. They spotted an enemy machine approaching from the German lines and, turning off the engine, Rees glided to meet what turned out to be the new Albatros C.1. The German opened fire first but missed. Hargreaves waited until they were closer and emptied half a drum. This caused the Albatros to break off and head for its own lines where it crashed on landing.

For these three engagements, Lionel Rees and James Hargreaves were awarded the Military Cross and the Distinguished Conduct Medal respectively. A week later, Rees and Hargreaves attacked an Albatros near Gommecourt causing it to dive for a cloud bank. As the German emerged, British anti-aircraft guns opened up and shot away the starboard wing. Although the Artillery claimed the German scalp, it was shown later that Hargreaves had shot the pilot dead before they could fire.

By October 1915, Major Rees had returned to the Central Flying School as instructor. Before long he was given command of a new squadron, No.32, equipped with the Vickers DH2, a new pusher-type single-seat scout machine. On 6 June 1916, they arrived at their new airfield at Treizennes near Aire.

On 1 July, the opening day of the Battle of the Somme, the squadron was out early accompanying a bombing raid against Don and Lille. As commander, Rees had been ordered not to cross the front line so he patrolled just behind the British line and waited for the bombers to return from their mission.

Rees began to patrol over the large slag-heap known as the 'Double Crassier' near Loos when he spotted what he thought was the British bombers returning from their raid. Climbing steadily, he planned to join the formation as they headed west. As he drew nearer, he took a look through his binoculars and realised that he was flying straight into a black-crossed formation of German two-seater aircraft, mostly Rumplers and Albatrosses. Despite being outnumbered ten to one, Rees continued his ascent and prepared to attack. The Germans saw him at the same time and felt confident they would soon claim another victory.

Rees later wrote: 'The Germans used their usual tactics of circling round and firing at an angle of 45 degrees between the tail and sideways. There were about ten machines flying in a ragged echelon – the leader well out to the front ... The machine I got closest to had a fuselage very like a Nieuport ...

'As I got nearer, at about Annequin, the second machine turned out of the position and dived towards me firing his guns. I waited until he came with convenient range and fired one drum ... After about the 30th round I saw the top of his fuselage splinter between the pilot and observer. The machine turned round and went home. This machine was marked with a big "3" and a small cross on the fuselage. I then went to attack a second machine. When he saw me he fired red Very's Lights, and three more joined him. They fired an immense amount of ammunition but were so far away they had no effect. The escort machines swooped down onto their own machine instead of me; and so shot past him and went out of action.

'When I got to a convenient position, I fired one drum. After about 30 rounds a big cloud of blue haze came out of the nacelle in front of the pilot. The machine turned and wobbled, and I last saw him down over the lines under control. It looked either as if a cylinder was knocked off or else the petrol tank punctured.

'I then saw five close together. They opened fire at very long range. I closed, and fired one drum at very long range at the centre and the five dispersed in all directions. I then saw the leader and the two second machines going west. I overhauled them rapidly and when I got near the lowest, he turned sharply to the left and dropped a bomb. He opened fire at long range. I closed, just as I was about to fire, a shot struck me in the leg putting the leg temporarily out of action. I fired another drum, but not having complete control of the rudder, I swept the machine backwards and forwards. I finished firing about 10 yards away, and saw the observer sitting back firing straight up into the air, instead of at me.

'I grabbed my pistol and dropped it on the floor of the nacelle and could not get it again. I then recovered the use of my leg and saw the leader going towards the lines. I got within long range of him. He was firing an immense amount of ammunition. Just before he reached the lines I gave him one more drum. Having finished my ammunition I came home.'

Succeeding in breaking up the German formation, Rees managed to land without further mishap and was rushed to No.2 Canadian Clearing House. From there, he was evacuated to England where it was found that the German bullet had caused more damage than previously thought and he spent the rest of 1916 recuperating. His daring confrontation with the German formation had been witnessed from the ground by the 22nd Anti-Aircraft Battery and it was later confirmed that Rees had downed two of the German machines. When the details were learned of Rees's solo fight with ten enemy aircraft, he was recommended for the Distinguished Service Order but Major General Hugh Trenchard insisted on the Victoria Cross. The nomination was approved and his citation appeared in *The London Gazette* on 5 August 1916. He had recovered sufficiently to attend the investiture at Buckingham Palace on 14 December.

Lionel Rees's days as a fighter pilot were now over. Fear of capture meant that Rees's new-found fame restricted his contribution to that of a military aviation advisor. Promoted to Lieutenant Colonel, he accompanied the Balfour Mission to the United States, where he remained until January 1918.

On his return, he was given command of No.1 School of Aerial Fighting at Turnbury in Scotland, where hundreds of British and American airmen were trained in the art of aerial combat. Incidentally, Turnbury was a golf course established around the turn of the century and commandeered by the Royal Flying Corps for the establishment of the flying school. It later became one of the British Open Championship courses.

Towards the war's end, the RFC was subsumed into the fledgling Royal Air Force. Wing Commander Rees was one of the senior officers who were sent to the RAF College, Cranwell in Lincolnshire. Recognised for his great experience, he was appointed the Assistant Commandant of the College in charge of flying training. On New Year's Day, 1925, he was promoted to group captain and appointed as an aide de camp to the King.

During October 1926, Rees took over the command of the newly formed Headquarters of RAF Palestine and Transjordan. Apart from some problems with the Druze in Syria, Rees became fascinated with the region and often visited the ruins of the ancient civilisations. This new-found interest in ancient history and archaeology led to Rees taking part in aerial photography to identify promising sites for excavation.

Not everybody shared his enthusiasm for archaeology and the Air Officer Commanding the Middle East was particularly scathing. As a result, Group Captain Rees was recalled and given command of No.21 Group Headquarters at Uxbridge. This dull chair-borne life did not suit him and he retired in 1932. Still hungering for adventure, he bought a ketch called *May* and spent some months learning how to handle her. He then sailed her down the Irish Sea and into the English Channel and wintered in the Solent.

Rees then thought about the possibility of crossing the Atlantic to the Caribbean and made plans through the winter. Finally, on 2 July 1933, he left Falmouth on his solo adventure. After thirty-three days, he reached the Azores, where he spent two weeks on repairs and replenishing his rations. Leaving the Azores, he ran into bad weather and learned of a hurricane approaching Cuba. He altered course for the Bahamas and, on 21 October, he dropped anchor in Nassau harbour.

His arrival caused great interest as a solo trans-Atlantic crossing was something of a rarity and he was reported in the London newspapers. Lionel Rees spent a couple of years sailing amongst the many islands that make up the Bahamas group. He also sailed south through the Caribbean to Trinidad. Deciding to buy a new boat more suited to the Caribbean, Rees plumped for a smaller ketch called *Aline.*

At the age of fifty-five, and with the probable outbreak of another war with Germany, Rees volunteered his services to the RAF. Finally, he was called back to London but had to take the lower rank of Wing Commander. Once again, he was posted to the Middle East as a station commander at RAF Helwan near Cairo.

In early 1942, he was replaced by a younger officer and instructed to return to London. The route chosen was to fly to West Africa, a distance of 4,000 miles, then to Gibraltar and then Britain. Rees reached Takoradi in the Gold Coast (Ghana) and decided to stay without any reference to higher authority. He found that the small section of the RAF Regiment was without a commanding officer, so he appointed himself as Station Defence Officer without pay. Finally, in November 1942, the bureaucracy caught up with him and he was replaced.

Having 'done his bit', Lionel Rees returned to the Bahamas, and spent his time sailing, farming and studying Old Testament archaeology. In 1947, he caused quite a stir amongst the white community in Nassau when he married Sylvia Williams, the eighteen-year-old daughter of a black family on the island of Andros. Over the years, they had three children. Sadly this new-found family life was cut short when Lionel Rees was diagnosed with leukaemia and forced to return to the UK for treatment. He came back to spend his last days in the Bahamas, where he died on 28 September 1955.

The Western Front was not the only area where the war was being fought in 1916. There were struggles going on in Africa, or the Near and Middle East, where the borders of colonial powers met. One such area was Mesopotamia, where the British had oil interests at Abadan on the Persian Gulf.

With Turkey's entry into the war on 29 October 1914, the British opened a new front in the remote Ottoman province of Mesopotamia (present day Iraq). Using an Anglo-Indian force, the British pushed the Turks back up the River Tigris and even threatened to take the capital, Baghdad. After General Charles Townsend, had captured the town of Kut-el-Amara on the River Tigris in September 1915, he was tempted to advance further towards the Mesopotamian capital. In a pyrrhic victory over the Turks at Ctesiphon, in which he lost 4,600 men, he decided to retreat back to Kut and await reinforcements. The Turks, who had started to pull back to Baghdad, learned of Townsend's retreat and turned about and went in pursuit of the British.

The weakness of the British-Indian position at Kut soon became apparent. The supply line was 340 miles long from their base at Basra and relied upon river transport. In contrast, the Turkish Army could be readily supplied with men, equipment and rations from Baghdad. The pursuing Ottoman forces reached Kut on 7 December 1915 and steadily increased their numbers. So began the infamous Siege of Kut. The Turks encircled the town and settled down to a 147-day siege. As the months passed, the situation in Kut worsened with hunger and sickness weakening the defenders. Occasional supplies were dropped by the few aircraft available and attempts were made between January and March to lift the siege without success. The British had advanced to Amarah on the Tigris about halfway between Basra and Kut. It was learned that rations had been cut to starvation level and that the city could not hold out for much longer.

Lieutenant General Fenton John Aylmer, commander of the Tigris Corps, had previously taken part in the relief of Chitral in 1891 and helped rescue Charles Townsend's garrison from the remote fort. For this he was awarded the Victoria Cross. Now he was asked to repeat the process with his command of 7th (Meerut) Division, the 12th Indian Division and other smaller units. He tried three times against the resolute Turkish Army, inflicting and receiving huge losses. Finally, Aylmer was dismissed and succeeded by Lieutenant General Sir George Gorringe who had little time to mount a relief expedition.

With time running out for the starving defenders of Kut, a final death or glory effort to bring supplies to Kut was made in which two posthumous VCs were awarded.

CHARLES HENRY COWLEY VC (1872-1916)
HUMPHREY OSBALDERSTON BROOKE FIRMAN VC (1886-1916)

The expression 'Forlorn hope' is generally applied to suicidal missions undertaken by the Army, but in 1916, it was especially apposite regarding an action undertaken by the Royal Navy in Mesopotamia.

Moored at Amarah was the 900 ton, 210-foot-long river steamer SS *Julnar*, which was used for shipping men and supplies along the Tigris. The naval commander of the Egypt and East Indies Squadron was Vice-Admiral Sir Rosslyn Wemyss, who had led the landing at Cape Helles and Suvla Bay the previous year. He thought there was only one more throw of the dice in getting supplies to Kut and that was by loading up *Julnar* and trusting the skill of the experienced river pilot, Charles Cowley, to get her through. It was definitely a long shot, for the Turks had forces lining the banks of the Tigris to block any attempt to relieve Kut.

Charles Henry Cowley was born on 21 February 1872 in Baghdad. His father was an Irishman who worked for Lynch Bros. as a riverboat captain and was married to a half-Armenian mother. Charles was educated in Liverpool, joining the training ship *Worcester* as a cadet in 1885. When qualified, he was apprenticed with the shipping company, McDiarmid & Co.

With the death of his father, the twenty-year-old Cowley returned to Baghdad and followed his father and grandfather into Lynch Bros., as a riverboat officer. Over the years his experience was rewarded by being made the company's senior captain. He came to be regarded by the Turks as one of their citizens whereas Charles thought of himself as thoroughly British and not as an Arabicised foreigner. This was a state of affairs that would seal his fate.

Cowley sailed the Euphrates and Tigris rivers and nobody knew them better. He was fluent in Arabic and used as an interpreter as well as a gatherer of intelligence. He was in command of the river boat *Mejidieh* and given the temporary rank of Lieutenant Commander RNVR in August 1915. This was something that angered the Turks who regarded this as an act of a traitor. He was regarded as a pirate and had been condemned to death by a Baghdad military court. When it was learned that there was to be one last attempt to supply Kut, and that there was no one else who had his navigational knowledge to guide the ship upstream at night, Cowley was a marked man. It was a brave decision to attempt such a dangerous mission particularly as he knew that would inevitably end in his death if captured.

Despite the obvious dangers, there was no shortage of volunteers, this group being trimmed down to 'bachelors only'. Another experienced river boat employee was William Reed, *Julnar*'s chief engineer, who was given the rank of Engineer Sub-Lieutenant. Also chosen were twelve ratings from the gunboats of the river flotilla.

A regular naval officer, Lieutenant Humphrey Osbalderston Brooke Firman, was put in overall command. Born in Kensington, London on 24 November 1886, Firman joined the Royal Navy as a cadet on 15 May 1901. He career followed the predictable path of a midshipman with service on battleships and in the Royal Yacht *Victoria and Albert*. He saw overseas service in the Persian Gulf and the Horn of Africa. With the outbreak of the war, he was appointed to the gunboats on the River Tigris. He saw action against the Turks in his first command, HMS *Greenfly* before being put in command of *Julnar.*

In preparation for its mission, *Julnar* was stripped of her cabins, saloon and upper-deck stanchions. Her masts were reduced in height and she was fitted with iron-plating and sandbag protection. This was all done without any secrecy and everyone knew her destination, including the Turks. The officers at Amarah began laying bets at 100 to 1 against success, which did little to raise morale. Despite this, the men on *Julnar* were filled with determination to get through to Kut.

On 21 April, *Julnar* left Amarah for her final staging post upstream at Fallahiya. After dining with Admiral Wemyss and his staff, Cowley and Firman took their leave and boarded the much-altered river boat.

At 20.00 hours on the evening of 24 April 1916, *Julnar*, loaded with 270 tons of supplies, slipped her berth and headed up steam against a Tigris in flood, which reduced her speed to just six knots. Under cover of an intense artillery bombardment to distract the Turk's attention, *Julnar* entered enemy territory. Within thirty minutes, the Turks sent up star-shells which illuminated the vessel and began to fire on her. The rifle bullets peppered the sheet metal and sand-bags and one or two penetrated the engine-room injuring a couple of stokers.

So far, they had made good progress and by 23.40 hours they had reached Es Sinn Bank. Here they came under intense fire from Turkish artillery. Although taking hits, she sailed on another twenty minutes to the fort at Margasis, situated on a sharp right-handed bend in the river. Here the Turks had made serious preparations.

Anticipating *Julnar*'s arrival, the Turks had stretched steel hawsers across the river. One snagged the ship's propellers and *Julnal* spun out of control and grounded on a sandbank. All the time artillery shells were raining down on the helpless vessel. One exploded in the boiler room and another hit the bridge, killing Lieutenant Firman.

There was little alternative but to surrender. Cowley had escaped with slight injuries and was separated from the rest of the crew when the Turks came aboard. He knew that his chances of being spared were non-existent as he was led away. His fate is unknown; the Turks say he was shot trying to escape, while others say his death sentence was carried out and he was executed. The surviving crew went into captivity and all later received gallantry awards ranging from a DSO for William Reed to CGM and DSMs for the rest.

Meanwhile, the Kut garrison expected *Julnar* to arrive at about 04.00 hours, but the sound of heavy gunfire to the south told them to expect the worst. When dawn broke, they could see the *Julnar* grounded four miles across the marshes from Kut and just eight miles away by river. This was the final blow and General Townsend surrendered two days later resulting in the worst military capitulation of the British Army up to that date.

Admiral Weymess recommended Cowley, Firman, as leader, and Reed for the Victoria Cross. Because so little reliable information was available, the Admiralty delayed any decision. Finally, they agreed to honour Firman and Cowley with the VC. Their joint citation appeared in *The London Gazette* dated 2 February 1917. The Turks buried their bodies but their whereabouts is not known. Their names, therefore, appear on the war memorial at Basra.

Chapter 45

First World War, 1917

Number of VCs awarded	173
Number of VCs awarded to officers	75
Number of VCs awarded to other ranks	98
Total awarded to Royal Navy	21
Total awarded to Royal Flying Corps	4
Total awarded to British Army	106
Total awarded to British Indian Army	2
Total awarded to Canadian Army	21
Total awarded to Australian Army	17
Total awarded to New Zealand Army	2

Origins of the War

The dreadful battle of Verdun in 1916 had drained French manpower. This was exacerbated by the mutinies that struck the French Army after the disastrous Second Battle of the Aisne in April 1917. The losses had deadened France's will to attack.

More was therefore expected of the British Army and, to boost the numbers required, conscription had been introduced in early 1916. The new fully-conscripted British Army had grown to two thirds the total numbers in the French forces and was required to shoulder the burden of fighting during 1917. This can be reflected in the doubling of Victoria Crosses awarded during that year. Another factor was that the Commonwealth countries, particularly Canada, New Zealand and Australia, contributed large numbers of men. This is apparent in the case of Canada whose forces had three VCs awarded in 1916. This rose dramatically in 1917 to twenty-one.

Field Marshal Douglas Haig made it clear that he wanted a more ruthless and aggressive attitude from the British Army. He understood the usefulness of medals. War-winning acts resulting in German casualties resulted in a great increase in the numbers of VCs and DCMs awarded.

Humanitarian acts like helping or rescuing wounded comrades that had made up much of the previous VC acts would not be rewarded with the Victoria Cross unless they were for exceptional circumstances. Instead, men who risked all to take out a block-house or a German trench were to be recognised with the Victoria Cross.

New tactics were tried with the introduction of the Machine Gun Corps and the Tank Corps; with the latter offering more mobility even if the results were not entirely successful. After the inconclusive Battle of Jutland, Germany switched her priority from capital ships to the submarine and in a short time caused Britain to suffer from this invisible blockade which hit her vital imports. In a bid to counter the U-boat threat Q-ships were employed and in 1917, and on these six Victoria Crosses were earned, including one to a New Zealander.

WILLIAM EDWARD SANDERS VC (1883-1917)

A first-generation New Zealander, William Edward Sanders was born to Edward, a boot maker and his wife, Emma Jane in Auckland on 7 February 1883. He was known as Billy at his school and, in 1897, he was apprenticed to a mercer. He stuck this job for two years before leaving to join a small coastal steamer, *Kapanui*, as a cabin boy. This life suited him and he gained his third mate's certificate in 1910. By 1914, he was serving as first mate on the barque *Joseph Craig*, which carried timber from Tasmania. Three days after Britain entered the war, *Joseph Craig* was wrecked on at Hokianga of the west coast of North Island. Mate Sanders showed great bravery in single-handedly steering a boat through heavy surf to shore to raise the alarm and save the crew.

Billy Sanders joined the Union Steamship Company, serving briefly on *Moeraki* before applying to join the Royal Naval Reserve. He was not immediately mobilised and signed on for three round trips to the Middle East and England on the troopships *Willochra* and *Tofua*. Impatient for a more active service, he worked his passage on the tramp steamer *Hebburn Jan* which sailed for Britain. The ship arrived in Glasgow in April 1916 and Sanders immediately applied to the Admiralty, which commissioned him as a temporary sub-lieutenant.

After a gunnery course at HMS *Excellent*, he was sent to Milford Haven in Wales for 'Special Service'. This shadowy term referred to the submarine decoy ships or Q-Ships which were designed to look like innocent merchant ships but carried concealed guns. When a German U-boat was sighted, the Q-Ship crew braced itself for incoming gun-fire. This would signal a staged 'panic' among some of the crew, resulting in those involved in abandoning ship – but leaving a small party concealed on-board who would play a dangerous cat and mouse game with the U-boat. Often the merchant ship would sustain more shell fire before the submarine felt confident that the ship was totally abandoned before moving in for the *coup de grace*. When she was in range, the guns would be un-masked and the submarine would often be sunk or damaged.

Promoted to acting lieutenant, Billy Sanders was chosen for his experience on sailing ships which looked an easy target for the enemy. Appointed second in command he joined the two-masted brigantine *Helgoland* as gunnery officer. The second day on patrol, the ship found itself becalmed and vulnerable to attack. Surrounded by three U-boats, *Helgoland* sighted one submarine and felt forced to reveal its identity but the engagement was inconclusive. Frustratingly, a similar action occurred in October but the ruse seemed to be working in enticing the German submarines to close in and sink their prey with gunfire rather than waste a precious torpedo.

VC Action

On 5 February 1917, Billy Sanders was given command of the Q-Ship HMS *Prize*, then being fitted out with two auxiliary engines and two 12-pounder guns. She was a topsail schooner and so named because she was the first German vessel taken as a prize on the outbreak of war. On 26 April 1917, Lieutenant Sanders and his crew, all wearing shabby work clothes, left Milford Haven to patrol the waters off the Irish west coast. For four days they saw no sign of enemy submarines and Sanders was considering leaving the area. However, as dusk approached on 30 April a submarine, *U-93*, was spotted about two miles away at a position about 180 miles south-west of Ireland.

In their well-rehearsed routine, the crew waited for the submarine to open fire. Then six men of the 'panic party' launched their small boat and rowed clear of the *Prize*. A total of sixteen shells continued to hit the seemingly helpless ship, some near the waterline and putting one of the engines out of action. Keeping a cool head, Sanders crept forward on his hands and knees to encourage the gun crews. Holding their fire, Sanders waited until *U-93* was just eighty yards away before ordering the gun screens dropped and to fire at will. At that range the submarine was an easy target.

Billy Sanders later recalled what happened next: 'A pause of barely two seconds elapsed and then both forward and after 12-pounder guns and the Lewis gun fired simultaneously. A shell from the after gun hit the enemy's forward gun, blew it to pieces, and annihilated the gun's crew. The forward gun missed. The Lewis gun swept about 25 men off the decks of the submarine. [This was an exaggeration]. The submarine then proceeded at full speed with helm hard a-starboard. As she started to move a second shot from the after gun blew the conning tower clean off.'

Kapitänleutnant Edgar Freiherr von Spiegel von und zu Peckelsheim, *U-93*'s captain, was standing by the rear gun when it was hit. The impact blew him overboard and he and three other crew members were picked up by the 'panic boat'. The submarine was down in the stern and in imminent danger of sinking. She managed to put some distance between herself and the stricken schooner while still taking some hits from *Prize*. Sanders was convinced that he had sunk *U-93* and turned his attention to his own ship. The German captain and three of his crew had been taken on board. Aware of the need to save the ship, the Germans offered to help. One of the Germans was a mechanic and managed to get one of the damaged engines started and *Prize* limped back to Kinsale, Ireland.

In a subsequent interview, Billy Sanders gave brief account of the fight: 'I have been in another good scrap, and I am still alive to tell the tale. I can give you no names, but it will give you some idea when I tell you we were only eighty yards apart. We are badly holed, and our internal fittings all smashed up; but the enemy is no more, so we are victors. My first command has been very successful, and it is now that I shall receive my decoration.'

Sanders was a little premature in his belief that he had sunk *U-93*. In one of the great stories of the sea, it later emerged that the U-boat had survived its terrible battering and despite being unable to submerge managed to evade Allied patrols and mines to reach Germany nine days later.

Billy Sanders was recommended for the Victoria Cross and his citation appeared in *The London Gazette* dated 22 June 1917.

After a refit, *Prize* resumed her role of submarine decoy. On 12 June, she encountered *U-75*. During the inevitable shelling, Sanders was blown across the deck sustaining two wounds to his arm. The Q-Ship replied at distance and the result was inconclusive. For his part in the action, Sanders was awarded the DSO.

By now, *Prize* was familiar to the Germans. Further patrols did not attract any U-boats and the strain began to tell on Billy Sanders. On 3 August, he requested to be relieved but before it was agreed, he undertook one more patrol. Freshly painted and flying the Swedish flag, *Prize* left Milford Haven with the British submarine HMS *D.6* in tow.

Once the patrol area was reached, *D.6* slipped her tow and was free to manoeuvre in the search for enemy submarines. On 13 August, *U-48* was sighted and began to close on the Q-Ship. *D.6* attempted to get into position but with darkness falling she could not locate the enemy. In the meantime, *Prize* opened fire registering one hit, which took away the signal mast. *U-48* submerged and about midnight fired two torpedoes, one of which struck Sander's ship causing a tremendous explosion. By the time *D.6* arrived there was no trace of the ship or her crew.

On 19 June 1918, in a ceremony in Auckland, the Governor-General to New Zealand presented Billy Sanders's VC and DSO to his father.

The Third Battle of Ypres is more emotively referred to as simply 'Passchendaele' – a name that has become synonymous with the folly and futility of war. It has gone down in history as being particularly horrific for the appalling loss of life and of men who had to fight in a quagmire of thick clinging mud and ominously deep water-filled shell holes. Perhaps the most telling reaction to this campaign was when General Sir Lancelot Kiggell, Haig's Chief of Staff, who had spent the battle at GHQ in Cassell, paid his first visit to the front. As his car bumped and slithered over the battlefield, he was reduced to tears muttering, 'Good God, did we really send men to fight in that?' It was pointed out to him that conditions were much worse at the actually front line.

The area in which the battle was fought was low-lying. The ground was drained by many steams, canals and ditches which had been destroyed after three years of shelling. The onset of early rains caused swampy conditions which reduced the effectiveness of the tanks that were to accompany the infantry.

Instead, for three and half months the British and Commonwealth soldiers struggled their way to the ridge at Passchendaele, losing 60,000 men and performing sixty-one acts that were deemed worthy of the Victoria Cross.

On 31 July 1917, the first day of the attack, thirteen VCs were awarded; one of the highest number for a single day. Amongst these was one to an officer who was roundly hated by his fellow officers but nevertheless managed to rally the remnants of three regiments to stem the overwhelming enemy counter-attacks.

BERTRAM BEST-DUNKLEY VC (1890-1917)

Bertram Best-Dunkley was born in York on 3 August 1890. He attended a military school in Germany before returning to Britain and joining the 4th Battalion Lancashire Fusiliers (Territorial Force) as a second lieutenant in 1907. A year later he was promoted to lieutenant. He qualified as a teacher and worked as assistant master at Tientsin Grammar School in China, which served the increasing number British ex-patriots who sought the business opportunities after the defeat of the Boxers.

When war was declared, Best-Dunkley returned to England and re-joined the 4th Lancashire Fusiliers. In May 1915, he was posted to the 2nd Battalion to fill the gap caused by the heavy casualties in the Second Battle of Ypres. He was then transferred to the King's Own Lancaster Regiment before moving back to 2/5th Lancashire Fusiliers, where he acted as adjutant.

Best-Dunkley was once described as a small and rather nondescript man who looked like a typical teacher, his chosen profession. He was also lacking in charm but made up for this with brusqueness and bad temper which he had in abundance, which did not endear him to his fellow officers. He did, however, have drive and ambition. In the Battle of the Somme he served with the 55th Division from July to September 1916. It may have been this experience that caused him to blink and twitch his nose as a result of shell shock.

Promoted to captain, Best-Dunkley was, shortly afterwards and at the young age of twenty-seven, given command of the battalion, an accident having removed the new colonel who arrived to take over command. Now a temporary lieutenant colonel, Best-Dunkley relished being in command and has been described as hard-driving and dedicated. Others were not always so charitable. In his book *At Ypres with Best-Dunkley*, a fresh officer named Thomas Floyd wrote: 'First impressions; he suffers from a swelled head; that he fancies himself as a budding Napoleon; that he is endowed by the fates with a very bad temper and most vile tongue, that he is inconsiderate of his inferiors wherever his personal whims and ambitions are concerned; and that he is engrossed with an inordinate desire to be in the good graces of the Brigadier-General, who is really, I believe, a very good sort.'

In fact, Floyd had a lot of time for his irascible commanding officer who he came to admire. Floyd later wrote: 'Throughout the whole summer of 1917 his whole heart and soul were absorbed in preparation for the coming push; never did a man give his mind completely, unstintingly and whole-heartedly to a project that B-D did to the Ypres offensive which was to have carried us to the Gavenstafel Ridge, into Roulers and across the plains of Belgium. He was determined to associate his name indelibly with the field of Ypres; he was determined to win the highest possible decoration on 31 July: he knew what the risks were … he was determined to stake life and limbs and everything on the attainment of his ambition and to cover himself with glory.'

During the hot spell of weather, the battalion set off on a training march. Unfortunately, Colonel Best-Dunkley took his eye off what was happening to his men and General Stockwell, the local commander, gave Best-Dunkley a most humiliating public dressing down for allowing his battalion to straggle on the march on a very hot day. This was observed by Floyd, who recalled the wording of the admonishment: "'These men have not had a long enough rest or anything to eat all day. If this is the way you command a battalion you're not fit to command a battalion. You're not even fit to command a platoon!"

'The General then said that the Colonel, the Adjutant and four company commanders could consider themselves under arrest … It was an extraordinary scene. Those who have writhed under the venom of Best-Dunkley in the past would, doubtless, feel happy at this turning of the tables as it were, a refreshing revenge … As it was General Stockwell's fault as much as Best-Dunkley's, he later modified his judgement. One of the consequences of the long hot march was the death of the Sergeant Major through heat apoplexy.'

On another occasion Best-Dunkley was invited for drink in 'B' Company's Mess but spoiled the moment by remarking that: 'It was a dirty mess, pointed out a match on the floor and, with his customary blink and twitch of the nose, asked how we dare ask him into such a dirty mess.'

When it was learned that a son and heir had been born to Best-Dunkley one officer opined: 'Poor little ……! To think that there's another Best-Dunkley in the world to look forward to!'

The battalion practiced its part in the forthcoming Third Battle of Ypres in the surrounding cornfields and vegetable fields. When it was suggested that the popular Major Brighton should lead the battalion with the colonel on 'battle reserve', Best-Dunkley saw his chance of impressing his superiors receding. He implored General Stockwell to allow him to lead the battalion and finally got his way.

In the days leading up to the attack, the battalion sustained very heavy casualties in the trenches through shelling and was left too weak to go into battle. Large drafts of reinforcements arrived to make up the numbers but the regiment was still numerically weak.

Lieutenant Floyd wrote: 'At 8 we were all standing behind the parapet waiting to go over. Col. B-D came walking along, his face lit up by smiles more pleasant than I have ever seen before …

'Eventually at 8 I got the signal to go on. Could you possibly imagine what it was like? Shells were bursting everywhere. It was useless to take any notice where they were falling, because they were falling all around; they could not be dodged; one had to take one's chance …Thus we advanced amidst shot and shell-fire, over fields, trenches, wire, fortifications, roads, ditches, and streams which were simply churned out of all recognition by shell-fire. The field was strewn with wreckage, with the mangled remains of men and horses lying in all over in a most ghastly fashion … just like any other battlefields I suppose … It was hell and slaughter.

'About 100 yards slightly to the right I saw Colonel B-D complacently advancing with a walking stick in his hand, as calmly as if he was walking across a parade ground.'

The official Lancashire Fusiliers account states: 'It was difficult to obtain a definite account of all the incidents that happened before Black Line was reached but great gallantry was shown by the officers and NCOs in rallying the men in the face of heavy fire. The Commanding Officer, Lt-Col. B-D put himself at the head of all men in his immediate vicinity and led them on through intense machine-gun fire.'

As a result of German counter-attacks and heavy British casualties, the attack stalled and was pushed back. Calling for an artillery strike to break up the counter-attacks, Best-Dunkley was mortally wounded, possibly by a British shell that fell short. He was carried to a dressing station but seemed mostly concerned with the opinion of his general and whispered that he hoped he had not been disappointed with his battalion. This brave but unloved battalion commander hung on for nearly a week before he succumbed, on 5 August, at the Proven Medical Clearing Station. He was buried at Mendinghem Military Cemetery, Proven, twelve miles north-west of Ypres.

Best-Dunkley was recommended for the Victoria Cross by General Jeudwine. His citation read: 'For most conspicuous bravery and devotion to duty when in command of his battalion, the leading waves of which, during the attack, became disorganised by reason of rifle and machine-gun fire at close range from positions, which. despite heavy losses, were carried. He continued to lead his battalion until all their objectives had been gained. If it had not been for this officer's gallant and determined action, it is doubtful if the brigade would have reached its objectives. Later in the day, when our position was threatened, he collected his battalion headquarters, led them to the attack and beat off the advancing enemy. This gallant officer has since died of his wounds.'

When Best-Dunkley's widow went with her new-born child to collect her husband's award, the King made a moving gesture in pinning the VC to the infant's shawl.

As the battle for Passchendaele ground-on, the British gradually inched their way forward. Haig had thrown both the Australian and then the New Zealand divisions forward in an attempt to penetrate the cordon of strongpoints that covered the approaches to Passchendaele.

Both divisions had been repulsed with a long list of casualties. Haig then sent the Canadians into the fray. It took a final heave by men of the Canadian Corps to take the devastated village of Passchendaele. During the period from 26 October to 6 November, nine Victoria Crosses were awarded to Canadian soldiers as the Germans were finally pushed off the Passchendaele Ridge.

CECIL JOHN KINROSS VC (1897-1957)

One of the war's more unconventional VC heroes was Cecil John Kinross. He was born the third of five children, at Dews Farm, Harefield in Middlesex on 17 February 1896. His parents were John Stirling Kinross, a tenant farmer, and Emilie (née Hull). By 1904, the family had moved to a farm at Lea Marston, near Kingsbury, Warwickshire, near where Emilie had come from.

In 1912, the Kinross family immigrated to Canada and settled on a prairie farm at Lougheed, Alberta, about ninety miles south-east of Edmonton. When the war broke out, the tall twenty-two-year-old Kinross enlisted in the 51st (Edmonton) Battalion Canadian Expeditionary Force (CEF) at Calgary on 21 October 1915. The following month he embarked for the UK.

After a short spell of training, he was posted to the 49th (Edmonton Regiment) Battalion CEF and was sent to France on 6 March 1916. He soon became known as something of an oddball character and a hard man to control. His scruffy appearance was often described as a disgrace to the platoon.

Kinross also had an attitude that bordered on insolence towards authority. As time went by, he also gained a reputation for being something of a jinx and acquired the nickname 'Hoodoo'. As his platoon's runner, he had attracted the enemy's fire but never received so much as a scratch. In contrast, it had become noticeable that several officers to whom he reported had become casualties.

Kinross was eventually wounded during the disastrous Canadian attack on Regina Trench on 9 October 1916, when the 49th took fifty per cent casualties.

When he had recovered, Kinross was part of the great Canadian victory on Vimy Ridge. There followed an interlude with the brigade engineers before he re-joined the 49th as they entered the final stages of the dreadful battle of Passchendaele. For three months, British and Australian troops had inched their way through acres of mud towards the German position on Passchendaele Ridge.

VC Action

On the morning of 30 October 1917, the Canadian 7th Brigade put in an attack on the north-west outskirts of what remained of Passchendaele village. The creeping artillery barrage was ineffective and there were many casualties, particularly from a well-sited enemy pill box.

By 06.30 hours, the attack had stalled and men were huddling for shelter in shell-holes unable to advance or retreat. Kinross found himself trapped in a hole close to the enemy strongpoint. After enduring the point-blank machine-gun fire, Kinross decided to do something about it. Stripping off the 170lbs of equipment that the attacking soldiers carried, he picked up his rifle and a bandolier and, braving the heavy fire, sprinted for the pillbox. Without stopping, he jumped through the doorway at the rear of the strongpoint, and shot, bayoneted and clubbed the six Germans before destroying the machine-gun. This single act of bravery enabled the Canadians to advance 300 yards and a week later, the battle was finally won.

Cecil Kinross was seriously wounded in the arm and head later in the day. Working his way through the casualty chain, he eventually reached the No.16 Canadian General Hospital at Orpington in Kent. As he was recuperating, he learned that he had been awarded the Victoria Cross. Even when he received his Cross at Buckingham Palace on 6 April 1918, trouble dogged him. He was detained by two military policemen who accused him of wearing a VC ribbon to which he was not entitled. Not until he produced the Cross and showed them his name engraved on the reverse were they convinced.

Kinross was posted to the 21st (Reserve) Battalion and remained in Britain until he was discharged in February 1919. He returned to Lougheed where the Canadian Government gave him 160 acres of land to farm. He did return to the UK to attend the House of Lords Dinner in November 1929. He was also presented to King George VI and Queen Elizabeth at Edmonton in 1939. A 10,000-foot high mountain in Jasper National Park was named in his honour in 1951.

Kinross eventually retired from farming and moved to the Lougheed Hotel, where he died on 21 June 1957 at the age of sixty-one. He was given a full military funeral which was the largest seen in the area. One of the pall bearers was a fellow Albertan VC, Alex Brereton.

Amongst the other areas of conflict was the Middle East. There the Palestine Campaign began when a German-led Ottoman force invaded the Sinai Peninsular in January 1915 with an intention of seizing the Suez Canal. The attack was foiled by a strongly held defence along the Canal and the Turks satisfied themselves with the occupation of Sinai.

With the failure of the Gallipoli Campaign, Britain withdrew most of her forces to Egypt and formed the Egyptian Expeditionary Force (EEF). In a series of battles, the EEF successfully ejected the Turks from Sinai and pushed into southern Palestine.

After a period of stalemate lasting from April to October 1917, General Edmund Allenby finally captured Beersheba. Having weakened the Ottoman defences which stretched from Gaza on the coast to Beersheba, the Battle of Hareira and Sheria was fought in which the Victoria Cross was awarded to one of those men who relished war but was hopeless in civilian life.

ARTHUR DRUMMOND BORTON VC (1883-1933)

Born on 1 July 1883 into a distinguished military family, Arthur Drummond Borton was raised at at Cheveney House, the family home in Yalding, Kent. His uncle was the Afghanistan War VC, Major General William John Vousden. His grandfather General Sir Arthur Borton had been the Governor and Commander in Chief at Malta, while his father, Arthur Close Borton, acted as his ADC. With so many 'Arthurs' to contend with, it is little surprise that the family sought a nickname and called the latest addition, 'Bosky'. He had an older brother who rejoiced in an equally *Boy's Own* nickname, 'Biffy', and together, the self-styled 'Brothers Borton' experienced a most extraordinary First World War.

Bosky followed a common path followed by the upper-class soldier, namely an education at Eton followed by the Royal Military College at Sandhurst. From there, he was commissioned into one of the elite regiments, the 60th Rifles (Kings Royal Rifle Corps), and served during the final year of the Boer War, taking part in operations in the Transvaal between March and May 1902.

After the war, Borton's regiment was posted to India and his letters home were filled with news of inter-battalion polo matches and, increasingly, appeals for funds. By 1907, probably a mixture of boredom and a state of insolvency drove Bosky to resign his commission and seek his fortune in the United States.

Bosky's relationship with his father declined in direct proportion to the number of times he had to be bailed out from the disastrous schemes with which he became involved. These ranged from a new bottle-stopper to the purchase of some northern lakes with the view to selling the ice that accumulated in winter. All of these projects were doomed to failure. Thus, the old Etonian was reduced to going without food and sleeping on park benches. When he did have money, he used it to feed his increasing taste for alcohol. Bosky now filled the role of the archetypal black sheep of the family.

With the outbreak of war, Bosky, anxious to redeem himself and to join the fight, returned home. After a cautious welcome, he convinced his father that he had turned over a new leaf by rejoining his old regiment, despite trouble with the medical board. With his brother, Biffy, gazetted flight commander in the Royal Flying Corps, Bosky volunteered for duty as an observer. Strings were pulled, allowing the two brothers to fly together. However, by early 1915 Bosky was transferred to the BEF in France. He later gave an account what it was like to fly in mid-winter as an observer: 'The cold was horrible, freezing hard on the ground, and my face was a sight on landing. My eyes and nose ran and it all froze solid. We chased a Hun machine and my fingers were so cold I couldn't reload my rifle after I'd used up my first clip.'

Borton did, however, have a success on 6 February, when he and his pilot, Lieutenant Wadham, shot down an enemy plane. An enthusiastic Bosky wrote: 'It was "some scrap"; at times we were within 50 feet of the blighter, blazing away at each other with automatics and rifles – great chunks flying out of both our busses. Finally we got him, and he took the floor about 15 miles behind their lines in a plough. It was a wonderful experience, but I cannot say I am keen on another go for a while.'

Just a month later, Bosky's flying career came to an end when his 'plane crashed on take-off. Miraculously both Wadham and Bosky survived the abrupt descent from an altitude of 150-foot, although the latter suffered a dislocated neck. After hospitalisation, he returned to Cheveney to convalesce.

Borton had only been there a couple of months when he was joined by his brother, Biffy, who had suffered a terrible facial wound during a dogfight. In an action similar to that experienced by William Rhodes Moorhouse, the first Air VC, Biffy was hit by a bullet from an enemy aircraft. The bullet entered his neck, passed below the tongue and exited through the left jawbone. Despite the pain and loss of blood, he managed to fly the twenty miles back to British lines under heavy anti-aircraft fire before landing. Unlike Moorhouse, however, Biffy had the extra responsibility of his observer's life. Biffy was promptly recommended for the Victoria Cross, but this was denied and he received the DSO instead.

As Biffy began his recuperation, so Bosky began to pester the authorities for another fighting appointment. Both the Army and RFC turned him down, but he managed to be accepted by the Royal Navy Volunteer Reserve. Such was his determination to put himself in danger that Bosky was to serve in all three services within the space of a year. He also chose this moment to marry, but plans for a honeymoon had to be shelved. Bosky and his new unit were ordered to the Dardanelles as part of the Royal Naval Division.

The doomed Gallipoli campaign had become stalled, so Lord Kitchener decided on another throw of the dice to break the deadlock. A force of 20,000 men, mostly new recruits who had answered Kitchener's call to arms, were put ashore further up the Gallipoli Peninsula at Suvla Bay in what was expected to have been an almost unopposed landing. Through inept leadership, a golden opportunity was squandered and the British force was soon pinned down within a precarious toehold. Bosky's letters veer from great enthusiasm to deep despair. On one occasion, for example, he observed that, 'As compared to the Turks, we are nothing but a bunch of amiable amateurs when it comes to scrapping in this kind of country'.

Flies, a scarcity of water, scorching sun by day and freezing nights, and the smell of decomposing bodies were just some of the discomforts suffered by Bosky and his comrades. The Turkish artillery dominated the heights and the compact British perimeter made an easy target, so casualties steadily mounted. Bosky spent thirty days on the front line before being relieved.

By December, Bosky, like the rest of the Mediterranean Expeditionary Force (MEF), was cold, dispirited and aware of the abject failure of the Gallipoli venture. He also bemoaned his lack of promotional opportunity: 'If only this show hadn't been such a fiasco, I might have been able to do a bit of good for myself, but am afraid as things stand that having been at Suvla will not be an open sesame for promotion.'

Finally, during the middle of December 1915 the troops at Suvla and Anzac were evacuated in what was about the only great success of the Gallipoli Campaign (the evacuation from Helles followed soon after, the last Allied serviceman leaving the Peninsula on 8 January 1916). Bosky's naval battery covered the evacuation and was one of the last to leave.

Borton returned to the UK and in May 1916 was awarded the DSO. After a few weeks at home, he once again became restless for action. The War Office suggested that he could rejoin the KRRC, as a subaltern. This did not receive favour from the volatile Bosky. Fortunately, strings were again pulled and by the end of June Bosky was appointed second-in-command of the 2/22nd London Regiment (The Queen's) and, as part of the 60th Division, sent to France. For several months, they occupied trenches in a 'quiet' sector, with only the occasional raid to capture prisoners to relieve the tedium.

To Bosky's dismay, the regiment was then ordered to the Middle East again. On 22 December 1916, the battalion arrived at the Greek port of Salonika to take part in a campaign notable for its total lack of results. The Germans later described the Salonika front as 'our largest prisoner of war camp', because hundreds of thousands of Allied troops were committed to a sideshow that was a waste of time and manpower.

The bleakness and discomfort of mountain warfare proved too much for Colonel Luck, the CO of the 2/22nd Londons, and he applied for a transfer. After a nerve-racking wait, Bosky was promoted to lieutenant colonel on 17 March 1917, and given command of the regiment. After months of desultory action, Bosky and his regiment were ordered to Egypt, where his brother has been stationed for several months. Once again, the Brothers Borton were reunited.

In between socialising with Biffy, who seemed to find time to drop supplies of cigarettes into Bosky's camp, the Queen's were put through some tough route marches and exercises in preparation for the new campaign in Palestine which was being planned by General Allenby. Biffy was given command of the 40th Wing RFC so the warrior brothers were about to take part in the same campaign.

On 1 November, Bosky led the Queen's into its first real battle and was elated with its success. He wrote: 'We worked our way up to about 500 yards of the enemy and lay "doggo" while our Artillery tried to cut gaps in the wire. This, however, they could not do as each shell raised such an awful dust that observation was impossible and we had to lie up for two hours under a very heavy fire in the open. It was darned trying, but the men were too wonderful. Our casualties during this time were pretty high – about 15%. The Brigadier then got a message to me to know whether we could go without the gaps being cut?

'It was the thing I had been hoping for, as I felt that no wire was going to stop us … I'd got a flag with the Queen's Badge on it, in my pocket, and when the time came (8-15am) arrived, I tied it to my walking stick and away we went. I never felt so damn proud in my life. The Flag was a surprise to the men and tickled them to life. We got in practically without loss; we cut the wire 25 yards behind our own barrage. This of course meant a few hits from our own guns, but not a soul in the trenches dared show his head, and the moment the guns lifted, we were into them with bomb and bayonet and scuppered the whole garrison.'

VC Action

An even greater victory followed on 6 December at Tel el Shiera near Beersheba, during which Bosky performed his VC deed. The citation that appeared in *The London Gazette* 18 December 1917 briefly read: 'For most conspicuous bravery and leadership. Under most difficult conditions in darkness and in an unknown country, he deployed his battalion for attack, and at dawn led his attacking companies against a strongly held position. When the leading waves were checked by a withering machine gun fire, Lt. Col. Borton showed an utter contempt of danger, and moved freely up and down his lines under heavy fire. Reorganising his command, he led his men forward and captured the position. At a later stage of the fight, he led a party of volunteers against a battery of field guns in actions at point-blank range, capturing the guns and the detachments. His fearless leadership was an inspiring example to the whole brigade.'

As usual, the citation carried just the bare facts. Bosky's letter to his father conveyed the raw emotion of being under fire: 'As the light grew better I found we were in a devilish awkward fix – we were swept by machine-gun fire from both flanks, and behind their artillery put down a barrage on top of us and if it had not been that the light was so bad – would have been wiped out in a matter of minutes. It was impossible to stay where we were, and hopeless to go back, so to go forward was the only thing to do. And we went!

'One of the men had a football. How it came to be there goodness knows. Anyway, we kicked off and rushed the first guns, dribbling the ball with us. I take it the Turk thought we were dangerous lunatics, but we stopped for nothing, not even to shoot, and the bayonet had its day. For 3000 yards, we swept up everything, finally capturing a field battery and its entire gun crews – The Battery fired its last round at us at 25 yards …

'We're all pretty beat tonight and are hoping for a day to reorganise tomorrow. I have had to send in my Christian names to Division this morning, so I hope it may mean a bar [to his DSO]. Anyway, they are pretty bucked about the show. My losses are, considering the two fights, very low, but I have lost 11 officers out of 20 since we started 10 days ago, and am pretty busy most of the time. But I wouldn't have missed it for the world.'

Without doubt, this was the highpoint of Bosky's life.

Biffy, whose aircraft had supported the advance, filled in more details that he had picked up from another battalion commander: 'Bosky called for 10 volunteers and went straight for the guns, which opened fire at 150 yards, with their fuses set at zero! They killed or captured the whole of their crews and, according to Bosky's account, the last gun fired when they were 10 yards from the guns and the man who pulled the string immediately flung up his hands and said in a broad German accent "I vas an Arab!", to which the voice at Bosky's elbow replied, "Arab, be damned!" and a bayonet disappeared in the region of the third button of the "Arab's" coat.

'Bosky, meanwhile, armed to the teeth with a walking stick and a stream of blasphemy (I should have said "armed to the Gums" as according to one account, he mislaid his teeth, so luckily no one knew what he was saying.) Anyhow, the whole thing seems to have been one of the finest done in the War! And now all I hope is that it will be recognised as such.'

Although those at home knew of Bosky's VC, the Brothers Borton did not hear of it until 21 December when yet another Borton arrived. This was their uncle, Neville, who was appointed Governor of Jerusalem until ill health forced him to relinquish the post.

Without a doubt, Saturday, 16 February 1918 was a day to remember for the Bortons and the residemts of Yalding. Bosky arrived at the small station and was cheered the mile-long route into the village. Accompanied by the peal of church bells, he drove up the decorated High Street and on to Cheveney. A guard of honour consisting of the local volunteers, Boy Scouts and wounded from the small local hospital, had been drawn up there. Bosky made a speech of thanks and, no doubt, when the villagers dispersed, many felt in appropriate to toast their hero's health in the five hostelries that were then in Yalding.

On Saturday, 23 February, Bosky and his wife went to Buckingham Palace, where he received both his VC and DSO from the King. Bosky then spent a few weeks being feted. He attended a civic reception at Bermondsey, the home of his volunteer regiment, and delivered speeches in support of the War Bond campaigns.

On 16 March, he embarked on his ship for the trip back to Palestine. Biffy also later returned to the Middle East in one of the great feats of aviation. In July, accompanied by a co-pilot, two mechanics and a small dog, he took off from Manston in a Handley-Page and flew to Cairo, the first ever flight to Egypt.

Bosky spent the next few months of the campaign as acting brigadier and was instrumental in cutting off the retreat of four Turkish divisions. When the Turks surrendered, he bemoaned the fact that he had got nowhere, despite being awarded the VC, DSO, Order of the Nile and commanded a brigade and the 22nd Londons. Ever anxious to fight and not to miss an opportunity to shine, he tried to get transferred to France. With the signing of the Armistice, even this avenue was closed. Instead, he applied for a position in the Egyptian Army, only to be turned down on the grounds of being too senior.

As peace broke out, Biffy further added his name to the record books by piloting the first flight to India. Meanwhile, within a few weeks of his return, the restless Bosky volunteered to join the Expeditionary Force to fight the Bolsheviks in North Russia. This confused and abortive campaign ended after six months and the British withdrew.

While he was in the Arctic region, Bosky befriended the polar explorer Ernest Shackleton and, through him, was given a job of local director of the Northern Exploration Company. This was yet another 'get rich quick' enterprise which had always attracted Bosky. He was posted to Spitzbergen, the new 'Eldorado of the Arctic', where rich mineral deposits had been found. For whatever reason, the scheme lasted just two months and Bosky was soon back in England.

There was one last military act he was asked to perform. He was one of the pallbearers at the Burial of the Unknown Warrior on 11 November 1920.

Bosky could not adjust to civilian life; he could not hold on to a job, drank heavily and ran up debts. He attended the VC reunion dinner held on 9 November 1929 at the House of Lords. When his father died in 1927, the estate passed to Biffy. Bosky was given a modest allowance and moved to Suffolk, where, at the age of forty-nine, he drank himself to death on 5 January 1933. His body returned to his home and he was buried in the small churchyard at nearby Hunton; a tragic hero who was only truly happy when at war.

Chapter 46

First World War, 1918

Number of VCs awarded	207
Number of VCs awarded to officers	97
Number of VCs awarded to other ranks	104
Total awarded to Royal Navy	11
Total awarded to Royal Marines	2
Total awarded to Royal Flying Corps	11
Total awarded to Royal Air Force	6
Total awarded to British Army	110
Total awarded to British Indian Army	2
Total awarded to Canadian Army	31
Total awarded to Australian Army	29
Total awarded to New Zealand Army	6

Origins of the War

The dawn of the last year of the Great War found the opposing armies similarly gloomy about the prospects for 1918. On the Allied side, the British were only just coming to terms with the enormity of their losses at Passchendaele which had sapped their strength and morale. The Army in 1918 was smaller than in 1917 and half the infantry were aged nineteen or younger. Enlistments had fallen from 1.28 million in 1915 to 820,000 in 1917. Large reserves of healthy manpower were no longer available. In 1917-18 only thirty-six percent of men examined were suitable for full military duties. The French Army, too, was exhausted and running out of replacements for its enormous list of casualties. To the Allies it seemed that Germany was on the front foot.

From a German perspective, the prospects were less than rosy. True, she was now able to transfer fifty divisions from the Eastern Front now that Russia had withdrawn from the war. But if she had one less enemy to deal with, it faced another – the United States. The Royal Navy's blockade of German imports was causing severe hardship and there were rumblings of civil unrest. Faced with the prospect of the war dragging on and further weakening the country, the two key German commanders, Field Marshal von Hindenburg and General Ludendorff, decided to launch an all-out offensive against the weakened Anglo-French defenders before the Americans arrived in force.

Dubbed the *Kaiserschlacht* – Kaiser's Battle – the Spring Offensive of 1918 consisted of four major assaults code-named *Michael, Georgette, Blücher-Yorck* and *Gneisenau*. It was, in effect, the last throw of the dice, for German manpower was as depleted as that of its enemies and losses could not be effectively replaced.

In February 1918, Allied intelligence learned of the build-up of German forces opposite perceived weak points on the British front. These were aimed specifically at the Fifth Army commanded by General Hubert Gough and General Sir Julian Byng's Third Army, which together held a forty-mile front between Arras and La Fere. The goal was to cut the BEF off from the French in the south and to wheel north-west to the Channel ports. With the prospect of a rare German offensive, the military authorities gave the war correspondents permission to warn the British public of the impending attack.

Most of the divisional commanders dismissed the reports as 'GHQ, has the wind up', convinced that they could contain the German attack. Some conceded that ground might have to be sacrificed to keep an unbroken defence line, which would be a bitter pill to swallow – the thought of surrendering all those hard-fought-for objectives for which so many had paid with their lives.

Field Marshal Haig's call for more reinforcements was not well received by the British Government who was loath to send any more after the Passchendaele slaughter. Haig also called upon General Philippe Pétain to send troops, but this was refused as the French were more concerned about protecting Paris. With no prospect of additional men, Haig was forced to tell Gough that he had to make do with what he had.

At 04.30 hours on 21 March 1918, the Germans launched Operation *Blücher-Yorck* with a five-hour barrage of gas and HE shells along a fifty-mile front. Their infantry advanced in dense fog, smashed through the British lines and, in the misty confusion, captured pockets of defenders who found themselves cut off from the main body. In spite of the seeming ease with which they advanced, the Germans were sustaining heavy casualties from the British rear-guard as they fought over the old battlefields of the Somme.

On that day, nine VCs were awarded including a posthumous one to a lone lance corporal whose determined action delayed the advance enough to influence German aspirations. In the confusion of the first few days of the *Kaiserschlacht*, the ramifications of this solo action were not recognised; even his regiment's historian omits mention of him. Despite being regarded as the 'forgotten VC', John Sayer was a man who helped change the course of the war.

JOHN WILLIAM SAYER VC (1879-1918)

On the pivotal 21 March 1918, a largely unknown two-hour lone stand had consequences which may have influenced the outcome of the Great War. This single-handed action was fought by John William Sayer, a middle-aged former seed merchant. Born in Ilford, Essex on 12 April 1879 to farmer Samuel and Margaret Sayer, John was brought up with agriculture in his blood at Wangye Hull Farm, Chadwell Heath. After his education, John stayed in agriculture and later ran a corn and seed merchants in Cricklewood.

John Sayer was conscripted and after a period of training, went to France in December 1916 as a machine-gunner in the 8th Queen's (Royal West Surrey) Regiment. In 1917 he was promoted to lance corporal and, in early 1918, his regiment was part of the 17th Brigade of the 24th Division positioned at the village of Le Verguier, five miles north-west of St Quentin. When the German attack was launched, the positions south of Le Verguier were overwhelmed and to the north the enemy broke through the front line but met heavy fire from the Rifle Brigade.

VC Action

Lance Corporal Sayer was defending a strategic position at Shepherd's Copse close to the German Hindenburg line north-east of Le Verguier. John Sayer's deed was witnessed by his platoon commander, Lieutenant Claude Lorraine Piesse, who, with the regiment's commander, Colonel Hugh Chevalier Peirs, later recommended him for a Victoria Cross.

In a letter Peirs described what had happened in the front line outposts, about a mile north-east of the Battalion's main position, on the morning of the German advance. Piesse's command at Shepherd's Copse in fact included three separate posts connected by trenches. These were initially defended by twenty-two men, although men from other positions (thick fog made it impossible for Piesse to record exactly how many) joined during the fighting.

Due to an earth mound which limited the eastward view, the Shepherd's Copse trench complex was not ideal for defence, even without the fog. Lieutenant Piesse noted the defenders had no grenades, only limited rifle ammunition and no palatable drinking water (supplies having been stored in kerosene drums).

The position which Sayer occupied at the junction of two communication trenches, although open to enfilade, provided the only effective sight on the advancing enemy. Fluctuating visibility meant fighting was frequently at close quarters and Piesse described how, in repulsing repeated attacks along the trench, Sayer single-handedly killed six attackers with his bayonet, while dropping others with his rifle. Lieutenant Piesse was wounded and semi-conscious as he was being carried away but counted nine bodies he believed had been killed by Sayer, almost certainly an underestimate of the actual total.

For most of the two hours Sayer endured a continuous hail of machine-gun fire and grenades in a manner Piesse found near miraculous: 'It was a wonder to me every minute that he did not fall. Sayer was defending against all attacks of the very much stronger enemy by bayonet and rifle with almost incredible bravery.'

Due to the dense fog, fighting was often hand-to-hand. Only at noon, with the fog clearing and Sayer badly wounded, were the Germans able to capture his position. Piesse reported: 'Although for two hours he was continually exposed to enemy machine gun fire and bombs, he used his own rifle as coolly as if at the butts. Sayer showed the utmost contempt for danger and the enemy and inspired everyone by his conduct.'

Sayer was badly wounded and captured. He lost his leg after amputation and died four weeks later in German captivity. Aged nearly forty, he left a widow and six children.

By midnight on the 21st, the dead and wounded totalled nearly 40,000 German and about 17,500 British. Another 21,000 British soldiers had been captured, making this one of the highest single day's casualty tolls of any war. The offensive had been intended to land a knock-out blow, but the maximum advance before the campaign's abandonment sixteen days later was about forty miles. Compared to the gains of the previous four years this was substantial, but not nearly enough to achieve the aim of driving the British back to the North Sea. German armaments and men far outnumbered British resources, and no one who experienced the ferocity of the onslaught ever forgot it. Winston Churchill described the five-hour salvo along the fifty-mile British front which preceded the German advance, as 'the most tremendous cannonade I shall ever hear'. It was said the guns could be heard 200 miles away in London.

John Sayer's VC citation appeared fifteen months later, on 9 June 1919: 'For most conspicuous bravery, determination and ability displayed on 21st March, 1918, at Le Vergoier [*sic*], when holding for two hours, in face of incessant attacks, the flank of a small isolated post. Owing to mist the enemy approached the post from both sides to within 30 yards before being discovered. Lance-Corporal Sayer, however, on his own initiative and without assistance, beat off a succession of flank attacks and inflicted heavy casualties on the enemy.

'Though attacked by rifle and machine-gun fire, bayonet and bombs, he repulsed all attacks, killing many and wounding others. During the whole time he was continuously exposed to rifle and machine-gun fire, but he showed the utmost contempt of danger and his conduct was an inspiration to all. His skilful use of fire of all description enabled the post to hold out till nearly all the garrison had been killed and himself wounded and captured. He subsequently died as a result of wounds at Le Cateau. He was also buried there.'

Overlooked Gallantry

Despite the importance of Sayer's solo action in delaying the German advance for two hours, the events of the Shepherds' Copse stand are virtually unknown. Sayer is also missing from most VC battle literature and most accounts of the First World War. The accounts that appeared in the 1920s contain errors, including an incorrect date for his VC deed. A search for any reference to Sayer in the obvious source, his regiment's official history, does not mention his name. Even the *History of the Queen's Royal West Surrey Regiment in the Great War*, by Colonel Harold Wylly and published in 1925, contains no mention of him or, indeed, of Shepherd's Copse. While other VCs are recalled on memorials, street signs or cigarette cards, Sayer is forgotten and the significance of his place in First World War history remains largely ignored.

Sayer's apparent invisibility is not helped by the lack of any record of his service career, which in fact included a previous act of exceptional bravery in August 1917. There is other evidence about both the strategic importance of Shepherd's Copse and the delayed advance on Le Verguier. Although the shelling of Le Verguier had commenced before the attacks on the outposts, the German assault proper on the village did not start until 15.00 hours. The only explanation for the lateness of the assault, and the one that Peirs later accepted, is the morning's hold-up at Shepherd's Copse, which was unknown to the defenders in Le Verguier at the time. The fog's persistence and the delayed attack had provided time for defensive regrouping, so that by noon men from abandoned outposts had moved to strong points in the village. By contrast the units on either side of the 8th Battalion (a battalion of the 66th Division on the left and the 3rd Rifle Brigade on the right) had been pushed back earlier, so that Le Verguier then stood, as Peirs later told Piesse, 'at the point of a narrow peninsula extending into enemy territory'.

Communication with Piesse's platoon had been lost very early on. Shepherds Copse was therefore assumed to be in enemy hands as, according to escaped survivors, were the other outposts. A captured Prussian officer was questioned and said that the German plan had been to take the village within two hours as a first step towards eventually pushing the British back to the coast. Le Verguier standing on high ground and containing numerous strong points was in fact eminently defendable in clear weather providing sufficient men were available to staff the forts. So the German timetable presumably depended on completing the attack under fog cover, which the Shepherds Copse hold-up had frustrated. The postponed attack had allowed the battalion to maintain its position for longer than any other unit on the entire British front, which had led to commendation in the Commander-in-Chief's despatches.

The existence of the Shepherds Copse stand had previously been unknown and its impact had therefore been uncalculated. Because communications with the outpost had been severed early the action, it was not included in the battalion's contemporary War Diary. Piers supported the recommendation for a VC nomination for Sayers. Although when Peirs wrote he was still awaiting full confirmation of Sayer's role, his letter indicates he believed the Shepherds Copse stand was the major reason for the delay in the German attack, which had preserved so many lives and enabled the twenty-four-hour resistance. So, it is curious that neither of these facts are included in Sayer's VC citation of June 1919. It is particularly puzzling that the delaying action and its life-saving consequences are not mentioned even though, in August 1918, Peirs had intended to recommend an award for Sayer centred on these dual effects.

Instead, the long delay can be explained by the fact that by the time Sayer's citation came to be written, all credit for the resolute defence had already been given to Peirs himself. He was awarded a second bar to his DSO in September 1918. His citation reads: 'For conspicuous gallantry and devotion to duty in defence of a village, when he fought until surrounded, and then made his way back under cover of a fog. It was entirely due to his great courage and fine leadership that the enemy offensive was delayed for nearly two days.'

Leaving aside the fact that the twenty-four hours had been stretched into two days, one might assume that the comprehensiveness of Peirs' citation precluded giving Sayer any credit for Le Verguier's lengthy resistance. Although strictly speaking Peirs' award should not have influenced Sayer's 1919 citation, it undoubtedly created complications.

The 8th Battalion's reputation in response to the 1918 Spring Offensive had become well-established without acknowledging Sayer. Their success had been applauded in British newspapers, notably *The Times* of 26 March which had praised them under the headline 'West Surreys Fight to Last Man'; they had been mentioned by General Haig; and their CO had been decorated for resistance 'entirely due to his great courage'. Announcement of the effects of Sayer's action would mean reapportioning credit, unsettling this cumulatively-built reputation.

Therefore, if Peirs was to get Sayer his award, which apparently met some opposition, the safer initial approach would be to limit any description of events to those Piesse had observed; not to extend it to the consequences the rest of the battalion had experienced. Neither Piesse nor Sayer's widow then knew that Sayer had died eleven months previously.

A month later the VC nomination was returned to Peirs by GHQ for removal of 'some paragraphs in which exceptions were taken'. This would suggest that the offending paragraphs may have mentioned Sayer's role in delaying the assault on Le Verguier. Sayer's nomination will also have received particularly lengthy scrutiny because it related to an award for an action which had culminated in his capture. Bravery medals weren't given in these cases, although exceptionally a VC could override the rule.

Piesse related conversations with German soldiers and civilians that had convinced him that the slide in German morale which cost them the war dated from 21 March, when things went wrong from the outset. German objectives for the Spring Offensive were over-ambitious, but the now forgotten twenty-four-hour delay in taking Le Verguier was clearly one of the factors which made the 21st a pivotal date in the last year of the war.

By 5 April, the Germans had advanced forty miles and were within range of Amiens – but they failed to take the city, thanks in no small part to the Australian Brigade, which made a surprise attack on Viller-Bretonneux, a village to the east of the town.

With this failure, the German advance began to run out of steam. There was still fighting for strategic objectives but the forward momentum had been lost.

With the American Expeditionary Force (AEF) arriving in increasing numbers, it was soon thrown into the front line. In June 1918, the third Battle of Aisne, the 5th US Marine Corps gained its battle honour for the Battle of Belleau Wood, just to the east of Château-Thierry.

For a month, Germany had pushed back the British and French until exhaustion and larger-than-expected losses forced another stalemate. Ludendorff's Operation *Blücher-Yorck* had been brought to a standstill. The Germans had punched three large holes in the Allied defences but had been unable to deliver the killer blow. The arrival of the Americans and the fact that they had made an immediate impact made a German victory unobtainable.

On 15 July, Ludendorff opened the Second Battle of the Marne, attacking both sides of Rheims. Initially, the Germans made great progress, pushing east towards Epernay. Foch and Pétain then ordered a counterstroke which threatened to encircle the Germans in the salient they had created. Realising the danger, Ludendorff ordered a withdrawal, so ending Germany's offensive. The effort had cost the Germans 200,000 casualties. The initiative had clearly passed to the Allies.

On 8 August 1918, the Allied fight-back commenced with General Rawlinson's Fourth Army and the French First Army attacking the Germans in early morning mist and taking the enemy by complete surprise. In two days about eight to ten miles had been re-taken with 24,000 prisoners and some 300 guns. The attack began with a four-minute hurricane barrage, followed by the infantry and tanks under a creeping barrage. The momentum was with the Allies and by the 27 August, they were back to their former line on the Somme. Ludendorff called it 'the blackest day of the German Army'.

The Allies were now advancing over familiar territory and re-occupying towns that had been largely reduced to rubble: Albert, Péronne, Merville, Armentières and passing over the Hindenburg Line. Sixty-four VCs were awarded between 8 August and 26 September, one of which was to a Lancashire Fusilier who would find himself in the same area again during the 'Phony War' of 1940, though his second visit would end in tragic circumstances.

EDWARD BENN SMITH VC (1898-1940)

Edward Benn Smith was born on 10 November 1898 at 1, North Quay, Maryport, Cumberland to Charles Henry and Martha Smith (née Benn). He was one of three brothers and two sisters. Both sides of the family were seafaring and several of his mother's family were lifeboatmen at Maryport. His father later served in the RNR and saw action in the Dardanelles during the First World War.

Maryport was the largest port on the Cumberland coast and was also a coal mining area. After attending the National School, Ned, as he was known, went to work at the nearby Oughterside Colliery. Life was tough and he had to learn to look after himself and he developed into a useful boxer. He also played as a front-row forward in the local rugby team.

On the outbreak of the First World War, Ned was anxious to enlist, but had to wait until he was seventeen. Turning his back on the family tradition of seafaring, Ned joined the Army Reserve until he was old enough to enlist in the Lancashire Fusiliers in July 1917. It is evident that Smith and the Army were well suited to each other. Despite his youth, he soon became an NCO in the 1/5th Lancashire Fusiliers, part of the 125th (Lancashire Fusiliers) Brigade, 42nd Division. He joined them as they were posted to the much-fought over area of Givenchy. There they were mostly involved in reinforcing the trench line, which followed the edges of the many mine craters that had been exploded since 1916.

Although the brigade had not been directly involved in the German breakthrough on 21 March 1918, it was in the forefront of the Allied counter-attacks in August. The Lancashire Fusiliers were in trenches in the Beaumont Hamel-Puiseux sector, infamous for the huge loss of life suffered during the Battle of the Somme in July 1916.

The Commanding Officer of the 42nd Division, Major General A. Solly-Ford, wrote the following report about Edward Smith: 'On 10 August, south-east of Hébuterne, this NCO led a daylight patrol. By skilful handling and use of cover he examined two points of the enemy line about which information was required. This information he obtained. When on the point of returning, Sgt. Smith noticed a party of forty of the enemy coming forward from their main line of resistance, obviously to take up night outpost dispositions. Sgt. Smith decided to wait for the enemy, and engage them, though outnumbered. He inflicted heavy casualties on the enemy, who at once scattered, His initiative and determination to inflict casualties on the enemy was a fine example.'

For this action, Sergeant Edward Smith, still only nineteen, was awarded the Distinguished Conduct Medal. Just ten days later, an even higher award was to be won.

VC Action

The Battle of Albert started on 21 August 1918, and the men of the 1/5th Lancashire Fusiliers had assembled in preparation for a major attack the following day. They had three main objectives: south of Puiseusx there was Hill 140 which, better known as The Lozenge, was a strongpoint bristling with machine-guns; to the east was an area of high ground; whilst, thirdly, there was a road junction named Beauregard Dovecot, which overlooked Miraumont and the Ancre River.

Leaving their trenches on the misty dawn of the 22nd, Smith and his comrades moved forward under a heavy creeping artillery barrage and managed to capture Hill 140 with only light casualties. Advancing on the high ground, they met stiffer resistance and suffered heavier casualties.

It was in the capture of the Dovecot that Edward Smith displayed his outstanding gallantry and leadership. His action was recognised with the award of the Victoria Cross and his citation reads: 'Sergt. Smith, while in command of a platoon, personally took a machine-gun post, rushing the garrison with his rifle and bayonet. The enemy, on seeing him advance, scattered to throw hand grenades at him. Regardless of all danger, and almost without halting in his rush on the post, this NCO shot and killed at least six of the enemy. Later, seeing another platoon requiring assistance, he led his men to them, took command of the situation, and captured the objective. During the enemy counter attack on the following day he led a section forward and restored a portion of the line. His personal bravery, skill and initiative were outstanding, and his conduct throughout exemplified magnificent courage and skill, and was an inspiring example to all.' At the time, he was said to be the youngest VC in the Army.

There was still much fighting to be done and the Lancashire Fusiliers were involved in the battles that finally brought about the end of the war. Just two days before the last round was fired, Sergeant Edward Smith stood to attention before King George V in the ballroom at Buckingham Palace to receive the Victoria Cross. He returned home on leave to Maryport to be hailed by a crowd of 6,000 townspeople. There was a civic reception, speeches and gifts, including £200 in War Bonds and, rather bizarrely, a Meerschaum pipe.

The Lancashire Division was demobilised in March 1919 and reformed again in April 1920. Ned, finding a return to the colliery unappealing, re-enlisted in May 1919 in the Cameron Highlanders. A year later, he transferred to his old regiment and was appointed Drum Major in the 1st

Battalion, Lancashire Fusiliers. He was the youngest VC in attendance at the Royal Garden Party at Buckingham Palace on 26 June 1920.

In 1924, he was promoted to company sergeant major. In 1926, he was detached and sent to South East Asia to instruct the Malaya Volunteer Forces, known affectionately as 'The Vultures'. This rather pleasant secondment lasted for three years, after which CSM Smith returned to a depression-hit Britain. A lifelong bachelor, he gained a reputation as a 'ladies man'.

On 29 July 1932, Smith was made regimental sergeant major and served with the battalion in Shanghai and Tientsin as part of a multi-national force to protect the International Settlement threatened by the Sino-Japanese clashes, which were a precursor to the Japanese invasion of China in 1937.

Second World War and Tragedy

In 1938, Ned Smith left the Army on a full pension and joined the Corps of Commissionaires in London. This new career was short-lived for, with the outbreak of the Second World War, Smith re-joined the Army and his old regiment, being granted a Short Service Commission as lieutenant and quartermaster. As in the First World War, the 2nd Lancashire Fusiliers was part of the 42nd (East Lancashire) Division and was sent to France as with the British Expeditionary Force.

The Germans did not invade France and Belgium until April 1940 and this lull before the storm was known as the Phoney War. Ned Smith, however, found it was deeply disturbing for, by a twist of fate, he found himself at Bucquoy – virtually at the same spot where he fought so gallantly twenty-two years earlier. Although nature had softened the ravages of conflict, the area still bore enough scars to re-awake terrible memories of fallen comrades.

On 12 January 1940, Edward Smith was found dead in his store with a single head wound – his revolver next to him. He left a note saying that he could not live through the horrors of yet another world war. His body was taken to the Beuvry Communal Cemetery, just east of Béthune, where it was buried (Plot 1, Row B, Grave 7).

The regiment decided to keep Smith's suicide a secret out of respect to the family and also because he was a well-regarded holder of the VC. Although the German Blitzkrieg did not commence until the spring, there were plenty of minor skirmishes on the frontier where fighting patrols from both sides frequently clashed. As his battalion was soon to be involved in the bitter rear-guard fighting back to Dunkirk, Smith's death could easily be covered up and it was accepted that he had been killed in action.

Ned's VC group was left to the regiment but, during the 1950s, his siblings requested their return. As the relevant paper work had been lost during the war, the regiment felt it could not refuse and the medals were passed to the family. Within a short time, the group had been sold to a private buyer but, in 1996, Edward Smith's exceptional VC group was purchased at auction and now form part of the Ashcroft Trust's collection.

Between 27 September and 1 October 1918, a most decisive battle was won by the British, French and Americans when they managed to cross the St Quentin Canal, one of the most formidable strong points on the Hindenburg Line.

More victories followed in quick succession. Between 14-19 October, the fighting saw the recapture or liberation of towns such as Courtrai, Roulers, Ostend, Bruges and Zeebrugge. It had been at the latter that one of the most daring naval raids had taken place the previous April – an operation that resulted in the award of eight Victoria Crosses, including one to a submariner.

RICHARD DOUGLAS SANDFORD VC (1891-1918)

During the last year of the Great War, the Zeebrugge Raid was the British attempt to hinder German submarine access to the North Sea via the canal from Bruges and Ostend. U-boat activity in the English Channel had successfully sunk many Allied vessels, merchant and naval, and a plan to seal off Zeebrugge, discussed since 1914, was finally approved in early 1918.

Vice-Admiral Roger Keyes took over command of the Dover Patrol on 1 January 1918 and set about planning a direct attack from the sea. The aim was to sink three block ships in the canal's entrance. In order that they could enter the harbour and make their approach, an obsolete heavily-armoured cruiser, HMS *Vindictive*, would disembark some 250 marines and sailors on the seaward side of the mile-long Mole and draw the enemy's fire. Heavy bombardment from monitors and a dense smokescreen would also help to keep the enemy's attention away from the block ships.

There was one other objective that was regarded as verging on the suicidal. The heavily defended stone Mole was connected to the shore by a 300-yard-long railway viaduct built on iron piers. This open lattice-work allowed the sea to scour out the entrance to the canal and prevent the harbour from becoming silted. It was intended to send in two obsolete submarines, each laden with five tons of Amatol explosive, and detonate them beneath the viaduct, thus isolating the Mole and preventing the Germans from bringing up reinforcements.

The suggestion was made by one of Admiral Keyes' staff, Lieutenant-Commander Francis Sandford, that submarines should be used rather than the original idea of using the hit and miss method employing rafts. He further suggested giving command of one of the submarines to his younger brother, Lieutenant Richard Sandford.

Early Life

Richard Douglas Sandford was born on 11 May 1891 at 15 The Beacon, Exmouth, Devon, the sixth and youngest son of the Venerable Ernest Grey

Sandford, the Archdeacon of Exeter and Ethel Marie (née Poole). He was educated at Clifton College, Bristol, before joining the training ship HMS *Britannia* at the age of thirteen.

Sandford qualified as a Midshipman in 1908 and served on the battleship HMS *Hibernia*. Following the orthodox career path, there was a series of appointments to other ships until in 1914, when he joined the fledgling Submarine Service. For nearly three years, Dick Sandford had spent much of his service ashore waiting for the construction to be completed of his new appointment only to be transferred to another posting.

In November 1916, Sandford had been transferred again to await the introduction of a huge revolutionary new design of submarine, the K-Class. This was a steam-driven turbine powered vessel of 1,980 tons, with a surface speed of twenty-four knots. Its concept, however, was doomed to failure. Numerous problems occurred during its development and the subsequent modifications did little to improve its performance. Four of these subs had already been lost through accidents during 1916 but still the navy took delivery of them. The submarines proved far more lethal to their crews than to the enemy, so much so that 'K' was said to stand for 'Kalamity'.

Sandford spent two months waiting for HMS *K-6* to be completed and joined her as a first lieutenant in February 1917. The shortcomings of the vessel restricted the crews to taking part in exercises and anti-submarine patrols. For Dick Sandford, the war had been one of boredom and inactivity. The first few months of 1918 would soon change that.

Isle of May Disaster

In January 1918, the ships at Rosyth were ordered to steam north to Scapa Flow to take part in a full-scale Grand Fleet exercise. On the afternoon of 31 January, around forty naval vessels left Rosyth and sailed out of the Firth of Fourth to the North Sea. By the time they reached the mouth near the Isle of May, the night was pitch-black with patches of mist.

The two K-Class flotillas were following, with some difficulty, behind their cruiser leaders. Suddenly out of the mist appeared a couple of minesweepers which had not been informed of the fleet's movements. The two leading submarines changed course and the third, *K.14*, veered to starboard to avoid colliding with them. In the process, her rudder jammed and she performed a complete circle and was rammed by the last submarine, *K.22*. The battle cruiser *Inflexible*, following the same course, then ploughed into *K.22*.

The leading cruisers turned back to assist and steamed straight into chaos. HMS *Fearless* rammed *K.17*, sinking her in eight minutes. The battle cruiser *Australia* narrowly missed *K.12*, which turned into the path of *K.6*, whose officer on watch was Dick Sandford. *K.6* tried to avoid her and rammed *K.4*, nearly cutting her in two. The seriously-damaged *K.4* was sinking, only to then be hit again by *K.7*. To complete the disaster, three following battleships and their destroyers passed through the area unaware of the tragedy and ran down survivors in the water.

Within seventy-five minutes, the submarines *K.17* and *K.4* had been sunk and *K.6, K.7, K.14, K.22* and *Fearless* had been damaged. In total, 270 men had perished in one of the worst naval disasters of the war. So embarrassing was the incident, that the facts were not generally admitted for more than sixty years.

An enquiry followed and several officers, including Dick Sandford, were sent for a course at HMS *Dolphin.* It must have been with a sinking heart that he was put in temporary command of *K.2* with little prospect of engaging the enemy or rescuing his stalled naval career.

The Zeebrugge Raid

Meanwhile, Admiral Keyes plan to block the Bruges Canal at Zeebrugge was gathering pace. His staff officer, Francis Sandford, had suggested using an obsolete C-class submarine to deliver the explosive charge against the railway viaduct. Regarded as a suicide mission, only unmarried crew were considered. As the captain of *C.3* was married, Francis recommended his bachelor brother as a replacement, knowing Dick was despairing of ever seeing any action.

Richard Sandford joined the rest of his crew at Portsmouth, where the two submarines, *C.1* and *C.3* were being fitted out for their special one-way voyage. Each submarine carried a crew of six; two officers and four ratings. With Sandford were his navigator, Lieutenant John Howell-Price (an Australian who had won the DSC), Petty Officer Walter Harner, Coxswain William Cleaver, Engine Room Artificer Alan Roxburgh and Stoker Henry Bindall. The raid's planners were able to refer to detailed drawings of the viaduct, these having been smuggled out by the Belgian engineers who had been involved in its construction of the viaduct. These drawings gave Dick Sandford a clear idea where to steer *C.3* and create the most damage

Although the attack was highly risky, it was not an outright suicide mission and the submarine crews had to be given every opportunity to escape. Each submarine was therefore equipped with a pair of motorised skiffs which were carried either side of the conning tower. Gyro steering gear was fitted so the crews could abandon the submarines before impact with the viaduct. A steam picket boat, commanded by Francis Sandford, would be on hand to pick up the escaping crews.

By the end of March 1918 all was ready. Most of the attacking force was assembled at Dover. These elements would rendezvous with *Vindictive, Iris, Daffodil* and the block ships, which were anchored off the Essex coast.

On 11 April, the armada sailed for Zeebrugge but thirteen miles from their objective, had to abandon the attack due to a change of wind which would have rendered the planned smokescreens useless.

Another attempt was made on 13 April but rough seas caused it to be postponed and the ships once again returned to port. The Admiralty was getting nervous that the Germans must have got wind that an attack was on the way and wanted to cancel the operation. Admiral Keyes successfully pleaded to be allowed to try again.

The next period of favourable tides began on 22 April and this was the date Admiral Keyes decided to launch the third attempt. The evening brought low cloud and rain, which was going to hamper the bombardment by the monitors *Erebus* and *Terror*, but there was no thought of another postponement.

The combined force met at the assembly point and set sail for their target. Lieutenant Sandford's *C.3* was towed by the destroyer HMS *Trident*; *C.1* by *Mansfield* and the rescue picket boat by *Phoebe.* About ten miles from Zeebrugge, the submarines were due to slip their tows and proceed to the railway viaduct.

VC Action

Four minutes had been allowed for the submarines and picket boat to assemble. Sandford waited, unaware that the towing cables of *C.1* and the picket boat had parted causing a lengthy delay. Sandford waited the allotted four minutes and decided to carry on alone. About eleven minutes from his target, Sandford saw the flashes as the monitors opened fire and heard the roar of the German's heavy coastal guns as they passed overhead in reply.

The smokescreen had masked Sandford's approach but now he was clear of the smoke and aiming for the viaduct. Because of a shift of wind, *C.3* found itself with a mile and a half still to travel. A tremendous cannonade of firing to port heralded the arrival of *Vindictive* at the Mole.

Suddenly a star shell burst overhead and illuminated the sea around *C.3*. The submarine's own smoke-making apparatus proved useless as the smoke blew out to sea. *C.3* was quite alone and very exposed. Several rounds landed around Sandford's vessel, but for some reason the firing ceased. Flares and explosions inside the harbour meanwhile exposed the silhouette of the viaduct's lattice-work and Sandford adjusted his course to hit the target at right angles. At this point, Sandford decided to dispense with the gyro steering apparatus and steer the vessel himself, further lessening his chance of survival.

With about 200 yards to go, the crew clustered around the conning tower, clearly hearing the Germans talking on the viaduct. A searchlight momentarily caught them in its beam but was switched off again. At a speed of around ten knots, *C.3* ran under the viaduct between two vertical piles and slid up the horizontal girder. This was the exact position Sandford had hoped for.

There was no time to lose. Sandford ordered the skiff to be lowered and the crew to make to make their escape. Firstly, Sandford went below and lit the three fuses. Then he clambered back on deck and joined the crew in the skiff. The engine was started, but the current pushed them back against the submarine and the skiff's propeller snagged against the exhaust pipe and killed the engine. Five precious minutes had elapsed and still they had not moved away from explosive-laden vessel. Bindall and Harner grabbed an oar each and strained to pull the heavy skiff clear.

By now the Germans had woken up and started firing at the skiff and water started to pour in through the bullet holes. Fortunately, Howell-Price, on the bilge pump, managed to keep the water at bay. Bindall was hit and his place was taken by Cleaver. Then Harner was shot and Roxburgh grabbed his oar. There were now only minutes before the fuses reached the explosive. Slowly, the skiff pulled further away.

Sandford, at the tiller, was then hit twice and Price scrambled to take his place. The crew was only 300 yards away, still well within the danger area, when *C.3* erupted with a tremendous explosion throwing a pillar of flame high in the sky. The blast threw debris as far as 800 yards; it was a miracle that though great lumps of metal crashed into the sea all around the tiny boat the crew emerged unscathed.

The defenders on the viaduct were either killed or wounded. A German cyclist corps that had been sent to reinforce the Mole garrison had disappeared over the 100-yard gap that had appeared in the viaduct. A further bonus for the attackers was that the electricity supply was cut and the searchlights extinguished.

Sandford's crew was still slowly rowing against the current when out of the darkness there appeared the lost picket-boat, which had made the greater part of the journey under its own steam. To Francis Sandford's delight, he found his brother alive but badly wounded. Fortunately, he was able to transfer the wounded men onto HMS *Phoebe* where they could receive treatment from the ship's doctor. Most of the ships had already left the area and were returning to Dover. *Phoebe* was one of the last to leave and provided Richard Sandford with a little more unsought excitement.

HMS *Phoebe* and *North Star* had been operating at the mouth of the harbour by the lighthouse at the end of the Mole. Both had come under very heavy fire, and towards the end of the raid, *North Star* received hits in her engine room which disabled her. *Phoebe* attempted to take her in tow but twice the cable parted. Under almost point-blank enemy fire, she took off the crew of *North Star* in a rescue that took nearly an hour. Incredibly, *Phoebe* survived the battering and was able to make its escape. Sandford and his crew had experienced a second miracle within two hours.

Dick Sandford languished in hospital for three months and heard strong rumours that the Victoria Cross was to be awarded to some participants of the raid. On his discharge, he learned that he was to receive the Cross along with Captain Edward Bamford RMLI, Lieutenant-Commander George Bradford RN, Captain Alfred Carpenter RN, Sergeant Norman Finch RMA, Lieutenant-Commander Percy Dean RNVR and Able Seaman Albert

McKenzie RN. After the Battle of Rorke's Drift, this was the highest number of Crosses awarded for a single action.

News of the raid had been received with great enthusiasm by a British public dismayed by the huge gains made by the German army in their Spring Offensive. In fact, audacious as the raid was, it did not inconvenience the Germans for long. The block ships had not sealed the exit from the canal and the U-boats were soon able to pass to and from their pens in Bruges.

Sandford's attack on the viaduct had caused a 100-yard gap between the shore and Mole but the Germans were soon able to rig a footbridge between the two. Despite the disappointment, Sandford and his crew had achieved their goal to perfection and Sandford's award was the most universally approved.

On 31 July 1918, Lieutenant Richard Sandford received his Cross from the King at Buckingham Palace. A month later, he was awarded the French *Legion d'Honneur*.

Sandford spent the remainder of the war at HMS *Lucia* on the Tees as relief CO of the submarine *G-11*. Tragically, within twelve days of the Armistice on 11 November, Dick Sandford died of a deadly combination of typhoid and Spanish flu in the Royal Navy Auxiliary Hospital at Grangetown. He was buried at Eston Cemetery, Middlesbrough (Plot J, Row U, Grave 709).

The war in the air had fluctuated as the opposing sides sought better aircraft, tactics and weapons. In the first half of 1917, the Germans held the upper hand with their Albatros D-series fitted with the twin synchronised machine-guns. The Royal Flying Corps suffered particularly heavy losses in April 1917 to the extent that they suffered a severe blow to their morale. A total of 275 aircraft were shot down with 207 aircrew killed.

During the latter part of 1917, the British Sopwith Camel and S.E.5a and the French SPAD fighters start to arrive in France and the air superiority pendulum swung back in the Allies' favour. In 1918, the death of the famed Red Baron, Manfred von Richthofen, coincided with the stalling of the German offensive and added to the perception that Germany was on the backfoot.

The Royal Flying Corps had been an arm of the British Army until it amalgamated with the Royal Naval Air Service to form a new service on 1 April 1918 called the Royal Air Force. The first RAF pilot to be awarded the Victoria Cross was a man who overcame adversity to lead a most varied and extraordinary life.

FERDINAND MAURICE FELIX WEST VC (1896-1988)

Born in Paddington, London, on 29 January 1896, to Lieutenant Francis Drake West of the East Lancashire Regiment and his French wife, Comtesse

Clemence de la Garde de Saignes, Ferdinand Maurice Felix West, who was generally known as 'Freddie', lived most of his formative life in Europe. When his parents married in 1894, Francis was twenty-eight and Clemence was eighteen. The West family thoroughly disapproved of the match, even more so when Francis gave up his Army commission when the regiment was posted abroad so he could be with his wife. With the outbreak of the Boer War, however, Francis volunteered and sailed for South Africa. In 1902, Francis was reported missing, probably killed.

With nothing to keep her in England, mother and son departed for Italy to stay near Clemence's sister, Mary, who was a nun in a convent in Milan. Freddie became an acolyte in the convent church and formed a strong bond with the Convent Chaplain, Monsignor Ratti. One day Ratti asked Freddie if he would like to try mountaineering. Obtaining permission from his mother, Freddie accompanied Ratti in climbing the 6000ft Mount Resegone at night in bright moonlight and reached the summit soon after mid-day. Flushed with success and admiration, Freddie told Ratti that he was sure he would become a bishop or even a cardinal. In the event Ambrogio Damiano Achille Ratti was created Pope Pius XI on 11 February 1922 and sovereign of Vatican City from its creation as an independent state on 11 February 1929 until his death on 10 February 1939.

When Freddie spent a long summer holiday in England, he started playing football for Xaverian College near Brighton and returned to Milan fired with enthusiasm for the game. He had soon organised a boys' team. There was nothing like it in Milan, nor indeed Italy. Soccer was about to be injected into the lifeblood of Italy and become its national sport. Freddie could justifiably claim to have introduced junior football to Italy.

At the beginning of 1914, Freddie enrolled at Genoa University to study International Law. When Britain declared war on Germany in August, Freddie returned to Milan determined to go to the UK to enlist. The British Consul gave him a letter for the French authorities in case he was stopped and questioned. On reaching Paris, he found that it was useless to attempt crossing the Channel owing to the large troop movements.

When Freddie finally reached Victoria Station, he was accosted by two burley men in uniforms who bullied him into a nearby recruiting office. As it was his intention to enlist anyway, it did not seem to be a problem. To Freddie's dismay, he found that he had been recruited into the Royal Army Medical Corps and sent to Aldershot where he spent six miserable months under canvas. One day Freddie spotted an item on the notice board. One of the officers was looking for anyone who could fence. One of the several sports in which Freddie was proficient was fencing and so he applied.

Major Pattison was a poor fencer but enjoyed the contests. The pair became friends and Freddie asked for help to transfer to a fighting regiment. Pattison agreed to help and recommended him for a commission. Reporting to the War Office for an interview, Freddie was asked if he was a Roman Catholic. As result, he was commissioned into the 2nd Battalion Royal Munster Fusiliers, a regiment that had suffered heavy casualties, particularly amongst the officers.

Second Lieutenant Freddie West arrived in France on 8 November 1915 to join his new regiment in the Loos Sector soon after the disastrous battle had ended. He found that the battalion, once 1,000 strong, had been reduced to just 250 men. All the majors and captains had been killed and Freddie's company commander was a Lieutenant.

The winter of 1915 was freezing and wet making life in the trenches unbearable. Freddie wrote: 'We crawled amongst human refuse and humane carnage. We never undressed. Our clothes became a sweat-caked skin upon us. We burrowed into the ground and slept there … Our trench section was narrow, and as we were at the bottom of a slope the rain infiltrated all the time. We wallowed in slime in which duckboards had long since disappeared.'

Winter also saw the beginning of mining on the Western Front. It came as little surprise when the Munsters learned that the Germans were burrowing beneath their trench. For weeks, the soldiers endured terrible suspense waiting for the mine to be detonated. Divisional Headquarters had a different take on the mine. They reasoned that the mine was not simply to blow up the front line trench but to create a hill with a crater on the top. The enemy would rush forward and occupy the summit of the new hill with machine-guns that could fire down on the trenches.

To counter this, a new formation was created; the 'Crater Party'. Upon the explosion of the mine, the Crater Party, led by a 'Crater Officer', was to quickly react and take the hill from the enemy. Freddie was appointed Crater Officer. He once recalled what followed: 'I can remember the beginning of the explosion. It started with a sudden heave under my feet, literally an earthquake, and then a rumble that grew with a thunderous crescendo. Then I knew no more … I came to, vaguely and slowly, in little pulses of consciousness. I realised that I was buried.'

Frantically grubbing away, Freddie managed to dig his way out. Concussed and disorientated, he tried to organise his Crater Party, but most had been buried. By the time he got a small number of the Party together, the Germans had taken the new mound. Having spent so much time digging his way out, Freddie was still reprimanded for failing in his duty as Crater Officer. As a punishment, he was appointed to guide to a battalion of the Black Watch who succeeded in ejecting the Germans from their new hill.

A visit to an airfield near Amiens and a chance to be taken on a flight fired Freddie with determination to apply for a transfer to the Royal Flying Corps. This did not go down well with his fellow officers in the Royal Munster Fusiliers and there were even hints of disloyalty. The application, however, was accepted and Freddie was sent to Brooklands in Surrey to start training as an observer.

In July 1917, having qualified as an observer/gunner, Freddie was assigned to No.3 Squadron which flew the Morane Parasol, a two seater monoplane reconnaissance aircraft. Clocking up some 225 flying hours, Freddie was notified that he had been selected for pilot training. His training began at Grantham, Lincolnshire, where his squadron commander was Major Trafford Leigh-Mallory. The training aircraft used was the Airco DH-6 known as the 'Skyhook'. At the end of five hours of dual control, Freddie made his first solo flight on 15 November.

A near disastrous crash-landing whilst attempting a forbidden loop-the-loop resulted in Freddie facing Leigh-Mallory's wrath. Chastened after threats of a court-martial, Freddie received his pilot's wings just before Christmas. On 4 January 1918, he was posted to France. Leigh-Mallory offered his congratulations and said, rather pointedly: 'I've had you posted to No.8 Squadron; you may be interested to know, West, that I have been posted to command it.'

When he arrived at his new squadron's aerodrome near Amiens, Leigh-Mallory greeted the new pilots with the encouraging words: 'You, gentlemen, are just the chickens the red German eagles are looking for.'

Leigh-Mallory's warning referred to von Richthofen, the Red Baron, and his squadron of red-painted Fokkers. It was on Sunday, 21 April that Freddie came upon the Red Baron in a dramatic manner. He was patrolling in the Amiens-St Quentin area when his observer spotted three red Fokkers. Expecting to be attacked, both men prepared their guns.

To Freddie's astonishment, one of the Fokker's gently glided to earth. Landing near the crashed enemy machine, he was greeted by a jubilant Australian artillery officer who said': 'We've had a bit of luck. Guess who we've shot down?' West inspected the dead pilot and was amazed to be looking at the Red Baron; 'quite calm in death – he might have died in bed'. Freddie telephoned his squadron commander with the news, to which Leigh-Mallory responded with: 'Don't go and ruin your reputation by originating sensational rumours'.

On 1 May 1918, Freddie and his observer, Lieutenant John Haslam, were noticed by General Rawlinson when they made a low-level bombing attack and recommended them for the Military Cross. Their citation dated 26 July reads: 'For conspicuous gallantry and devotion to duty. While on patrol he, and another officer, observed fifteen enemy motor lorries. As these could not be engaged by our artillery by zone call, they flew 8,000 yards over the enemy line at a height of 3,800 feet. In the face strong opposition from the ground, and dropped four bombs, obtaining direct hits on the lorries and doing considerable damage to their personnel. They then proceeded to attack them with machine-gun fire as they sought cover.

'A fortnight later they carried out, as a height of 150 feet, a reconnaissance of their corps front, on which an attack was expected.

Despite the fact that the clouds were at 200 feet, and there was a thick mist, they obtained most valuable information.

'During this flight they directed and located the fire of our artillery on a concentration of enemy infantry. Throughout the operations their work in co-operation with our artillery was always of the greatest value, and their enterprise in attacking enemy troops and transport with bombs and machine-gun fire was splendid.'

On 19 June, Freddie was promoted to captain and given command of a flight. No.8 Squadron was equipped with the Armstrong Whitworth FK-8, a two-seater biplane known as 'Big Acks'. It was a sturdy reconnaissance airplane, ideal for photographing enemy positions. By the beginning of August 1918, the squadron had supplied an accurate photographic plan of the sector as the British prepared for a mass assault along the Amiens front.

The British Army began its attack at dawn on 12 August. At the same time, Freddie and Haslam took off to find where the enemy reinforcements were massing. The weather was poor with low cloud and mist. Flying low to avoid enemy aircraft, they looked for openings in the mist. Suddenly, Freddie spotted one and saw a huge concentration of troops, transport and tanks at the edge of a wood.

Diving, he flew low over the enemy trying to accurately pin-point their position. Freddie was so engrossed that he was oblivious to the heavy ground-fire. He pulled up into the mist but decided to make another low-level run to re-check the position.

Freddie recalled the second pass: 'As I dived, two aircraft seemed to pass in front of me, like ghosts, through shallow vapour, and then I felt a burning pain in my right foot. At the same moment, the staccato rat-tat-tat of machine-gun fire came to me from close to. I looked at my instruments. My wireless transmitter was smashed …

'I was temporarily lost. Then it was there again, to port, a large funnel of a hole; just what I wanted. I wheeled and dived for it and spotted the woods again. There was no mistaking their position now and the Army must have the vital information quickly. With my transmitter gone I had double reason for getting home safely.'

Two more German aircraft appeared and opened fire, and Freddie felt a tremendous pain in his left leg. Behind, Haslam, blasting away, drove the enemy off. Freddie, though, was in a very bad way. His left leg was almost severed by an explosive shell and he desperately sought to stem the bleeding from his femoral artery with an improvised tourniquet.

'I realised that I would never reach the aerodrome,' he later recalled. 'I must land somewhere but safely. I must free the rudder bar for better manoeuvre or I might come to grief. My left leg was in the way. It was useless. I lugged and heaved at it, pulling it clear of the controls.'

Despite feeling light-headed and in excruciating pain, Freddie managed to cross the front line and saw an open field. He succeeded in touching down, despite the close attention of one of the German fighters which kept firing along the length of the Big Ack. Soon there were Canadian soldiers running towards the machine. A section was cut out of the side of the cockpit and they lifted the grievously wounded pilot out causing him to lose consciousness several times.

On reaching the field hospital, and lapsing in and out of consciousness, Freddie managed to deliver his report on the concentration of enemy troops before passing out. When he awoke, the pain in his legs had gone and replaced by violent pins and needles.

'I threw back the blankets and sheets to reach for my feet. One leg was gone … yet I wanted to scratch my foot, which was itching badly.'

When he gained some strength, Freddie was transferred to the London Hospital in Whitechapel. It was there, on 9 November 1918, that he learned he had been awarded the Victoria Cross, the first to a member of the newly-formed Royal Air Force. Two days later came even better news with the declaration of the Armistice.

In December, Freddie was sent to Roehampton to be fitted with an artificial limb. It turned out to be a clumsy wooden leg which he could only manipulate with the aid of crutches. Using £50 of the £250 compensation the Air Ministry paid him for the loss of his leg, Freddie visited Paris. There he found a shop that sold artificial limbs and bought a much-improved leg. But still it did not solve the problem of moving without crutches. Freddie knew that the RAF would not keep him and he was resigned to returning to his law studies.

A chance meeting with a precision tool manufacturer changed his life. Marcel and Charles Desoutter had formed a company, Desoutter Brothers, at Baker Street, London. Marcel had lost his limb in a flying accident at Hendon Aerodrome in 1913 and together with his brother they had designed, and then manufactured, a lightweight articulated limb that did away with the use of crutches. Freddie was completely sold on the idea and the thought of remaining in the RAF spurred him on. In a few weeks, Freddie was confident enough to have an interview with Air Vice-Marshal Sir Hugh Trenchard, commander of the RAF. He received a sympathetic hearing from Trenchard who offered him a new position as the RAF liaison officer with the Foreign Office as the first Air Force diplomat.

On 1 March 1919, a couple of weeks before he took up his appointment at the Foreign Office, Freddie travelled to Buckingham Palace where he received his Victoria Cross and Military Cross from the King. When he reported for duty at the Foreign Office, his naval colleague explained that he was now in a 'cloak and dagger' department.

'He added that he had something in common with me,' said Freddie, 'and he then got up from his chair and, taking a stick by his side, tapped what was obviously a wooden leg. He then introduced me to the Army member and he too revealed a wooden leg. So there we were three of us representing a department supposed to be shrouded in secrecy, all stumping about on wooden legs.'

In August, the expected cuts for the RAF were announced. At the end of the war there had been 30,000 officers, a number which was drastically reduced to just 200. Fortunately for Freddie, he was one of the lucky ones to be spared.

Indeed, 1919 was a lucky year for Freddie West for he also met, fell in love with and became engaged to Winifred 'Wynne' Leslie. They waited until 19 January 1921, by when Wynne had reached her nineteenth birthday, before getting married at Westminster Cathedral.

On 26 June 1920, Freddie attended the VC Garden Party held at Buckingham Palace and was part of the Unknown Warrior's VC Guard of Honour during the inaugural Remembrance Day on 11 November 1920.

By this time, Freddie had ended his tour of duty with the Foreign Office, had passed his Civil Service Commission examination in French and Italian and was qualified as a first-class interpreter. In February 1921, Freddie was posted to RAF Uxbridge. Although he was not employed on flying duties, he took every opportunity to fly with one of the instructors. One day, he managed to badger the instructor into letting him take over the controls and he once again enjoyed the thrill of flying. It was only a short step to taking a machine up for a solo flight. He found the strain on his back and leg painful but after several flights, he felt at home. In 1923, Freddie moved to the RAF Staff College at Andover before being posted to No.17 Squadron at Hawkinge, flying Woodcock and Grebe fighter aircraft. In 1927, Freddie was transferred to the Central Flying School at Upavon and year later posted to Malta. He took up the post of adjutant to the seaplane base at Kalafrana.

On a visit to Rome, Freddie managed to get an audience with his old mentor Monseignor Ratti, now Pope Pius XI. Taking the opportunity to see his mother, he and Wynne travelled to Milan. There Freddie had his pocket picked and he sent Wynne after the thief and engaged him in conversation while he summoned the police. The thief was arrested and turned out to be a dangerous internationally known criminal wanted in several countries.

From 1929 to 1933, Freddie was posted to the School of Army Co-Operation at RAF Old Sarum, near Salisbury. The main task was the development of efficient air/ground communication under operational conditions, principally between Army officers, including those of the newly-formed armoured forces and the pilots and observers of the RAF Army Cooperation Squadrons. This was just the sort of operation that Freddie had experienced during 1916-18.

From 1933 to 1936, Freddie was Squadron Leader OC of No.4 Army Cooperation Squadron at Farnborough. It was while attending a race meeting at Goodwood that he bumped into the Chief of Air Staff, Sir Cyril Newall, who told him that he had been with No.4 Squadron long enough and offered him another posting.

Freddie was appointed as the first Air Attaché to Finland, Estonia and Latvia. He took advice from the Air Attaché in Moscow that the RAF uniform was quite unsuitable for the freezing temperatures he could expect in a Baltic winter. Although it was against regulations, he created a new uniform with an emphasis on warmth. Freddie attended official functions wearing a grey and white fur hat with the RAF badge in the centre and a thick fur-lined blue overcoat and riding boots. One of his great achievements during his three-year appointment was to persuade the Finnish Air Force to buy the Bristol Blenheim instead of the German equivalent. War with Germany seemed inevitable and Freddie was recalled to command No.50 (Army Cooperation) Wing at Odiham.

On the afternoon of 3 September 1939 when the outbreak of war was announced, Freddie was ordered to take his command immediately to France. The squadrons on No.50 (Army Cooperation) Wing were stationed in the Amiens, Arras and St Pol areas. This was the Phoney War period with little operational flying. On Christmas Day, Freddie felt very ill and was advised to return home. When he finally examined in hospital, it was found that he had a burst stomach ulcer and had lost half his blood. After a couple of months, he had recovered sufficiently to agitate for a new appointment.

Having lost his command in France, Freddie was pleased to accept the appointment of Air Attaché in Rome. This did not last long, as Italy sided with Germany in June 1940 and Freddie was ordered to join the British Legation in Berne, Switzerland, regarded as the 'window on Germany'. Very soon after arriving in Berne, Freddie helped a Bulgarian diplomat out of a scrape and in return learned that the Nazis were planning to get rid of him. A chance meeting in a restaurant provided him with a formidable bodyguard, a White Russian named Serge Ovsievski, who became his chauffeur/minder.

Besides providing the Air Ministry with daily weather reports from Central Europe, Freddie became involved with escapees from amongst the air crews shot down over France and Germany or had escaped from PoW camps. Using secret routes through Vichy France, most managed to reach Spain and returned to the UK. The Nazis tried to infiltrate this route by imposing a stooge as a Norwegian member of RAF aircrew, but Freddie was able to unmask him and return him to Germany.

A real intelligence coup came about when a businessman contact in Italy arrived at Freddie's office bearing a large parcel. The donor had been in his garden when he saw a German 'plane falling from the sky. He ran to the wreckage and found the pilot dead. There was no fire, so he searched the aircraft and found a tin trunk with the painted words *Geheim* (Secret). Grabbing the trunk, he hid it in a ditch until the search party concluded their examination of the wreckage. When he thought it was safe, he wrapped the contents in brown paper and travelled to Berne.

Freddie recalled: 'Inside was a carefully docketed card-index file with some three hundred cards and several files of documents and correspondence. One of the first letters I read was over the signature of Field Marshal Kesselring. The correspondence dealt with the existing German Air Force dispositions in Italy and their urgent reinforcement requirements. Hurriedly I scanned through the card-index. It listed the locations and situation reports, machines, crews, casualties, reinforcements and shortages, as far as I could see, of every German squadron in Italy. British Intelligence was naturally overjoyed.'

When Italy capitulated in 1943, escapers arrived over the Alps in their hundreds. The Swiss set up holding camps for the three Services. The number of British officers and men who found their way to Switzerland from Italy eventually reached 5,000. They had to remain until they could be repatriated in September 1944. When the Allies landed in the south of France on 16 August 1944, the British in Switzerland, with their close contacts in the French Resistance, were able to supply intelligence to the Allied Headquarters.

Eventually, Freddie and Wynne were able to leave Switzerland for the first time since June 1940. They travelled to the recently liberated Paris and met up with his old CO, Trafford Leigh-Mallory, now C-in-C Allied Expeditionary Air Force. Sadly, two months later on 15 November, Leigh-Mallory's transport aircraft crashed in the Alps near Grenoble killing all on board.

By the summer of 1945, Freddie's war assignment in Switzerland came to an end and he returned to London. He was given a department at the Air Ministry but was easily persuaded by the Rank Organisation to retire and take up a senior position in their new offshoot, J. Arthur Rank (Overseas) Film Distributors. He then became Managing Director of Eagle-Lion Film Distributors. Other directorships followed, including chairmanship of a betting shop group.

In 1956, Freddie attended the centenary of the Victoria Cross at Hyde Park and was active in both the Victoria Cross and George Cross Association and his local branch of the RAF Association. In 1971, he finally retired to his home in Sunningdale. He died on 2 July 1988, just a month after Wynne passed away. He was the last surviving VC of the First World War.

Returning to the events of 1918, hostilities came to an end with the armistice with Turkey on 30 October, Austro-Hungary on 3 November and that with Germany on 11 November. The fighting of the Great War, the 'war to end all wars', had some to an end.

It was a war that had led to the awarding of 626 Victoria Crosses, by far the highest number in any conflict.

Chapter 47

North Russia Campaign, 1919

Number of VCs awarded	5
Number of VCs awarded to officers	3
Number of VCs awarded to other ranks	2
Total awarded to Royal Navy	3
Total awarded to British Army	2

Origins of the War

The Armistice of November 1918 ended four years of slaughter that left the participant nations exhausted and their populations weary of war. Servicemen returned to their homes to pick up the pieces of their shattered lives and left the politicians to tidy up the mess that had been left.

One such mess was the unresolved problem of Russia and the revolution that was threatening to engulf the Baltic States. During the war, Britain had supplied vast amounts of material to help keep Russia in the war but, with the Bolsheviks' revolution in November 1917, Lenin negotiated a separate peace with Germany. In September 1918, the British decided to send a force to the ports of Murmansk and Archangel in Northern Russia to reclaim the supplies left at the docks. In doing so, she became embroiled in a short, fruitless and largely forgotten conflict which, none the less, saw five VC actions.

The cessation of hostilities did not bring peace to Europe but stirred up struggles for social change and national identity. The struggle for Russia between the Communists and the White Russians had encouraged the Baltic States of Estonia, Latvia, and Finland, all former imperial provinces, to declare their independence in 1917. Their new-found independence, however, depended on which side they supported during the long and bitter civil war.

Lloyd George's government was undecided as to how to react to events in Russia. Germany was still perceived as the main enemy and it therefore backed the side that would keep Russia fighting on the Eastern Front. There was little sympathy or support for the deposed Tsarist regime but the anti-Bolshevik White Russians seemed the lesser of the two evils and were given half-hearted support. The Allied decision to send forces to intervene in the Russian Civil War, just as the Great War was drawing to a close, was driven by two objectives. The first was to prevent the Allied war material stockpiles from falling into Bolshevik hands. Secondly, in Winston Churchill's words, 'to strangle at birth the Bolshevik State', by supporting the Pro-Tsarist White Army.

The campaign, coming so soon after the desperate fighting of the past four years, was deeply unpopular. This was voiced in the *Daily Express* of January 1919 which echoed Bismarck's earlier statement that 'the frozen plains of Eastern Europe are not worth the bones of a single grenadier'.

In the wake of the Russian Revolution of 1917, the British despatched a force known as the North Russia Expeditionary Force. Its purpose was to help train the anti-Bolshevik White Army and to protect the large quantities of military supplies that had been sent to Russia, most of which lay stored at the ports of Murmansk and Archangel. By March 1919, it was clear that the Red Army had the upper hand and that the White Russians were, at best, unreliable. It was decided to withdraw from the conflict.

A force, known as the North Russia Relief Force, had to be quickly recruited to cover the withdrawal and retrieve the military stores. Recruitment began amongst many of the troops awaiting demobilisation, including members of the Australian Imperial Force (AIF). Most were waiting for transport to return them to Australia, which would take until 1920 to complete. About 150 AIF men volunteered but had to be discharged in order to join the British Army for a period of one year.

The AIF undertook to repatriate them after they returned from Russia. The Australian volunteers served mainly in the specially-formed 45th and 46th service battalions of the Royal Fusiliers and the 201st Machine Gun Battalion. During August 1919, two Australian soldiers of the 45th Royal Fusiliers, Samuel Pearse and Arthur Sullivan, were awarded the Victoria Cross for gallantry in the fighting south of Murmansk.

As the increasingly bitter civil war grew in ferocity, the Bolsheviks began to show their true colours. Foreigners were regarded with great suspicion and were frequently attacked. Finally, the Foreign Office closed its embassy, thus silencing any reliable news from the Bolshevik centre of Petrograd (St Petersburg).

It was in this small area that a Royal Navy junior officer and his five companions conducted secret operations under the noses of the Bolsheviks and dealt a damaging blow to their navy for which he was awarded the Victoria Cross. Later, he was involved in the audacious attack on the Russian Fleet in Kronstadt Harbour, which netted the Royal Navy another two VCs.

AUGUSTUS WILLINGTON SHELTON AGAR VC (1890-1968)
Augustus Willington Shelton Agar was the youngest of thirteen children produced by Irish-born John Shelton Agar, a tea planter, and his Austrian wife, Emily. Augustus, or Gus as he was generally called, was born at Kandy, Ceylon on 4 January 1890. A combination of excessive childbirth and tropical climate carried away Emily soon after Gus was born.

Gus' father was left to bring up his large family as best he could. He did this by sending each child to Europe for their education – the boys to English boarding schools and the girls to either Vienna or Germany.

Gus' turn came when he became eight and he was sent with his brother John on the long voyage to England. After an idyllic childhood of being looked after by servants in a lush tropical paradise, young Gus came down to earth with a thud when he joined his first boarding school in East Anglia in mid-winter. Cold, miserable and inept at sports, Gus somehow adjusted to his new life. During holidays, he and other fellow boarders whose parents were abroad were sent to vicarages near the seaside. There he got his first taste of the sea and enjoyed sailing and the occasional trip in a fishing boat.

Having been sent to Framlingham Collage in Suffolk, soon after Gus learned of the death of his father from cholera while visiting China. Gus had not seen his father since he left Ceylon and it fell to his crippled eldest brother, Shelton, to take over the responsibility of raising Gus who became more like a father to him.

Without consultation with Gus, it was decided by Shelton and the Trustees that he should go into the Navy. He had no particular inclination to do so, but showed willing to please his beloved oldest brother. Leaving Framlingham College, Gus was sent to a 'crammer', Eastman's Naval Academy. At the age of thirteen, he passed his entrance exam and entered HMS *Britannia,* the last batch to go through this illustrious old training ship before all cadets moved onshore to Dartmouth College. There he found the family he had lacked and he revelled in Navy life.

In 1905 Gus passed his examinations and received his first sea-going appointment to HMS *Prince of Wales*. Between 1906 and 1910, Gus served on four ships. In 1911, he scraped through his exams and became a sub-lieutenant in the 'Small Ship Navy', which was regarded as rather unglamorous. Gus, however, enjoyed serving on a series of torpedo boats and destroyers, which were more independent and relaxed than the more rigid regimes of the capital ships. He was commissioned as a sub-lieutenant on the torpedo destroyer, *Ruby.*

In 1913, Gus attempted to become an aviator and joined the Central Flying School at Upavon. Rather surprisingly, the Admiralty had given their blessing to those officers who wished to learn to fly, with the proviso that 'there was no flying on Sundays'. On his way to attaining his pilot's license, Agar wrote off three aircraft without seriously injuring himself. On being transferred to Commander Samson's section, the new leader of the RNAS decided Agar should return to sea duties, as he was not keen to let him loose on his precious aircraft. Despite this rebuff, Agar remained a firm advocate of a naval air arm. This was more than could be said for the then Secretary of State for War who declared that the government 'do not consider that aeroplanes will be of any possible use for war purposes'.

Augustus Agar was promoted to lieutenant in 1912 and in September 1913, joined the old battleship HMS *Hibernia*. When war broke out in August 1914, *Hibernia* sailed north to join the Grand Fleet at Scapa Flow and the anticipated imminent battle with the German High Seas Fleet. To his disappointment, *Hibernia* was regarded as too venerable to be of much use in the expected clash and was sent to Rosita where Gus fretted with frustration.

Fortunately for him he was not destined, like so many of his contemporaries, to sit out the war at the huge anchorage of Scapa Flow waiting to do battle with the German High Seas Fleet. Instead, his ship was sent to the Dardanelles in the early summer of 1915. For two months, *Hibernia* cruised up and down the Turkish coast firing salvoes from her 6-inch guns. For the first time in his life he experienced incoming fire when a Turkish field gun sent a shell through one of the funnels. Apart from this, the thrill of being in a war zone wore thin as it became apparent that the campaign was a costly failure. Finally, a decision was made to pull out of Gallipoli and *Hibernia* helped to cover the evacuation from Anzac, Suvla and Cape Helles.

Returning to British waters, *Hibernia* was anchored off Sheerness to protect the Thames Estuary, a monotonous and thankless duty which Gus endured for a year until he joined yet another aging vessel. In early 1917, Agar was serving as second in command on the light cruiser *Iphigenia*, which was sent to the Northern Russian port of Murmansk to act as a floating base for the fleet of British minesweepers which were keeping the sea lanes clear of German mines. The British were sending large supplies of war material for the Russian Army, which was suffering from huge losses and shortage of armaments. Soon he witnessed the consequences of the Russian Revolution which had just broken out.

Adjacent to their anchorage was the five-funnelled Russian cruiser, *Askold*. Gus saw the spectacle of sailors mutinying against their officers, most of who were taken ashore and shot. The sailors stayed on board listening to revolutionary speeches and generally loafing about until all the food and drink was expended. The ship was then abandoned and within a couple of months *Askold* had become a rusting derelict.

The British had orders not to intervene as the new Social Revolutionary Government under Alexander Kerensky had promised to continue the war against Germany, which was all that concerned the Allies. The supply of materials from Britain continued even though they remained piled on the dockside where they were either looted or rotted. Finally, word came that the Kerensky Government had been ousted by the Bolsheviks and that another spate of civil war had broken out. The new regime wanted to gain complete control without the distraction of fighting the Germans and began to negotiate a separate peace. At the end of February 1918, *Iphigenia* sailed out of the White Sea, following a Canadian icebreaker through the thick ice, and headed for her home port of Chatham. There she would find one last glorious task waiting for her.

After a short leave, Agar was summoned to the Admiralty, where he found he had been selected to do a special course in mining, as he had had some experience during his service on *Iphigenia*. It turned out that this was just part of his appointment. A new and exciting warship was about to enter service and Gus's rather low-key war was about change. He was transferred to a new and secret naval establishment being constructed on Osea Island, which stands at the mouth of the Blackwater River in Essex.

This isolated position was chosen as the base for two special high-speed craft known as Coastal Motor Boats (CMBs), which had been developed by Sir John Thornycroft. They had a hydroplane–type hull, which skimmed over the water when driven at high speed (forty knots) and which gave them a shallow draft of about three feet. At these speeds, they could travel over minefields with impunity, unless they hit a mine that had come adrift. They could be armed with a torpedo, depth charges or used as mine layers and could reach enemy targets which conventional ships could not. There were two sizes; the smaller 40ft carried one torpedo, while the 55ft could take two.

It was planned that Agar would command a flotilla to carry and lay the top secret magnetic mines outside the enemy harbours in Belgium. A mining course at Portsmouth followed with a few weeks at Dunkirk, where he learned how to operate these revolutionary boats. He was at Dunkirk when the famous St George's Day Raid on Zeebrugge was ordered. The CMBs were selected to lay smoke screens outside the Zeebrugge mole to cover the escape of the crews of the blockships. One of the blockships that had been sunk at the entrance to the canal was Agar's old ship, *Iphigenia*. Although he did not take part in the actual raid, Agar viewed the attack from one of the spare boats.

By May, Agar joined the Osea Island base and he and his colleagues exercised amongst the Essex mudflats. Plans were then made for the CMBs to mount a raid on the High Seas Fleet, lying in anchor in the Tershilling Roads, but before that could be put in to operation, the Armistice was declared. Although Agar was happy to be attached to the CMBs, he felt somewhat deflated that he had not had a chance to taste the thrill of battle and there was a sense of anti-climax amongst the Osea Island men.

Mysterious Visitor

One mid-winter day, the Osea Island establishment received a visit from an unnamed be-monacled naval commander who walked with a pronounced limp. He was most interested in the performance and capabilities of the CMB and asked Agar several questions, but gave nothing away as to the purpose of his visit.

The civil war in Russia dragged in the reluctant Allies, who had the more pressing problems to deal with. Nonetheless, the British sent a large force to Murmansk and Archangel to secure the huge stores still piled on the dockside including a flotilla of CMBs.

In February 1919, Agar received a summons to report to the Naval Intelligence Division at the Admiralty. He was offered a special mission in the Baltic Sea, which he readily accepted. That established, he was then taken to Horse Guards and, after a walk through a maze of corridors, which culminated with a rooftop walk, he ended up in the office of Mansfield Cummings. On entering, he recognised the mystery naval officer, who had visited Osea Island a few weeks previously. This was the legendary 'C', who was the first Chief of the Secret Service from 1909 until his death in 1923. Seasickness had marred his naval career and he had spent a decade at Southampton developing boom defences and other special duties.

Secret Service Duties

Agar was asked to undertake an undercover operation for the Secret Service, which would be highly dangerous. 'C' explained that communications with their top man in Russia had broken down and it was essential to restore them. Agar was told only that the agent was an Englishman (Paul Dukes), who was known by the code 'ST25'. Agar's task was to go to the Baltic with two CMBs and ferry couriers to and from the coast near to Petrograd. It was further explained that Agar and his companions would no longer belong to the Navy but transferred to the Secret Service. They should adopt civilian identities and wear civilian clothes. The proviso was, with such clandestine operations, that the British Government would deny responsibility if they were captured.

Agar was told to handpick five unmarried men. When Agar returned to Osea Island, he selected Sub-Lieutenant J. Sindall, Midshipmen J. Hampsheir and R.N. Marshall. In addition, he took two mechanics, one for each boat; Beeley for *CMB 4* and Piper for *CMB 7*. Two days later, Agar was back in 'C's office and explaining his plan.

Finland

Agar had decided to make one of the innumerable inlets on the Finnish coast his base and to run the couriers across the thirty to fifty miles of the Gulf of Finland to the Estonian shore. From there the courier would have a long and difficult journey into Petrograd. This seemed the only logical route as the Bolsheviks had Petrograd defended by the Baltic Fleet base at Kronstadt, on the island of Kolin in the middle of the narrow approaches to the city. Extending either side of the island was a series of forts with submerged breakwaters between them.

'C' handed over £1,000, the names of local agents who would assist and a concession that Agar and his men could carry their naval uniforms, into which they could change if the worst came to the worst. Agar was also given the coded identification 'ST34'.

Agar and his companions travelled as a sales team for pleasure craft and the 40ft CMBs were painted white to look like power boats for the rich. After a search for a suitable base, Agar decided on the disused former Imperial Yacht Club at a place called Terrioki, a tiny sheltered cove close to the Russian border. He further saw that it would be possible to run the CMB between the chain of forts on the north side of the channel as the Bolsheviks would not be expecting anything so daring.

It now became important to report to Admiral Sir Walter Cowan. Cowan commanded the British blockading fleet in the Gulf of Finland which had been sent to counter any move by the Bolsheviks out of Kronstadt. Agar could not have wished for greater support and Cowan was to become a major player in the events that followed. Before he left the admiral, Agar asked for two torpedoes. London had told him specifically to avoid any hostile act, but Agar thought that they might come in useful in self-defence. He promised that if they did use them, then they would unfurl the White Ensign and don their uniforms.

It was now June and the period of 'white nights', when twilight extends into the night and early morning, left only a short period of darkness in which to evade the sentries in the forts. At last, the first courier, Peter Petrovitch, arrived and a local smuggler/pilot was paid to guide the CMB through the safest route. Leaving at 10.00 hours, Agar's CMB cast off and headed towards the forts some fifteen miles away. The pilot directed the boat between Forts 6 and 7, which were nearer the Finnish shore. Slowing down to eight knots, the craft slid silently past the sinister forts, 100 yards on either side. Soon they were clear and able to open up to full speed towards the distant lights of Petrograd.

In a quarter of an hour, they had reached the mouth of the Neva River and stopped the boat a few hundred yards from the shore. A small skiff was lowered into the water, a brief handshake then Peter disappeared into the darkness. Agar waited until Peter signalled with his torch that he had landed before making the return journey undetected.

A few nights later, Agar repeated the nerve-wracking journey and collected Peter and his precious despatches from ST25 (Paul Dukes) who had decided not to come out but to remain in Petrograd one more month until the 'white nights' were over. For the time being, the CMB courier service was on hold.

Agar learned that there was a counter-revolutionary plot in Petrograd designed to synchronise with a mutiny in the fortress of Krasnaya Gorka, which lay on the Estonian coast, about ten miles south from Kronstadt. On 10 June, the garrison revolted against its Communist commander and hoisted the White Russian flag.

This was a signal for the British flotilla to come to their assistance, but Admiral Cowan was unable to do this for two very good reasons. The Bolsheviks had laid a deep minefield that had made any approach to the eastern end of the Gulf of Finland almost impossible. He had, in fact already lost several ships to mines. Secondly, the Bolsheviks, with two battleships and heavy cruisers, considerably out-gunned the British, who had only light cruisers and destroyers.

Kronstadt

From a nearby church steeple, Agar watched through binoculars as two Bolshevik battleships, *Petropavlosk* and *Andrei Pervosvanni,* with their screen of destroyers, lay just out of range of the guns of Krasnaya Gorka and pounded the fortress with impunity. Unable to stomach this unequal contest any longer, Agar took the long and uncomfortable overland route to where the British fleet was anchored at Bjorki Sound.

Ushered into Cowan's cabin, Agar told him he was prepared to attack the Russian battleships that night, but needed to clear it with 'C'. The reply soon came back: 'Boats to be used for Intelligence purposes only unless specially directed by Flag Officer.' So, the buck was passed to the admiral, who said he could not direct Agar to attack but would give him his full support. That was good enough for Agar, who immediately returned to Terrioki to prepare his boats and crews for an audacious attack.

Sindall and Agar worked out their tactics and decided to concentrate on just one target as it would be better to fire two torpedoes into one ship with a greater chance of sinking her rather than chancing each torpedo against a separate target. Leaving at about midnight, the two craft sped across the fifteen or so miles with ensigns flying and the crews wearing leather coats and uniform caps.

All went well for the first half an hour, until Sindall's boat hit an underwater obstruction, which broke the propeller shaft. There was nothing left to do but abort the attack and Agar towed the damaged CMB back to Terrioki. Sindall's boat would be out of action for at least a fortnight. Agar had to decide whether to risk the remaining boat on a solo attack which would put at risk bringing out ST25 or leave the Russians free to take Krasnaya Gorka. Agar decided that the latter was the most pressing and prepared to attack the following night.

From his vantage point on the church steeple, Agar saw that the two battleships were returning to Konstadt and were replaced by the heavy cruiser *Oleg*. It later transpired that the battleships had run out of ammunition. Towards the late afternoon, *Oleg* recommenced the bombardment of the fortress.

Agar later wrote of that evening's events: 'As on the previous evening, Hampsheir, Beeley and I waited in our CMB in the shelter of the harbour until just before midnight, when, once more, we set out and headed for the

Tolbuhin lighthouse. This time we were alone and the object of our attack was the cruiser *Oleg*. Arriving off the lighthouse, we could clearly see the destroyer screen ahead of us. It was necessary to pass through it in order to reach a position from which we could fire our torpedo at the cruiser. I slowed down to minimise the risk of noise and spray which, with a strong wind dead ahead of us and a high speed, was being thrown up over our heads. We were now creeping through the destroyers in precisely the same way as we crept through the forts on our way the Petrograd, and all seemed to be going well, when I suddenly felt the whole boat quiver and shake. I thought we had hit something and stopped. Hampsheir appeared from below the hatch with an agonised look on his face. "The charge has fired, sir", he said.

'I must explain here that we had an ingenious device for firing the torpedo by ejecting it from the stern with a hydraulic rammer. The impulse by means of which this rammer was propelled was supplied by firing a small cordite cartridge in a cylinder, which created a pressure against the head of the rammer. Somehow or other, in loading the cartridge, Hampsheir had accidentally fired it, and it was this that caused the shock we had felt.

'Fortunately, in addition to these mechanical arrangements, there was also fitted in the boat two stout iron stops operated by a lever near the steering wheel, which held the torpedo in the boat, irrespective of the rammer, provided the stops were down. Fortunately, I placed this lever in the "down" position so that when the cartridge prematurely fired, the only result was a severe concussion to the hull of the boat and a tremendous shock to Hampsheir, who must have injured his hand.'

The concussion was severe enough to shatter the unfortunate Hampsheir's nerves for he spent many weeks in a sanatorium and invalided home.

'I ordered Beeley to help him extract the fired cartridge and put in another one – a difficult operation with the boat rolling in the sea. It was dark and their hands were cold. I waited for what seemed an interminable time, although it must have been only ten or fifteen minutes. All though this time of intolerable suspense my eyes were on the destroyers on either side of us, now distant only two to three hundred yards. Ahead, I could dimly see the silhouette of our target, the cruiser Oleg, which I was about to attack.

'We might at any moment be seen, as it was then just before one o'clock in the morning and the first streaks of early dawn were due to appear. Beeley remained wonderfully calm. There was nothing to be said. It was a time for deeds, not words. At last, Hampsheir popped up from the hatch. "It's all right, sir, we have reloaded."

'With a sigh of relief, I slipped the clutch. Throwing all caution to the winds, I put on full speed and headed straight for the Oleg, which was now clearly visible, and in a few moments, we were nearly on top of her. I fired my torpedo less than five hundred yards away, just as the first shot from her guns was fired at us in return. Then I quickly put the helm over, turning a complete circle. And, with the sea now following us, headed back westward towards the same direction from which we had approached.

'We looked back to see if our torpedo had hit, and saw a large flash abreast of the cruiser's foremost funnel, followed almost immediately by a huge column of black smoke reaching up to the top of her mast. The torpedo had found its mark.

'We tried to give three cheers, but could scarcely hear ourselves for the din of the engines. Yet we could hear the whistle of shells overhead, telling us that both the destroyers and forts were firing at us, but in the uncertain light just before early dawn, speed made us a very difficult target to hit. We carried on in the direction of Biorko Sound (where the British Fleet was based) as I wanted the forts to think that was where we had come from instead of Terrioki, and we did not turn round to the northward until we were out of sight of them.'

Two days later, Agar managed to arrange for a Finnish aircraft to fly him over the spot where he had fired his torpedo. Descending to two thousand feet, he could hardly suppress his feelings when he saw quite clearly, the hulk of *Oleg* lying on her side like a large dead whale on the bottom of the sea. His elation turned to dismay as the aircraft then flew over the fortress of Krasnaya Gorka and saw, instead of the White Russian flag, the red banner of the victorious Communists fluttering from the battlements. The loss of *Oleg*, however, caused much consternation amongst the Bolsheviks and there was a real fear that the sailors at Kronstadt would turn against their Communist Commissars.

After the sinking of *Oleg*, there was a suspension of operations. Agar and his men made use of this lull to service their craft at Helsingfors and the British Navy base at Biorko Sound. Admiral Cowan, who was fulsome in his praise for Agar's exploit, called the young lieutenant to discuss a plan he was hatching. Buoyed by the success of Agar's solo attack, Cowan proposed that the idea of bringing a flotilla of CMBs from the UK for a full-scale attack on the Russian fleet in Kronstadt harbour.

Sporadic raids by one or two boats were not good enough. Something on a larger scale was wanted if the Bolshevik fleet was to be put out of action and it had to be something totally unexpected. He had as his model the attack on Zeebrugge, which had shown the value of surprise. The Admiralty gave approval to the plan and set about supplying Cowan's requirements, which would take until August to arrive.

Augustus Agar now had both of his CMBs ready for further courier runs and called on the Admiral to let him know that he was going to pick up agent ST25 and Gefter on the night of 8 August. Cowan responded by informing the young lieutenant that he had submitted his recommendation for the Victoria Cross for the sinking of *Oleg*.

Admiral Cowan's planned raid on the Russian Fleet at Kronstadt was not welcomed by MI6. Major Scales, the chief of northern Europe operations had been critical of Gus Agar's exploit in sinking *Oleg*, and felt that the courier-running operation was being compromised. Nevertheless, the Admiralty had given their full support to the attack and supplied Cowan with all that he needed to carry it out.

The plan was to approach the harbour through the chain of forts to the north of Konin Island, through which Agar and his team had delivered the couriers. The flotilla would pass round the south of the island and enter the harbour from the Petrograd direction. The approach was to be further disguised by a bombing raid by the RAF.

Leading the raid was Commander Claude Congreve Dobson who wrote: 'I left HMS *Vindictive* with eight CMBs and proceeded to a rendezvous off Inonemi Point. Owing to the darkness it was impossible to see how many boats were keeping in company and all signalling was strictly forbidden. I arrived at Inonemi Point ten minutes before the appointed time of leaving, and stopped. The remainder of the flotilla joined up about midnight. I then proceeded towards the North Channel at nineteen knots, Lieutenant Agar proceeding independently according to plan. I passed to southward of Fort No.4 and then between forts No.8 and 10. By this time I was a little late on programme time and the air raid had commenced, so I should have liked to have increased speed, but the difficulties of navigation were so great that I had to reduce rather than increase.

'No signs of Lieutenant Agar and *CMB 24* and I could only see two boats following me, Nos.79 and 88. These two boats had kept perfect station the whole time. However, as the air attack was in full swing, I determined to press on with the boats I had, rather than wait on the off chance of being able to pick up stragglers.

'I found the Petrograd Canal and proceeded up it. Lieutenant Bremner on 79 taking station ahead of me, as arranged. We found a flotilla leader guarding the entrance to the Middle Harbour. But no one on deck; No.79 left her on the starboard hand and turned and entered the basin causing me to stop to avoid confusion at the entrance. 70 carried out his orders and torpedoed the submarine depot ship. I then entered the basin and Lieutenant McBean succeeded in hitting the Pervozanni with two torpedoes. I then saw No.88, who had followed me into the basin, put one torpedo in the Andrei Pervosanni and one into the Petropaylova. Machine gun and rifle fire being very hot by this time; all three boats started to retire and appeared all right.

'Lieutenant Gordon Steele described what happened in No.88, commanded by Captain Dayrell-Reed ... Nothing seemed to happen, however, and we arrived at the dock entrance without a shot being fired at us. We stopped engines to give the two boats ahead of us (Bremner and MacBean) time to get in.

'Suddenly a huge bump and a dull thud were felt – I knew a ship had been torpedoed. The next instant a high column of water could be seen rising from the side of the cruiser with three funnels and two masts. She was quite close to us.

'Bremner (No.1) had found his target and the Pamiet Azova listed rapidly on her side. After this there was a silence and still no sign of life. The air bombardment had obviously driven everybody underground. We entered the harbour. Then fire opened upon us from the direction of the dry dock, and afterwards from other sides. We followed behind Dobson, heading for the corner where our objectives, the battleships, were berthed.

'Almost simultaneously we received bursts of fire in the boat from the batteries and splashes now appeared on both sides. Morely and I instinctively ducked for a moment as the bullets whistled past; when I looked up, I could see splashes everywhere in the basin. I turned round and was just about to remark to Dayrell-Reed, "Where are you heading?" (as we were making straight for a hospital ship), when I noticed that, although still standing up and holding the wheel, his head was resting on the wooden conning tower top in front of him.

'I lowered him into the cockpit, at the same time I put the wheel hard over and righted the boat on her proper course. We were now quite close to the battleship Andrei Perosvanni. I must fire now or never. In a few seconds, it would be too late. Throttling back the engines as far as possible I fired both torpedoes at her after which I stopped one engine to help turn the boat quickly.

'Almost as I did this, we saw two columns of water rise up from the side of the battleship and heard two crashes. I knew they must have been Dobson's torpedoes which had found their target. We now headed for our "waiting billet", which was close to the hospital ship but, while turning, there was another terrific explosion nearby. We received a great shock and douche of water. Looking over my shoulder, I realised the cause of it was one of our torpedoes exploding on the side of the battleship. We were so close to her that a shower of picric powder from the warhead of our torpedo was thrown over the stern of the boat, staining us a yellow colour which we had some difficulty removing afterwards, when we reached Biorko.'

With the Bolshevik defences now fully alert, Dobson gathered the surviving CMBs and, with the crippled Howard in tow, managed to return to Biorko. Agar was the last to leave and headed back to Terrioki just as dawn broke. Photographic reconnaissance undertaken the next day revealed the success of the raid. Both battleships lay on their side and *Pamiat Azova* had heeled over resting on the bottom. *Rurik* and the dry dock had escaped damage, as did *Gavriel,* which had survived two torpedo attacks. Retribution followed, however, when she was sunk by a mine laid in the main Petrograd Channel by Agar.

Both Commander Dobson and Lieutenant Steele were gazetted for the Victoria Cross on 11 November 1919. Gus Agar had the DSO added to his VC and all the rest of the men and officers received decorations for this daring raid.

The MI6 agent, Paul Dukes, who after a circuitous and dangerous route managed to reach safety, later recalled: 'At King's Cross, representatives of the Foreign Office, the Admiralty, the War Office and the Secret Service met me on the platform. Once more I was driven to Whitehall and whisked up to the roof-labyrinth into the presence of "the Chief". The grand old man gave me a warm welcome, "The King wishes to see you at once", he said, "he wants to hear your story from you personally".

'One day, soon after, when I was leaving the Chief's office, I met a young naval officer on the threshold. To judge by his looks, he was about twenty-five years of age, of medium height, very handsome, with wavy hair, and a frank and most engaging smile. For a moment neither of us spoke.

'"Hullo". He said finally, "are you Dukes?"

'"Yes. Agar?"

"'Yes."

'Thus we met – instead of at midnight one mile south of the Elagin lightship … Failing the Elagin lightship, there was only one fitting place for us to meet – in our Chief's office, as we did. And the Chief, standing by, leaning on his stick, smiled happily.'

Entering the King's private study, Gus was invited to sit and relate the whole story. The King mentioned that Paul Dukes, too, deserved the Victoria Cross as well as Agar but the conditions of the award precluded him from receiving it. Instead, Dukes received a knighthood on 1 January 1920, the only time that an agent received one for a specific operation.

At length, the King presented Agar with his Cross, taking care to look on the back to make sure that the date was correctly inscribed on it. He also presented him with the DSO for his part in the Kronstadt raid. That evening, 'C' gave a small dinner party at the Savoy Hotel, in honour of his two 'top mates', Agar and Dukes.

Promoted on 30 June 1920, Lieutenant Commander Augustus Agar VC, DSO, married a month later. He had met the twenty-year-old Mary Francis Petre, Baroness Furnivall, when he attended a series of power boat races at Monte Carlo. Within months they were married at Westminster Cathedral in one of the great Society weddings of the year. Sadly, they were not suited to each other and the marriage ended in 1932.

In time the CMB squadron was disbanded and Gus was appointed to the Royal Yacht *Victoria and Albert*, something the King had promised during their private meeting. The years between the wars were filled with much foreign travel and another marriage, this time to Ina Hirst in Bermuda during February 1932. His new life was almost cut short six months later when a small seaplane in which he was a passenger crashed during a squall. Both the pilot and other passenger were killed, while Gus suffered serious injuries and was not expected to recover. When he was well enough, he attended a Senior Officer's course at Greenwich and was promoted to captain in December 1933.

In 1937 he was given command of the cruiser *Emerald* and then, in late 1941, *Dorsetshire,* famous for its part in the sinking of the *Bismarck.* Within a few months, Agar's new command was involved in the sinking of the German commerce raider *Python* in the South Atlantic. From there, *Dorsetshire* was sent to escort a convoy of reinforcements bound for Singapore. Unfortunately, most of these troops were destined to become prisoners of the Japanese, who soon swept aside the mixed British, Indian and Australian army in Malaya before capturing Singapore. *Dorsetshire* became involved in evacuating personnel from the island and escorted the last convoy to leave before the surrender on 15 February 1942.

The Royal Navy pulled its warships back to Ceylon, where they were organised into the Eastern Fleet. It was expected that the Japanese would target the ports of Colombo and Trincomalee so, when a reconnaissance aircraft reported that a Japanese fleet was heading west from the Strait of Malacca, *Dorsetshire* and *Cornwall* were sent to join the aircraft carriers *Formidable* and *Indomitable* to counter the Japanese.

Unfortunately, on Easter Saturday they were spotted by a Japanese reconnaissance 'plane and soon the two ships were attacked by a strong force of dive-bombers. The anti-aircraft guns were too light and too few to ward off the attack; soon *Dorsetshire* was crippled by a succession of hits. Within six minutes of the first bomb hitting, she sank, as did *Cornwall.*

Captain Agar had been hurled into the sea as the ship heeled over and he was dragged down with the suction. He managed to resurface, but one of his lungs had been badly damaged. Rescuers dragged him onto one of the two whalers and he organised the gathering in of all the survivors until they formed a large circle. He then set as many of the stronger survivors as possible to swim around the circle to frighten the gathering sharks away. In this way, they survived the night and most of the following day until they were spotted by an RAF aircraft, which guided the cruiser *Enterprise* and two destroyers to their rescue. Within a short time 1,122 survivors from *Dorsetshire* and *Cornwall* were taken on board the three ships, but 442 officers and men had lost their lives in the brief but deadly air attack.

Gus avoided a medical examination and was on active service for a further two years before his collapsed lung caused him to be invalided out of the Navy. He finished his career as Commodore-President of the Royal Naval College at Greenwich. Gus then retired to Alton in Hampshire and became a strawberry farmer and even wrote a book on the subject. In 1960, there was a touching compliment paid to him. For years, his old *CMB 4* had languished out of sight on the banks of the Thames at Molesey until it was rescued and transported to the Thorneycroft Boatyard at Southampton to be restored. It was arranged that the transport would divert past Agar's home. As his old boat, in which he had such adventurous times, passed by, Gus stood to attention at the roadside and saluted.

On 30 December 1968, Augustus Agar died at his home, Anstey Park House, aged seventy-eight. He is buried with his wife in Alton Cemetery (Section R, Grave 238). Unique amongst naval VCs, Agar's vessel, *CMB 4*, in which he performed his VC exploit, is on display at the Imperial War Museum, Duxford.

Chapter 48

The Arab Revolt – Iraq, 1920

Number of VCs awarded	1
Number of VCs awarded to officers	1
Total awarded to British Army	1

Origins of the War

After the First World War, the newly-formed League of Nations created 'mandates' of the territories formally controlled by the defeated Central Powers. At the San Remo Conference in April 1920, the mandates were shared between the victors; Great Britain was awarded Mesopotamia and Palestine, while France was granted Syria. The final carving up of the Ottoman Empire has left a bloody legacy, with Iraq, formally Mesopotamia, Palestine and Syria involved in protracted civil unrest which still involves the victorious Europeans.

The theory behind the mandate policy was that the territories would eventually become independent under the guidance of Britain and France. The populations of these former Ottoman provinces saw things differently and feared that there had been a swop from one imperial power to another. The people of Mesopotamia particularly feared that they would become part of the British Empire. The British writer, archaeologist and political officer, Gertrude Bell, drew up the borders of present day Iraq, which combined the provinces of Basra, Mosul and Baghdad, a potent mix of different religious beliefs.

Although she stated to an Arab nationalist leader that complete independence was what the British ultimately wished to give, he replied that 'complete independence is never given; it is always taken'. The British added to the discontent by supporting a new administration and installed the friendly Sunni, Faysal ibn Husayn, as the King of Iraq. This led to a prominent Shia *mujahid* issuing a *fatwa* calling for mass meetings and demonstrations to oppose British rule.

In late June 1920, an armed revolt broke out and soon gained momentum. There was unprecedented co-operation between Sunni and Shia Muslims, something that did not last long. The British garrisons in the mid-Euphrates region were lightly held and soon the armed rebels controlled this area, encouraging the revolt to spread. In response, the British War Secretary, Winston Churchill, authorised immediate reinforcements and the deployment of two RAF squadrons. The use of the latter played a great role in successfully stifling the revolt which ended in October 1920. The casualty list of this short-lived revolt was high; between 6,000 and 10,000 Iraqis killed and over 2,000 British and Indian troops killed or wounded. There was one Victoria Cross awarded early on in the uprising to an exceptionally brave officer who had an outstanding record in the Great War.

GEORGE STUART HENDERSON VC (1893-1920)

George Stuart Henderson was born at East Gordon Farm, near Gordon, Berwickshire on 5 December 1893 to Robert Henderson, a farmer and auctioneer, and his wife, Mary (née Ross). At the age of ten, he was sent as a boarder to Rossall School, Fleetwood, Lancashire, and in 1912, entered the Royal Military College Sandhurst.

In January 1914, having passed out fifty-first amongst over 200 cadets, Henderson was commissioned into the 1st Battalion, Manchester Regiment, and posted to the Punjab. Henderson was in India for just six months before the First World War started on 4 August. The regiment, which made up part of the Lahore Division, was shipped to France and went into the line at Ypres. On 9 November, Henderson was promoted to lieutenant and six days later was wounded in the arm. Evacuated to Britain, Henderson recovered in six weeks and returned to the front where he received his first award, a Mention in Despatches.

During the Second Battle of Ypres in April 1915, George Henderson was awarded the Military Cross, the citation of which appeared in *The London Gazette* on 3 July 1915: 'Near Ypres on the 26th April 1915 after his company-commander had been wounded, he led his company up to within seventy yards of the enemy's trenches with great gallantry and determination, and held on through several hours of daylight, and finally established himself there. Throughout the operations he set a fine example, after most of the senior officers had become casualties.' Henderson was also promoted to temporary captain.

In November 1915, the 1st Manchesters left the Western Front for Mesopotamia and arrived in Basra on 8 January 1916. The Manchesters were still the only British battalion in the 8th Indian Brigade of the 3rd Lahore Division and travelled with their Indian comrades to fight against the Turkish Army. The Indian regiments had not fared well on the Western Front and had suffered badly from the climate. They were rushed to Mesopotamia to relieve the 6th Indian Division besieged at Kut-el-Amara.

Double DSO

On 8 March 1916, the Kut Relief Force attempted to capture the Dujeilah Redoubt, an important defensive position blocking the way to the besieged town. The twenty-three-year-old George Henderson added to his growing list of awards when he was awarded the Distinguished Service Order. His citation, dated 31 May 1916, read: 'On entering the (Dujeilah) Redoubt he organised and led bombing parties which cleared out the enemy, of whom he personally shot five. He subsequently covered our withdrawal and was one of the last to leave the Redoubt.'

There was some suggestion that he was originally recommended for the Victoria Cross. Sadly, the attack proved to be a failure and it was virtually the last throw of the dice to relieve Kut, which fell on 29 April 1916.

In January 1917, the British began extended operations which spelt the end of Turkish occupation of Mesopotamia. The 1st Manchesters attacked on a 200-yard front at the critical battle of the Khadairi Bend on the Tigris River. Once the soldiers entered the Turkish trenches they were able to push forward until they were confronted with an overwhelming force that counter-attacked. As the company commanders were either killed or wounded, it was left to Captain Henderson to steady the troops and withdraw them to safety. Ultimately, the British succeeded in putting the Turks to flight which turned out to be the turning point in the campaign. For his coolness in a potentially disastrous situation, Henderson was awarded a clasp to his DSO.

On 12 January 1918, George Henderson left the Manchesters, having volunteered for a secret composite force made up of officers and NCOs for special duties. It was named the 'Dunsterforce' after its commanding officer, Major General L.C. Dunsterville, who was the inspiration for Rudyard Kipling's adventure story *Stalky and Co*. The role of this force was to organise and lead any elements of the Russian Army of the Caucasus or of the civilian population of Trans-Caucasia who were ready to continue resistance to the Turks in the mountainous country to the south and west of the Caspian Sea. In the event, it was not a glorious campaign for it was carried out during a severe famine bedevilled by civilian corruption and incompetence.

With the signing of the Armistice in November 1918, George Henderson returned to the UK and a brief reunion with his family before joining his regiment in Tipperary. His time in this troubled island was brief for he was ordered to return to Mesopotamia, or Iraq as it came to be named after the defeat of the Ottoman Empire. A serious Arab insurrection had broken out and threatened the small force left behind after the war. Henderson must have wished he had seen the last of this flat, poverty-stricken land but found he was to retrace the routes the Manchesters took in the recent war. Arriving in Basra on 13 March 1920, Henderson was in command of 'D' Company made up largely of untried recruits.

On 21 July, the Manchesters arrived at Hillah on the Euphrates, about sixty miles from Baghdad. The plan was to send a relief column to Kufa about twenty-five miles south-west of Hillah, where the small garrison was holding out against a much larger force of insurgents. In fact, the whole area south of Hillah was full of unreliable tribesmen. With water in short supply, the column made first camp for the night in a poor condition, suffering from the heat and lack of water. The next day they marched about two miles to the Rustumiyah Canal, making camp at 12.45 hours and finding drinkable water. The medical officer advised that the men needed to rest for twenty-four hours due to heat exhaustion and dehydration.

VC Action

The column was now about fourteen miles from its base at Hillah; too far to reach in a hurry and too weak to defend itself. In the early evening of the 24th heavy firing was heard to the south and in the gloom it could be seen that thousands of tribesmen had approached without being spotted and encircled the camp. After being pinned down for a few hours, the decision was taken to fight their way out and return to Hillah. It was during this chaotic night-time retreat that George Henderson earned his Victoria Cross. His citation reads:

'On the evening of 24th July 1920, when about fifteen miles from Hillah the company under his command was ordered to retire. After proceeding about 500 yards, a large party of Arabs suddenly opened fire from the flank causing the company to split up and waver. Regardless of all danger, Captain Henderson at once reorganised the company, led them gallantly to the attack, and drove off the enemy.

'On two further occasions this officer led his men to charge the Arabs with the bayonet and forced them to retire. At one time, when the situation was extremely critical, and the troops and transport were getting out of hand, Capt. Henderson, by sheer pluck and coolness, steadied his command, prevented the company from being cut up, and saved the situation.'

Quartermaster Sergeant A. Smith was with Henderson when he was killed. During a charge against the enemy firing from behind an embankment, they surprised the Arabs who tried to scramble away. Henderson ordered his men to fire down on them until their magazines were empty. As they re-joined the column, Henderson was shot in the leg but hobbled on. Another burst of firing followed and Henderson fell to the ground. Smith could see that the wound was fatal but still Henderson issued orders and reached for his revolver, firing off a couple of shots. His final words were: 'I'm done now; don't let them beat you.'

The defeated Manchester column reached Hillah the following morning. It had taken a bad beating, losing 179 killed and sixty wounded. Captain George Henderson was posthumously recommended for the Victoria Cross. His sister, Jess, received it from the King on 8 March 1921. His exceptional medal group is on display in the Manchester Regiment Museum.

Chapter 49

North-West Frontier, 1915–1936

Number of VCs awarded	6
Number of VCs awarded to officers	4
Number of VCs awarded to other ranks	2
Total awarded to British Army	1
Total awarded to British Indian Army	5

Origins of the War

Field Marshal Lord Roberts VC once accurately described the troublesome North-West Frontier as 'the robber-haunted No-man's Land which lies on our immediate frontier'.

The great uprising in 1897/8 did not neatly end with the disbanding of the various British-led field forces. Low-key troubles were constantly flaring up and dealt with by troops stationed locally. By the early twentieth century the British were satisfied to maintain a fragile state of equilibrium on the Frontier which they had established covering some 300 miles in length and 100 miles in depth. They had learned something of the nature of the Pathans and felt disinclined to impose full imperial rule in this region; instead the Frontier served as a useful buffer between British India and Afghanistan. The Amir of Afghanistan had indicated that he would do nothing to cause trouble on the Frontier while Britain was occupied with the war in Europe.

In early 1915, Turkey's decision to fight on the side of Germany against Britain inevitably led to trouble with the Muslim Frontier tribes, many of whom saw the Sultan of Turkey, Abdul Hamid, as 'Khalifa' (successor to Muhamed). The result was a series of raids by tribesmen across the Durand line into British India with some connivance on the part of the Afghan army.

It was an inhospitable mountainous area of extreme temperatures, savage customs and dangerous people, part of whose creed was absolute loyalty to those they had sworn to protect, vengeance against those who had 'dishonoured' them and a love of raiding, fighting and looting. The role of the Frontier Force was to maintain a military presence within the Frontier region to control the excesses of the tribes, such as the Mahsuds and Wazirs; to punish any tribesmen who raided across the official line into what constituted British India (where the rule of law was strictly imposed) and to keep control of the roads leading across the border. Officers in the Frontier Force regiments had to be men of character and courage. The very best of these were taken from their parent regiments and attached to the Frontier Scouts.

The Scouts was a militia corps composed of Frontier tribesmen led by young British officers and experienced Indian officers. The idea was to take the tribesmen's knowledge of the Frontier and their fighting skills and to use them to good effect to control their peers; the principle being that of poachers turned gamekeepers. The Scouts was not in fact part of the Indian Army but came under the control of the political arm of the British administration in India. There were close to 2,000 men in each Militia Corps, with only six British officers: a commandant, an adjutant/quartermaster (who also commanded the mounted infantry of approximately 150 sowars) and four 'wing' officers.

British officers attached to the Frontier Scouts had to be tough. They had to be able to command the respect of tribesmen who from their birth had been imbued with a warrior cult which mixed honour with great savagery and ruthlessness.

They were volunteers for what was likely to be an exciting life, albeit, a dangerous one.

One such officer was Eustace Jotham, who was awarded his Victoria Cross in 1915. Most VC histories and lists include him as a Great War recipient, presumably because of the date, but his exploit was a typical Frontier action and only peripherally involving the Central Powers.

EUSTACE JOTHAM VC (1883-1915)

Eustace Jotham was born in Kidderminster, Worcestershire, on 28 November 1883. His father, Frederick Charles, was a wine merchant who had married into the Harvey family of Bristol Cream fame. Eustace was educated firstly at Lucton School, Hertfordshire and, latterly, Bromsgrove School. He entered the Royal Military College Sandhurst in 1902 and was commissioned into North Staffordshire Regiment in April 1903.

Prospective officers for the Indian Army had first to go to a British regiment and spend a year 'acclimatising' with them in India. If they showed an aptitude to learning the local language and had the right attitude towards their men, they could transfer to the Indian Army. The level of competence required of officers in the Indian Army was relatively high because there were fewer British officers in each battalion and the men required leaders of strength and tact. Jotham was transferred to the 2nd Battalion North Staffordshire Regiment prior to its embarkation for India in

October 1903. He was then duly transferred to the 102nd King Edward's Own Grenadiers in 1905.

By 1908 Jotham's career had progressed further; he had transferred to the 51st Sikhs, a regiment of the Frontier Force, and served on the North-West Frontier. In 1911, Jotham was attached to the North Waziristan Militia (NWM) and he was promoted captain in April 1912; his role was that of adjutant and quartermaster. The NWM was based at Miranshah, a bleak, flea-ridden place, too hot in the summer and freezing cold in the winter. The Militia patrolled a large area of rocky, mountainous land and manned eighteen posts along the sixty-mile-long east-west road from Bannu to Datta.

In 1913 Jotham visited home on leave for the first time in ten years. Returning from a fishing trip to Scotland, his train was involved in a night-time collision at Ais Gill, Westmoreland, when it was hit in the rear by the Edinburgh express, resulting in several deaths. In addition to the derailment of the rearmost carriages, fire broke out and those trapped and injured were in danger of being burnt alive. Jotham, who was uninjured, set about rescuing the passengers trapped in the derailed carriages.

His actions were noted by a fellow passenger, Major Walter St. Hill, an officer of the Royal Fusiliers, who reported Jotham's conduct to the War Office: 'I noticed a man working with ceaseless energy and pluck and always in the right directions. He was on top of the compartment, already a mass of flames, handing out the poor people as we could extricate them. All the while talking to them as if nothing was at stake and cheering them with kind words. He actually, to my certain knowledge, handed out four himself, his hair singed, his coat and cap on fire, working quite unconcernedly to the last.'

In September 1913, Jotham returned to his duties in India and one year later was seemingly in the wrong place for a career officer when war broke out in Europe. He wrote to a friend that it was hard 'to be shut up in a mud built, sun-baked fort when I longed to be in France'. It would have been even more galling for Jotham to know that his parent regiment, the 51st Sikhs, had been sent for war service overseas, but Jotham could not be spared from the Frontier.

Although Habibulla, the Amir of Afghanistan, had sought to control his own army in the hopes of obtaining total independence from Britain, there were elements that joined forces with the turbulent tribesmen who raided across the Durand line into British India.

In November 1914, Jotham was granted the chance to experience the action for which he craved. A raiding party consisting of several thousand Mahsud and Wazir tribesmen, with soldiers of the Afghan army, attacked the *serai* at Miranshah. This was a walled enclosure about 300 yards long by 200 yards wide with walls of mud about twenty feet high and the interior divided so that bazaars could be held. The NWM received advanced warning and withdrew to their fort which was about 600 yards away. A determined group of twenty-three civilian *chewkidars* (watchmen) refused to leave the *serai* and grimly held out in one of the watchtowers against the raiders. They fought until the arrival of Jotham's Militia, who dug their way through the walls of one of the towers to rescue them. Jotham and his men then set about the raiders; at one point he led a bayonet charge, to disperse them.

Following an uneasy Christmas, on the evening of 6 January reports were received that a large tribal army was approaching the post at Boya. A small force of thirty-seven mounted infantry was dispatched from Miranshah to scout ahead, and a force of 300 infantry was ordered to follow. Captain Clement Smith was placed in command of the scouting party and was accompanied by Lieutenant Prendergast and Captain Jotham. It was in the action which followed that Jotham was to gain his Victoria Cross.

VC Action

By the morning of 7 January 1915, Clement Smith's party reached Boya and found that the Khostwals had advanced to the post at Spina Khaisora about ten miles distant. The Khostwals were tribesmen from the Khost region on the Afghan side of the border and had been swayed by the fanatical teaching of their mullahs to cross the frontier and attack the post at Spina Khaisora. As the NWM approached the post, it was seen to be surrounded by an estimated 7,000 to 10,000 belligerent tribesmen. The Scouts dismounted from their horses and climbed the steep side of the valley leading to the post, to observe precisely what was taking place. It was clear that the post was still being held by the Militia garrison, consisting of some sixty men. Had the tribesmen taken the fort and captured the soldiers their fate would have been cruel and unmerciful. Therefore, the men inside were fighting with a courage borne of desperation.

It was with this in mind that the advance force led by Clement Smith opened fire. The hope was to distract the tribesmen from their attempts to take the post and then to force their way in to help the defenders until relieved. The small command opened fire on the Khostwal tribesmen, among whom were a number soldiers of the Afghan army.

After harrying the tribesmen with their Lee Enfields for some time, the Scouts decided to advance up the valley to the post. This they managed to do under the leadership of Jotham, taking up a second position on the valley side after forcing their way through some determined resistance. They were now about 800 yards from the post and attempted a third dash forward up a side *nullah* which was a cul-de-sac. As they rode to the end of this deep *nullah*, they realised they were in danger of being trapped. Tribesmen immediately surged down the sides of the valley, firing at close range, some from as close at fifty yards.

It was a desperate situation with forty men being attacked by 1,500 and the only escape was to turn and ride back. After a brief consultation between the officers, three parties were formed, each containing a third of the men.

First to leave were thirteen sowars led by Captain Clement Smith; second to make its escape was Prendergast's party, and last to leave was Jotham and his group. One can imagine the fear the men in Jotham's party must have felt as they attempted to mount their horses, which were spooked and skittish as bullets flew around them, and the terror at being caught alive by the Afghans.

The clearest account of what happened next comes from Lieutenant Prendergast in a letter to Jotham's father: 'As I left the *nullah* I turned and saw your son seated on his pony saying, "Are you all ready – gallop." At this time we must have been under fire from about 1500 rifles, scores of whom were running up to within 50 yards. I myself knew nothing further, as my pony was shot and I had to run, very shortly after starting. What I do know is that when I started, your son and his party were mounted and ready to leave. The rest of the story comes from two men who escaped from his party and left after I did.

'It appears that a sowar [Lance Duffadar Mersal] at the last moment had his own horse hit or frightened, in any case it broke from him and your son stopped, pulled him up behind and started off. The delay, however, in helping his comrade, and the extra weight on his pony, allowed the enemy to approach within a matter of a few yards, and this glorious attempt to help another man when in fearful danger and in a perfect hail of bullets, cost your son his life.

'I got back later with reinforcements and found that he and the man he had stopped for managed to get a hundred yards or more down the *nullah*, and had evidently put up a magnificent fight against quite impossible odds.'

'It seems possible that Jotham could have escaped but when he saw one of his men was unhorsed he stopped to save him. This was done instantly and without heeding the danger to himself; such was his loyalty to those under his command.'

In *The Frontier Scouts*, Charles Chevenix Trench states that Jotham was armed only with a sword, providing a most heroic picture of a British officer, sword in hand, going to the aid of his trooper. Sir George Roos-Keppel, Chief Commissioner North-West Frontier Province, later informed Jotham's father that before his death his son had 'personally accounted for seven of the enemy', Roos-Keppel's official correspondence reveals the grisly information which was kept from Jotham's father: 'the bodies were indescribably mutilated'.

Jotham's remains were buried at Miranshah and the news of his death was received in Kidderminster on the 11 January. The award of the Victoria Cross was announced in *The London Gazette* of 24 July 1915.: 'For the most conspicuous bravery on 7 January, 1915, at Spina Khaisora (Tochi Valley).

During operations against the Khostwal tribesmen, Captain Jotham, who was commanding a party of about a dozen of the North Waziristan Militia, was attacked in a *nullah* and almost surrounded by an overwhelming force of some 1500 tribesmen. He gave the order to retire and could have himself escaped, but most gallantly sacrificed his own life by attempting to affect the rescue of one of his men who had lost his horse.' The medal was received by Jotham's father from King George V on 29 November 1916.

A similar action took place on 5 September 1915, at Hafiz Kor, when Private Charles Hull of the 21st Lancers saved the life of his officer.

The First World War produced a great leap forward regarding the instruments of war. Now there were reliable machine-guns, armoured cars and aeroplanes which the Pathans describes as 'White Eagles'. With the ending of the war, Amir Habibulla claimed that he had largely controlled his soldiers and there had been relative peace on the Frontier. The British were not unsympathetic to his request for independence to pursue his country's own foreign affairs but before an agreement could be reached, Habibulla was assassinated and his place was taken by his son, Amanulla. Afghanistan experienced an upsurge of nationalism which mirrored events in India.

In April 1919, Brigadier General Rex Dyer ordered his troops to open fire on a prohibited assembly in Amritsar. This drastic action resulted in the deaths of 379 civilians and deeply shocked Indian public opinion. Amanulla sensed his country could take advantage of this outrage and condemn the British for their insensitivity to the Indians who had supported their cause in the recent war. He then ordered his army to move to the Durand Line, a provocative move that the British could not ignore.

The Afghan occupation of the western end of the Khyber Pass resulted in the British hurrying reinforcements to the Khyber forts. Learning that an insurrection was planned in Pershawar in support of the Afghans, the British surrounded the city and nipped the uprising in the bud. By 9 May, shots were exchanged and the Third Afghan War began in earnest.

The British forces were weak compared with the Afghan regular army, which could muster 50,000 men with an additional 80,000 tribesmen they could expect to support them. In contrast, the British-led Indian forces had been weakened by the Great War and their ranks were filled with untried recruits. The British relied on men from the Territorial Army who had served in India to release the regular regiments to fight in France. What was lacking in manpower quality was made up with motor transport, wireless communications and the RAF. Two months of manoeuvring and fighting finally brought about an armistice in June and a peace treaty in August. The Afghans obtained the independence they sought which they would have received without a war.

The Third Afghan War was over but it had stirred up unrest along the Frontier, in particular Waziristan, and there were to be years of disorder and fighting before peace returned to the region. In October 1919, a convoy was attacked and a posthumous Victoria Cross was awarded to an Indian Medical Service's captain, Henry Andrews. In operations against the Mahsuds in January 1920, Lieutenant William Kenny with just ten men of the Garhwal Rifles fought off repeated attacks by vastly superior numbers for four hours until all were killed. He was awarded a posthumous Victoria Cross.

Two Infantry brigades and three Mountain Artillery batteries were formed into the Derajat Column. In a fighting sweep of just over three months, the Column achieved its target in forcing the Mahsuds in to submission. The Wana Wazirs continued to give trouble and in November 1920, another punitive expedition was formed and called the Wana Column. Although they successfully occupied Wana, the Wazirs continued to raid. In one such ambush, the first Victoria Cross awarded to a Sikh was gained for an outstanding sequence of gallant acts.

ISHAR SINGH VC (1895-1963)

Ishar Singh was born on 30 December 1895 at Nenwan in the Punjab. When he was eighteen he enlisted in the 28th Punjabis, on 13 December 1913, and was sent to Ceylon. When war was declared on the Turks, he was sent to serve in the Mesopotamian Campaign in 1915. He spent the rest of the war in Palestine and Egypt. In 1921, he was serving closer to home in Waziristan with the Wana Column.

On 10 April 1921, he was part of an escort of transport that was attacked at Haidari on the Shahur Zam River. His outstanding acts of bravery are well described in the citation published in *The London Gazette* dated 25 November 1921: 'When the convoy protection troops were attacked, this Sepoy was No.1 of a Lewis-gun Section. Early in the action he received a very severe gunshot wound in the chest, and fell beside his Lewis gun. Hand-to-hand fighting having commenced, the British officer, and Indian officer, and all the halvildars of his company were either killed or wounded, and his Lewis gun was seized by the enemy. Calling up two other men, he got up, charged the enemy, recovered his Lewis gun, and although bleeding profusely, again got the gun into action.

'When his Jemedar arrived he took the gun from Sepoy Ishar Singh and ordered him to go back and have his wound dressed. Instead of doing this the Sepoy went to the medical officer, and was great assistance in pointing out where the wounded were, and in carrying water to them. He made innumerable journeys to the river and back for this purpose. On one occasion, when the enemy fire was very heavy, he took a rifle off a wounded man and helped to keep down the fire. On another occasion he stood in front of the medical officer who was dressing a wounded man thus shielding him with his body. It was over three hours before he finally submitted to be evacuated, being then too weak from loss of blood to object. His gallantry and devotion to duty were beyond praise. His conduct inspired all who saw him.'

Ishar Singh received his Victoria Cross from the Prince of Wales, later King Edward VIII, at Rawalpindi on 10 March 1920. He was promoted to Jemedar in 1926, Subadar in 1928 and Subadar Major in 1936. In the same year, he was appointed the King's Indian Orderly and awarded the Royal Victorian Medal and the Order of British India.

In 1942 he was promoted to lieutenant and appointed to a Special Training Team. He retired as Honoury Captain and Sirdar Bahadur in 1944. He died in his home town of Nenwan on 2 December 1963 and his impressive VC group is displayed at Lord Ashcroft's Gallery in the Imperial War Museum.

The twentieth century saw many outbreaks on the turbulent North-West Frontier, most of which are consigned to the footnotes of history. One such short-lived and forgotten war happened in 1935 and is memorable for producing the only Victoria Cross recipient during the reign of King Edward VIII, as well as being the last occasion the Cross was awarded for an action on the North-West Frontier.

There was barely a time during the 1930s when there was not the sound of gunfire somewhere on the Frontier. These campaigns and short-lived uprisings went almost unreported in the British newspapers, but for the men involved in the fighting, they were vicious affairs.

The Khudai Khitmatgars or 'Servants of God', recruited young Pathans for the fight against British rule. Mostly poor and unable to afford a uniform, they dyed their shirts with brick dust and hence became known as the Red Shirts. Their moment of fame, or notoriety according to your point of view, lasted from April through to October 1931.

Anarchy threatened the area until troops supported by aircraft finally brought about peace of a kind. The truculent Mohmands tribe came out in belated solidarity with the Red Shirts. They were particularly opposed to the building of a military road through the Gandab Valley.

In August 1935, some 2,000 Mohmands began to attack construction of the hated military road and to destroy the completed section running through their territory. By 15 August, they were joined by many more tribesmen. It was clear that a major operation had to be mounted to reopen and keep clear the road. It was during this operation that a further Victoria Cross was added to the many that had been awarded over the years for gallantry on the Frontier.

GODFREY MEYNELL VC (1904-1935)

Godfrey Meynell (pronounced Mennell) was born to Brigadier Godfrey Meynell and his wife Edith (née Cammell) at the family seat of Meynell

Langley, Derbyshire, on 20 May 1904. He came from a military family that contained a great-uncle who had served in the 75th Regiment during the Crimean War and had died on attachment to the Turkish Amy on the Danube. His father had fought in the Tirah Campaign of 1897-8 and commanded the 171st Brigade in the First World War, finally commanding the King's Own Shropshire Light Infantry (KSLI) before retiring in 1926.

Young Godfrey attended Norris Hill School before going to Eton in 1917 as a King's Scholar. Choosing a military career, Godfrey entered Sandhurst and, on 31 January 1924, passed out thirteenth in his year. He was commissioned into his father's regiment, the KSLI and posted to India. Within two years he had qualified as a first-class interpreter in Hindustani and later in Pushto. In 1926, he was promoted to lieutenant and decided to transfer to the Indian Army.

Taking advantage of a couple of months' leave, he joined the Corps of Guides on their bi-annual march to Chitral and soon he fulfilled his wish to be posted to this elite regiment. In 1929, he went on detachment to the Tochi Scouts and gained his first taste of action on the Frontier in Waziristan. During a mounted night patrol, which was suddenly attacked by hostile tribesmen, Meynell – who was riding a white pony and wearing a solar topi (pith helmet) – was easily recognised as a British officer, which drew enemy fire while his men retired. He received a bullet in the back but managed to stay in the saddle for the seven miles back to base without dismounting.

Meynell was recalled to his regiment where he was appointed adjutant on 16 April 1931. The regiment was involved in another minor outbreak and Godfrey was awarded the Military Cross for carrying out a successful ambush against Bajauri tribesmen at Bangadai on 14 September 1932. Six months later, now promoted to captain, he married Sophie Patricia Lowis in the Guide's church at Marden in the Punjab.

VC Action

When the Mohmands began their attacks on the military road in August 1935, Captain Meynell's Guides made up part of two brigades, the Nowshera and Pershawa, which combined to be known as Mohforce. The two brigade commanders rose to become prominent leaders in the Second World War – Brigadier the Honourable Harold Alexander and Brigadier Claude Auchinleck. By 25 August, the force had advanced into the tribal territory. On 17 September, the Nowshera Brigade was given the task of moving up the Gandab Valley to secure the Nahakki range and hold a dominant feature, Point 4080. This move was duly completed and the brigade made camp on the floor of the valley with Point 4080 in sight to the north.

The numbers of Mohmands, however, had been seriously underestimated and the terrain extremely tough. The brigade was constantly on alert as the tribesmen fired into the camp each night and attacked a Guides piquet on the twentieth.

One of Meynell's fellow officers was twenty-three-year-old Second Lieutenant Geoffrey Hamilton, who wrote an unpublished personal account of the events of 29 September: 'There were no bugles that morning on the 29 September 1935. One o'clock. No lights in the camp, of course, and no moon yet. No noise either except for the shuffle of sandals on loose stones, the muttered curses and the snorts of shackle mules sniffing the cold night air: all the age-old sounds of infantry girding themselves for battle in the dark.

'We had been told what to expect the previous evening in the mess-tent ... A Petromax lamp was on the table and Godfrey had his map propped up against the tent-pole. He was dedicated and intelligent Eton scholar of about thirty-two with a short sandy moustache and a ready, if cynical, sense of humour that played constantly round the corners of his half shut eyes. We liked him well for his bravery and his deep knowledge of our Jawans and their dialects, several of which he spoke fluently...

'Godfrey began to give his orders which boiled down to the Nowshera Brigade, of which we were part, having to capture a 1500 foot high ridge of rocky peaks ending at a cross of a T with the hill-top, PT.4080, at the junction of the two ridges. The Guides were to do it, supported by the 2/15 Punjab Regiment.'

The official account of the battle must now briefly take over. It states that: 'Rendell (Tony) with 3 and 4 Platoons of Company reached the highest point of the eastern face of Pt.4080 but were held up by the fire of the enemy who were occupying a number of small spurs in the vicinity. Good (Syd) now moved forward behind Rendell with 1 and 2 Platoons and took up a position on the left (eastern) shoulder of Pt.4080 facing the ridge running south. Meynell, the Adjutant, had at this point gone forward to ascertain the situation. It was much lighter and the enemy fire was increasing and inflicting heavy casualties ...

'Good (Major Syd Good, the acting CO) now called up the two platoons (11 and 12) of C Company from their covering position on the ridge. These two platoons were unable to get up onto the higher slopes of Pt.4080 and took up a position on the left of 1 and 2 Platoons, facing south below a large wall of rock just above the junction of the ridge and the main feature.

'In the meantime, Meynell had reached the forward platoons on and around the main objectives and found them involved in a terrific struggle.'

Lieutenant Anthony Rendell had been killed and Meynell assumed command of 3 and 4 Platoons of 'A' Company, which were now, to all intents and purposes, isolated, only to be killed himself in a fierce hand-to-hand fight a few minutes later.

Major Good managed to signal to Lieutenant Hamilton to bring forward his company where they found the area crowded with wounded. There was also no battalion headquarters, as it had foolhardily advanced with the six leading platoons. Hamilton was shot in the stomach as he led his men forward and the heavy enemy fire pinned down his company for two hours. It was clear that there were no Guides left alive on Pt.4080. Finally, the artillery started to shell Pt.4080 and but by that time it was only occupied by the dead and wounded. The battle was over.

Geoffrey Hamilton's account concluded: 'For some extraordinary reason a counter-attack was never launched, but the Mohmand tribes had had enough for the time being and sued for peace the following day. The headless bodies of Tony and Godfrey and the bodies of twenty other Guides were collected and either buried or burnt. The eight wounded men of the Regiment who were captured on Pt.4080 were duly returned unharmed … So ended another military disaster which never should have happened.'

The Guides' casualties were two British officers killed and three wounded, two NCOs killed and two wounded, nineteen ORs killed, thirty-nine wounded. It was estimated that Mohmand casualties were at least 144 killed for they surrendered the following day.

Captain Godfrey Meynell was recommended for the Victoria Cross, the announcement of which appeared in *The London Gazette* on 24 December 1935. Part of the citation reads: 'Captain Meynell had at his disposal two Lewis guns and about thirty men. Although this party was maintaining heavy and accurate fire on the advancing enemy, the overwhelming numbers of the latter succeeded in reaching the position. Both the Lewis guns were damaged beyond repair and a fierce hand to hand struggled commenced. During the struggle, Captain Meynell was mortally wounded and all his men either killed or wounded … The fine example Captain Meynell set to his men, coupled with his determination to hold the position to the last, maintains the traditions of the Army and reflects the highest credit on the fallen officer and his comrades.'

Godfrey Meynell's body was recovered and buried at the Guides' Cemetery, Marden. Meynell's widow received his Cross on 14 July 1936 at Buckingham Palace from King Edward VIII – the only one during his short reign. She was quite unimpressed by the King, who was not very well briefed about her husband's bravery.

In 1961, Queen Elizabeth II visited Meynell's grave during an official visit to Pakistan.

Chapter 50

The Second World War, 1940

Number of VCs awarded	16
Number of VCs awarded to officers	11
Number of VCs awarded to other ranks	5
Total awarded to Royal Navy	5
Total awarded to Royal Air Force	5
Total awarded to British Army	6

Origins of the War

The defeat of Germany in the First World War was followed by a decade of civil unrest, partly because of the punitive reparations payments inflicted under the 1919 Treaty of Versailles. A decade of civil unrest led to the rise of the National Socialist German Workers Party, the Nazis, under the leadership of Adolf Hitler. The Nazis came to power under the promise of a strong central government based on racial cleansing, increased *Lebensraum* (living space), and the retaking territory they had lost in the Great War. To most of the German people who had suffered hyper-inflation, recession and the lingering humiliation of defeat, the Nazis assumption of power in 1933 offered what appeared to be a way of regaining national pride and wealth.

Still in a dire economic mess, Hitler launched a massive public works project which included the secret reviving of Germany's armed forces. By supporting General Franco's Nationalists in the Spanish Civil War, the Germans were able to use the conflict to try out their new military equipment, particularly their armoured units and air force. This was followed by the invasion of Czechoslovakia, to reclaim the German-speaking Sudetenland, and the Anschluss of Austria.

On 28 March 1939, Madrid surrendered to General Franco's Nationalists so ending the civil war, the repercussions of which would rumble on for decades. Three days later, Britain and France, finally awaking from self-delusion, opposed Nazi expansion by pledging aid to Poland in the event of a threat to its independence by Germany. This followed Germany's annexation of the Czech territories of Slovakia, Bohemia and Moravia on 15 March. Then, on 22 March, camee the seizure of the Baltic port of Memel from Lithuania. On 7 April, Italy got in on the act by over-running the small Balkan state of Albania. It was now abundantly clear that the forces of fascism were on the move.

It came as a shock to the British and French governments when they learned that Germany and the Soviet Union had signed a non-aggression pact on 23 August. What was not revealed until later was the intention to divide Poland between them. A week later, Germany invaded Poland.

In order to have a legitimate reason for going to war, the Nazis staged a cynical exercise to show that Poland had instigated an attack on German territory. Taking ethnic-Poles from concentration camps, they dressed them in Polish uniforms and shot them at the border town of Gleiwitz, claiming they had fired the first shots. On 3 September, Britain and France declared war on Germany, so setting in motion the devastating six-year long Second World War, a truly global conflict.

In a move similar to the start of the First World War, Britain sent an Expeditionary Force to France but, unlike the earlier conflict, there followed an eight-month long period of inactivity known as the 'Phoney War'. It was not until the spring of 1940 that Germany turned from her conquest of Poland in the east to confront the Allies in the west.

As a result, practically all of the early fighting involving Britain was carried out at sea. When the UK declared war against Germany in September 1939, its merchant ships became easy targets for pocket battleships like *Admiral Graf Spee,* which was operating in the South Atlantic. One of her supply ships was the tanker *Altmark* and prisoners from sunken merchantmen were transferred to her for transportation back to imprisonment in Germany.

On 14 February 1940, *Altmark*, carrying 303 British prisoners of war, was permitted to travel through Norwegian waters. According to international rules any non-combatant vessel from a warring nation could seek shelter for some time in neutral waters if permitted. When a group of British destroyers appeared on 16 February, *Altmark* sought refuge in a Norwegian fjord. Ignoring international rules and Norwegian neutrality, HMS *Cossack* entered the fjord and attacked *Altmark*, boarding it, killing seven German crewmen and liberating the prisoners. This violation of their neutrality angered the Norwegians, and briefly there was some anti-British feeling.

Norway, though neutral, was considered strategically important to both Britain and Germany for two main reasons. Firstly there was the importance of the port of Narvik, from which large quantities of Swedish iron ore, on which Germany depended, were exported; this route was especially important during the winter months when the northern part of the Baltic Sea was frozen over. Narvik is only about fifteen miles from the Swedish border and linked with the iron-ore region by rail. Secondly,

Narvik became of greater significance to the British as the ports in Norway could serve as a hole in the Royal Navy's blockade of Germany, allowing the enemy access to the Atlantic Ocean.

Hitler had earlier considered invading Norway and his invasion plan found a new sense of urgency after the *Altmark* Incident. The main goals of the invasion were to secure the ports and ore fields, with Narvik as a priority, and to establish firm control over the country to prevent collaboration with the Allies. It was to be presented as an armed protection of Norway's neutrality.

The plan called for the capture of six primary targets by amphibious landings including Trondheim and Narvik. The plan was designed to quickly overwhelm the Norwegian defenders and occupy these vital areas before any form of organized resistance could be mounted. It was during this phase that the first Victoria Crosses of the Second World War were awarded posthumously to two destroyer captains in the freezing waters off Norway.

GERARD ROOPE VC (1905-1940)
BERNARD ARMITAGE WARBURTON-LEE VC (1895-1940)

On 5 April, the Home Fleet sailed from Scapa Flow in Operation *Wilfred* – a plan for the mining of waters off Norway. The 1,345-ton destroyer HMS *Glowworm* left with the Narvik group consisting of the battle cruiser HMS *Renown* and three other destroyers. For two days, the seas around Norway were whipped up by a ferocious storm, during which time rumors went around that the Kriegsmarine was heading for the same area. Amongst the German invasion forces were the ships of *Gruppe 1* bound for Narvik. This omprised of ten destroyers: *Wilhelm Heidkamp* (flagship), *Hans Lűdemann, Hermann Kűnne, Diether von Roeder,* and *Anton Schmitt* (these were 2,400 tons and completed in 1939), *Erich Koellner, Georg Thiele, Wolfgang Zenker, Bernd von Arnim, Erich Giese* (these were 2,200 tons and completed in 1937/38). *Gruppe 2*, meanwhile, was bound for Trondheim and comprised of the heavy cruiser *Admiral von Hipper* and a destroyer escort.

Additionally, the battle cruisers *Scharnhorst* and *Gneisenau* would escort *Gruppe 1* and *Gruppe 2* as they travelled together, and there would also be several echelons of tankers carrying additional troops, fuel and military equipment.

The captain of HMS *Glowworm* was Gerard Broadmead Roope. He was born on 13 March 1905, at Hillbrook Trull, near Taunton, Somerset, to Gerard, who was described as a 'gentleman of independent means', and his mother Florence (née Broadmead). When he was thirteen, Roope entered the Royal Naval College, Dartmouth and on 15 January 1923, was appointed midshipman in the gunroom of the battle-cruiser HMS *Revenge.* As a sub-lieutenant, he served on board *Concord* and *Caledon* until he was promoted to lieutenant and joined *Marlborough* in 1928.

On 22 July 1938, Roope took command of the G-class destroyer, HMS *Glowworm*. This 1,345-ton ship had been launched at the Thorneycroft Shipyard in Southampton on 22 July 1935. She was armed with four 4.7-inch guns; seven anti-aircraft / machine guns; ten 21-inch torpedo tubes and depth charges, and she carried a complement of 145.

The first posting was to the Mediterranean for escort duty during the latter months of the Spanish Civil War. It was during this period that *Glowworm* developed a habit of colliding with other vessels. During a night exercise in 1939, she hit a sister ship, HMS *Grenade*, and then, in early 1940, collided with the Swedish ship *Rex*. Both accidents resulted in extensive repairs.

Roope was regarded as a competent officer and was well-liked and respected by his crew who, nevertheless, anointed him with the nickname 'Rammer Roope'. He also rejoiced in another epithet, 'Old Ardover', for his habit of altering course at a moment's notice, which must have caused consternation in the ship's galley.

At the outbreak of the war, *Glowworm* was ordered back to home waters and started patrolling the Channel. In March 1940, she was sent to Scapa Flow in anticipation of the German moves to occupy Norway. On the morning of 6 April, it was discovered that a torpedo man had been swept overboard during the night. A signal was made to *Renown*, and *Glowworm* was given permission to look for the missing man. For two days, *Glowworm*, was involved in a fruitless search in the heavy seas and finally abandoned the attempt. She then set a course to catch up with the Narvik group.

VC Action

On the dawn of the 8th, and in poor visibility, *Glowworm* ran into the German *Gruppe 2* and came under immediate fire from *Hipper*. Instead of trying to escape from the unequal contest, Captain Roope signaled that he was engaging the enemy. This was the last communication received from *Glowworm*.

Hipper opened up with her eight 8-inch guns and immediately scored direct hits on *Glowworm*. Roope responded by steaming straight for *Hipper* to bring his own guns in range. All the while, *Hipper* was causing considerable damage and casualties, including the entire medical team. Another casualty was Roope's dog, who had been sitting between his master's legs when it was killed by a shell fragment. One of the shells brought down part of the main mast and the wireless aerials tangled with the siren on the funnel, causing it to continuously wail, giving the impression of a wounded beast in agony.

Roope managed to fire off a spread of five torpedoes, all of which missed, one but narrowly. *Hipper* laid a smoke screen, which only enabled *Glowworm* to steam ever closer. As she emerged, she crossed *Hipper*'s bow from port firing off another five torpedoes to no effect. Turning sharply to starboard, and with the banshee scream of the siren, Roope ran *Glowworm* full tilt into the Hipper's starboard side, tearing away about 100 feet of armored plating, damaging some torpedo tubes, and puncturing two fresh-water tanks.

The battered fire-swept hulk of HMS *Glowworm* pulled clear and lay off about 400 yards. After firing one last salvo from the only undamaged aftermost gun, the stricken ship began to settle down by the bows and list to starboard. With steam pressure gone, Roope gave the order to abandon ship. As the ship began to capsize, a few men were photographed from *Hipper* standing on the upturned hull.

One of these men was Gerard Roope, who turned to his Torpedo Officer, Lieutenant Robert Ramsey, and spoke his wonderfully understated final words: 'I don't think we'll be playing cricket for a long time yet.' With all the survivors in the water, the hulk of *Glowworm* began to sink, finally cutting off the screech of the siren, leaving an eerie silence. Men struggled to get clear of the area for fear of being sucked down or blown up by the store of depth charges. A heavy slick of oil covered the sea, causing further distress to the exhausted sailors.

The commander of *Hipper*, Kapitän zur See Hellmuth Heye, chivalrously maneuvered his ship to allow the sea to float the survivors towards their rescuers. Germans, who moments before had been trying to destroy their enemy, were now pulling oil-caked survivors to safety. One of these was Lieutenant Commander Roope, who managed to reach the side of the huge battle cruiser. A rope was thrown to him, but he was unable to tie it around him. Having no strength left to hold on and be hauled up, he released his grip and fell back exhausted into the water where he perished. In those early days of the war, there was considerable respect shown by both sides and prisoners were generally well treated. The Germans congratulated the thirty-one survivors on a good fight.

Kapitän zur See Heye went even further, when he sent a message through the International Red Cross recommending Roope for the Victoria Cross. This was the first time that the award of a VC had been recommended by the enemy. There were two other examples. One was made by U-boat captain Oberleutnant Klemens Schamong for the action of Flying Officer Lloyd Trigg RNZAF whose whole crew was killed in the sinking of *U-468* on 11 August 1943. The other was the recommendation of Sergeant Thomas Durrant by a German destroyer captain during the raid on St Nazaire.

Meanwhile, in the Norwegian Campaign, with both sides unaware of the other's moves, they proceeded as planned. HMS *Renown* arrived at Vestfjords and maintained position near the entrance, while the mine-laying destroyers proceeded to their task. The German *Gruppe 1* continued towards Narvik; each of its ten large modern destroyers carrying 200 mountain troops and equipment. In addition, four U-boats were to be stationed along the 100 miles from the open sea to Narvik. The first direct contact between the two sides occurred the next morning without either side's intention.

The Admiralty contacted *Renown* and her escorts, ordering them to go and investigate the *Glowworm* incident. Thus, no British ships stood in their way, and the ten German destroyers entered the Vestfjords area unopposed. By the time they had reached the inner area near Narvik, most of the destroyers had peeled off from the main formation to capture the outer batteries of Ofotfjord.

In addition to the German landings in south and central Norway, the Admiralty was also erroneously informed, via press reports that a single German destroyer was in Narvik. In response to this they ordered the 2nd Destroyer Flotilla to engage. This flotilla, under the command of Captain Bernard Warburton-Lee, had already detached from *Renown* being ordered to guard the entrance to the Vestfjord.

Bernard Armitage Warburton-Lee was born on 13 September 1895 at Broad Oak, Redbrook, Marlor, Flintshire to Joseph and Eva. His father was a barrister and later the High Sheriff of Flintshire. At an early age, Bernard wanted a naval career and, after preparatory school, he attended the Royal Naval College at Osborne, Isle of Wight, before going to Dartmouth, where he passed out top of his term in 1912.

His first posting was HMS *Hyacinth* and he saw his first action in 1914 against the German cruiser *Königsberg*. In 1916, he joined a series of destroyers, which became his favoured class of warship. He was universally known as 'Wash' and became a close friend of Commander Lord Louis Mountbatten.

Between the wars, he moved from one command to another and was posted to the Royal Naval Staff College, the Imperial Defence College, and was clearly destined for higher things. He was also an outstanding sportsman, excelling at tennis and polo. His reports described him as an exceptional leader … strong, clever and a stickler for efficiency.

As flag-captain, he took command of HMS *Hardy* as OC 2nd Destroyer Flotilla on 28 July 1939. With the outbreak of war, his first task was to participate in the search for *Admiral Graf Spee* in the South Atlantic. Recalled to Scapa Flow, the 2nd Destroyer Flotilla rendezvoused with HMS *Renown* and sailed for Vestfjord.

At 16.00 hours on 9 April, Warburton-Lee sent two officers ashore at the pilot station at Tranøy, fifty miles west of Narvik, and learned from the locals that the strength of the German force was between four to six destroyers and a U-boat. Warburton-Lee reported these findings back to the Admiralty, concluding with his intention to attack the next day at 'dawn, high water', which would give him the element of surprise and protection against any mines. This decision was approved by the Admiralty.

In order to time his dawn attack precisely, Warburton-Lee led his flotilla westwards towards the open sea. One of the German U-boats spotted this move and reported the news to the German commander, Kapitän zur See und Kommodore Friedrich Bonte. This gave the Germans the mistaken notion that the threat of a British attack was receding and, as a consequence, they dropped their guard.

VC Action

At 23.30 hours, the British turned back towards the fjord and headed for Narvik. Heavy snow reduced visibility to zero for much of the journey as they made their way cautiously up the narrow fjord. This worked to their advantage as there were three U-boats guarding the approaches. Shortly before dawn, the flotilla entered Ofotfjord, where the expanse of water widened. Its luck further increased when the German guard ship, *Dieter von Roeder*, returned to Narvik, leaving clear the approach to the harbour.

At 04.30 hours, Warburton-Lee arrived at Narvik harbour and entered along with HMS *Hunter* and HMS *Havock,* leaving behind HMS *Hotspur* and HMS *Hostile* to guard the entrance and monitor the shore batteries. The fog and snow were extremely heavy, allowing Warburton-Lee's force to approach undetected. When it arrived at the harbour itself, the British found five German destroyers and numerous cargo ships.

Firing off a spread of torpedoes, *Hardy* started the First Battle of Narvik. In this opening salvo, a torpedo struck Bonte's flagship, *Wilhelm Heidkamp,* causing an explosion in the magazine. The stern was blown off and three guns were hurled into the air. Crucially, Kommodore Bonte, the *Gruppe 1* commander, lost his life, which added to the chaos that ensued.

Warburton-Lee's flotilla then left the harbour, almost untouched. It made another pass but did not enter the harbour, being joined by *Hotspur* and *Hostile,* who added to the mayhem. The British sank two destroyers, disabled one more, and sank six supply ships, all without suffering any damage.

The Germans, for all their apparent superiority, were in a very vulnerable position. All the destroyers were low on fuel and there was only one tanker, *Jan Wellem,* which had a slow pumping capacity. Consequently, none of the German warships had been refueled by the time the British attacked with such devastating effect.

Pulling back a couple of miles, Warburton-Lee debated whether or not to risk a third attack. He had plenty of torpedoes left and the Germans seemed in no position to counter-attack. Fatally, Warburton-Lee decided on a third pass. Belatedly, three German destroyers, *Wolfgang Zenker*, *Erich Griese* and *Erich Koellner* had been able to sail out of their anchorage in nearby Herjangsfjord and catch Warburton Lee's flotilla as it completed its third attack and was making its way back to the entrance of the Vestfjord. To complete the trap, a few minutes later two more destroyers, *Georg Thiele* and *Bernd von Arnim*, having sheltered in Ballangen Bay, arrived in front of them, thus surrounding Warburton-Lee's force.

The leading German ship was of such a size that it was mistaken for a cruiser and Warburton-Lee ordered an immediate withdrawal. The German gunnery was most accurate and quickly found its range. HMS *Hardy* was the first ship to be hit and her bridge was destroyed and a mortally wounded Warburton-Lee was amongst the casualties. With *Hardy* taken out of action, one of her surviving officers managed to beach her and her crew able to scramble ashore. Warburton-Lee was found to be dead and his body was later laid to rest in the nearby cemetery at Ballangen.

Local residents gave refuge to the 140 surviving crew members, who were later picked up by a British ship and returned to Britain. Captain Warburton-Lee was posthumously awarded the Victoria Cross, which was presented to his widow on 2 July 1940.

HMS *Hunter* was the next ship put out of commission, coming to a dead halt in the water after several hits. *Hotspur* was then hit and received damage to her steering system, causing her to crash into *Hunter*. Several more hits were registered on the pair until *Hotspur* was able to reverse out of the wreck.

Hostile and *Havock*, having raced ahead, turned about and came back to aid the retreat of *Hotspur*. The German ships having received a few hits and, more importantly, being critically short of fuel, were not able to pursue. As they exited Ofotfjord, the three British destroyers managed to sink the German supply ship *Rauenfels*.

Vice-Admiral Whitworth received orders from the Admiralty to send a larger force to Narvik and finish the job that Warburton-Lee had started. Force 'B' consisted of eight destroyers – *Bedouin, Punjabi, Eskimo, Cossack, Kimberley, Foxhound, Hero and Icarus*. In a bold decision, the old battleship HMS *Warspite* was also sent despite the narrowness of the fjord. She was commanded by another VC from the First World War, Captain V.A.C. Crutchley VC, DSO, and Whitworth transferred his flag to her from *Renown*.

On the morning of 13 April, Admiral Whitworth's force entered Vestfjord using *Warspite*'s scouting aircraft to guide the way. Aside from locating two of the German destroyers, the scouting aircraft also sank an enemy U-boat, the first such occurrence. *Warspite*'s destroyers travelled three miles in advance of the battleship and were the first to engage their German counterparts, which had come to meet them. Though neither side inflicted notable damage, the German ships were running low on ammunition and were gradually pushed back to the harbour.

By that afternoon, most attempted to flee up the Rombaksfjord, the only exception being *Hermann Künne* which beached itself as it made for Herjangsfjord and was destroyed by HMS *Eskimo*. Four British destroyers continued to chase the German ships up through Rombaksfjord and *Eskimo* was soon damaged by the waiting opposition. However, the German situation was hopeless. Having run out of fuel and ammunition, by the time the remaining British ships arrived the enemy crews had abandoned and scuttled their ships. By 18.30 hours the British ships were making their way out of the now cleared fjord.

The consequence of the complete destruction of the German flotilla contributed to Hitler's reluctance to invade Britain until his naval losses could be replaced. The German occupation of Norway, however, was to prove a thorn in the side of the Allies during the next few years. Long-range aircraft based there meant that several squadrons of British fighters had to be kept in the north during the Battle of Britain, and German commerce raiders used Norway as a staging base to reach the North Atlantic with impunity. Likewise, the battleship *Tirpitz,* although largely confined to sheltering in the labyrinth of fjords, was such a threat that a large naval force had to be kept in northern waters just to counter any movement she made. After Germany invaded Russia in 1941, air bases in Norway were also used to attack the Allied arctic convoys heading there, inflicting painful losses to shipping.

The 2nd Destroyer Flotilla's action in Ofotfjord was the last of the old fashioned naval actions where opposing sides were evenly matched and fought within sight of each other. A mixture of skill and luck favored Warburton-Lee's ships. If he had not attacked the Germans when he did, they would have all been refueled and resupplied. The outcome could have been so different and Hitler would have pressed ahead with the invasion of Britain.

Despite the efforts of the Royal Navy, the efforts to put troops ashore at Namsos to stop the Germans moving on Narvik were a costly failure. Lack of artillery and aircraft led to an almost immediate withdrawal from Norway. One of the reasons was the unfolding Battle of France, which was considered the priority, with operations in Norway being regarded as a side-show.

The quick German advance into northern France had split the Allies, and the British found themselves falling back on the port of Dunkirk and its surrounding beaches. Between 15 to 31 May, five Victoria Crosses were awarded during the retreat, these being those to Second Lieutenant Richard Annand, Lance-Corporal Harry Nicholls, CSM George Gristock, Lieutenant The Honourable Christopher Furness and Captain Harold Ervine-Andrews.

Having successfully evacuated 338,226 Allied soldiers, though often minus their equipment, Britain faced the might of the German Luftwaffe during August and September. In an epic battle for Britain, the Royal Air

Force inflicted enough damage on the Germans to discourage any immediate thought of invasion.

Surprisingly, only one fighter pilot was awarded the Victoria Cross and this was because of the intervention of King George VI. Though Flight Lieutenant James Nicolson's recommendation had been for the Distinguished Flying Cross, the King crossed it out and upgraded it to the Victoria Cross. One factor was that Britain had just been saved by the bravery of her fighter pilots and, if ever there was good opportunity to bestow a Victoria Cross on a member of Fighter Command, it was then. Nicolson was the only VC of Fighter Command during the Second World War.

Chapter 51

The Second World War, 1941

Number of VCs awarded	22
Number of VCs awarded to officers	13
Number of VCs awarded to other ranks	9
Total awarded to Royal Navy	2
Total awarded to Royal Air Force	4
Total awarded to British Army	7
Total awarded to British Indian Army	2
Total awarded to Canadian Army	1
Total awarded to Australian Army	3
Total awarded to New Zealand Army	3

Origins of the War

With Britain still recovering from her military losses from the Fall of France and enduring daily bombing raids on her towns and cities, there might reasonably be expected a period of rallying to regain her strength. Any further involvement on the Continent was out of the question. Instead, a threat on the fringes of her Empire occupied the Government's attention.

The aim of the Italian dictator Benito Mussolini was to continue to persecute his plan for a Mediterranean and African Empire. He had already proclaimed his 'Italian East African Empire' in 1936 having occupied Ethiopia, Eritrea and Italian Somaliland, which he added to the North African colony of Libya. This occupation of most of the land on the west side of the Red Sea constituted a threat to British supply routes through the Suez Canal. With Britain preoccupied with home defence, her African possessions seemed easy prey.

The Italians in Libya were massing on the border and succeeded in advancing to Makitila, where they dug-in, fortified their positions and awaited reinforcements and supplies before marching to the Nile. The Italian newspapers announced that 'Nothing can save Britain now'. Facing the Italians was General Wavell's force in Egypt which numbered 30,000. Opposing them were approximately 150,000 Italians.

Against the odds, Wavell's Desert Force, augmented by soldiers from Australia and New Zealand, defeated the Italians taking 130,000 prisoners and appeared to be on the verge of overrunning the last of Mussolini's forces in Libya. On the point of expelling the Italians from Libya, Wavell was ordered by Churchill to halt his advance and send troops to Greece, which was being threatened by the Axis.

Wavell disagreed with this decision but followed his orders with disastrous results. The rush to reinforce the Greeks had deprived Wavell of 60,000 troops he could ill afford to lose. In the hasty and doomed Greek campaign, the Anzac/British force lost 15,000 men killed or captured and all their equipment destroyed. Britain's foot-hold in Europe was gone.

The Allied troops were evacuated to the island of Crete – but the Germans followed them. On the first day of the German invasion of the island the Allied defenders managed to inflict heavy casualties on Hitler's airborne forces. A breakdown in communications led to Allied confusion and the advantage swung to the Germans who managed to occupy the north of the island allowing the British forces to evacuate from the south.

This disastrous campaign saw the award of the Victoria Cross to three men – Petty Officer Alfred Sephton RN and two from the New Zealand Expeditionary Force, Second Lieutenant Charles Upham (the first of his double VC) and Sergeant Clive Hulme.

ALFRED CLIVE HULME VC (1911-1982)

Decades after the Battle of Crete, one of New Zealand's VC heroes was accused of war crimes by three academics. Sadly, it has become the norm these days to resurrect events that may have been acceptable at the time but are now frowned upon. The hero in question was Alfred Clive Hulme. Born in Dunedin on 24 January 1911, he attended Eastern Hutt School. Clive, as he preferred to be called, was a tough and powerfully built youth who developed into a talented wrestler. In 1934, he married Rona Marjorie Murcot and had two children, Anita and Denny. Working as a farm labourer in Nelson, he enlisted in the 2nd New Zealand Expeditionary Force and posted to the 23rd (Canterbury-Otago) Battalion.

Sent to the Eastern Mediterranean Hulme was appointed Provost Sergeant to the 2nd New Zealand Division's field punishment centre at Platanias on the island of Crete. The precipitous retreat from Greece to Crete, some sixty miles from the mainland, was initially thought to be a staging point on the division's way to Egypt. About 32,000 soldiers, including the bulk of 2nd New Zealand Division, soon learned that they were to spend more time on Crete than they had prepared for with no air cover or artillery.

The New Zealand soldiers were responsible for the western sector of the island, which included the all-important Maleme airfield, the towns of Platanias and Canea, and the village of Galatas. For nearly a month, the troops were anticipating an attack. Finally, as the prisoners were having breakfast on the morning of 20 May 1941, the German airborne assault began. Quickly issuing rifles and ammunition, the prisoners were released to join in the fight against the German invaders with the promise that those who survived would be granted the remission of their sentence.

VC Action

Sergeant Hulme re-joined the 23rd Battalion as it battled the German paratroopers who had jumped from the dozens of Junkers Ju 52 transports that filled the sky over Maleme. He led several groups and succeeded in keeping the Germans at bay.

In an interview after the war, Hulme admitted that he was haunted by the killing of one particular German paratrooper he found rummaging amongst the papers at the punishment centre. Hulme shot him between the eyes and for some reason, given the numbers he killed, this affected him: 'I never felt so sorry to kill a German.'

Hulme took possession of the paratrooper's camouflage blouse and cap, as well as a Mauser sniper's rifle equipped with telescopic sights. He also picked up a couple of Luger pistols. Now suitably equipped, he started to stalk the Germans, even if meant suffering summary execution if caught.

While he was moving about behind enemy lines, he came across a small party of New Zealand engineers which had been captured and were guarded by a single sentry. Wearing his paratroopers smock and cap, Hulme approached the unsuspecting sentry and despatched him with his bayonet.

After a two-day fight, the New Zealanders were forced to relinquish Maleme airfield, which gave the Germans a supply base to push east and squeeze the Allies from the island. On 25 May, the Germans attacked the strategically important village of Galatas and soon occupied it. Despite increasing casualties, Brigadier Kippenberger organised a counter-attack, in which Sergeant Hulme took part. With the support of two British light tanks, the New Zealanders pushed their way back into the village. The advance was held up by a machine-gun in a schoolhouse. Hulme went forward alone and attacked the building with hand grenades, which either killed or caused the Germans to retreat.

Following up with another soldier, Hulme saw a German run into a nearby house and gave chase. When they entered, they could not find the enemy soldier but noticed that a trapdoor in the floor was slightly opened. While the other soldier help open the door, Hulme threw in a couple of grenades. Tragically, the cellar was occupied by the women and children from the village who were either killed or wounded. It was to have a deep and lasting impression on Alfred Hulme for the rest of his life. That night, Hulme donned his smock and went in pursuit of the enemy on the outskirts of the village.

The next day, 26 May, Alfred Hulme learned of the death of his brother, Corporal 'Blondie' Hulme of the 19th Battalion. Filled with a need to avenge his brother's death, Hulme stayed hidden as the 23rd Battalion withdrew from Galatas. He took up a position overlooking a food dump and waited until an enemy patrol appeared, shooting three and forcing the rest to withdraw.

Later, the 23rd acted as rear-guard and, after a gruelling march, reached Stylos where the weary men slumped to the ground in exhaustion. A couple of officers made a quick reconnaissance and spotted a party of Germans approaching about 400 yards away. The company commander called Sergeant Hulme to lead his men up the hill before the Germans could reach the summit. Hulme sprinted ahead and beat the Germans by fifteen yards. Hurling grenades and firing, Hulme drove off the enemy but was wounded in the arm.

The battalion's history records that: 'Hulme was to be seen sitting side-saddle on the stone wall, shooting at the enemy on the lower slopes. His example did much to maintain the morale of the men whose reserves of nervous and physical energy were nearly exhausted.'

The next day, German snipers fired at some senior officers at 5 Brigade's headquarters. Hulme volunteered to go out and deal with them. Donning his German disguise, he managed to climb undetected until he was behind the five snipers, pretending to be part of their group. Singling out the leader, Hulme shot him. The other four snipers looked round to see where the shot had come from. Hulme also turned his head as if searching for the shooter and then shot and killed two more in quick succession. The other two snipers realising they were the next targets attempted to escape but Hulme nailed them as well. All this was witnessed by Hulme's company commander, Major H.H. Thompson, who was following the action through his binoculars.

Another withdrawal followed, as well as another daring act by Alfred Hulme. The Germans began shelling the rear-guard as it held an important ridge with a heavy mortar. Once again Hulme penetrated the German lines and killed the mortar crew, putting the mortar out of action. On the same day, he killed three more snipers, bringing his tally to thirty-three in one week.

While he stalking another sniper, he was shot through the shoulder and forced to go to the rear. The wound was serious but he stayed in the Stylos area, directing traffic and organising stragglers into section groups. By now the Allies were making their way over the mountains that divided Crete to the evacuation port of Sphakia and on 30 May, Alfred Hulme was on his way back to Egypt.

His outstanding solo actions during the retreat had been noted by four officers including Brigadier Hargest, who wrote: 'Sgt. Hulme, during the whole of the fighting up till the moment of being wounded, conducted himself with such courage that the story of his exploits were on everyone's lips. From my own personal observation I knew he showed such a complete contempt for danger that it amounted to recklessness … The effect his actions had on all the men in his unit is incalculable, and he at once became almost legendary. I sincerely hope that the recommendation will be accepted.'

The recommendation was indeed accepted. The announcement of the award of the VC appeared in *The London Gazette* on 10 October 1941. Sergeant Hulme received his Cross from the Governor General of New Zealand at Nelson on 7 November 1941.

Later Life

As a result of his wound, Alfred Hulme was medically discharged in 1942. The wound subsequently wasted the muscles in his forearm, but it was the post-traumatic stress that caused him the most torment, particularly the incident of the grenades in the cellar at Galatas. After the war, he lived at Pongakawa near Te Puke on the north coast of North Island, running a small farm and trucking business.

His son, Denny, learned to drive a truck while sitting on his father's lap and by the age of six was driving solo. Alfred encouraged Denny's passion for driving and was rewarded when his son won the Formula One World Driver's Championship in 1967. Alfred Hulme died on 2 September 1982.

In 2006, a book by two military historians who attacked Hulme for committing 'acts of perfidy' in winning the Victoria Cross was published. The claim gained support amongst a number of other academics; one even stated that Sergeant Hulme's actions were 'unsanctioned murder' and that the New Zealand government should apologise to the families of the Germans he killed: 'Killing soldiers while wearing their uniform was prima facie a war crime.' The New Zealand public thought otherwise and the furore soon died down.

In 2007, Hulme's medal was amongst the nine VCs stolen from the National Army Museum at Waiouru, New Zealand – part of a haul of ninety-six medals taken from locked, reinforced glass cabinets in the museum. On 16 February 2008, New Zealand Police announced that all of the medals had been recovered as a result of a NZ$300,000 reward offered by Lord Ashcroft and New Zealand businessman Tom Sturgess, a former United States Marine.

The hasty evacuation from Crete followed by the swift German advance convinced the Vichy French in neutral Syria to throw in its lot with Germany. Britain concentrated in overcoming the threat that the Axis forces posed for the vital Suez Canal. General Wavell's Western Desert Force had pushed the Italians back to Benghazi in Libya. In desperation, Mussolini called upon help from Hitler, who despatched a motorised force termed the Afrika Korps under the command of General Erwin Rommel. They were ordered to reinforce their Italian allies and to defend against any further British advance. Instead, Rommel discovered just how weak the British advance was and went on the offensive. By the end of April, the weakened Western Desert Force had been pushed back to the Egyptian border.

On 15 June 1941, General Wavell launched Operation *Battleaxe* in an effort to clear eastern Cyrenaica of German and Italian forces. It was also hoped to relieve the siege at Tobruk held by the Australians. The initial assaults against Rommel's strong defensive positions resulted in the British loss of half her tanks on the first day. By the third day, the British narrowly avoided a complete disaster by withdrawing just ahead of a German encircling movement which would have cut them off from retreat. The result of this failure spelt the end for Wavell, who was replaced by General Claude Auchinleck.

The new commander launched a new offensive in November called Operation *Crusader* resulting in the relief of Tobruk and forcing Rommel to retreat. Unfortunately, this was a false spring for the Axis forces turned and in six months had pushed the British forces back into Egypt. As a consequence of his failure, Auchinleck was replaced by General Sir Harold Alexander and, in command of the Eighth Army, General Bernard Montgomery.

Chapter 52

The Second World War, 1942

Number of VCs awarded	31
Number of VCs awarded to officers	20
Number of VCs awarded to other ranks	11
Total awarded to Royal Navy	10
Total awarded to Royal Air Force	4
Total awarded to British Army	7
Total awarded to British Indian Army	1
Total awarded to Canadian Army	1
Total awarded to Australian Army	5
Total awarded to New Zealand Army	2
Total awarded to South African Army	1

Origins of the War

Another front was about to open in the Far East. The Japanese army invaded Malaya just after midnight on 8 December 1941. In a co-ordinated plan, an hour later the Japanese attacked the American naval base at Pearl Harbor, Hawaii, which saw the USA join the Allies.

By 16 February 1942, Japan had forced the surrender of Singapore and overrun the Dutch East Indies. She now turned their attention to Burma, then part of the British Empire. In what became Britain's longest continuous campaign of the war, the operations in Burma were undertaken by a combination of British Commonwealth forces against the Japanese determination to invade India. The campaign was fought in dense mountainous jungle with few roads but many rivers, with a climate that took more lives than any fighting. Another limiting factor for both sides was the heavy and persistent monsoon rain, which effectively allowed campaigning for only six months each year.

Undoubtedly, 1942 was a bad year for the British in Burma. The Japanese occupied Rangoon in March and, in a retreat that resembled the events in Malaya, Allied troops fell back to north-east India. With the Middle East being Britain's immediate priority, the forces in the Far East were starved of men and resources. There were additional crises to attend to, not least the disastrous famine that struck Bengal which left 3,000,000 dead. Another drain on the British was the violent protests to 'Quit India', which took large numbers of British troops to suppress. In this state of unpreparedness, the British launched a small offensive into the Arakan in west Burma. Unable to penetrate very far, the attack was repulsed and the beaten army retreated to India.

In North Africa, Rommel's Afrika Korps was just 150 miles from Cairo at the small railway halt of El Alamein. The new Eighth Army commander, Bernard Montgomery, had fresh troops, increased armour and artillery and air supremacy. He also was very close to his source of supplies – Cairo – whereas Rommel's supply route had been extended to breaking point.

The Battle of El Alamein in October 1942, saw Rommel's forces begin a retreat through Libya to Tunis. It was a significant turning point in the war and the first major victory for the British Army against the Germans.

In January 1942, the powerful German battleship *Tirpitz* moved from the Baltic, through the Kiel Canal to Trondheim on the Norwegian coast. There was very real danger that she would break out into the North Atlantic and attack the Atlantic convoys. The only port capable of handling a ship of her size was the Brittany port of St Nazaire, which lay six miles from the mouth of the River Loire. A plot was hatched by the Planning Division in the Admiralty to destroy the Normandie dry dock which was the only one that could accommodate *Tirpitz*. The idea was taken to Vice-Admiral Louis Mountbatten, who had recently become Chief of Combined Operations. Time was critical for the mouth of the Loire is full of shifting sandbanks and a high spring tide would enable an invasion force to overcome these obstacles.

The raid that followed has, with some justification, been called the 'Greatest Raid of All'. It led to a lavish round of gallantry medals which included five Victoria Crosses, these being those to Lieutenant Commander Stephen Beattie, Commander Robert Ryder, Able Seaman Bill Savage, Sergeant Thomas Durrant and Lieutenant-Colonel Charles Newman.

AUGUSTUS CHARLES NEWMAN VC (1904-1972)

Augustus Charles was born on 19 August 1904 to Bertram and Margaret Newman of Buckhurst Hill, Chigwell, Essex. He attended Bancroft's School, Woodford Green, and left in 1922 at the age of eighteen. He joined a small civil engineering firm at Buckhurst Hill called W.C. French, which was to be his sole employer for his working life.

Newman joined the Territorial Army, which also had an enjoyable social attraction; he always took his golf clubs to camp. Being an engineer, he first joined the Engineer and Railway Staff Corps, but later transferred to the 4th Battalion Essex Regiment.

In 1928, Newman married Audrey Hickman and together they produced a large family of five girls and a son.

Charles, as he preferred to be known, kept a small notebook filled with his small neat handwriting. In this he kept a record of the events that led up to the 'Greatest Raid of All'. Before then, he had, under the heading 'And so to Germany', written: 'It was a strange coincidence that the first intimation of my "call-up" should have been through the Press. I remember I was in the printing works of "The Evening Standard" at the time. I was, in civil life a Contractor and my firm were rebuilding these works. War was looming ahead and, being a Territorial, one was daily expecting things to happen. On this particular afternoon, I chanced to call in to have a chat with the Editor, who told me that information had come through that the Territorials, or part of them, were going to be employed. As I was on the first call-up list of my Battalion, called the 'Key Party', I guessed this meant – ME!

'I'd better tell you that I was a Major in the Essex Regiment. I've been a Territorial for sixteen years having started for year as a Private Soldier, and loved every minute of it … The one desire was to soldier with one's friends, to have under one's command all those lads from Barking, East Ham and outer London whom we had trained from raw recruits. We knew all their families and loved them all and now was a chance to fight with them … How strange, in fact, it all turned out that in my case, it was fated that I should not see my Battalion in action.'

After weeks of training and being moved from one billet to another, Newman ended up in Northumberland. His CO, Colonel Gibbs, called him to HQ and asked him, '"Would you volunteer for a dangerous job?" "Yes, sir!" (I didn't know what he meant but I supposed one did these things).

"'You have been selected to Command a composite volunteer force to be paired from the Division to go to a place unknown, to carry out a job unknown for an unknown length of time. Would you like to go?"

'Well, I ask you! I was given a free hand to choose one officer and twenty men, all to volunteer, from the Battalion to go with me. 21 men from 1000 – what a job!'

It was March 1940 and Newman had been selected to lead No.3 of the newly-formed Independent Companies, the forerunner of the Commandos. With the addition of selected personnel from the Royal Engineers, Signals and Service Corps, they numbered about 150 men.

Norway

Newman and his comrades were issued with equipment such as snow shoes, skis and ropes, so it was deduced that Norway was to be their destination. Also, £4,000 in banknotes was to be taken to help buy food, horses, carts, cars etc. Their initial purpose was to operate behind enemy lines, but this was altered to assist the main British force as it withdrew northwards, by harassing the Germans on their flanks.

After a most uncomfortable voyage across the North Sea, they were landed at Bodö, about sixty miles inside the Arctic Circle. The Germans were anxious to capture the ports of Narvik and Trondheim, which were ideal bases for their Atlantic raiders. Lacking the manpower, the British were steadily pushed northwards.

After much marching and counter-marching, Newman's command did have a fierce fire fight with the advance guard of the enemy. While they were covering the retreat of the Scots Guards, No.3 Independent Company took up a position overlooking a bridge. At length about 100 German soldiers on bicycles approached accompanied by a lorry. Waiting until they were only 150 yards away, Newman gave the order to open fire, with devastating effect.

'What a sight! Over they went like ninepins – steel helmets roll over the road – the first burst shattered the windscreen of the lorry which charged off the road – bicycles everywhere – talk about a suicide squad – darn good shooting!'

The bridge was blown up and the first fatality occurred when a soldier was hit by a piece of flying girder from over 400 yards. Another long and dreary retreat was ordered, with German 'planes constantly strafing them. All kit had been lost including greatcoats and blankets. The mountain top, where they were positioned, was swept by sleet and freezing winds. The men thought so much of their officer that they would take it in turns to cover him with their bodies so he could keep warm and get some sleep. Finally, they reached Bodö again.

'The sight of Bodö, that picturesque little town that we had seen so few days ago, was now nothing more than a smouldering ruin – absolutely flat.'

They embarked on a British destroyer, which was to take them eventually as far north as Tromso. Orders came for them to transfer, mid-ocean, to the ill-fated *Lancastria* and return to Britain. The Norwegian campaign was at an end.

After a few days back in Scotland, everyone was wondering how soon they could get back to their own units. Newman was told that there were other jobs ahead for the Independent Companies and he was to sort out those who would re-volunteer. About 150 did and were sent up the West Coast to Traigh House near Arisaig.

'The new policy was explained to me – I was to get the Company up to strength with new volunteers from the Division and train for new duties. "Raids on the French Coast" was the order!

'The inspiration and leader of this training and Independent Companies was that famous veteran Admiral of the Fleet, Sir Roger Keyes, and he came to Traigh telling us of the job we were going to do. (His title was Director of Combined Operations).'

The men trained extensively in landing from the sea, mountaineering, demolition and long marches lasting several days and nights resulting in a tough and very fit unit. There was a period of frustration after the Battle of Britain when Newman's company was detailed for defensive duties at Dungeness in Kent in anticipation of an invasion.

'About this time, I was besieged with cables from West Africa where my old Battalion had gone, to re-join them … I did not know what to do as I liked this irregular soldiering and was very fond of my Company, but the ties to the old Battalion were very strong.

'The decision was made in a very odd way. I was summoned to Sandwich to meet a Colonel Glendenning who informed me that Independent Companies were being disbanded forthwith; they were all combining into Special Service Battalions and the raiding theme was going to be carried out on a much larger scale. That meeting with Willie Glendenning was a momentous one for me "I want you to be my Second in Command." I replied, "I'm on!"'

Most of the men chosen had to accompany Newman to Dartmouth where they were formed into No.1 Special Service Battalion. Another nine Special Service Battalions were being formed all over the country: 'As No.1, we naturally felt the Senior Battalion! Our training here was very much tied up with the Royal Navy … and trips were arranged to visit destroyers, submarines and anything that came in to the Dart. I had a day or two at sea on HMS Jupiter with Captain 'D' Lord Louis Mountbatten.'

Training was continuous, but whenever an operation was in the offing, it was cancelled. There was another plea from his old CO to join the Essex Regiment in West Africa but, again, the decision was made by another change.

'5/4/41. It had been found that for the type of soldering we were to do, the Special Service Battalions were too large and an order came from above that they would all be dissolved but new units, smaller, would be formed to be called 'Commandos'. My chance came when No.1 Special Service Battalion split – No.1 Company became No.1 Commando with Willie Glendenning in command and No.2 Company forming No.2 Commando, whose command I was given. This meant promotion to Lieutenant Colonel … This change started the ball rolling for the happiest and most exciting part of the war for me.'

Early in 1942, Charles Newman was ordered once more to the War Office. Admiral Sir Roger Keyes had been replaced as Director of Combined Operations by Lord Louis Mountbatten.

'Was this to be another false alarm or had our time come at last? … I went along to the DCO's office and was handed an Intelligence file of St Nazaire … a very illuminating document of the docks showing the new Dry Dock and its workings and many photos of the Normandie being built in the Dock. Apart from being very interesting, I was not much enlightened until the Brigadier (Charles Haydon, head of the Special Service Brigade) arrived and told me of the proposed plan to carry out a raid in these docks with the idea of smashing them up. Not only was it the biggest raid yet attempted but No.2 Commando were to provide the fighting troops for it! This was something like it! … the next few days were probably the most momentous in any life. One office to myself (literally locked in for security reasons) a marvellous model of St Nazaire – a large scale aerial photograph – the Intelligence summary and many meetings at which the plans were discussed.'

After a planning meeting on 26 February, Colonel Newman was introduced to his opposite number on the naval side, Commander R.E.D. Ryder, nicknamed 'Red'. Ryder had been asked to attend the meeting and was startled when Mountbatten sprung on him the news that he was to lead the naval force in what was called Operation *Chariot*.

While Newman was involved in the planning, he sent instructions to Scotland for his second-in-command, Major Bill Copland, to proceed with training in night-time street fighting.

The object of Operation *Chariot* was to render the huge dry dock at St Nazaire inoperable for Germany's last remaining battleship, *Tirpitz*. The means decided upon was the ramming of an explosive-packed destroyer into the huge lock gates and detonating it with time-delay fuses. The Commandos were to land and destroy the pump house and winding gear for opening and closing the enormous caissons. The intensive training included setting the explosive charges by touch as they would be working in pitch darkness. The date set was the night of 27/28th March – barely a month away.

On Friday, 13 March, as Newman was about to leave London to travel to Falmouth to meet up with his command, he was called back by Lord Mountbatten, who had some very forthright comments to make. Emphasising that the operation was of the highest importance, he added that he did not expect any of them to return.

'If we lose you all, you will be the equivalent to the loss of one merchant ship, but your success will save many merchant ships. We have got to look at the thing in those terms.'

Meanwhile, 'Red' Ryder had been organising the fleet of motor launches that would deliver the Commandos to their target. He and Newman travelled to Portsmouth to view the destroyer which was to be rammed into the dock gates. This was an obsolete US destroyer, the former USS *Buchanan*, which was renamed HMS *Campbeltown*. The destroyer was moved to Devonport to have extensive modifications made, these being completed in just nine days.

The sixteen motor launches, each carrying about fifteen Commandos, were not ideal troop-carrying craft. With the naval crew, they were very crowded and the installation of an extra 500-gallon fuel tank on the upper deck did not make conditions easier. Two extra small ships were included; a Motor Torpedo Boat (*MTB 74*) and a Motor Gun Boat (*MGB 314*), the latter acting as the HQ boat and carrying both Newman and Ryder to St Nazaire.

HMS *Campbeltown* underwent a complete facelift. The four funnels were reduced to two and their tops raked to give them the superficial appearance of a German Möwe-class destroyer. Her draft was reduced and the main guns and other excess weight removed so she could negotiate the shallow Loire estuary. The most important alteration was the explosives sited near the original forward gun position. This consisted of twenty-four Mark VIII depth charges enclosed in steel tanks and concrete and totalling an explosive charge weight of 3.17 metric tonnes.

Campbeltown was commanded by Lieutenant Commander Stephen Beattie, who, for some reason, was known in the Royal Navy as 'Sam'. The number of men involved in attack was 611, of whom 257 were Commandos. The Commando force was divided into three groups, two on the motor launches and one on *Campbeltown.* These were further divided into demolition and protection squads. The former carried 60 to 90lbs of demolition equipment, including axes and sledgehammers, so they were armed only with pistols. The protection squads were fully armed with Thompson machine-guns, hand grenades and Bren guns.

Because the raid would be at night and identification difficult, Newman ordered all webbing to be scrubbed white. They were also issued with the new rubber-soled boots, and Newman told his men that 'if you hear anybody whose boots are crunching, you can shoot him – he'll be a German'. He also made up the password, which would be difficult for Germans to pronounce correctly – 'War Weapons Week' – to which the reply was 'Weymouth'.

As the attack date approached, Newman gathered his men together and went through the whole plan again. He then relayed the message that Mountbatten had given him on the steps of the Admiralty – that he was sure they would do the job but that their chances of getting home again were negligible. He gave the men the last opportunity to stand down if the wished to, with no stain on their record, but not a single man took up the offer.

It was planned that the RAF would mount a diversionary air raid on St Nazaire to protect, for as long as it was possible, the flotilla's approach up the Loire. There was some rancour about this plan as Bomber Command needed all available aircraft for its own operations and was reluctant to use the numbers of aircraft that Mountbatten wanted. Also, Winston Churchill refused permission to bomb the town itself for fear of damaging relationships with the French. The forecast predicted deterioration in the weather and Ryder suggested they brought forward the attack one day to 26 March.

At 14.00 hours, under a sunny sky, the flotilla set sail from Falmouth, escorted by the destroyers *Atherstone* and *Tynedale,* following a long circuitous route to their target. There were a couple of alarms. A distant U-boat was spotted and attacked. Although she escaped, she had reported that the British ships were mine-laying. Soon after they came upon a fleet of French fishing trawlers but once it was ascertained that there were no enemy observers aboard, they were allowed to go.

At 20.10 hours on 27 May, they spotted the signal flashes from the submarine HMS *Sturgeon* which was acting as a navigational beacon to get a pin-point for the final run in. Finally, after a thirty-six hours' voyage, it was time to transfer from the destroyer to *MGB 314*. Once they had manoeuvred into formation, with *Campbeltown* astern and two columns of motor launches on either side, *MGB 314* led the final leg of the journey; seventy-five miles to St Nazaire. The two destroyers turned away and began their night patrol off the mouth of the Loire to wait for any surviving boats.

At half-past midnight, the small force entered the Loire estuary just as the diversionary bombing raid began. Unfortunately, it was premature and desultory and had the effect of putting the German defences on alert. The flotilla was now in dangerous shoal waters and speed was reduced to minimise *Campbeltown*'s draft as much as possible. She was also flying the German ensign in an effort to buy time if spotted but just two miles from their target, they were discovered.

A large searchlight suddenly illuminated the whole formation and a there was a burst of machine-gun fire in front of the bows of *MGB 314*. The British had been prepared for this and a long, delaying message in German complete with a genuine call sign and a Very-light recognition signal bought some precious minutes with scarcely a mile to go.

After minutes of indecision, the Germans opened a heavy fire and the British ships responded. Sam Beattie, on *Campbeltown*, ordered full steam-ahead and the hoisting of their battle ensign. This was the signal for all the small boats to do the same. The night became a wild pattern of criss-crossing fire and briefly, the British seemed to have subdued the German defences.

On *MGB 314*, Able Seaman Bill Savage, manning the forward pom-pom, managed to silence the harbour defence ship that stood off the East Jetty directly blocking the course the British were taking. The brief respite was temporary as the German defences concentrated a murderous fire on *Campbeltown* which was repeatedly hit but Beattie kept her on course and increased her speed to twenty knots.

Four minutes late, at 01.34 hours on 28 March, *Campbeltown* struck the massive caisson dead centre with such a force that she rode up so her bows were resting on top of the gate. The six-hour delay fuses had been set shortly before she had come under fire. Covering fire from *Campbeltown*'s Oerlikons covered the Commando teams as they quickly disembarked and headed for their targets. The protection teams landed first and silenced four gun positions which enabled the demolition teams to reach their targets and successfully destroy them. Amazingly, these were all completed within half an hour of *Campbeltown* embedding itself in the caisson.

Just before *Campbeltown* had accelerated towards its target, *MGB 314*, which was still leading, veered to starboard and circled around to land Newman and his HQ team at the wooden jetty on the south side of the Old Entrance. At about 01.40 hours and with a handshake, Ryder and Newman parted, not to see each other again for three and a half years.

The MGB then crossed to the north side of the Old Entrance to pick up survivors from *Campbeltown*. The MTB also entered and fired its torpedoes at the outer lock-gates of the Old Entrance, before taking on survivors. Both vessels then headed for home through the carnage and wreckage of the badly mauled motor launches. In fact, seven of these flimsy craft had been destroyed, drastically reducing the number of Commando parties to be landed.

The Old Mole, on which most of the Commandos were to have landed, proved to be so heavily defended that it was impossible to put them ashore. Those who were not killed were frustrated when the motor launch commanders were forced to abort and fight their way downstream to the open sea.

When Newman landed, he was unaware of the destruction of the motor launches and the failure to land at the Old Mole. He had selected a building near Bridge G at the far end of the Old Entrance to be his headquarters and led his HQ group towards it. He found the building apparently deserted and began to look for the entrance. As he walked around a corner, he 'bumped helmets' with a German and instinctively said: 'Sorry'.

The German hurriedly surrendered and divulged that the building was being used as a HQ of sorts by the Germans. He ordered the German to go in and bring out his comrades with their hands up. Before this could be done, the HQ party was spotted and fired upon. They took cover behind the building and there established their HQ.

About 113 Commandos had been landed, of whom forty were only armed with pistols. They had little difficulty in dealing with the superior numbers of enemy troops, but were almost helpless under the concentrated fire from the fixed gun positions and the ships in the harbour, some of whom were firing at close quarters. Despite the withering fire, there were some telling fights with the German troops who started pouring into the area known as the Old Town inland from the Old Mole.

Gradually, these dispersed small units gathered at the HQ. Colonel Newman's calm and jovial manner was remarked upon by many of his men and had the effect of reassuring everyone. He still did not know of the disaster that had destroyed most of the landing motor launches, and he joined his Number 2, Major Bill Copland, in making for the quayside to organise re-embarkation. When they emerged from the maze of building and saw the river around the Old Mole, they were horrified. The water was on fire and the wreckage of motor launches littered the river.

'Well, Bill, there goes our transport', Newman wryly remarked, for gone were the hopes of a safe return to the UK. The first task was to rally his men and work out a new strategy. Having rejected surrender, despite being almost completely surrounded, Newman ordered his men in to groups of twenty. They were to force their way across Bridge D at the head of the Southern Entrance leading to the Submarine Basin, fight their way through the town to open country and make for the Spanish border and thence to Gibraltar – a mere 1,000 miles.

Leaving the warehouse area, the Commandos began fighting their way towards the girder bridge, taking casualties all the way. Finally reaching the bridge, they barely hesitated before charging over in the face of machine-gun and rifle fire. The Germans were so astonished at this seemingly suicidal charge that they fired too high and were forced to retreat. The machine-gun nests were put out of action as the Commandos raced away.

Suddenly a motor-cycle combination and an armoured car appeared at the cross-roads ahead and Newman knew at once that units of the German Army had arrived. If they had arrived fifteen minutes later, the British would have reached the marsh country outside the town and stood a chance of escape.

With the area now effectively sealed by this unwelcome increase of enemy forces, the Commandos split in to smaller parties and began what was later termed the 'St Nazaire Obstacle Race'. To keep clear of the streets, the Commandos clambered over back walls, through chicken coops and even through houses in an effort to evade capture. Newman recalled going head-first into a parlour with the breakfast things already laid out on a blue check table cloth. It was noticed that the Germans were very jumpy and shooting at anything that moved, frequently hitting their own men.

As dawn approached, Newman decided to lie up during the day and led fifteen men, most of whom were wounded, into a spacious cellar equipped as an air-raid shelter complete with mattresses. A few hours later, they were discovered and Newman dashed upstairs and offered surrender to prevent any possibility of a grenade being pitched amongst his men.

They were roughly pulled from their refuge and marched across the road and taken into the house opposite which turned out to be the German headquarters. During the course of the morning, more individuals and small groups were picked up and, despite their plight, their spirits were high. The only thing that worried them was that the time that *Campbeltown* was due to blow up had passed and doubts appeared as to whether the time fuses had failed.

The Germans also could not understand the purpose of the raid. So many lives and effort expended for so little gain. *Campbeltown* had become the centre of attraction and dozens, maybe hundreds, of Germans and their female companions wandered around the strange enemy wreck.

At about 10.35 hours there was a great roar and the building shook as if hit by an earthquake. While the Germans rushed around in panic, the prisoners let out a great cheer. *Campbeltown* had exploded.

The effects were even more devastating than planned. Between 100 and 300 Germans were blown to pieces and their grisly remains scattered about the dock area. The already tense Germans were further unnerved when the torpedoes that had been fired at the Old Entrance lock exploded the following afternoon. Sabotage was suspected and period of indiscriminate firing against the French followed.

All the prisoners were moved to the nearby seaside town of La Baule where Sam Beattie was among the naval personnel who joined the Commandos. Then, after more interrogation, the able and slightly wounded prisoners were sent to a prison camp, *Frontstalag 133*, at Rennes, which was in a filthy condition. It was there that Newman received a visit from a German naval officer who wished to report the outstanding bravery of one of his men. This was Sergeant Tom Durrant, who had engaged a German destroyer during the withdrawal down the Loire. Durrant had continued to fire a Lewis gun, despite being mortally wounded. The German officer related his captain's report and mentioned the gallant conduct of a sergeant, 'as you may wish to recommend him for a high award'. This was also corroborated by a survivor of *ML 306*.

Fortunately, they were soon moved from Rennes on to less unpleasant camp at Sandbostel in Germany. A most unusual event occurred there.

The camp commandant, an old German admiral, ordered a special parade. He called Colonel Newman forward along with Sam Beattie. The old admiral announced that Sam had been awarded the Victoria Cross to the delight of all the prisoners. In fact, both Ryder and Beattie were gazetted on the same day, 21 May 1942, along with Able Seaman Bill Savage, who received a posthumous VC.

In time, the prisoners were again moved. The naval personnel were sent to *Marlag und Milag Nord* near Bremen, while Newman and fellow officers went to *Oflag X1A* near Kassel. Newman remained there until the camp was liberated in 1945.

When Colonel Newman returned to Britain, he put forward Tom Durrant's name for the Victoria Cross. He himself received the same honour and they were both announced in *The London Gazette* dated 19 June 1945. His citation reads: 'On the night of 27/28 March 1942, Lieutenant-Colonel Newman was in command of the military force detailed to land on enemy occupied territory and destroy the dock installations of the German controlled naval base at St Nazaire. This important base was known to be heavily defended and bomber support had to be abandoned due to bad weather [*sic*].

'The operation was therefore bound to be exceedingly hazardous, but Lieutenant-Colonel Newman, although empowered to call off the assault at any stage, was determined to carry to a successful conclusion the important task which had been assigned to him. Coolly and calmly he stood on the bridge of the leading craft, as the small force steamed up the estuary of the River Loire, although the ships had been caught in the enemy searchlights and a murderous cross- fire opened from both banks, causing heavy casualties.

'Although Lieutenant-Colonel Newman need not have landed himself, he was one of the first ashore and during the next five hours of bitter fighting, he personally entered several houses and shot up the occupants and supervised the operations in the town, utterly regardless of his own safety, and he never wavered in his resolution to carry through the operation upon which so much depended. An enemy gun position on the roof of the U-boat pen had been causing heavy casualties to the landing craft and Lieutenant-Colonel Newman directed the fire of a mortar crew against this position such an effect that the position was silenced. Still fully exposed, he then brought machine gun fire to bear on an armed trawler in the harbour, compelling it to withdraw and thus preventing many casualties in the main demolition area.

'Under the brilliant leadership of this officer the troops fought magnificently and held vastly superior enemy forces at bay, until the demolition parties had successfully completed their work of destruction. By this time, however, most of the landing craft had been sunk or set on fire and evacuation by sea was no longer possible. Although the main objective had been achieved, Lieutenant-Colonel Newman nevertheless was determined to try and fight his way out into open country and so give all survivors and chance to escape. The only way out of the harbour area lay across a narrow iron bridge covered by enemy machine-guns and although severely shaken by a German hand grenade, which had burst at his feet, Lieutenant-Colonel Newman personally led the charge which stormed the position and under his inspiring leadership the small force fought its way through the streets to a point near open country, when, all ammunition expended, he and his men were finally overpowered by the enemy.

'The outstanding gallantry and devotion to duty of this fearless officer, his brilliant leadership and initiative, were largely responsible for the success of this perilous operation which resulted in heavy damage to the important naval base at St Nazaire.'

On 11 December 1945, Charles Newman, accompanied by his mother, went to Buckingham Palace to be presented with his VC by King George VI. Also receiving their Crosses that day were Ian Fraser and James Magennis of X-craft fame.

Newman kept in touch with his old comrades, who felt much affection for him. One of his men, Captain Micky Burn MC, wrote of him: 'Numerous heroes and born leaders came my way in the Commandos .... Charles Newman is the one I am most thankful to have had as our Colonel. He was thirty-eight, a Territorial officer with sixteen years in the Essex Regiment, by profession a building engineer, in politics Conservative and very "sound", married, unlike nearly all of us, with a family, convivial, gregarious, a non-intellectual, ringside, rugger-playing hearty, who also played jazz and music-hall on the piano. The Commando became an extension of his family.

'To me Charles remained volunteer, almost civilian ... He imposed discipline, but lightness bubbled up; sternness came out of a necessary tap. I do not say that he made war fun. The purpose of a soldier in war is to kill and not be killed. But I reckon that he saw training as a kind of playing-field: not for him at Eton, on which the battle of Waterloo may or may not have been won, but somewhere more gritty, familiar to those his Essex Regiment had trained in peacetime.'

With the post war boom in building and construction, W.C. French prospered and expanded and Charles grew with it. After forty-six years with the company, in which he saw this little Essex firm grow in to a large international company, he retired as Chairman in 1969. Charles and his wife moved to Sandwich, Kent, where he was naturally drawn to the famous St George's Golf Club. His retirement was sadly short for he died just three years later on 26 April 1972 aged sixty-seven. He was cremated and his ashes scattered in the Garden of Remembrance at Barham Crematorium. His medal group is displayed at the Ashcroft Gallery, Imperial War Museum.

Churchill had returned from a meeting with Joseph Stalin in Moscow, where the Russian leader urged the Allies to open a second front to divert German troops to the west. Unwilling and unready for a full-scale invasion of France, Churchill was persuaded by the Director of Combined Operations, Admiral Lord Louis Mountbatten, of his plan for a 'reconnaissance in force' on Dieppe. The success of the raid on St Nazaire encouraged Mountbatten to launch another Combined Operation assault on mainland Europe.

With Churchill's blessing, Mountbatten pushed through the raid over the objections of other senior officers who thought the plan was ill-advised and flawed. The idea of landing such a small force on the beaches of Dieppe, have them destroy some coastal defences, hold the town for two tides and then withdraw seemed not only foolhardy but would in no way alleviate the pressure on Russia.

The amphibious landing would be the greatest since Gallipoli in 1915 and would match it as a disaster. Three VCs were awarded for this debacle; two to members of the Canadian forces and one to a British Commando officer, Patrick Porteous.

Despite the setbacks, the Allies saw victories in North Africa, at Stalingrad and America's entry into the war. There was now a detectable shifting of the balance away from the Axis powers.

Chapter 53

The Second World War, 1943

Number of VCs awarded	25
Number of VCs awarded to officers	16
Number of VCs awarded to other ranks	9
Total awarded to Royal Navy	3
Total awarded to Royal Air Force	6
Total awarded to British Army	8
Total awarded to British Indian Army	4
Total awarded to Canadian Army	1
Total awarded to Australian Army	2
Total awarded to New Zealand Army	1

Origins of the War

With the fall of Singapore and defeat in Burma, Britain retreated into India to reorganise and build up her forces. Although there was an abortive advance in the Arakan area of western Burma which ended with defeat, Britain pulled back to her border positions in the remote area of north-east India. As Britain's influence in the Far East declined with her attention focused on Germany, Australia turned to America as her principal defender. The Americans planned to use Australia and New Zealand as bases from which they could launch attacks on the Japanese in the Pacific. Despite the fact that not all Australians were happy about accepting American military assistance, the Australian Prime Minister, John Curtin, appointed General Douglas MacArthur as Supreme Commander of the South West Pacific Area which gave him direct command of the Australian military.

Attention focused on Port Moresby, the capital of New Guinea, about 500 miles north-east of Queensland. The Japanese had made Port Moresby an essential objective as it would give them a base from which they could strike north and eastern Australia. They had already invaded the north and eastern part of New Guinea and were ready to advance across the Owen Stanley Mountain Range, via the Kokoda Track, to take Port Moresby.

The Japanese managed to get within thirty miles of Port Moresby but exhaustion and lack of ammunition forced them to retreat. It had been a close-run thing, but the ill-equipped Australians had managed to prevent the all-important capital from being captured.

The terrain of New Guinea precluded large-scale overland movements which forced MacArthur to use attack aircraft to bomb and strafe the Japanese positions north of the Owen Stanley Mountain Range. For the Royal Australian Air Force its involvement resulted in the posthumous award of the Victoria Cross to one of its most daring pilots.

WILLIAM ELLIS NEWTON VC (1919-1943)

William 'Bill' Ellis Newton was born on 8 June 1919 at St Kilda, Melbourne, Australia, the only son of Minnie Newton (née Miller) – the second wife of dentist Charles Ellis Newton. He was educated at Melbourne Church of England Grammar School, before moving to St Kilda Park Central School when the family's income was drastically curtailed due to the effects of the Great Depression in the 1930s. There were fewer clothes and family meals were less grand as fewer patients attended Charles's surgery.

In 1934 at the age of fifteen, the now six-foot-three-inches, sixteen stone and stocky schoolboy returned to Melbourne Grammar to continue his studies. Even at his young age he was certainly determined and worked hard in his studies, earning 100 per cent in his exam and winning the school's Latin prize. He excelled in sport and was considered to be an all-rounder; his skills in leadership, coupled with a strong temperament were spotted by his schoolmasters – qualities that would be displayed with devastating precision in his later life. He represented the school in cricket, football and swimming. A natural candidate for being the senior prefect, he also led younger boys as a sergeant in the school's cadet corps. Any dreams of future careers he may have fostered had to be suppressed for the time being as tragedy hit the Newton family when his father died suddenly of a heart attack at just fifty-one in September 1936. The family was split up with Bill staying with his mother and the others going to other family members.

Newton's stint as a sergeant in the cadet corps propelled him to join the 6th Battalion, Royal Melbourne Regiment of militia on 28 November 1938. His immediate ambition, though, was to join the RAAF.

When war was declared in September 1939, Newton joined the RAAF on 5 February 1940. On 14 March 1940, after eight hours of instruction, he completed his first solo flight; he became a pilot officer on 28 June 1940, just three weeks after turning twenty-one. Because of his flying aptitude, he was selected to become a flight instructor; something he did not seek.

On 9 May 1942, after two years as an instructor, Newton managed to obtain a posting to an operational unit – 22 (City of Sydney) Squadron at Richmond RAAF base – and was promoted to flight lieutenant. His arrival coincided with the delivery of new Douglas Boston bombers sent to replace the now obsolete Wirraway.

New Guinea

Between July and September 1942, the squadron was engaged in convoy escort and anti-submarine patrols off Sydney before taking its Bostons to Townsville, Queensland. No.22 Squadron was then tasked with a dangerous form of aerial attack, diving low over the objective and bombing and strafing the target. The Boston was a tough dependable aircraft with an excellent reputation for speed and manoeuvrability.

By November 1942 the squadron was deployed to Port Moresby, Papua New Guinea, under the leadership of No.9 Operational Group, RAAF. With the approach of Christmas 1942, Bill went home on leaveto see his mother. With a hint of fatalism, as Bill left, he told his mother that if he did not return, 'not to make a fuss'.

Before the entry of Japan into the war in December 1941 the majority of Australia's forces had been fighting alongside the British in North Africa. Things changed in 1942 with the start of the New Guinea Campaign. Prior to the Second World War the north-east part of the island of New Guinea was controlled by the Australians. Papua in the south was an Australian colony and the Dutch held the western part of the island. Strategically, New Guinea was crucial to the Australians as it sits immediately to the north. Due to the flatness of the land it provided ample room for land, air and naval bases.

In early 1942, clashes between Allied and Japanese forces began with a Japanese attack on Rabaul – which became a springboard for other Japanese attacks, including the Battle of Buna-Gona. Newton's 22 Squadron had assisted in attempting to prevent the Japanese creating a beachhead in the Buna-Gona area of Oro Bay at New Guinea.

Only a small brigade was stationed at Port Moresby on the south coast. Although smaller garrisons on the north coast and the Solomon Islands were withdrawn when the Japanese attacked, holding onto Port Moresby was deemed essential as any Japanese attack at this location could have easily reached Queensland on the Australian mainland.

After Rabaul, the Japanese had fixed their attention on at the large town of Lae and the small administrative town/port in Salamaua on the north coast of New Guinea. In March 1942, the Japanese occupied Salamaua, originally meant to be a springboard for attacks on Port Moresby. When these proved fruitless they turned the port into a key supply base. These two towns became a battleground between the Allies and the Japanese. Casualties were heavy – 5,700 Australian and 2,800 US – with three time as many suffering from sickness in the malarial jungles.

Air support was vital in the fight for places like Kokoda and the Kumusi River, where Japanese defences were overcome with the aid of bridging materials that were dropped by air. Australian and USAAF air units upheld a relentless barrage of bombing raids in this area and meeting heavy accurate fire from well-sited Japanese anti-aircraft batteries.

As January1943 dawned, Newton undertook the first of fifty-two operational sorties under the command of Squadron Leader Keith Hampshire. Lae proved to be one of the last bastions of Japanese resistance; the enemy was intent on holding onto it and assembled a huge sixteen-ship convoy to protect it. During January and early February, 22 Squadron's records show an impressive tally of successful sorties. Newton had gained a formidable reputation at diving headlong onto the targets, swooping low to just above tree level, taking advantage by bombing any target he could. This had earned the fearless Newton the nickname 'Firebug', for leaving his target in flames and he often returned with a bullet-riddled aircraft. On one mission, ninety-eight bullet holes were counted on his aircraft. Flying these sorties, Newton cut an instantly recognisable figure for his wearing a blue soft cricket cap.

VC Action

At 06.45 hours on 2 March 1943, Newton, in one of six Boston aircraft from 22 Squadron, flew down the Markham Valley and again attacked Lae airfield, dropping fifteen bombs along the full length of the runway and straffing the assembled Japanese fighters. This hampered the Japanese as they were now unable to operate their fighter aircraft which gave the Allied bombers free-rein in what became known as the Battle of the Bismarck Sea.

On 16 March his objective was to hit supply dumps near McDonald's Road. The flight report was typically modest and did not recant the full impact, merely stating: 'Stores and buildings of foreshore of Salamaua bombed .... Remaining bombs covered target area, starting four fires, which were converging into one general fire covering practically the whole area ... Flames were rising several hundred feet.'

Newton's VC citation states: 'He dived through intense and accurate shell fire and his aircraft was hit repeatedly. Nevertheless he held his course and bombed his target from a low level. The attack resulted in the destruction of many buildings and dumps including two 40,000 gallon fuel installations.'

Although accurate, the attack on the Salamaua Isthmus was nothing short of death-defying – though this drama is not captured in the citation. The Japanese ground fire had peppered the fuselage of Newton's Boston, damaged both wings, repeatedly holed the fuel tanks and near killed the right engine. He had run the gauntlet through 800 metres of fanatical anti-aircraft fire, and he had to fly straight towards the guns as the battery protecting the target was in line with the best approach to the target. At this point, Newton had a choice (the aircraft had suffered four direct hits), either to fly to Dobodura forty miles away to refuel or a 180-mile flight back to base at Ward's Field. He chose the latter.

Though the trip back was uneventful more headaches ensued as one of the bomber's tyres had been damaged and on touchdown the Boston ran off the runway, though no injuries were recorded. Newton landed at 10.05 hours.

It was on the strength of the 16 March sortie and other similar exploits that Newton's CO recommended him for the VC: 'Despite this harassing experience, he returned next day to the same locality. His target this time was a single building, was even more difficult but he again attacked with his usual courage and resolution.'

Thursday, 18 March saw Newton's Boston, coded A28-3, and five other bombers leave Ward's Field, Port Moresby, at 09.02 hours to bomb an objective at Salamaua. Reports of the day show that the bombing was accurate, starting many fires in stores and buildings. Eyewitness accounts attest to fires burning brightly, if only for a short duration. Sadly, on lifting over his target the anti-aircraft ground fire struck lucky and raked the fuselage and wings of Newton's Boston.

RAAF records recount the next few desperate seconds: 'Aircraft A28-3 seen smoking after leaving target area, later caught on fire and landed in water approximately 1.5 miles south of Lapui Point and one mile out to sea and sank in a few seconds.'

It is believed that Bill still had use of the aileron rudder plus engine control as he flew low south-east. Newton had battled to get his craft to the shoreline and away from the enemy so that his crew had a fighting chance at survival. The belly of the 'plane hit the sea at over 120mph, skimmed the water for about 150 yards, finally coming to rest around 900 yards from the shore. The aircraft sank in a matter of seconds.

On reaching shore Newton and his wireless-operator, Flight-Sergeant John Lyon, ran into some natives who agreed to lead them to safety. It is unknown why the two flyers broke from their guides. One theory is that they may have seen friendly aircraft – which had flown around the area for over two hours. They branched out on their own to find their way to friendly forces. Luck finally ran out for the pair as they were captured by a troop from the Japanese No.5 'Sasebo' Special Naval Landing Force, and sent to Lae for interrogation.

War Crime

The Japanese instantly recognised their prize (due to his cap) and he was interrogated by the feared Japanese military police, the *Kempeitai*. On the orders of Rear Admiral Ruitaro Fujita, Newton was sent back to Salamaua and into the hands of the 51st Infantry Division of the Imperial Japanese Army.

As one account states, 'the modus operandi of Japanese wartime interrogation was torture … with physical violation of the worse kind for almost a week. John & Bill had no training whatsoever … and it is doubtful they resisted for more than three days.'

John Lyon was executed by bayoneting through the back. Newton's fate was to be spun out even further until 29 March.

In 1943, the Australia government appointed Sir William Webb to investigate allegations of Japanese war crimes. In his first report he wrote of the fate of William Newton based on a captured diary from a Japanese eyewitness soldier entitled 'Blood Carnival' which Webb assumed was genuine. Sections of the diary entry record:

'29/3/43: All four of us assembled in front of HQ at 15.00 hrs … one of the … Douglas crew … had been under cross examination by 7 Base Force for some days … it has been decided to kill him. Tai Commander (Uichi) Komai (9) … he was going to kill the prisoner himself with his favourite sword. The prisoner … is given his last drink of water … the prisoner with his arms bound and his long hair cropped and close, totters forward … he is more composed than I thought he would be. (He is then taken on a truck for twenty minutes). I glance at the prisoner: he has probably resigned himself to his fate … he looked about … and seems deep in thought. (The truck stops). Komai says "we are going to kill you" … Prisoner says a few words in a low voice. Apparently he wants to be killed by one stroke of the sword. Commander replies "yes".

'Prisoner is made to kneel on the bank of a bomb crater filled with water (at Kila Point). He is apparently resigned … but remains calm. He even stretches out his neck, and is very brave. It (sword) glitters in the light and sends a cold shiver down my spine. He taps the prisoner's neck lightly … then raises it … and brings it down with a sweep … In that moment I closed my eyes … With a sound as though something watery has been cut out, body falls forward. The head detached from the trunk, rolls in front of it … The dark blood gushes out. All is over. A seaman … takes a sword … intent on paying off old scores … cuts his abdomen open … It is pushed over into the crater at once and is buried …This will be something to remember all my life.'

The body of the twenty-three-year-old Newton lay in the unmarked bomb crater in Salamaua until September 1943 when the Allies finally took the town from the Japanese. His body was located in the water-logged crater about thirty feet from the sea by an Australian local: 'I drained the crater and discovered the remains. It was lying on its stomach and arms outspread and was missing the head. I recovered every bone except the head. The remains were dressed in slacks and shirt.'

Bill Newton's family were understandably distraught. His nephews recalled: 'The family were devasta1ted to learn of Bill's death. More so when the circumstances and manner of his death became known. I know it left an indelible mark of sadness on my father [Bill's step-brother] for the rest of his life … many times he would confide in me how much he thought about Bill.'

The man who executed him, Lieutenant Uichi Komai, was killed in the Philippines soon after and the senior Japanese commander, Ruitaro Fujita, committed suicide at the end of the war.

Bill's body was initially interred with full military honours at Salamaua Military Cemetery. It was exhumed and moved to Lae War Cemetery, Papua New Guinea in January 1946. The VC recommendation was first made on 17 August 1943 by the Australian Governor General, Lord Gowrie. Newton was the only Australian airman to be awarded the Victoria Cross in the South West Pacific theatre.

The citation that appeared in *The London Gazette* on 19 October 1943 stated, the following, the full facts yet to be revealed: 'With great skill he [Newton] brought his blazing aircraft down on the water. Two members of the crew were able to extricate themselves and were seen swimming to the shore, but the gallant pilot was missing. According to other air-crews, who witnessed the occurrence, his escape hatch was not opened and his dinghy was not inflated.'

Some two and a half years after his death, William's mother, Minnie Newton, was presented with her son's VC by HRH the Duke of Gloucester in a ceremony at Melbourne. Interestingly the date engraved on the reverse of the VC shows the date when the submission was signed by the King, and not the date of the action. His medals were presented to the Australian War Memorial in January 1966.

In North Africa, the reinforced and well-supplied Eighth Army had beaten the Afrika Korps at the Battle of El Alamein. The RAF and the Royal Navy had gained the upper hand as the German and Italian armies retraced their steps across Libya. With his supply route stretched with few natural harbours along the North African coast, Rommel had little choice but to retreat to Tunisia, the closest to Axis-occupied Sicily.

In November 1942, Operation *Torch* saw the Americans and Allies land in Algeria with the intention of occupying Tunisia from the west. The advance was delayed, which gave the Axis time to build up their forces in Tunisia and the fight for that country became increasingly difficult for the Allies. The French had constructed a defence system in the south called the Mareth Line to counter any Italian invasion from Libya. The Germans occupied these formidable strongpoints to meet the British advance. To the west rose the Atlas Mountains which dominated the few passes from Algeria. To add to the Allies' problems the winter brought torrential rain that grounded their aircraft and turned the roads into quagmires.

In February 1943, Rommel's forces inflicted a heavy defeat on the inexperienced and poorly-led American troops at the Battle of Kasserine Pass. As the weather improved, a series of battles was fought which gradually dislodged the Germans, pushing them back to the ports of Tunis and Bizerte. The ferociousness of these battles can be gauged by the number of Victoria Crosses awarded between 20 March and 28 April. The ten awards were those made to Lieutenant Colonel Derek Seagrim, Second Lieutenant Ngarima, Subadar-Major Lalbahadur Thapa, Private Eric Anderson, Lieutanant Colonel Lorne Campbell, Company Havildar Major Chhelu Ram, Captain Lord Lyell, Major John Anderson, Lieutenant Sandys-Clarke and Lance Corporal John Kenneally.

JOHN KENNEALLY VC (1921-2000)

Leslie Jackson had just about the most unpromising start in life. He was born the illegitimate son of eighteen-year-old Gertrude Noel Robertson, the daughter of a Blackpool pharmacist on 15 March 1921. In those days, a pregnant unmarried daughter of a respectable middle class family was a social stigma, so Gertrude was sent off to a family friend in Birmingham and told never to darken their door again.

The other half of this liaison was Neville Leslie Blond, the Jewish son of a wool manufacturer, who had served as an officer in the Royal Horse Guards during the First Word War and been awarded the *Croix de Guerre*. He later married the daughter of Simon Marks of Marks & Spencer Ltd.

Christened Leslie, he was given Gertrude's new surname of Jackson. His mother made her living as a dance hall hostess and a high-class prostitute. Gertrude managed to obtain a maintenance order against Neville and she started a ladies' hairdressing business. In 1932, her son gained a scholarship place at King Edward's Grammar School, where he was an average scholar but exceeded in sports. He also enjoyed the Army cadets and later joined the Boy Scouts.

Life was still unsettled at home and money tight. Gertrude's business failed and she took a series of poorly-paid jobs. In 1938, Leslie matriculated and left school, working in an office before taking a job in a garage.

Enlists in the Army

In early 1939, Leslie and a friend joined the Territorial Army and took the advice of an old soldier, 'Don't join the bloody infantry, all that muck and mud and you march everywhere. Join the Royal Artillery and you will ride.'

By the time war was declared, Leslie had received a thorough training and, on 3 September 1939, graduated to a regular soldier. However, he became increasing disillusioned with the Royal Artillery, particularly when he was posted to the Honourable Artillery Company in London instead of going with his battery to France. In a rebellious mood, he extended a five-days leave to nine and was court martialled. Because of his previous good record, he was sentenced to just one month's detention at Wellington Barracks, near Buckingham Palace, the home of the Brigade of Guards.

The regiment occupying the barracks at that time was the Irish Guards and it made an immediate impact on him to the extent that, when his sentence was completed and he returned to the HAC, he put in a transfer request to join the Irish Guards. This was turned down flat. Instead, he was posted to a Light Anti-Aircraft Battery defending the RAF aerodrome at Waltham Abbey.

Change of Identity

Overlooked for promotion because of his blemished record, Leslie put in for another transfer to the Irish Guards, which was again refused. This time he was assigned to the Motor Transport Section, which entailed him driving around London and making deliveries to the scattered gun sites. This made him a free-agent and led to the biggest change of his life.

In one of the cafés he frequented during his rounds he met and befriended a group of Southern Irishmen, who had come over to do manual work, such as demolition, clearing bomb debris and blacking-out factories. They were each issued with an identity card which expired after six months. Under wartime regulations they were then eligible for call-up.

As the gang was going to Glasgow to work, he was invited to a farewell drink. Towards the end of the evening a fight broke out between servicemen and civilians; a not uncommon occurrence. It was broken up by the local constabulary and military police and he and his friends narrowly evaded arrest. In the cold light of the following morning, he saw that the bruises and ripped uniform would lead to further punishment when he returned to HQ. Also, in the fight he had lost his cap showing his name and number.

It did not take a lot of persuasion to accept the offer of joining the Irish gang and go to Glasgow under a fresh identity; John Patrick Kenneally. This was the name of a worker who had returned prematurely to Ireland and did not need his identity card.

New Name, New Regiment

After four weeks' working in Glasgow, his Irish friends returned to Ireland and Leslie travelled to Manchester as John Kenneally to enlist in the Irish Guards. He took easily to his new life and was very proud to become a Guardsman. After intense training, initially at Caterham Barracks, then at tough training areas around the country, he was appointed to No.1 Company, 1st Battalion Irish Guards.

In February 1943, the regiment embarked on the P&O troopship *Strathmore* bound for North Africa. *Strathmore* survived a German air attack, including torpedoes, off the coast of Tunis before arriving at Bône on 13 March.

The Bou

When the Germans were forced to retreat from the Mareth Line, they occupied a line of hills that barred the way to the plain beyond and so on to Tunis. The steep and rocky terrain meant that tanks could not operate effectively and that the job of clearing the way was left to the infantry. The initial advance successfully pushed the Germans off the first ridge line.

On the way, the Irish Guards passed the remnants of a company of Scots Guards which had been involved in fighting on their left flank. Their

Company Commander, Lord Lyell, had been killed and later received a posthumous Victoria Cross.

The main German position was on the massive rock-strewn feature called the Djebel Bou Azoukaz, simply referred to as The Bou, which dominated the approaches to the plain. It was essential to the final thrust on Tunis that this feature should be captured and held. On the afternoon of 27 April, the Irish Guards began their advance. Instead of setting off under cover of darkness, orders had been changed at the last minute and the Guards had to cross a mile of cornfield in the heat of the sun and in full view of the enemy. Greeted with sustained artillery and mortar fire they suffered heavy casualties. Instructions had been given to mark the spot of the fallen with their rifle and bayonet so they would not be crushed by the following tanks.

John Kenneally wrote of this terrifying advance: 'It seemed that all the artillery in the German army was having a go. As we entered the cornfield, the fire seemed to intensify. We plodded on grimly, our eyes fixed on Captain Chesterton and Lieutenant Eugster, who were leading. I was dazed and shocked; the noise was devastating, the hot blasts from explosions scorching my face, patches of corn were burning fiercely, stones and earth thrown up by shell bursts were rattling down on my steel helmet, machine gun bursts were scything down the corn like a reaper and down with the corn went officers and men alike. It was a bloody massacre.'

Taking shelter in an olive grove, Kenneally's Company Commander, Captain Chesterton, gathered together the remnants of Nos. 1 and 4 companies, which had lost all their officers and senior NCOs. Just as they were about to continue their advance to take Points 212 and 214, Lieutenant Eugster was killed. As dusk was falling, Captain Chesterton led the depleted force to its target and forced the Germans to retreat.

The high ridge of The Bou stretched some 1,500 yards between Points 212 and 214. It consisted mainly of solid rock for about twenty-five yards each side of the slope. It then tapered down into barren scrub. Only 173 men had survived to reach the summit and their situation was about to get worse.

Lance Corporal Kenneally was appointed second-in-command to Sergeant Fanning. Taking half a dozen men, he went in search of supplies that were supposed to have been dumped by carriers at the bottom of The Bou. They did not find any dumps but found instead a carrier that had hit a mine. Taking sacks of bread, tins of bully beef and a quantity of .303 ammunition, Kenneally also decided to include a couple of land mines from the stricken carrier. Because of the high slopes, it had not been possible to bring up the heavy mortars and machine-guns nor the cumbersome No.19 radio set. This meant that Points 212 and 214 were both isolated and out of touch with Brigade HQ. To add to their problems, the Germans had virtually surrounded them.

At noon, the Germans began a three-hour-long heavy barrage followed by an attack on Point 214. A runner was sent to Point 212 to ask for reinforcements, so Kenneally took nine men and ran over to 214. About 100 Germans were sheltering amongst the rocks fifty yards away, firing semi-automatics and throwing stick grenades. Setting his Bren on single shot, Kenneally accounted for enough of the enemy to make them fall back and retreat through the cornfield. He then returned to his own Company at 212.

VC Action

As the day wore on, so thirst and the heat of the African sun became a real hardship. Towards dusk, the enemy shelling increased and the Germans once again put in an attack on 214. This time, despite fierce resistance, they overran the position and headed along the ridge towards 212. Fortunately, a 3-inch mortar with twenty bombs had just arrived and the bombardment put the Germans to flight. By the morning of 29 April, there were just fourteen men left of No.1 Company. Kenneally moved to a position on the forward slope from which he could see trucks and armoured vehicles disgorging infantry at the bottom of the lower slope. An increase in the shelling kept his head down. When the firing eased, he again looked but had lost track of the enemy reinforcements.

Kenneally recalled: 'I could not see them but I could hear them. There were two large boulders about ten yards in front of me so I ran to them and took cover. A German voice was very clear now. I left the Bren behind the boulders and crawled through the scrub. The ground fell away into a deep gully and there they were. Most of them were squatting round a German officer. He was holding an 'O' [orders] group and was pointing here and there. Some were lying down taking a breather and they were bunched like a herd of cattle. What an opportunity!

'I crawled back to the boulders and quickly took off all my equipment – speed was to be of the essence in this operation. I put a new magazine on the Bren and one in each pocket. "Here goes", I said to myself. I took a deep breath and belted forward, firing from the hip. I achieved complete surprise. I hose-piped them from the top of the gully. They were bowled over like ninepins and were diving in all directions. I had time to flip on another magazine and gave them that too. Enough was enough, and I fled back to the boulders and safety.'

This was not the only action he saw that day. Later that morning, he was sent down the hill with three men to find if any supplies had been dumped during the night. Half way down, he met Company Quartermaster Sergeant Mercer, who had left a carrier packed with supplies further down. The three men were sent down to collect everything they could carry while Mercer and Kenneally walked back to 214.

On the way, they walked slap bang into four Germans setting up a machine-gun position. Kenneally gave them a quick burst with his Bren, hitting two of them. The other two began to lob stick grenades, making life very uncomfortable. Kenneally kept them occupied with his Bren, whilst CQSM Mercer worked his way above the Germans and took them out with his Sten gun.

In the afternoon, the Germans began another attack on 212, this time supported by three tanks in single file. With no anti-tank guns and all the 3-inch mortar ammunition expended, there looked no way to repel this attack. The two mines that Kenneally had rescued from the wrecked carrier were improvised into anti-tank shells by tying a hand grenade with a seven-second fuse to each mine; they were hurled into the path of the leading tank. The two huge explosions did no damage but it was enough to deter the tanks, who thought that the British had anti-tank guns.

The following morning, 30 April, was relatively quiet and they were able to take stock of the situation. There were now only ten left of No.1 Company, including Kenneally and Sergeant Fanning. In all, just eighty men held The Bou.

Final Assault

At about 11.00 hours, the Germans commenced a fierce barrage as the prelude to the last attempt to retake The Bou. Kenneally was in the same OP as the previous day with a Sergeant Salt of the Reconnaissance Corps. As the enemy disappeared into the gully below, Kenneally told Salt of his success there. Approaching quietly, they dashed forward, Kenneally firing his Bren and Salt his Sten. They each emptied a magazine, spraying bullets all around. As the Germans climbed out of the gully, they returned fire, killing Sergeant Salt and hitting Kenneally in the leg. Meanwhile No.1 Company had advanced and put the Germans to flight.

While this was going on, Point 214 was being overrun, so all available men crossed the ridge to help. Kenneally, with the aid of another Guardsman, hopped over with his Bren. It was touch and go, with much close combat until, suddenly, the enemy was no longer around. They had started to break and were chased off the hill by the Micks. They never came again; the battle was over. Over 700 Germans lay dead on the slopes of The Bou and just eighty men of 1st Battalion Irish Guards remained.

A medal and a portrait

Kenneally was flown to the General Hospital at Algiers, where the bullet was removed from his calf. After a short convalescence, he re-joined his unit by hitching a ride in a Royal Artillery truck. As luck would have it, he was recognised by one of the crew from his days in the RA and had to explain that he had transferred to the Guards.

The battalion was at only company strength and it would be several months before it had four rifle companies again. Awards were given for the recent campaign including an MC for Captain Chesterton. Kenneally was slightly miffed at being overlooked but did receive promotion to lance corporal and was sent away for a month's course at the Allied School of Infantry in Constantine. It was mid-August and the last week of the course when the Allied forces network news came over the radio. The final news item was that His Majesty King George VI had awarded the Victoria Cross to Lance Corporal John Patrick Kenneally!

A special parade was held on 27 August at which General Alexander presented John Kenneally with the VC ribbon. The battalion was formed up on three sides of a square under a very hot sun. After General Alexander had inspected the parade, Kenneally was marched through the battalion by RSM McLoughlin to be presented with his VC ribbon. He then joined the general at the saluting base as the battalion marched past.

A few days later, Kenneally presented himself to General Alexander's HQ to sit for his portrait painted by the war artist Captain Henry Carr. For the next twelve days, he sat for two or three hours until it was completed. Although Kenneally was not particularly fond of it, the painting is now in the Imperial War Museum.

Anzio

On 7 December 1943, the 1st Battalion Irish Guards landed at Taranto in southern Italy. Seven weeks later, on 22 January 1944, it was part of the Guards Brigade that landed unopposed at Anzio. Days of inaction by the American Commander, Major General Lucas, allowed the Germans to rush reinforcements to the area and put the Allies under siege. Constant shelling in miserable wet and cold conditions led to heavy casualties. Kenneally was now in the HQ Company so was spared the initial onslaught but did have a close encounter with the enemy.

The battalion had been depleted after three to four days of heavy fighting so Kenneally was detailed to drive down to the beachhead to pick up any reinforcements if they had arrived. He found one guardsman and drove back up into the hills. As he rounded a bend there was a loud crack and the newcomer slumped across him, stone dead, causing Kenneally to swerve into a ditch. As he laid the dead soldier on the ground, there was another sharp crack as a bullet ploughed into the dead man's leg. Kenneally dived for cover under the truck and tried to work out from where the firing came. It appeared that the only likely place was a clump of pine trees about 250 yards above and to the left. Cautiously, Kenneally managed to remove his Bren gun from the cab and sprinted ten yards to a deep irrigation gully.

From there, Kenneally crawled about 100 yards and then worked his way through undergrowth until he was about seventy yards from the trees. Watching for what seemed like an age for a sign of the sniper, he was rewarded by the slightest of gleams from the end of a telescopic sight. He eased the butt of the Bren into his shoulder and blasted the whole magazine off into the trees. In the silence that followed, he waited and then heard a loud rustling in the trees as the dead sniper fell through the foliage and landed in a crumpled heap in the long grass.

Kenneally debated whether or not to continue on to HQ or return to the beachhead. He decided on the latter but soon ran into an enemy barrage concentrated on a transport convoy. He pulled up behind an RAMC ambulance and dashed across the road to a cemetery and took shelter in a substantial looking lodge. There he found an RAMC corporal who asked him to help him move the four people he had in his ambulance. Besides two wounded British soldiers, there was a heavily pregnant girl accompanied by an elderly woman.

During a lull in the shelling, they managed to move them all into the lodge. The bombardment began again and a number of shells exploded in the cemetery, which terrified the women. It had the effect of sending the girl into labour and the corporal delivered a baby boy. To celebrate the birth, Kenneally suggested a drink and made his way back to his truck, which was lying on its side. Fortunately, the bottle of cognac was intact but, as he made his way back though the cemetery, another shell landed amongst the graves and a chunk of marble embedded itself in his wrist.

Post War

This was the end of the Italian campaign for John Kenneally and he was evacuated to the main hospital in Naples. When he had recovered, he joined his battalion as it sailed for the UK and Chelsea Barracks. On 24 May 1944, he went to Buckingham Palace to receive his Victoria Cross.

Kenneally received praise from Winston Churchill in a rather ironic way. While denouncing Eamonn de Valera, the Irish premier, for 'frolicking' with the Germans, Churchill said that all bitterness for the Irish race 'dies in my heart' when he thought of Irish heroes like Kenneally.

After the surrender, Kenneally considered leaving the Army and joining the police, especially as he was now a family man with a son. Instead, much to his wife's dismay, he signed on for a further five years and trained as a parachutist in the 1st Guards Parachute Regiment. In April 1947, he was sent to Palestine during that turbulent period that led up to the establishment of the state of Israel.

The British troops were tasked with keeping the Arabs and Jews apart and, in the process, became targets for both sides. Kenneally, being half Jewish, was delighted to be given the job of organising the defence of a kibbutz in northern Galilee. Thanks to his efforts and tactical skills, the kibbutz survived a major Arab night attack. As a result, he was tempted by an offer to remain in Israel and join its army, but with thoughts of his family, which had increased with the birth of another son, he declined.

At the conclusion of this particularly unpleasant tour of duty, Kenneally was persuaded by his wife to purchase his discharge (£120). He marched out of Pirbright Camp on 22 July 1948 as a civilian.

Civvy Street

Moving back to the Midlands, Kenneally used his pre-war interest in cars to open a car showroom in Solihull and settled in the village of Lapworth near Birmingham. During a period when the car business failed, he was employed by Unigate as a security advisor. When he resigned from this post, he again started selling cars until he finally retired.

Kenneally lived out his life in Lower Rochford, near Tenbury Wells in Worcestershire. In 1987, he went with a party of Irish Guards veterans to visit the Tunisian battlefields and to see the scene of his VC exploit. On St Patrick's Day 1998, in the presence of the Queen Mother, John Kenneally was given the singular honour of distributing shamrock to the regiment at a ceremony at Wellington Barracks.

John Kenneally died on 27 September 2000 and was buried in St Michael's and All Angels churchyard, Rochford. His medals are displayed at the Guards Museum, Wellington Barracks, London.

When the Germans were finally driven from Tunisia, there was a pause in until July when Sicily was invaded. By September, the island had been taken and Italy surrendered. The Germans resorted to defending the mountains that ran down the centre of Italy in a series of well-prepared strong points like the Gustav and Gothic Lines. The cost in lives was the highest of any campaign fought in the west: some 60,000-70,000 Allied dead and 60,000-150,000 Germans killed.

Meanwhile in the Far East, after the failed attempts by the Allies to mount offensives into Burma, the Japanese prepared to invade India.

Chapter 54

The Second World War, 1944

Number of VCs awarded	52
Number of VCs awarded to officers	28
Number of VCs awarded to other ranks	24
Total awarded to Royal Air Force	7
Total awarded to Canadian Air Force	2
Total awarded to British Army	24
Total awarded to British Indian Army	14
Total awarded to Canadian Army	3
Total awarded to South African Army	1
Total awarded to Fijian Military	1

Origins of the War

The balance of the war in Burma shifted decisively in 1944, thanks in the main to the battles of Imphal and Kohima. Also, there were improvements in the Allied leadership in the shape of Lieutenant General William Slim who oversaw the raising of the morale the men of the 14th Army through better training and equipment. Some of the most severe fighting in South East Asia, involving the 14th Army, occurred with the attempts by the Japanese Army to invade India though the remote areas of north-east Burma.

On 8 March 1944, the Japanese began crossing the Chidwin River, pushing back the 17th and 20th Indian Divisions. General Slim removed troops from the Arakan and transported them to the bases at Imphal and Dinapur, the objectives of the invading Japanese.

By early April, Imphal had been encircled and under siege. Fifteen thousand troops of the Japanese 31st Division then turned their attention to the important supply base at Dinapur. In their way was the small hill station of Kohima, on the important supply road between Imphal and Dinapur, which, instead of isolating it, General Kotoku Sato chose to capture.

One of the units flown in to reinforce the Manipur region was the 4th Battalion Royal West Kents, which became closely associated with what is often described as the 'Stalingrad of the East'. Sent to Kohima, they joined 3,500-strong Kohima garrison. Besides being an important supply artery, Kohima lay at the summit of a pass that offered the Japanese the best route into India.

By 4 April 1944, some 15,000 Japanese troops confronted the small garrison which occupied the high ground on features with names like FSD Hill, GPT Ridge and Garrison Hill. Within four days, the first Victoria Cross had been won by a nature-loving man from an unusual family.

JOHN PENNINGTON HARMAN VC (1914-1944)

John Pennington Harman was born in Beckenham, Kent on 20 July 1914. He was the first child of Martin Coles Harman and his wife Amy Ruth (née Bodger). There followed three more additions; Albion, Ruth and Diana. The family lived at Deans Place in Chaldon near Caterham, Surrey.

At an early age, John was sent to the Clifton Pre-Preparatory School in Bristol, which he hated. He was particularly distressed by the sounds from the nearby Zoo, which perhaps represented, for him, unwelcome captivity and restraint, even in his tender years. Twice he ran away from school, until his parents brought him back to the new family home at Heathfield in Sussex. There he was in his element, for he loved the countryside and wildlife. In 1925, he was sent to board at the progressive school, Bedales, near Petersfield, Hampshire. There he found more freedom and thrived on the liberal time he was allowed out of doors.

John's father, Martin Coles Harman, had been born in 1885, one of six sons and five daughters. Educated at Whitgift School in Croydon, he left and developed a talent as an entrepreneur and financier. Like John, he was a lover of the countryside and encouraged his rather problematical son to pursue his enthusiasm for nature. In 1925, Martin put into practice his passion for remote natural beauty when he bought Lundy Island from the Christie family for £15,000. A wildlife haven, the island, which is three miles long by half-a-mile wide, lies off the North Devon coast in the Bristol Channel.

John and Albion accompanied their father to spend Christmas on the island at the elegant Millcombe House and from that time Lundy held a special fascination for them. Martin proclaimed himself 'King of Lundy' and later issued an independent Lundy currency of Half Puffin and 1 Puffin coins. This resulted in a prosecution for illegal coinage and he was fined. Lundy was a huge challenge and had to be self-sufficient. Crops were sown and sheep introduced. Soon, however, this bucolic idyll was shattered by a double blow.

In 1931, John's mother died at the early age of forty-seven. This had followed the loss of the family fortune in the Great Depression. Martin was bankrupted, but he had had the foresight to put Lundy in trust, which gave the children a base during this distressing period.

In this fallow time, John spent the next few years travelling in Australia, New Zealand, South Africa and Spain. He tried his hand at lumber jacking, gold prospecting and sheep farming. John was always able to live rough if necessary and would explore any natural place he found himself in. On his return in 1935, he applied to the Air Ministry for a Short Service Commission but, when the letter came back requesting details of his maths qualification, he had to give up any hope of joining the RAF.

Army Life

John enlisted in the Army on 29 November 1941 and joined the Household Cavalry. It became obvious from the start that military life did not suit him, as can be gleaned from his comments in letters to his family. For example: 'I have now completed three weeks training: drill comes easier with physical improvement. Life is just bloody hell – dirty, noisy, crude and inefficient. I heartily wish I had never joined up. There is no time to do anything after set tasks are done – except clean equipment for the following day.'

John continued to criticise Army clothing and equipment, which he described as 'crude and inefficient'. He replaced the blankets with his Icelandic sleeping bag.

Air Crash

To his obvious delight, on 26 May 1942, John was granted a month's agriculture leave to assist work on Lundy. He immediately undertook the planting of 5,000 cabbage plants.

Six days later, on 1 June, a Whitley bomber crashed on the cliffs on the west side of the island in patchy fog. The aircraft involved, a Mk,V from 77 Squadron, serial number AD698 and coded KN/R, was returning from an anti-submarine patrol when it crashed into the 300 feet high cliffs.

John quickly arrived on the scene and, with help, made fast the fuselage of the Whitley with ropes. He then crawled out along to the tail, which was suspended over the cliff edge, and managed to drag the rear gunner, Sergeant Oswald A. Jones, to safety. Unfortunately, it was found that Jones had been killed on impact.

The rest of the bomber's crew had perished when the burning mass of the cockpit had plummeted onto the rocks below. The bodies of Sergeant John E. Veal (pilot), Sergeant Reginald Ellis (pilot), Sergeant Eric Hampson (observer), Sergeant Harry Hannah (Wireless Operator) and Sergeant Young J. Markham (air gunner) were never found, recovered or identified, and they are all commemorated on the Runnymede Memorial.

John soon returned to duty and his liturgy of complaints continued. Evidently, the Household Cavalry agreed with John, for they gave up trying to make a soldier of him and transferred him out of the regiment. In September, John was sent to a drafting station near Worcester to become a private in the Worcestershire Regiment. His stay with his new regiment was brief for on 3 December 1942, he was transferred to the Royal Fusiliers at Kenley. On 28 January 1943, the 20th Battalion Royal Fusiliers was on its way to India, which it reached on 22 March. John's brother, Albion, was already serving there as an officer in the Royal Engineers, but they never had to the opportunity to meet up.

Burma

Just before Christmas, Harman was part of a draft transferred to the 4th Battalion Queen's Own Royal West Kent Regiment for the offensive in Burma. John was assigned to the newly-formed 'D' Company under the command of Major Carey. The men had just one week's training as a company before being moved into the line.

The advance south through the Arakan province was most dangerous. The mountainous and rugged terrain heavily favoured the Japanese defenders. Every position had to be wrested from the enemy in fierce hand-to-hand fighting.

For three months, the regiment was continually engaged in the fighting and none more so than 'D' Company. John appears to have relished this release from the daily drudgery he had endured for the past two years. He was recognised as having a fine fighting spirit, always volunteering for patrols and often going out on his own for several hours to return claiming to have killed several Japanese.

Kohima

On 22 March 1944, the West Kents were relieved by the South Wales Borderers and sent north with the 5th Indian Division to the Naga Hills. A huge Japanese army was threatening to invade India by way of this remote region on the Burma-China border and the British rushed in all available forces to counter this threat. On 5 April, the West Kents took up position at the vital road junction at Kohima. The men arrived under fire from the surrounding hills and within a short time, they were surrounded by the Japanese 31st Division. So began the epic Siege of Kohima.

John Harman, who had impressed his superiors during the Arakan fighting, had been promoted to lance corporal. He immediately showed his contempt for the enemy by taking little notice of the snipers and his self-confidence encouraged his comrades. It may well have been at this time that he told his company commander, Major Donald Easten, of the prediction he had received that he would live until he was at least seventy. According to his sister, John had an open mind regarding the spiritual and was quite taken with the mysteries of unexplained phenomenon.

The perimeter that the West Kents was defending was small and the Japanese had closed to within a matter of yards. The defence was concentrated around the District Commissioner's bungalow and surrounding area and, because of the terracing of the slopes, the fighting was at platoon and section level.

The Japanese attack began in earnest on the night of the 6th and was repulsed. The following morning, 'D' Company put in a counter-attack, in which some seventy of the enemy were killed. Harman was in the thick of it and he seized and brought in a wounded Japanese officer. He was one of the three or four men who dashed into the bakery and threw grenades the Japanese who had taken shelter in the six ovens.

VC Action

The next day, John performed the first of two outstanding acts of gallantry. During the night, the Japanese had established a machine-gun nest within fifty yards of the British positions – which enabled them to sweep the ground with a heavy fire. The terracing on Detail Issue Hill made direct fire impossible, so Harman crawled out of his position, slowly ran forward and, gathering momentum, he flung himself down at the very mouth of the Japanese post. He then took a grenade, pulled the clip, counted to three and threw it into the opening. The two occupants were killed and John returned with the machine-gun.

On the 9th, five Japanese with machine-guns and automatics were on a nearby ridge that overlooked the whole British position. John ordered a comrade on a Bren gun to give him covering fire as he dashed down the slope. Pausing, he aimed his rifle and shot one of the Japanese. He then moved on and shot another. By this time he was under automatic fire from the remaining three.

Fixing his bayonet, John crossed the valley floor and dashed up the slope toward the Japanese position, ignoring the heavy incoming fire. By some miracle, he reached the post unscathed. Leaping down on them, John bayoneted all three and held the machine-gun up to the cheers of his comrades, before flinging it away amongst the trees.

Harman then made his way back, half-running, half-stumbling. Urged on by his comrades, John was seemingly so exhausted by his uphill charge that he did not take precautions or use cover. As he approached the safety of his own lines, a burst of machine-gun fire hit him in his side. A comrade dragged him into cover where his last words were: 'I got the lot. It was worth it'. Five minutes later, Harman had succumbed to his wounds. He was buried on the spot. For this action, and that of the previous day, John Harman was recommended for the posthumous award of the Victoria Cross.

The siege at Kohima was raised on the 20th, but the fighting went on in the area for a further two months, before the Japanese withdrew. In this epic battle, about 500 Kentish Territorials together with Indian troops had held at bay some 13,000 highly-trained and experienced Japanese.

This was the high water mark of the Japanese invasion. From that moment, they were in retreat. Lord Mountbatten reinforced the point in a speech when he said: 'The Battle of Kohima will probably go down as the greatest battle in history. It was in effect the battle of Burma.'

Harman's Victoria Cross was gazetted on 22 June 1944 and his father received it from the King at a Buckingham Palace investiture. He is buried in the Kohima War Cemetery, which is sited on what was known as Garrison Hill. Part of the cemetery encompasses the tennis court, which featured so prominently in the battle, and is marked out on the ground.

In June 1949, a memorial to John was unveiled on Lundy in a disused granite quarry, now called VC Quarry. This is in an entirely appropriate position facing the sea and one John would have approved of. On 13 August 1952, Martin Harman gave his son's Cross to the regiment and the complete group can now be viewed at the Regimental Museum in Maidstone, Kent.

Back in the Mediterranean theatre, the Allies, having achieved victory in Sicily, were surprised that they met no opposition from the Germans when they crossed the short distance to mainland Italy. Instead the Germans had fallen back on a previously-constructed series of defensive lines across Italy, all of which took much hard fighting to overcome.

Perhaps the most formidable was the Gustav Line, which wounds its way from west to east through the Apennine Mountains. The centre of the line crossed the main route north to Rome which followed the Liri Valley and was anchored around the mountains behind the town of Cassino. Dominating this crucial highway was Monte Cassino on which was situated an old monastery – a location which came to symbolise the intense fighting that went on in the surrounding area. Many awards for gallantry were awarded in this long and grim battle, but only one Victoria Cross.

FRANCIS ARTHUR JEFFERSON VC (1921-1982)

Francis Arthur, only child of James Holmes Jefferson and Ethel Haley, was named after his grandfathers, Francis Jefferson and Arthur Haley, but was known by his family and friends as Frank. He was born on 18 August 1921 at 70 Sunderland Terrace in Ulveston, Cumbria, on the edge of the Lake District. He attended Dale Street Infant School and Lightburn Council School, completing his education at Victoria Senior School. When he left school, he trained as a bricklayer and was employed by Messrs. Baker and Foster, Contractors.

Frank was called up for war service in February 1942 and completed his initial training with the South Lancashire Regiment. In May 1943, he was posted to the 13 Platoon, 2nd Battalion, Lancashire Fusiliers. He joined the battalion in North Africa, but was too late to see any action.

The 2nd Battalion was part of the famous 8th Army, which landed on Sicily on 10 July 1943 and immediately captured Syracuse. After a month's heavy fighting, the Allies secured the island.

The 8th Army landed troops at Taranto on the heel of Italy and advanced up the Adriatic side of the country. By 17 September they had captured

Foggia with its valuable airfields and on 3 October, the town and port of Termoli was taken. The 8th Army then began a slogging advance as it met stubborn resistance, progressing from one defended ridge to another. There followed two fierce battles to secure bridgeheads on the rivers Trigmo and Sangro. The latter was an outpost of the immensely strong Gustav Line, which was to hold up the Allied advance for many costly months.

On 31 December 1943, Lieutenant General Sir Oliver Leese took over command of the 8th Army from General Bernard Montgomery. This marked the conclusion of the 8th Army's winter offensive.

By March 1944, the 8th Army, with the exception of 5th Corps, which was left in the Adriatic sector, had been switched west across to the central sector for the drive up the Lire Valley.

Monte Cassino

The Lancashire Fusiliers had their first glimpse of the ruined monastery on Monte Cassino when they went into the line in March. Corpses from the previous battles lay on the slopes and the smell of death pervaded the surrounding area. Food and water had to be transported by mule to a distribution point then carried by Indian porters at night.

The Germans had fortified the line with gun pits, concrete bunkers, turreted machine-gun emplacements, tank-traps, barbed-wire and minefields. Approximately fifteen German divisions were employed in its defence. From 17 January to 18 May there were four assaults by the Allies before the Germans were finally driven from their positions. One officer vividly described the terrain when he stated that 'The monastery brooded over the battlefield like a curse'.

VC Action

For weeks, the Lancashire Fusiliers endured constant shelling, suffering dysentery in cold and wet weather. The ground was too rocky to dig trenches so the men had to find what cover they could in small stone shelters while the Germans bombarded them with accurate artillery and mortar fire directed from the monastery.

Fusilier Frank Jefferson was the man in charge of his platoon's Projectile, Infantry, Anti-Tank, a weapon known simply as the PIAT. This was a dubious honour for it was heavy and bulky to carry and needed two men to cock it. It also had a fearsome kick if fired from the shoulder. The PIAT, despite its drawbacks, was quite an effective weapon and extensively used against not only against armour but also enemy strong points and bunkers.

The fourth battle for Monte Cassino began on 11 May 1944 with an artillery barrage along a twenty-mile front. Over the following days, the British, Canadians and Poles edged their way forward. On the morning of 16 May, the Lancashire Fusiliers advanced behind the protection of tanks from the 17th/21st Lancers. With the armour soon held up by anti-tank obstacles, the infantry went on unsupported. They took their objective of two houses that were used by enemy machine-guns, but before they could consolidate their positions, the Germans launched a counter-attack. About twenty infantry, supported by two tanks, wiped out a platoon and forced the other to fall back.

Frank Jefferson, on his own initiative, went forward. He was followed by Fusilier Nunn who carried a case of PIAT bombs. Taking up a position behind a bush until the leading enemy tank was near, Frank stepped out and, despite heavy fire, aimed and fired at the tank at a range of twenty yards. The recoil knocked him down. Nunn exclaimed: 'Hey Frank, you've hit the bastard.'

Jefferson had scored a fatal hit at the base of the turret and the tank burst into flames; ammunition stored inside exploded, killing the entire crew. Frank reloaded but the following tank retreated before he could get within range.

Frank Jefferson later recorded his recollections of the Italian campaign and his exploit on 16 May which resulted in the award of the Victoria Cross: 'During the first attack our company's objective was two small farmhouses which were being used by the Germans as strong machine-gun posts. The tanks (17/21st Lancers) were to go in first and we were to follow on behind, on foot and under heavy fire from mortars, machine guns and 88-millimetre shells, but due to an anti-tank obstruction our tanks had great difficulty in covering the ground. This, however, didn't stop them engaging the enemy's heavy tanks. But with our tank support unable to advance we had to push forward on foot in the face of heavy German fire, which had already knocked out several of our tanks.

'My Company was one of the leading companies and after a bit of a do, we took our objective, silencing the machine-guns and taking many prisoners. After making sure that no Germans were left, we started to dig in. But before we finished this, the Germans launched a counter-attack with tanks and infantry coming at us from two directions.

'We had one platoon in each house and the other platoon was soon in a bad way. They had been shot up very badly and were falling back, so our position drew all the enemy fire. We took what cover we could and by the time the leading German tank was about 50 yards away I thought it was time that something was done about it. As I was the only PIAT man in the platoon, I knew it was up to me to do it.

'So, getting to my feet, I went forward and when the tank was about 20 yards away I fired one shot which hit it around the turret. The recoil of the PIAT knocked me flat on my back but when I got up I saw the tank was done for. It was burning fiercely with the cracking of bullets exploding inside.

'I went back to my Number Two and reloaded but saw the remaining tanks all turn tail and retire. After this, our tanks succeeded in overcoming their obstacles and we reformed and continued our push forward.

'Major Kevin Hill then ordered the remaining men to charge the retreating Germans and all twenty enemy soldiers were killed.'

The following day, a flag appeared on top of the monastery signalling that Monte Cassino had fallen and the Germans were in retreat. The main highway to Rome was now open and the Allies entered the capital on 4 June. During the pursuit that followed, Jefferson was wounded in the shoulder by shrapnel and was hospitalised.

Frank Jefferson was promoted to lance corporal and recommended for the Victoria Cross which was gazetted on 13 July 1944. In a ceremony that included another Monte Cassino VC, Captain Richard Wakeford, Jefferson received his crimson ribbon from a visiting King George VI.

Homecoming

Frank Jefferson returned home on leave but this shy man had to endure an outpouring of public adulation from the citizens of Ulverston. A crowd of 2,000 filled the square outside Coronation Hall to honour Frank as he acknowledged the cheers from a balcony. Once he could get away, Frank headed to his favourite pub, where he was the undefeated darts player, and joined his old drinking companions.

Now stationed back in the UK, Frank was gave morale-boosting talks to factory workers all over the country, something he found more frightening than facing the German tanks. He received his actual Victoria Cross from the King at Buckingham Palace on 12 December 1944.

Frank was demobbed at the end of the war and returned to his old job as a bricklayer. He married Betty and moved to Preston Street, Barrow-in-Furness and soon had two sons. The fact that Frank was a national hero brought few privileges, a fact born out when he applied for a council house and found that he was number 10,965 on the waiting list.

In 1951 Frank and his family emigrated to the United States. They were sponsored by a Mr Ashley T. Cole, a retired lawyer from New York, who had begun an exchange of correspondence when he had asked for Frank's autograph. Frank stated that the move was to seek a better lifestyle, but close friends believe he emigrated to escape the continuing publicity of his heroism.

The family moved to the steel town of Buffalo in upstate New York and lived at 205 Griffiths Street. Initially, things went well with Frank getting employment bricklaying and enjoying the respect he received for his war service. In June 1956, he attended the Centenary of the Victoria Cross in London. Before he left, the ex-pat community organised a lavish send-off for Frank. On 5 May 1956, a Grand Victoria Cross Ball was held at the Hotel Buffalo in his honour.

Sadly, as the years passed Frank's marriage began to fail. He ceased bricklaying and took a job as night manager of a small hotel in Buffalo. In 1974, he and Betty divorced, at which point Frank too the decision to return to England.

Last Years

Frank went to live with his widowed mother at 16 Luton Street, Bolton. At that time, he was receiving a weekly VC pension of £1.92 and despite two offers to buy his medals for £15,000, he refused. His Victoria Cross was his most treasured possession.

In January 1982, a burglar broke into Frank's home and stole his VC. A part of him died that day and in the following nine months he sank into a deep depression and started to drink heavily. Although the Lancashire Fusiliers presented him with a replica medal group, Frank's depression could not be lifted.

On the evening of 3 September, he went drinking at the King William, his local pub, and had to be assisted home. Early the following morning, he went to his mother's bedroom in tears and told her that he had nothing to live for. He kissed her on the cheek and thanked her. Later that morning he walked to Burnden Junction, Bolton, and threw himself in front of a train. Frank Jefferson died of multiple injuries.

The circumstances of his death shocked the public and he was afforded a full military funeral at Bolton's Overdale Crematorium. Amongst the many who attended was Ian Fraser VC. His ashes were scattered in the Lancashire Fusiliers Memorial Garden of Wellington Barracks, Bury, Lancashire.

In the North Atlantic the war's longest continuous campaign was still being fought. The Battle of the Atlantic pitted the German U-boats against the vital supply convoys, moving Winston Churchill to later observe that 'the Battle of the Atlantic was the dominating factor all through the war. Never for one moment could we forget that everything happening elsewhere, on land, at sea or in the air depended ultimately on its outcome.'

By 1943, the threat from U-boats had lessened as improved Allied aircraft, weapons and tactics began to bite. The Germans had countered these moves, for example by increasing the firepower on the decks of the newer U-boats making them a formidable target for any attacking aircraft.

One such incident took place near the Arctic Circle and resulted in the Victoria Cross being awarded to a resilient RAF Pilot.

JOHN ALEXANDER CRUICKSHANK VC (1920 –)

RAF Coastal Command was formed within the RAF in 1936 and was its maritime arm. Having established this new command, the Air Ministry then denied it all of the resources it needed to develop properly. With the outbreak of war, all concentration of material focused on Fighter and Bomber Commands. Coastal Command had to make do with inadequate aircraft of limited range and performance and it was little surprise that it was referred to as the 'Cinderella Service'.

By 1943, the U-boat threat was so great that Coastal Command finally received the investment it needed. Long-range seaplanes like the Sunderland and the Consolidated Catalina were entering service and enabled the crews to conduct patrols of ten hours or more. Radar-equipped long-range aircraft enabled the Command to hunt down and destroy U-boats with greater efficiency. In particular, they were able to cover the 'Atlantic Gap' in the central Atlantic where the U-boats had previously operated almost with impunity.

By mid-1943, a large number of U-boats had been sunk with little loss to Allied shipping. The following year, after the D-Day landings, the Germans lost their submarine bases on the French coast and were forced to relocate to Norway and Germany.

Early Life

John Alexander Cruickshank was born on 20 May 1920 at 14, Foothill Road, Aberdeen to James Crane and Alice Cruickshank (née Bow). He was educated at Aberdeen Grammar School before completing his schooling at the Royal High School and Daniel Stewart's College in Edinburgh. When he left school in 1938, he joined the Commercial Bank of Scotland as the start of a banking career. The following year, at his father's suggestion, he joined the Territorial Army as a gunner in the Royal Artillery. With outbreak of war, Cruickshank was called to service with the 129th Field Regiment, Royal Artillery with whom he stayed until 1941.

Applying for a transfer to the RAF, he joined the aircrew reception centre on 19 July 1941 and began basic instruction at No.11 Initial Training Wing. He was posted to Toronto, Canada for elementary pilot training and then to the US Naval base at Pensacola for advanced instruction. He completed his course and was awarded his 'wings' on 9 July 1942, and the following day commissioned as a Pilot Officer, RAFVR. After over a year in North America, Cruickshank arrived back in the UK where he was posted to No.4 (Coastal) OTU at Invergordon for operational training.

Coastal Command

On 25 March 1943, Cruickshank was promoted to flying officer and sent to 210 Squadron, which was initially based at Pembroke Dock and then Poole Bay. The squadron was equipped with the Consolidated PBY Catalina flying-boat, which had an exceptionally long-range, was dependable and popular with the aircrews who flew it.

Cruickshank recalls that 'the operations we carried out were anti-U-boat patrols, almost all in the Bay of Biscay. This period was interrupted with a two-month detachment to Gibraltar, where we carried out similar anti-U-boat patrols in the Atlantic Ocean, west of Portugal. On one of these patrols I sighted my first U-boat. Visibility was good, so we too were sighted by the U-boat and it submerged before we could mount an effective attack.'

Cruickshank's Crew

In early January 1944, Cruickshank's squadron moved to Sullom Voe in the Shetland Islands. John soon got into the routine of long patrols with little or no contact with the enemy. The patrols covered fixed areas and it took crews with exceptional patience to scan the hundreds of square miles of empty sea in the hopes of spotting an enemy vessel. Cruickshank had completed forty-seven full operational patrols in sixteen months with only one abortive contact with the enemy. His crew all regarded the 6ft-3in Cruickshank as an exceptional pilot and on 5 July, he was promoted to flight lieutenant.

On the morning of 17 July 1944, Cruickshank made preparations for his forty-eighth operational sortie. His ten-man crew included his old friend and navigator, Flying Officer John Dickson, who had flown with Cruickshank in all the previous forty-seven missions. The second pilot was Flight Sergeant Jack Garnett and a young 'rookie' pilot, Sergeant Ian Fiddler, was brought along to gain experience. The flight engineer was Flight Sergeant S.B. Harbison, whilst the two wireless operators were Warrant Officer W.C. Jenkins and Flight Sergeant H. Geershenson, both of whom doubled as gunners. The mechanic and radar operator was an Australian, Flight Sergeant John Appleton, with Sergeant R.S.C. Proctor and Flight Sergeant A.I. Cregan completing the crew.

VC Action

Cruickshank's Catalina, JV928 DA/Y, lifted off from the waters of Sullom Voe soon after 13.00 hours on 17 July 1944. It headed for the Arctic waters north-west of the Lofoten Islands in the hope of spotting one of the U-boats now forced to operate from bases in Norway. As the Catalina droned along at ninety-five knots, the journey took five hours.

Eventually reaching their allotted patrol area, the crew began the monotonous scanning of the dead flat ocean, hampered by sea-mist that reduced visibility to about 600 feet. After about three hours of fruitless search, John Appleton detected a signal about forty-three miles away on the radar-screen. Alerting Cruickshank, the aircraft turned towards the target.

Nobody was getting too excited for it was known that the Royal Navy was operating in the area. Also the target could be a trawler or even wreckage. At their low-speed, it took about twenty minutes to sight the target – at which point it was identified as a German U-boat. The Catalina's crew clambered to their stations in preparation for an attack. Flying Officer Dickson, for example, left his navigatior's desk and crawled into the bomb-aiming compartment in the nose of the aircraft.

Cruickshank pulled the Catalina into a complete circuit around the U-boat and descended to fifty feet as he commenced his attack. The Germans had already responded with a heavy barrage of flak. Despite their fire, the German gunners' aim was off and the Catalina swooped low over the submarine.

Dickson announced that the bombs were released as Cruickshank broke away. Appleton recalled: 'I immediately went aft, absolutely certain that I would see the destruction of a U-boat. When I got there I saw a couple of irate crew member (the mid-section gunners) and I said "What's the matter? What's the matter?" They said, "Look", and they pointed to the two wings and there were the six depth charges still there: the depth charges had failed to drop.'

Appleton went forward and reported to Cruickshank, who felt considerable anger and demanded to know the reason. Dickson checked but could not find why the release had failed. Cruickshank announced that they were going for another attack, this time he would operate the bomb release from the cockpit.

Turning back, they noticed that the U-boat had stopped to give its gunners a steadier platform. With the element of surprise lost, the German submariners were now prepared to lay down an accurate blanket barrage as the slow-moving Catalina approached.

'A wall of black anti-aircraft fire in front of us but we flew straight through it,' continued Appleton. 'As we flew straight through this lot and it was quite obvious that we had been hit.'

Despite taking hits, Cruickshank kept the flying boat steady and released all six depth charges close to the U-boat. Cruickshank, however, had been hit in the legs and chest and he recalled: 'I remember feeling the impact of the exploding shells but whatever effect there was from this did not deflect my mind.'

At the same time one of the shells exploded in the middle of the forward compartment, instantly killing Dickson and wounding Harbison in the foot; Garnett was hit in the left hand and John Cruickshank had sustained a further wounding.

The Catalina was soon enveloped in the sea-mist leaving behind the rapidly sinking *U-361*. John Appleton remembered: 'Paddy Harbison had noticed, as they pulled away, a violent explosion which we suspect was one of the submarine's own torpedoes going off because the explosive content of a torpedo was more than of a depth charge. '

Gruelling Return

As the Catalina gained height and turned towards home, Appleton began to bandage Garnett's left hand. He glanced at Cruickshank and saw that his face had turned deathly pale and his trouser legs were blood-soaked. From the first-aid kit he found a large pair of scissors and was able to cut away one of Cruickshank's trouser legs. At this point, Cruickshank collapsed.

Garnett took over the controls as Appleton and Fidler managed to half-carry their skipper through the bulkheads to mid-ships where they lay him on a bunk. 'He was obviously in terrible shape and I realised he must be in terrible pain,' added Appleton. 'I could see blood starting to soak through even though all his flying gear and pullovers and so on, but he hadn't mentioned any of this at all. He was lapsing between consciousness and unconsciousness. He was obviously in very bad shape. I thought he was mortally wounded and I wanted to make him as comfortable as possible.'

Fidler returned to the cockpit to help Jack Garnett, while Appleton bathed Cruickshank's face, bandaged his legs and tried to keep him warm. Asking about casualties, Appleton had to tell Cruickshank that his best friend, 'Dicky' Dickson, had been killed, which was a further blow to the already traumatised skipper.

'I thought he must be terrible pain and inside the first-aid kit there were tubes of morphine ... But John Cruickshank was alert enough to see what I was doing and quite firmly said, "No, no, no, no".' Cruickshank himself later recalled that, 'I declined morphine as it might impair my judgement.' He was concerned that Garnett had never landed a flying boat and would need clear-headed instruction. Appleton later said that this act was 'captaincy of the highest order'.

Ian Fidler made some calculations and was alarmed to find that fuel consumption was higher than expected and that it was not likely they would reach base. It was later discovered that one of the fuel pipes had been hit and they were haemorrhaging fuel.

For six hours Cruickshank lay bleeding profusely, lapsing in and out of consciousness as the Catalina limped towards Sullom Voe. Appleton informed his captain and he insisted on being helped back to the cockpit. This proved to be an agonising struggle. Once he was sat in the co-pilot's seat it was clear that there were limitations to what he could do. It was too dark to risk a landing so the aircraft circled and all excess equipment was jettisoned to lighten it as much as possible.

Finally, after about forty minutes, Cruickshank decided it was just light enough to land on the waters of Sullom Voe. As they made their approach, Cruickshank was telling Garnett, 'Lower, lower. Not so low. Take it easy. Too much power, not enough power', and so on.

Fortunately, the water was calm as Cruickshank headed the aircraft towards a stretch of beach near the landing-stage designated as an emergency beaching area. Garnett eased the flying boat onto the surface and it bounced back into the air. Cruickshank called out, 'I have control' and managed to guide the Catalina back on to the water and run it up the emergency beach.

Aftermath

There were many dinghies waiting and one of the first to reach the Catalina was the medical team led by the base medical officer, Patrick O'Connor. As O'Connor boarded the aircraft, he immediately realised that only a blood transfusion on the spot would give Cruickshank any chance of survival. Using such limited equipment as he had available, O'Connor stabilised the wounded man sufficiently to move him to hospital. Only then did O'Connor appreciate the full extent of Cruickshank's seventy-two separate injuries.

John Cruickshank remained on the danger list in hospital for the next ten days. This was followed by two months' recuperation.

On 1 September 1944, *The London Gazette* announced that Cruickshank had been awarded the Victoria Cross. On 21 September, accompanied by his parents, he was presented with his Cross by King George VI at Holyrood Palace, Edinburgh. Also present was Jack Garnett, his co-pilot, who was awarded the Distinguished Flying Medal. When he had fully recovered, Cruickshank spent the remainder of the war at Coastal Command HQ at RAF Northwood, Middlesex until he was discharged on 13 September 1946.

Cruickshank returned to banking and international finance and worked for Grindley's Bank until he retired in 1977. At the time of writing, he is the sole surviving VC from the Second World War.

Chapter 55

The Second World War, 1945

Number of VCs awarded	33
Number of VCs awarded to officers	11
Number of VCs awarded to other ranks	22

Total awarded to Royal Navy	2
Total awarded to Canadian Navy	1
Total awarded to Royal Marines	1
Total awarded to Royal Air Force	1
Total awarded to South African Air Force	1
Total awarded to British Army	10
Total awarded to British Indian Army	8
Total awarded to Canadian Army	3
Total awarded to Australian Army	6

Origins of the War

The end of the war was in sight. In all theatres, the enemy was in retreat but still managed to fight back. In Western Europe, the Allies finally crossed the Rhine and struck out into the heart of Germany. In Italy, the last pockets of resistance were mopped up. In Eastern Europe, the Soviet Army was steamrolling its way towards Berlin, exacting a devastating retribution upon the German population as it went. In South East Asia, the Japanese were in retreat with the Americans island-hopping ever closer to Japan itself.

There was an understandable reluctance to risk one's life with victory an increasingly forgone conclusion. But still men did continue to perform outstanding acts of bravery and it is of little surprise that during the final phases of the war, nineteen VCs were awarded posthumously, including those to Ian Liddell and, the final VC of the war, Robert Gray.

IAN OSWALD LIDDELL VC (1919-1945)

Ian Liddell's VC action, as an example of cool, cold-blooded courage, is one of the most outstanding awards made at any time and yet is relatively unknown. He was a young man, born into privilege and luxury, newly-married, with every prospect of a bright and comfortable future ahead of him, who took a calculated decision to place himself in extreme danger simply because it was what was needed to resolve a difficult situation. Indeed, many would say that he must have realised that his decision to carry out this act of extreme bravery was almost certain to result in his death. Rarely can any gallantry award have been so well-deserved. Reading the details of his actions on the Ems river bridge in April 1945, one can only marvel that he survived absolutely unscathed.

Early Life

Ian Liddell was born in Shanghai on 19 October 1919, where his father was a partner in Liddell Brothers, one of the leading trading companies in China, which had been founded by his grandfather in the late nineteenth century. One of five children, he began his education in Shanghai before being sent to England to St Andrews School in Eastbourne and later, to Harrow School. Like his older brother, David, he excelled in music and had a love of animals which determined his choice of career and, when he had completed his formal education, he began to train as a veterinary surgeon.

In the 1930s, the family moved back to England and bought Mounton House, near Chepstow, which was ideally situated, being only two miles from Shirenewton Hall, where Ian's grandfather, Charles Liddell, the founder of Liddell Brothers, was living. On the outbreak of war in 1939, Ian was called up for service in the Shropshire Light Infantry in May 1940.

Coats Mission

Liddell's education and background obviously made him a candidate for a commission and he attended the Royal Military College at Sandhurst where he was given an emergency commission in the Coldstream Guards and posted to the Holding Battalion at Regents Park Barracks in London. The battalion's main function was to provide a base for officers and men who had completed their training but who had not been posted to a service battalion.

In addition, it was given extra duties which included the provision of a small detachment to an organisation known as the Mobile Detachment which had been formed on 3 July 1940, under the command of Major J.S. Coats, MC, to provide protection for the members of the Royal Family in the event of invasion. If the invasion threat materialised, these officers were to convey the King, Queen and the two princesses to one of four houses located in different parts of the country – Newby Hall in North Yorkshire, Pitchford Hall in Shropshire, Madresfield Court in Worcestershire and Bevere Manor in Worcestershire – and guard them.

On 9 October 1940, the Mobile Detachment was formally constituted and named the Coats Mission. It consisted of five officers and 124 men, with a headquarters at Bushey in Hertfordshire. Most of its time was devoted to exercises with various locally-based military units, preparing for the possibility of German invasion. In addition, the unit provided a regular rota of duties at Sandringham when the Royal Family was in Norfolk. There the Mission's members, particularly the officers, became part of the Royal household and became well-known to the Royal Family.

Ian Liddell was promoted to acting lieutenant and posted to the Coats Mission in February 1941, where he remained until November 1942. He became a favourite with both the other Mission members and with the Royal Family who took to his lively personality, humour and ability to get stuck in to any project. The Mission was eventually disbanded in January 1943.

MT Officer

When Liddell's tour of duty with the Coats Mission ended on 27 November 1942, he returned to the Holding Battalion and was immediately posted to the 5th Battalion Coldstream Guards. This battalion had been formed at Elstree School in October 1941, under the command of Lieutenant Colonel Lord Stratheden, and in May 1942 was placed in 32 Guards Brigade of the Guards Armoured Division, providing the lorry-borne infantry which operated alongside the tanks. When Liddell joined, the battalion was stationed at Mere, near Warminster.

There followed a lengthy period of intensive training, moving to various parts of the country, before eventually heading south to Eastbourne in May 1944, ready for D-Day. During this time, perhaps because of his youth and the relatively comfortable war he had endured in the Coats Mission, Liddell was not thought to be the ideal officer to command a rifle company and was given command of the battalion's motor transport platoon, responsible for the organisation, care and maintenance of the lorries used to transport the whole battalion.

Having landed in Normandy, 5th Coldstream camped outside Bayeux on 25 June, the last unit to arrive being the transport under the command of Liddell. The battalion was soon involved in action, coming under attack from the 12th SS Panzer Division 'Hitlerjugend'. The battalion was rarely out of the line for the next few weeks until the remains of the German forces in Normandy managed to withdraw. The British and Canadian armies pursued the enemy north-eastwards, capturing and destroying numerous V-1 rocket sites.

Crossing the old battlefields of the First World War, they eventually reached Brussels. It was from there that Liddell wrote: 'From here we made another dash, this time to Brussels. You can gather from my description that the French gave us a pretty good reception, but what the Belgians gave us I am incapable of describing. All I can say is that I have never seen or imagined such heartfelt joy and thankfulness as the Belgians showed … Without exaggeration at all I can truthfully say that I was nearer killed by the joy of the people of Brussels than I have been since we landed [in Normandy].'

The Coldstream Guards took part in Operation *Market Garden*, the attempt to seize the Rhine bridges between the Dutch frontier and Arnhem, moving through Eindhoven and coming under American control for the assault over the Waal River. On 23 September, it launched an attack on Vokel, then, two days later, moved north to guard the Nijmegen to s'Hertogenbosch road, before being pulled out of the line for a month's rest at Hatert.

Liddell took his leave and got married. He returned and re-joined 5th Coldstream which was by this time stationed at Opheylissem and Neerheylissem in Belgium. Two days after his return the battalion, supported by the tanks from the Welsh Guards, resumed the attack across the trenches and obstacles of the formidable Siegfried Line.

Combat Company

After one of the officers became a casualty, Liddell was transferred from motor transport to take command of No.3 Company. On 2 April 1945, the Division turned east into Germany. The Scots and Welsh Guards fought their way to the River Ems at Shepsdorf, near Lingen, where two sections managed to cross the river before the bridges were blown and they had to withdraw to the west bank.

Plans were then drawn up for an assault across the river. The Coldstream was brought forward to defend the northern flank of the assault crossing and by the morning of 3 April was busily preparing its positions near Mittellohne. At 14.30 hours, a Household Cavalry patrol reported finding a bridge intact over the Ems and 1st (Armoured) Coldstream Guards and 5th Coldstream Guards, were ordered to try and seize it. Liddell was detailed to take No.3 Coy and accompany 1st (Armoured) Coldstream Guards.

Ems Bridge

The Germans had prepared the Ems Bridge for demolition by the placing of a series of eight aerial bombs, both on the road surface and below. These were then wired up to a detonation point somewhere on the far bank. In addition, a large barrier had been placed across the western end to prevent tanks from rushing onto the bridge. In addition, the bridge was covered by three 88mm guns, two 20mm anti-aircraft guns and several well-placed machine-gun posts. No doubt thinking of what had happened at the previous river crossings, the officers considered what to do next. Liddell volunteered to attempt to cut the demolition wires and borrowed a pair of wire cutters from a fellow officer.

VC Action

Having made the decision to single-handedly cross the bridge and try to disarm the bombs, Liddell then had to wait for the support to be put into place. The tanks of 1st (Armoured) Coldstream Guards were positioned on the edge of a wooded escarpment, from where they could fire at the bridge some 400 yards away and put down a smoke screen.

Liddell had calculated that the Germans would certainly blow the bridge if they saw the tanks coming towards it, or if an attempt was made to cut the detonation wires. But he reasoned that they would be unlikely to detonate the bombs if they saw just one man on the bridge; he would be a much better target for small-arms fire. He must also have calculated that, with no cover available to him on the bridge itself, it would only be a matter of seconds, or perhaps a minute, before he was hit. If the Germans thought that there seemed to be any possibility of him actually disarming the bombs, they would almost certainly detonate them rather than present the British with an intact crossing of the river.

All of this took time. The battalion's War Diary makes no record of how long the preparations took, only that the first report of the intact bridge arrived at 14.30 hours and that by 19.00, the bridge had been captured; a period of over four hours. For Liddell this must have been an anxious wait.

Lieutenant Laurie described what happened next: 'The whole circus started. We started the battle and the thundering fire came over and the Typhoon rockets … All hell was let loose, so much so that you couldn't think really. And Ian, as he promised, climbed over the road block on the end, and I had a full view of him, and I noticed he'd dropped his precious Tommy gun getting over the barricade.

'We all had Sten guns but Ian had a Tommy gun … he ran like a lamplighter across the bridge and cut the wires on the enemy end and back again and cut the wire at our end, climbed back onto the road block thing. So Lump's platoon, then off they went … mine was the second platoon. Lump was already going through the position on the left, I turned to go right where actually I was very lucky, there was not very much to compete with.

'Ian was standing on the end, unarmed because he had dropped his Tommy gun and I saw a German soldier coming out of a trench. I didn't know whether he was armed or what his intentions were, but he was behind Ian, and Ian was between me and him, so I said, "Ian, look behind you!" … he saw this chap coming out, so he flung the wire cutters at him and hit him, and both the soldier and the wire cutters disappeared below ground. That's how they got lost, and I expect some German family has still got them as a souvenir now. I've always remembered saying it was so typical of Ian. He hadn't got anything (I suppose he had got a .38, but that was tucked away). He just turned round and belted those really heavy wire cutters.'

Unknown to Liddell, or to the men on the bank, the Germans had wired the bombs in series so that, when the wires on the first bomb were cut, all the bombs were disabled. When the Germans realised what he was doing, they would undoubtedly have tried to detonate the bombs, but by that time it was too late. As for Liddell, his courage in rushing to the German end of the bridge to cut the wires on the second bomb was unnecessary and his survival unscathed is little short of a miracle. During the action to capture the bridge, only one Coldstream Guard was killed. On the German side, forty men had been killed and forty-two taken prisoner, including the commander of the position, who explained why he had failed to blow the bridge. When Liddell began his dash onto the bridge, the German captain had been in the wrong dugout and had been unable to get to the detonator. When he did manage to reach it, it was too late; Liddell had already cut the first wire and broken the circuit.

At 20.00 hours, No.2 Company and another squadron of tanks arrived to strengthen those units already holding the bridge and in the early hours of the following morning, 185 Brigade captured Altenlingen and crossed the Dortmund–Ems Canal and was heading south towards Lingen.

Liddell and his company mounted an attack on a large number of German troops positioned in the barracks and surrounding pillboxes, many of them members of the Brandenburg Regiment, an elite unit. At noon on 5 April, the company was relieved and sent to re-join the battalion.

During the next two weeks, Liddell and his men were at the forefront of the Guards Armoured Division as it advanced. By 14 April, the division had reached the village of Emstek, some 110 miles from the Rhine crossing. After a short rest, the Coldstreams were again on the move, heading north-east, fighting their way through towards the town of Rotenburg. Accompanied by tanks of 1st (Armoured) Coldstream Guards, they pushed along the road (Veersebrücker Straße) towards Rotenburg to carry out a reconnaissance.

Moving cautiously forward through heavily wooded countryside, they came to a level crossing and a road block which was too well defended to enable them to advance further. Some skirmishing took place while messages were sent through to Rotenburg, trying to secure the town's surrender. No response was received.

The following morning, 21 April, a full-scale assault on Rotenburg was prepared. No.3 Company, accompanied by No.3 Squadron, took part in clearing the woods and the level crossing that was captured, along with 150 prisoners, by noon. Amongst the casualties, though, was Ian Liddell, who had been shot by a sniper.

Lieutenant Laurie recalled what he saw: 'Philip Rashleigh [Lieutenant P.S. Rashleigh] had just joined as a replacement; he was looked after by Ian who went forward and took his platoon position to see that he got dug in alright and was in a slit trench with Philip when a sniper got them both. Now, I was always told that the bullet ricocheted off Philip … and killed Ian, although he was actually said to have died of wounds although he was as good as dead.'

The award of the Victoria Cross to Ian Liddell was gazetted on 7 June 1945. After the restoration of peace, it was decided to consolidate many of the smaller war cemeteries into larger regional cemeteries for ease of administration and maintenance. The graves of Ian Liddell and the other five men at Söhlingen were moved to a new cemetery at Becklingen, on a hillside overlooking Luneberg Heath, where Field Marshal Montgomery had accepted the surrender of German forces on 4 May 1945.

Though there was now peace in Europe, the bitter fighting in the Far East raged on – leading to further VCs. A mentioned, the last of the Second World War was that awarded posthumously to Robert Gray.

ROBERT HAMPTON GRAY VC (1917-1945)

The awarding of the Victoria Cross to a member of the Royal Canadian Navy, as well as the Fleet Air Arm, concentrated the minds of the Admiralty's Honours and Awards Committee in the weeks that followed the end of the Second World War. They had to examine the case of a posthumous award to a Canadian-born pilot attached to the Fleet Air Arm, at the same time considering a memo sent by Vice-Admiral Sir Philip Vian (Flag Officer Commanding, First Aircraft Carrier Squadron, British Pacific Fleet) to the Commander-in-Chief, British Pacific Fleet.

Dated 13 September 1945, the memo read: 'In recommending the award of the Victoria Cross Posthumous to the late Temporary Lieutenant R.H. Gray, DSC, RCNVR, I have in mind his brilliant fighting spirit and inspired leadership, an unforgettable example of selfless and sustained devotion to duty without regard to safety of life and limb:

'Secondly, that you may think as I do that a Victoria Cross is the just due of the gallant company of Naval Airmen who have from December last have fought and beat the Japanese from Palembang to Tokyo and:

'Thirdly, that the award of this highly prized and highly regarded recognition of valour may fittingly be conferred on a native of Canada, which Dominion has played so great a part in the training of our Airmen.'

The question was clear. Should a VC be awarded to a naval airman because he was a Canadian and serving in the Fleet Air Arm?

Early Life

Robert Hampton Gray, nicknamed Hammy, was born 2 November 1919 in Trail, British Columbia, a town, just ten kilometres from the United States border. He was the oldest of three children born to Boer War veteran John Balfour Gray and his wife, Wilhelmina. The family later moved to another border town, Nelson, where Hammy enjoyed an unremarkable but happy upbringing. He graduated from high school in 1936 and enrolled at the University of Alberta, then transferred to the University of British Columbia in 1939, intending to go on to McGill University for medical training.

In the summer of 1940, Gray decided to enlist and applied to join the Royal Canadian Naval Volunteer Reserve (RCNVR) as an officer cadet to serve on loan to the Royal Navy. On arriving in the UK, he saw that the road to officer status would be a long one, so when he saw an opportunity to transfer to the Royal Navy's Fleet Air Arm as an officer pilot, he seized the moment.

Gray was joining at the right time for the Fleet Air Arm was rapidly expanding and needed aircrew. Despite never previously expressing an interest in flying, Hammy began his basic flying training at HMS *St Vincent* at Gosport in Hampshire. He was commissioned as a sub-lieutenant and was awarded his wings on 6 October 1941. He was sent to HMS *Daedulus* and HMS *Heron* for advanced training and operational preparation. Finally, on 10 March 1942 he joined 757 Naval Air Squadron. It would be three long years, however, before he saw any action.

Active Service

Gray was almost immediately transferred to 789 Naval Air Squadron based at HMS *Afrikander*, a shore base at Simonstown in South Africa. The newly-formed squadron operated Albacores, Sea Hurricanes, Swordfish and Walruses and was in South Africa to protect against any moves the Imperial Japanese Navy might make. After the American success at the Battle of Midway, the threat to South Africa eased and Hammy was reassigned to Kilindini in Kenya with 795 Naval Air Squadron.

Yet more transfers saw Gray move through 803 to 877 Naval Air Squadrons. The latter flew Sea Hurricanes from HMS *Illustrious*. With the transfer, he was promoted to lieutenant and second in command. His final transfer was to *Illustrious*'s sister-ship, HMS *Formidable*, as senior pilot with 1841 Naval Air Squadron. After four years of training and operational flying, Hammy was finally going to see some action.

The target was the German battleship *Tirpitz*, still at anchor in Kaa Fiord in northern Norway after a daring X-craft attack the previous September. A series of carrier-born strikes were planned but poor weather caused them to be cancelled. Operation *Goodwood III* finally got under way on 24 August 1944. The aircraft carriers *Furious*, *Indefatigable* and *Formidable* launched forty-eight bombers and twenty-nine ground attack aircraft in an attack that resulted in just two hits that caused minor damage. One bomb did penetrate the upper and lower armour decks and came to rest in the No.4 switchboard room. Its fuze, however, had been damaged and it failed to explode.

Hammy took part in a second raid five days later, but poor visibility prevented any accurate bombing. He did lead a close-in attack on the anti-aircraft batteries and received a hit on his rudder. His gun camera showed just how close he was in his attack on the German flak defences. He also led an attack on three enemy destroyers at anchor. For this display of bravery, he was Mentioned in Despatches: 'For undaunted courage, skill and determination in carrying out daring attacks on the Tirpitz.'

Pacific 1945

By early 1945, the naval war against Germany was virtually won, allowing a number of Royal Navy ships to be transferred to the Pacific. In April, HMS *Formidable* joined the British Pacific Fleet as the Japanese 'Greater Eastern Co-Prosperity Sphere' steadily deflated. Leaving Sydney at the end of June, *Formidable* and four other carriers joined the US Navy's Third Fleet.

The enemy still held some nasty surprises and HMS *Formidable* was on the receiving end of one of them. In operations south of Okinawa in July, the Japanese launched a series of *kamikaze* attacks on the Allied warships. In one of these, a *kamikaze* hit the flight deck of *Formidable*. Fortunately, her armoured deck withstood the impact and there was little interruption to her aircraft's operations against Japanese targets.

Almost constantly in the air, the aircrew losses were heavy – the British carriers lost forty-seven aircraft to enemy fire and other causes. In July, Hammy led strafing missions against enemy airfields and on 24th led a strike against shipping and airfields in the Inland Sea area. On the 28th, he headed a strike against the naval base at Maisuru and achieved a direct hit on a destroyer (it was later reported sunk). His leadership against such well-defended targets led to a recommendation from Admiral Vian for an immediate award of the Distinguished Service Cross.

VC Action

On 30 July 1945, the Fleet withdrew for a couple of days for replenishment. This became extended due to a succession of typhoons that hit the operational area. It also coincided with the dropping of the atomic bomb on Hiroshima on 6 August, around the time that Hammy's squadron returned to operations against Japanese targets. Captain Ruck-Keene, the carrier's commander, cautioned the pilots to avoid taking unnecessary risks and to restrict themselves to just one attack run on each target.

On 9 August, a second atomic bomb was dropped on Nagasaki – it could only be a matter of days before the Japanese surrendered.

The 9th was also the day that 1841 Naval Air Squadron was tasked with three sorties against enemy airfields, for there was still the fear of *kamikaze* strikes. Participating on one of these missions, Hammy took off with seven other Corsairs and climbed to 10,000 feet. Each aircraft carried a pair of 500lb bombs in addition to four .50-inch wing-mounted machine-guns.

They flew the 150 miles from the carrier to landfall at the mouth of Onagawa Bay and Hammy noted two destroyers and two escorts at anchor. Continuing inland the pilots found their intended target, only to discover that it had been destroyed by other Allied aircraft.

As there seemed no point in wasting bombs on an airfield that was no longer operable, Hammy radioed that instead he intended to attack the ships he had seen in Onagawa instead. All eight Corsairs turned towards the bay and their approach was covered by the surrounding hills. As they cleared the hills in a 400mph dive down to almost sea level, they were met by heavy anti-aircraft fire from dozens of guns sited on the hillsides and the naval ships.

Hammy aimed at one of the ships, *Amakusa*, an escort frigate, and closed at full speed, jinking to avoid the enemy fire. One of his bombs was shot off and he was taking hits. Undeterred, he managed to release his remaining bomb and hit *Amakusa* below the after gun turret, which detonated the ammunition locker and blew out the side of the ship. Very quickly, she foundered and then sank.

Hammy Gray, his Corsair on fire, continued flying for a few seconds. Then his 'plane rolled over, hit the water at high speed and broke up. The rest of the group continued its attack. Another Corsair burst into flames as its port wing petrol tank exploded and it too crashed into the sea. Reforming, the group made another attack and badly damaged two of the other warships, before returning to the carrier. Sadly, they were to lose another pilot, who crashed while attempting to land back on *Formidable*'s deck.

Just six days later, on 15 August 1945, Japan surrendered.

Captain Ruck-Keene wrote to Hammy's father, concluding with the words that he was: 'The best and bravest fighter pilot in the ship and everybody loved him. The tragedy is all the worse coming so close to the end.'

VC Award

The Admiralty's Honours and Awards Committee debated the issue that similar cases had been considered and rejected. At length, they reached agreement that, in view of the success of the attack, Lieutenant Gray should receive a posthumous Victoria Cross. Gray's citation appeared in *The London Gazette* on 12 November 1945. His Cross was presented to his family in February 1946 by the Governor General, the Earl of Athlone, in Ottawa. His medal group is today held by the Canadian War Museum.

In Onagawa Bay, next to a memorial to those Japanese servicemen killed on 9 August (150 died), stands the only foreign military memorial on Japanese soil – a memorial to Robert Gray VC. This was placed by the Japanese military to honour what they saw as an extreme act of heroism. During a 2006 visit to Japan, members of the Canadian warship HMCS *Ottawa* placed a wreath at the memorial in Hammy Gray's honour.

Chapter 56

The Korean War, 1950–53

Number of VCs awarded	4
Number of VCs awarded to officers	3
Number of VCs awarded to other ranks	1
Total awarded to British Army	4

Origins of the War

On 25 June 1950, some 75,000 soldiers of the North Korean People's Army poured across the 38th Parallel to invade the pro-Western Republic of Korea. This was the first military action of the Cold War between Communism and Western Democracy.

The invasion came as a complete surprise to the Americans who realised that this was not just another border dispute between two unstable dictatorships. The North Koreans easily swept aside the inept South Korean Army and the Americans were forced to step in. They were quickly supported by the United Nations; a total of twenty-one member states contributed forces for the defence of South Korea.

After a UN counter-offensive at Inchon near the 38th Parallel, the North Koreans retreated and were pushed north to the Yalu River, which marked the border with China. On 27 November 1950, a numerically superior Chinese Army intervened and pushed the UN soldiers back to a front line close to the 38th Parallel. There the UN forces dug in and the fighting soon resembled the trench warfare of the First World War, with men huddled together in freezing fox-holes and facing the costly mass attacks of the enemy. Faced with a stalemate, the fighting ceased on 27 July 1953. The two sides met at the border town of Panmunjom and an armistice agreed. This remains in place today as no peace treaty has been signed.

The Korean War has been described as one of the worst conflicts fought in modern times. Although it was relatively short, it was exceptionally bloody with nearly 5,000,000 dead. The civilian casualty rate was higher than in the Second World War. The US Secretary of State, Dean Acheson, observed: 'If the best minds in the world had set out to find us the worst possible location in the world to fight this damnable war, the unanimous choice would have been Korea.'

It was felt that a stand had to be made to dissuade the Communists from trying to occupy one place after another. The Korean War became a symbol of the global struggle between East and West and there was a very real fear that the war would lead to Soviet aggression in Europe and the deployment of nuclear weapons.

Four Victoria Crosses were awarded for actions undertaken in this conflict. The recipients included Major Kenneth Muir of the Argyll and Sutherland Highlanders, who had withstood not only mass attacks by the North Koreans but also 'friendly fire' in the shape of a napalm attack by three US Mustang fighter bombers until he was killed by a burst of automatic fire. Probably the most celebrated Korean War VC is Bill Speakman, who fought off waves of attacks with hand grenades and, as is often said, but erroneously, beer bottles. His exploits and subsequent notoriety made him a favourite with the media. Colonel James Carne, meanwhile, commanded the Gloucestershire Regiment and always claimed to wear the Victoria Cross on behalf of all the officers and men of his regiment. The forth VC was a young platoon lieutenant who died performing two acts of outstanding gallantry.

PHILIP KENNETH EDWARD CURTIS VC (1926-1951)

Philip Kenneth Edward Curtis was born on 7 July 1926 at 43, Pembroke Street, Devonport, Devon. He was the only child of John Curtis, a general labourer and his wife Florence Richards. Philip was educated at Tamar High School in Plymouth, which was destroyed during the Blitz on the city. While part of the school was evacuated to Truro, Curtis remained in Plymouth and acted as a messenger for the Air Raid Protection wardens. He was desperate to join the RAF but was rejected because of his age.

In 1944, he was accepted into the Army but, to his disappointment, was not posted overseas. In 1946 he was given a Regular Army Emergency Commission into the Duke of Cornwall's Light Infantry (DCLI), although he never actually served with the regiment. While still stationed in Cornwall, he married a local Devonport girl, Joan Hayes, and later had a daughter, Phillipa Susan.

Bravery in Palestine

Curtis was then attached to the Royal Army Service Corps and sent to Palestine. It was there that he first displayed his coolness in a dangerous situation. One of his fellow officers and a close friend had been ordered to dispose of a room full of 2lb slabs of gun cotton which had dangerously deteriorated and were highly unstable. As he gingerly loaded a 3-ton truck, having warned the camp to evacuate, he was joined by Curtis who volunteered to help with the loading and disposal. With Curtis walking ahead searching for bumps and potholes, the truck slowly made its way to a nearby emergency landing strip. Choosing a collection of abandoned mud building at the end of the strip, they unloaded the gun cotton. Curtis had brought along some detonators and Cordex to set off the explosion. Once the explosive was in place, Curtis applied the end of his cheroot to the fuse and the two men made a hasty retreat but still got covered in debris.

Philip Curtis was demobbed in 1948 and placed on the Reserve of Officers. He took a job with Roneo, the duplicator company, but found the work depressingly dull. In 1950, he suffered a tragedy when his wife died in childbirth and he was left with a young infant to raise. To add to his woes, the Korean War broke out and he was recalled to the much-reduced Army to serve in the United Nations force being sent to Korea. Again, he was destined to serve with a different regiment; this time the Gloucestershire Regiment. Leaving his daughter with her-in-laws, he re-joined the Army.

Korea

In March 1951, he was sent to join 'A' Company and commanded No.1 Platoon of the Glosters. Within weeks, he was involved in one of the epic actions of the twentieth century – the Battle of the Imjin River. The Glosters were part of 29 Brigade, which included the Royal Northumberland Fusiliers and the Royal Ulster Regiment, the men being deployed along hills and ridges lining the south bank of the Imjin River about thirty miles north of Seoul.

Curtis befriended Lieutenant Terrance Waters of the West Yorkshire Regiment, another attached officer, who led No.2 Platoon. 'A' Company was sent to occupy Castle Hill which overlooked a ford over the river; the most likely direction the enemy would take. It was situated out on a limb with the nearest support nearly 3,000 yards away. Previously the Americans had occupied the area and had built a bunker as an observation point which would play an important role later.

The days before 22 April 1951 were quiet and the patrols found no sign of the enemy. Then on the night of the 22nd, the Chinese Army began to wade across the Imjin. Wave upon wave swept up the slopes of Castle Hill only to be met with devastating fire from machine-guns and mortars. By dawn on the 23rd, Castle Site, which was occupied by 2 Platoon commanded by Curtis's friend, Terry Waters, was on the point of being overrun having borne the brunt of the night fighting. Lieutenant Curtis was ordered to mount a counter-attack to ease the pressure.

VC Action

Curtis cautiously led his men towards the OP bunker when suddenly the Chinese stood up behind the bush-wood they had been carrying and opened a point-blank fire. The machine-gun fired from the bunker made any movement impossible. Despite this, Curtis moved forward and began lobbing hand grenades at the bunker's opening until he was struck in the head and fell a few yards from his target.

Captain, later General, Anthony Farrar-Hockley wrote an account of Curtis and his VC action: 'Phil is badly wounded: he drops to the ground. They drag him back through the wire somehow and seek what little cover there is as it creeps along their front. The machine-gun stops. Content now that it had driven them back; waiting for a better target when they move into the open again. "It's all right sir," says someone to Phil. "The Medical Corporal's been sent for. He'll be here in a minute."

'Phil raises himself from the ground, rests on a friendly shoulder, then climbs with great effort on to one knee. "We must take Castle Site", he says, and gets up to take it … "Just wait until Papworth has seen you, sir" – But Phil has gone: gone to the wire, gone through the wire, gone towards the bunker … And so it seems as if, for a few breathless moments, the whole of the remainder of that field of battle is still and silent, watching amazed, the lone figure that runs so painfully forward to the bunker holding the approach to the Castle Site: one tiny figure, throwing grenades, firing a pistol, set to take Castle Hill.

'Perhaps he will make it – in spite of his wounds, in spite of the odds – perhaps this act of supreme gallantry may, by sheer audacity, succeed. But the machine-gun in the bunker fires into him: he staggers, falls, and is dead instantly; the grenade he threw a second before his death explodes after it in the mouth of the bunker. The machine-gun does not fire on three of Phil's platoon who ran forward to pick him up; it does not fire again through the battle: it is destroyed; the muzzle blown away, the crew dead.'

Taking advantage of the lull in the fighting and the destruction of the machine-gun, 'A' Company withdrew from Castle Hill and joined the rest of the regiment on Hill 235. Over a four-day period from 22 to 25 April 1951, this single British battalion, gallantly assisted by 'C' Troop, 170th Independent Mortar Battery, held back thousands of advancing Chinese soldiers intent on reaching the South Korean capital. Seventy-nine per cent of the total strength of the Glosters' Battalion Group was taken prisoner, and only nine per cent escaped, but the extraordinary heroism of the men defending the position against seemingly impossible odds ensured that Seoul was never reached by the enemy. This feat resulted in worldwide commendations for the stand of the Glorious Glosters.

When the Glosters were fnally overrun, the survivors went into a wretched captivity. Philip Curtis's friend Terry Waters was awarded a posthumous George Cross for his leadership and fortitude despite the barbarous treatment he suffered at the hands of the North Koreans.

Philip Cutis's body lay where it fell and was not recovered for another six weeks. It was later interred at Busan UN Memorial Cemetery, South

Korea. One wonders if the recent death of his wife had coloured his decision to mount his almost certain suicidal charge.

Certainly, there are other examples of VCs who had suicidal feelings when they performed their outstanding acts – Paul Kenna of the 21st Lancers and John Beeley, KRRC, for example.

It was not until Colonel James Carne was released from captivity that he was able to recommend the Victoria Cross to Lieutenant Philip Curtis. On 6 July 1954, as is the practice with posthumous awards, the Queen held a private audience with Curtis' mother and mother-in-law and presented the VC to his seven-year-old daughter, Susan.

Chapter 57

Indonesia-Malaysia Confrontation, 1963–66

Number of VCs awarded	1
Number of VCs awarded to other ranks	1
Total awarded to British Army	1

Origins of the War

The violent conflict between Russian-backed Indonesia and the fledgling federation of Malaysia was seen as another Communist attempt to overthrow former Western colonies and install regimes favourable to Soviet Russia and China. As part of her withdrawal from the Far East, Britain created Malaysia, an amalgamation of the Federation of Malaya, Singapore and the British protectorates of North Bornea and Sarawak on the island of Borneo.

In 1960, Indonesia's first president, Sukarno, embarked on a series of aggressive anti-colonial policies and was drawn increasingly to the communist bloc who supplied him with military aid. Having seen off the Dutch in Netherlands New Guinea in August 1962, Sukano turned his attention to the British-supported Federation of Malaysia, claiming it was plot to undermine Indonesia. Despite some support from leftist political elements in British Borneo, the majority welcomed the establishment of the new country.

The subsequent confrontation was in effect an undeclared war. Most of the action took place in the border area on the island of Borneo. The frontier followed a 1,000-mile-long ridge-line of jungle-covered mountain ranges occasionally interrupted by a few roads or tracks. Initial Indonesian attacks into East Malaysia (North Borneo and Sarawak) relied on local volunteers trained by the Indonesian Army and as the number of incursion increased, the infiltration forces became larger and better organised. The main targets for attack were border villages and police stations.

The confrontation escalated and reached further afield with a wave of bombings which hit Singapore and the Malaya Peninsula. Sukarno hoped this would encourage an uprising but instead it galvanized the British Government and the local authorities into action. The Malaysian Army with support from British forces, including the Gurkhas, kept the infiltrators largely at bay. Initially the Australian and New Zealand governments were reluctant to involve their forces but by 1964 they sent infantry and some special forces, who mounted covert cross-border operations into Indonesia.

In 1964, Sukarno gave a speech in which he declared the following year as 'the year of living dangerously'. His choice of naming 1965 was prophetic. In September 1965, the Indonesian Communist Party (PKI) attempted a coup which was heavily crushed by the Indonesian Army. President Sukano, whose support base lay with the PKI, was forced to transfer power to General Suharto. There followed a mass murder of PKI members and it was estimated that over 1,000,000 Indonesians, including ethnic Chinese, were killed in the power struggle. On 11 August 1966, Suharto signed a peace treaty with the prime minister of Malaysia so ending the confrontation.

In this cat and mouse conflict fought by small units, one Victoria Cross was awarded for an outstanding feat of life-saving under almost point-blank fire.

RAMBAHADUR LIMBU VC (1939 –)

Born on 8 July 1939, in the village of Chyangthapu in East Nepal, Rambahadur suffered great loss and sadness in his childhood. As he later related: 'It was not that there was no love for me in the family, but it was evident that Death was determined to wipe out my whole family in no time. A large family of ten members died one by one within a short span of time, leaving only three young brothers.'

Limbu's older brother assumed the role of head of the family but, tiring of subsistence farming, the fifteen-year-old Rambahadur ran away with his cousin to join the British Army. The adventure that he sought eluded him in the routine of the recruitment camp and he decided to leave and return home. When he was nearly seventeen, he again left the village and went to neighbouring Sikkim to find work as a lumber-jack. He also met a girl he wanted to marry and, when his brother came to see him and persuade him to return home, he promised he would come back for his loved one. His elder brother was pleased that Rambahadur was about to settle down and encouraged him to return to Sikkim as soon as possible.

Rambahadur's younger brother was then old enough to join the British Army and was about to make the journey to the recruiting depot. The route was on the same direction to Sikkim, so the brothers travelled together. En-route, and plied with *rakshi* (local rice wine), Rambahadur forgot about the girl and re-joined the Army! The only fear that he had in re-joining was that he would be recognised as the boy who deserted. As he had grown and filled out, his fear was unfounded.

On 1 November 1957, he stood as a full soldier with the number '10' painted on his bare chest. He later learned that he was now enlisted in the 10th Princess Mary's Own Gurkha Rifles.

Two months later, Limbu and his fellow recruits arrived at their training camp in Malaya. There followed a ten-month long period of hard training at the end of which Rambahadur joined the 2nd Battalion, which was involved in the hunting down of the last terrorists from the Malayan Emergency. After two years of operating in the jungle, during which time there was no contact with the enemy, Rambahadur returned home on leave.

In March 1961, he married Tikamaya, a girl from his village, but because he was too junior in the battalion, he was not entitled to a place in the married quarters. A few months later, when he was stationed in Singapore, he received a letter from home telling of the birth of his first son, Bhakte. Promoted to lance corporal, he went on his second leave at the beginning of 1964. He was now entitled to bring his wife and son to married quarters in Singapore but soon had to leave them as he had to join his battalion in the island of Borneo in November 1964.

VC Action

The 10th Gurkhas had been involved in clashes with Indonesian forces which had crossed the border into Sarawak. President Sukarno opposed the establishment of the emerging independent country of Malaysia and sought to seize Sarawak, that country's part of Borneo. Rambahadur Limbu and his comrades were involved in many jungle operations in extremely tough conditions.

Heat, humidity and sudden enemy contact were the lot of the men of the 10th Gurkhas throughout 1965. Rambahadur recalled the action that resulted in him being awarded the Victoria Cross: 'My two gunners, Riflemen Kharkabahadur Limbu and Bijulparsad Rai cooked their food in the mess tins. They were unusually silent that morning … and ate very little. This was very unusual … I clearly noticed that something was wrong because he (Bijuliparsad) looked unusually sad and uncomfortable.

'That afternoon when we were advancing towards the enemy position, Bijulparsad was on my right-hand side. He was hit the first time the enemy opened fire. I saw blood on his face. As soon as I saw his blood, my own blood began to boil. I swore that the enemy would pay for this with their own blood. Blood for blood and nothing but blood could settle this account.

'For a few moments I could think of nothing else. But when I saw Kharkabahadur and Bijuliparsad lying wounded, I immediately rushed to them. I had to take them away into safety otherwise they were going to be an easy target for the enemy. I was more than ready to gamble my own life for those of these, my young Riflemen. The enemy had already seen me and knew my intention. They directed fire at me.

'The bullets whizzed past over my head. Fortunately, the bullets always tend to travel higher if not correctly aimed and it is not always easy to aim correctly in real action at moving human targets. A man with small stature like me has, therefore, some advantage. It took some time but I was able to take my two Riflemen into safety and I immediately joined my friends who were exchanging fire with the enemy. Within an hour we killed them all. At the end of the battle, four of them had tried to escape but they could not escape from our bullets.'

Vivid though his first-hand account is, Rambahadur omitted many details. It is in his lengthy citation that one can appreciate the sheer gallantry of the man. Not all accounts are as detailed as Rambahadur's official citation that appeared in *The London Gazette* on 22 April 1966:

'On 21 November 1965 in the Bau District of Sarawak, Lance Corporal Rambahadur Limbu was with his Company when they discovered and attacked a strong enemy force located in the Border area. The enemy were strongly entrenched in Platoon strength, on top of a sheer hill, the only approach to which was along a knife-edge ridge allowing only three men to move abreast. Leading his support group in the van of the attack he could see the nearest trench and in it a sentry manning a machine gun. Determined to gain first blood, he inched himself forward until, still ten yards from his enemy, he was seen and the sentry opened fire, immediately wounding a man to his right. Rushing forward, he reached the enemy trench in seconds and killed the sentry, thereby gaining for the attacking force a first but firm foothold on the objective. The enemy were now fully alerted and, from their positions in depth, brought down heavy automatic fire on the attacking force, concentrating this onto the area of the trench held alone by Lance Corporal Rambahadur Limbu.

'Appreciating that he could not carry out his task of supporting his platoon from this position, he courageously left the comparative safety of his trench and, with a complete disregard for the hail of fire being directed at him, he got together and led his fire group to a better fire position some yards ahead. He now attempted to indicate his intentions to his Platoon Commander by shouting and hand signals but failing to do so in the deafening noise of exploding grenades and continuous automatic fire he again moved out into the open and reported personally, despite the extreme dangers of being hit by the fire, not only from the enemy but by his own comrades.

'It was at the moment of reporting that he saw both men of his own group seriously wounded. Knowing that their only hope of survival was immediate first aid, that evacuation from their very exposed position so close to the enemy was vital, he immediately commenced the first of his supremely gallant attempts to rescue his comrades. Using what little ground cover he could find, he crawled forward, in full view of at least two enemy machine gun posts who concentrated their fire on him and which, at this stage of the battle, could not be effectively subdued by the rest of his platoon.

'For three full minutes he continued to move forward but when almost able to touch the nearest casualty, he was driven back by the accurate and intense weight of fire covering his line of approach. After a pause, he again started to crawl forward but he soon realised that only speed would give him the cover which the ground could not. Rushing forward he hurled himself on the ground beside one of the wounded and calling for support from two LMGs, which had now come up to his right in support, he picked up the man and carried him to safety out of the line of fire.

'Without hesitation, he immediately returned to the top of the hill determined to complete his self-imposed task of saving those for whom he felt personally responsible. It was now clear from the increased weight of fire being concentrated on the approaches to and in the immediate vicinity of the remaining casualty, the enemy were doing all they could to prevent any further attempts at rescue. However, despite this, Lance Corporal Rambahadur again moved out into the open for his final effort. In a series of short forward rushes, and once being pinned down for some minutes by the intense and accurate automatic fire which could be seen striking the ground all around him, he eventually reached the wounded man.

'Picking him up and unable now to seek cover, he carried him back as fast as he could, through the hail of enemy bullets. It had taken twenty minutes to complete this gallant action and the events leading up to it. For all but a few seconds, this young NCO had been moving alone in full view of the enemy and under the continuous aimed fire of their automatic weapons. That he was able to achieve what he did against such overwhelming odds without being hit, was miraculous. His outstanding personal bravery, selfless conduct, complete contempt of the enemy and determination to save the lives of the men of his fire group set an incomparable example and inspired all who saw him.

'Finally re-joining his section on the left flank of the attack, Lance Corporal Rambahadur was able to recover the LMG abandoned by the wounded and with it won his revenge, initially giving support during the later stage of the prolonged assault and finally being responsible for killing four of the enemy as they attempted to escape across the border. This hour long battle, which had throughout been fought at point blank range and with the utmost ferocity by both sides, was finally won. At least twenty-four enemy are known to have died at a cost to the attacking force of three killed and two wounded. In scale and in achievement this engagement stands out as one of the first importance and there is no doubt that, but for the inspired conduct and example set by Lance Corporal Rambahadur Limbu at the most vital stage of the battle, much less would have been achieved and greater casualties caused.

'He displayed heroism, self-sacrifice and devotion to duty and to his men of the very highest order. His actions on this day reached a zenith of determined, pre-meditated valour which must count amongst the most notable on record and is deserving of the greatest admiration and the highest praise.'

The two battalions of the 10th Gurkhas between them eliminated more enemy and won more gallantry awards than any other regiment of the Brigade of Gurkhas.

The Borneo Campaign came to an end with a peace agreement signed in August 1966. The 10th Gurkhas returned to Singapore where Rambahadur found that his wife was ill. She had suffered from stomach pains after the birth of their second child and was admitted to the British Military Hospital. Rambahadur was at her bedside when she died on 6 February 1966, leaving him a grieving widower with two small children.

Distraught, he told his superiors that he intended to leave the Army. In the middle of his mourning and pain, he became aware that he was to receive an award for gallantry although he was too numb to take it in. At length, he learned that he had been awarded the Victoria Cross and was to travel to Britain to receive it from Queen Elizabeth II.

London Investiture

Accompanied by his Company Commander, Captain C.E. Maunsell, and later joined by his five-year-old son, Bhakte, Rambahadur was the centre of much media attention and feted everywhere he went. On 12 July 1967, he attended the investiture at Buckingham Palace. Afterwards, the Queen invited her newest VC and his little son to a private audience, where the latter embarrassed his father by showing complete indifference to Her Majesty.

On his return, Rambahadur went on leave and remarried. It was while he, his family and another Gurkha officer and family were travelling by train through India to re-join the regiment that another disaster occurred. Despite sleeping together in a locked first class compartment, thieves somehow managed to break in and steal their entire luggage, which included his newly-presented Victoria Cross. Fortunately, a replacement was specially collected by his Colonel from the UK and brought to Hong Kong where it was less formally presented.

In 1971, Rambahadur was promoted to sergeant and again in 1976 to company sergeant major. During that period, the regiment served briefly in Cyprus and then back to Hong Kong, with spells in Brunei. He was appointed a Member of the Royal Victoria Order in 1984 for his service as Queen's Gurkha Orderly Officer. When Rambahadur retired in on 25 March 1985 as Honorary Captain, he was employed to serve in the Sultan of Brunei's Gurkha Reserve Unit, which acted as a bodyguard to the Sultan.

Limbu retired in 1992 and returned to his farm in the village of Chayang Thapu. Since his retirement, Rambahadur has been a regular visitor to Britain to attend the bi-annual reunion of the VC and GC Association.

Chapter 58

Vietnam, 1959–75

Number of VCs awarded	4
Number of VCs awarded to other ranks	4
Total awarded to Australian Army	4

Origins of the War

The end of the Second World War in the Far East heralded the beginning of the anti-colonial conflicts in the countries that had been occupied by the Japanese. The weakened British bowed to the inevitable in India and left in 1947. Likewise, Malaya and Singapore, after suppressing communist guerrillas, gained their independence. The Dutch, after a brief opposition, left Indonesia to its turbulent birth.

One country that tried to re-impose its colonial presence in Indo-China was France, which embraced the counties of Vietnam, Cambodia and Laos. After its surrender in 1940, Vichy France was established as a client state of Nazi Germany. The French authorities in Indo-China collaborated with the Japanese and continued to run the countries' affairs, although the ultimate power resided with the Japanese. Ironically, during this period the United States and Nationalist China supported the independence group, the Viet Minh, in their struggle against Japan.

Once the war against the Japanese ended, Ho Chi Minh and the Viet Minh declared the independent Democratic Republic of Vietnam in the north. The major Allied victors, the United States, the United Kingdom and the Soviet Union, agreed that the area should return to the French, who began sending forces to re-occupy the region. Very soon the Viet Minh began its guerrilla campaign culminating in the Battle of Dien Bien Phu in 1954, which ended France's rule in Indo-China.

The country was divided along the 17th parallel according to the Geneva Conference, with the Russian communist north under Ho Chi Minh facing the ruthless dictator, Ngo Dinh Diem, supported by America, in the south. Thus, the die was cast.

The northern forces known as the Viet Cong began to make incursions into the south encouraged by the unpopularity of Ngo Dinh Diem. America, having employed advisors, increasingly had to prop up the regime by sending more troops in what became a bloody and unpopular war. America and the West were concerned about the 'domino effect' which held that a communist takeover in Vietnam would lead to a chain reaction in neighbouring countries.

America sought allies, including Australia, who initially sent thirty military advisors in 1962. Within three years its strength had increased to 7,672. By the time the last Australian soldier left in 1972, approximately 50,000 men had served in Vietnam.

While helping the British during the Malayan Emergency, the Australians had gained valuable experience in jungle-warfare and counter-insurgency, something the American Army lacked. A new unit called the Australian Army Training Team Vietnam (AATTV), made up of officers and senior NCOs, was sent to train the South Vietnamese Army and the Montagnard tribesmen in the Central Highlands. Operating in dangerous jungles with troops who were often unreliable put a huge burden on these men and it is little surprise that four Victoria Crosses were awarded for feats of outstanding gallantry.

The first and second were posthumously awarded to Warrant Officer I Kevin Wheatley and Major Peter Badcoe, for actions in 1965 and 1967 respectively. The other two were awarded in the same month, May 1969, to Warrant Officer II Keith Payne and Warrant Officer II Rayene Simpson.

RAYENE STEWART SIMPSON VC (1926-1978)

Rayene Stewart Simpson was born on 16 February 1926 at Chippendale, an inner-city suburb of Sydney, the third child of a family that boasted two boys and four girls. Ray's parents, Robert William Simpson and mother Olga Maude (née Montgomery), lived on the poverty line and 1920s Australia was particularly tough for the Simpsons. Finally, between 1930 and 1931 Olga deserted the family and left her husband to manage their large brood. Unable to cope, Bob Simpson sent five-year-old Ray to the Weslyn Dalmar Children's Home at Carlingford. He continued his education at Carlingford Public School near to Dalmar. It appears that when he was eleven-years-old he worked as a farm hand on a dairy farm on Dumaresq Island in the north coast of NSW near Taree and may have continued his education at the Dumaresq Island Public School. Up until the age of eighteen little is known about his formative years except on leaving school he seemed destined to follow his father's occupation as an unskilled labourer.

When Ray was old enough he volunteered for service in the Australian Imperial Force, enlisting on 15 March 1944. He was duly transferred to the 41st/2nd Infantry Battalion (a 'holding' unit for soldiers under the age of nineteen).

Ray's first combat experience came on home ground. On 5 August 1944, his unit was part of reinforcements sent to assist garrison troops at Cowra after 1,104 Japanese PoWs attempted to escape. During the ensuing manhunt, four Australian soldiers and 231 Japanese prisoners were killed. Ray manned No.1 Vickers machine-gun, identical to the No.2 gun which, several hours earlier, had been defended to the death by Private Hardy and Private Jones; both men were posthumously awarded the George Cross.

During April 1945, Ray Simpson trained in jungle warfare in Queensland with the Australian Recruit Training Battalion before seeing out the war in Morotai, Tarakan, Rabaul, New Guinea and Borneo. He had postings with the 2/3rd Pioneer Battalion, AIF and later with the Advanced Ordnance Depot and the 26th Battalion (New Guinea), AIF. At the close of 1946 he was back in Sydney with the General Details Depot (Eastern Command) and the Services Training Centre. On 9 January 1947, he was officially demobilised.

'Civvie Street' proved unfulfilling. Up until 1951 he moved from one job to the next, living a 'roustabout's' itinerant life and never really settling in one place. Variously, he tried his hand at tram conducting, labouring, sugar-cane cutting and going to sea as a merchant seaman.

When the Korean War began in July 1950, Australia responded to the United Nations' call to send a contingent. Ray Simpson re-enlisted on 17 January 1951, initially joining up under his brother Robert's name due to a number of disciplinary charges against him from the Second World War. He came clean with his CO and wrote out a statutory declaration after which his correct name was used. After five months, he joined the 3rd Battalion, Royal Australian Regiment (RAR) and, on 10 July 1951, arrived in Korea.

Ray's previous experience led to promotions to lance corporal on 30 November 1951, rising to corporal on 21 January 1953, temporary sergeant on 4 February 1953 and culminating in his appointment as sergeant on 1 July 1955.

Simpson, as part of 'A' Company 3 RAR in October 1951, saw some of the fiercest fighting of the war. He was present at Hill 317 (better known in Australia as the Battle of Maryang San). It was there, incidentally, that Private Bill Speakman performed his VC act.

During the Korean War a senior officer once said of Simpson: 'He was the most outstanding soldier among an elite bunch of men. He is a rough and tough sort of a bloke, who knows more about soldiering than anybody I know. He's pretty much a loner, a man who knows what he's doing.'

Soldiers often took long compulsory leave in Japan after they had satisfied certain tenure in Korea. It was during his leave in February 1952 that he met and fell in love with Shoko Sakai, a young Japanese working at the US Leave Centre in Tokyo. She was a single mother with one daughter, Harumi. Although they had known each other for less than a month they married on 5 March 1952 in a Japanese Shinto ceremony. On or around 2 January 1953 they may have had to marry again officially as a Shinto marriage was not officially recognised by the Australian Military. Despite the fact that they could not have children, the marriage endured for a very happy twenty-seven years.

Sergeant Simpson was posted to the 2nd Battalion RAR and served in Malaya until 6 November 1957 after which he spent five years with the 1st Special Air Service Company (RAR).

Vietnam

With the conflict intensifying in Vietnam, Ray volunteered his services and as instructor to the South Vietnamese Army. On 16 July 1962, Sergeant Simpson joined the (AATTV), known simply as 'the Team', in the post of assistant instructor, arriving in Saigon on 3 August. His first tour of Vietnam was comparatively uneventful with the training of South Vietnamese troops in the art of jungle warfare, enlivened with the occasional skirmish.

Ray returned to Saigon in July 1964 with a promotion to Temporary Warrant Officer II. He was instantly seconded to a mixed group of US and Vietnamese Special Forces. Amongst the recruits were the indigenous Montagnard tribesmen (known as 'Yards') from the mountainous jungle areas of the Central Highlands. Ray was a key figure in setting up a patrol base near the village of Ta Ko, its main purpose being to monitor any infiltration by the enemy, as well as accompanying platoons on reconnaissance missions near to the base.

On 16 September 1964, he formed part of a patrol under the command of a Vietnamese officer. Ambushed and seemingly outnumbered by the enemy, the officer was shot and Simpson took a bullet in his right leg rendering him incapable of standing. Despite rapidly losing blood he assumed command of the beleaguered platoon and organised the men into a defensive perimeter. He called for back-up and by sheer will and determination repelled attack after attack by a persistent enemy. Reinforcements arrived sometime later, but not before ammunition supplies were severely depleted and Ray's near fainting from loss of blood and exhaustion. Thinking of others before himself he refused to be evacuated before those around him had left and the position was secure. Only then did he leave by helicopter to be taken to the 6th Field Hospital at Nha Trang.

Ray was transferred to the Zama Hospital in Tokyo on 20 October 1964, where he convalesced until discharged on 14 May 1965. During his convalescence, he punched an unpopular officer during a raucous evening when a smoke bomb was exploded in the officer's mess. A court martial would have ended his Army career but he was defended by an officer and the charges were dropped.

The wound in his leg, however, had caused irreparable damage and, after successive operations, it the Army decided that Ray was unfit for service in Vietnam. Ray returned to Australia in June 1965 and received the

Distinguished Conduct Medal for his inspiring leadership and bravery during the ambush.

Disappointed and angry at the decision to deny him further service in Vietnam, Ray rejected the invitation to Government House to receive his medal and suggested it be posted to him. As a result, he was seconded to the 1st Royal NSW Regiment on 26 January 1966 (better known as I Commando Company – a Citizens Military Force), but to him soldiering in Australia was tedious. His Army record showed that on 16 May 1966 he left, having requested his discharge because of his downgraded medical classification.

In 1964, Shoko returned to Tokyo to look after her infirm mother. The fare to Tokyo from Australia was expensive which meant trips were infrequent. The return to civilian life did not suit Ray and within a year he had paid his own fare back to Saigon and managed to re-enlist with 'the Team' on 2 May 1967. Though acutely embarrassing for the Australian Army, his many contacts smoothed the way and he was accepted back into the fold, for his third tour, and secured permanent promotion to WOII one year later on 1 May 1968.

VC Action

The Victoria Cross awarded to Ray Simpson was bestowed for sustained action over a period of two separate days. Undoubtedly, 1969 was a watershed year for the US in Vietnam. January had seen the inauguration of Richard Nixon as US President with a mandate to scale down US participation. After the Tet Offensive the South Vietnamese had clawed back key territories from the communist North.

The area of Ben Het in Kontum Province on the Vietnam-Cambodian-Laos border was a major route for the Viet Cong. In March 1969, it had seen the only tank battle between the US and North Vietnamese forces.

On 6 May 1969, Simpson was in command of indigenous Montagnard tribesmen who comprised the 232nd Mobile Strike Force Company of the 3rd MFB Company, which was part of a larger battalion tasked with finding Viet Cong routes of infiltration and eliminating any enemy using them by means of ambush. The 231st and 233rd were also in attendance. Their objective was to act as a search-and-clear force which brought them west of Ben Het, less than two miles from the Cambodian-Laos border.

Hampered by rugged terrain, steep hills, torrential rain and poor visibility Ray led his men cautiously forward, dodging old bomb craters and weapons pits from previous confrontations. The one consolation afforded by the atrocious weather was that the raid deadened the noise of the troops, thereby not alerting the enemy, as they slipped or brushed against bamboo.

It was at 14.30 hours on the 6th that Simpson's platoon made contact with North Vietnamese troops. As part of the leading company, his men were the first to face a barrage of heavy fire from a well-concealed enemy.

The Montagnards took cover and returned fire. This allowed Simpson to move forward to work out what to do next.

By 15.30 hours a second platoon had joined the action. Simpson's immediate response was to initiate a swift counter-attack using the accompanying reserve platoons. With little regard to the obvious danger, he stood in full view of unseen fire and led an assault. A criss-cross motion was adopted as Simpson and his men moved through the bamboo trees, all the time Ray rallied his men with words of encouragement.

Fully exposed, he made for an easy target and as a result attracted intense fire. Unlike the Montagnards, the NVA were superior troops who knew exactly what jungle warfare entailed. Well trained, they set up a flank position and were holding fire until maximum damage could be inflicted on the enemy. As Simpson's platoon neared their position they were met with more fire. WOII M.S. Gill, one of Simpson's platoon commanders, was badly wounded in the assault and the Montagnards began to retreat.

Ray's VC citation states: 'W.O. Simpson, at great personal risk and under heavy enemy fire, moved across open ground, reached the wounded W.O. and carried him to a position of safety. He then returned to the C.O. where, with complete disregard for his own safety, he crawled forward to within ten metres of the enemy and threw grenades into their position.'

Knowing the seriousness of the situation Simpson tried furiously to kick start the battle – conversing in Montagnard dialect and some good old Aussie patter to get his men fighting. Unfortunately, the inexperienced Montagnards refused to leave their cover. Still refusing to believe the cause was lost, Simpson moved forward to a bomb crater within a few metres of the enemy bunker and began to throw grenades. It was soon clear that he and his unit were hopelessly outgunned so he gave the order to withdraw to safety. To cover the withdrawal, he hurled phosphorus grenades into the trees.

Simpson's own report into the assault lacked any of his own heroic deeds, but was more scathing of his Company: 'At 16:50hrs the remainder of the Company moved to assist 1 & 4 platoon as the sit [situation] was developing to NVA advantage. During the ensuing fire fight 232 Company sustained 5 WIA, 2 of them serious.

'The performance of the Company was a damned disgrace both during the contact and subsequently at the LZ. Men refused to manoeuvre or shoot and many in fact moved off position to the rear … At 21:00hrs one wounded (Gill, AATTV) died … At first light 7 May the Company moved and joined up with the remainder of the platoon.'

In addition to this Simpson had also tried to organise a landing area to allow a rescue helicopter to put down and airlift out casualties. This was again hampered due to the inability of his men to form a perimeter. He mentions in his report: 'The dust-off received fire and refused to land. A slick attempted to recover the wounded and was shot up. The evacuation was aborted.'

On 11 May, Simpson's company was roused at dawn and given orders. By 07.30 hours three platoons were moving forward. Once again progress was slow as the platoons climbed the steep hills and pushed through dense undergrowth. Simpson's 232nd Company trailed the 231st. Captain Green was at the head of the column and before long heavy fire rained on the troops. WOII Kelly (AATTV advisor) was hit and Captain Green killed outright. Attempts to push the Montagnard troops into a left flank assault position proved fruitless.

Unwilling to move closer to the scene of firing, Simpson's own platoon of indigenous soldiers reacted in the same way as earlier occasions. Attached to the platoon was Sergeant P. Holmberg of the USSF (US), and nearby, WOII Walsh of 231st Company. The situation was now becoming desperate. WOII Kelly was lying in an exposed position next to the dead body of Captain Green. Two objectives now presented themselves: to rescue Kelly and keep the enemy at bay. Accompanied by Sergeant Holmberg and WOII Walsh, Simpson moved forward to place himself between the enemy and the wounded Kelly whilst at the same time allowing Holmberg and Walsh opportunity to get to the officer.

The VC citation picks up the story: 'From his position he fought on and by outstanding courage and valour was able to prevent the enemy advance until the wounded were removed from the immediate vicinity. WOII Simpson's gallant and individual action and his coolness under fire were exceptional.'

Simpson added that, 'At approx.. 11.30 hours firing was heard from 231 Company location and Kelly reported that Green was dead and that he was wounded himself. I ordered Holmberg with 3 Platoon to re-join the Company and be prepared to move with myself and 2 squads from 1 platoon to assist Kelly. Firing at this time was sporadic.'

Whilst throwing grenades and firing at the enemy, and receiving some close-range fire himself, Simpson was able to keep the Viet Cong at bay long enough to allow Holmberg, who examined Green's body, to confirm death.

'Sgt Holmberg administered to Kelly and the seriously wounded,' continued Simpson in his report. 'The watch, ring and necklace were removed from Green's body. Also his claymore bag contained notes, locations and S01. Orders were given to prepare to take out the casualties.'

Difficulties with his inexperienced soldiers still persisted: 'The Yards [Montagnards] refused to obey their leaders or their advisors. They were completely demoralised. Eventually because of the noises i.e.: orders being shouted from the centre where the body of Green and the advisors were located, the enemy concentrated his main fire power … From this time on the Yards had had enough.' (Simpson's Report)

Walsh and Holmberg, despite asking the 'Yards' for help, had to create a makeshift stretcher for Kelly to move him to safety, by themselves. At the same time, Captain Rothwell (an AATTV staff officer at Special Forces HQ at Nha Trang) was attempting to make a clearing amongst the jungle thicket to allow a helicopter to land. Though the helicopter was unable to land due to enemy fire Rothwell was able to keep the enemy at bay to allow the injured to be moved to a position further from the fighting. In an interview, later, Rothwell felt he deserved the VC rather than Ray Simpson. Instead he had to make do with a Mentioned in Despatches.

Simpson, in his own report concluded: 'Finally we moved from point of contact and reached the LZ [Landing Zone]. It was hell's own job trying to get the Yards to assist in carriage of wounded or to maintain flank and rear security. Eventually we returned to company position and evacuated wounded at approx. 19.30hrs.'

Helicopter support was eventually forthcoming. The CO of the AATTV in Vietnam, Lieutenant Colonel R.D.F. Lloyd, had witnessed at first-hand the inadequately-trained Montagnards and personally flew to see the US Commander of 5th Special Forces Group to voice his disdain about everything from poor intelligence on enemy activity in the area to low morale which resulted in reckless waste of life.

The Australian Task Force Commander, Major General R. Hay had summoned Simpson and other advisors to a conference in Saigon on 21 August. Before the meeting, Hay announced to him that he had been awarded the Victoria Cross, much to Simpson's incredulity. Typically, Ray played down his own part in the action and congratulated Peter Holmberg who had been so instrumental in 11 May battle saying: 'He was with me on those actions they gave me the VC for. He's a beauty.'

Ray was given a new advisory post at the Mekong Delta district – training villagers in the art of defending their territories. However, important though this task was, Army life was fast losing its appeal to Ray. The decision to leave had been coming over a period of months. Shoko had been caring for her invalid mother and Ray wanted to join her as they had spent too many years apart. He flew to Saigon on 9 April 1970 and requested his discharge papers.

On 1 May 1970, nearly a year after his outstanding gallantry, Australia's most highly decorated soldier topped his impressive array of medals with a VC. This was personally conferred on him by HM The Queen at Government House in Canberra. Ever blunt, Ray wrote to his CO at the AATTV pointing out that if his wife could not be present at the investiture then they could post the medal to him. In the event, the Army made sure Shoko was present at his investiture. Three days later he took his discharge from the Army.

As all his earnings were sent back to Shoko, he found employment as a kitchen hand working in various Army unit messes around Sydney. Once again, the authorities were embarrassed by the spectacle of a recent VC recipient working as a mess hand in front of other soldiers. Alternative employment that befitted his status was sought and found. A position was secured for him with the Australian Embassy in Tokyo in January 1972 as an administrative officer (stationery, printing and supplies co-ordinator). He also managed the Embassy's 'Bunker Bar', but, running true to form, he remained his own man: 'His hard drinking habits and laconic attitude did nothing to endear himself with the gin & tonic set, and attitudes towards him hardened still further after an altercation during which he hauled an official across the bar and administered some summary justice to him.'

In June 1976 Ray received the Long Service Good Conduct Medal from Prime Minister Fraser on a visit to Japan. This was swiftly followed by the Queen's Silver Jubilee Medal at the Australian Embassy in 1977. One of his last public appearances was in London in early 1978 when he attended a bi-annual reunion of the VC and GC Association in the presence of the Queen.

On 18 October 1978, Australians woke up to the news that one of their military heroes had died. For a period of eighteen months he had borne the pain of malignant cancer of the lymph glands – the final six months being particularly painful. Never one to fuss, he told few people of his condition. He was fifty-two-years old and died at the University of Tokyo Medical Clinic. The official cause of death was double pneumonia.

Two days later a funeral service was held in Tokyo with a requiem mass at the St Ignatius Church, Sophia University. At the request of his family, Ray's body was cremated, with half his ashes interred at the Yokohama War Cemetery and the other half residing with Shoko.

Even in death Ray Simpson still proved a thorn in the side of officialdom. Widows of serviceman were normally entitled to a war pension. Though Shoko was a naturalised Australian (since 1961), she had lived in Tokyo most of her married life. The authorities stated that she had not lived in Australia long enough to meet the criteria and, therefore, no pension could be granted. Pressure from the Ex-Serviceman's Association, relatives and the media resulted in an inadequate pension being paid to Shoko, who suffered from arthritis and deafness. By 1980 a job as a cleaner was offered at the Australian Embassy – much to the disgust of media and relatives alike. The Australian War Memorial (AWM) who normally only accepted medals as gifts agreed to buy Ray's collection for a well-below market price of $12,000. After an outcry in the media the figure was raised to $15,500.

Nearly three years after his death – in May 1981 – a War Widow's pension was given to Shoko Simpson. Though pneumonia may have killed Ray, it was the lymphoma that caused the pneumonia – and it is probable that the chemical *Agent Orange* may have caused the cancer. Records show that in three long tours of duty in Vietnam exposure to areas soaked in the defoliation chemical was highly likely. The Repatriation Review Tribunal could not prove that the chemical did not start the chain of events that led to Ray's demise and finally a pension was granted. Ray Simpson VC is now honoured in Canberra and in the Hall of Heroes, Fort Bragg, North Carolina.

Chapter 59

Falklands War, 1982

Number of VCs awarded	2
Number of VCs awarded to officers	1
Number of VCs awarded to other ranks	1
Total awarded to British Army	2

Origins of the War

The windswept Falkland Islands in the South Atlantic have a complex history which stretches back over 500 years. Although the islands were first sighted in the early 1500s it was not until 1690 that the English explorer John Strong landed and named them after the Admiralty Commissioner, Viscount Falkland. France established a naval base there in 1764 but agreed to sell it to Spain. There followed a dispute between Britain and Spain over who owned the islands which was settled with Spain retaining Puerto Soledad on the West Island and Britain keeping Port Egremont on East Island.

Due to the pressure of the American War of Independence, this agreement did not last, for Britain decided to evacuate many of her overseas settlements including the Falklands. On her departure, the British left a plaque asserting British dominion. She left the islands to a few seal hunters until they were ejected by the Spanish. The Napoleonic Wars occupied the attention of the European nations leaving, the Falklands to become little more than the domain of sealers and whalers.

It was not until 1829 that Argentina made its first claim for the islands, which she called the Malvinas. In the leisurely manner that countries responded before the advent of the telegraph, Britain re-established control of the islands in 1833. By 1840, Britain had established a colony on the Falklands and Port Stanley becomes an important harbour for ships rounding Cape Horn. In 1850, Britain and Argentina signed a 'Settlement of Existing Differences and the Ee-establishment of Friendship', which effectively ceded the Falklands to Britain. Since then the Falklands have remained a British possession.

Periodically, Argentina made claims to the islands believing them to be its territory, but it took the desperation of a military junta to provoke the largest and most severe armed conflict between Britain and Argentina. By 1982, Argentina was suffering a devastating economic crisis with a huge foreign debt and chronic inflation leading to civil unrest. The succession of military dictatorships responded by waging the Guerra Sucie, or Dirty War, which was described by the military as the 'Process of National Reorganization'. During an eighteen-year period, around 13,000 government opponents 'disappeared'.

Britain had its share of economic problems and appeared to be indifferent about the far-off Falkland Islands. A new Argentine junta headed by General Leopoldo Galtieri, Brigadier Basililio Lami Dozo and Admiral Jorge Anaya calculated that Britain would never respond militarily if Argentina could quickly occupy the islands.

They felt that such an action would not only divert attention away from the terrible problems the country suffered, it would also bolster the junta's standing.

Despite repeated warnings from the Royal Navy, the British government made plans to withdraw the Antarctic patrol ship, HMS *Endurance*, the only naval presence in the South Atlantic, thus sending the junta a clear signal that Britain would not defend the Falklands.

After occupying South Georgia on 19 March 1982, Argentina mounted an almost unopposed landing on the Falklands on 2 April. Britain responded by launching Operation *Corporate*, the codename for military operations to wrest the islands from Argentine occupation. A motley fleet was rapidly put together using whatever vessels were available. Besides various Royal Navy ships, including the aircraft carriers *Invincible* and *Hermes*, their destroyer screens, six submarines and Royal Fleet Auxiliary vessels, the Task Force requisitioned ships of the Merchant Navy. These included the liners SS *Canberra* and *Uganda*, RMS *Queen Elizabeth II* and eight Roll-on-Roll-off ferries (RORO), numerous container ships, freighters, tankers and other support ships.

Despite the logistical difficulties of operating 8,000 miles from the UK and the general air of pessimism expressed by the three Services, the Ministry of Defence (described by Admiral Sandy Woodward as all 'initially suspected the operation was doomed'), the 127-strong Task Force sailed for the South Atlantic.

Just one month later on 1 May, Britain made its first attack on the Falklands when a Vulcan bomber dropped bombs of the runway at Stanley. Finally, on 21 May, the British landed on the beaches around San Carlos Water, a force which included men of the 2nd Battalion Parachute Regiment (2 Para) from the RORO ferry *Norland* led by their commanding officer, Colonel H. Jones. Jones was soon to be awarded the most controversial Victoria Cross of the post-war era.

HERBERT JONES VC (1940-1982)

Herbert Jones was born in Putney on 14 May 1940, the eldest of three sons born to Herbert, a wealthy American artist, and his Welsh wife, Olwen. Young Herbert attended Eton for five years and, finding his name inappropriate, changed it to a simple 'H' – Bert Jones was not suitable for Eton. His school record was not impressive but he managed to enter the Royal Military Academy Sandhurst.

On 23 July 1960, Jones was happy to be commissioned in the Devonshire and Dorset Regiment, having spent most of his life around the River Dart area. This county regiment was his home for nearly twenty years. He served in Cyprus and Northern Ireland but despite taking part in numerous exercises, never faced any enemy fire. Described as a loner, he did cultivate close and loyal friends. His Army reports describe him as being impatient and highly strung, which could lead to a loss of temper over minor irritants. He certainly did not suffer fools gladly.

The regiment was sent to Northern Ireland where H's impetuosity and impatience became apparent. The so-called Battle of the Falls involved a mob throwing petrol bombs, grenades and other missiles at the Devon and Dorsets. H, to his immense frustration, was held in reserve at Battalion HQ and could barely contain his impatience at missing out on some real action. The sound of gunfire acted as a magnet and he had to be restrained from leaving his post to join in to fight.

Always ready with a memorable quote, Field Marshal Sir Garnet Wolseley, the Victorian Commander-in-Chief of the British Army once declared: 'The first business of an ambitious young officer is to try and get himself killed … All other pleasures pale before the intense, the maddening delight of leading men into the midst of an enemy, or to the assault of some well defended place.' This prophetically described H's desire to lead his men from the front.

Any criticism aside, Jones was regarded as an energetic officer and he steadily climbed the promotion ladder. In the late 1979, he was appointed for a position on the Staff and was appointed lieutenant colonel and General Staff Officer Grade 1 at United Kingdom Land Forces HQ at Wilton.

In 1981, Jones hoped to return to his old regiment as its commander, but he had upset too many people for him to be considered. Instead he was given instead command of 2nd Battalion, the Parachute Regiment.

The 2nd and 3rd Para were among the battalions chosen as part of the Task Force sent to eject the Argentine forces from the inhospitable Falkland Islands. On the night of 21/22 May, 2 Para duly landed at Bonner's Bay, San Carlos Water, and dug in on Sussex Mountain protecting the south of the beachhead. For four days, the regiment suffered the biting wind with no sign of the enemy. Finally, the fifty-mile cross-country advance on the capital, Stanley, was given the green light. Its success depended on the capture of the Lafonia area to the south the Argentine soldiers were dug in on the narrow Darwin-Goose Green isthmus.

The closest British troops able to undertake the task was 2 Para; the task of capturing this position was therefore given to Colonel H. Jones and his 500 men. Arrayed against them was approximately 750 enemy infantry who were well dug in across the one-and-a-half-mile-wide peninsula. Conventional military wisdom states that the attacker needs a three-to-one superiority over the defender, something the Paras patently did not have. The terrain was sodden peat with low tussock-covered hills and gorse filled valleys. With little cover, any approach in daylight was ruled out. The Paras had to make a night attack and left their position on Sussex Mountain having marched with heavy packs thirteen miles from San Carlos to the start line. The main reason for this exhausting march was the loss of the valuable support helicopters that sank with *Atlantic Conveyor.*

For some reason, Colonel Jones delayed giving his orders for four hours, thus reducing the number of hours of darkness available – something that nearly resulted in the enemy halting the Para's advance. Support fire from HMS *Arrow* signalled the start of the attack at 03.35 hours on the morning of 29 May. The Paras pushed the outlying enemy defences back to Darwin Hill and Darwin Ridge, which covered the width of the isthmus. There the attack stalled.

With dawn breaking, 'A' Company was in a perilous situation with no artillery support and sheltering in the gorse at the base of Darwin Hill. It had taken several casualties, mainly from the accurate fire of an Argentine sniper. H learned that both his flanking companies were also pinned down and that the enemy would have to be dislodged frontally. Throwing a couple of smoke grenades, H left his HQ and ran the 100 yards to 'A' Company's position.

VC Action

On arriving and assessing the situation, H showed his frustration and was critical of 'A' Company's failure to carry the enemy position. He saw that all efforts to assault the enemy, securely embedded on top of the Ridge, had ended with casualties. After about forty-five minutes, frustration drove H to lead an assault.

As John Geddes wrote in his book, Jones called: "'Come on A Company. Get your skirts on. Follow me!" None of them did. They were in no mood for public school gestures or gung-ho cries from a *Commando* comic book.'

Jones charged out of the Gorse Gully, round a spur and up a re-entrant. He was followed by two of his body-guard who recounted what happened. Noticing a trench to his left and above him, 'H ran at it firing his SMG [Sterling Machine Gun] and then rolled down the slope, changed his magazine and then ran back at the trench again.'

As H approached the trench he was hit by rounds fired from a trench to the right of the re-entrant. He had, however, penetrated the enemy defences deeper than any of his men and fell a few yards short of the enemy trench, mortally wounded. H's charge had been seen by few witnesses and did not galvanise 'A' Company. What did was a nerveless feat of bravery performed shortly afterwards by Corporal Dave Abols. Exposed to enemy fire, Abols, armed with a light anti-tank rocket launcher, stood and fired into the enemy command bunker. This determined the outcome of the impasse on Darwin Hill and the Argentines began to surrender. This did not mean the battle was over for it lasted a further twelve hours.

British casualties amounted to seventeen killed, whilst the enemy lost between forty-five and fifty-five dead.

At the end of 29 May, the Argentines locally accepted terms and 114 Goose Green civilians were freed. The men of 2 Para had won the first battle of the Falklands Campaign by fighting a numerically superior defending force to a standstill.

The British public needed a hero from this daring but vulnerable Task Force, where the Royal Navy had been taking severe punishment from the Argentine Air Force. H. Jones was originally nominated for a posthumous Distinguished Service Order but the Prime Minister, Margaret Thatcher, suggested the Victoria Cross instead. This has sparked off a controversy that resonates today: should H. Jones have made his lone brave, but fruitless, charge or should he have maintained his overall command at his HQ? Without the prestige of the Victoria Cross, Jones's action would now be almost forgotten. The change from DSO to VC is reminiscent of King George VI's decision to alter a DFC to a VC in the case of Flight Lieutenant James Nicolson for downing of an enemy aircraft during the Battle of Britain. A heroic figurehead was needed at that moment when the threat of defeat was still a possibility.

Colonel H. Jones was buried with other comrades at Blue Beach Military Cemetery by San Carlos Water. His Victoria Cross group is displayed to the National Army Museum.

As the British closed in on Stanley, two well-defended mountains had to be taken – Mount Tumbledown and Mount Longdon. It was on the latter that another posthumous VC was awarded to Sergeant Ian McKay of the 3rd Battalion the Parachute Regiment. In a move reminiscent to H. Jones, Sergeant McKay led a charge that dislodged the Argentines and carried Longdon. In doing so, McKay was shot and killed.

For the next twenty-five years, there has been something of a hiatus regarding the awarding of the Victoria Cross. Although there was conflict in regions such as the Balkans and other smaller theatres of war, there were no more Victoria Crosses awarded. This did not mean that there was no activity from an administrative perspective for there were some important changes.

The most significant was the replacement of the Imperial Victoria Cross with the creation of Crosses for Australia, New Zealand and Canada. In the last sixty years, these Commonwealth countries have introduced their own honours systems separate from the British Honours System. In January 1991, Australia was the first to introduce the Victoria Cross for Australia which, along with New Zealand, is identical to the Imperial VC and still made by Hancocks the jewellers in Burlington Arcade, London.

The Cross for New Zealand does make for the provision of awarding it to civilians operating under the military.

The Canadian Victoria Cross is different in that it is only partly made from the bronze supplied by the UK, to which other Canadian metals including copper, zinc and lead are added. This has enabled a lighter and easier-flowing alloy to produce sharper detailing, including the addition of the fleurs-de-lis, an acknowledgement to the French-Canadians, a more stylised lion guardant, and replacing the wording 'For Valour' with 'Pro Valore'. A broader definition of the term enemy was extended to armed mutineers, pirates and terrorists.

In 1992, the Governor General said at the unveiling: 'Canada wanted its own Victoria Cross, a Cross that would resemble the British VC but would better reflect who we are.'

The Governor Generals of all three nations are vested with the responsibility of awarding the Victoria Cross on the recommendation of their own honours committees. Since its inception, the new Commonwealth VCs been awarded to one New Zealander, Corporal Willie Apiata of the New Zealand SAS, and four Australians. Of the latter, the first was to Trooper Mark Donaldson in 2008, followed by two in 2010 – the recipients being Corporal Ben Roberts-Smith and Corporal Daniel Keighran. In 2013, a posthumous Australian VC was awarded to Corporal Cameron Baird.

In Britain, a second level gallantry award was created in 1993; the Conspicuous Gallantry Cross. To date, fifty-nine have been awarded, most for actions that previously warranted the awarding of the Victoria Cross. In consequence, the bar for the Victoria Cross has been raised even further.

It was under John Major's government that this new award was unveiled and it was the Prime Minister who significantly raised the pension for VC holders. Major mentioned Second World War VC, Umrao Singh, at the Conservative Party Conference held shortly after the VE Day celebrations in 1995. He had been amazed to learn from Umrao Singh that the pension had been set at £100 per year since the end of the Second World War and so took steps to have it raised to £1,300 per annum. Since then, Chancellor George Osborne raised the pension further to £10,000 in the 2015 budget.

Chapter 60

Aghan War, 2001–14

Number of VCs awarded	3
Number of VCs awarded to other ranks	3
Total awarded to British Army	3

Origin of the War

On 24 December 1979, the West was caught unawares as Soviet tanks crossed the Amu Darya River so starting the ten-year-long Soviet-Afghan War, often described as Russia's Vietnam. A pro-Soviet government had seized power in Afghanistan the previous year and quickly suppressed opposition from the traditional Muslim Afghans. This resulted in a country-wide rebellion and by December 1979 the government had lost control of territory outside the cities. The Soviets responded for calls of assistance by sending in her Army to put down the rebellion, despite an overwhelming UN General Assembly resolution to withdraw.

The Americans saw an opportunity to frustrate and oppose the Soviets by proxy. The CIA gave material support to the Islamist fighters. The vicious guerrilla war against the Soviets led to their departure in February 1989. The unpopularity of the war amongst the Russian population added to the final fall of the Soviet Union on 26 December 1991.

The left-wing Afghan government's forces continued to fight the Mujahedeen but in 1992 it was overthrown. There followed a civil war between the various Muslim factions resulting in the Pakistan-sponsored ultra-conservative religious Taliban seizing power in 1996. The Taliban government quickly established an extreme form of Sharia law. Women were forced to wear the burqa at all times in public and were not allowed to work or be educated after the age of eight. Punishments and executions for any violation of Taliban law were frequent and barbaric, and included stoning and public beheadings. Pressure built in the West to intervene and overthrow this brutal regime. Finally, America and her allies entered Afghanistan to fight what was initially called the 'Good War'.

Britain and America found themselves fighting two separate wars at the same time, both with the same object in mind; the second was the so-called War on Terror. Triggered by the 11 September attacks, America identified Afghanistan, with its ultra-fundamentalist government, as providing sanctuary for Al-Qaeda, the perpetrators of this outrage. Ironically, it was the US who materially supported the Mujahedeen against the Soviets, an organisation which later morphed into the Taliban. All appeals to the Taliban to handover Osama bin Laden were rejected, accelerating the West's intervention.

On 7 October 2001, American-led NATO forces began to bomb Taliban and Al-Qaeda bases. The Afghan United Front (Northern Alliance), aided by American Special Forces, overthrew the Taliban, which retreated to the wild frontier of their sponsor, the semi-autonomous Pakistan Tribal Areas. These lands were familiar to Britain in her prolonged policing of the North-West Frontier during the days of the Raj. Despite her 150 year-long bruising encounters with the Afghans, Britain again sent her military into Afghanistan as part of the International Security Assistance Force (ISAF) with the aim of establishing a democratically elected government under the presidency of Hamid Kazai.

Generous humanitarian aid and reconstruction was funded by the Americans, but corruption, along with the failure to halt the production of opium, thwarted the West's target of bringing Afghanistan into the modern world. By 2005, the Taliban had reasserted itself in Afghanistan through the combination of funding from sponsors from the Persian Gulf and the millions made from the cultivation and sale of opium. The Taliban also changed its tactics and adopted those employed in Iraq, namely suicide bombs and improvised explosive devices (IED). They avoided pitched battles and became adept at ambushes which resulted in a steady stream of allied casualties.

In one such encounter, a posthumous Victoria Cross was awarded to a paratrooper for two acts of outstanding gallantry.

BRYAN JAMES BUDD VC (1977-2006)

Bryan James Budd was born in Belfast on 16 July 1977, one of twins; the other being his sister Tracy. At an early age, the family moved to England and Bryan was educated at the Thomas Sumpter School in Scunthorpe, Lincolnshire. In December 1995, he enlisted in the Parachute Regiment and, after serving in Northern Ireland, applied to join the Air Assault Brigade's Pathfinder Platoon. This group, besides being a reconnaissance force, also was skilled in HALO parachuting (High Altitude Low Opening) and establishing drop zones in enemy territory.

The Pathfinder Selection Cadre is open to soldiers of all cap badges, although the majority are from the Parachute Regiment. After a rigorous selection program, Budd served in the elite unit for ten years, undertaking tours in the Balkans, Sierra Leone, Macedonia and during the Second Iraq War. During this time, he met and married Lorena, a clerk in the Royal Artillery at Catterick. They set up home in Ripon, North Yorkshire and had a daughter who was born in 2004.

Corporal Budd re-joined his regiment, 3 Para, in Helmand Province, Afghanistan in early June 2006 during Operation *Herrick IV* (Operation *Herrick* was the codename under which all British operations in Afghanistan were conducted). The plan was for the British Army to provide security for 'hearts and minds' reconstruction operations. Instead they became increasingly involved in combat with the Taliban who vehemently opposed such humanitarian strategies.

Corporal Budd was deployed with 'A' Company in the District Centre of Sangin, which was under almost constant attack. On 27 July, whilst on a routine patrol, his section came under fire from two enemy gunmen on the roof of a building who managed to wound two of Budd's men. One was seriously injured and lay in the open as bullets struck the ground around him. Realising that the gunmen must be removed he led an attack under fire and chased off the two Taliban, who were killed as they ran across an open field. This prompt action enabled the wounded soldier to be evacuated and successfully treated.

VC Action

One of the features of the 2006 Helmand conflict was the use of platoon houses or blockhouses, which, manned by small numbers of British soldiers, frequently became Taliban targets. One such was an isolated outpost in the Sangin area where 'A' Company was based. A comrade of Bryan Budd recalled the events of 20 August:

'We were sent out to protect some Royal Engineers who were blowing holes in a compound 500 metres away from the platoon house. This was so we could cut through the compound quickly and avoid enemy fire when we were out on patrol. There were three sections of us out, a total of 24 guys, all spread out in a head-high cornfield around the compound.

'Bryan was the first to spot the Taliban approaching, really close to us, only about 50 metres away. With just hand signals, he led his section in a flanking manoeuvre round to the cornfield's outskirts to try and cut them off. but the section was spotted by the enemy before they could get there and they opened fire on the lads. Then a load more Taliban behind a wall further back also opened up on the section.

'The guys were taking heavy fire from two positions. The enemy were just blatting away, their AK47s above their heads, and rounds were coming in from all over the shop. One lad got a bullet in the shoulder and another was shot in the nose. Everyone was kneeling or lying down trying to take cover. It was mayhem.

'That's when Bryan made his move. He knew how dangerous it was but he obviously decided it was his responsibility to destroy the threat, because the enemy were cutting us to pieces. He got up and rushed straight at through the corn in the direction of the Taliban just 20 metres away. We heard Bryan's rifle open up on them on fully automatic mode but that was the last anyone heard of him. All contact was lost with Bryan. Straight afterwards, the enemy's fire lessened and allowed the rest of the section to withdraw back to safety so casualties could be treated.'

There was pause while air support was called in and the whole of 'A' Company was able to push their way forward, beating the Taliban back.

'About an hour later some of the lads found Bryan's body beside two dead Taliban. It was obvious he was the one who wasted them but he was obviously hit at the same time – by either them or the fighters behind the wall. He was badly wounded and he had no pulse. The company sergeant major rushed forward on a quad bike to get him and carried Bryan back to the platoon house, but there was nothing anyone could do for him by then and he was declared dead.'

All fatalities are tragic but Bryan Budd's death was particularly poignant. He was due to return to the UK five days later to be with his wife who was expecting their second child. It was felt that Corporal Budd's double action warranted the Victoria Cross and his citation appeared in *The London Gazette* on 14 December 2006. Then more distressing news followed: the shot that killed Budd came from a NATO 5.56 round which meant he was killed by 'blue on blue' or friendly fire. He had been hit in the pelvic region below his body armour which severed several arteries including the femoral artery causing certain death. A coroner's report confirmed this as a tragic accident caused by crossfire.

On 7 March 2007, Leona Budd received her husband's Cross from Queen Elizabeth II during a private audience in Buckingham Palace. His VC is displayed at the Parachute Regiment and Airborne Forces Museum at the Imperial War Museum, Duxford, Cambridgeshire.

In 2009, the Americans sent 11,000 Marines to reinforce the British presence in Helmand province. The British had been under pressure because of the 'platoon house' strategy which saw troops tied down in remote outstations. These posts attracted sustained and intensive Taliban attacks and many remained under siege for long periods. The number of fatalities continued to rise, due mainly from the use of IEDs (Improvised Explosive Devices), which accounted for more than sixty-six per cent of coalition deaths. The 'Good War' was rapidly losing support with the public as it was revealed that the Afghan government was misappropriating America's largess, condemning it to being the second most corrupt in the world.

In October 2014 the British government decided to withdraw from this unwinnable and unpopular war with its mounting casualty list. Until the troops could return home, however, the British Army continued to mount patrols and operations together with US and Afghan forces. It was for one soldier's actions during one of these final routine operations that resulted in another VC.

JOSHUA MARK LEAKEY (1988 –)

Born in Hampshire in 1988, Joshua Mark Leakey is the eldest son of Air Commodore Mark Leakey and his mother, Rosemary. As the son of a serving RAF officer, Joshua was liable to be moved during his education. He attended Witham Hall preparatory school near Stamford, Lincolnshire, before completing his education from 1999 to 2006 at Christ's Hospital, also called the Bluecoat School, near Horsham in West Sussex. He was accepted by the University of Kent at Canterbury to sit a degree in military history but dropped out after just one term to join the Army. His mother recalled that Joshua rang her up after eight weeks and said; 'Mum, I'm fed up of reading about wars. I'm going to go and be in them.'

In 2007, Leakey joined the Army and was posted to the 1st Battalion Parachute Regiment, which is the main contributor to UK's elite Special Forces Support Group (SFSG). By joining the Army, he was following in the footsteps of his second cousin twice removed; Sergeant Nigel Leakey who was awarded a posthumous VC against the Italians in Ethiopia in May 1941.

The men of 1 Para served three tours of duty in Afghanistan during Operation *Herrick* – in 2009, 2011 and 2013. It was during the latter tour that Lance Corporal Joshua Leakey was awarded the Victoria Cross.

On 22 August 2013, in what was supposedly a routine joint operation commanded by US Marines, the combined force was flown by Chinook helicopters to the village of Bar Nowzad in northern Helmand province to search for illegal weapons. Leakey's helicopter landed on a hill overlooking the village, where he and three other paratroopers and an Afghan soldier were to provide covering support while the rest of the patrol entered the village. The US Command Group landed behind the hill and almost immediately came under Taliban fire from machine-guns and RPGs (rocket-propelled grenades).

VC Action

From his position on the lee of the hill Leakey heard over the radio that someone had been shot. He recalled: 'When you hear there's a man down, the hairs on the back of your neck stand up. Clearly then your plans change.'

Running across the barren hillside to the top of the hill, he saw the wounded man and, being the group closest to him, he gathered his four comrades and dashed down the hill to help the fallen soldier. The wounded man was lying in a rubble compound, which offered sparse cover to the two machine-guns and mortar team. He also saw that about twenty Taliban had pinned down the men in the compound rendering their fire-power ineffective. Under heavy fire, Leakey reached the wounded Marine Corps officer, Captain Brandon Bocian, giving first aid before dashing back up the hill to retrieve a machine-gun his section had left on the hill. All the time, the Taliban were firing at him as he made his way back encumbered by his 60lb pack. Picking up the machine-gun and, with bullets ricocheting off the weapon, he ran back down the hill. While his comrades opened fire on the enemy, Leakey again dashed up the hill to collect the other machine-gun and returned to open fire.

Leakey soon realised that he was in a poor firing position in the compound, so he grabbed his weapon and yet again ran up the hill where he could fire his machine-gun more effectively. Meanwhile, the wounded officer had been pulled to safety and was airlifted on a Black Hawk helicopter to hospital. Leakey's exhibition of outstanding bravery inspired his comrades and it was the turning point in the battle, which lasted forty-five minutes. When the shooting died down, eleven insurgents had been killed and four wounded.

In rather leaden militarise, Joshua Leakey's citation dated 26 February 2015 records the following: 'Between May and December 2013, Lance Corporal Leakey was deployed in Afghanistan as a member of a Task Force conducting operations to disrupt insurgent safe-havens and protect the main operating base in Helmand province. The majority of operations took place in daylight in non-permissive areas, attracting significant risk. On 22 August 2013, Lance Corporal Leakey deployed on a combined UK/US assault led by the United States Marine Corps into a Taliban stronghold to disrupt a key insurgent group.

'After dismounting from their helicopters, the force came under accurate machine gun fire and rocket propelled grenades fire resulting in the Command Group being pinned down on the exposed forward slope of a hill. The team attempted to extract from the killing zone for an hour, their efforts resulting in a Marine Corps Captain being shot and wounded and their communications being put out of action. Lance Corporal Leakey, positioned on the lee of the hill, realising the seriousness of the situation and with complete disregard for his own safety, dashed across a large area of barren hillside which was now being raked with machine-gun fire. As he crested the hill, the full severity of the situation became apparent: approximately twenty enemy had surrounded two friendly machine gun teams and a mortar section rendering their critical fire support ineffective.

'Undeterred by the very clear and present danger, Lance Corporal Leakey moved down the forward slope of the hill, and gave first aid to the wounded officer. Despite being the most junior commander in the area, Lance Corporal Leakey took control of the situation and initiated the casualty evacuation. Realising that the initiative was still in the hands of the enemy, he set off back up the hill, still under enemy fire, to get one of the suppressed machine guns into action. On reaching it, and with rounds impacting on the frame of the gun itself, he moved it to another position and began engaging the enemy.

'The courageous action spurred those around him back into the fight: nonetheless, the weight of enemy fire continued. For the third time and with full knowledge of the extant dangers, Lance Corporal Leakey exposed himself to enemy fire once more. Weighed down by over 60 lbs of equipment, he ran to the bottom of the hill again: a round trip of more than 200 metres on steep terrain. Drawing the majority of enemy fire, with rounds splashing around him, Lance Corporal Leakey overcame his fatigue to re-site the gun and return fire. This proved to be the turning point. Inspired by Lance Corporal Leakey's actions, and with a heavy weight of fire now at their disposal, the force began to fight back with renewed ferocity.

'Having regained the imitative, Lance Corporal Leakey handed over the machine gun and led the extraction of the wounded officer to a point from where he could be safely evacuated. During the assault 11 insurgents were killed and four wounded, but the weight of enemy fire had effectively pinned down the command team.

'Displaying gritty leadership well above that expected of his rank, Lance Corporal Leakey's actions single-handedly regained the initiative and prevented considerable loss of life, allowing a wounded US Marine officer to be evacuated. For this act of valour, Lance Corporal Leakey is highly deserving of significant national recognition.'

When the award of the Victoria Cross to Leakey was announced at a ceremony at Lancaster House, General Sir Nicholas Carter, Chief of General Staff, gave Joshua Leakey a handshake and a rather awkward hug. On 14 April 2015, Leakey was presented with the Cross by the Queen in the quadrangle at Windsor Castle. It was the sixth VC the Queen had given to a living recipient, leading her to remark that she does not give this one out very often. In addition, Leakey received the City of London's highest honour to become a Freeman of the City.

The wounded soldier he treated, Captain Brandon Bocian, made a full recovery. On hearing of the award of the VC to his rescuer, he said: 'The fact that he chose to leave his position to help me speaks of his courage and character. I am happy to hear that he is being formally recognised.'

Chapter 61

The Second Iraq War 2003–11

Number of VCs awarded	1
Number of VCs awarded to other ranks	1
Total awarded to British Army	1

Origins of the War

The origins of the Second Iraq War lie in the events leading up to the Gulf War of 1990-91. The main source of friction was between Iraq and Kuwait, both major oil producers. Kuwait had been the province of Basra under the Ottoman Empire until 1922, when Britain drew the border between the two countries thus making Iraq virtually land-locked. Iraq continued to claim that Kuwait was rightfully its territory. Relations between the two countries worsened when Kuwait was accused of exceeding the OPEC (Organisation of the Petroleum Exporting Countries) quotas for oil production, depressing the desired price, which exacerbated Iraq's desperate financial woes. The Iraqi government described it as a form of economic warfare and responded by moving 30,000 troops to the Kuwait border.

Finally, the Iraqi Air Force bombed Kuwait City on 2 August 1990 and her troops occupied the country. The invasion was condemned by the United Nations and months of talks began. An ultimatum was issued demanding that Iraq withdraw by 15 January 1991. Meanwhile America, along with her Coalition allies, began massing its armed forces on the Saudi border. With no sign that Iraq intended to withdraw, the Coalition forces launched a massive air offensive that soon destroyed the Iraqi Air Force and her anti-aircraft facilities.

This was followed by the invasion which liberated Kuwait and chased the Iraqis back to their own country. The long convoy of retreating Iraqi troops along the main Iraq-Kuwait highway was bombed so extensively that it became known as the 'Highway of Death'. Soon after, President Bush declared a ceasefire as Kuwait had been freed. Unfortunately, this brief war only served to bring about a long, destructive war with huge loss of life some twelve years later.

The continuing rise of Al-Qaeda, the militant Sunni Islamist global terrorist organisation, and the spectacularly awful destruction of the World Trade Centre in New York in 2001, once again focused attention on Iraq and its leader, Saddam Hussein.

During the post-Gulf War period, Saddam had brutally suppressed the rebellions that had broken out in Iraq, particularly those of the Kurds in the north and the Shi'ite Muslims in the south. Despite his defeat, Saddam became popular amongst many Arabs for standing up to the West, especially America.

As a fellow Sunni Moslem, Saddam was suspected of having links with Al-Qaeda, but this has been subsequently discounted. After the destruction of the Twin Towers, America was looking to build a case against Iraq, who was seen as supporting terrorism, and the new US president, George W. Bush, found a ready ally in British Prime Minister, Tony Blair.

Faulty, or manipulated, intelligence, claiming that Iraq possessed weapons of mass destruction, gave the Anglo-Americans the perfect excuse to topple Saddam Hussein and his Ba'ath Party. During the 1980s, Saddam had been condemned internationally for deploying chemical weapons against Kurdish and Iranian civilians. Iraq was known to have pursued an extensive biological and nuclear weapons program and the United Nations Special Commission (UNSCOM) oversaw the destruction of the biological weapons after the Gulf War. No nuclear device was found or even built. The former UN weapons inspector, Scott Ritter, categorically stated in June 1999:

'When you ask the question, "Does Iraq possess viable biological or chemical weapons?" the answer is "No!" Can Iraq produce today chemical weapons on a meaningful scale? No! Can Iraq produce biological weapons on a meaningful scale? No! Ballistic missiles? No! It is "no" across the board … Iraq today possesses no meaningful weapons of mass destruction capability.'

Despite the evidence to the contrary, President Bush and Prime Minister Tony Blair formed a Coalition to 'disarm Iraq of weapons of mass destruction, to end Saddam Hussein's support for terrorism and free the Iraqi people.' Without a mandate from the United Nations, the invasion went ahead. Effective air strikes preceded the coalition forces' invasion in late March 2003. By 1 May all major military action had ceased.

The military occupation that followed attempted to install an Iraqi Interim Government and rebuild the country's infrastructure. Their efforts were considerably slowed by the rise of militant Iraqi insurgency which erupted into a sectarian civil war, primarily between the Sunni and Sh'ite factions, with the Coalition forces regarded as the enemy by both.

After America, Britain contributed the largest number of personnel, who were deployed in Basra province in the south of the country. It was there in 2004 that the first Victoria Cross was awarded to a living recipient in the British Army since the Indonesian-Malaysia Confrontation in 1965.

JOHNSON GIDEON BEHARRY VC (1979-)

Johnson Gideon Beharry was born on 26 July 1979 in the village of Diego Piece on Grenada, the southernmost island in the Lesser Antilles. His parents being Florett Beharry and Michael Bhola, Johnson was one of seven children brought up in an impoverished environment dominated by their volatile, alcoholic father. They all lived in a wooden hut without running water and comforts were few. In his book, *Barefoot Soldier*, Johnson recalls that it was not until he attended school that he wore shoes. Leaving his primary school at the age of thirteen, Johnson seemed destined for a life as a builder's labourer or odd job man.

When he was twenty, he left Grenada to come to Britain and found work as a builder's labourer. When a group of his friends said that they were going to join the Army, he decided to do the same but was rejected on the grounds of his dreadlocks and hash smoking. After six months of cleaning up his act, he applied again and was accepted.

Johnson joined the British Army on 6 August 2001. After completing his training at the Infantry Training Centre, Catterick, he joined the 1st Battalion Princess of Wales's Royal Regiment in March 2002 as a rifleman and, because he showed a mechanical aptitude, was trained as a driver of the Warrior armoured personnel carriers (APC). On 15 February 2002, he married his childhood sweetheart and fellow Grenadian, Lynthia, who worked as a clerk for the MoD.

The regiment were soon deployed overseas, serving six months in Kosovo and three months in Northern Ireland. Following the invasion of Iraq, Johnson and his comrades of 1 PWRR were deployed to southern Iraq in April 2004 on a six-month tour of duty. Within two months he was called upon to perform his acts of valour.

In an exceptionally active period, the regiment was involved in a total of 850 attacks, which averaged a relentless six a day for five months. One particular saw the regiment endure a staggering 109 attacks. It is small wonder that 1 PWRR was awarded the highest number of gallantry awards to date in Iraq – the total number of awards was thirty, consisting of one VC, two Conspicuous Gallantry Crosses, two DSOs, seven Military Crosses, fifteen MiDs, one Queen's Commendation for Valuable Service and two MBEs.

Official VC citations tended to be dry and lack the essence of the act they describe. Johnson Beharry's citation is an exception and is one of the longest and most detailed of all citations:

'Private Beharry carried out two individual acts of great heroism by which he saved the lives of his comrades. Both were in direct face of the enemy, under intense fire, at great personal risk to himself (one leading to him sustaining very serious injuries). His valour is worthy of the highest recognition.

'In the early hours of the 1st May 2004 Beharry's company was ordered to replenish an isolated Coalition Forces outpost located in the centre of the troubled city of Al Amarah. He was the driver of a platoon commander's Warrior armoured fighting vehicle. His platoon was the company's reserve force and was placed on immediate notice to move. As the main elements of his company were moving into the city to carry out the replenishment, they were re-tasked to fight through a series of enemy ambushes in order to extract a foot patrol that had become pinned down under sustained small arms and heavy machine gun fire and improvised explosive device and rocket-propelled grenade attack.

'Beharry's platoon was tasked over the radio to come to the assistance of the remainder of the company, who were attempting to extract the isolated foot patrol. As his platoon passed a roundabout, en route to the pinned-down patrol, they became aware that the road to the front was empty of all civilians and traffic – an indicator of a potential ambush ahead. The platoon commander ordered the vehicle to halt, so that he could assess the situation. The vehicle was then immediately hit by multiple rocket-propelled grenades. Eyewitnesses report that the vehicle was engulfed in a number of violent explosions, which physically rocked the 30-tonne Warrior.

'As a result of this ferocious initial volley of fire, both the platoon commander and the vehicle's gunner were incapacitated by concussion and other wounds, and a number of the soldiers in the rear of the vehicle were also wounded. Due to damage sustained in the blast to the vehicle's radio systems; Beharry had no means of communication with either his turret crew or any of the other Warrior vehicles deployed around him. He did not know if his commander or crewmen were still alive, or how serious their injuries may be. In this confusing and dangerous situation, on his own initiative, he closed his driver's hatch and moved forward through the ambush position to try to establish some form of communications, halting just short of a barricade placed across the road.

'The vehicle was hit again by sustained rocket-propelled grenade attack from insurgent fighters in the alleyways and on rooftops around his vehicle. Further damage to the Warrior from these explosions caused it to catch fire and fill rapidly with thick, noxious smoke. Beharry opened up his armoured hatch cover to, clear his view and orientate himself to the situation. He still had no radio communications, and was now acting on his own initiative, as the lead vehicle of a six Warrior convoy in an enemy-controlled area of the city at night. He assessed that his best course of action to save the lives of his crew was to push through, out of the ambush. He drove his Warrior directly through the barricade, not knowing if there were mines or improvised explosive devices placed there to destroy his vehicle. By doing this he was able to lead the remaining five Warriors behind him towards safety.

'As the smoke in his driver's tunnel cleared, he was just able to make out the shape of another rocket- propelled grenade in flight heading directly towards him. He pulled the heavy armoured hatch down with one hand, whilst still controlling his vehicle with the other. However, the overpressure from the explosion of the rocket wrenched the hatch out of his grip, and the flames and force of the blast passed directly over him, down the driver's tunnel, further wounding the semi-conscious gunner in the turret. The impact of this rocket destroyed Beharry's armoured periscope, so he was forced to drive the vehicle through the remainder of the ambushed route, some 1500 metres long, with his hatch opened up and his head exposed to enemy fire, all the time with no communications with any other vehicle. During this long surge through the ambushes the vehicle was again struck by rocket-propelled grenades and small arms fire. While his head remained out of the hatch, to enable him to see the route ahead, he was directly exposed to much of this fire, and was himself hit by a 7.62mm bullet, which penetrated his helmet and remained lodged on its inner surface.

'Despite this harrowing weight of incoming fire Beharry continued to push through the extended ambush, still leading his platoon until he broke clean. He then visually identified another Warrior from his company and followed it through the streets of Al Amarah to the outside of the Cimic House outpost, which was receiving small arms fire from the surrounding area. Once he had brought his vehicle to a halt outside, without thought for his own personal safety, he climbed onto the turret of the still burning vehicle and, seemingly oblivious to the incoming enemy small arms fire, manhandled his wounded platoon commander out of the turret, off the vehicle and to the safety of a nearby Warrior. He then returned once again to his vehicle and again mounted the exposed turret to lift out the vehicle's gunner and move him to a position of safety. Exposing himself yet again to enemy fire he returned to the rear of the burning vehicle to lead the disorientated and shocked dismounts and casualties to safety. Remounting his burning vehicle for the third time, he drove it through a complex chicane and into the security of the defended perimeter of the outpost, thus denying it to the enemy. Only at this stage did Beharry pull the fire extinguisher handles, immobilising the engine of the vehicle, dismounted and then moved himself into the relative safety of the back of another Warrior. Once inside Beharry collapsed from the sheer physical and mental exhaustion of his efforts and was subsequently himself evacuated.

'Having returned to duty following medical treatment, on the 11th June 2004 Beharry's Warrior was part of a quick reaction force tasked to attempt to cut off a mortar team that had attacked a Coalition Force base in Al Amarah. As the lead vehicle of the platoon he was moving rapidly through the dark city streets towards the suspected firing point, when his vehicle was ambushed by the enemy from a series of rooftop positions. During this initial heavy weight of enemy fire, a rocket-propelled grenade detonated on the vehicle's frontal armour, just six inches from Beharry's head, resulting in a serious head injury. Other rockets struck the turret and sides of the vehicle, incapacitating his commander and injuring several of the crew.

'With the blood from his head injury obscuring his vision, Beharry managed to continue to control his vehicle, and forcefully reversed the Warrior out of the ambush area. The vehicle continued to move until it struck the wall of a nearby building and came to rest. Beharry then lost consciousness as a result of his wounds. By moving the vehicle out of the enemy's chosen killing area he enabled other Warrior crews to be able to extract his crew from his vehicle, with a greatly reduced risk from incoming fire. Despite receiving a serious head injury, which later saw him being listed as very seriously injured and in a coma for some time, his level headed actions in the face of heavy and accurate enemy fire at short range again almost certainly saved the lives of his crew and provided the conditions for their safe evacuation to medical treatment.

'Beharry displayed repeated extreme gallantry and unquestioned valour, despite intense direct attacks, personal injury and damage to his vehicle in the face of relentless enemy action.'

After treatment at the Shaibah Field Hospital, south-west of Basrah, Beharry was evacuated to the Royal College of Defence Medicine in Selly Oak, Birmingham. He lay in a coma and his chances of survival were not high. There he underwent a neurosurgical reconstructive survey, which resulted in a series of delicate operations. This was followed by a long period of convalescence and rehabilitation.

On Wednesday, 27 April 2005, Private Beharry received the Victoria Cross from Her Majesty the Queen, an investiture many thought would never occur again. He became the first non-posthumous UK Armed Forces VC recipient since Rambahadur Limbu in 1965. Any fear that Johnson might feel somewhat overawed by the august company was dispelled, for he was joined by seven of his PWRR comrades, who were receiving their own awards: 'I was just thinking about everyone else who helped me, because I didn't do it myself and I am happy that these guys are here today to see me receive it.'

Indeed, Beharry and his Warrior APC colleagues have become the most decorated armoured vehicle crew in the history of the British Army.

At the ceremony, as the VC outranks all other honours, Private Beharry was first in the line of 113 recipients to receive an award. Not since she awarded the Australian Ray Simpson and Keith Payne during her visit to Australia in 1970 has the Queen pinned a Cross on the breast of a recipient.

'I don't get to the chance to do this very often; you're very special,' she told Beharry.

Shortly after his memorable day at Buckingham Palace, came the announcement that he and his wife were separating. It was implied that Johnson's wounds had caused a personality change but the fact is they had amicably agreed to part before the events of the previous year. For the sake of good PR, they kept together until after the investiture.

Johnson's wounds cause him constant headaches and pain in his shoulder and back. Like many soldiers, he was beset with dreams and visions of his time in Iraq – 'the soldier problem' – and on a December night in 2008, he decided to end his life by driving his sports car at 100mph into a lamp post. Luckily, he survived the crash unharmed.

Too many soldiers unable to cope with the vivid flashbacks to the horrors of war have chosen suicide as a way out. Some recipients found the VC an unwelcome burden, meeting untimely ends, or were so damaged by their gallant act that their lives were changed for the worse. Thankfully now the condition is recognised as post-traumatic stress disorder and attempts are made to treat the sufferer.

Fortunately, Beharry has been well treated by the Army despite his wounds and now serves as a lance-sergeant in a public relations role with the Household Division. He has become something of a media celebrity with his appearance on TV's *Dancing on Ice*, carrying the FA Cup onto the field for the final between Manchester United and Chelsea in 2007; unveiling a memorial plaque in Madeira to Cecil Buckley, the first gazetted VC, and various other public duties. He married again in 2013 and his wedding was featured in *Hello!* Magazine, quite possibly making him the most recognisable recipient of the Victoria Cross.

After defeating the Iraqi army, the Coalition found that fulfilling its post-conflict resolution was not so easy. Embarrassingly, the British High Command misjudged the scale of the job they it been given and had to be rescued by the Americans. This was all the more humiliating as the British had been saying that that they were much better with dealing with a post-conflict situation than the Americans.

The British Army was hampered by the cut-backs in man-power and equipment. The hopes to install democracy in Iraq became a vain hope as the country threatened to fragment. Large swaths of northern Iraq were taken over by the so-called Islamic State, which took advantage of the Syrian civil war and Iraq's fragile government. Also in the north, the Kurds determination to establish a homeland on the Turkish and Iranian borders shows signs of succeeding and another possible flashpoint to add to the many in the Middle East. The final main withdrawal of the Coalition left the country it had hoped to set free in a state of chaos.

Index